Renaissance Revit
Creating Classical Architecture with Modern Software

Paul F Aubin

with Foreword by Andy Milburn

G3B
PRESS

Renaissance Revit—*Creating Classical Architecture with Modern Software (Color Edition)*
Part of The Aubin Academy Master Series
By: Paul F. Aubin

© 2013 Paul F. Aubin

ALL RIGHTS RESERVED. No part of this work covered by the copyright herein may be reproduced, transmitted stored or used in any form or by any means graphic, electronic, or mechanical including but not limited to photocopying, recording, scanning, digitizing, taping, Web distribution, information networks, or information storage and retrieval systems, except as permitted under Section 107 or 108 of the 1976 United States Copyright Act, Without the prior written permission of the publisher.

Autodesk, AutoCAD, Revit®, Revit® Architecture, and the Autodesk logo are registered trademarks of Autodesk.

ISBN-13: 978-1492976592

ISBN-10: 1492976598

G3B Press
c/o Paul F. Aubin Consulting Services
P.O. Box 223
Oak Lawn, IL 60454
USA

To learn more about titles by G3B Press, the book's authors and other offerings by Paul F Aubin Consulting Services, please visit **www.paulaubin.com**. Updates are posted to the blog section of the site. Please use Contact link to send email.

Notice to the Reader

Publisher does not warrant or guarantee any of the products described herein or perform any independent analysis in connection with any of the product information contained herein. Publisher does not assume, and expressly disclaims, any obligation to obtain and include information other than that provided to it by the manufacturer. The reader is expressly warned to consider and adopt all safety precautions that might be indicated by the activities described herein and to avoid all potential hazards. By following the instructions contained herein, the reader willingly assumes all risks in connection with such instructions. The publisher makes no representations or warranties of any kind, including but not limited to, the warranties of fitness for particular purpose or merchantability, nor are any such representations implied with respect to the material set forth herein, and the publisher takes no responsibility with respect to such material. The publisher shall not be liable for any special, consequential, or exemplary damages resulting, in whole or part, from the readers' use of, or reliance upon, this material.

The views expressed herein are solely those of the authors/presenters and are not those of Autodesk, Inc., its officers, directors, subsidiaries, affiliates, business partners, or customers.

Contents at a Glance

Contents at a Glance	iii
Contents	v
Foreword	ix
Preface	xi
Chapter 1 • Revit and Classical Architecture	1
Chapter 2 • Understanding the Revit Family Editor	11
Chapter 3 • Scaling and Proportion	35
Chapter 4 • Constraining Curves	59
Chapter 5 • The Tuscan Base, Capital and Pedestal	111
Chapter 6 • Completing the Tuscan Order	143
Chapter 7 • Managing Graphics	177
Chapter 8 • The Doric Column	209
Chapter 9 • The Doric Entablature	243
Chapter 10 • The Ionic Order	279
Chapter 11 • The Massing Environment	309
Chapter 12 • The Column Shaft	341
Chapter 13 • The Corinthian Capital	379
Chapter 14 • File Management Techniques	431
Conclusion	447
Appendix	449
Bibliography	452
Index	455

Contents

Contents at a Glance iii

Contents v

Foreword ix

Preface xi

Welcome xi • Features in This Edition xi • Prerequisites xi • Style Conventions xii • Units xii • Revit Versions xii • Book Dataset Files xii • We Want to Hear from You xiii • About the Author xiii • Dedication xiii • Acknowledgments xiv • Credits: xiv

Chapter 1 • Revit and Classical Architecture 1

Introduction 1 • Objectives 2 • Understanding the Orders 2 • Traditional Vs Massing Families 4 • So which Enviroment are we using? 6 • Levels of Detail 7 • Resources 7 • Synergy 8 • Summary 10

Chapter 2 • Understanding the Revit Family Editor 11

Introduction 11 • Objectives 11 • Basic Family Editor Skills 11 • Create a Sandbox 12 • Create a Simple Parametric Box 12 • Set the Units 13 • Create Reference Planes 14 • Flex the model 16 • Repeat the Process 16 • Add Geometry 16 • Load into a Project 17 • Creating "Seed" Families 18 • Type and Instance Based Seed Families 19 • Create Custom Family Template Files 21 • Face-Based or Free-Standing 21 • Create a Face Based Family Seed 23 • Adding Reference Planes 23 • Dimension and Constrain the Reference Planes 24 • Solid and Void Form Geometry Types 26 • Creating Complex forms 26 • Working with Solids and Voids 27 • Create a Void Form 29 • Create a Revolve Form 29 • Profile Families 30 • Apply a Profile Shape to an existing Sweep 31 • Create a Custom Profile Shape 31 • Create a Swept Blend using Profiles 32 • Summary 34

Chapter 3 • Scaling and Proportion 35

Introduction 35 • Objectives 35 • Understanding Scale and Proportion 35 • The Revit Scale Command 36 • Proportional Parameters 38 • Adding Formulas to Parameters 38 • Base Diameter Parameter 39 • Grouping Parameters 40 • Creating a Simple Column 41 • Create a Base Family 42 • Create a Capital Family 42 • Create a Shaft Family 43 • Nested Families 47 • Create a Schematic Column Family 48 • Adding Nested Components 49 • Associate Family Parameters 51 • Reporting Parameters 53 • Family Types Parameters 55 • Test in a Sandbox 55 • Alternative Scaling and Proportion approaches 56 • Summary 58

Chapter 4 • Constraining Curves 59

Introduction 59 • Objectives 59 • Curvature in the Traditional Family Editor 59 • Constraint and Parameter Direct Attachment 60 • Create a Parametric Circle 60 • Create a Parametric Ellipse 62 • Center Mark Visible 64 • Automatic Sketch Dimensions 64 • Enable Center Mark 64 • Enable Automatic Sketch Dimensions 64 •

Quarter Round and Half Round (Astragal and Torus) 67 • Locking Endpoints 67 • Controlling Rotation 70 • Create a Door Family with Variable Swing 70 • Create and Constrain a Reference Line 70 • Add a Swing Parameter 73 • Create the Door Panel Geometry 74 • Rotating a Curve 74 • Build the Reference Lines and Parameters 74 • Create Geometry on the Rotating Curve 75 • Arches 76 • Create a Parametric Segmental Arch 76 • Gothic Arch 79 • Elliptical Arches 80 • Compound Curves 80 • Profile Families 81 • Ovolo 81 • Using trigonometry to model traditional molding forms 82 • Using a nested rig to model traditional molding forms 85 • Cavetto 85 • Cyma 88 • Cyma Reversa 91 • Cyma and Cyma Reversa Rigs 92 • Proportional Scaling Strategies 92 • Corona 93 • Scotia 94 • Create a Variable Corona Profile 95 • Controlling a Spline 99 • Combining Strategies 101 • Three Center Arch 101 • Compound molding profile 104 • Arched Door Family 105 • Summary 110

Chapter 5 • The Tuscan Base, Capital and Pedestal 111

Introduction 111 • Objectives 111 • Tuscan Setup 111 • Build the Tuscan Capital 112 • Add Reference Planes 113 • Add Dimensions and Parameters 114 • Import Profile Families 115 • Explore the Ovolo Profile 116 • Create the Abacus 117 • Create the Ovolo Molding 117 • Create the Corona Molding 119 • Build the Tuscan Base 124 • Add Reference Planes, Dimensions and Parameters 124 • Add the Formulas 127 • Create the Plinth 127 • Create the Revolve Molding 127 • Build the Tuscan Pedestal 130 • Planning the Family 130 • Configure Reference Planes, Dimensions and Parameters 131 • Create the Lower Molding Geometry 134 • Using Trajectory Segmentation 137 • Copy and Modify a Molding 139 • Summary 142

Chapter 6 • Completing the Tuscan Order 143

Introduction 143 • Objectives 143 • Parts of the Tuscan Order 143 • The Tuscan Shaft 144 • Creating the Framework 145 • Create the Astragal Molding 147 • Create the Shaft as a Sweep 149 • Load the Profile and Create the Sweep 152 • Assemble the Tuscan Column 154 • Reload Families from Project Browser 154 • Creating Optional Items 156 • Load the Pedestal Component 156 • Make the Pedestal Optional 157 • Adding an If Statement 158 • Add Family Types 159 • Load into a Sandbox File 160 • Creating the Tuscan Entablature 161 • Layout the Entablature Extents 161 • Import Molding Profiles 164 • Add a Sweep Profile 165 • Copy Additional Sweep Profiles 169 • Add a Spline to the P3 Profile 172 • Create Family Types 174 • Add the Entablature in a Sandbox File 174 • Summary 176

Chapter 7 • Managing Graphics 177

Introduction 177 • Objectives 177 • Column Plan Display 177 • Make the Column Solid 179 • Intercolumniation 181 • Placing Columns 182 • Reference Plane "Is Reference" Setting 184 • Plan Regions 185 • Placing Beams 187 • Shift the Z Justification 188 • Using Column Top Offset 190 • Alternate Approaches for Entablature 193 • Wall Sweeps 193 • Slab Edges 196 • Working with Levels of Detail 196 • Other Detail Levels and Schematic Lines 200 • Materials 200 • Test the Completed Tuscan Column 202 • Customize the Entablature 204 • Summary 208

Chapter 8 • The Doric Column 209

Introduction 209 • Objectives 209 • Introduction to the Doric Order 209 • Create the Schematic Doric 210 • Rename all Nested Families 210 • Adjust the Proportions of the Nested Families 211 • Adjust the Heights and Reload 213 • Create the Doric capital 214 • Configure the Existing Moldings 216 • Add the Necking 218 • Create a Void Sweep 219 • Cyma Reversa Profile Adjustments 223 • Create the Doric Shaft 224 • Adjust the Doric Shaft Profile 224 • Adjust the Shaft Astragal 227 •

Create the Doric Base 229 • Add an Extruded Core 230 • Adding Sweep Moldings 231 • Create the Doric Pedestal 235 • Configure the Profile Type Parameters 236 • Configure Profile Offset Parameters 237 • Configure Pedestal Moldings 238 • Load into Sandbox 240 • Summary 242

Chapter 9 • The Doric Entablature 243

Introduction 243 • Objectives 243 • Line Based Options 243 • Beams 243 • Walls 244 • Slab edges 246 • Curtain Walls 246 • Line based families 246 • Railings 247 • Adaptive component 249 • Creating a Complex Profile 250 • Create the Cornice Cyma 251 • Completing the Profile 253 • Create a Line-Based Family 257 • Build a Rotation Rig 258 • Adding Geometry 260 • Preliminary Sandbox Test 262 • Mutules, Triglyphs and Metopes 263 • Place and Position the First Components 264 • Create a Parametric Array 267 • Adjust the Y Position 270 • Load into Sandbox 272 • Using Railings 273 • Summary 278

Chapter 10 • The Ionic Order 279

Introduction 279 • Objectives 279 • the Ionic Capital 279 • The Ionic Schematic Capital 280 • The Ionic Volute 281 • Understanding the Approach 281 • Create the Volute Profile Family 283 • Add Reference Planes with Equality Dimensions 286 • Create the Inner Fillet Edge 288 • Complete the Profile 291 • Create the Second Volute Profile 292 • Create the Ionic Capital 294 • Adjust the Abacus 295 • Create the Volute Sweeps 296 • Create the Scrolls 299 • Import the Profile Families 299 • Create the Scroll Forms 300 • Editing Sweep and Swept Blend Paths 301 • Adding the Collar 303 • Copy and Adjust 305 • Completing the Order 307 • Summary 308

Chapter 11 • The Massing Environment 309

Introduction 309 • Objectives 309 • Accessing the Massing Environment Tools 310 • Changing the Category of Massing Families 311 • Shared or Non-Shared 312 • Setting Work Planes in 3D 313 • Object Selection in the Massing Environment 314 • Creating Form 315 • Save a Simple Massing Seed Family 317 • Traditional Techniques in the Massing Environment 318 • Creating a Massing Profile 319 • Load a Massing Profile and Create Form 322 • Reference Lines and Points 323 • Spline Through Points 324 • Hosted Points 326 • 3D Snapping 327 • Lofting 329 • Building Rigs 330 • Using Divide and Repeat 334 • Basic Dentil Molding 335 • Round Colonnade 336 • Create an Adaptive Component Family 337 • Summary 340

Chapter 12 • The Column Shaft 341

Introduction 341 • Objectives 341 • Shaft Height Proportions 341 • Entasis and Diminution 342 • Build a Smooth Shaft with Elliptical Entasis 343 • Fluting In the Traditional Family Editor 349 • Fluted Doric Shaft (Greek Inspired) 350 • Create Stacked Swept Blends 352 • Fluted Doric Shaft (Palladian) 355 • Use the Fluted Shaft as the Fine Detail Version 357 • Fluting In the Massing Family Editor 358 • Understanding the Approach 358 • Create a Massing Profile 359 • Using a Divided Path to Aid in Spacing 363 • Create Hosted 3-Point Arcs 366 • Create the Shaft Form 367 • Using Voids for Fluting 371 • Medium Detail Alternative 374 • Draw Lines on 3D Surfaces 375 • Using a Divided Surface for Medium Detail 376 • Summary 378

Chapter 13 • The Corinthian Capital 379

Introduction 379 • Objectives 379 • The Corinthian Dataset Files 379 • Understanding the Medium Detail Version 381 • Save a Fine Detail Version 382 • The Abacus and Drum 382 • Using GM Profiles for both Path and Shape 383 •

• Creating Classical Architecture with Modern Software •

Building the Path with a Massing Rig 385 • Acanthus Leaves 390 • The Leaf Path 390 • Adding Hosted Point Rigs 392 • Create Parameters and Adjust Profiles 395 • Create the Lofted Form 397 • Create the Tall Leaf 400 • Corinthian Volutes 401 • Add Hosted Profiles to a Path 403 • Create Forms 406 • Create the Small Volute 408 • Cauliculi 410 • Flouret 411 • Create 3D Splines 411 • Adjust Points with Gizmo Controls 415 • Add Hosted Points and Profiles 417 • Create Forms from GM Profiles 420 • Scaling Families with the Planting Category 422 • Assemble the Capital 425 • Load into Project 428 • Summary 430

Chapter 14 • File Management Techniques 431

Introduction 431 • Objectives 431 • Managing File Size 431 • Two-Dimensional Model Families 436 • Export to CAD to Create a 2D Version 436 • Building a Two-Dimensional Elevation Version 438 • Create a Captial Family using the 2D Planting Families 440 • Import the 2D Family and Load it into a Project 441 • Saving Options 443 • Backups 443 • Previews 444 • Summary 446

Conclusion 447

Appendix 449

Introduction 449 • Molding types 449 • Trigonometry resource 449 • Trigonometry Cheat Sheet for Revit 450 • Creating the Cover Rendering 451

Bibliography 452

Books and References 452 • Websites and Blogs 454

Index 455

Foreword

I had a fairly traditional Grammar School education in the north of England. Then at some point in my mid to late teens I decided that self-directed, life-long education made more sense. It was a quiet personal rebellion at first, but it chimed with the spirit of the times in the late 60s and eventually blossomed into a series of adventures that have greatly enriched my life. During this journey, drawing has been my constant companion and one of my primary learning tools. I have been drawing for as long as I can remember: thinking things out in visual terms, taking my pencil for a walk across the paper, searching for new discoveries.

In my mid-thirties I discovered the world of CAD and was especially excited by the three dimensional capabilities of this new tool. For someone who had laboured for long hours constructing a perspective by hand, 3D CAD was a revelation. Here was power and fluency beyond our wildest dreams. It may be hard for those who have grown up playing with computer games to grasp how mind-blowing this was for us old timers. But there was more to come, and over the next decade or so various programmes contributed to the approach which is now called BIM. You can read a lot of nonsense about BIM, but it does herald a fundamental shift in the way that the construction industry will work. I use the future tense, because BIM is very much a work in progress. The good news is that this means you can contribute to the process while it is still fluid. From my perspective BIM is another pencil. Yes it is also a database and a management tool, which is great, but I am a visual thinker. It's in my bones and Revit is my current tool of choice. Revit gives me the power to explore building designs with a speed and fluency I would never have believed 40 years ago when I was sitting at a drawing board with my Rotring pen. The fact that you are reading this foreword suggests that you too are excited by what Revit can do. Take my advice. Grasp the nettle. Don't look back.

Classical Architecture has roots that go back almost three thousand years to the Mediterranean world of ancient Greece and Rome. From austere Doric Temples to flamboyant Corinthian Public Baths, myriad variations flourished around a strong, unifying central theme. After the collapse of the Roman Empire, the mystique faded and Europe explored the more organic & muscular approach that we have labeled Gothic. Some centuries later, when new economic forces had pulled the focal point away from the inland sea and towards the Atlantic rim, the classical mode experienced a dramatic rebirth. It became the unifying style of European civilization during its remarkable and somewhat scary rise to dominance. As a result, classical buildings can be found almost anywhere in the world: New York, Chicago, Delhi, Cape Town, Mexico City, Auckland, Lagos, Saigon ...

Paul Aubin has carved out a distinctive niche in the overlapping worlds of BIM, Revit & Education. He offers support to self-directed learners who have caught the BIM bug and are seeking greater fluency & deeper knowledge. To a large extent I think his success is rooted in his own eagerness to explore and learn; plus his ability to share that enthusiasm with others. In this book he has taken that approach to a new level, seizing on one of his long-term interests, embarking on a journey of discovery, and sharing the results with his audience.

Copy-paste architecture is rarely successful, and I would caution the reader against this approach. We don't necessarily explore the classical tradition in order to copy it. Le Corbusier was hugely enthusiastic about Greek temples and Roman amphitheatres. He drew them from life and enthused about the play of masses in light & shade. Then he took this inspiration and transformed it into buildings like the Villa Savoye and the chapel at Ronchamp. Take that lesson to heart and use the classical style as a source of deep inspiration rather than a treasure chest to be pillaged.

By taking this journey with Paul as your guide, you will come to a much deeper and richer understanding of classical form. To maximize this experience you should open your eyes to the world around you. Look at classical buildings with new eyes, take out a book on Palladio or Brunelleschi. Wren, Jefferson, Bullfinch … there is no shortage of examples. And as you explore, you will realise how rich and subtle are the variations. It is difficult to find two columns that are identical in size and proportions, except for those standing side by side on the same building. It is a constant marvel to me how the classical style maintains this impression of unity while allowing such room for experiment and elaboration. Perhaps that is the secret of its appeal, down the centuries and across the continents. And there is no better way to deepen your insight than to build your own versions of the classical orders using a programme like Revit.

Around 40 years ago I went to see Buckminster Fuller speak in London. It was a riveting experience. At some point in that immense monologue he spoke about synergy. In a way it's like chemical reactions. Put two substances together and sometimes they will just sit there minding their own business. But other combinations will smoulder, fizzle, change colour, explode, and give birth to something entirely new. I think Paul has hit upon an explosive combination. Let him draw you in and take you on two rides for the price of one. Let the synergy generated by the disparate worlds of software & history drive your learning experience forward. You may well find that, like a child, you learn new skills and knowledge in an effortless riot of exploratory play.

So buy the book, make the journey and take your BIM pencil for a walk across the virtual pages of history.

Andy Milburn is an architect and BIM addict, currently living in Dubai. He spent his twenties laying bricks and playing in a rock band, his thirties as a teacher and curriculum developer in newly independent Zimbabwe, returning to Architecture at the age of 40. He is an active member of the global Revit/BIM community, an associate at GAJ Architects and a lifelong believer in open learning. Check out his blog on **www.grevity.blogspot.com**

Preface

WELCOME

This book is primarily a book about the Revit Family Editor. The examples are drawn from classical and renaissance architecture, but the techniques are thoroughly modern and fully leverage the power of Revit's parametric change engine. So whether or not your professional practice involves traditional form making, I am certain you will find many tools, tips and techniques herein that have universal appeal. If you work does involve the classical orders, it is my hope that you will find the techniques and content herein suitable for your work and true to whatever source material you may be following such as Palladio, Vignola, Chambers or Gibbs. For all Revit content authors; those building contemporary forms and those building traditional forms, the pages that follow are packed with procedures, methods and tools that I am certain will provide a worthy addition to your existing toolset. So if you are ready to put your Revit "pencil" to the task of exploring classical architecture, then let's get started.

FEATURES IN THIS EDITION

This book's format is tutorial based. Chapter 1 presents an overview of the book and its goals. Each chapter following this presents a series of tutorial lessons. All required files are provided as a digital download for you to follow along with as you perform the exercises. To get the most out of this book, you are encouraged to read the entire book from start to finish. However, several catch-up files are provided at key points in each lesson. So you can pick up at any point using the catch-up file if you get behind or if you wish to skip certain topics. Just look for the banner indicating a catch-up file:

> **CATCH UP!** The completed file has been provided: *Sample Family.rfa*.

Please see the "Book Dataset Files" topic below for instructions on how to access catch-up files. Registration is required.

PREREQUISITES

The content in this book is intermediate to advanced level in most lessons. It is assumed that you have an understanding of Revit essentials before attempting the lessons in this book. If you are new to the family editor, the basic family editor skills are covered in Chapter 2. But we will move pretty quickly after that. If you need to review the essentials before attempting this book, consider getting a copy of my other Revit Architecture book: *The Aubin Academy Master Series: Revit Architecture 2013 and beyond*. I also have several video courses available at www.lynda.com/paulaubin. You might want to consider *Revit Essential Training, Revit Family Editor* and *Advanced Modeling in Revit Architecture*. All of these will provide an excellent foundation for the lessons in this book.

STYLE CONVENTIONS

Style Conventions used in this text are as follows:

Item	Formatting
Step-by-Step Tutorials	1. Perform these steps.
Menu picks	**Application menu > Save As > Project**
Dialog box and palette input	For the length, type **1.000**.
On screen input	For the length type: **0.526**. For the name input: **Name**.
File and Directory Names	*C:\RenaissanceRVT\Chapter01\Sample Family.rfa*

UNITS

This book makes only a few references to units. Units are addressed early in Chapter 2 and set to a decimal format. From that point, no mention is made of units, so while the dataset files are technically in imperial feet, we will be working in decimal feet, so that the specific unit is effectively moot. You will be asked to input numbers in decimal format with no mention of units. The main focus of the lessons is on the concepts and maintaining scale and proportion. Therefore I have tried to make the unit inconsequential. As such, a separate metric dataset and references are not needed nor are they provided.

Most content in this book is built to be fully scalable. Therefore, if you typically work in metric units, upon completion of any exercise, you can resave the file and change the units to metric. After doing so, simply edit the "Family Types" and change the Base Diameter to the desired metric size. All proportions will be maintained.

REVIT VERSIONS

This books was authored using Revit 2014 Building Design Suite. You can use either the suite version or Revit Architecture. Revit LT can also be used for many lessons, but LT does not support the massing environment. Therefore you will be unable to complete the lessons in Chapters 11 through 14. If you have a copy of Autodesk Vasari, which is essentially a standalone version of the Revit massing environment, you can attempt Chapters 11 through 14 in Vasari, but please note that I have not tried any of the lessons in this book in Revit LT or Vasari nor have I attempted to open them in those programs either. So while I foresee no issues with doing so, I cannot guarantee that they will work properly outside of the full version of Revit.

If you are using Revit 2012 or 2013, I have created a 2012 version of the book's dataset files. The 2012 version contains nearly all of the same files provided in the 2014 version. A few files have been left out where I encountered difficulties in replicating the files. Also in cases where a feature was not available in 2012, I built the file as close as possible as I could to what is described in the book's lessons. There are a few footnotes that mention these differences, but I have not given detailed instructions in those cases. If you have 2014, I recommend you use those files. If you have 2013 or 2012 only, then please use the 2012 version.

BOOK DATASET FILES

Files used in the tutorials throughout this book are available for download from **www.paulaubin.com**. The collection of files; which contains mostly Revit family and project files, will be referred to as the book's dataset files. This dataset is provided in two packages. The basic package contains *only* the minimum files required to begin each lesson. It does not include any of the catch-up or completed files.

Package two contains the catch-up and completed files. If you wish to download the catch-up and completed files, you must register at the site and provide your email preference. Registration simply asks for your name and email address so that I can keep you informed of any edits or updates to the book's content. You are of course entitled to opt-out of the email list if you so choose. Complete details are available at the site.

> **Note:** Please note that the accompanying dataset contains *only* Revit files (RVT, RTE and RFA) and other related resource files necessary to complete the tutorial lessons in this book. The provided dataset does *not* contain the Revit software. Please contact your local reseller if you need to purchase a copy Revit.

To access and install the book dataset files, please do the following:

1. In your web browser, visit: **http://www.paulaubin.com/dataset/renaissance-revit-1ed/**
2. Follow the instructions on that page to access the basic or expanded dataset downloads.
3. There may be more than one item to download. Click each item and follow the instructions of your browser to download each one.
4. Run the WinZip EXE file and unzip the files to your C Drive.

The default unzip folder is named *C:\RenaissanceRVT* on your hard drive. Unzipped files will utilize approximately 542 MB of disk space.

WE WANT TO HEAR FROM YOU

We welcome your comments and suggestions regarding *Renaissance Revit: Creating Classical Architecture with Modern Software*. Please visit **www.paulaubin.com**. Use the contact form at the top of the page to send an email with your comments and questions. I am very interested in your feedback on this project. So please drop me a line.

ABOUT THE AUTHOR

Paul F. Aubin is the author of many CAD and BIM book titles including the widely acclaimed: *The Aubin Academy Mastering Series*: *Revit Architecture, AutoCAD Architecture, AutoCAD MEP and Revit MEP* titles. Paul is also the author of Revit video training for lynda.com **www.lynda.com/paulaubin**. Paul is an independent architectural consultant who travels internationally providing Revit® Architecture and AutoCAD® Architecture implementation, training, and support services. Paul's involvement in the architectural profession spans over 20 years, with experience that includes design, production, CAD management, mentoring, coaching and training. He is an active member of the Autodesk user community, and has been a top-rated speaker at Autodesk University (Autodesk's annual user convention) for many years. Paul has also spoken at the Revit Technology Conference (RTC) in both the US and Australia and other regional events such as the Central States Revit Workshop and CAD Americas. His diverse experience in architectural firms, as a CAD manager, and as an educator gives his writing and his classroom instruction a fresh and credible focus. Paul is an associate member of the American Institute of Architects and a member of the Institute of Classical Architecture. He lives in Chicago with his wife and three children.

DEDICATION

This book is dedicated to my wife Martha. Thank you for your boundless love and support.

ACKNOWLEDGMENTS

Thank you to Aaron Maller who served as technical editor for this edition. Aaron's many though provoking and insightful suggestions helped to make this book even better. Thanks Aaron!

Any project like this requires the help and support of many individuals. The following people have provided valuable insight, support, expertise and/or opinions on this book and its contents. To each of them I am eternally grateful.

David Abair, Ron Bailey, Dave Baldacchino, Harlan Brumm, Butts David, Koch David, Matt Dillon, Tabor-Hanson Donnia, Chau Dorian, Carla Edwards, Stenstrom Eric, Bixler Erich, Mertens Gregory, Luke Johnson, Talamantez Joseph, Shari D. Kamimori, Durham Kevin, Trey Klein, Zach Kron, Schwalb Laurie, Kelcey Lemon, David Light, Brian Mackey, Dezi Mackey, Aaron Maller, Stachoni Matt, Andy Milburn, Klaus Munkholm, Takehiko Nagakura, Membreno Philip, Jeffrey Pinheiro, Deutsch Randy, Naab Richard, Davis Scott, Marcello Sgambelluri, Jim Smell, Steve Stafford, Kelvin Tam, Tim Waldock, Patty Wines, Robert Yori, Jay Zallan

I published a survey early in the planning process for this book. My thanks goes out to all those who answered the survey anonymously. Your responses helped me a great deal. One of the questions I asked was for suggestions on the book's title. I got lots of great suggestions, all of which I am grateful for. But I would like to thank Trey Klein for his suggestion which ultimately became the inspiration for the final title.

CREDITS:

Technical Editor: Aaron Maller

Cover Design: Michael Brumm

Cover Renderings: created by author

Author Illustrations: Ron Bailey

Photographs throughout the books, in Chapter 1 and on the summary page of each chapter are taken by the author. Most were taken in the summer of 1989 during a semester study in Europe while attending Catholic University of America. Photos of Corinthian columns in Chapter 1 were taken in Chicago this past year. Ionic column on the summary page for Chapter 10 was taken at MIT this past year.

Chapter 1
Revit and Classical Architecture

INTRODUCTION

Welcome!

This is the most exciting book that I have ever written. This book will look at a topic that has always held great interest for me: Classical Architecture. This may seem a surprising interest for someone who makes their living mastering and teaching the latest technology like Revit. Why not a book on the latest innovations in architectural form? Well, I am certain that would be an excellent subject for a book as well, but what interests me about classical form is actually perfectly well suited to tools like Revit. For starters, classical architecture is steeped in geometry, proportion, scale and rational form making. All of these are things that computers in general, and Revit in particular facilitate. This book for me is as much about finding a vehicle for learning and teaching the potentials and possibilities of Revit as it is a way to explore the specifics of a genre like classical architectural form.

My first book was written about Architectural Desktop software and was published in 2001. This was right around the time that Autodesk started updating its software annually, so little did I know at the time that I would need to rewrite the book just a few short months later. I have published at least one book per year and in some years several books per year since that time. At last count I have about 27 volumes (I had to look it up) to my name. These started with Architectural Desktop, which became AutoCAD Architecture and then gave way to Revit. In its years with Autodesk, Revit has been referred to as Revit, Revit Building, Revit Architecture and now back to just "Revit" again. At an average of 800 pages per book, I am now responsible for the publication of around 22,000 pages of content on Autodesk building design software! Hard for me (and I am sure my college roommates) to believe given how much I grumbled about having to write just 50 pages for my college thesis.

So why is this volume that you now hold in your hands the "most exciting" that I have written? Well, the prior 27 volumes have been essentially the same. They were how-to manuals on the tools available. Examples I used were deliberately kept simple and in most cases generic enough to appeal to as wide an audience as possible. I realize that with this book, I may immediately loose those folks who do not share my interest in classical form. While I certainly understand this possibility, I hope it will not be the case. This is also a "how-to" manual in the sense that I will provide plenty of tutorials explaining exactly how I built each of the Revit families and forms that we will be discussing. However, all the examples will be classical forms. That being said, it is my hope that even those readers who may not be particularly interested in classical form will be able to see beyond the specific example to underlying techniques. The fact is that in this book, we will look at practical examples of how to approach many common Revit challenges, such as:

- Strategies to planning and building reusable family content
- How to control scale and proportion reliably
- How to parametrically control curves like arcs, ellipses and compound curves
- Strategies for working with appropriate levels of detail
- Approaches to effectively managing repetitive elements
- Building rules, relationships and design intent into your content
- Strategies to use two-dimensional geometry instead of 3D

Reading this introduction you may also notice another point. I have decide to write this manual in the first person. I made this decision partly because of the very personal nature of the subject matter and also because so much of the content that follows is like a case study of sorts. By presenting it in first person I feel that it will convey my intent a little more; which is to share as much my journey through this process as the techniques that I settled on along the way.

So if you want to know how to create a classical column family in Revit, rest assured you have come to the right place and I will walk step-by-step through the process. However, I will also share some other narrative along the way. I might share how I arrived at a particular technique, or discuss some of the issues encountered and even show the failures and half successes. I think that all of this can be a valuable learning resource.

Andy Milburn in his excellent foreword (for which I am humbled and grateful) likes to say that Revit is his current "pencil of choice". Architects have always used the pencil as an extension of the brain and a way to explore ideas and understand forms and relationships. How do we understand the built environment around us? We go out with a sketchpad and draw. So even if you have no need for classical forms in your current work, I would argue that the lessons in this book are just as relevant to you as to someone who intends to create a completely faithful classically themed design. Using Revit as your pencil, and creating the forms discussed in this book will allow you that critical insight into what the masters who came before us were thinking. We can dissect the forms, understand the relationships and gain better insight into the history that binds us all together. I hope that you will join me now as we explore classical forms in Revit; our current pencil of choice.

OBJECTIVES

This chapter sets the stage. Topics in this chapter include:

- A look at the goals of this book
- An overview of the Revit tools that we will explore
- A discussion of the strategies and approach

UNDERSTANDING THE ORDERS

I'd like to begin with a quick definition of what the classical "orders" are. If you are an Architect or have training in architecture or building design, you have no doubt some familiarity with the classical orders. Nonetheless, I could hardly skip the topic altogether now could I? At the very least you probably are curious what I think the orders are. So understanding the orders and defining a few terms is a good a place to start as any.

As I began to write this passage, a very basic question popped into my head. Why are they called "orders"? So naturally I went to Google for a quick answer. Choosing to skip over the obligatory Wikipedia article that came up first, the next site is one that I have visited on many occasions: **http://theclassicalorders.com/**

The definition given on the home page of this site cut right to the chase: and order "orders" architectural form. Simple, concise. I like it. Here is the complete quote:

> All classical architecture of the Greco-Roman tradition is composed, or written, in one language of forms. These elements of classical architecture include specific Moldings and assemblages of moldings called an Order. An Order is an accepted way of assembling a column (supporting element) with an entablature (spanning element) while imparting a certain character. In short, an Order orders a design. Orders are never applied after the building is designed, as they are generative.
>
> Over time the canon has come to include five Orders: Tuscan, Doric, Ionic, Corinthian, and Composite.
>
> (The Classical Orders.com n.d.)

I love this definition because it touches on many of the salient points that I believe are critical to the undertaking at hand. First, the analogy to classical architecture's being a language. When you learn a language, you learn vocabulary, grammar and style. It is not enough to know just a bunch of words. You have to know how to put those words together into meaningful sentences to covey complex thoughts and ideas. When you learn a language, you learn how to communicate, not how to merely recite back some words and sentences. A simplistic way to look at classical architecture is to think of it static forms that scale proportionally based on the diameter of the column's base. But there is much more nuance to it than that. I have seen this in the development of the Revit orders that I will share with you here. By sketching them, molding them, flexing them in Revit, I have gained a much more thorough understanding than I could by simply reading about them or looking at them. I suppose we can extend the language analogy further by equating it to the differences between reading, speaking and writing. While all rely on the vocabulary and grammar, writing is a very different skill than reading or speaking.

Next our definitions identifies the two dominant components in the classical vocabulary: the column and the entablature. These are our nouns and verbs. The best part of the definition however is the note that the orders are not "applied" but rather "generate" the form. The classical language is not simply wall covering and paint. It defines a methodology of form. There are rules implied in its forms and proportions. Some of these can be bent, some broken. We see this throughout history as the orders evolved and each new master made them their own. One of my favorites at this was the renaissance master Michelangelo. Michelangelo worked in the height of the renaissance where he and other masters were rediscovering and redefining the language that the ancients had left to them.

Michelangelo is best known for his paintings and sculpture, but he was also a brilliant Architect. My favorite of his architectural works is the Piazza del Campidoglio. This is his reworking of the Capitoline Hill in Rome. It is a brilliant space and if you have never seen it, you should definitely look it up (see Figure 1.1).

FIGURE 1.1
Piazza del Campidoglio by Michelangelo

Photo by the author

One of the first orders I attempted to build was an Ionic capital. With the Campidoglio being one of my favorite works, I based this capital on the ones used there. (This was actually built a few years before I started using Revit in AutoCAD Architecture—see Figure 1.2).

Michelangelo took some liberties with the forms, particularly at the capital in the volutes, necking and other details. I incorporated some of these nuances in the form of the horns behind the volutes, but only captured a small fraction of the subtly. Upon closer examination, I discovered that the horns and even the volutes actually vary quite substantially from one another at different points along the façade. I did not notice this subtly at first. It took me some long sessions of investigation to fully appreciate these nuances. The work of Michelangelo is certainly appreciated by many, and even scorned by a few. But despite how you might feel about him and his work, it is hard to argue that the Capitoline Hill is anything short of a masterpiece.

FIGURE 1.2
My first Ionic capital model built in AutoCAD Architecture

Some may argue that Michelangelo did not practice classical architecture at all; perhaps even that none of the Renaissance masters did. That their brand of classicism was something new entirely. I will leave such discussions to works and authors more capable of doing the subject justice than I. For the purposes of this work, let me return to the original question: just what do we mean by classical architecture?

For the basic defining principal behind this work, I will keep the goals relatively modest. My focus is primarily on the classical orders fashioned on the Roman and perhaps more specifically Renaissance tradition. I will show how to create four of the five orders: Tuscan, Doric, Ionic and Corinthian. I have chosen not to do a Composite order at this time, but by combining the strategies I outline for Ionic and Corinthian, one could readily be devised using the procedures outlined herein. For each order, there will a base, shaft and capital. For a few of the orders, I will also create pedestals and I discuss approaches to the entablature and intercolumniation. I will also devote some attention to arches, moldings and a few other accoutrements. Furthermore, the proportions of all the families presented will be based on the size of the diameter of the column as measured just above its base. Formulas, linked parameters and other techniques will be used to ensure that everything flexes properly and as expected. These will be fully parametric families.

TRADITIONAL VS MASSING FAMILIES

As you may know, Revit families are built in an environment called the Family Editor. The family editor is an environment where instead working in a project file, you work directly inside of a family file. The family editor saves files with an RFA extension. There are a few ways to enter the family editing environment. First there is the so called "traditional family editor." This environment has been available in Revit the longest and is where most of the commonly used components like doors, windows, columns, furniture and equipment are created. The traditional family editor environment has a project browser similar to the project environment and all forms are sketch-based forms that must be sketched on a 2D work plane. Reference planes are the primary element used to establish work planes. The traditional environment has five forms: Extrusion, Blend, Revolve, Sweep and Swept Blend. The same five forms can be used to create both solids and voids see the top of Figure 1.3). By combining the two, you can create complex three-dimensional forms.

While it is possible to create the shapes required by most everyday items using the simple 3D forms available in the traditional family editor, there are limitations. A few years ago, the massing family environment was introduced to Revit. The massing environment is similar to the traditional environment in a few ways. It is a separate environment and it saves RFA files. But there are far more differences than similarities. The most notable difference is that the massing environment is a three-dimensional work environment. Instead of working and sketching exclusively in 2D views and using 3D views just to study final results (as is the case with the traditional family editor), in the massing environment, you can work directly in 3D. This includes work planes (visible only in 2D views in the traditional family editor) which display in 3D space in the massing environment. Reference lines also play a prominent role in both establishing work planes and creating 3D form. Perhaps the most notable difference however is the way that you create form in the massing environment. In the massing environment, there is a single "Create Form" button on the ribbon (see the bottom of Figure 1.3). By creating lines and edges for use as both the "sketch" of the form and its (sweep or rotation) path as appropriate, you can create nearly any kind of form without being required to enter a dedicated sketch mode. This approach allows for the creation of some kinds of forms that are not easily replicated in the traditional environment such as lofted forms and freeform shapes.

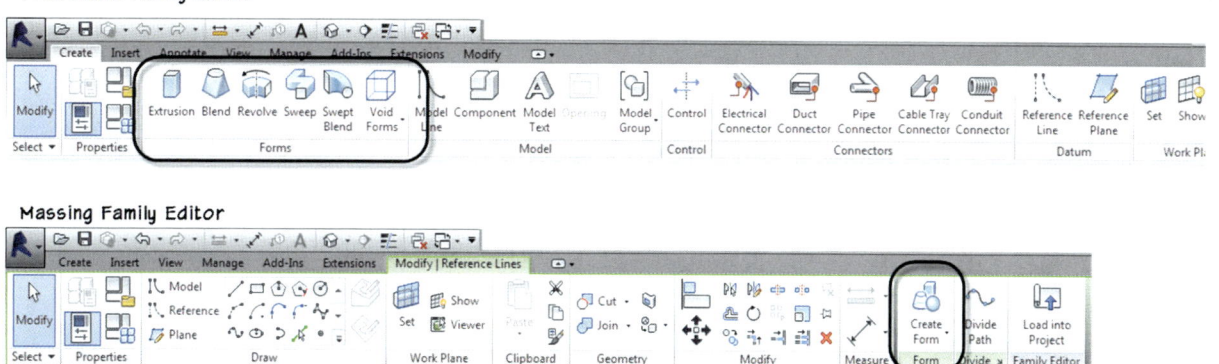

FIGURE 1.3

Comparing the two family editor environments

The massing environment is robust and nuanced. Mastering it takes a considerable amount of time and effort. For those who have invested the time, would argue that it is time well spent and that the advantages afforded by the environment are well worth it. It is not my aim to refute this assertion; the massing environment does have many useful and powerful benefits. However, there are some down sides as well. I would like to highlight just two for now: categories and file size/performance.

Families created in the massing environment default to the Mass category. It is possible to create families in the environment of other more useful categories, but you must ensure that start the family correctly in order to do this. Families created from the *Mass.rft* template cannot have their category changed to anything other than Mass. The Mass category is only useful as a "clay model" or "study model" in your projects. The intention is that the mass family will serve the purpose of helping you shape the form of walls, roofs and other geometry in your project and eventually the mass will be hidden or removed.

> TIP: Do not use the *Mass.rft* template for any of the exercises in this book.

• *Creating Classical Architecture with Modern Software* •

To use the massing environment to create families of other standard "component" categories, you have to start with one of the following templates:

- *Curtain Panel Pattern Based.rft*
- *Generic Model Adaptive.rft*
- *Generic Model Pattern Based.rft*

The two pattern based templates are designed to create a component that can be used in conjunction with a divided surface on another massing family. So while you can change the category of these, unless you are using divided surfaces, they are probably not your best choice. That leaves *Generic Model Adaptive.rft*. The subject of adaptive components could fill an entire book of its own. The main use for adaptive components is creating flexible components that adjust to the locations of a series of placement points. When you insert an adaptive component, you are prompted to click points to locate its placement points. This can occur in 3D space, not just on a single plane. The component will "adapt" to the shape defined by these placement points. It is the only element in Revit that behaves this way and it is very powerful. However, even if you do not have the need for the "adaptive" feature, adaptive components have one other special advantage. They can be assigned to many standard component categories including but not limited to: Casework, Columns, Doors, Furniture, Generic Models and Specialty Equipment. This feature means that you can use an adaptive component to create a freestanding element that is built using all of the features of the massing environment but is categorized with an appropriate category. So if you don't mind using an adaptive component and changing its category, you can use the massing environment to create nearly any type of component family.

Before going this route with content that you are building, consider the other potential pitfall. Adaptive components tend to be larger (often significantly so) than their counterparts created in the traditional family editor. File size by itself does not immediately mean poor performance, but large families can certainly contribute to poorly performing project files. Other factors involve the complexity of the families, formula usage, associated family parameters, levels of nesting, etc. So don't just focus on file size exclusively, but do have it in the back of your mind. My first Corinthian column weighed in at 130 MB. This certainly impacts performance. The one we will create in this book is still pretty large but is about a tenth of the size of my first attempt. So much better, but still huge.

There are plenty of other much more subtle differences in the two family editor environments. For example, using the TAB key to cycle through selections is different: chain selection is the default in the massing environment, where it is second in the project environment. Selecting an object like a reference plane automatically sets it as the active work plane. If you are not paying close attention, this can cause issues. Careful attention must be paid to the order that you build hosted elements. Profile families cannot be used to create form, but Generic Models can be used in almost the same way. You cannot copy and paste between traditional and massing. You can nest traditional families into massing families, but *not* vice versa. The list goes on. Practice certainly does make perfect here, but while you are learning and even long after, the subtle differences can be frustrating.

SO WHICH ENVIROMENT ARE WE USING?

So after the detailed discussion on the two family editor environments, you may be wondering which one will be covered in the lessons that follow? The answer is both. The book will start with the traditional family editor. Given some of the issues already discussed, my preference for component families is to create them in the traditional family editor wherever possible. However, I am certainly not against using the massing environment and adaptive components where useful or necessary to do so. So we will approach the book this way. Orders like Tuscan and

Doric are very easy to create using traditional form making in the traditional family editor. As a consequence, they will be simpler to build, more lightweight and will be able to be readily nested into other families and/or projects.

On the other hand, given the complexity of the forms and shapes in the Corinthian order, many of its forms will be created as adaptive components. This will give us much nicer results but at a cost of higher file size and some of the other limitations already discussed.

The bottom line is that both environments give us many features and benefits. If you are not already familiar with both, you should try to become so. Both tools will certainly have a place in your daily Revit workflow.

LEVELS OF DETAIL

Not to be confused with Level of Development (LOD) from AIA document E202. Level of detail in Revit is the three display options of Course, Medium and Fine. The benefit of these is that you can build a family that incorporates elements that will only display in one or two of these levels. So when planning a complex family, you can decide to only show a simple schematic rendition in Course, a slightly more complex rendition in medium and a fully detailed version in Fine. The families that we will build here will utilize all three levels of detail (see Figure 1.4). This will be done primarily to manage performance and drawing quality. If you are showing your classical column in a 1/16"=1'-0" [1:200] scale elevation, is it really necessary to show each turn of the spiral on the volutes of your Ionic column or all of the leaves of your Corinthian? Furthermore, you can use a similar strategy to draw a different representation in plan views than in elevation or 3D.

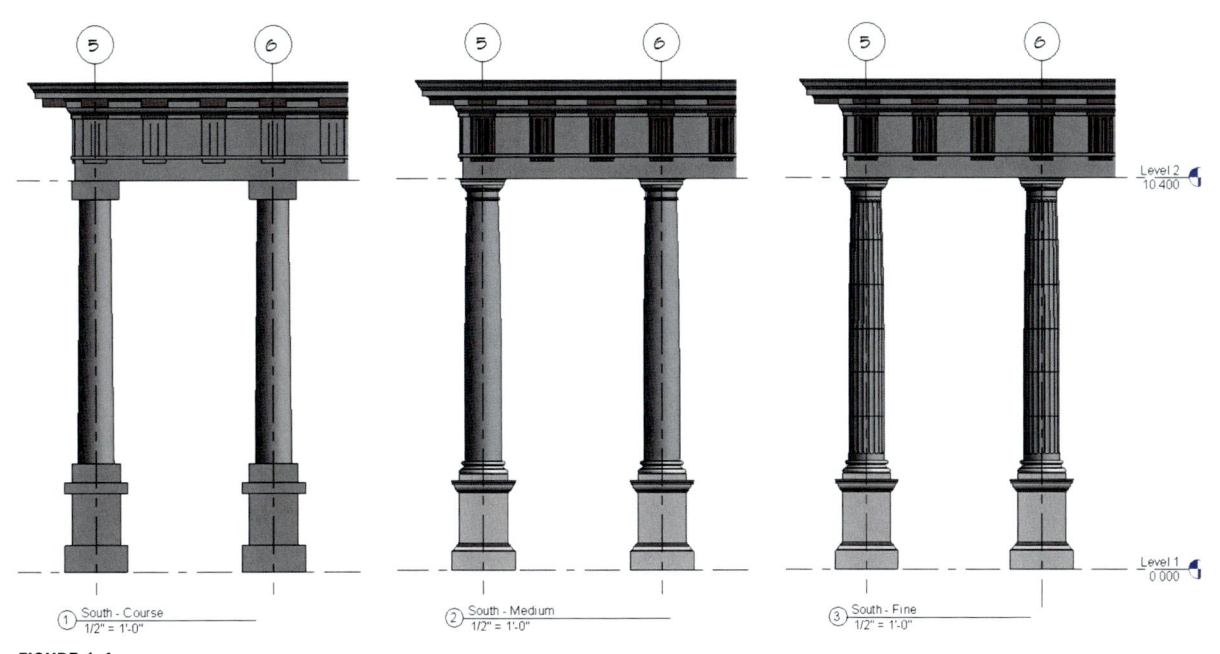

FIGURE 1.4
Most of the content in this book will be produced in three levels of detail

RESOURCES

I have several source materials that I use for reference when determining the proportions and forms, but my "go to" resource is: *The Classical Orders of Architecture*, by Robert Chitham (Chitham 1985, 2005). In it, Chitham details how to construct many traditional forms including the five architectural orders (Tuscan, Doric, Ionic, Corinthian and Composite) as well as many common moldings, balustrades and other forms. I highly recommend the book and it has been an invaluable resource in developing the ideas in this book. The book was first published on cusp of the computer age and therefore focused on traditional techniques to construct the orders using hand drafting methods. Chitham has extensive plates throughout the book and does side-by-side comparisons of each order as outlined by the masters in many previous architecture treatises such as Vitruvius, Palladio, Gibbs and Chambers. The book is unfortunately out-of-print, but you can still get a Kindle edition or perhaps find a copy in the second hand market.

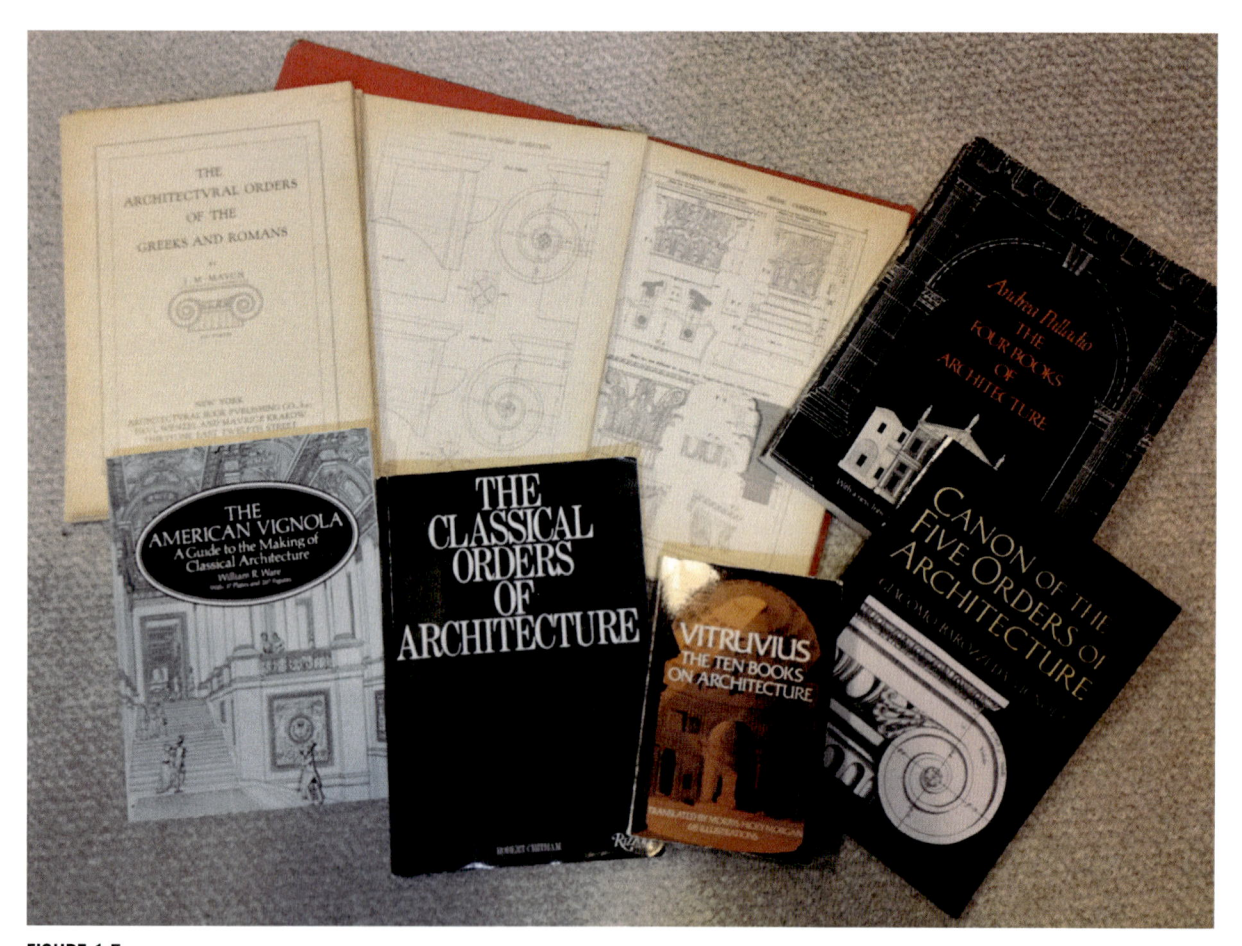

FIGURE 1.5
A selection from my library

Throughout the book I will discuss many of my source materials where appropriate (see Figure 1.5). I have also included a bibliography at the end.

SYNERGY

I studied Architecture at Catholic University in Washington DC. Classical architecture graces nearly every corner of the nation's capital. In my fourth year at CUA I took a semester in Europe. We spent months visiting ancient cities and ruins with sketchpad in hand (see Figure 1.6). I am simply awestruck when I contemplate the monuments that dot the landscapes and try to imagine the lives of the people who built them. I have a great love of history and of architecture and of making things. When I combine those loves with my love of technology like Revit, a project like the one you hold in your hands just seems like a natural to me. For me this has been a "pet" project for some time. Over ten years ago, I got the idea to try to create a classical column capital in the software that I was using in my day job every day. The results of that first exploration are shown in Figure 1.2 above. I would sometimes work on the project intensely for a period until "real" work got in the way and it would slip to the back burner again, sometimes for months at a time. But I always returned to it sooner or later and made steady progress. Recently I decided it was time to revisit all of my previous attempts and document my efforts. The result is the book you now hold in your hands. I have devoted a great deal of time and energy to this endeavor. I believe that the methods I am detailing here will have universal appeal to anyone using Revit to create architectural form; both traditional and modern. Put another way, I find classical architecture a fascinating and challenging vehicle from which to explore and push the possibilities of Revit and its powerful family editor environment. In that spirit I hope you will take this journey with me and along the way find yourself to be much more proficient at Revit family content creation.

FIGURE 1.6
Some pages from my sketchbook

SUMMARY

Now that you have some idea of the background and goals of this book, here is a summary of what you can expect to find in the coming chapters:

- ✓ Early chapters will cover an overview of the family editor environment.
- ✓ Basic strategy, references, parameters and form making.
- ✓ Each order will include a separate base, shaft and capital. Some will include a pedestal.
- ✓ Each order will contain a course level of detail schematic version.
- ✓ Most will contain both medium and fine versions as well.
- ✓ The diameter of the column as measured just above the base (Base Diameter) will be the primary driving parameter for all families.
- ✓ Each order will be fully parametric, scaling proportionally based on the value of Base Diameter.
- ✓ All geometry will be native Revit geometry. No imported geometry.
- ✓ Tuscan, Doric and Ionic will be built in the traditional family editor.
- ✓ Corinthian will be built in the massing family editor.

BRAMANTE'S TEMPIETTO
Photo by author

Chapter 2
Understanding the Revit Family Editor

INTRODUCTION

This book is not intended to give a comprehensive look at the Revit Family Editor. I assume that if you are reading this book, this is not the first time that you have tried your hand at creating Revit family content. However, I do feel that some review of the basic concepts and skills in the Revit family editor are in order. If you are an expert in the Revit family editor, you may be tempted to skip this chapter. That is understandable, but do consider at least skimming its contents. You may find some items in here that are valuable to you despite your existing expertise. Furthermore, we will build a few templates and rigs in this chapter that will be reused throughout the rest of the book. So familiarizing yourself with this chapter's contents will help you to understand the basic assumptions being made in later chapters.

If the Family Editor is new to you, then this chapter is a **must read**. I will cover some of the most basic skills required to be successful building family content. As I noted, I am not attempting to cover *every* family editing tool and skill; I am focusing on those that are required to build the families we will be discussing in this book. So if you want a more comprehensive introduction to the Family Editor, consider supplementing this chapter with other resources such as my video course at lynda.com: Revit Architecture: The Family Editor (Aubin, Revit Architecture: The Family Editor 2011).

OBJECTIVES

Being successful building classical architectural families requires many basic family editor skills. In this chapter we will focus on the traditional family editor and look at the essential skills required to successfully create family content such as:

- Starting with the best choice of template
- Establishing reference planes and work planes
- Using dimensions, constraints and parameters
- Building geometry
- Flexing your model
- Creating seed families
- Working with profiles

BASIC FAMILY EDITOR SKILLS

This is going to be a hands-on chapter. So if you have not already done so, please download the dataset files provided with this book. You can visit the "Book Dataset Files" topic in the Preface to learn how to download the files.

There are many kinds of families we can create. There are 2D families and 3D families, parametric and static families, model and annotation families. All of these are important to understand to get the fullest potential out of Revit. The focus in this book is on parametric 3D model families. In this chapter, we will start with a simple

12 | Chapter 2

parametric box; controlling the length, width and height. We will use the framework of this example to create several starting point families that will become the seeds for all future content created in this book. We'll end the chapter with a look at the kinds of geometry we can create in the traditional family editor and an exploration of profiles.

CREATE A SANDBOX

If you were going into the shop to build some cabinetry, you'd want to make sure you had all the tools you needed and that the shop was in order before you started. Let's do the same in Revit.

1. If Revit is not already running, launch it now.
2. From the Application Menu (big "R"), or on the Recent Files screen, choose **New > Project**.
3. Choose the standard **Architectural Template** and then click OK.

    If you don't have access to the standard Architectural Template, you can click the Browse button. Navigate to the folder where you downloaded the book's dataset files. Double-click the *Templates* folder and select the file named: *default.rte*. Click Open and then OK.

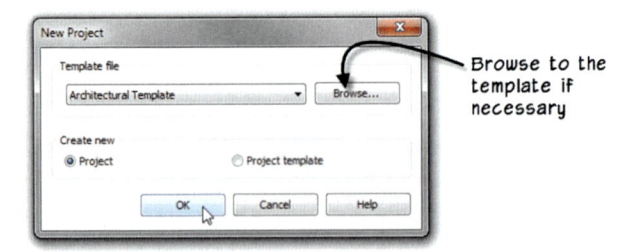

FIGURE 2.1
Create a new Sandbox file from the default Architectural Template

4. From the Application menu, choose **Save As > Project**.
   ⇨ Browse to the location where you downloaded the book's dataset files and open the *Chapter02* folder.
   ⇨ Name the file: **Sandbox** and then click Save.
   ⇨ Minimize the view onscreen.

The project file will remain open as we work through the next several lessons. As you build Family content, you will want to test if frequently. Having a project file open in the background is an excellent way to do this. I like to minimize it so that it stays out of my way till I need it. For this example, we have created an empty sandbox file based on the out-of-the-box architectural template file. There is nothing special about a "sandbox". It is purely for testing your content. In real work, you can open your standard office template, add a few Walls and other items and save it as a sandbox. *It is that simple.*

CREATE A SIMPLE PARAMETRIC BOX

It all starts with a box. A box you say? Yes a box. The first thing you need to learn to build in the Family Editor is a simple box. But not just any box, we'll be building a **Parametric** Box. *Ooo ahh.* In all seriousness a simple box really is the basis for so many other common forms (see Figure 2.2).

> **Note:** This lesson will explain each step. If this is your first time in the Family Editor, pay close attention to explanatory text between the numbered steps to gain insight on the process as we go. If you are familiar with the family editor and have built family content before, simply focus on the numbered steps instead.

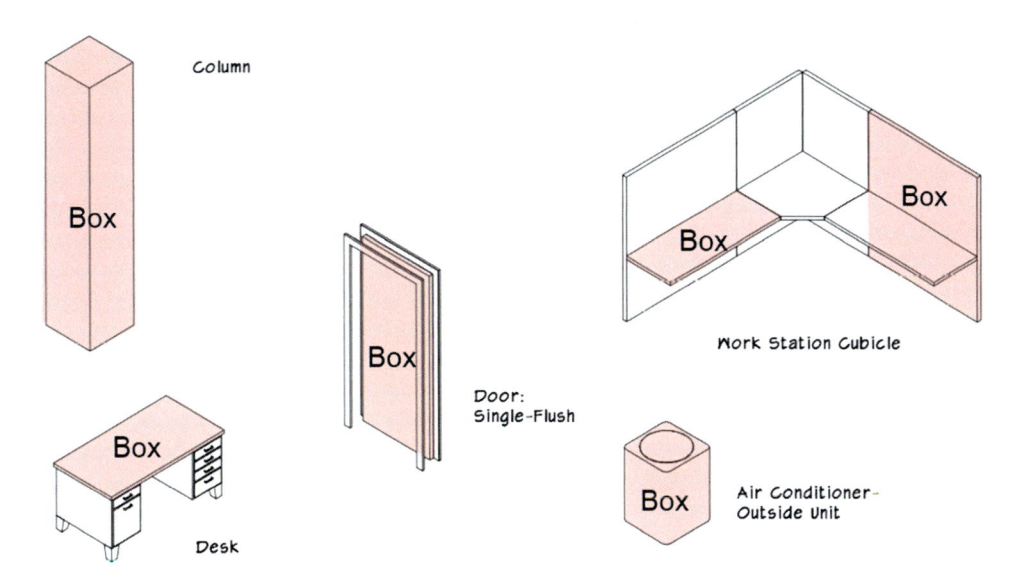

FIGURE 2.2

A simple box is the basis for many more complex forms

1. From the Application Menu (big "R"), choose **New > Family**.

The "New Family – Select a Template File" dialog will appear. Template files do some very important things to get you off to a good start in your Families. For now, we will just choose Generic Model. (Don't be fooled by this choice however. Template choice is very important and should be given careful consideration in each new family that you create).

2. Select *Generic Model.rft* from the list and then click Open.

    A copy of this file is provided in the *Template/OTB* folder with the book's dataset files.

3. Type WT and then ZA.

4. From the Application Menu choose **Save** and name the file *Box.rfa*.

These two keyboard shortcuts tile the windows (View tab, Windows panel) and zoom them all to fit the available space (Navigation Bar). If you are not using keyboard shortcuts, you should consider learning some. Big time savers! Just remember, type only the letters, do *not* follow a shortcut with the ENTER key.

SET THE UNITS

For these examples, I am going to keep the units generic. I will be using decimal feet here. This means we can simply input simple numbers to three decimal places. This will avoid the need for two sets of numbers in the instructions. If you prefer, you may use whatever unit you choose instead, but to avoid confusion, I recommend using decimal feet as I have.

1. On the Manage tab, click the Project Units button.

2. Next to Length, click the button to change the setting.

3. For Units, choose **Decimal Feet**. For Rounding choose **3 decimal places**.

4. Click OK twice to finish (see Figure 2.3).

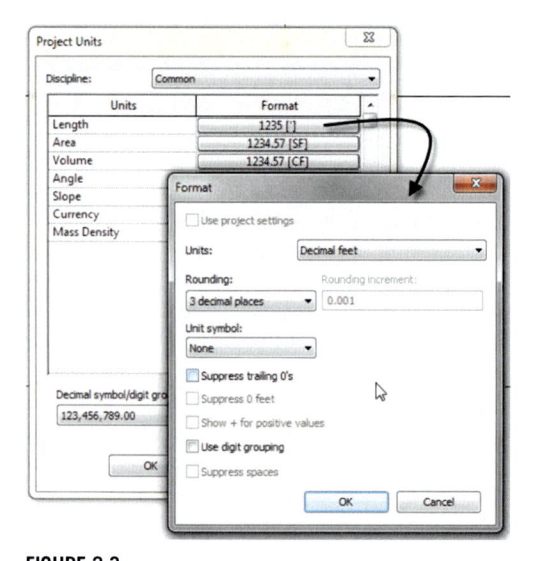

FIGURE 2.3

Set the units in your seed family

CREATE REFERENCE PLANES

Reference planes give our family its structure. Think of it as the skeleton of your family. Always start with reference planes.

1. On the Create tab, on the Datum panel, click the Reference Plane (*not* Reference Line) button (or type RP).

2. Draw a vertical reference plane to the left of the centerline. Edit the dimension to make it **3.000** from center. Repeat to create a horizontal one below at **2.000** from center (see Figure 2.4).

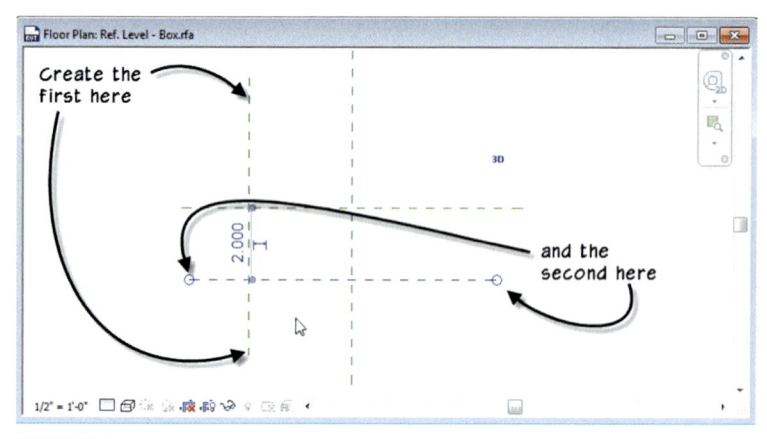

FIGURE 2.4

Draw a horizontal and vertical reference plane

3. Select one of the reference planes, click the Mirror Pick Axis tool and mirror it about the center reference plane. Repeat for the other one.

You should now have four reference planes forming a rectangular shape centered on the original two reference planes. To use a reference plane as a work plane, name it. To name a reference plane, select it and on the Properties palette, type in the Name field.

4. Select the one on the left, and on the Properties palette, name it: **Left**.

5. Repeat for the other four naming them **Right**, **Front** and **Back** (see Figure 2.5).

• Renaissance Revit •

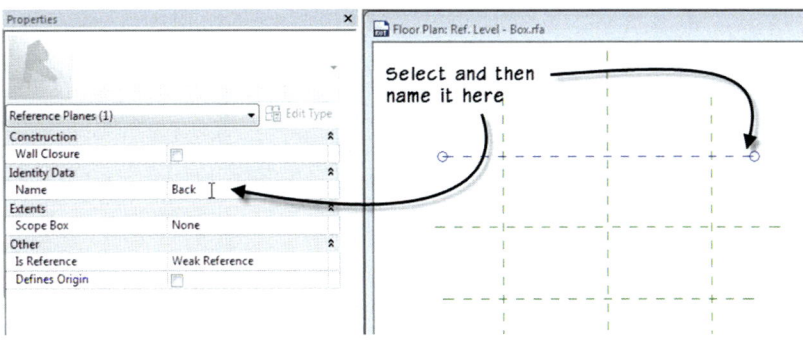

FIGURE 2.5
Name the four new reference planes on the Properties palette

6. Add dimensions (Modify tab or type DI) to each group of reference planes. Two vertical and two horizontal. There should be an overall and a continuous string including the centerline in each direction (see Figure 2.6).

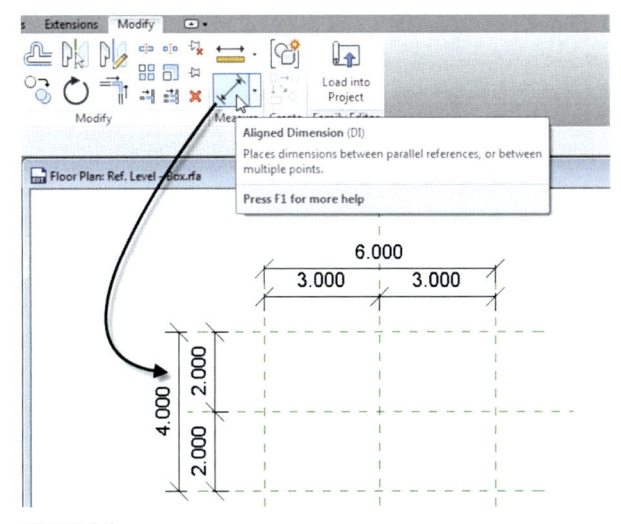

FIGURE 2.6
Add dimensions

7. Select each of the continuous strings and toggle on the Equality (click the small EQ icon).

8. Select the 6.000 overall dimension onscreen and then on the Options Bar, click the Label dropdown and choose **<Add Parameter>**.

⇨ In the "Parameter Properties" dialog that appears, name the new parameter **Width**, choose the **Instance** radio button (do *not* check "reporting") and then click OK (see Figure 2.7).

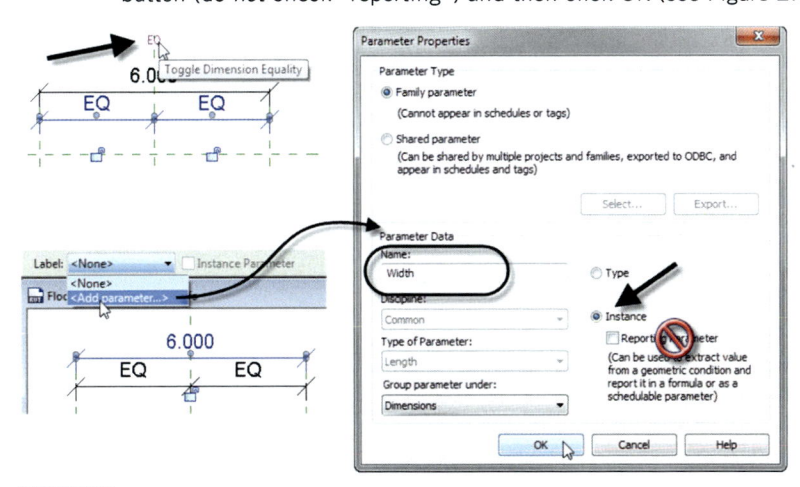

FIGURE 2.7
Toggle dimension equality and then create a new parameter label

• *Creating Classical Architecture with Modern Software* •

9. Repeat for the other dimension calling it **Depth** and also an Instance parameter.

FLEX THE MODEL

What we have so far is a rectangular formwork defined by the reference planes. The two labeled dimensions are "parameters" that will allow these dimensions to be flexible. The two "EQ" dimensions will constrain the model in such a way as to keep everything centered. Let's test it out. When you test your flexible Family, it is called "flexing" the model.

1. On the Create tab (or the Modify tab), click the Family Types button (see Figure 2.8).

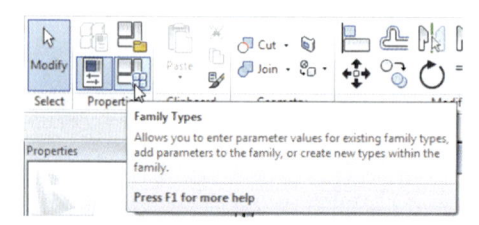

FIGURE 2.8
Open the "Family Types" dialog to flex the model

2. Input a different value for both the **Width** and **Depth** fields and then click the Apply button.

The locations of the reference planes should adjust but stay equally spaced from the center. If it does, congratulations, you have completed your first set of correctly configured parameters.

3. Reset the Width to **6.000** and the Depth to **4.000** and then click OK.

REPEAT THE PROCESS

Now we'll shift to elevation and add a reference plane to control the height.

1. In the *Front* elevation view, create another reference plane running parallel to and **3.000** off the ground.
2. On the Properties palette, name the new reference plane **Top**.
3. Add a dimension between the new reference plane and the Ref Level already in the file.
   ⇨ Label the dimension with a new parameter and call it **Height**.
   ⇨ Make it an **Instance** parameter (not reporting).
4. Flex the family.

> **CATCH UP!** If you get behind, look for these boxes. I have saved versions of the files at various stages of completion. You can open the file completed to this point in the *Chapter02* folder named: *02_Box_A.rfa*.

ADD GEOMETRY

How about some geometry? With a good framework in place, you are ready to add your first solid form to the Family. Since this is a simple box, all we need is an extrusion.

5. Click in the *Plan* view to make it active.
6. On the Create tab, click the Extrusion button (item 1 in Figure 2.9).
   ⇨ On the Modify | Create Extrusion tab, on the Draw panel, click the Rectangle shape (item 2 in Figure 2.9).

Understanding the Revit Family Editor | **17**

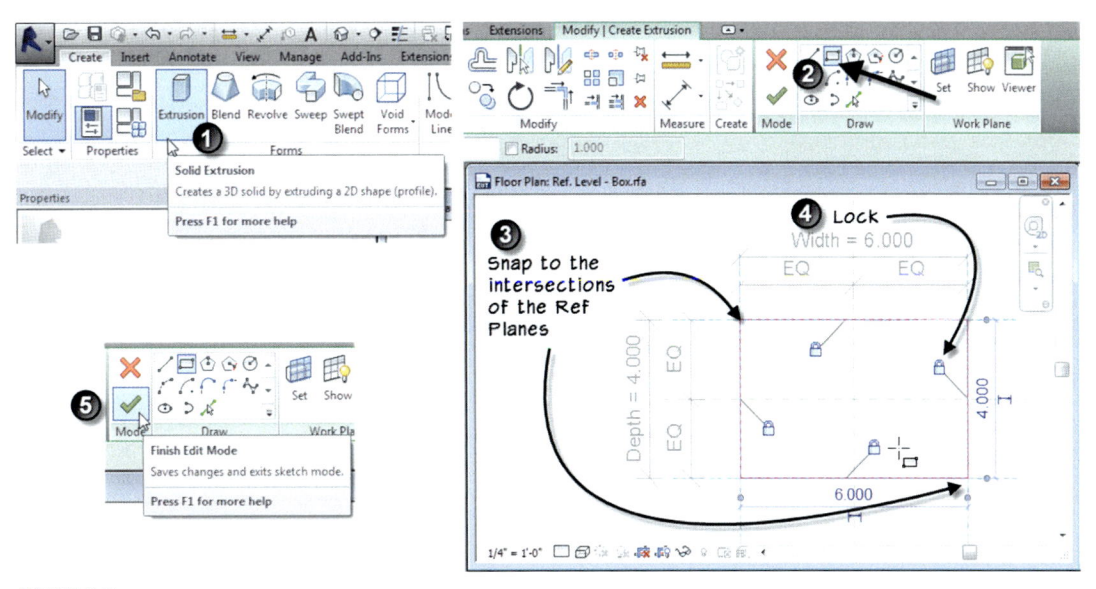

FIGURE 2.9

Draw a rectangular shaped extrusion

- Snap to the intersection of two of the reference planes for the first corner, and then snap to the opposite intersection for the other corner. Lock all four sides (items 3 and 4 in Figure 2.9).

- On the ribbon, click the big green checkmark button to finish (item 5 in Figure 2.9).

7. Zoom the 3D view to fit. You can do this quickly by clicking a corner of the ViewCube. Turn on Shading in the 3D view.

8. In an elevation view, select the box. Drag the triangle shape handle grip at the top and snap it to the reference plane. Lock it (see Figure 2.10).

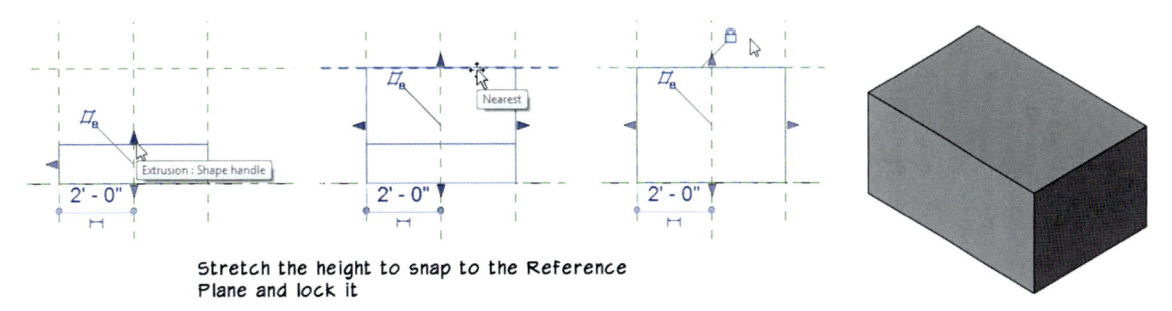

FIGURE 2.10

Lock the height of the extrusion to the Top reference plane

9. Flex the family to ensure that it is working properly.

10. Save the family.

LOAD INTO A PROJECT

The best way to flex any new Family is to load it into a project. This is where the Sandbox file we created earlier comes in.

> **CATCH UP!** You can open the file completed to this point named: *02_Box_B.rfa*.

If you did not create and minimize the *Sandbox.rvt* project file earlier, please refer to the steps above and do so now.

1. With your Box family active, on the ribbon, click the Load into Project button (see Figure 2.11).

• *Creating Classical Architecture with Modern Software* •

18 | Chapter 2

FIGURE 2.11

Load the family into the sandbox project to test

The sandbox file will maximize and the Modify | Place Component ribbon will be active.

- ⇨ Place it anywhere inside the building.
- ⇨ Make a couple copies and try moving or rotating them.

2. On the Properties palette, edit the Width, Depth and Height.

Notice each instance can have its own dimensions (this is because we used Instance parameters). Expand the *Families* branch of the Project Browser. Under Generic Models you will see the Family listed (see Figure 2.12).

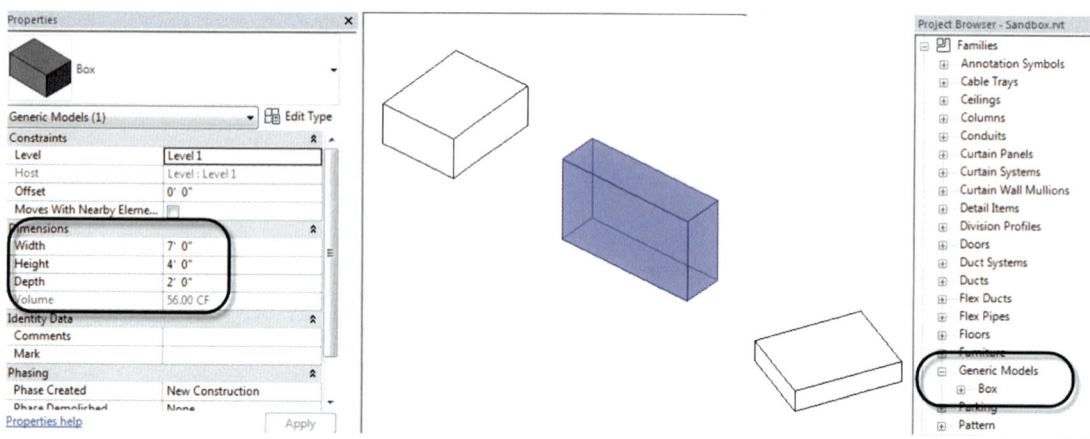

FIGURE 2.12

Load the family into the sandbox project to test

3. Save the sandbox project and then minimize it.

> TIP: When closing family files, choose **Close** from the Application menu instead of the close (X) icon in the upper corner of the view windows if you want to preserve the windows that were open the next time you reopen the file.

Congratulations. You have created your first parametric model Family. Granted it is just a simple box, but that simple box can become lots of useful things as we'll see moving forward.

CREATING "SEED" FAMILIES

There are many ways that we could start our explorations. No one approach is necessarily more correct than others in many cases. The best thing you can do is try a few techniques and then in each situation, choose the best technique(s) that suite the needs of the specific family that you are trying to create. Now that we have completed our simple box family, we can take it to the next level. There will be many common aspects that you will use in various families. For example, the basic parametric rectangular formwork of reference planes built in the previous exercise is useful in a variety of families. Other characteristics can be easily reused as well. If you create a few starting

• Renaissance Revit •

families with these characteristics already built-in, it can save you time and effort when you build each new family. We will call such starting families "seed" families.

TYPE AND INSTANCE BASED SEED FAMILIES

Let's start with the family we created above. Our basic *Box.rfa* family has the reference planes and basic parameters required. However, you may want to think about if the parameters should remain instance based or if it might be useful to have them as type based instead. This thought process changes if the Seed Family is shared, as well.

Make sure that you have the *Sandbox.rvt* and *Box.rfa* files open. If you closed, them, reopen them now.

1. In the *Sandbox.rvt* file, select one of the instances of the *Box* family.

Let's consider family types first. In the previous exercise, we only built the basics into the family. One of the things that we did not add to the family was any types. If you do not add a type, Revit will create a default type for you. The default type will have the same name as the family, which can be considered undesirable. In this exercise, we will name the default type (see Figure 2.13).

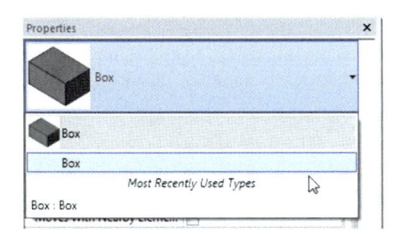

FIGURE 2.13
The default type name matches the family name

2. From the Switch Windows dropdown, switch to the *Box.rfa* family file. (If you closed it, select an instance onscreen and then click the Edit Family button).

3. On the Create tab click the Family Types button.

    ⇨ In the "Family Types" dialog, click the New button.

There are many strategies for naming. In families that are dominated by type based parameters, it often makes the most sense to name the type in a way that describes the values of the type parameters. For example in the out-of-the-box Single-Flush door family, types are named for the width and height such as 36" x 84" or 30" x 80". So we could name this new type 6 x 4 x 3. But the parameters here are instance parameters, so while we could name them this way, it is easy for the end user to change the sizes without renaming the type. Furthermore, these are seed families. This means that we will reuse them in a variety of ways and later will nest them into other families and drive the parameters with associated family parameters. Therefore I prefer a more generic name. I have begun using the name: FLEX. This is just a placeholder name that tells me that this is the default type that is used to flex the family. You can use a different name if you prefer. The specific name is not important. All that matters is that you name your default family type and that you choose a logical name that you use consistently.

⇨ In the "Name" dialog, type **Flex** and then click OK twice.

4. From the application menu choose **Save As > Family**.

    ⇨ Name the new file: **Family Seed (Instance Based)** and then click Save.

5. Load the family back into the sandbox and place an instance.

6. Click on the new instance and look at the Type Selector again (see Figure 2.14).

20 | Chapter 2

FIGURE 2.14

The new version has a type named Flex

We still have the original Box family here, but we now have our new one with its named type as well. Later we can purge the other out if desired. For now it can stay. Let's save another copy where we change the instance parameters to type parameters.

7. Minimize the Sandbox file to return to the Family Seed file.

8. Open the "Family Types" dialog.

9. Select the Width parameter, and on the right side, click the Modify button.

⇨ In the "Parameter Properties" dialog, on the right side, chose the Type radio button and then click OK.

⇨ Repeat for the other two parameters (see Figure 2.15).

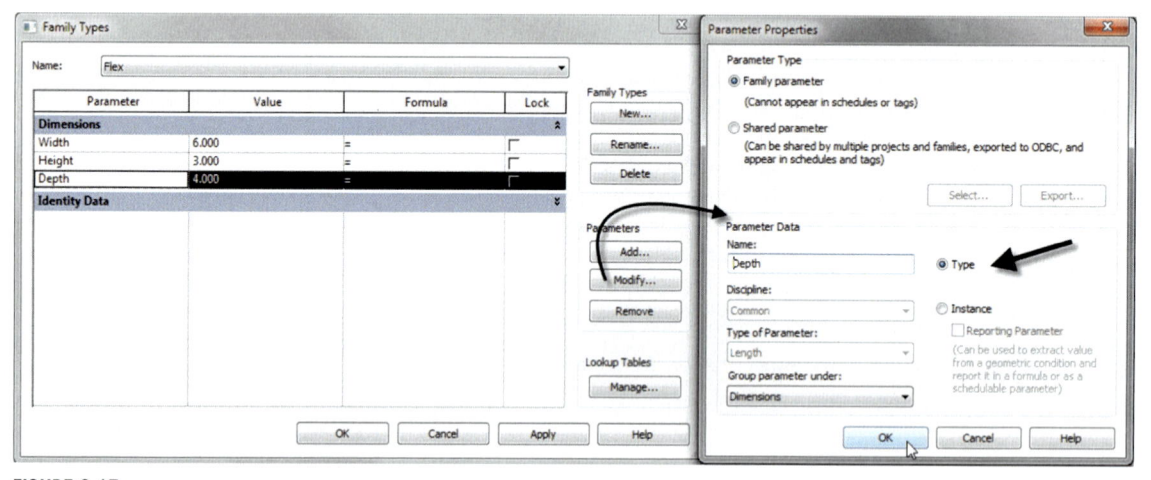

FIGURE 2.15

Change all three parameters to type based

At this point, we can optionally rename the Flex type and then create additional types of different sizes. However, since this is a seed family, we do not really know exactly how it will be utilized yet. Therefore, I am going to leave the type called Flex in the seed file. Later when we use this family to create new families, we can edit the types then.

10. Click OK to dismiss "Family Types".

11. Save the family as and name it: **Family Seed (Type Based)**.

12. Load it into the sandbox and place an instance.

When you select this one and look at the Type Selector, it will appear much like the other with its only type being named: Flex. However, this time to see the Width, Height and Depth parameters, you have to click the Edit Type button.

13. Save the sandbox.

• Renaissance Revit •

...have been provided completed to this point named: ...ily Seed (Instance Based)_A.rfa and 02_Family Seed (Type Based)_A.rfa.

CREATE CUSTOM FAMILY TEMPLATE FILES

So we now have two seed families. When we want to create a new family from them, we can do is in two ways. The easiest thing to do is to open the seed family RFA file and then Save As to a new name. The only potential down side here is that we might forget to save as and then accidentally save over our seed family. The other option is to create a custom family template file. This can be done just by renaming our seed family with the RFT extension.

To do this, just open Windows Explorer. In Explorer, make sure that files extensions are turned on. Browse to the folder that contains your seed families and then rename the files. Remove the RFA extension and replace it with RFT. That's it. Now you can open the Application menu and choose **New > Family**. Browse to the folder that contains your new templates and choose one. A new family will be created from the template that starts with the seed family! You will get a new family with a generic name like "Family 1".

If you decide to make the custom RFT files, make sure you delete the box geometry first. Once you rename the file as an RFT file, Revit will no longer let you delete the box geometry. So unless you *always* want the box, delete it before renaming.

> TIP: To make it even easier to use the seed families, consider moving them to the default family template folder. To locate this folder, from the Application menu, choose Options. Then click the File Locations tab. There you can find the Default path for family template files.

FACE-BASED OR FREE-STANDING

I alluded to the importance of family templates above. Family templates establish several critical characteristics of your new family file. They establish its category, they determine if the family will require a host when inserted and they often have other specialized behaviors as well. So choosing the template is an important first step in the planning phase. Categories can be changed after the family is created, but the sooner you establish the correct category the better. This is because many of the special behaviors for a family come from its category. The hosting behavior on the other hand cannot be changed. So this decision must be made carefully. Hosted families can be very powerful and useful, but free standing families can also be useful. So you really need to think about how the family will be used and remember that this feature cannot be changed later. So take a little extra time in the beginning to think through all the desired behaviors and use cases. I one day hope to do a full inventory of all family templates, but time and space do not allow for it at this time. Consequently, I will consider just a few of the most common templates here (copies of these files are provided in the *Template/OTB* folder):

- *Generic Model.rft*
- *Generic Model wall based.rft*
- *Generic Model face based.rft*

Each of these is very similar. They use the Generic Model category and you can use them to model most anything. Naturally the major difference is that the face-based one will be hosted to a surface (or face) of another object in your model. The wall-based one will be similar, but the face *must* be the surface of a wall. No other object type will be allowed. The *Generic Model.rft* family is free-standing and requires no host. Using the face-based template and inserting a family on the faces of other geometry can be very useful, and unlike the more restrictive "wall-based",

22 | Chapter 2

"ceiling-based" and "roof-based" versions, face-based allows the object to be inserted on *any* kind ceiling, roof or even the faces of other component families. You can even insert it on the face determined by planes like grids and reference planes. The face hosting makes the family automatically orient itself to the face of on which you insert it, but by not requiring a certain kind of face, it is nearly as flexible as its free-standing brethren.

There is one more very useful feature of the *Generic Model face based.rft* template. This template includes a built-in parameter called: Default Elevation. When you insert a face based component, this Elevation parameter controls its height. By default, this is measured from the level of insertion to the origin point of the family. The default origin of the family is the intersection of the two center reference planes. However you can change this (see Figure 2.16).

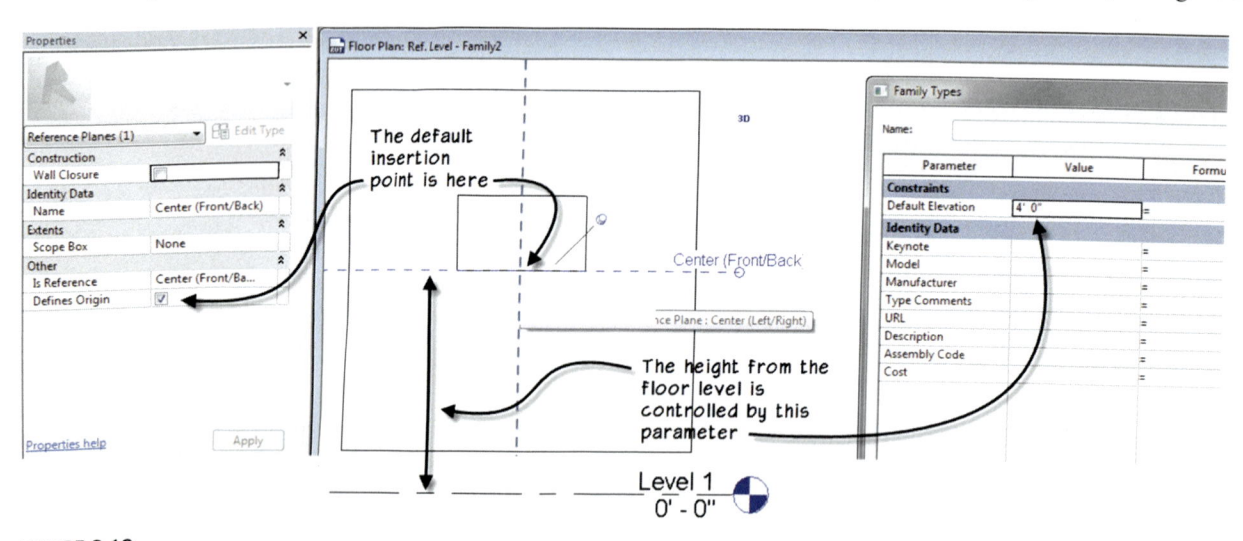

FIGURE 2.16

The Default Elevation parameter can control the height of insertion in a face-based family

If you plan your geometry with respect to this location and behavior, it can be very useful. For example if you plan to insert on a vertical face, plan it so that the Default Elevation locates the object to the top or bottom edge as appropriate. On sloped or horizontal surfaces, the measurement is still to the insertion point of the family, only now it is the "Z" direction within the family. In other words, the host surface in the family editor should be planned as the bottom of the object (see Figure 2.17).

Note also in the figure that unlike other hosted families, a face-based family can become "disassociated" from its host face without being deleted. Notice the top most insertion is above the wall plane. Its Default Elevation is still measured from the level, but the Host will show as <Not Associated>. Could all of this be achieved with a wall-based template instead? Mostly. But there are a few differences. The wall-based template does not have the Default Elevation parameter built right into the template. Instead it has a system parameter that is very similar called simply: Elevation. This parameter does not show up in the family editor but does appear when the family is inserted. It is measured from the level to the lowest geometry in the family. So it *can* move if you edit the geometry of the family! The other major difference is that the object must be inserted on a wall and while it can be moved off of the wall like the one in the figure, if the wall is deleted, the hosted element will also be deleted. It cannot become disassociated from its host. Both the wall-based and face-based can be good choices for an item that attaches to another surface, such an arch family. (We'll explore some arch families in a later chapter).

Understanding the Revit Family Editor | 23

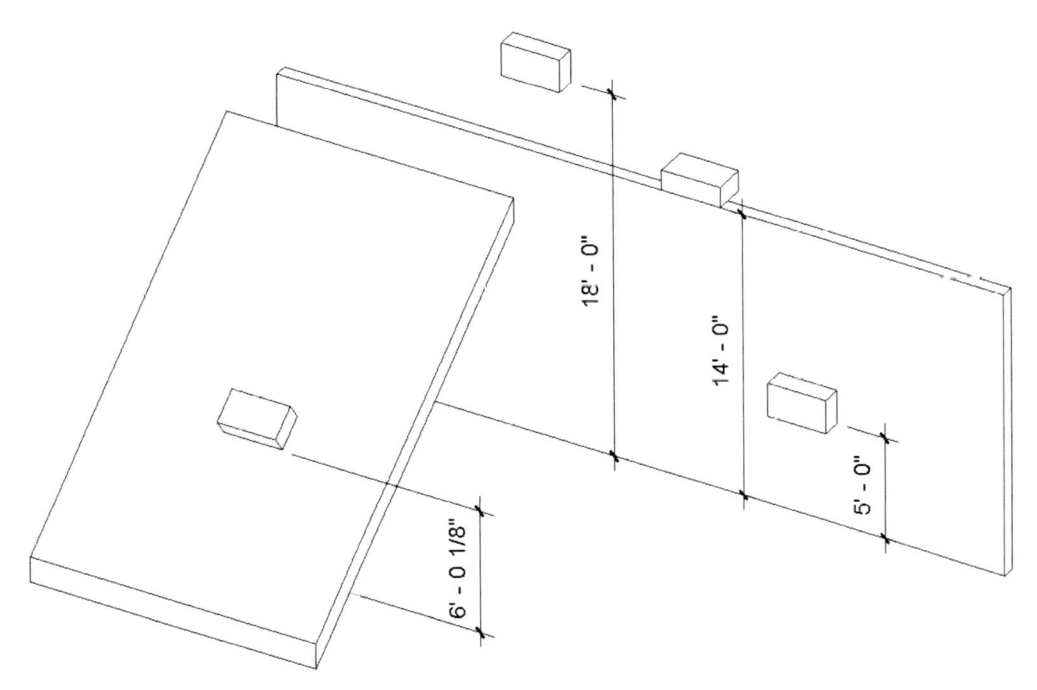

FIGURE 2.17

The Default Elevation parameter as measured in different insertion conditions

The seed families we built above are free standing families. They do not require a host. But the bottom line is that having a face based family seed will be a valuable addition to our collection of seed families. We cannot however, simply use save as like we did above. The face based seed must be built from scratch.

CREATE A FACE BASED FAMILY SEED

As we saw above, the basic steps to create a new family involve choosing an appropriate template, adding reference planes, dimensions and geometry. We also saw the value in creating some of these basic elements ahead of time and saving them in a "seed" family or customized family template file (RFT). In this lesson, we will create another family seed. This one will start from the *Generic Model face based.rft* template.

If Revit is not already running, launch it now.

1. From the Application Menu (big "R"), or on the Recent Files screen, choose **New > Family**.

   ⇨ Select the file named: *Generic Model face based.rft* and then click Open.

   A copy of this file is provided in the *Template/OTB* folder with the book's dataset files.

   ⇨ Type WT and then ZA.

2. Following the steps outlined above in the "Set the Units" topic, set the units to decimal feet at three decimal places.

3. Save the file as: **Family Seed (Face Based)**.

ADDING REFERENCE PLANES

We'll add the same basic reference planes and some parameters for width and length like we did in the other seed families above.

1. Starting in the upper left quadrant, about 1 unit away from the centerline, click the start point.

2. Draw it straight down vertically.

• *Creating Classical Architecture with Modern Software* •

24 | Chapter 2

3. Mirror the reference plane to the other side.
4. Mirror them both along a 45° angle to create four total.
5. Name each one: **Left**, **Right**, **Front** and **Back** (see Figure 2.18).

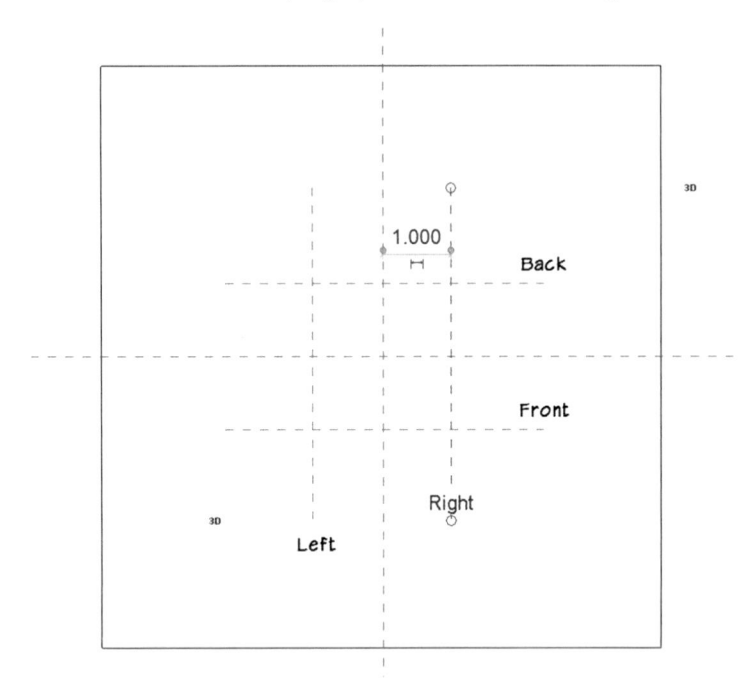

FIGURE 2.18
Create and name the reference planes

> **Note:** Even though we are using names like Left, Right, Front and Back, with face based families, these may not always be the orientations. If you place a face based family on a vertical surface for example, these might all be rotated 90°.

DIMENSION AND CONSTRAIN THE REFERENCE PLANES

Next we'll add the basic linear dimensions.

1. Using the Aligned Dimension tool (DI), click the first witness line on the reference plane Left, then Center (Left/Right) and then Right.
   ⇨ Click a point to place the dimension and then toggle ON the equality.
   ⇨ Create a second one with witness lines at left to right only.
2. Repeat both dimensions in the vertical direction as well (see Figure 2.19).

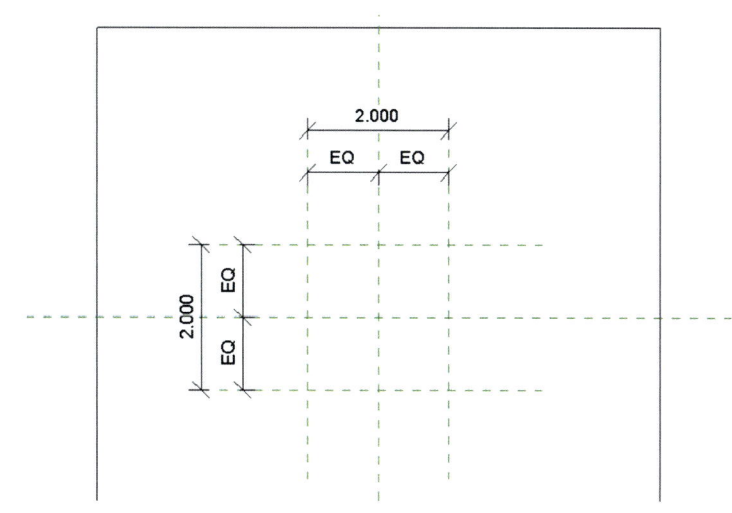

FIGURE 2.19
Add dimensions

3. Select the horizontal dimension and label it with a new Instance-based parameter named: **W**.

4. Select the horizontal dimension and label it with a new Instance-based parameter named: **D** (see Figure 2.20).

> **Note:** If you prefer, you can write out the names as "Width" and "Depth". The reason I did not do so here is because with a face based family, the orientation can vary based on the face on which you insert it. So I prefer to keep the names a little more generic on this seed family. Ultimately the names you choose are a matter of preference.

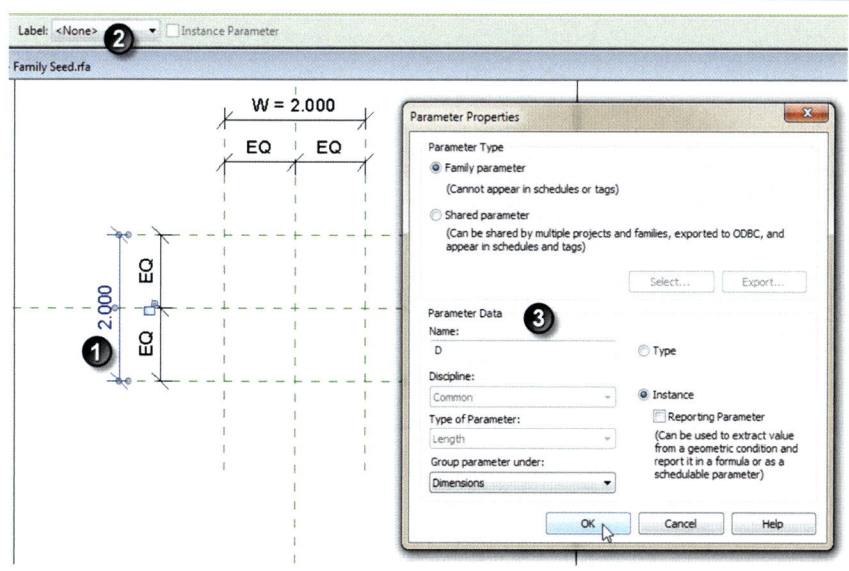

FIGURE 2.20
Create and assign parameters

5. On the Project Browser, open the *Front* elevation view.

⇨ Create a reference plane parallel to the Ref Level. Name it **Top**.

⇨ Add a dimension, label it with a new parameter called **H**.

If you like you can add a simple extrusion locked to the reference planes and then flex again. However, including the geometry is not necessary for our seed family.

6. Open the "Family Types" dialog. Flex it to test it out.

• *Creating Classical Architecture with Modern Software* •

Stay in "Family Types" and add a type.

7. Beneath "Family Types," click the New button.
   ⇨ Name the new type: **Flex** and then click OK twice.
8. Save the file when everything is working correctly.

If you added some solid geometry, you can load it into the sandbox to test it out. You will be prompted to place it on a face, but on the ribbon, you can also change this to Work Plane to place it flat on the level or a reference plane if you wish. If you did not add any solid geometry, then testing in the sandbox will not yield any useful results. It's also a good idea to change the scale of the views in your seed templates. This will make the dimensions easier to read when things get close together.

> **Catch Up!** Files have been provided completed to this point named: *02_Family Seed (Face Based).rfa*

SOLID AND VOID FORM GEOMETRY TYPES

Geometry in families consists of solid and void forms. Solid forms represent the actual physical parts of the family and void forms are used to carve away portions of the solid forms. For example, you could create a solid form box, and then use a void form to cut a hole in it like a donut. Both solid and void forms come in five varieties. These include: Extrusion, Blend, Revolve, Sweep and Swept Blend (see Figure 2.21).

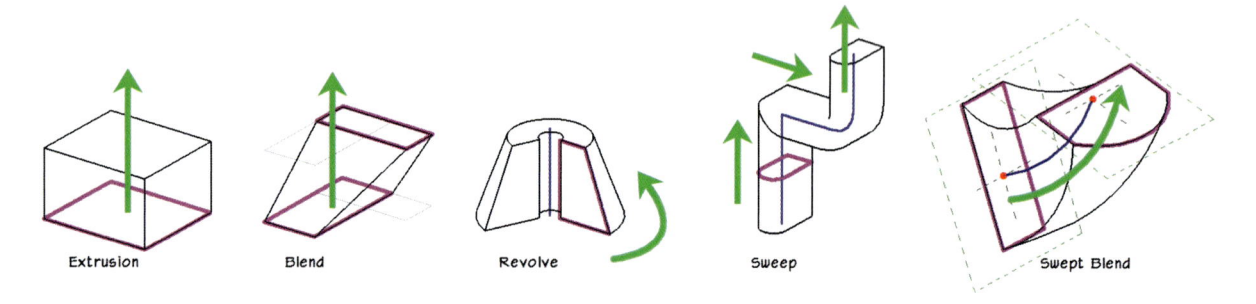

FIGURE 2.21
Five form types are available as solids or voids in the traditional family editor

An extrusion is a sketched shape pushed along a distance perpendicular to the sketch plane. A blend is similar accept that instead of a single shape, you have both a top and a bottom shape and the 3D form transforms (or blends) from one to the other along the perpendicular height of the form. A revolve spins a sketch shape around an axis. A revolve can be a full 360° or a partial arc. A sweep pushes a shape (sketch or loaded profile) along a path. The shape is perpendicular to the path. The path can be sketched in a 2D plane, or picked from a series of continuous edges on 3D elements. A swept blend combines features of both the blend and the sweep. The form morphs between two profiles or sketches as in a blend, but can follow a non-linear path. Unfortunately unlike the sweep, the swept blend path can only contain *one* segment. This means that complex forms require a spline path, or several consecutive swept blends. Bear in mind however that spline paths can affect performance.

CREATING COMPLEX FORMS

Since we have just the five shapes, you have to be clever about how you construct your 3D geometry. If you look at any object around you, you can start to imagine how it could be broken down into smaller parts. Your job is to figure out how to make each of those smaller parts from one of the five standard forms. Keep in mind that we also have voids. So sometimes it is easier to think "additive" and build up two or more solid forms. Sometimes it is easier to think "subtractive" and start with a solid and then carve away from it with one or more voids.

Let's consider a simple example. Suppose we needed to model a simple molding around perimeter of a board or slab. The board or slab part can be a simple extrusion built in much the same way that we constructed our seed families. To add the molding, we can apply a sweep. Depending on how we approach it, we could add the sweep as a second solid form, or we could carve the sweep away from the solid using a void form (see Figure 2.22).

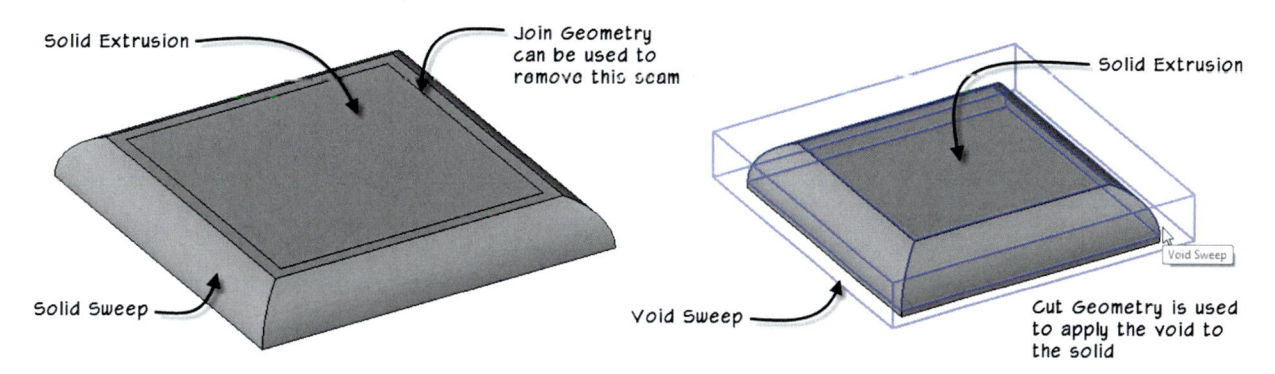

FIGURE 2.22

Your approach to form building can be either additive or subtractive

There are pros and cons to each approach, but the end results can end up largely similar. Solids can be joined together using the Join Geometry tool on the Modify tab. When you create a void, if it intersects a solid, Revit will automatically apply it to that solid(s). If they do not intersect, you can move it into position and then use the Cut Geometry tool to apply it selectively to one or more solids. For certain modeling tasks, using a void is the only way to create the desired form. We'll see a few examples below. In other cases, like the example shown here, you can achieve the desired form using only solids or both solids and voids. In such cases, I tend to favor solids and minimize the use of voids. But this is really just a preference based on simplicity and not any limitation of voids. There is some evidence to suggest that voids can impede performance, but overall I have not run into too many situations where concern over performance kept me from using a void if it was appropriate or desirable to do so to solve a particular modeling challenge. Voids can be a little trickier to control parametrically, but again, not to the extent where I would feel compelled to recommend against their use. So I am not discouraging the use of voids, rather make an effort to understand all of the pros and cons to each approach you can take to solve whatever modeling task you have at hand and you will be equipped to make the best choice for each situation.

WORKING WITH SOLIDS AND VOIDS

Let's look at a few simple solid and void modeling examples.

1. From the File menu choose **Open**.
2. In the *Chapter02* folder, select *Bracket (Start).rfa* and then click Open.

This Family is a wall mounted bracket. It makes use of each of the five 3D forms as solids and also has a few void extrusions as well. You can move your mouse around the screen and pre-highlight any of the forms to see a tool tip indicating the type of form used for each solid and void (see Figure 2.23).

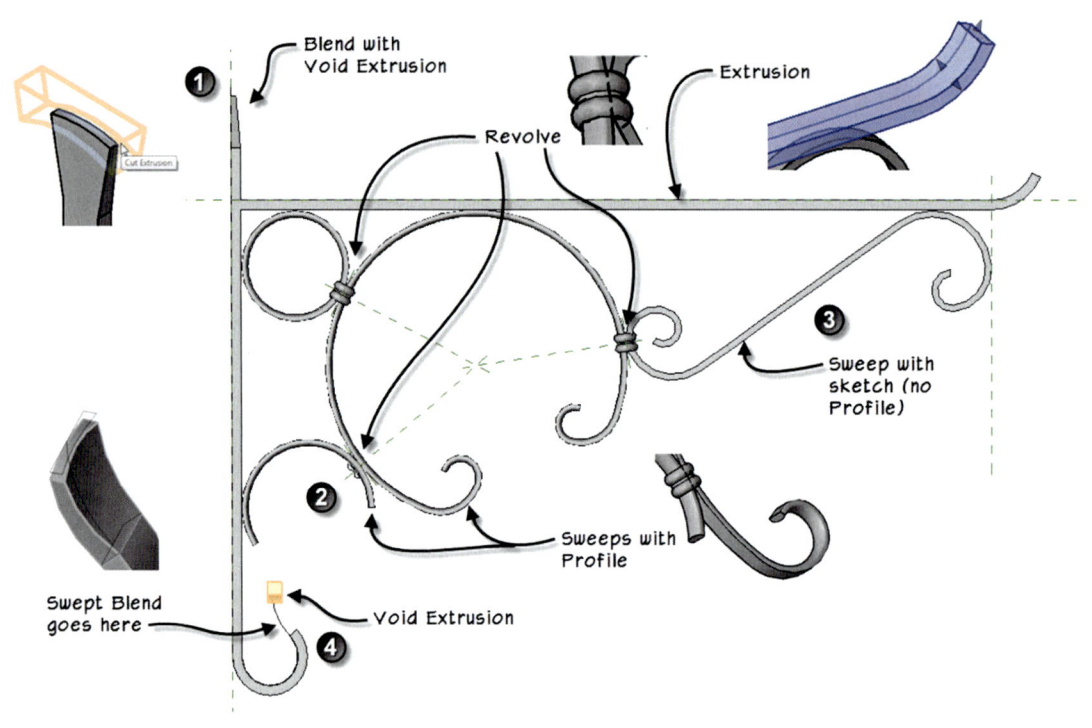

FIGURE 2.23

The Bracket Family uses each of the solid form shapes and a few voids

3. Zoom in on the location labeled as number 1 in the figure.

    There is a solid Blend form in this location and some Model Lines.

4. Select the solid Blend.

    ⇨ Take note of the settings in the Constraints grouping on the Properties palette (see the left side of Figure 2.24).

The Work Plane is the plane on which the top and base sketches are drawn. First End and Second End are offsets for each sketch measured from this Work Plane.

5. On the ribbon, click the Edit Base button.

    Take note of the sketch.

6. On the ribbon, click the Edit Top button (see the right side of Figure 2.24).

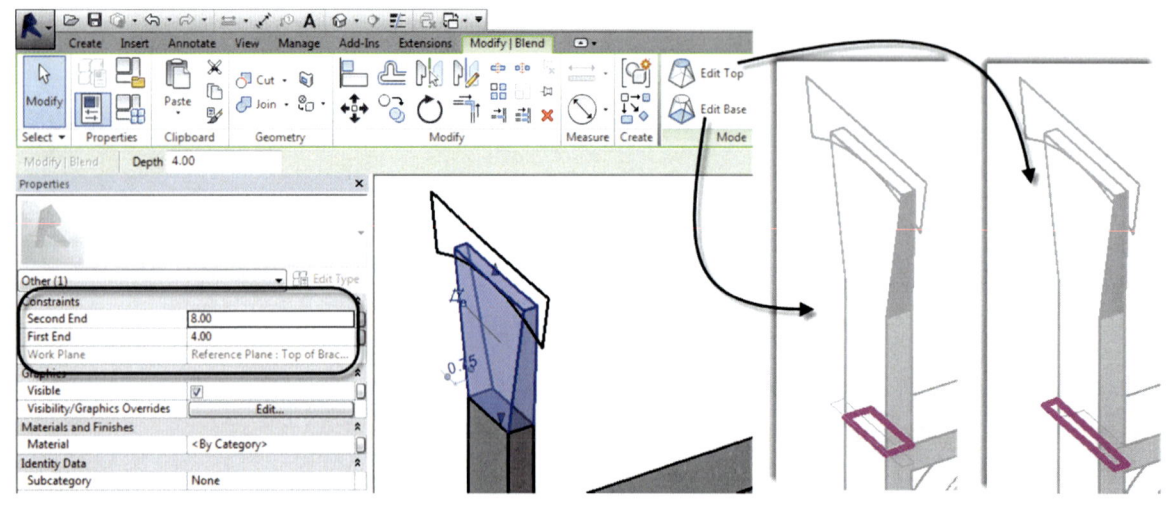

FIGURE 2.24

Edit the Blend form to see the sketches used to define its top and base

• Renaissance Revit •

The two sketches are just simple rectangles, but since they vary in size and proportion, the result is an interesting form that makes the top of the bracket look like it has been hammered flat at the end. Let's round off the corners by applying a void.

7. On the ribbon, click the Cancel Edit Mode button (big red "X"). In the warning dialog, click Yes to confirm.

When you discard a sketch, all edits in that mode are lost. So Revit asks to be sure.

CREATE A VOID FORM

To simplify our task, some model lines have been placed in the template. We'll use these to create a void.

1. On the Create tab, on the Work Plane panel, click the Set button.
   ⇨ From the Name list, choose **Reference Plane: Center (Front/Back)** and then click OK.
2. On the Create tab, on the Forms panel, click the Void Forms dropdown and choose **Void Extrusion**.
3. On the Draw panel, click the Pick Lines icon and then click on each of the Model Lines near the top of the blend (3 straight lines and one arc – see Figure 2.25).

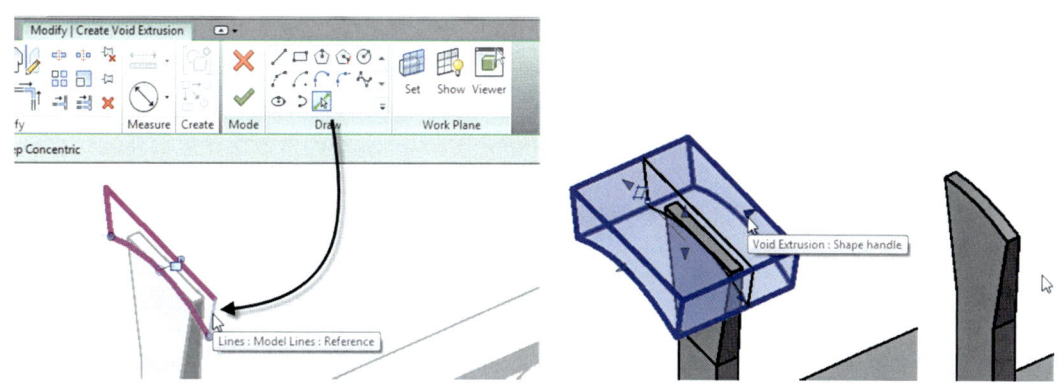

FIGURE 2.25
Use Pick Lines to create the sketch

4. Click the Finish Edit Mode button (green checkmark).
5. Use the grips to adjust the depth of the extrusion so that it intersects the blend.
6. Delete the model lines.

CREATE A REVOLVE FORM

We'll create a revolve solid form next. There are two complete ones already in the family. Feel free to start by editing them first to see how the work.

1. On the Project Browser, open the *Right* Elevation view.
   ⇨ Zoom in on the area labeled 2 in Figure 2.23 above.
   Some model lines have been provided here as well.
2. On the Create tab, on the Forms panel, click the Revolve button.
   ⇨ Again using Pick Lines, click on each of the model lines (3 lines, 3 arcs).
3. On the Modify I Create Revolve tab, click the Axis Line button.
   ⇨ Using the Pick Lines tool again, click the reference plane named Axis C. (It is parallel to the sketch).
4. Click the Finish Edit Mode button (see Figure 2.26).

• *Creating Classical Architecture with Modern Software* •

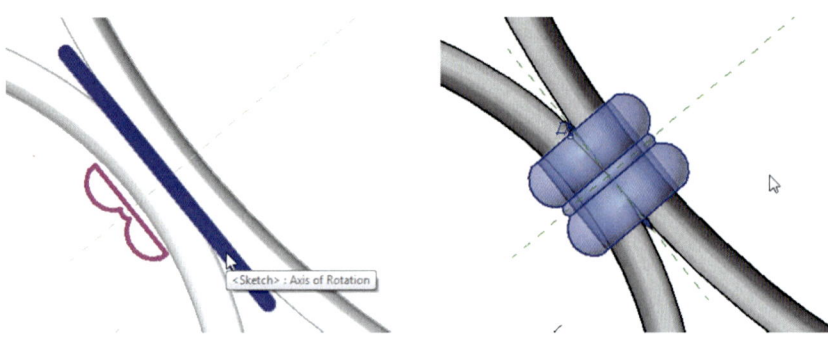

FIGURE 2.26

Create the Axis Line and then finish the Revolve

These first three forms: Extrusion, Blend and Revolve all use sketches to determine their shape. The last two forms: Sweep and Swept Blend can use sketches or Profile families to determine their form. In the next topic, we'll consider profile families.

PROFILE FAMILIES

Profile families contain simple two-dimensional shapes that when nested into other 3D families are used to produce more complex three-dimensional geometry. For example, when you create a sweep in a family or project, you can sketch the shape of the cross-section to be swept, or you can use a pre-defined profile instead. The use of profiles gives a few advantages:

- They are simple families drawn outside the project and can be saved as RFA files and used in any project or family.
- Like other families, a profile family can contain flexible parameters and locked constraints. This allows more power and control over the profile shape than a simple "one-off" sketched shape would allow.
- Like other families, a profile family can contain multiple types.
- Profile families behave like other nested families in most respects. Since they are self-contained, they will not distort in unexpected ways when the parent family flexes.

Several profile family templates are provided including: Mullion, Rail, Reveal and Stair Nosing. There is also a generic "Hosted" template and finally a simple *Profile.rft* template to use if none of the others is appropriate. So if you are creating a profile for use on stair treads, you would use the stair nosing template. Use the mullion template if creating a custom curtain wall mullion shape and so on. Otherwise, you would choose the basic profile template instead. You can even choose the basic one and then later change the usage to something more specific.

When you work in the Family Editor, there are two solid forms that can use a nested profile family rather than a sketched shape. These are the Sweep and the Swept Blend. Using a profile to build these forms affords many of the same benefits listed above. To use a profile in a model family that you are creating, first create a new family based on the *Profile.rft* template. Draw your shape (it must be a single closed loop of lines); add any parameters, constraints and types. Save the family and then load it into the model family that you are creating. Once the profile is loaded, you can use it to create solid forms.

Sweeps and Swept Blends can be used in place of Extrusions and Blends in almost all cases. You can even build a sweep that closely approximates a Revolve, making it theoretically possible to make almost any form using a nested profile family. Let's look at a quick example.

APPLY A PROFILE SHAPE TO AN EXISTING SWEEP

Continuing in our bracket family, there are a couple sweeps in the file. Most of them already use a profile family. One of them: the fancy "S" shaped form at the leading edge of the bracket (the area labeled 3 in Figure 2.23 above), currently uses a sketch for its profile cross-section instead. Let's substitute that with the predefined profile shape utilized by the other sweeps instead.

1. Select the "S" shaped sweep.
2. On the Modify I Sweep tab, click the Edit Sweep button.
3. On the Modify I Sweep tab, click the Select Profile button.

    Notice that on the dropdown next to the Select Profile button that the sweep currently shows: <By Sketch> for the profile (see Figure 2.27).

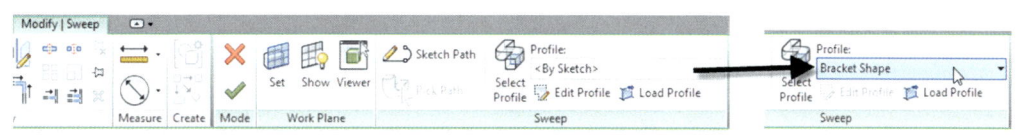

FIGURE 2.27
The Sweep currently uses a sketch instead of a Profile Family

   To use a profile instead of a sketch, simply choose the profile you wish from the dropdown menu. If the profile you need is not loaded into the project/family, click the Load Profile button first to load one.

4. Click on <By Sketch> and then choose **Bracket Shape**.
5. On the ribbon, click the Finish Edit Mode button.

Notice the sweep change. It now has a rounded shape like the other sweeps in this family.

CREATE A CUSTOM PROFILE SHAPE

For this next exercise, we'll create a new swept blend. Like Sweeps, Swept blends can also use profiles or sketches. In the previous exercise, the profile was already loaded and in use in the family. This made the process of applying it to the sweep easy. In many cases, you will have to first load a profile from the library (be sure to explore the collection of profile Families provided out-of-the-box before creating your own) or create one yourself. Creating a new profile Family is easy.

6. From the File menu choose **New > Family**.
7. Select the *Profile.rft* template and then click Open.

    A copy of this file is provided in the *Template/OTB* folder with the book's dataset files.

    Two Ref Planes appear on screen marking the insertion point. Draw your shape relative this intersection. For this exercise, we will create a very simple shape to illustrate the process.

8. On the Create tab, click the Line tool.
   - Click the first point on the Center (Left/Right) reference plane.
   - Move straight up along the reference plane and then type **0 3** and press ENTER. (That is zero SPACEBAR three).
   - Zoom in and move the line from its midpoint and snap it intersection of the two reference planes.
9. Draw two horizontal lines starting from endpoints of the vertical line.

• *Creating Classical Architecture with Modern Software* •

32 | Chapter 2

⇨ Click the first point snapped to the endpoint, move directly to the right, then type **0 .4** and press ENTER (That is zero SPACEBAR point four).

You can also simply draw a horizontal line, and then come back and adjust the length with the temporary dimensions.

10. Finish the shape with a Start-End-Radius arc.

11. Snap the start and end points to the ends of two horizontal lines.

12. For the radius, move the mouse to the left so that it curves in toward the vertical line. Type in the radius of **0 9** and then press ENTER (zero SPACEBAR nine) (see Figure 2.28).

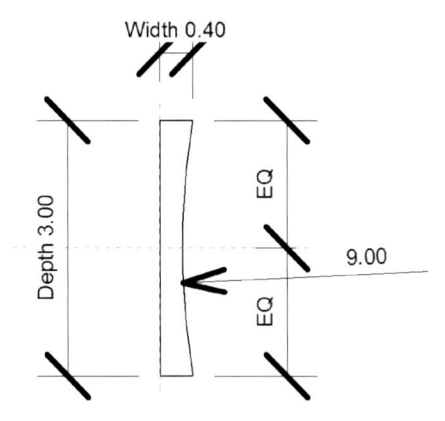

FIGURE 2.28
Draw a profile shape using Lines and Arcs (Dimensions and labels in the figure are for reference, you do not need to create them)

13. Save the Family as: **Bracket Finial Profile1** and then click the Load into Projects button.

This will load it into the *Bracket (Start).rfa* file.

> **CATCH UP!** Files have been provided completed to this point: *02_Bracket.rfa* and *02_Bracket Finial Profile1.rfa*.

CREATE A SWEPT BLEND USING PROFILES

Now that we have a custom profile, we will use it in conjunction with another that is already loaded in the bracket family to create the final solid form our bracket needs—a small finial at the bottom of the bracket wall support.

Continue in your *Bracket (Start).rfa* file or use the catch-up file.

1. Open the *Right* elevation view.

2. On the Create tab, on the Forms panel, click Swept Blend tool.

A swept blend requires two profiles and a single segment path (it can be straight, curved or even a spline) but it must be just one segment. The profiles can be sketched or use nested profile families as we are doing here. For this example, a model line is provided in the location required to make drawing the path easier. In your own work, you can choose either the Sketch Path or Pick Path buttons to create the path. Here, we will choose the Pick Path option.

3. On the Modify | Swept Blend tab, click the Pick Path button and then click the small arc that appears at the bottom of the bracket.

A sketch line will appear matching the shape of the provided arc. Two work planes will appear automatically at either end. These are where the two shapes will be drawn for the blend.

4. Click the Finish Edit Mode button (green checkmark).

5. On the Modify | Swept Blend tab, click the Select Profile 1 button.

⇨ From the Profile list next to this button, choose **Bracket Finial Profile 1**.

⇨ On the Modify I Swept Blend tab, click the Select Profile 2 button.

⇨ From the Profile list next to this button, choose **Bracket Finial Profile 2**.

6. On the Project Browser, beneath the *3D Views* branch, double-click to open the *View 1* 3D view.

7. On the Modify I Swept Blend tab, click the Finish Edit Mode button (green checkmark).

Study the model in the 3D view. A void extrusion has been included in the dataset that we can use to round off the top of the finial as a finishing touch. When you create a void form, Revit attempts to apply it automatically to any intersecting solid geometry. In this case however, since the void was created before the solid, we need to apply it manually.

8. On the Modify tab, click the Cut Geometry tool. Select the swept blend first, and then click the void (see Figure 2.29).

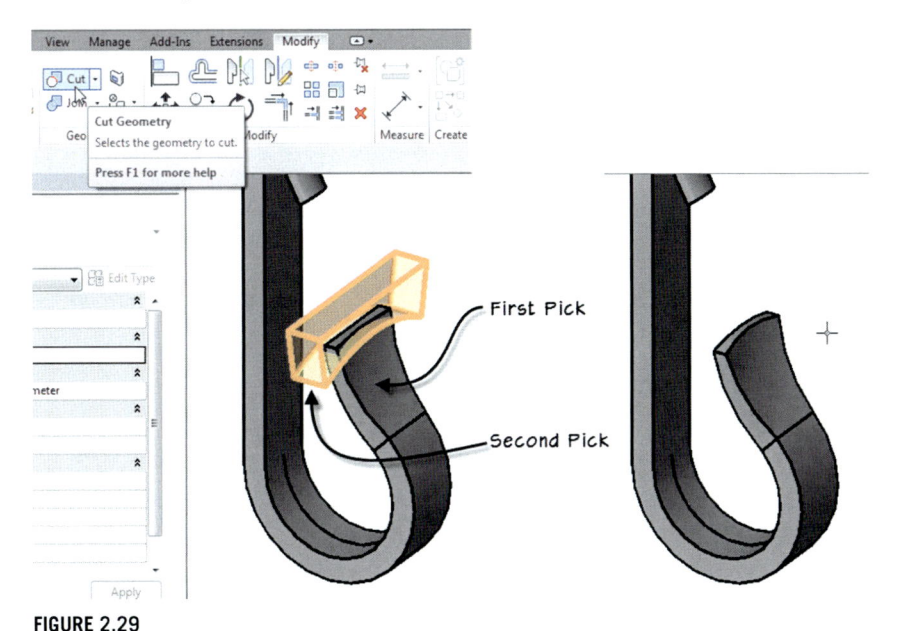

FIGURE 2.29
Cut the swept blend with provided void

The top of the swept blend should now appear curved and the void is invisible unless you hover your mouse over it. This completes the bracket Family.

9. Save the *Bracket (Start).rfa* file.

CATCH UP! The final file has been provided completed to this point: *02_Bracket (Finish).rfa*

The focus of this family was to give you a little practice with each of the five forms available in the traditional family editor. The bracket family is not parametric. This means that you cannot flex it to different sizes or configurations. Not all families need to flex, so this is a perfectly legitimate approach for many content items. However, many families do benefit from having flexibility built into them, so creating flexible or parametric families will be one of the main goals of the tutorials in the remainder of this book. Feel free to experiment with this or any of the other families we worked on in this chapter before continuing.

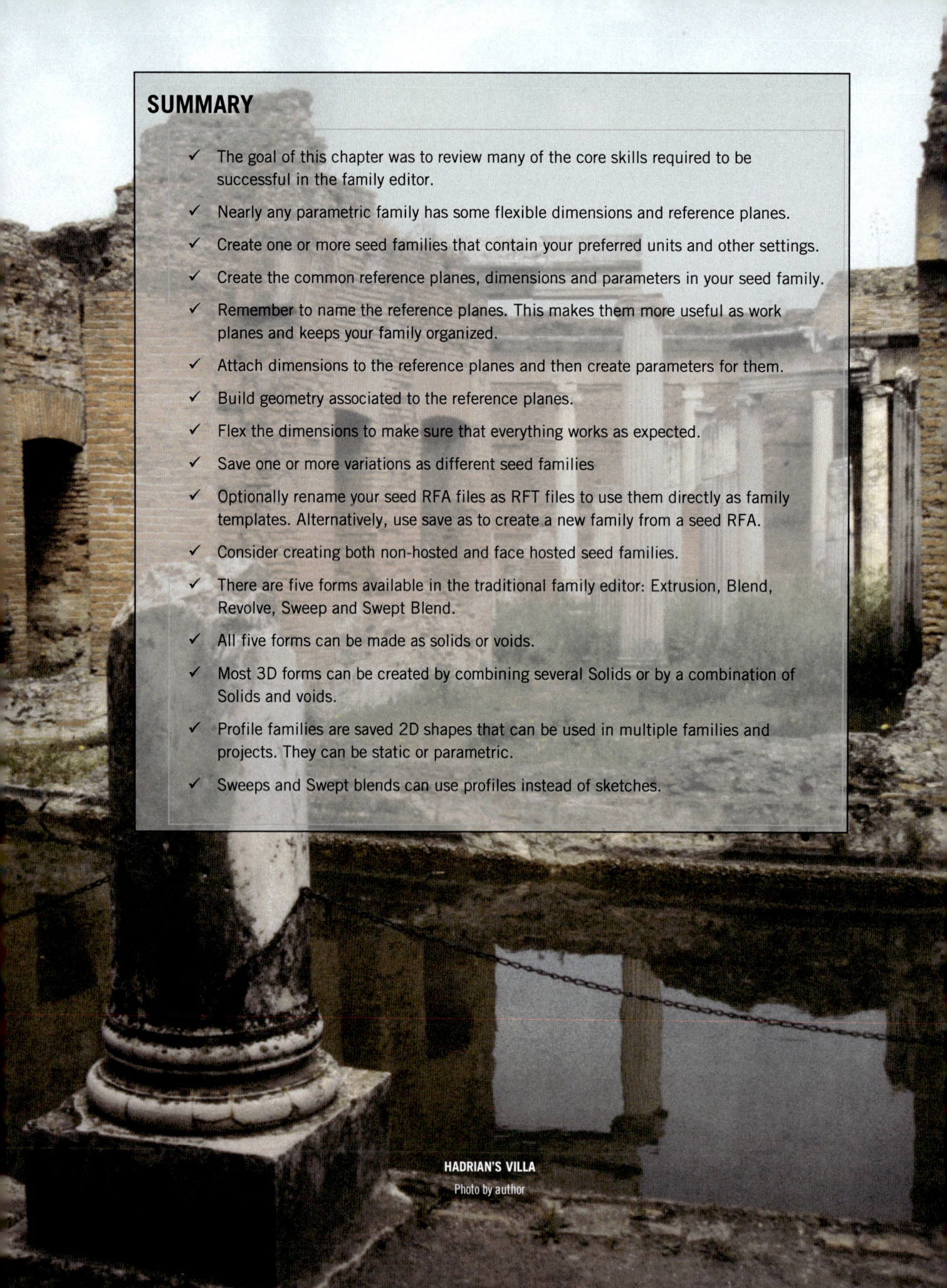

SUMMARY

- ✓ The goal of this chapter was to review many of the core skills required to be successful in the family editor.
- ✓ Nearly any parametric family has some flexible dimensions and reference planes.
- ✓ Create one or more seed families that contain your preferred units and other settings.
- ✓ Create the common reference planes, dimensions and parameters in your seed family.
- ✓ Remember to name the reference planes. This makes them more useful as work planes and keeps your family organized.
- ✓ Attach dimensions to the reference planes and then create parameters for them.
- ✓ Build geometry associated to the reference planes.
- ✓ Flex the dimensions to make sure that everything works as expected.
- ✓ Save one or more variations as different seed families
- ✓ Optionally rename your seed RFA files as RFT files to use them directly as family templates. Alternatively, use save as to create a new family from a seed RFA.
- ✓ Consider creating both non-hosted and face hosted seed families.
- ✓ There are five forms available in the traditional family editor: Extrusion, Blend, Revolve, Sweep and Swept Blend.
- ✓ All five forms can be made as solids or voids.
- ✓ Most 3D forms can be created by combining several Solids or by a combination of Solids and voids.
- ✓ Profile families are saved 2D shapes that can be used in multiple families and projects. They can be static or parametric.
- ✓ Sweeps and Swept blends can use profiles instead of sketches.

HADRIAN'S VILLA
Photo by author

Chapter 3
Scaling and Proportion

INTRODUCTION

Classical Architecture is all about scale and proportion. With our overview of basic Family Editor skills and features behind us, it is time to discuss the topics of scale and proportion since they have great relevance to the project at hand. When I set out to create my first classical column model over ten years ago, my goals were simple: create an accurate model faithful in its details, and be able to reuse it at any scale and size. Since I began the project in AutoCAD, the second part was easy; AutoCAD has a scale command. But when I moved the project over to Revit, I realized that scaling would become more of a challenge. Now you may be thinking, well Revit has a scale command too. This is true, but unlike AutoCAD, the scale command in Revit does not work on most elements like 3D geometry. I would have to find other ways to scale my models in Revit. There are a few methods that will do the job. In this chapter we'll take a look at some of the possibilities that I have explored.

OBJECTIVES

Revit does not allow you to simply scale 3D geometry. Scaling your models has to be accomplished deliberately: you have to build your scaling into the model. Topics in this chapter include:

- Understanding Scale and Proportion
- Using Parameters
- Using Formulas
- Other options

UNDERSTANDING SCALE AND PROPORTION

Classical architecture is defined by proportions that are all derived from the diameter of the column as measured from the base. Depending on the treatise that you reference, this Base Diameter might be divided into 30 parts or 60 parts. One of the ingenious innovations that Robert Chitham introduces in *The Classical Orders of Architecture* (Chitham 1985, 2005) is a decimal (rather than fractional) based proportion system. To derive his decimal equivalents, Chitham carefully compares the fractional proportions proposed by each of the masters (specifically: Vitruvius, Serlio, Vignola, Palladio, Scamozzi, Perrault and Gibbs) and creates a series of comparative orders. (Seeing each one side by side really illuminates the great variation that is possible in the orders). From his comparison, Chitham creates an idealized order based on a unique set of decimal proportions. I have adopted the proportions proposed by Chitham as my primary source for this book. They are used extensively in the examples that follow. (I have deviated in a few cases, and I will site my sources at those times).

Regardless of the exact system you choose to adopt for your own work, and despite the variation from one master treatise or historical work to the next, what all of the orders by any of the masters have in common is a tightly controlled set of proportions.

When setting out an order by hand, the draftsperson would be required to construct each part of the order carefully to achieve the desired proportions. It would not have been easy to make a slight adjustment to the dimensions without requiring a great deal of re-drafting. Such modifications in a computer are much simpler. With proportions built into the system, changing a dimension and scaling several elements is easy to achieve. This would seem to make computers the ideal tool for exploring classical architecture. (It is a shame they did not have them 100 or more years ago).

So before we get into the specific techniques, allow me to quickly define what I mean by scale and proportion. I did a quick Google search for Scale. There are many dictionary sites, Wikipedia and countless other references. Visiting: http://dictionary.reference.com/browse/scale I found 24 definitions for the word "Scale". Naturally as Architects, we are interested in a very particular type of scale. Consider this definition from the URL noted here:

> **Scale** (Noun): a series of marks laid down at determinate distances, as along a line, for purposes of measurement or computation: the scale of a thermometer.

And this one:

> **Scale** (Verb): to adjust in amount according to a fixed scale or proportion (often followed by down or up): to scale down wages.

Both of these are close to the meaning that we think of in an architectural context. Let's take a look at what the same site had to say about proportion. I have quoted a definition here or you can find the complete listing here: http://dictionary.reference.com/browse/proportion

> **Proportion** (Noun): comparative relation between things or magnitudes as to size, quantity, number, etc.; ratio.

Other definitions are listed as well, but the meanings are all similar. In an architectural context, looking at both definitions, the two terms are tied closely together. In fact, you can see the word proportion used in the definition of scale above. So how will we apply these concepts to our work in Revit? In Revit or most other computer graphics software, scale tends to be equal in all directions (at least by default). So if you scale a two-dimensional form, the amount it scales in the X direction is the same as the Y direction. If it is a three-dimensional object, the Z direction also scales the same amount. Technically, the amount you scale can be described as the proportion. If you scale X, Y and Z the same amount, it is said to be "fixed proportion" or simply: "proportional scaling." In Revit, the scale command is always fixed proportion. This means that there is a single scale factor property that is applied in all directions. Scaling occurs from a single point in space. If you put in a scale factor smaller than one, the object gets smaller (all points get closer to the fixed point), input a value greater than one, the object enlarges (all points move away from the fixed point).

However, as we will see in the next topic, proportional scaling of 3D forms in Revit is not always easy to achieve, but is in fact a very important aspect of classical architecture and the creation of classical Revit families.

THE REVIT SCALE COMMAND

Returning to the present day, and thinking specifically of Revit, let us remember that the scale command is not available for 3D geometry. All you need to do is read the tooltip of the scale command to learn the specific limitations (see Figure 3.1).

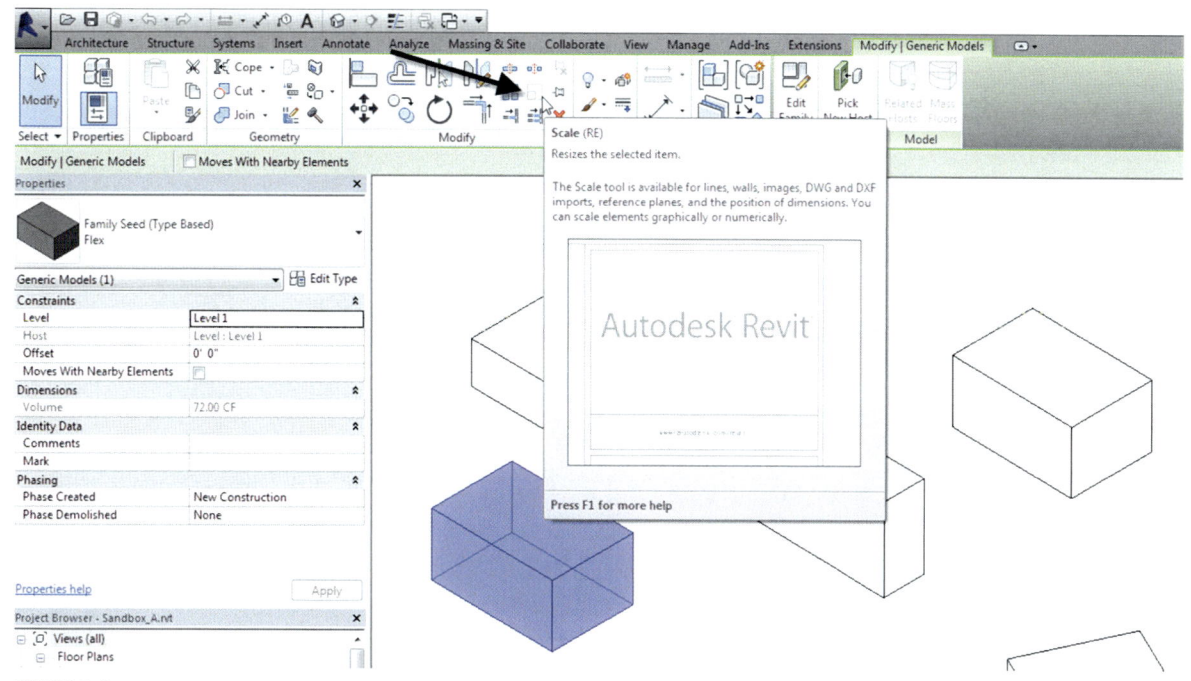

FIGURE 3.1

The Scale command only works on certain Revit elements

Ironically, as you can see in the figure, the scale command works for DWG imports! So you can carefully build your complete classical column capital in Revit, export it to a DWG file, (or build it directly in AutoCAD) and then import it back into your Revit project. Once imported, you can select the import instance and use the scale command on it. It almost doesn't seem fair (see Figure 3.2).

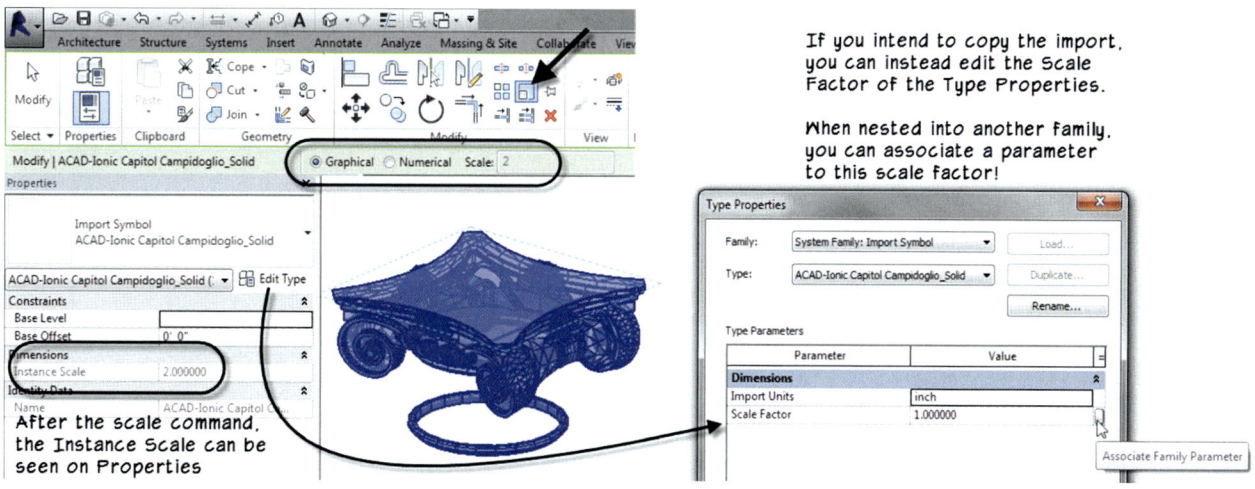

FIGURE 3.2

DWG imports can be scaled with the scale command or a Scale Factor parameter in their Type Properties

If you look at the left side of the figure, you can select the import instance and its current Instance Scale will show on the Properties palette. This cannot be changed directly on Properties. But you can now access the scale command. It will no longer be grayed out. Simply scale the element and the new Instance Scale will be reflected on the Properties palette when you are done.

Another way to scale an import is to edit its Type Properties. There you will see a Scale Factor property. If you nest the DWG into a family, you can even associate this scale factor to a family parameter! Definitely not fair.

• *Creating Classical Architecture with Modern Software* •

Well, this is all very interesting, but I assume that you did not buy a book on creating classical architecture in Revit only to be told that we have to export the geometry to AutoCAD, so as interesting as this technique is, it feels way too much like cheating to me. Besides, the DWG format imports with lots of tessellation lines (all those triangles) and generally hampers performance. So this will not be our approach.

PROPORTIONAL PARAMETERS

Most of the out-of-the-box Revit families do not use proportional scaling. Consider a typical door or piece of furniture. Most objects like this have a Width, Height and Depth or Thickness parameter. However, you are free to flex any one of these parameters completely independently of the others. For example, you may have a door family with several types whose Width varies, but the Height of all them remains a standard value. In most cases, this behavior matches the need of the door object which reflects the standard sizes that are typically available for purchase. But what if you always wanted the Height of the door to be twice as tall as the Width? Or maybe you want to the shape of the door to always make a golden rectangle. You could pull out your calculator, do the math to determine correct values of Height and Width, or much easier, you could build the math into the family.

To build the math into the family, we edit the family and in "Family Types" we can add a formula to one or more of the parameters to establish the desired relationship. How about a simple example?

ADDING FORMULAS TO PARAMETERS

For this example, we will open a simple door family and create a relationship between its Width and Height.

1. From the *Chapter03* folder, open the family file named: *03_Single-Flush (Formulas).rfa*.

This family is a copy of the out-of-the-box Single-Flush door family. However, for this example, all of the family types have been deleted. A single type named: Flex is included (see the "Type and Instance Based Seed Families" topic in Chapter 2 for discussion on this choice of name). The units have also been changed to decimal feet as we did in the "Set the Units" topic in Chapter 2. As noted in that topic, units are not critical to the discussion and you can work in any units you prefer.

2. Open the "Family Types" dialog.

3. In the Formula column next to the Height parameter, type: **Width * 2**.

> **Important:** Formulas are case-sensitive. You must type parameter names exactly when using them in formulas. Check your spelling carefully.

4. Now edit either the Height or Width parameter and then click Apply (see Figure 3.3).

FIGURE 3.3

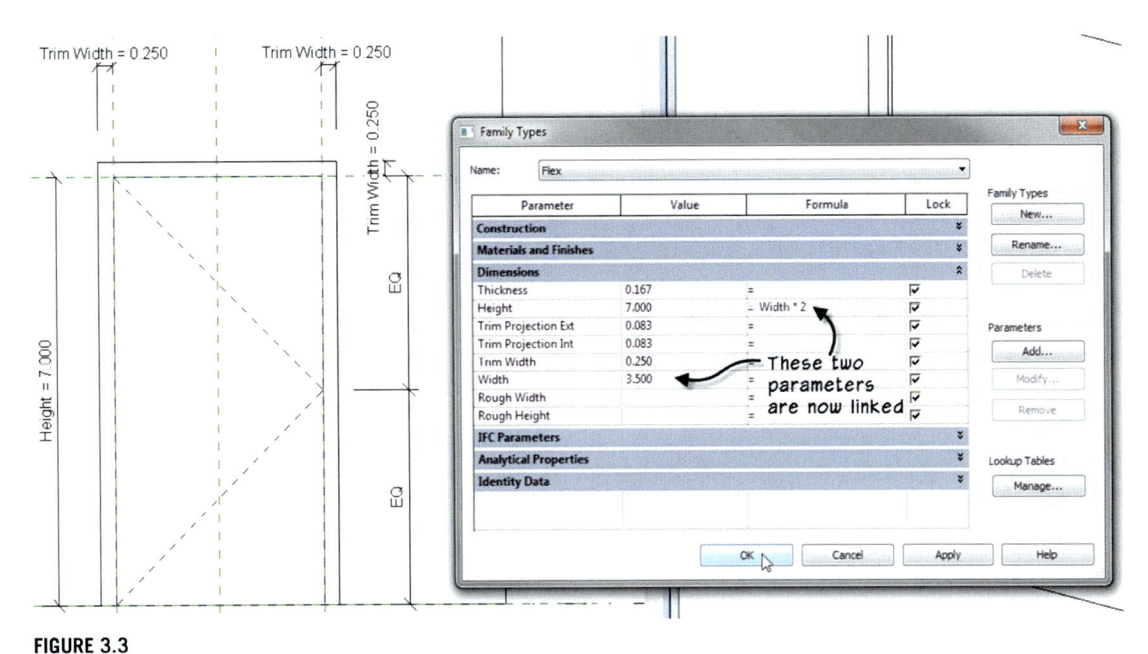

Add a formula to the Height parameter

Notice that you can change either Height or Width and the other will change accordingly. This is true for any arithmetic formula. To do addition, use the plus (+) sign. Use the minus (-) sign for subtraction. For multiplication use and asterisk (*) and for division use a slash (/).Keeping this in mind, do not use any of these characters in the names of the Parameters, as Revit will get confused when you try typing a formula.

To achieve the same result, we could have typed Height / 2 in the Width formula field. (Just be sure to remove the other formula first. If you want to shape the door to the golden ration, type: **Width * 1.618** in the formula field for Height. Click apply to see the result.

> **Note:** There is a nice website that lets you experiment interactively with the golden ratio. You can visit it at: http://www.mathsisfun.com/numbers/golden-ratio.html. Use the interactive tool on the site to explore the golden ratio.

5. When you are done experimenting, you can close the family. It is not necessary to save it.

The golden ratio may not be the most practical for door families, but the concept of using a formula and a ratio is the important aspect to grasp here. This is really the cornerstone of many of the tutorials that follow.

BASE DIAMETER PARAMETER

We have now seen how we can easily create formulas that using simple arithmetic will tie together two or more parameters. Let's take this concept a little further. Remember that the proportions of the moldings and subcomponents of a classical order form a very intricate set of proportions derived from the diameter of a column as measured from its base. Therefore, in creating our collection of parametric classical Revit families we will want to establish the Base Diameter as a parameter. This single parameter can then be used in the formulas of all of the other parameters giving us a single parameter that drives the scale and proportion of the entire order! (One parameter to rule them all…)

The best place to do this is to add the Base Diameter parameter to our seed families created in the previous chapter.

40 | Chapter 3

> **Note:** You can work in your own versions of the seed families created in the previous chapter if you prefer. Or you can open the copies noted here. Remember, if you previously renamed your versions to the RFT extension in Windows Explorer, you will need to rename them back to RFA, edit them, and then once you are finished, you can rename them back to RFT file again. Revit will not open RFT files directly.

1. From the *Chapter03* folder, open the family file named: *03_Family Seed (Type Based)_Start.rfa*.
2. Open the "Family Types" dialog.
3. Beneath "Parameters" on the right, click the Add button.

⇨ Verify that you are creating a Length parameter, make it Type and name it: **Base Diameter** (see Figure 3.4).

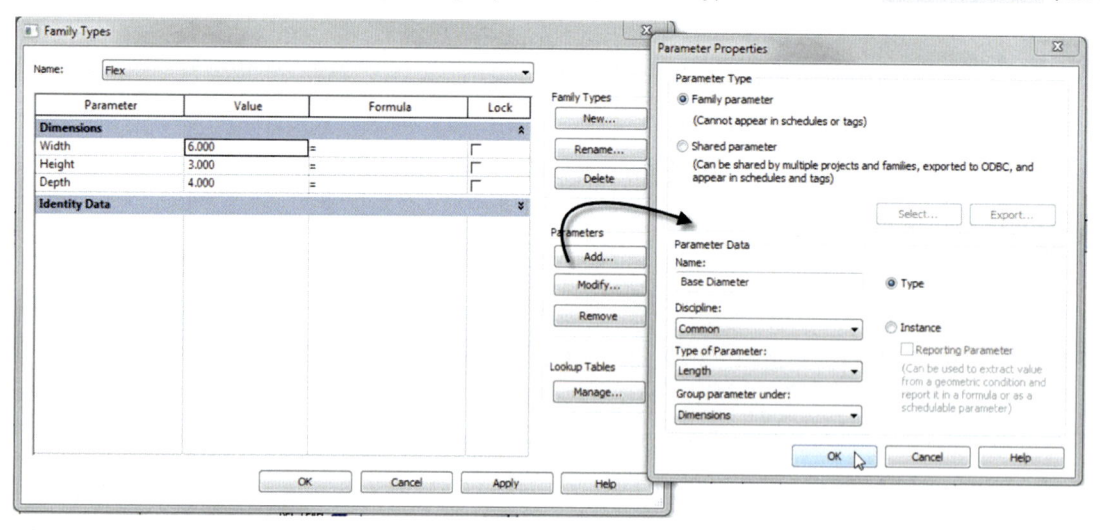

FIGURE 3.4

Create a Base Diameter parameter

4. Click OK and then in the Value field, set the Base Diameter to **1.000**.

Base Diameter will quite literally represent the size of our column's diameter measured at the bottom or base. In this case we have set the default to 1 unit. This family seed uses decimal feet as its units, so this is essentially 300mm. If you prefer to work in metric, you can make the appropriate adjustment to the units.

GROUPING PARAMETERS

By default when you create a new Length parameter Revit groups it under Dimensions. This is fine if you like it that way. The grouping is really just for organization and has no bearing on how the family behaves. However, I prefer to vary these groupings based on how I intend to use the various parameters. We cannot make our own custom groupings, but you can decide from the several available groupings where you want to store each of your parameters.

I like to put parameters that I intend to have my end users modify in the Dimensions grouping. For parameters that control the shape and form of the family but that my user will not directly input the values, I tend to put them under Constraints, Construction or General. I have other conventions that I follow as well, like the standard best practice of putting parameters I do not want edited in the Other grouping and using Identity Data for schedule properties, etc.

As I noted, changing the groupings is just a matter of preference, but can make families easier to use if you follow a strategy consistently. So before resaving our seed families, I would like to change the grouping of a few of our parameters. Let's move Width, Depth and Height to Constraints.

• Renaissance Revit •

1. If you closed "Family Types" reopen it now.
2. Select the Width parameter and on the right beneath "Parameters" click the Modify button.
   ⇨ From the "Group parameter under" list, choose **Constraints** and then click OK.
   ⇨ Repeat for Height and Depth (see Figure 3.5).

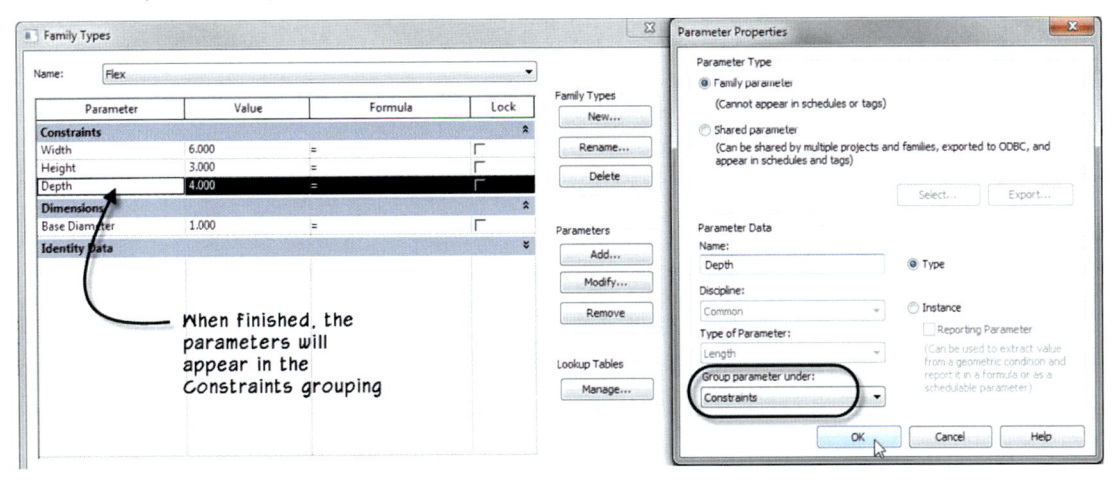

FIGURE 3.5

Move several parameters to the Constraints grouping

Let's now resave our seed family

3. From the Application menu, choose **Save As > Family**.
   ⇨ For the new name input: **Family Seed (Type Based)** and then click Save.
   ⇨ From the Application menu, choose **Close**.

> **CATCH UP!** Files have been provided completed to this point. They are in a separate folder in the dataset named: *Seed Families*. The files in that folder are named:
> *Family Seed (Instance Based).rfa* and
> *Family Seed (Type Based).rfa* and
> *Family Seed (Face Based).rfa*
>
> There are also RFT versions provided:
> *Family Seed (Instance Based).rft* and
> *Family Seed (Type Based).rft* and
> *Family Seed (Face Based).rft*.

CREATING A SIMPLE COLUMN

Let's focus for now just on the overall form and proportions. In the next few exercises we will create a very rough schematic form for a column. We will break it into three pieces: base, shaft and capital. The base of all five Roman orders has the same basic overall proportions: the width and depth are equal to each other and are 1.340 times the size of the Base Diameter. The height of the base for all five orders is half the size of the Base Diameter. For this exercise we will therefore create a box whose width and depth are 1.340 and whose height is 0.500.

Since the Width and Depth are equal, you could set one equal to the other by simply typing Width in the formula field for Depth or vice-versa. However, we would still need to tie these back to the Base Diameter. So instead we will input the same formula for both Width and Depth. The end result will be the same, but I feel tying everything back to Base Diameter is easier and straighter forward.

CREATE A BASE FAMILY

We'll build the base first.

1. From the *Chapter03* folder, open the family file named: *03_Family Seed (Type Based)_Start.rfa*.

This is the file you created above. If you prefer, you can use the catch-up file instead. As indicated in the previous catch-up box, this file is located in the *Seed Families* folder named: *Family Seed (Type Based).rfa*.

2. On the Create tab, on the Properties panel, click the Family Types button.
3. In the "Family Types" dialog, in the Formula field next to Width, type: **Base Diameter * 1.340**.

⇨ Type this same formula in the Depth field.

> TIP: You can also select the formula, press CTRL + C to copy it to your clipboard, then click in the next formula and press CTRL + V to paste it. Edit after pasting if required.

⇨ In the Formula field next to Height, type: **Base Diameter * 0.500**.

⇨ Click the Apply button (see Figure 3.6).

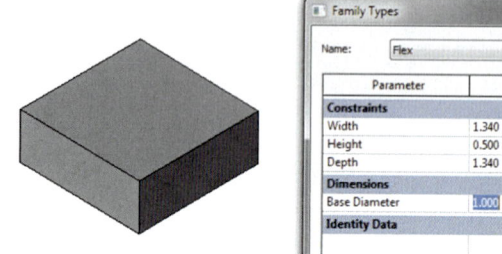

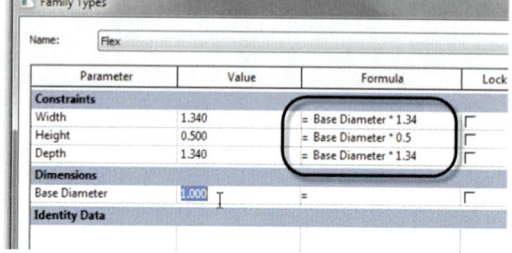

FIGURE 3.6
Input formulas to tie all the dimensional parameters to the Base Diameter

To flex the family, you now simply try a different value for the Base Diameter.

4. For the value of Base Diameter, try a few different values like **1.500**, **2.000** and **0.750**. Apply after each.

⇨ Return the value to **1.000** when finished flexing.

5. Click OK to dismiss "Family Types."
6. From the Application menu, choose **Save As > Family**.

⇨ For the new name input: **Base (Schematic)** and then click Save.

CATCH UP! The file has been provided completed to this point: *03_Base (Schematic).rfa*.

CREATE A CAPITAL FAMILY

Let's move to the capital and shaft next. We will simply save the file as and modify the formulas to achieve the desired proportions. While the bases of each of the orders use essentially the same proportions, there are variations in the proportions among each of the orders for the capital and shaft. So let's use the proportions for the Tuscan order for the rest of this exercise. The height is the same as the base: half the Base Diameter. The width and depth are Base Diameter times 1.250. The other variation that we want to make for the capital is to measure the height down from the Ref Level rather than up.

1. Start with your previously saved family: *Base (Schematic)*.

If you prefer, open the catch-up file: *03_Base (Schematic).rfa*.

2. From the Application menu, choose **Save As > Family**.
3. For the new name input: **Capital (Schematic)** and then click Save.
4. Open the *Front* elevation view.
5. Select the Top reference plane.
   - On the Modify | Reference Planes tab, click the Move tool (or type MV).
   - Click anywhere for the base point, move the mouse straight down (90°), type **1.000** and then press ENTER.

The reference plane should move below the Ref Level and still have the Height labeled dimension attached. If the dimension becomes invalid and is deleted, you can add it again and then label it with the Height parameter (see Figure 3.7).

TIP: Alternatively, you can select the reference plane, then click in the dimension, type **-0.5** and press ENTER.

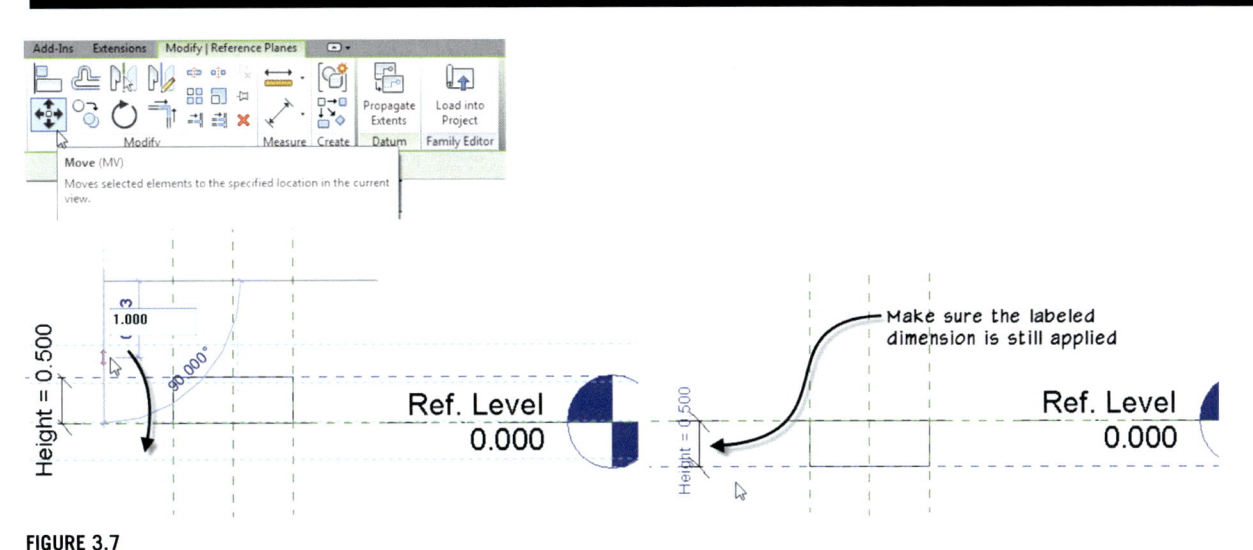

FIGURE 3.7
Move the Top reference plane down below the level

6. Keep the reference plane selected. On the Properties palette, change the name to: **Capital Bottom**.
7. Open the "Family Types" dialog.
   - Change the Formula next to Width and Depth, to: **Base Diameter * 1.250** and then click Apply.
8. Click OK to dismiss the dialog, and then save the family.
   - From the Application menu, choose **Close**.

CATCH UP! The file has been provided completed to this point: *03_Capital (Schematic).rfa*.

CREATE A SHAFT FAMILY

Now let's repeat the process to make the shaft. In keeping with the idea of building a very rough schematic, we will keep the form of the shaft simple. We could simply flex the box to make it the correct height. We could also change the shape to a circle instead of a box. Shafts on classical columns diminish in thickness as they move up. This is referred to as diminution or entasis. The two terms are not actually the same. Entasis bulges out slightly about one third the way up and then tapers back to become smaller at the top. This means that the widest point of the column is actually above the base. With diminution the diameter is constant for about the first third and then slowly tapers

44 | Chapter 3

to a narrower diameter at the top. Entasis can be seen in ancient Greek buildings like the Parthenon. Diminution is more common in the Roman and Renaissance traditions. Later in this book we will discuss techniques to model the diminution very accurately. For this simple schematic example, we will do a very simple taper. This can be achieved by replacing the extrusion with a blend.

1. Start with your previously saved family: *Base (Schematic)*.

    If you prefer, open the catch-up file: *03_Shaft (Schematic).rfa*.

2. From the Application menu, choose **Save As > Family**.

3. For the new name input: **Shaft (Schematic)** and then click Save.

4. Open the *Ref. Level* plan view.

5. Create four new reference planes forming an inner rectangular shape (see Figure 3.8).

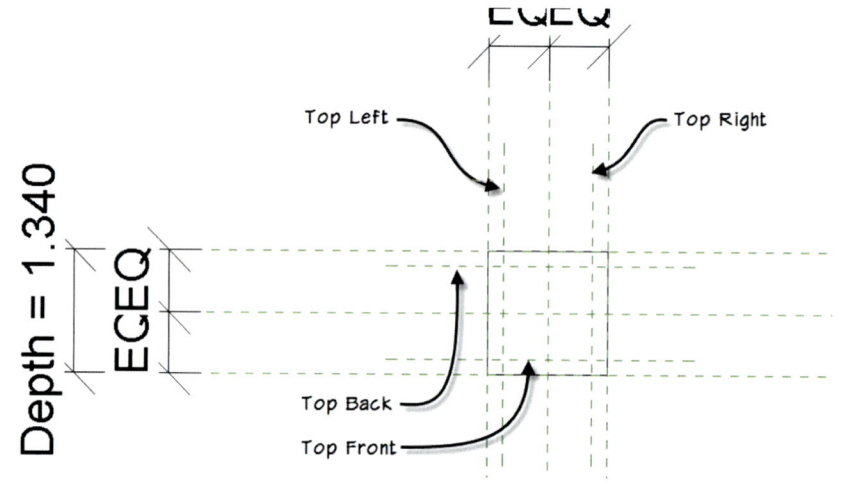

FIGURE 3.8

Create four new reference planes inside the originals

⇨ Name the four reference planes as indicated in the figure.

6. Add dimensions; an equality and overall in each direction.

7. Select both of the overall dimensions and label them with a new parameter (see Figure 3.9).

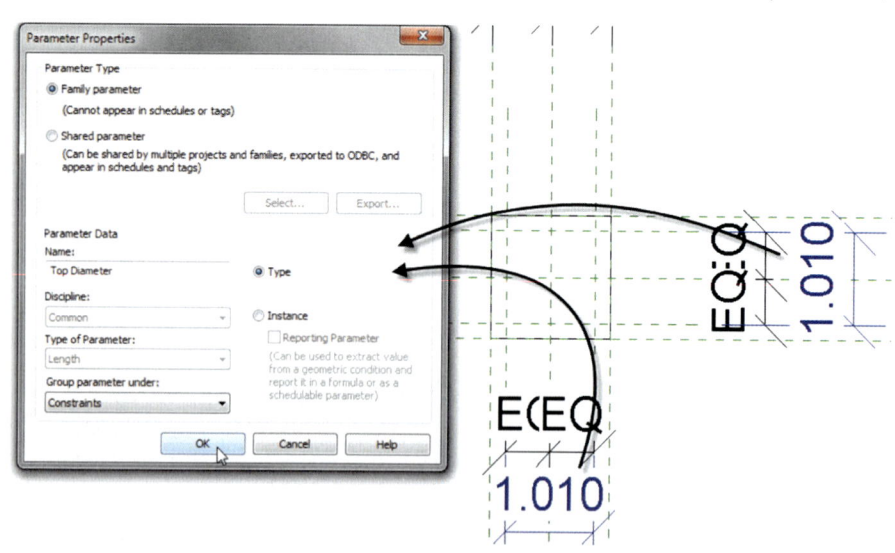

FIGURE 3.9

Label the two overall dimensions with a new parameter

• Renaissance Revit •

8. Name the new parameter **Top Diameter**, leave it set to **Type**, and group it under **Constraints**.

⇨ Click OK to complete the parameter.

9. Open the "Family Types" dialog.

⇨ Next to Top Diameter, input a formula of **Base Diameter * 0.850** and then click Apply.

At this point, we have a decision to make about how to deal with Width and Depth. Since this is the column shaft family, the Width and Depth parameters will end up being equal to Base Diameter without any multiplier. This means that we can simply input Base Diameter as the formula (making the value of Width and the value of Depth equal to Base Diameter) or we can delete the Width and Depth parameters and label their dimensions directly with the Base Diameter parameter. In general, fewer parameters will be easier to manage and can help improve performance. So let's delete Width and Depth and apply Base Diameter directly.

10. If you closed "Family Types" reopen it now. Select the Width parameter and on the right side beneath "Parameters" click the Remove button.

    Revit will warn you that the parameter is currently used by one of your dimensions (see Figure 3.10).

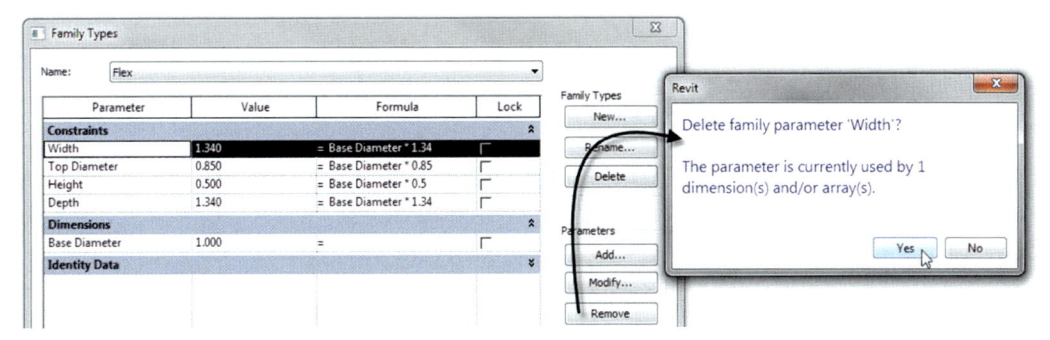

FIGURE 3.10

Remove the Width and Depth parameters

⇨ Click the Yes button to confirm removal.

⇨ Repeat for the Depth parameter and then click OK.

The two previously labeled dimensions will revert to displaying the numerical values only without a label. They are no longer driven by parameters. Let's reassign the Base Diameter to them now.

11. Select the two overall dimensions.

12. On the Options Bar, label them with the Base Diameter parameter (see Figure 3.11).

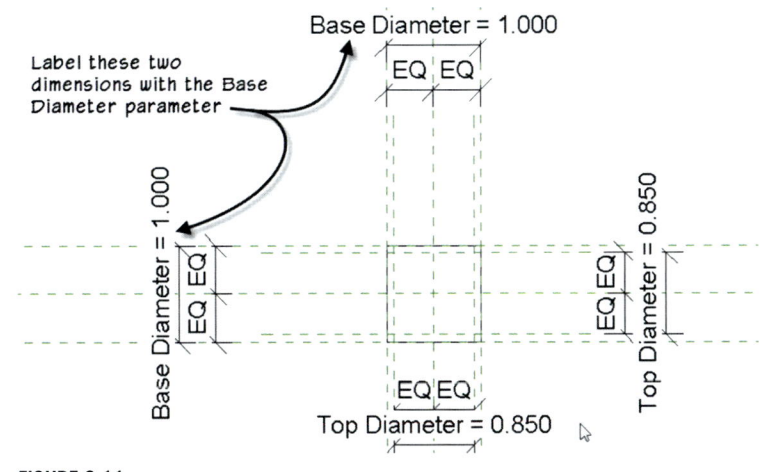

FIGURE 3.11

Apply the Base Diameter parameter directly to the reference planes

• Creating Classical Architecture with Modern Software •

The extrusion will immediately flex as the reference planes adjust to match the new value of the Base Diameter parameter. The last step is to replace the extrusion with a blend.

13. Select the extrusion onscreen and delete it.

14. On the Create tab, click the Blend button.

We created each of the five forms in the "Working with Solids and Voids" topic in Chapter 2. If you need to, please review that topic now. With the blend we need to create two sketches, the one for the blend's base, the other for its top.

⇨ On the Modify | Create Blend Base Boundary tab, click the rectangle icon.

⇨ Snap to the corners of the outer reference planes (the ones dimensioned with Base Diameter parameter).

⇨ Close all four lock icons (see the left side of Figure 3.12).

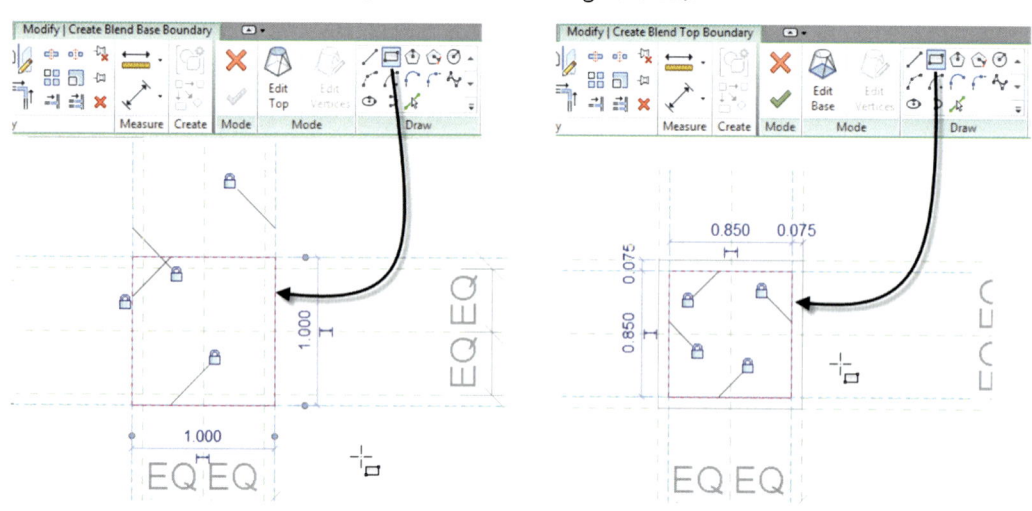

FIGURE 3.12
Sketch the base and top of the new blend

15. Click the Edit Top button.

⇨ Draw another rectangle snapped to the corners of the inside reference planes (the ones dimensioned with the Top Diameter parameter).

⇨ Close all four lock icons (see the right side of Figure 3.12).

16. On the ribbon, click the Finish Edit Mode button.

17. Open the *Front* elevation view.

We need to make a few adjustments to the height. First we need to attach the top of the blend to the reference plane and then adjust the formula that drives the height.

18. Select the blend onscreen.

⇨ Drag the shape handle grip at the top down until it snaps to the Top reference plane and Lock it (see Figure 3.13).

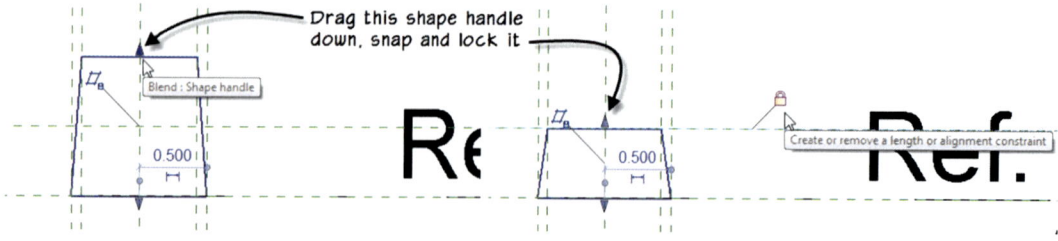

FIGURE 3.13
Lock the top of the blend to the reference plane

19. Open the "Family Types" dialog.

⇨ Change the formula for Height to **Base Diameter * 6** and then click Apply.

20. Click OK to dismiss the dialog, and then save the family.

⇨ From the Application menu, choose **Close**.

> **CATCH UP!** The file has been provided completed to this point: *03_Shaft (Schematic).rfa*.

We are using a multiplier of six here for the height. The Tuscan order is typically drawn at a height of seven diameters. In *The Classical Orders of Architecture*, Chitham includes a nice comparison of each of the orders as proposed by several of the masters throughout history. With the exception of Serlio, nearly all of the other masters keep the height of the Tuscan at or close to seven diameters (Chitham 1985, 2005). So when we subtract the height of our base and capital, we arrive at our multiplier of six.

NESTED FAMILIES

Let's finish our schematic column by combining the three families together into a column family. Like the other families we could begin this one with one of our seed families. However, since we are building a column here, it will be better to start with the out-of-the-box *Column.rft* family template.

1. From the Application menu, choose **New > Family**.
2. In the "New Family – Select Template File" dialog, choose the *Column.rft* template and then click Open.

   A copy of this file is provided in the *Template/OTB* folder with the book's dataset files.

A single view window will open to the *Lower Ref. Level* floor plan view. Notice that there are four reference planes already in this file with Width and Depth parameters already as well. The reference planes even have the same names as the ones in our seed families.

3. Open the *Front* elevation view.

Notice that there is a second reference level in this file as well called Upper Ref. Level.

4. On the Create tab, on Properties panel, click the Family Category and Parameters button.

Notice that the category here is set to Columns (see Figure 3.14).

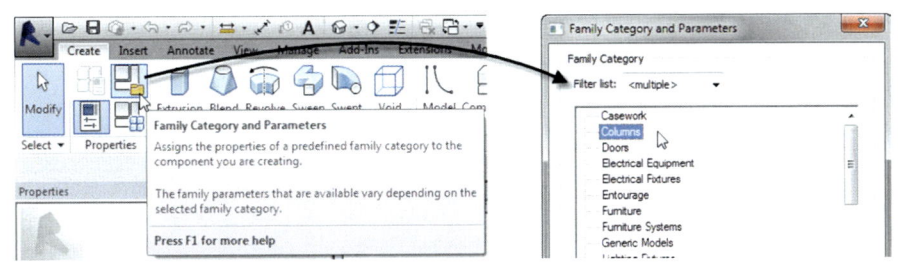

FIGURE 3.14
Check the category of the family

5. Click Cancel to dismiss the "Family Category and Parameters" dialog.

As you can see, even though we did not start with our seed template, the settings and starting parameters in this family closely match what we built into our seed family, but we are using the correct category: Column in this case. It is possible to create our family first from the seed family and then change the category. However, we would not have the Upper Ref. Level if we did it that way. As we will see below, having this second level will be quite useful.

48 | Chapter 3

> **Note:** There is a generic family template that contains two levels. It is named: *Generic Model two level based.rft*. You could use this one instead and later change its category to Column. Either way, having the two reference levels will be important to creation of fully functional column families.

CREATE A SCHEMATIC COLUMN FAMILY

We need to perform a few setup steps before we begin constructing our column family. Since we did not start with the seed family, our units need to be adjusted.

1. Follow the steps in the "Set the Units" topic of Chapter 2 to set the units to Decimal Feet at three decimal places.

2. Open the *Front* elevation view. On the View tab, click the Tile button (or type WT).

   ⇨ Zoom all windows to fit (type ZA).

3. Select the Upper Ref. Level and change its height to **7.000**.

4. Open the "Family Types" dialog.

   ⇨ Following the steps above in the "Base Diameter Parameter" topic, create a new Base Diameter parameter.

   ⇨ This time make it an **Instance** parameter and set the value to: **1.000** (see Figure 3.15).

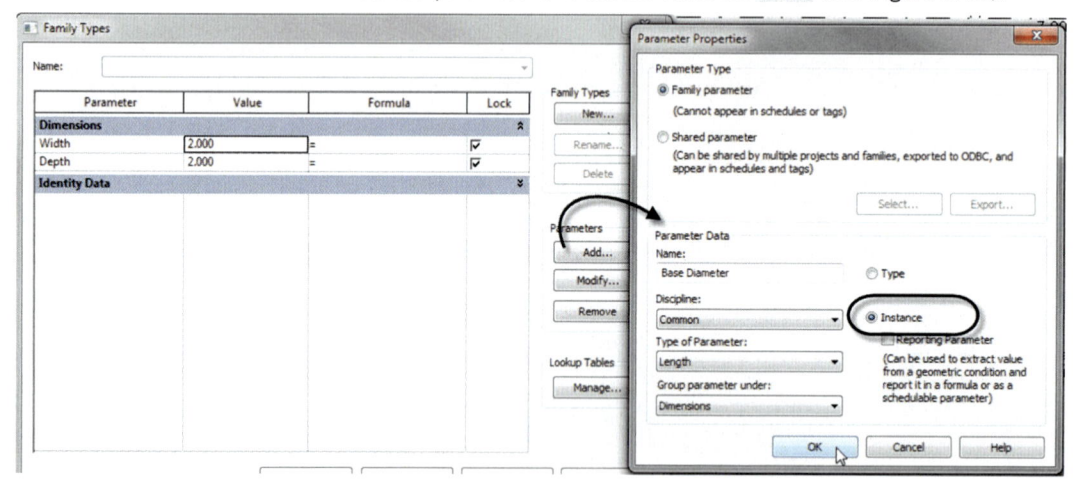

FIGURE 3.15

Create the Base Diameter parameter

5. Following the steps above in the "Create a Shaft Family" topic (steps 10 – 12):

   ⇨ Remove the Width and Depth parameters here and click Yes when asked to confirm.

6. Remain in "Family Types" and create a new Length parameter called **Shaft Elevation**. Make it an **Instance** parameter and group it under **Constraints**.

   ⇨ Add the formula: **Base Diameter * 0.500** to the Shaft Elevation parameter.

7. On the right, in the "Family Types" area, click the New button to create a new type named: **Flex** (see Figure 3.16).

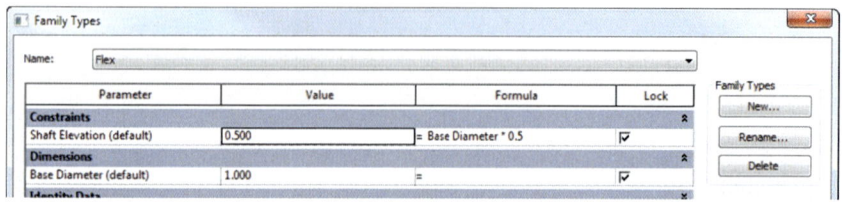

FIGURE 3.16

Add parameters, a formula and a default family type

• Renaissance Revit •

8. Click OK to dismiss the "Family Types" dialog.

9. Switch to the *Lower Ref. Level* floor plan view.

⇨ Select both dimensions and label them with the **Base Diameter** parameter.

10. From the Application menu, choose **Save As > Family**.

11. For the new name input: **Column (Schematic)** and then click Save.

> CATCH UP! The file has been provided completed to this point: *03_Column (Schematic)_A.rfa*.

ADDING NESTED COMPONENTS

With our column family configured and saved, we are ready to nest in the other components we built earlier in the chapter. Just like you can add components to a project, you can add them to a family as well. Use the same Component command on the ribbon. When you load other families into a family, they are considered "nested" families.

Continue in the *Lower Ref. Level* floor plan view.

1. On the Create tab, on the Model panel, click the Component tool.

Revit will display a message stating: "No Component family is loaded in the project. Would you like to load one now?"

2. In the message window, click Yes.

⇨ Browse to the *Chapter03* folder, and select your *Base (Schematic).rfa* family. (If you prefer, you can load the catch-up version instead: *03_Base (Schematic).rfa*).

⇨ Click the Open button to load the family.

⇨ Place the instance at the intersection of the Center (Right/Left) and Center (Front/Back) reference planes (see the left side of Figure 3.17).

⇨ Click the Modify tool or press ESC twice to cancel.

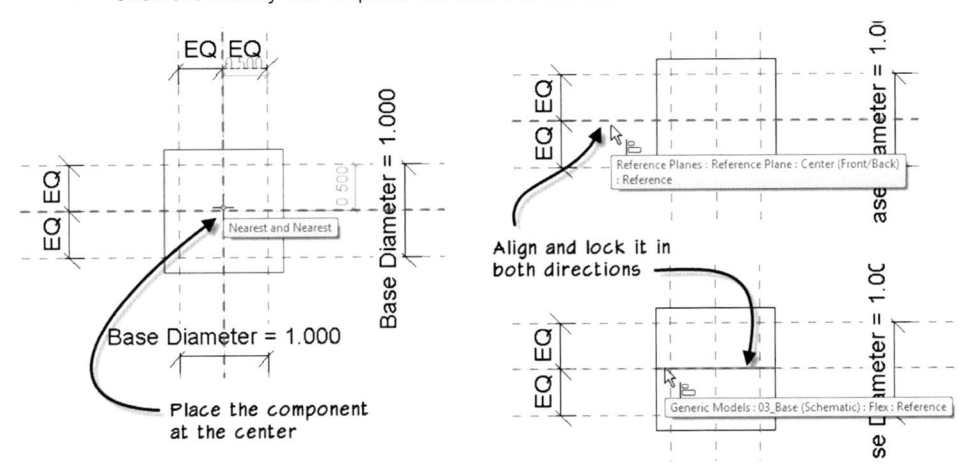

FIGURE 3.17

Place an instance of the base family centered on the reference planes, align and lock it

3. Using the Align tool, align and lock the component in both directions to the center reference planes (see the right side of Figure 3.17).

4. On the Create tab, click the Component tool again.

50 | Chapter 3

This time, since there is a component family loaded, it will not prompt you to load one. Instead, Revit will be ready to place another instance of the existing Base (Schematic) family. However, we can always manually click the Load Family button to choose a different family.

5. On the Modify | Place Component tab, on the Mode panel, click the Load Family button (see Figure 3.18).

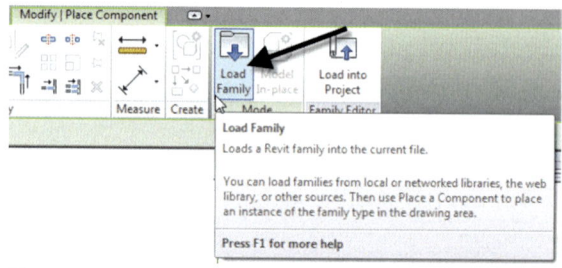

FIGURE 3.18

Use the Load Family button to load in a different family

⇨ Browse to the *Chapter03* folder and load the *Shaft (Schematic)* family this time.

Choose your version or the catch-up file.

⇨ Place it onscreen nearby where we want it (don't snap directly to the reference planes). Then use the align tool to align and lock it to the intersection of the center reference planes in both directions. (Be sure you are aligning the Shaft).

Important: As you align and lock, pay close attention to the tooltips onscreen. Corresponding messages also appear on the Status Bar at the bottommost corner of your Revit application window. The message in both locations indicates which object and reference you are selecting *before* you click. For example, above on the right side of Figure 3.17, tooltips indicate for the first click that we are selecting the reference plane Center (Front/Back) and then for the second click, that we are selecting the nested reference in the Base (Schematic) family.

Get in the habit of watching these tooltips. If the message does not display what you expect, press TAB until it does.

6. Repeat the entire process once more by clicking Load Family again and choose the *Capital (Schematic)* family this time.

⇨ Place it snapped to the center as before.

The component will not be visible as you place it and a warning will appear indicating that the family is not visible in the floor plan (see Figure 3.19).

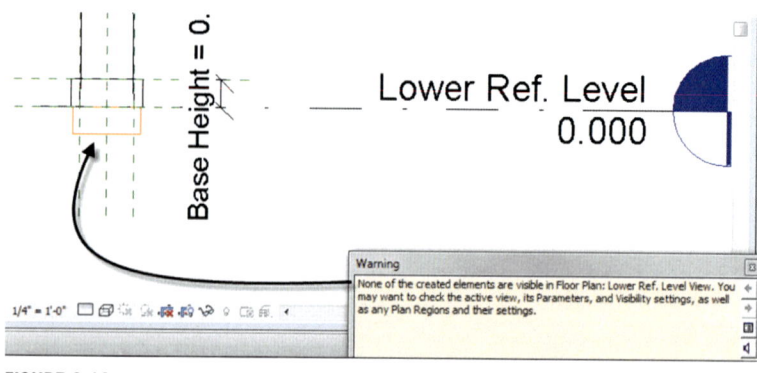

FIGURE 3.19

Place an instance of the base family centered on the reference planes

• Renaissance Revit •

7. Switch to the *Front* elevation view.

Recall above that we moved the reference plane in the *Capital (Schematic)* family and the geometry is now below the Ref. Level instead of above it. In the *Front* elevation view, you can see the issue very clearly. The geometry of this family falls below the Lower Ref. Level. The floor plan uses the same View Range settings as you would have in a project. We could change these settings, but there is no need since we actually need to move this family up anyhow.

8. On the ribbon, click the Modify tool and then in the *Front* elevation view, select the *Capital (Schematic)* component.

   ⇨ On the Properties palette, from the Level list, choose: **Upper Ref. Level**.

The family instance will move up to the location of the upper level. You should now see the component in the floor plan as well.

9. In the *Lower Ref. Level* floor plan view, align and lock the *Capital (Schematic)* in both directions. (Be sure you are aligning the Capital).

> **CATCH UP!** The file has been provided completed to this point: *03_Column (Schematic)_B.rfa*.

ASSOCIATE FAMILY PARAMETERS

We have almost all of the pieces properly positioned. Looking at the Front elevation we see that the shaft family needs to be adjusted vertically. Since we don't have a level for the shaft we cannot use the same approach we used above for the capital. Family templates have one level or two levels. You cannot add more. This is one of the many reasons it is important to start with a good choice of family template. (As we discussed above, if you need two levels, *Column.rft* and Generic *Model two level based.rft* are your options). To move the shaft to the correct height, we will use the Shaft Elevation parameter we created above.

Continue in the *Column (Schematic)* file or open the catch-up file.

1. Select the shaft component.

On the Properties palette, next to several properties on the right side you see some small gray buttons. These are called "Associate Family Parameter" buttons. They allow you to link up the selected property from the nested family to a parameter in the host family. The host family can thereby drive the parameter value of the nested family parameter.

2. On the Properties palette, next to Offset, click the small "Associate Family Parameter" button (see Figure 3.20).

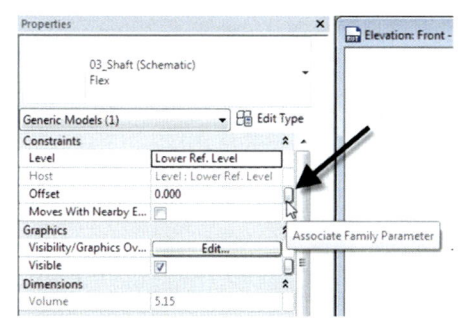

FIGURE 3.20
Associate the Offset of the shaft with the Shaft Elevation family parameter

3. In the "Associate Family Parameter" dialog, choose the Shaft Elevation parameter and then click OK.

A small equal (=) sign will now appear on the Associate Family Parameter button on the Properties palette. The shaft moves up to the correct location. If you were to flex the family right now, two items would flex as expected: the width and depth parameters and their associated reference planes since they are tied directly to the Base Diameter and the location of the shaft since it is now tied to Shaft Elevation which is in turn controlled by the Base Diameter. Go ahead and try it if you like.

This is a good start, but we also want the size and proportion of the three nested elements to flex when we adjust the Base Diameter parameter. Remember, the goal is for Base Diameter to drive the scale and proportion of the entire family! Associate Family Parameter to the rescue.

4. Select the *Base (Schematic)* family instance onscreen.

⇨ On the Properties palette, click the Edit Type button.

⇨ Next to the Base Diameter parameter, click the Associate Family Parameter button (see Figure 3.21).

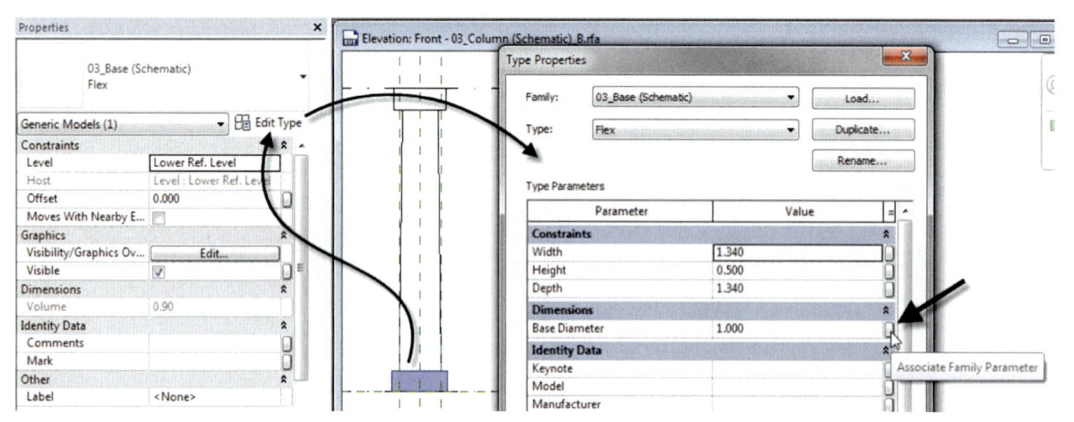

FIGURE 3.21

Associate the Base Diameter parameter to the nested families

⇨ In the "Associate Family Parameter" dialog, choose the Base Diameter parameter and then click OK.

5. Repeat the steps on the shaft and capital families, linking the Base Diameter to each family.

6. Open the "Family Types" dialog and flex the Base Diameter parameter.

⇨ For the value of Base Diameter, try a few different values like **1.500**, **2.000** and **0.750**. Apply after each.

⇨ Return the value to **1.000** when finished flexing.

> **CATCH UP!** The file has been provided completed to this point: *03_Column (Schematic)_C.rfa*.

We're almost there. Let's ignore the fact that the level height did not flex with the rest of the family. We will address that in the next topic. The really interesting feature here is that we were able to drive type-based parameters in the nested families with an instance-based parameter in the host! This is powerful indeed. You do have to be careful with this concept. If you try to do the same thing within a single family (no nesting), it will not work. Typically instance-based parameters cannot drive type-based ones. There is an issue of the hierarchy. You would end up with a single instance trying to change a type which could cause circular references. If you try it, Revit will display an error and prevent you from continuing. But in this case, it works because of the nesting and because the nested families are *not* set to "Shared."

A "Shared Family" is a family that behaves like an instance in the host project even though it is nested inside of another family. It is *shared* between the family and project. You may have seen examples of this with tables and chairs. You place the single table and chairs family, but then you can use TAB to select individual chairs. Individual chairs also show up on the furniture schedule. So in this case, if we need to be able to individually select or schedule our bases, shafts and capitals, we would set them to "Shared." But in doing so, we would break the association of the family type-based parameters. Fortunately, we do not need the nested components set to Shared. If we did, the solution would be to edit each of the nested families and change all the nested parameters to instance-based. Some would argue that we should do that anyhow. Since our intention is to drive these parameters with a host family, why use type-based parameters? I started using type-based as a management tool. I gain two advantages with this approach. First, the nested parameter is kind of buried. To edit it, the end user would have to open two families and then edit the Family Types. Second, we are dealing with simple boxes right now. But as our nested components become more complex, we will want to flex often while working in the nested families. I find flexing quicker and easier using types. Choose one of your types, apply, and then choose Flex again to set it back. This way I don't have to worry about forgetting to reset the values after flexing. I arrived at this after building *lots* of these families. Your results may vary.

In summary, if you don't need "Shared" nested families, you can use either type-based or instance-based parameters and still have the host family drive them with associated family parameters. I tend to prefer type-based where possible, but some prefer to stick to all instance-based. The choice is really up to you. I encourage you to experiment before deciding. Ultimately, consistency is the most important recommendation: once you decide on type or instance-based, stick to it. You can learn more in the "Shared or Non-Shared" topic in Chapter 11.

So, consistency you say? Well then, you may be wondering why did we switch to instance-based here in the host family? Excellent question. The answer is that we are going to make the distance between the two levels in this family drive the whole thing. To do that, it had to be instance-based. In the next topic we'll see how to do it.

REPORTING PARAMETERS

As discussed in the previous passage, the nested families can use either instance-based or type-based parameters depending on what you plan to do with them (will they be Shared or not) and what your personal preferences are. I chose type-based for the nested components for the reasons outlined above. Everything worked fine when we flexed except the overall height. The capital is associated with the Upper Ref. Level and the other components are associated with the Lower Ref. Level. This family does *not* have a height parameter. It does not need one since it has two levels. For our final exercise in this chapter, we will walk through a method to use the distance between the two levels to drive our Base Diameter parameter (which in turn drives the rest of the family parameters). To do this let's discuss "Reporting Parameters."

The parameters that we have worked with so far "drive" the geometry in our families. A reporting parameter "reports" a value in the family. It is similar to taking a measurement. Imagine you are asking your family how big an item is or how far apart two items are. This is what a reporting parameter can do. The value will show up as a read only value on the Properties palette for the family. Reporting parameters have lots of utility for schedules. You can use them to get lists of varying values of several instances of a family in a project.

If your reporting parameter is attached to host references, then it can actually be used in a formula of another parameter. This means it can actually help drive geometry. The key is "Host References." A host reference is a reference that is built into Revit. It can be a reference plane, a reference line, a point element (in the massing environment) or a level. The levels in our Column (Schematic) family are host references.

In this exercise, we will complete our Column (Schematic) family by adding a reporting parameter between the levels and then use it to calculate the Base Diameter.

54 | Chapter 3

Continue in the *Column (Schematic)* file or open the catch-up file.

1. In the *Front* elevation view add a dimension between the two levels.

    Make sure the tooltip for each witness line says "Levels" (see Figure 3.22).

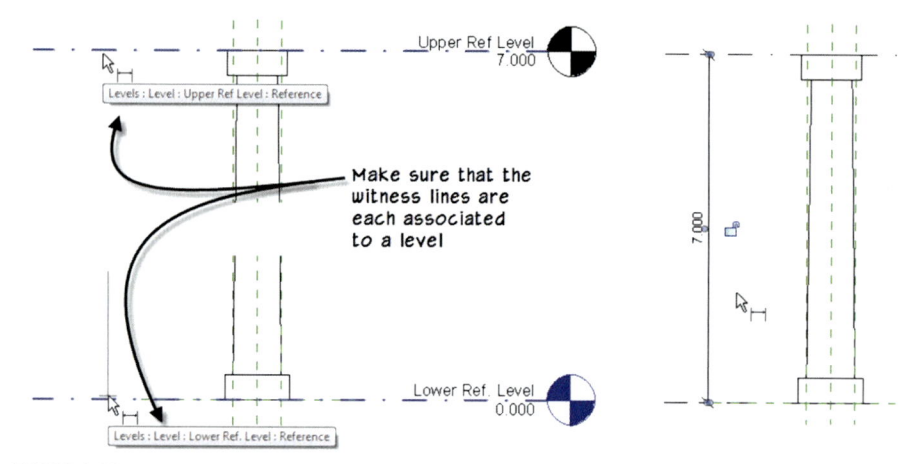

FIGURE 3.22
Add a dimension between the two levels

2. Click the Modify tool and then select the dimension.

    ⇨ Label it with a new parameter.

Notice that in the "Parameter Properties" dialog, the choices for Type and Instance are grayed out. Instance is selected and beneath it there is a checkmark in the "Reporting Parameter" checkbox. When you place a dimension between host references like these two levels, the only valid parameter type is a reporting parameter. This is because if you tried to make a driving parameter for this relationship, it would over-constrain the family.

⇨ Name the parameter: **Column Height** and group it under **Identity Data** and then click OK (see Figure 3.23).

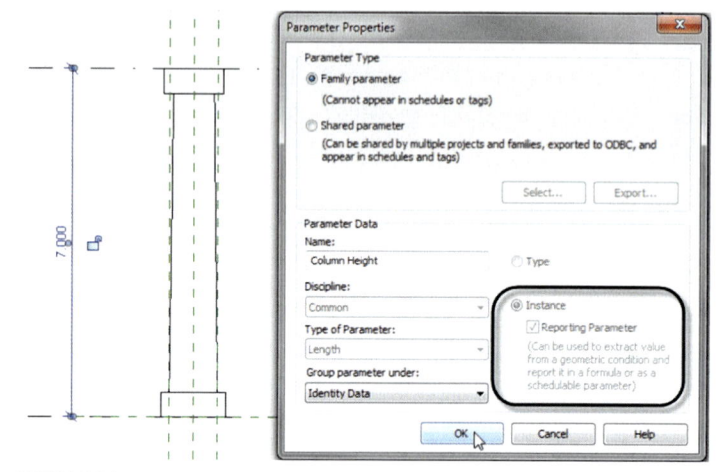

FIGURE 3.23
Add a reporting parameter

3. Open the "Family Types" dialog.

4. Expand the Identity Data grouping.

You will see the new Column Height parameter listed there. It will have the work (Report) next to it to let you know that his is a reporting parameter. It will also be grayed out indicating that it is read only.

5. In the Formula filed next to Base Diameter, type: **Column Height / 7** and then click OK (see Figure 3.24).

• Renaissance Revit •

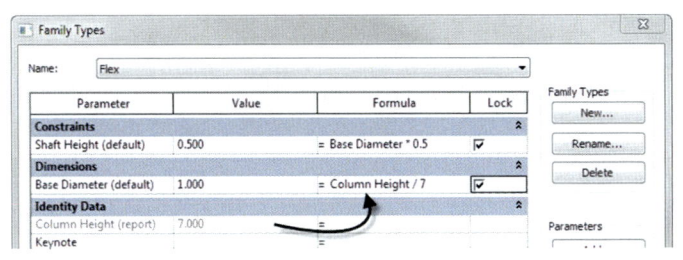

FIGURE 3.24

Use the reporting parameter in the formula for Base Diameter

That's it. Let's test it out. We are going to flex this one both inside the family editor and in a sandbox project.

6. Select the Upper Ref. Level and edit its height.

    Try any value you like. Try a few values and then set it back to **7.000** when finished.

7. Save the family file.

> **CATCH UP!** The completed file has been provided: *03_Column (Schematic).rfa*.

FAMILY TYPES PARAMETERS

A Family Types parameter is a parameter that allows you to swap out the type of a component nested within a family. You can use them to build flexibility into your parent family. For example, in the case of our classical families, you could contemplate using Family Types parameters to allow a single host family to have interchangeable base, shaft and capital components. I once built an example that had several orders built into a single family. By choosing the Doric type for example, the base, shaft and capital would all swap out to the Doric nested families and the height of the overall column would adjust accordingly. As a proof concept it worked pretty well, but in practical terms the family became very large and unwieldy. As I worked through the content for this book, I fully expected to create some of the content using Family Types parameters. However, in the end, I just did not find a suitable place to introduce the concept. As such, the content created in this book will not make use of family types. It is a powerful feature and can be quite useful. I just found other ways to manage the variations in this exercises that follow. If you want to learn more about family types, you can find a paper that I wrote for Autodesk University that discusses the topic at my website (Aubin, Autodesk® Revit® Families: Step-by-Step Advanced Concepts 2012, 24-31).

TEST IN A SANDBOX

Now let's try it out in a sandbox file. Remember that a sandbox is just a project file that we use for testing. One has been provided in the *Chapter03* folder.

1. From the Application menu, choose **Open > Project**.

    ⇨ Browse to the *Chapter03* folder and open the *03_Sandbox.rvt* file.

2. Switch back to the family file, and then on the ribbon, click the Load into Project button.

    Revit will switch back to your sandbox with the Column command active and ready to place an instance.

    ⇨ Click anywhere three times to place three instances.

    ⇨ Click the Modify tool to cancel.

This file has four levels in it. Level 1, Level 2 and Level 3 are each 10 units apart. Level 4 is 8 units above Level 3. You can see this in one of the elevation views if you like.

3. Select one instance of the column.

⇨ On the Properties palette, change the Top Level to **Level 3**.

⇨ Repeat for one of the other instances changing its Top Level to **Level 4** (see Figure 3.25).

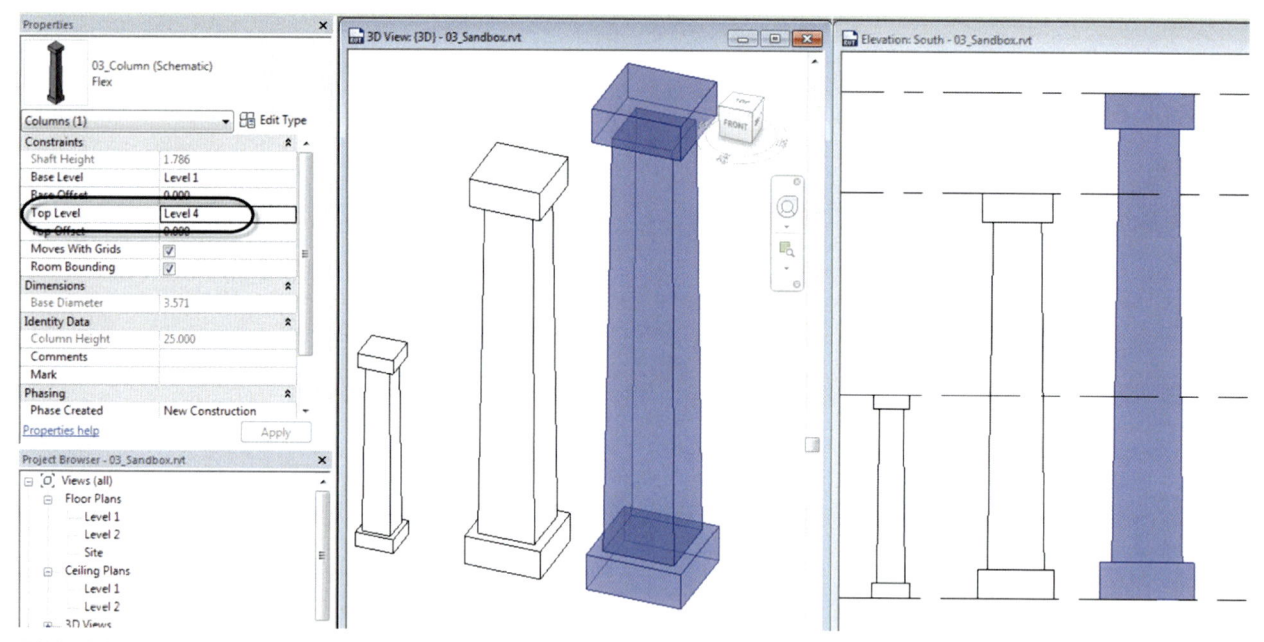

FIGURE 3.25
Load the family into a project and test it out

As you can see, the overall height of the column is now driving the entire family and all its nested components! I added some dimensions to the figure to show that the proportions are all adjusting properly. Level 4 is at 28.000 units. So this is four times larger than the numbers we used to construct the family.

Naturally, the approach we used here is not the only way that we can set this family up. The possibilities are nearly endless, but the goals of these exercises was to give you some idea of how we can systematically build family content with scale and proportion built in. Other approaches abound. But much of the content we will build in this book will build on the foundation laid in this chapter. We will explore some other methods to be sure. The next topic summarizes some of them.

ALTERNATIVE SCALING AND PROPORTION APPROACHES

I would like to end this chapter with a brief discussion on some of the other methods that are available for controlling scaling and proportion in Revit families, some of which will be utilized in tutorials in future chapters. When you have geometry that is more complex than the simple boxes we have been using, you might find that managing them with nested parameters become cumbersome. I have some examples that use dozens of nested parameters all tied back to the Base Diameter. It works, but when something breaks, it can be very difficult to pin down where the problem lies. When building Tuscan and Doric orders, and even Ionic, we can mostly rely on the techniques covered in this chapter (see Figure 3.26). But later when building the Corinthian, we will definitely be interested in simplifying things wherever possible. The three approaches that I would like to briefly discuss here all take advantage of a built-in behavior in each of the elements mentioned. We can think of these built-in behaviors as the "super power" of the element.

The first alternative approach to achieving proportional scaling is the special built-in behavior of splines. Splines can be added to the sketch of any solid or void form. As we will see in the "Controlling a Spline" topic in the next chapter, the super power of splines is they have a special property whereby the spline's shape will scale proportionally just by stretching the endpoints. This means that we can attach a parameter to the ends of the spline and by flexing just one or two parameters, we can scale the entire shape proportionally. For certain forms, this can be very effective. I have seen this technique used to shape molding profiles and even entire columns (Sgambelluri 2013, 7-14). However, I have some concerns about the accuracy of the curve and practical usage in such examples. I have used splines quite successfully to build the entasis into the column shaft profile and for many pieces of the Ionic and Corinthian capitals. These uses take advantage of isolated elements that are part of the overall form. They don't need to be dimensioned on their own and start and end with clear terminations. I will share the details of these examples in a later chapters.

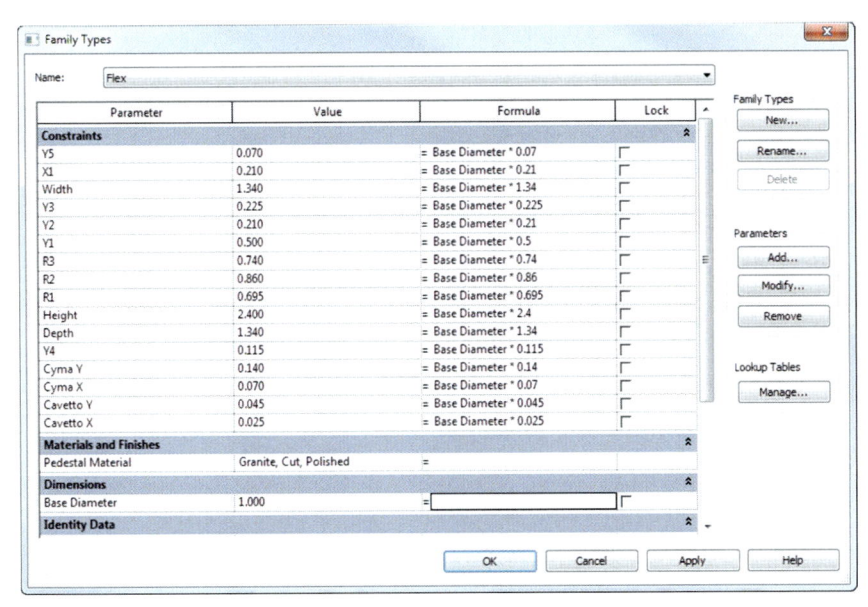

FIGURE 3.26
Using the approach shown here, you can end up with dozens of nested parameters all tied back to the Base Diameter

Another approach that has been circulating on the blogosphere and Revit conferences lately is the use of a planting family. The super power for the planting category is that the entire family scales proportionally based on its built-in Height parameter of this category (Tam 2013). The end result will be similar to what we achieved here with the Column family, only with fewer nested parameters and constraints. I will share some examples of this technique in the "Scaling Families with the Planting Category" topic in Chapter 13.

The third technique is available in the massing environment. The massing environment has many features that could be described as super powers; but the one that is most useful for proportional scaling is the concept of building a "scale rig" (Milburn 2013) (Kron 2012) (Light 2009). This approach involves creating a series of interconnected reference lines and points. You can build 2D and 3D rigs that are as simple as a rectangle to shapes that are much more complex. Regardless of the complexity of the rig, the idea is the same on all of them: cascading hierarchical relationships. The super power comes in the "Normalized Curve Parameter" measurement type. This setting is really just a percentage value from 0 – 100. If the length of the host curve changes (like when you flex the main control parameter) the normalized curve parameter remains constant at its percentage along the line or curve. If you host geometry on these points, you gain proportional scaling for "free!" We'll see some examples of this in the "Adding Hosted Point Rigs" topic in Chapter 13.

As you can see from this brief inventory, there is no shortage of approaches to challenge of proportional scaling. With a little practice, you will no doubt discover which your favorite approach is. But I think all are worth mastering as they each gives a little something that the others do not. So please be read on. There is plenty more to discuss.

SUMMARY

- Most Revit elements cannot simply be scaled with the scale command. They require that scaling behavior be "baked" in.

- Scaling and Proportion can be built into family content and controlled parametrically.

- Classical orders use a series of proportions derived from the diameter of the column measure directly above the base. This Base Diameter can become the master parameter used to scale all other family parameters proportionally.

- A simple schematic family can be used as a starting point and seed for future more detailed versions.

- Nesting family components together is an effective way to build the overall column family.

- Nested families can be shared or not shared. Shared families existing hierarchically at the same level as their host in the project. They can be selected and scheduled independently of their hosts.

- Type parameters in a nested shared family cannot be driven by parameters in the host.

- Type parameters in a nested family that is not shared *can* be driven by instance parameters in the host.

- Reporting parameters measure distances in the family and report the actual values.

- Reporting parameters associated with host elements in a family can be used to drive formulas. Reporting parameters to non-hosts cannot drive formulas.

HADRIAN'S VILLA
Photo by author

Chapter 4
Constraining Curves

INTRODUCTION

Families like straight lines. I don't have this on absolute fact, but rather on personal experience. Controlling the location of straight lines is easily accomplished in the Family Editor using simple reference planes or reference lines. When you introduce curves: arcs, circles and ellipses it becomes a little more difficult to control them parametrically in a reliable and stable way. Techniques and procedures designed to address this issue are what this chapter is all about.

OBJECTIVES

In this chapter we will explore several exercises designed to assist you in understanding how curves and rotation behave and then how to ensure that when you introduce curved forms or rotating elements into your family content that you can control the curvature and rotation predictably and reliably. Topics in this chapter include:

- Understand the challenges inherit in curves
- Apply parameters directly to curves
- Explore when to use references and rigs
- Understand how to apply complex formulas
- Learn to effectively use profile families

CURVATURE IN THE TRADITIONAL FAMILY EDITOR

This chapter focuses on techniques in the traditional family editor environment. Lessons in the chapter are cumulative from the lessons in the previous chapters. If you are not familiar with the basics of the traditional family editor, establishing reference planes, creating labeled dimensions and parameters and building 3D forms and voids, you are encouraged to review the previous chapters before continuing. This chapter will not explore the massing family editor environment. As such, when we speak of curvature in the family editor in this chapter, we are speaking of two-dimensional curves confined to the active work plane that include: circles, ellipses, arcs (portion of a circle), elliptical arcs (portion of an ellipse) and splines (Bezier splines with control handles) (see Figure 4.1).

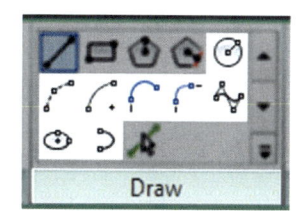

FIGURE 4.1

Curves available in sketch mode for solid and void forms in the traditional family editor

These are the shapes you can use in the five solid and void forms available to us in the traditional family editor. (Examples of each of the five forms were showcased in the previous chapter). Throughout the lessons in this chapter, we will explore several isolated scenarios first and then combine techniques together to create more complex forms.

CONSTRAINT AND PARAMETER DIRECT ATTACHMENT

The general rule-of-thumb in family creation is to create a clear and consistent hierarchy between the references, constraints and geometry. Typically this means that you would want to lay down your reference planes and reference lines first. You would next apply constraints and parameters to these references and flex them to be sure that they function properly. Finally, you would build your geometry and lock it to this properly flexing armature of references. This is the so-called "bones, muscle and skin" analogy. It is my experience that this is often the best approach in most situations. However, as with any rule or guideline there are always exceptions. In the next few lessons, we'll look at a few examples where the dimensions (be they constraints or parameters) will be applied *directly* to the geometry instead of a reference. The general rule should still be followed: if you can dimension your reference lines or reference planes first, and then attach geometry to them, it is generally preferred. But as we will see, this is not always possible or desirable, particularly when curves are involved.

CREATE A PARAMETRIC CIRCLE

Two forms that will use the direct attachment method will be circles and ellipses. To parametrically flex and or reliably constrain these elements, we typically need to apply the dimensions directly the forms.

1. From the Application menu, choose **Open > Family**.
2. Browse to the *Seed Families* folder, select the file named: *Family Seed (Instance Based).rfa* and then click Open.
   ⇨ Type WT and then ZA.
3. Save the file in the *Chatper04* folder as: **Circle**.

All solid and void forms in the Family Editor can use circles. So you can perform the following procedure on any kind of form. To keep the exercise simple, we'll use an extrusion, but feel free to practice the steps on other forms as well later on. Since the seed already contains an extrusion we can simple edit it.

    Work in the Ref. Level floor plan view

4. Select the extrusion onscreen.
   ⇨ On the Modify I Extrusion tab, click the Edit Extrusion button.
   ⇨ Select and delete the four existing sketch lines.
5. On the Draw panel, click the Circle icon.
   ⇨ Draw the circle centered on the reference planes in the file. Snap the size of the circle to the width and depth defined by the reference planes (see Figure 4.2).

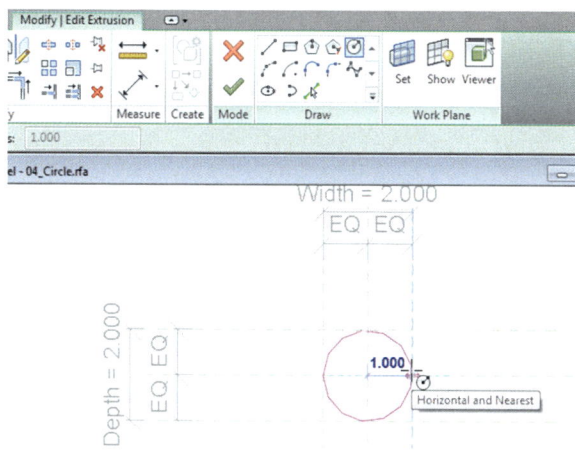

FIGURE 4.2

Draw a circle and snap it to the reference planes

Even though we snap the circle to the reference planes, it will not flex when the parameters flex. Try it out if you like. Instead we have to add another parameter to make our intentions known to Revit. We will add a radius dimension and parameter directly to the circle.

6. Click the icon beneath the dimension to make the temporary dimension permanent. Click the Modify tool to cancel.
7. Label this dimension with a new instance based parameter and call it: **R** (see Figure 4.3).

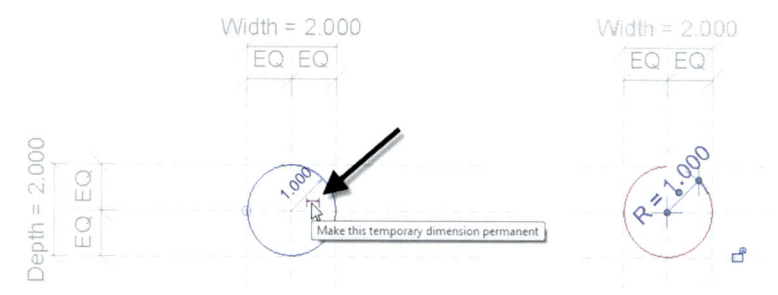

FIGURE 4.3

Create the dimension and a radius parameter

8. Finish the extrusion.

We could flex the extrusion now to be sure that it works, but since we already have the Width and Depth parameters that represent the overall extents of the circle, let's add a few simple formulas in the "Family Types" dialog to tie all three parameters together so they flex in a logical way. We want Width and Depth to be equal, and R to be half of Width and Depth.

9. Open the "Family Types" dialog.
10. In the Formula column next to Width, Type: **Depth**. For the Formula next to Depth, type: **R * 2** (see Figure 4.4).

62 | Chapter 4

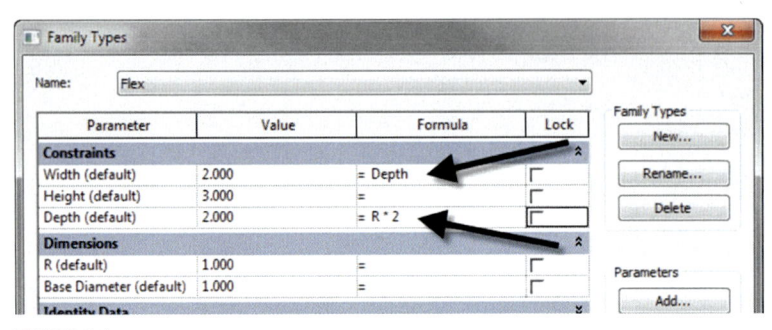

FIGURE 4.4

Link the three parameters with formulas

> **Note:** We are ignoring the Base Diameter parameter for the time being. If you prefer, you can set the Width and Depth equal to Base Diameter times a multiplier.

11. Flex the family.

The circle should change size as you flex the radius. The width and depth should also flex with the radius.

> **Note:** If you prefer, you can use the Diameter dimension tool on the circle and thereby eliminate the need for the formula based on the R parameter. In this case, the diameter can be set equal to the either the Width or Depth parameter directly.

> **CATCH UP!** You can open a file completed to this point named: *04_Circle.rfa*.

CREATE A PARAMETRIC ELLIPSE

Creating a parametric ellipse is very similar. For this one, we'll tie the width and depth separately to each ellipse axis. Otherwise, the procedure is nearly the same.

Continue in the previous file or open the catch-up file.

1. Save the file as: **Ellipse**.
2. Open the "Family Types" dialog.
   ⇨ Clear the formulas.
3. Select the R parameter and then click Modify.
   ⇨ Rename it to: **X** and then click OK. For the Formula, type: **Width / 2**.
4. Add another instance based Length parameter named: **Y**.
   ⇨ For the Formula, type: **Depth / 2** and then click OK (see Figure 4.5).

Constraining Curves | 63

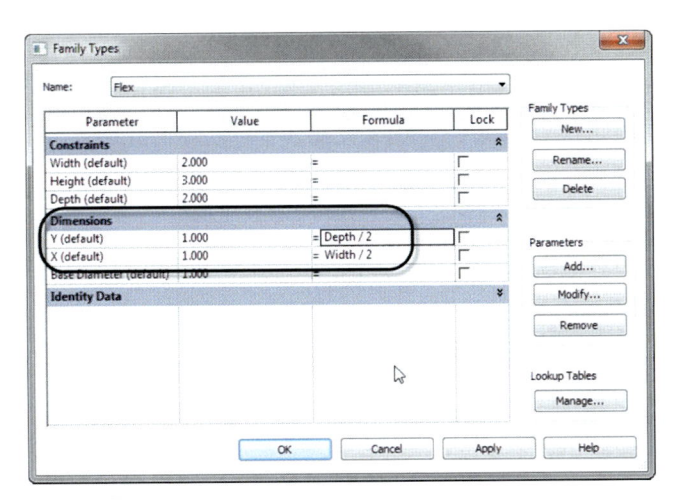

FIGURE 4.5

Edit the parameters to prepare them for the ellipse

The parameters are now ready, let's edit the extrusion next.

5. Select the circle extrusion and then on the ribbon, click the Edit Extrusion button.

⇨ Select the circle sketch and delete it.

6. On the Draw panel, click the Ellipse icon and then click the center point at the center of the square.

7. Snap the first ellipse axis to the intersection of the Center (Front/Back) and Right reference plane. Snap the other axis to the intersection of the Center (Left/Right) and Back reference planes.

8. Make both dimensions permanent (see the left side of Figure 4.6).

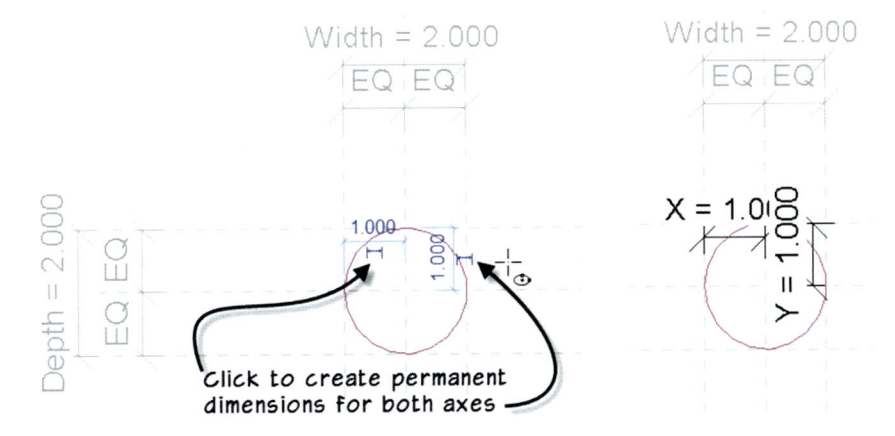

FIGURE 4.6

Draw an ellipse and make the dimensions for both axes permanent

At the moment, this ellipse looks like a circle. Mathematically, a circle is really just a special case of an ellipse. So you can actually use an ellipse all the time if you prefer and when you need a circle just flex it so that both axes are equal. Let's finish it and flex.

9. Label the vertical dimension with the Y parameter and the horizontal one with the X parameter (see the right side of Figure 4.6).

10. Finish the extrusion and then open the "Family Types" dialog and flex.

You should be able to input values for any of the four parameters. If you make the width and depth different, you will get an ellipse. Make them the same to get a circle.

• *Creating Classical Architecture with Modern Software* •

64 | Chapter 4

> **CATCH UP!** You can open a file completed to this point named: *04_Ellipse.rfa*.

CENTER MARK VISIBLE

For curved objects like circles and ellipses you can display the center mark. This can be helpful to ensure that the element flexes in the way you expect and intend. Any curved object has this setting including arcs. For ellipses, you can also display the foci. To display either, look for the checkbox on the Properties palette (see Figure 4.7).

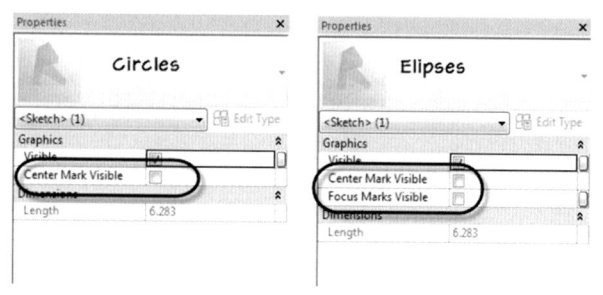

FIGURE 4.7
Enable the Center Mark or Focus Marks for Circles and Ellipses on the Properties palette

We'll look at some examples in the next topic.

AUTOMATIC SKETCH DIMENSIONS

You may have noticed that when you flex Revit families certain parts may be constrained automatically. Sometimes it behaves exactly as you want and expect, but not always. Revit does not always automatically constrain the points you expect. So how do you determine what automatic constraints are applied? The answer is "Automatic Sketch Dimensions." Automatic Sketch Dimensions can be made visible in the Visibility/Graphics Overrides dialog. Use the VG shortcut to open the dialog just like you would in a project. Once there, the Automatic Sketch Dimensions are a sub-component of Dimensions.

ENABLE CENTER MARK

1. Open the file: *04_Circle.rfa*.
2. Tile the windows and then save the file as: **Circle (Sketch Dims)**.
3. Open the "Family Types" dialog. Clear the formulas and then click OK.

This means that the width and depth parameters are no longer linked together.

4. Make the *Ref. Level* Floor Plan active.
5. Select the extrusion onscreen and then on the ribbon, click the Edit Extrusion button.
   ⇨ Select the circle onscreen. On the Properties palette, check Center Mark Visible (shown above in Figure 4.7).
   ⇨ Deselect the circle, but do not finish the extrusion yet.

ENABLE AUTOMATIC SKETCH DIMENSIONS

6. On the View tab, click the Visibility/Graphics button (or type VG).
   ⇨ Click the Annotation Categories tab.
   ⇨ Beneath the Dimensions category, check the Automatic Sketch Dimensions checkbox and then click OK (see Figure 4.8).

Constraining Curves | **65**

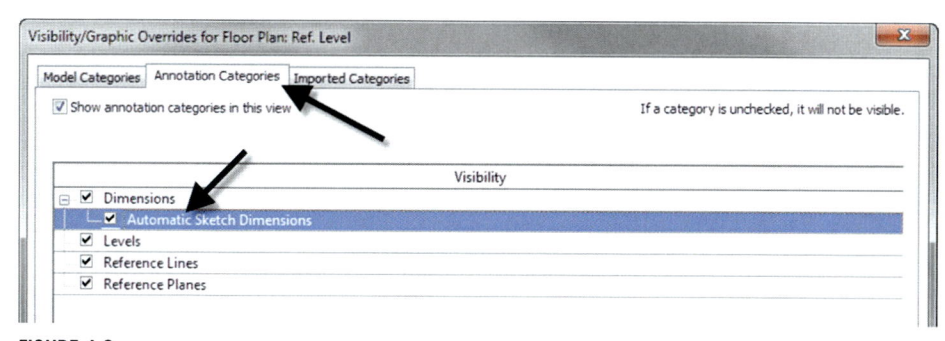

FIGURE 4.8

Enable the display of Automatic Sketch Dimensions

Notice the two blue dimensions near the center of the circle. These are the Automatic Sketch Dimensions and by default have associated the center of the circle to the intersection of the two reference planes at the origin of this family (see Figure 4.9).

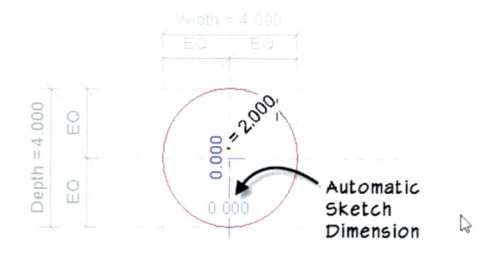

FIGURE 4.9

Automatic Sketch Dimensions display in a blue color

7. Return to the "Family Types" dialog and flex the Width and Depth parameters.

    As noted above, without the formulas, these two flex independently.

8. Flex the radius (R) parameter.

    Notice that the circle stays centered on the reference planes.

9. Click OK to dismiss the "Family Types" dialog.

Revit is always looking to establish logical relationships in your families. It does this by placing Automatic Sketch Dimensions in logical locations. In this case, Revit assumed we wanted to keep the center of the circle aligned to the reference planes at the origin (maintain a zero distance in each direction). This may seem pretty logical. For a circle, there aren't too many other logical assumptions to make, so constraining the center is a good bet. However, this simple example does not tell the whole story. Automatic Sketch Dimensions are not identical to constraints. They will adjust on-the-fly as you edit your family. Let's try another example.

10. Drag the circle down about **0.500** units (it does not have to be exact, but if you drag more than .5, the Automatic Sketch Dimension will shift).

Notice that the vertical Automatic Sketch Dimension no longer reads zero, but now displays .5 or whatever amount you dragged it. If you flex now, it will keep the center of the circle offset from the reference planes by this amount. Again, this may be your intent and may seem logical, but in some cases it may not be what you wanted.

11. On the ribbon, click the Finish Edit Mode button.

12. Close the family without saving changes.

• *Creating Classical Architecture with Modern Software* •

66 | Chapter 4

Let's return to our Ellipse family and see another example.

13. Open the file named: *04_Ellipse (Sketch Dims).rfa* and tile the windows.
14. Open the "Family Types" dialog.

    Note that the formulas here have already been removed.
15. Flex the Width and Depth parameters.

Notice that this time, the object does not stay centered. Let's edit the extrusion and take a look at the Automatic Sketch Dimensions. They have already been turned on in this file.

16. Select the extrusion onscreen and then on the ribbon, click the Edit Extrusion button.

Notice that the Automatic Sketch Dimensions are attached to the left side horizontally and to the center vertically. Logical? Perhaps; perhaps not. The point is, that if you do not like the assumptions that Revit makes with the Automatic Sketch Dimensions, you cannot edit them directly. Instead you have to add your own constraints and dimensions to make your intent known to Revit. As soon as you add a dimension or constraint of your own, the Automatic Sketch Dimension will be removed. You cannot simply delete them. You *must* add your own constraints or parameters to override (and therefore make unnecessary) the automatic behavior.

17. Select the ellipse onscreen. On the Properties palette, check Center Mark Visible (shown above in Figure 4.7).
18. Using the Align tool, align and lock the Center Mark to the Center (Left/Right) and Center (Front/Back) reference planes.

Notice that as soon as you lock the alignment, the Automatic Sketch Dimension disappears. The same is true if you add your own permanent dimension; even if you don't lock it. Any dimension, constraint or parameter will have a higher priority than the corresponding Automatic Sketch Dimension and as a consequence will disable it.

19. Flex the ellipse after aligning and locking and note that it now flexes around the intersection at the origin.
20. Finish the Edit Mode, and close the Ellipse file. You do not need to save.

Automatic Sketch Dimensions are an important factor in being successful in the Family Editor. If you are unaware of them, it can make your work in the Family Editor frustrating as you make guesses on how to force Revit to behave the way that you need. There are a few schools of thought on the use of Automatic Sketch Dimensions. The first is to have the goal of eliminating them in all families. To do this, you would need to add your own constraints and parameters at all locations where Automatic Sketch Dimensions appear. This can be easy to accomplish in simple families, but in more complex ones, it can become quite difficult to achieve. So an alternate approach is to replace only those Automatic Sketch Dimensions that run counter to your design intent. In other words, if the family is flexing properly with the Automatic Sketch Dimensions, you can leave them alone. It is really up to you.

> TIP: In general, I prefer to eliminate the Automatic Sketch Dimensions where possible, but try not to become consumed by the task. If Revit insists on applying some Automatic Dimensions and they are not preventing my family from flexing properly, then I leave them alone. Your results may vary.

> **Note:** As you work in the Family Editor, you may find yourself enabling and disabling the display of Automatic Sketch Dimensions frequently. While tempting to leave them on all the time, sometimes they get in the way, so you'll want to turn them on and off as needed. However, going in and out of Visibility/Graphics can get tedious. If you are familiar with the Revit API, you can use a macro to toggle the display of the Automatic Sketch Dimensions. There is a terrific blog devoted to the Revit API complete with many code snippets for you to try. It is called Boost Your BIM (Mattison 2013).
>
> Here are some links to the code and instructions on how to make a macro from it to toggle the Automatic Sketch Dimensions:
>
> http://goo.gl/65XH1I
>
> http://goo.gl/rgF5gP
>
> http://goo.gl/hsbfi7

QUARTER ROUND AND HALF ROUND (ASTRAGAL AND TORUS)

If you have successfully constrained, parameterized and flexed a circle or ellipse, you might next want to do the same for an arc. Arcs can be very similar to circles, but they do introduce an additional wrinkle; they have endpoints. If your center remains at a fixed location, arcs are pretty easy to control. If the center moves, you have the additional challenge of parameterizing the movement of the center. Let's consider the case where the center is fixed first.

LOCKING ENDPOINTS

1. From the *Seed Families* folder, open the file: *Family Seed (Sketch Dims).rfa*.
2. Tile the windows and then save the file to the *Chapter04* folder as: **Arc (Centered)**.

This file is a copy of the seed families created in the previous chapter. It has the all of the starting parameters and has Automatic Sketch Dimensions enabled. There are no formulas in Family Types.

To keep this example quick and easy, we'll build a model line. This way we can focus on just the arc instead of creating an entire form.

   Work in the *Ref. Level* plan view.
3. Delete the extrusion.
4. On the Create tab, click the Model Line tool.
   ⇨ On the Draw panel, click the Center-ends Arc tool.
5. For the center, click at the intersection of the Center (Left/Right) and Center (Front/Back) Reference planes.
   ⇨ Snap the first endpoint to the intersection of the Center (Front/Back) and Right Reference planes.
   ⇨ Snap the other point to the intersection of the Center (Left/Right) and the Back Reference planes.

Two lock icons will appear. Do not close them (see Figure 4.10).

68 | Chapter 4

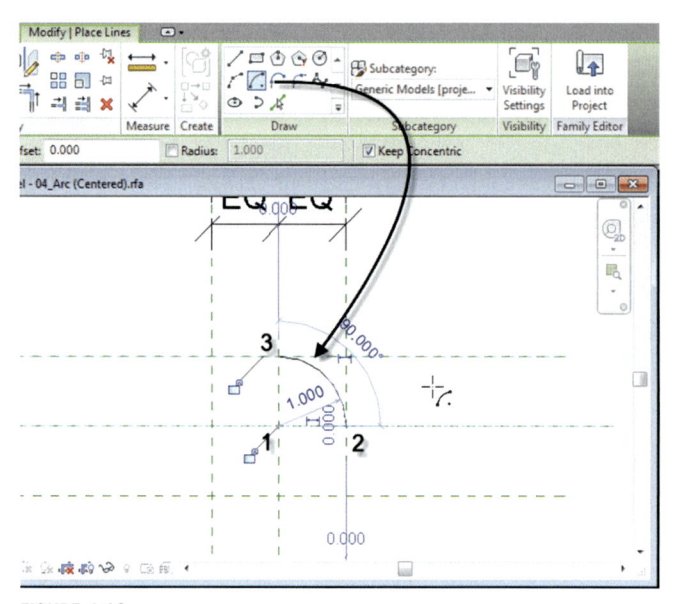

FIGURE 4.10
Create a Model Line arc centered on the reference planes

Notice all of the Automatic Sketch Dimension that appear. As noted above, the Automatic Sketch Dimensions try to anticipate how you intend to flex the object. They take into account the kind of geometry that you have. So in this case, since we have an arc, Revit is assuming we want to constrain the center point.

The more dimensions and constraints that you apply, the fewer automatic dimensions will be required. Of course there is a fine line we walk here. If you are not careful, it is easy to get the dreaded "this would over constrain the sketch" error.

   6. Add a radius dimension to the arc.

This removes one of the Automatic Sketch Dimensions. Let's add a parameter to the radius so we can flex the size of the curve.

   7. Select the radius dimension and label it with the existing Depth parameter (see the left side of Figure 4.11).

Notice how the center remains fixed as the arc's radius increases. Revit tends to favor the center point location.

   8. Delete the arc and then add it again. This time, close the lock icons.
   9. Add the radius dimension and again label it with the Depth parameter (see the right side of Figure 4.11).

Notice that this time, since we applied the locks, the center ends up moving when you flex it. Chances are, the first behavior was a little more expected than the second one. But both had their issues.

• Renaissance Revit •

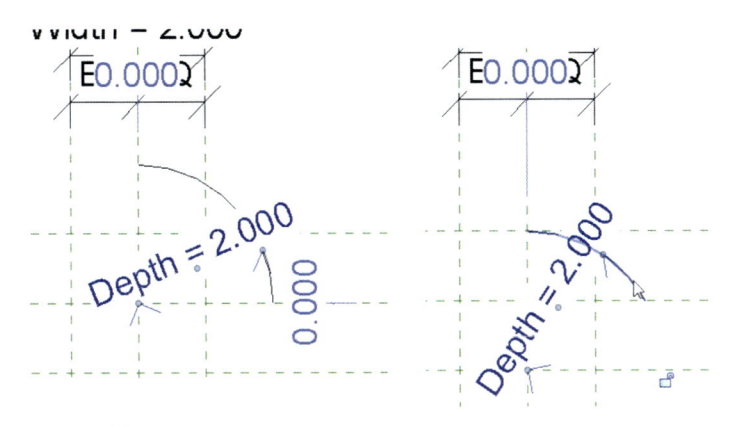

FIGURE 4.11

Relying on automatic dimensions vs. applying locks

I tend not to use the locks that Revit displays when drawing a shape. I use the Align tool instead to be more precise about where and what I am locking. With the Align tool, I see each lock being applied one at a time. I find this much more predictable then relying on the assumptions that Revit makes and offers.

10. Delete the arc and then add it one more time. Do not close the lock icons.

11. On the Modify tab, click the Align tool.

   ⇨ For the reference for alignment, click the back reference plane.

   ⇨ For the entity to align, click the endpoint of the arc. Lock it (see Figure 4.12).

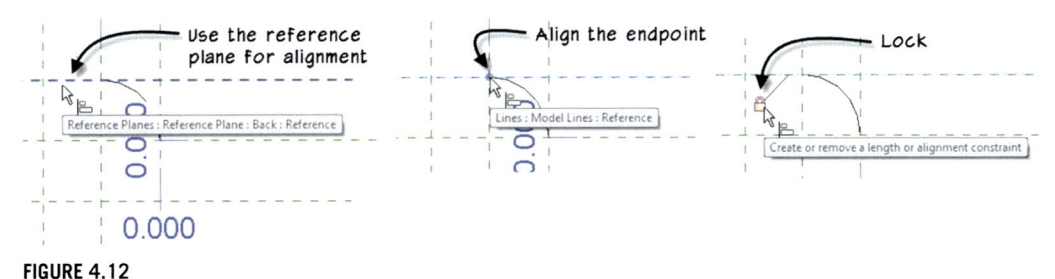

FIGURE 4.12

Align and lock endpoints

12. Repeat on the Center (Left/Right) reference plane and the same endpoint and again in both directions for the other endpoint. (This will be four alignments total).

Notice that as you finish aligning in all four directions, all of the Automatic Sketch Dimensions will disappear. The endpoints of the arc will now remain at the intersections of the reference planes.

13. Add the radius and label it with the Depth once again.

Were the results as you expected? This time, the center point moved. Considering that we just locked the endpoints to the intersections of the reference planes, there is really nothing else that could flex. I suspect however, that this may not be what you expected. It is likely that we would want the center to stay at the intersection of the two central reference planes and instead for the width and depth to flex. We can achieve this with a simple formula as we did in the last chapter.

14. Undo the application of the label to the radius, but keep the radius dimension.

15. Label it with a new instance parameter instead and call it: **R**.

16. Open the "Family Types" dialog and add a formula to both Width and Depth: **R * 2**.

17. Flex the family.

• *Creating Classical Architecture with Modern Software* •

Notice that now when you flex the radius, it stays confined to the upper right quadrant defined by the reference planes. So depending on the specific behavior you require, the precise approach you use is a matter of preference.

You can also try dragging the arc's endpoints to produce a different angle. 90° increments should be very stable. But even other angles should work well since the main controlling parameter here is the radius. To add even more stability, turn on the center mark (see above) and then align and lock the center in both directions to the reference planes. With both center and endpoints locked, you don't actually need the radius dimension. The width and depth and flex the arc and the alignments will be maintained. Feel free to experiment further before continuing.

You can use the previous techniques to create an astragal, a torus, quarter-round and half-round shapes. You can also use the half-round shape to create Roman arches.

> **CATCH UP!** You can open a file completed to this point named: *04_Arc (Centered).rfa*.

CONTROLLING ROTATION

While not directly related to curves, controlling rotation in a family reliably is another important skill. Many families require rotational parameters. Reference planes do not rotate reliably. To add an angular parameter to a family, you need to use a reference line instead of a reference plane. Even though reference planes appear on screen to have a start and end point, they are really infinite. This makes it difficult to use them to control rotation in a family. A reference line on the other hand has a finite length and both a start and end point. You can assign angle parameters to them. Also, reference lines have built-in work planes, so you can also use them to control the rotation of other elements within a family. A very common application for this is to control the swing of a door. However, we can also use this technique in conjunction with the previous lesson to control the angle of a variable arc at both its start and end points.

In order to use a reference line to control a rotation parameter effectively, you need to establish two things: first, you must constrain the end of the reference line that you wish to be the point of rotation. If you do not, the rotation parameter will behave unpredictably. Second, you must set one of the work planes of the reference line current and then add your solid geometry to this plane. Alternatively, you can lock geometry to the rotating reference lines in some cases as well. Reference lines can be drawn in a variety of shapes. However, a simply linear reference line is the most useful for rotational parameters.

CREATE A DOOR FAMILY WITH VARIABLE SWING

Many families can benefit from parametrically controlled rotation. But perhaps one of the most common is a door with variable swing. The following steps show a simple example.

1. From the Application menu (big "R"), or on the Recent Files screen, choose **New > Family**.
2. Select the template named: *Door.rft* and then click Open.

    A copy of this file is provided in the *Template/OTB* folder with the book's dataset files.

3. Save the file as: **Door w Variable Swing**.

CREATE AND CONSTRAIN A REFERENCE LINE

In this tutorial, we will create an angular parameter and associate it to a reference line for purposes of defining a variable door swing parameter in the door family. The trick to making the reference line work properly is being sure that you apply the constraints and parameters to it very carefully. In the Family Editor, it is sometimes easier to do this if you hide some of the geometry.

1. Select the Wall and on the View Control Bar, from the Temporary Hide/Isolate pop-up, choose **Hide Element**.
2. Repeat for the Frame/Mullion component.

There are three horizontal reference planes remaining on screen where the wall was. One is at the center and one each for the two edges of the wall. These two are named: Exterior and Interior. This is a standard feature of the *Door.rft* template (see Figure 4.13).

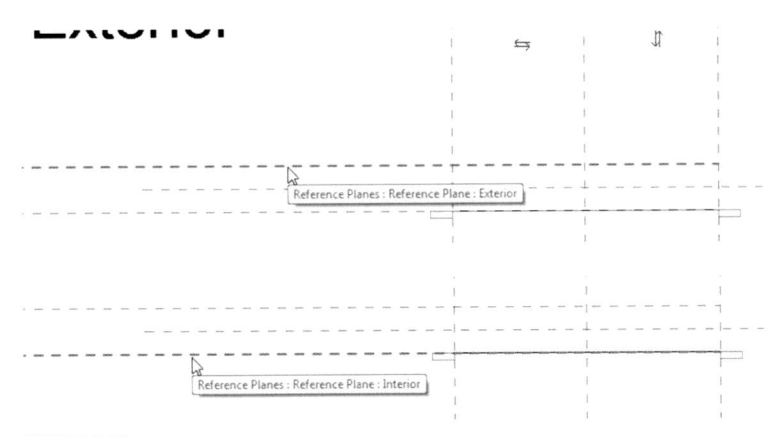

FIGURE 4.13
Reference planes are included at the faces of the wall

We need to decide where we want the door's hinge point to be. If you want the hinge to always be at the face of the wall, we can use one of these two reference planes. Otherwise, you would want to create a new reference plane for the hinge.

The point of considering this issue is to realize that there can be much deliberation that goes into the creation of any family. For simplicity's sake and to focus on the rotation parameter, we will use the Exterior reference plane for our hinge point in this exercise. Once you understand the procedure outlined here, you can take the technique and apply it differently in your own families.

The basic process required is as follows: draw a reference line, lock one endpoint to the intersection of two reference planes (this is the location of the hinge point). Then assign a rotation parameter to the reference line. The easiest way to do this is to draw the reference line at an angle first.

1. Draw a 45° reference line starting at the intersection of Left and Exterior reference planes. Make it **3'-0"** long (see Figure 4.14).

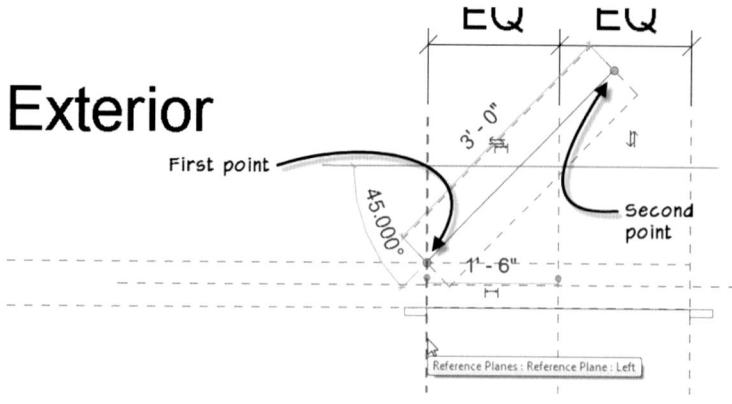

FIGURE 4.14
Draw a reference line from the hinge point at 45°

The order that you click the two points determines the direction of the face normal of the work planes (see Figure 4.15).

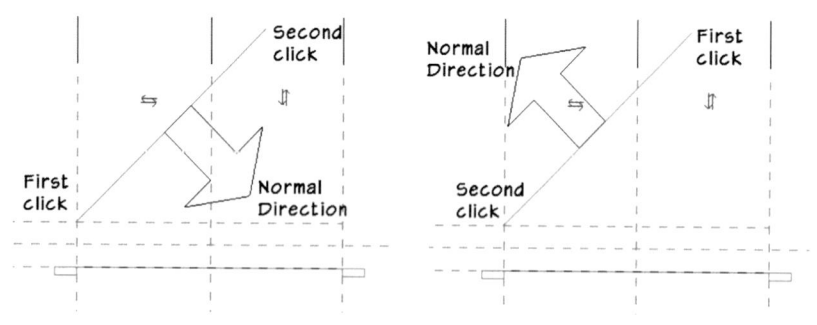

FIGURE 4.15
The normal direction (positive direction) of the faces of the reference line is determined by the direction you draw it

2. Select the reference line. On the temporary dimension that appears, click the small icon to make the temporary dimension permanent.

Adjust the position of the dimension if you like.

3. Select the new dimension and from the Options Bar, label this with the existing **Width** Parameter.

4. Use the Align tool and the TAB key technique to align and lock the end of the reference line to the Ref Plane: Left (see Figure 4.16).

5. Repeat on the Ref Plane: Exterior.

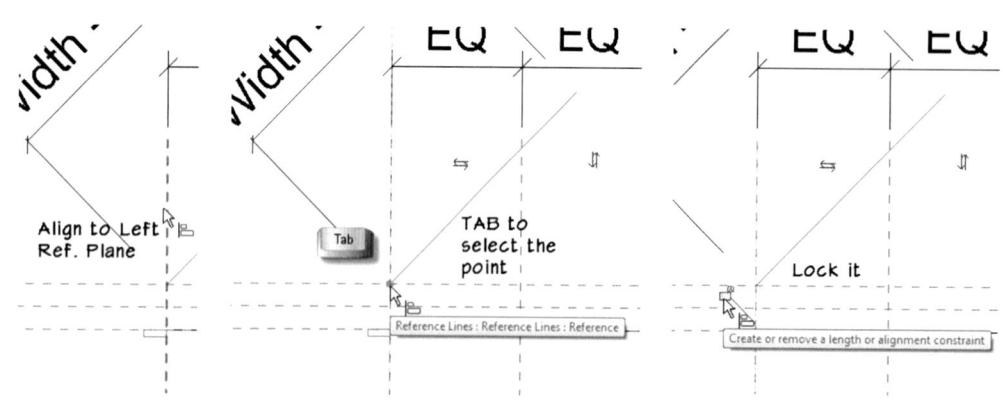

FIGURE 4.16
Align reference lines to lock them to the reference planes

This step is important. By locking the end point (hinge point) of the reference line in both the horizontal and vertical directions we ensure that the hinge point of the Door will move with the Door as expected. Having applied the Width parameter above further ensures that the reference line will flex as expected with the rest of the Door.

6. Flex the model. Modify the Width and then set it back to 3'-0" before closing the "Family Types" dialog.

ADD A SWING PARAMETER

The final step is create the rotation parameter.

1. On the Modify tab, on the Measure panel, click the drop-down on the dimension too and choose **Angular Dimension**.
2. Click on the Reference Plane:Exterior first and then click the reference line.
3. Place the Dimension (See Figure 4.17). Cancel the command.

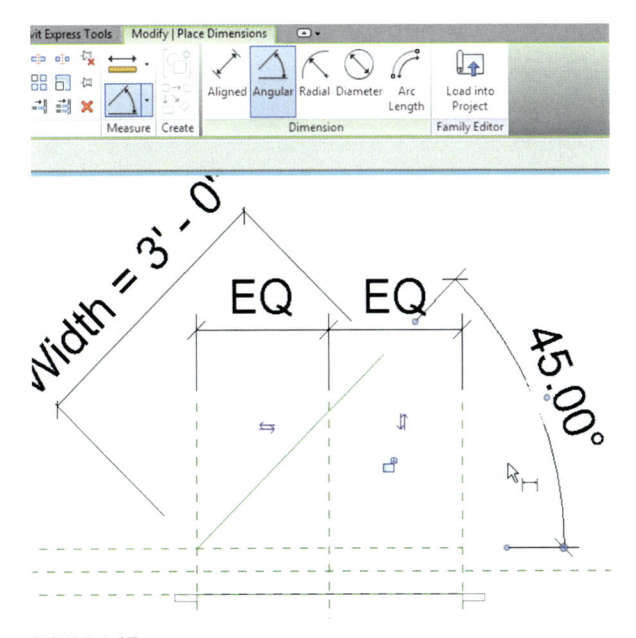

FIGURE 4.17

Create an angular dimension between the Exterior reference plane and the reference line

4. Select the angular dimension and then on the Options Bar, from the Label drop-down, choose **<Add parameter>**.
5. Name the parameter **Door Swing**, group it under **Graphics**, make it an **Instance** parameter and then click OK.

Group Under can be anything. We chose Graphics here, but if you prefer another grouping it will not affect its behavior at all. It is a matter of personal preference and/or office standard. Likewise, this parameter will function equally well as either a Type or Instance parameter. You can decide which will serve your needs best.

6. Flex the Model. Try different Widths and different Swing angles.
7. When satisfied that everything works properly, reset the Width to **3'-0"** and the Door Swing to **45°**.

> **CATCH UP!** You can open a file completed to this point named: *04_Door w Variable Swing.rfa*.

The main focus of this chapter is on techniques to control curvature in families. Therefore, we will just give a brief summary of the steps to follow next to create the solid geometry required for a door panel. This should give you the basics you need to complete the door family if you wish. Otherwise, the technique outlined above can be used to control rotation of nearly any element. (We will also create a more complete door later on in the "Combining Strategies" topic below).

CREATE THE DOOR PANEL GEOMETRY

To draw door geometry and constrain it to the reference lines is simple. The reference line has four integral Work Planes (see Figure 4.18). There is one horizontal, one vertical and one at each end point. You simply click the Set Work Plane tool, choose the "Pick a Plane" option and then select the plane upon which you wish to draw. It is recommended that you leave the reference line oriented at 45° for this. Cut a section at 45° as well, parallel to the reference line. Then open this view to work. If you work in one of the orthographic views, you can accidentally constrain your geometry to other nearby Ref Planes and geometry making it difficult to later flex the model. If you build your door panel extrusion on the 45° you can easily avoid this. Another technique often employed is to nest in another family for the door panel. The choice is a matter of personal preference and/or office standards.

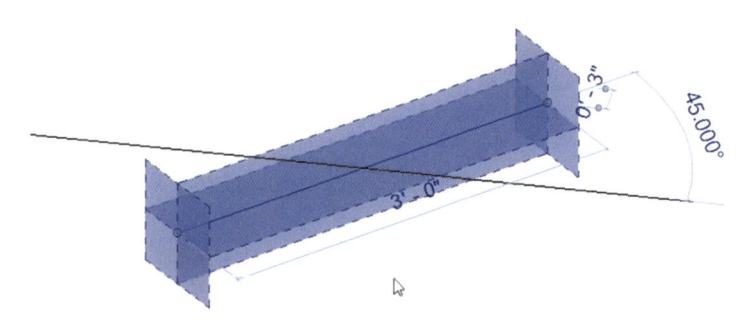

FIGURE 4.18
Reference lines have four integral Work Planes

Create the section, open it and then set the vertical work plane of the reference line current. Draw a solid extrusion on this plane. Snap it to the ends of the reference line. Use the Thickness parameter for the extrusion end property. To create a 2D plan version, draw Symbolic Lines using the pick lines option and constrain them to the edges of the solid extrusion.

ROTATING A CURVE

Combining the techniques covered in the two previous topics, we can create a parametrically controlled arc that allows us to set a start angle and an end angle. The basic process involves creating two parametrically rotating reference lines and then constraining the arc between them.

BUILD THE REFERENCE LINES AND PARAMETERS

1. From the *Seed Families* folder, open the file: *Family Seed (Sketch Dims).rfa*.

2. Tile the windows and then save the file to the *Chapter04* folder as: **Rotating Arc (Centered)**.

3. Delete the extrusion onscreen.

4. Following the procedure in the "Controlling Rotation" topic above, create a 45° reference line starting at the two center reference planes and make it **2.000** units long.

5. Make the temporary dimension permanent and label it with the **Depth** parameter.

6. Align and lock the endpoint at the center.

7. Add an angular dimension and label it with a new instance parameter named **A**.

8. Repeat the procedure creating a second reference line at 135° (see Figure 4.19).

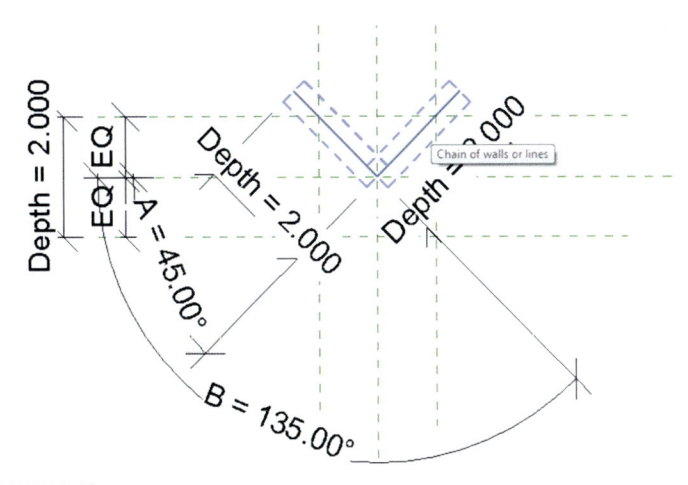

FIGURE 4.19

Create two reference lines constrained at the center with length and angle parameters

Be sure to perform all of the steps before flexing. Then flex everything and make sure it is working. For the geometry, we can make a Model Line again, or build an extrusion, or even create a curved path for a sweep.

> **CATCH UP!** You can open a file completed to this point named: *04_Rotating Arc (Centered).rfa*.

CREATE GEOMETRY ON THE ROTATING CURVE

Whichever type of geometry you decide to build, the process is similar. Make sure that the arc is centered on the reference planes (at the rotation points of the reference lines). Turn on the center marks, align and lock in both directions. Constrain the radius using the existing Depth parameter. Lock the endpoints of the arc to the reference lines (see Figure 4.20).

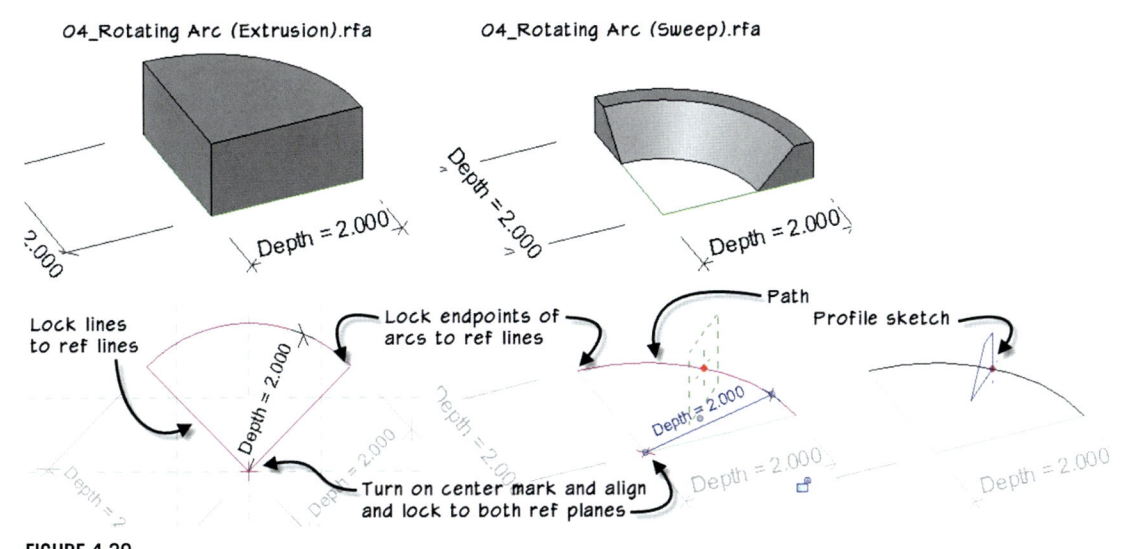

FIGURE 4.20

A variety of forms can be built on this armature such as extrusions or sweeps

You can construct any form this way. I made a pie slice with an extrusion and a simple curved sweep in the figure. But you could experiment with other forms if you like.

> **CATCH UP!** You can open files completed to this point named: *04_Rotating Arc (Extrusion).rfa* and *04_Rotating Arc (Sweep).rfa*

76 | Chapter 4

ARCHES

The previous examples all had the center point located at and constrained to two reference planes. But what do you do when the center of your arc does not land on such a convenient location? This is the case for many types of arches (see Figure 4.21) (Realtor 2001). Look around the town you live and you are bound to find many different types of arches used in the buildings; and not just the classical ones, but you will see plenty of arches on those as well.

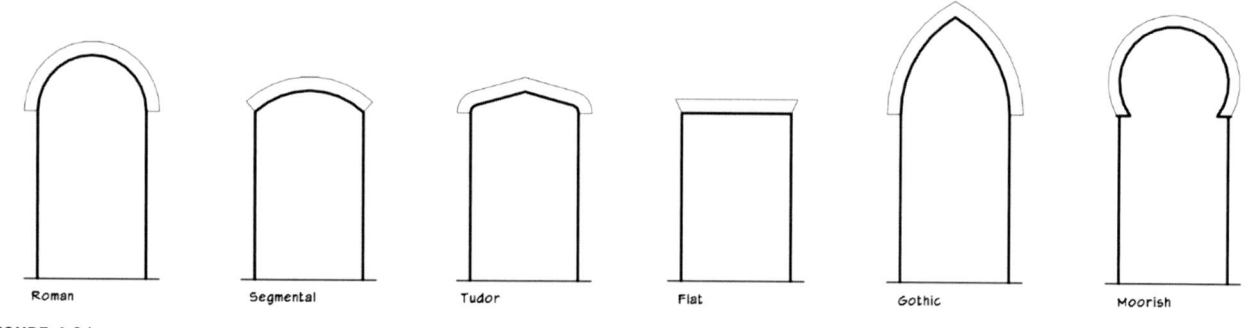

FIGURE 4.21
A selection of arches

CREATE A PARAMETRIC SEGMENTAL ARCH

We could do an entire chapter or maybe several on the subject of arches alone. I won't have time and space to do all of them, but let's consider a few common shapes. Starting with a Roman arch. To build a Roman arch you can simple use the techniques covered above. A Roman arch is a semicircle, so the techniques discussed above will work well. Just turn on the center mark, align and lock it to reference planes and then lock the endpoints of your arc on both sides as well. You can flex its shape with standard width and depth parameters (although you might want to think of the depth as height in the case of an arch) and add a radius parameter if desired.

If you have one of the other forms, you might have a tougher time making the arch behave as it flexes. For example, let's consider a Segmental arch. This one has an eyebrow shape and as its name implies is a segment of a circle. The main issue with such an arch is that the center point moves as the arch flexes. So since the techniques above relied on locking the center point, they will not yield good results. Let's look at what must be done to make a segmental arch behave. Here we must break our rule about keeping constraints applied only to references again. The key to success is applying the labeled dimension directly to the geometry of the curve (like the circle and ellipse above) rather than the traditional approach of dimensioning the reference planes and then letting them flex the geometry. (I should note that it is possible to stay true to the traditional approach and dimension only references. It would require formulas to calculate where the references need to be to give the correct curve. We will see examples of this below).

One last preliminary point. Back in the "Face-Based or Free-Standing" topic in Chapter 2, we discussed the face based family template and create a face based seed family. I think that in many cases, you will find a face based template a good choice for an arch. This makes it easy to place them on or in existing walls. You can of course use your free-standing template instead. All of the steps that follow should work fine in either one. But I have chosen our face based seed here.

1. From the Application menu, choose **Open > Family**.
2. Browse to the *Seed Families* folder, select the file named: *Family Seed (Face Based).rfa* and then click Open.

• Renaissance Revit •

⇨ Type WT and then ZA.

3. Save the file in the *Chatper04* folder as: **Segmental Arch**.

Our seed families all have the two default reference planes at the center. In this case, let's use the Center (Front/Back) reference plane (the horizontal one in the middle) as the spring line of the arch, so we'll need to delete the bottommost one.

4. Delete bottom reference plane. Also delete the extrusion.

When you do this, you will be left with a single unlabeled vertical dimension.

5. Select the vertical dimension.

⇨ On the Options Bar, label it with a new instance parameter and call it: **Rise**.

6. Select the top reference plane and on the Properties palette, rename it to **Arch Top**.

7. Flex the family to ensure everything is working. Set the Rise to: **0.750** (see Figure 4.22).

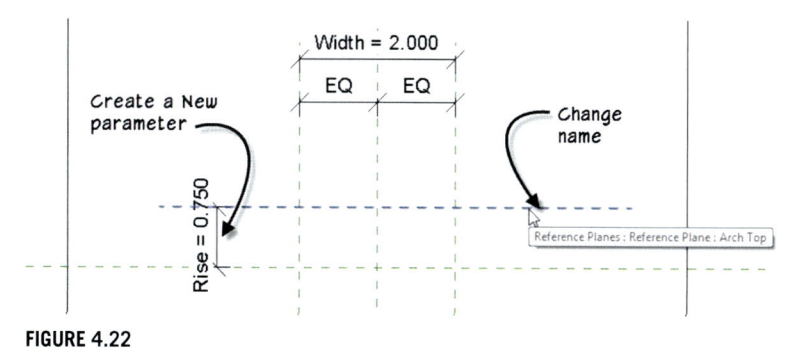

FIGURE 4.22
A selection of arches

With this framework in place, we are ready to build our geometry. While it is possible to use an extrusion here, it takes a little more effort to constrain it. This is because an extrusion would require two parallel curves. Instead, let's create a sweep. It is the path of the sweep that will form the arch shape.

8. On the Create tab, click the Sweep button. Choose the Sketch Path option on the ribbon.

9. From the Draw panel, choose the Start-End-Radius arc.

10. Snap the start and end points to the intersections where the left and right reference planes cross the Center (Front/Back) reference plane (see points 1 and 2 in Figure 4.23).

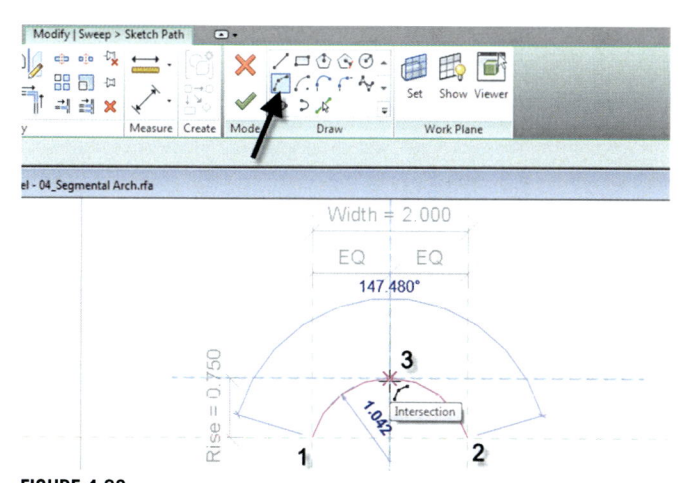

FIGURE 4.23
Create the path of the sweep with a start-end-radius arc

• *Creating Classical Architecture with Modern Software* •

78 | Chapter 4

> ⇨ Snap to the intersection of the Top and Center (Left/Right) reference planes for the radius (see point 3 in Figure 4.23).
>
> 11. Using the Align tool, align and lock the start and end points of the arc to the reference planes in both directions (see Figure 4.24).

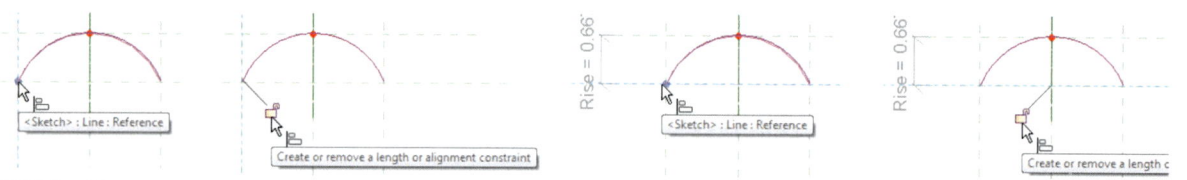

FIGURE 4.24
Align and lock the endpoints of the arc to the reference planes in both directions

Aligning and locking works fine for the endpoints. Unfortunately we cannot align and lock the midpoint of the arc. But just the same we always want the midpoint of the arc to stay with the top reference plane. To do this, we'll dimension the sketch line directly.

> 12. Create an aligned dimension. For the first witness line, click the Center (Front/Back) reference plane.
>
> ⇨ Click directly on the arc next to add the second witness line (see Figure 4.25).

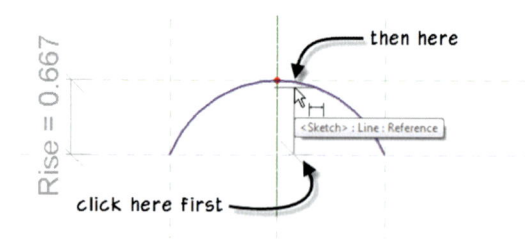

FIGURE 4.25
Dimension the arc directly

> 13. Label this dimension with the existing Rise parameter.
>
> ⇨ Flex the family.

That's it! The arch can now have nearly any rise value you like to create segmental arches of various shapes and proportions. If the value of Rise is equal to half of the Width parameter, you will get a Roman arch. If you go larger than this it will make an arch that has a Moorish shape. An arc must be curved, so you cannot use a value of zero. Therefore, to make a jack arch simply make a separate family with a rectangular form.

To complete the arch, just edit the sketch for the sweep profile and create a simple rectangle. If you prefer, you can use a more complex shape, but a rectangle will do the trick for now (see Figure 4.26). We'll do a more complex arch toward the end of the chapter.

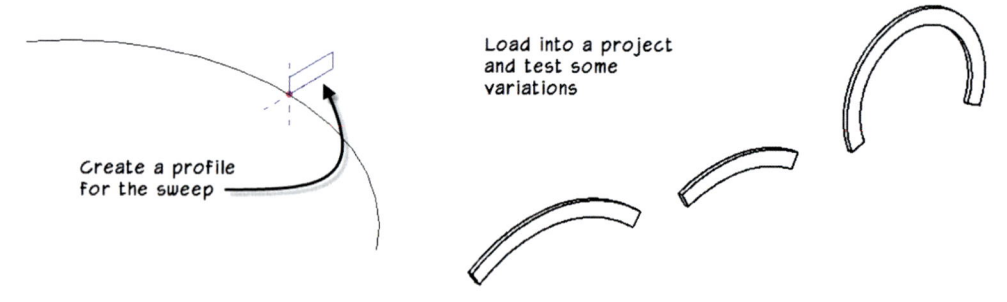

FIGURE 4.26
Complete the arch family and load it into a project

> **CATCH UP!** You can open a file completed to this point named: *04_Segmental Arch.rfa*.

GOTHIC ARCH

As noted, the previous family will yield many of the common arch forms, but not all. To create some of the others, we can leverage the same basic concepts. For example, a gothic shaped arch can be achieved by taking two segmental arch rigs and placing them in a triangular construct. I won't detail all of the steps here, but instead simply describe the overall process (see Figure 4.27).

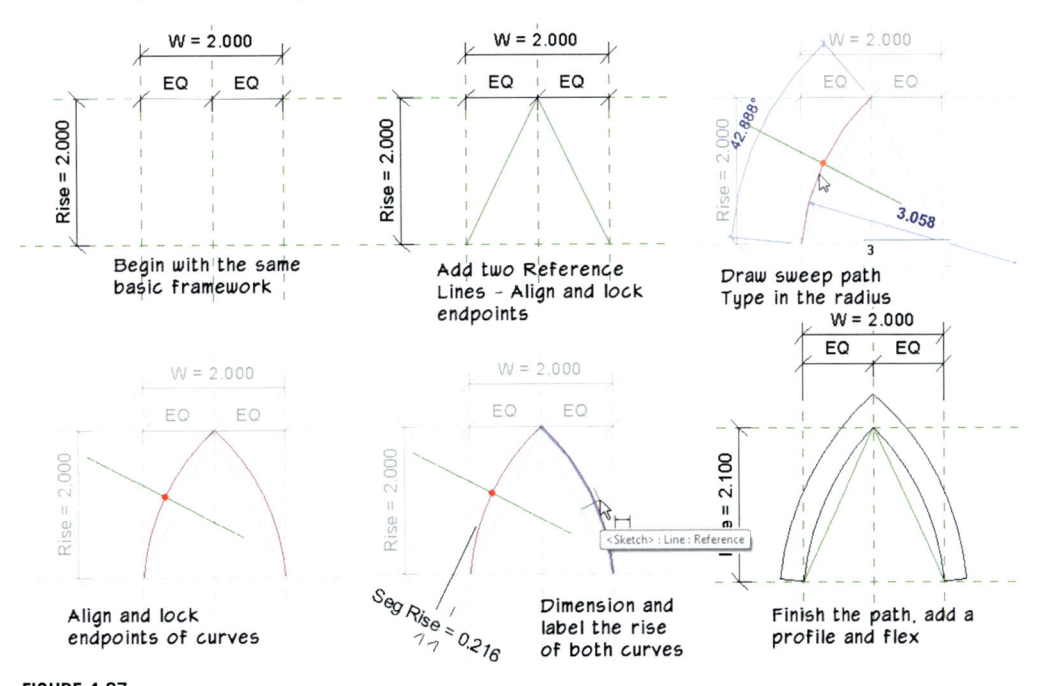

FIGURE 4.27

A gothic arch can be formed using essentially two segmental arches

Start with the same seed family and set it up the same way. You can even save the Segmental Arch family as a new name and just delete the sweep. Usually a gothic arch will have a higher rise, so flex the rise parameter to at least the same value as Width (shown as W in the figure). Draw two reference lines (*not* reference planes) forming a triangle. This will form the spring lines of each side of the arch. Use the Align tool to align and lock the endpoints of the reference lines to the intersections of the reference planes. Make sure you align and lock all four endpoints in both directions (eight total). It is a good idea to flex at this stage.

> **Note:** Sometimes when aligning and locking, Revit will complain that locking will over constrain the sketch. If you see this message, just click Cancel. No need to pursue it further as this message should be indicating that no further constraints are necessary at the location. Remember that having Automatic Sketch Dimensions displayed during this task can be very helpful in determining if you need to continue aligning and locking.

Begin your sweep and choose the Sketch Path option. Draw two Start-End-Radius arcs. The endpoints should snap to the ends of the reference lines. The radius can be anything, but they should be the same for both arcs. You can begin eyeballing the curve, and before clicking, type in a whole number value based on the temporary dimension displayed. This makes it easy to get the same radius on both sides. I used a value of **3** in the figure. Align and lock the endpoints of the curves to the reference planes.

Create a new dimension between the *reference line* and the rise of each arch. Make sure to set the first witness line at the reference line, then click the curve. Label each of these with a new parameter called: **Seg Rise**. Flex and then Finish the path.

• Creating Classical Architecture with Modern Software •

Finally, sketch the profile. You can also load in a profile family for the profile if you prefer. (We will explore profiles below). Flex the completed form. Be careful in flexing as certain combinations of Rise, Seg Rise and Width will cause it to fail, but it should work well for many combinations.

> **CATCH UP!** You can open a file completed to this point named: *04_Gothic Arch.rfa*.

ELLIPTICAL ARCHES

If you would rather use an ellipse to form the path of your sweep, much of the process remains unchanged. You draw the ellipse using the partial ellipse shape on the Draw Panel, align and lock its endpoints just like the arc. However, when you try to dimension the elliptical arc, Revit will stubbornly refuse to highlight it like it did for the arc. So instead of placing the dimension with the Aligned Dimension tool, the trick is to first select the partial ellipse onscreen, then click the small "Make this temporary dimension permanent" icon. This will make the dimension for you and then you can label it. All else will work the same way (see Figure 4.28).

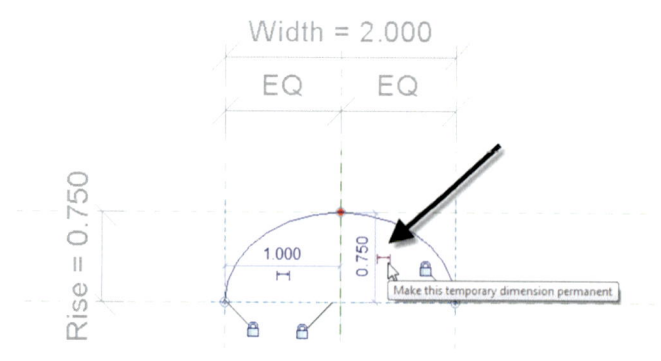

FIGURE 4.28

Make the temporary dimension permanent to create a flexible elliptical arch

All of the steps from the previous few examples are the same. Set up the same reference planes and parameters, or start with your segmental arch and save as. For the path of the sweep, draw a partial ellipse. Lock the endpoints and then select the elliptical arc and make the temporary dimension permanent as shown in the figure. Sketch the profile as a simple rectangle like the others and then flex it when finished.

> **CATCH UP!** You can open a file completed to this point named: *04_Elliptical Arch.rfa*.

COMPOUND CURVES

All of the examples so far have been single curves; in other words, there has only been one curve that we were trying to flex. In such cases, if you ensure that you constrain and/or parameterize the key geometric aspects of the curve, you will usually get good results. For example, with a circle or arc, if you constrain the center and radius, it will usually flex properly. With an ellipse, the center and axes usually give good results. However, as the forms that you wish to flex become more complex in shape, sometimes even constraining the center and radius will not be enough.

Consider situations where there is more than one arc segment making up a compound curve. Or even situations with a curve meeting a straight line at a tangent. There are endless possible examples. In this topic we'll consider a few of the more common examples. In similar fashion to the examples above, the key is going to be carefully constraining the curves so that you remove any ambiguity. **You want to make it very clear to Revit what your intentions are.** If you do this, everything *should* flex properly.

PROFILE FAMILIES

In the "Profile Families" topic in Chapter 2, we discussed profile families and applied some examples to simple sweep and swept blend forms. Several advantages of profile families were discussed in that topic. Perhaps the most important benefit of profile families is that we can use them in several forms and families. For the task of creating complex flexible curved forms, it is much easier to build a profile family and get the shape flexing properly, and then apply it to any 3D forms required. The remaining examples will use profile families.

Some challenges do exist. Profile families can contain reference planes, but *not* reference lines. Since we discussed the importance of using reference lines above when making a family that requires parametric rotation, this presents us with a bit of challenge.

There are some acceptable solutions. For example, you can use trigonometry to derive X and Y coordinates from any angle. This is very effective and very stable, however, trig can be challenging and introducing many formulas can have a detrimental effect on overall performance. Another solution that we will explore is using a nested rig family. Nesting can also be detrimental to performance, so you will have to consider each use case carefully. We'll see several examples below.

OVOLO

Let's start with some common molding shapes. I have previously cited the excellent book on classical architecture: *The Classical Orders of Architecture* (Chitham 1985, 2005). In Plate 76, Chitham details the construction of many common moldings. In Figure 4.29 I have reproduced the first two moldings we will consider: the ovolo and cavetto. Both use a single curve, but constructing them introduces a challenge (an offset center point) that once solved, will help us create the more complex compound curves that follow.

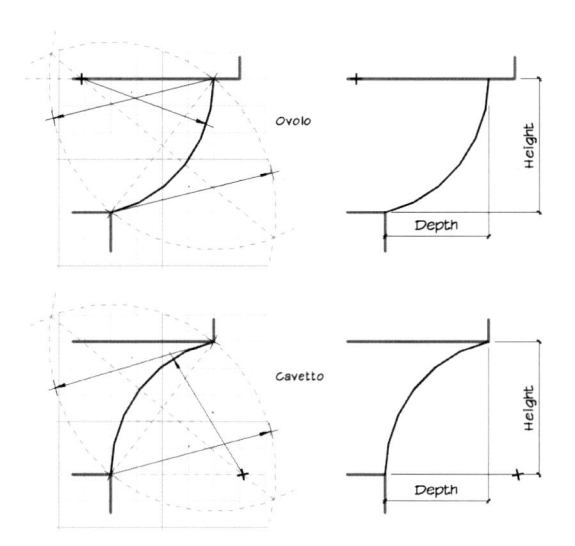

FIGURE 4.29
Constructing Ovolo and Cavetto profiles

Consider the shapes shown in Figure 4.29. The left side comes from Chitham and shows how to construct the curves using traditional drafting tools. The most likely way to describe the size of a molding like this and therefore the most likely way to flex this curve would be to ask for the depth and the height of the curved portion of the molding. This is shown on the right side. As you can see in the image, this width and depth of the curve portion are normally not equal, (A quick trip to your local lumber yard will allow you to verify this) meaning that the construction axes are along angled paths and as the dimensions flex. This also means that the center point is not always in the same location. As we mentioned above, reference lines are the best choice for controlling angles in families. However, reference lines are not available in profile families, so we could abandon our use of profiles and resort to building each molding with its own integral sketch. This would not be ideal since we would lose all benefits of using profile families. One of the most important being that they can be reused in multiple families. Therefore, if we can define them once in a good flexible profile family, we can then reuse them in almost unlimited ways in other content. So to build it as a profile family, we will have to resort to other techniques to control the shape of this family and ensure that it flexes properly.

USING TRIGONOMETRY TO MODEL TRADITIONAL MOLDING FORMS

As noted at the start of this topic, there are two viable options here. In the examples that follow, we'll look at both. Let's start with trigonometry. Depending on the complexity, the trig might be simple or complex. In this case, we have a simple case of similar triangles. You will be asking your user to input the desired height and depth of the molding. We will call these X and Y in the profile family. When you make a triangle from X and Y, you can easily derive the hypotenuse which we will call D (for Diagonal). Using trig, and these values, we can easily derive one of the angles which we will call A. Since we know all three sides, we have lots of options to choose from (Munkholm 2011) (also see Appendix A). For this example I went with the ATAN function performed on X and Y: **ATAN(Y/X)** to arrive at A. This new angle, coupled with half of D (we'll call this HD) can be applied to the second triangle. Finally with this information, the COS function will give us the length of the radius: **HD / COS(A)** (see Figure 4.30).

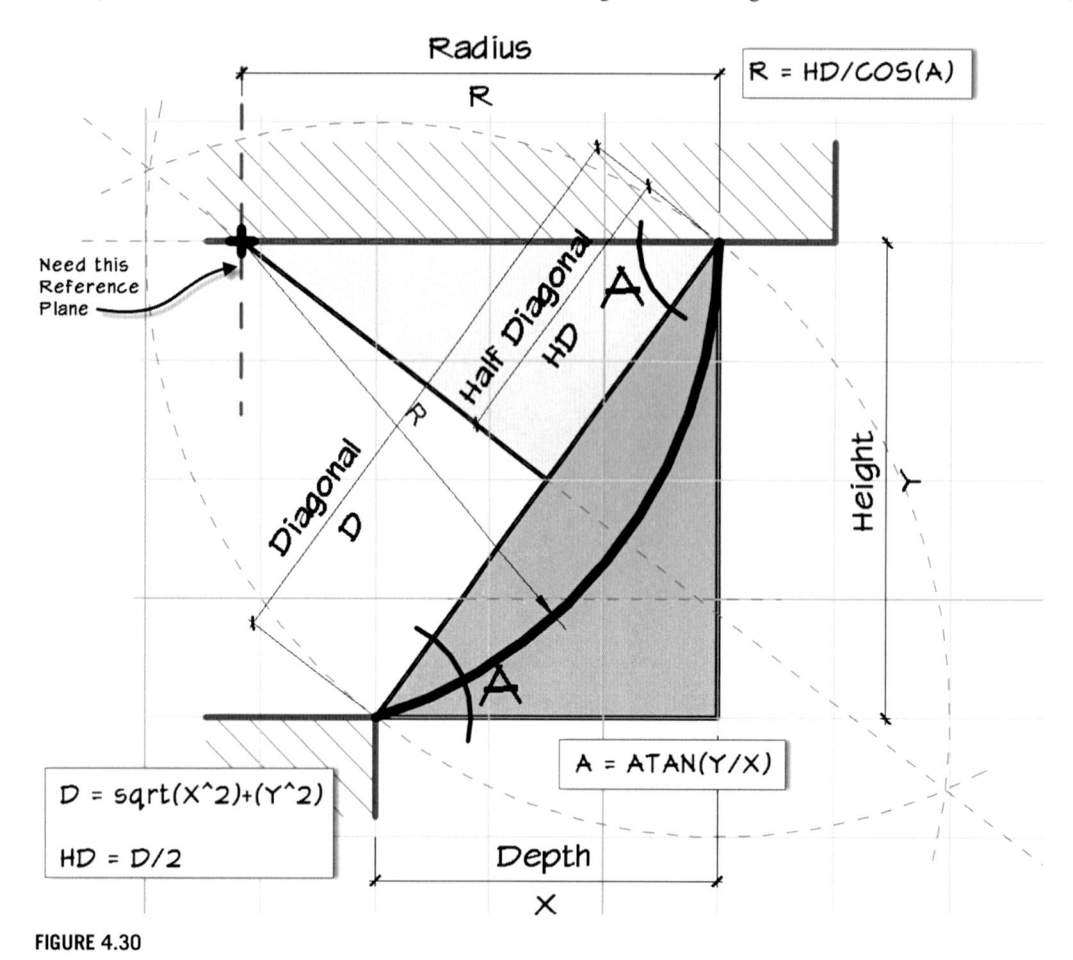

FIGURE 4.30
Applying trigonometry to locate the required reference planes

Provided with the dataset is a seed file for a profile family. It has the two default center reference planes positioned at the lower left corner. Two additional reference planes named: X Mid and X Max, and Y Mid and Y Max are placed above and to the right of these. They are dimensioned and constrained already. To this framework, we need to add a vertical reference plane to left for the radius location indicated in the figure. Our formulas will help us locate it.

1. From the Application menu, choose **Open > Family**.
   - Browse to the *Seed Families* folder, select the file named: *Family Seed (Profile).rfa* and then click Open.
   - Save the file in the *Chatper04* folder as: **Ovolo Profile**.
2. To the left of the Center (Left/Right) reference plane, draw a vertical reference plane. Name it **Radius**.
   - Add a dimension between the X Max reference plane and Radius.
   - Dimension and Label it with a new Type parameter called **R**.
3. Open the "Family Types" dialog.
4. Using the Add button on the right, create two new Type-based Length parameters: **D** and **HD**. Also create one Type-based Angle parameter called **A**.

   Group all of these under Constraints.
5. Input the formulas as follows (see Table 4.1):

TABLE 4.1

Parameter	Formula
D	sqrt((X ^ 2) + (Y ^ 2))
HD	D/2
A	atan(Y / X)
R	HD / cos(A)

6. Flex the family by creating a few Family Types (see Figure 4.31).

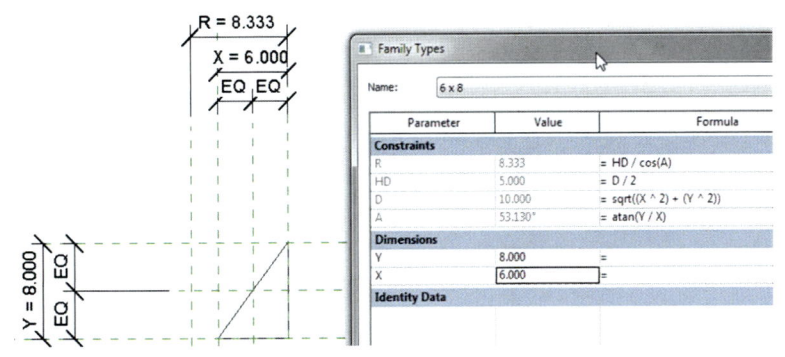

FIGURE 4.31

Create the parameters and Family Types

There is a simple triangle in this family already just to facilitate flexing. We can now delete this and draw the actual profile shape that we need.

7. Delete the triangle onscreen.

CATCH UP! You can open a file completed to this point named: *04_Ovolo Profile (Ref Planes).rfa*.

84 | Chapter 4

8. On the Create tab, click the Line tool.

9. For the right side, draw a Center-ends arc with the center at the intersection of the Y Max and Radius reference planes.

   Be sure to turn on the center mark, align and lock the center in both directions as well as the endpoints.

10. Draw vertical and horizontal lines locked to the reference planes for the leftmost edge and the top and bottom (see Figure 4.32).

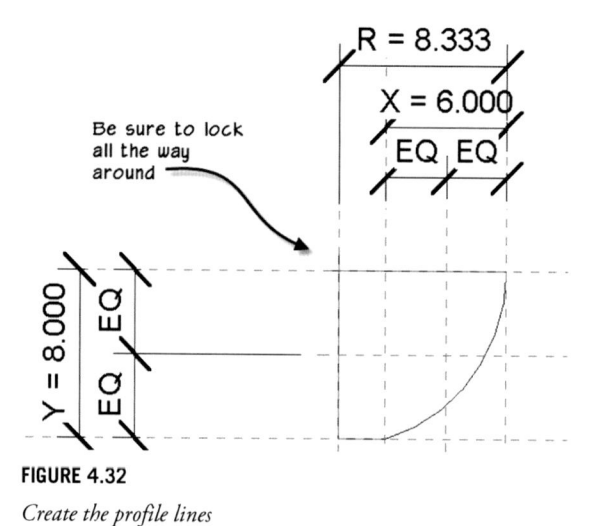

FIGURE 4.32
Create the profile lines

CATCH UP! You can open a file completed to this point named: *04_Ovolo Profile.rfa*.

11. Flex the completed version when done.

You can load this profile into any project or family now and use it shape anything from sweeps, to wall profiles to railings. A simple family file is provided here to test it out.

12. From the *Chapter04* folder, open *04_Ovolo Sweep Flex.rfa*.

A version of the profile family is already loaded, but if you prefer, you can load your version instead.

13. Select the sweep and edit it. On the ribbon, click the Select Profile button and then from the drop-down list, choose one of the types you previously defined.

14. Finish the sweep and flex the family (see Figure 4.33).

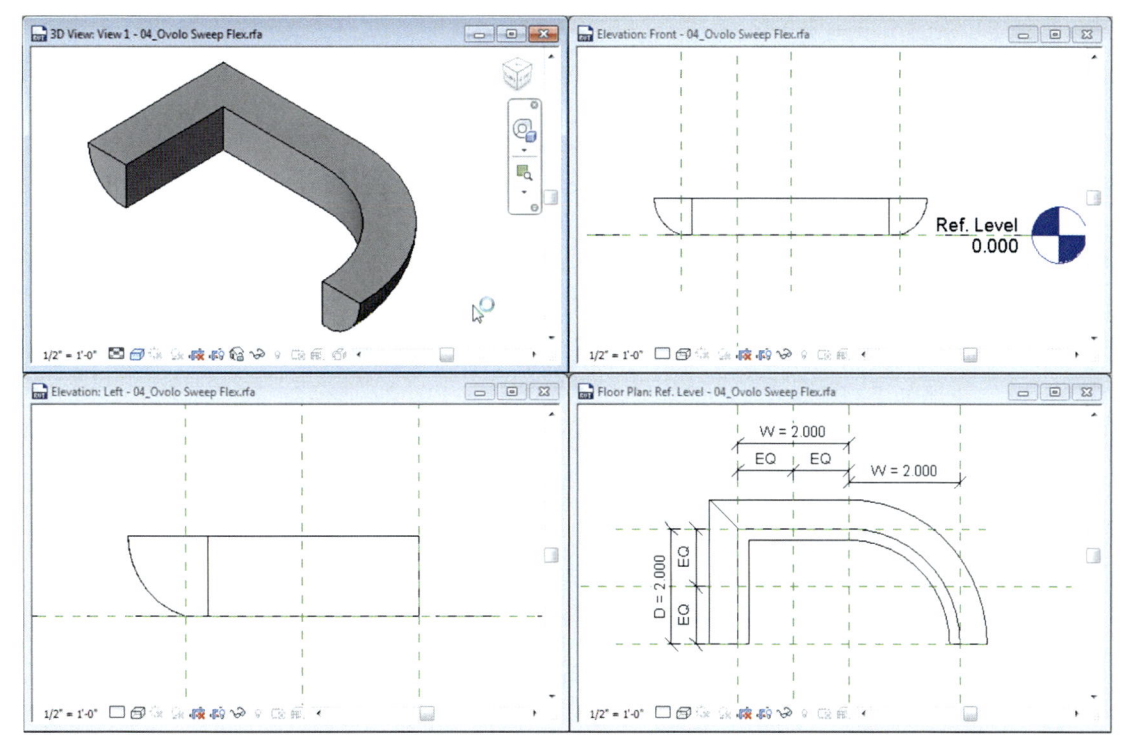

FIGURE 4.33
Apply the profile to the sweep form

This "flex" file that we have open is like a sandbox file. We are using it just to test out the profile and ensure that it works as expected. The family has two simple parameters: W and D. If you flex them, you will see the shape of the sweep path adjust. You can see by doing this how your profile follows along both straight and curved path edges. If you want to change the profile, edit the sweep again and pick a different type from the list. Using the technique we explored in the "Associate Family Parameters" topic in Chapter 3, we can even edit the type of the nested profile family and link up the X and Y parameters with driving parameters here in the host family. I will not go into the steps at this time, but feel free to experiment with this if you like.

15. Close both family files.

USING A NESTED RIG TO MODEL TRADITIONAL MOLDING FORMS

The previous example used formulas and trigonometry to locate the shifting center point of the curve. This allows us to have just two user inputs: X and Y and let the curve adjust to those inputs. For various reasons, you may wish to avoid formulas. Some folks find them cumbersome and complex. They also can impact performance if there are many of them in use. An alternative is available to formulas. We can build a separate "rig" family and then nest it into our profile family. This will help us overcome the limitation of not having reference lines to control rotation.

CAVETTO

In this example, we will look at the cavetto curve. It is exactly the same construction as the ovolo with the curve reversed. So the radius reference plane needs to be on the right with the center of the curve at the intersection of the radius and Center (Front/Back) reference planes. In all other ways, we could use the same strategy and formulas. But in this example, we'll look at an alternative: using a "rig" on which to build the curve form.

The starting family in this case uses the same seed we used for the ovolo profile above. It has one extra reference plane to control the depth of the form.

86 | Chapter 4

1. From the *Chapter04* folder, open the file: *04_Cavetto Profile (Rig)_Start.rfa*.
2. Save the file as: **Cavetto Profile**.

We'll also need our rig family. This one is a Detail Item family. We cannot use reference lines in Profile families. And while we can use reference planes, as we noted above, they do not work well in controlling angles. So instead of reference lines, we will simply draw lines instead. However, if we draw the lines directly in the profile family, they will be seen by Revit as part of the profile. If we instead draw our guide lines in a Detail Item family they can be used for our framework or "rig" and not be seen as part of the profile.

3. From the *Seed Families* folder, open the file named: *Family Seed (Detail).rfa*.
4. Save the file in the *Chapter04* folder as: **Single Curve Rig**.

This seed was created from the *Detail Item.rte* template. Reference planes were added and a few dimensions and parameters to save time. (The original *Detail Item.rte* template is provided in the *Templates/OTB* folder).

5. On the Create tab, click the Line tool. Snap the first point to the intersection of the Left and Front reference planes and the second point to the Right and Back reference planes.

   ⇨ Align and lock the endpoints to the reference planes in both directions on each end.
   ⇨ Flex to be sure it adjusts with the width and depth.

6. Draw a second line starting at the midpoint of and perpendicular to the first line. Make it approximately the same length as the other one.

   ⇨ Select the line and then click the small "Make this temporary dimension permanent" icon for both the length and angle dimensions (see the left side of Figure 4.34).

7. Select the new linear dimension and label it with the parameter called P (already in the file).

   ⇨ Lock the angle dimension (see the right side of Figure 4.34).

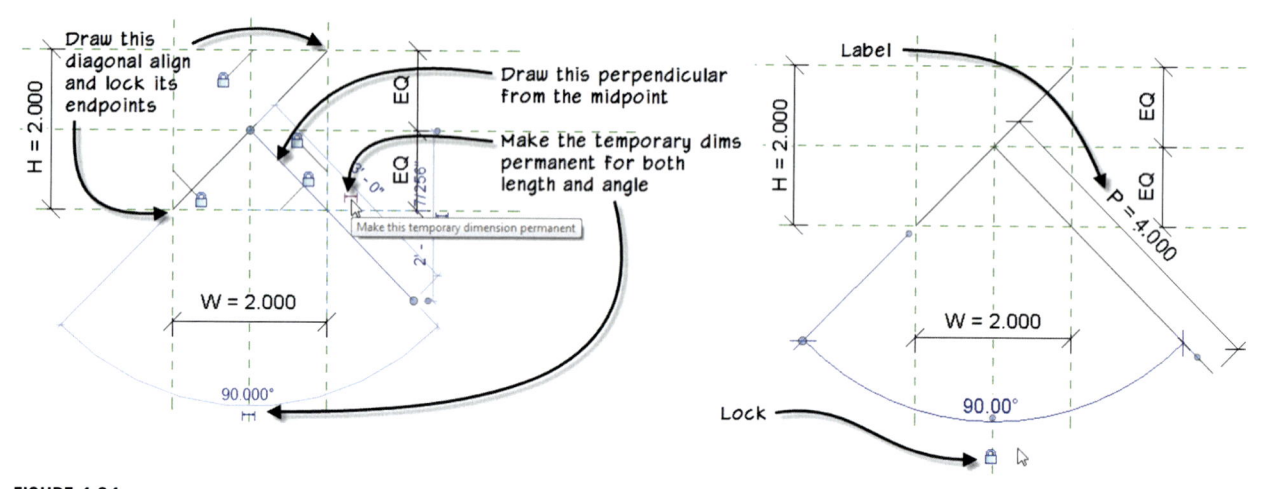

FIGURE 4.34
Build the rig in a Detail Item family

Optionally you can open Object Styles and create a new subcategory. Call it Guide Lines and then set the color to a light blue. This will help the rig stand out when nested into other families.

8. Save the family.

> **CATCH UP!** You can open a file completed to this point named: *04_Single Curve Rig.rfa*.

9. Click the Load into Project button.

⇨ Click to place it onscreen. Align and lock it on all four sides.

For each alignment, first click one of the reference planes in the host family, and then click the nested shape handle edge in the detail item family. Use TAB if necessary to get shape handle each time (see left and middle of Figure 4.35).

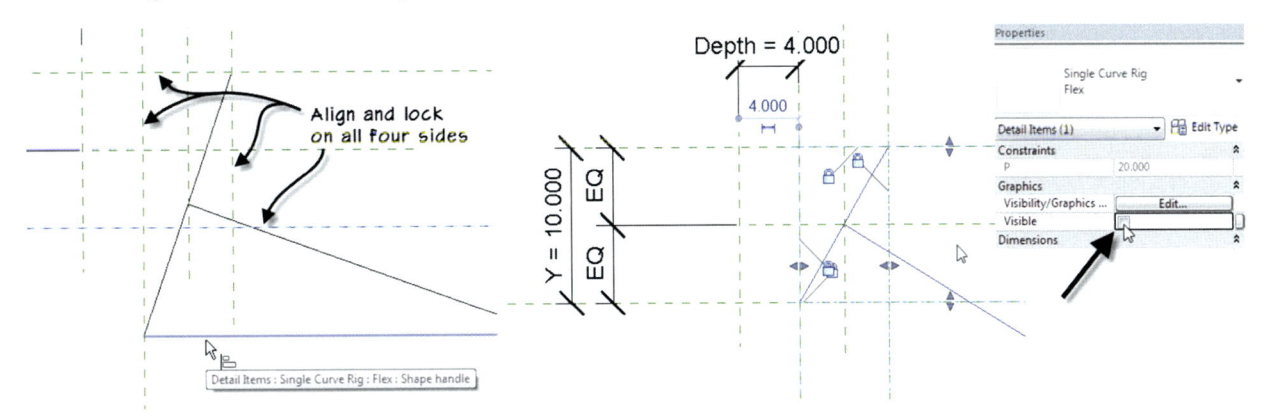

FIGURE 4.35
Nest in the rig, align and lock it on all four sides

10. Flex the family.

Notice that the nested detail item family changes shape with the host family. The diagonal line stays aligned with the flexing reference planes and the perpendicular line remains perpendicular. The intersection of the perpendicular line and the Center (Front/Back) reference plane is the center of our curve for this profile.

11. Select detail item and on the Properties palette, uncheck the Visible checkbox (see the right side of Figure 4.35).

This makes the rig invisible in all families that use the profile; we will only see it here were it is needed.

> **CATCH UP!** You can open a file completed to this point named: *04_Cavetto Profile (Rig)_A.rfa*.

With the rig in place, we draw the lines that make the profile shape next.

12. Draw the curve as we did above for the ovolo. Use the intersection of the perpendicular line and the Center (Front/Back) reference plane as the center.

13. Align and lock the endpoints of the curve.

> **Important:** Pay attention to the Status line as you align. You want to align to the reference planes in the profile family, *not* the references or shape handles in the nested family. Use TAB as necessary.

Notice that after you align and lock the endpoints in both directions, that all of the Automatic Sketch Dimensions will disappear. As such, you do not have to turn on the center mark or align and lock the center. However, it is a nice extra precaution. Furthermore, even though in most previous examples we aligned in the X and Y direction, you can actually enable the center mark and align it horizontally to the Center (Front/Back) reference plane and then align it again to the diagonal line in the nested family.

14. On the left, top and bottom, draw straight lines. Align and lock anywhere an Automatic Sketch Dimension appears (see Figure 4.36).

FIGURE 4.36

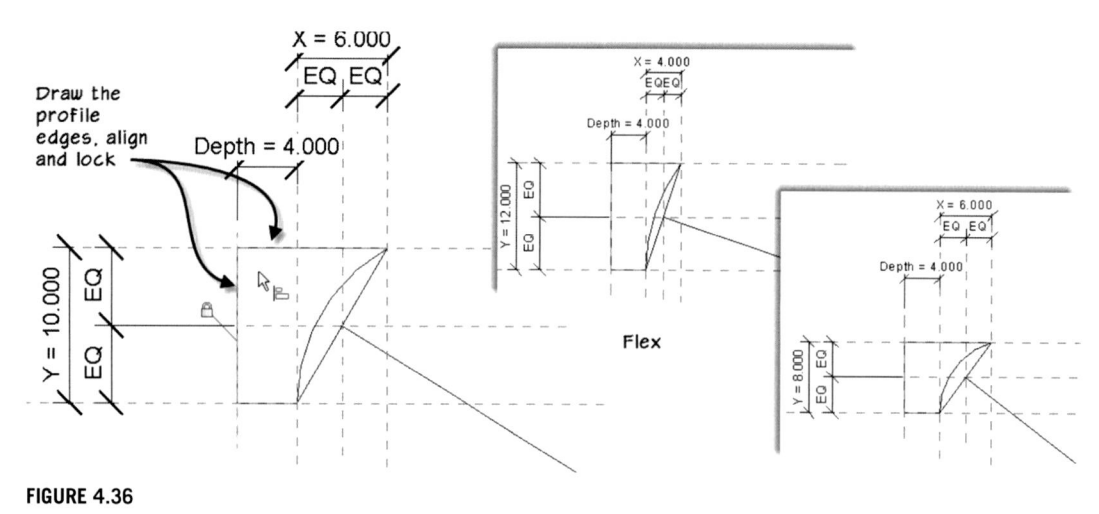

Create the profile shape and align and lock as necessary

> **CATCH UP!** You can open a file completed to this point named: *04_Cavetto Profile (Rig).rfa*.

15. Flex the family and then load it into the *04_Cavetto Sweep Flex.rfa* file to test it out in a sweep.

There are pros and cons to each approach. If you get the formulas right using formulas and trigonometry is very stable. But as noted, it can impede performance. Using the rig is a clever work around to some built-in limitations. It can be quite stable as well, but you have to be careful about which points you align and lock and make sure you do not inadvertently create bad references that prevent the families from flexing. You are encouraged to try both approaches and compare and contrast your results. With these techniques in hand, let's move on to more complex curves: the Cyma and Cyma Reversa.

CYMA

Figure 4.37 shows the way that the Cyma and Cyma Reversa profiles are constructed, a circle is created whose diameter matches the diagonal between the X and Y (Height and Depth). This circle is intersected with two arcs of the same radius which, when intersecting perpendiculars are drawn, creates four equal segments along the diagonal. The points where the arcs intersect the circle are the centers for the arcs used to create the Cyma profile (Chitham 1985, 2005). Once again, we will asking our user for Width and Height inputs.

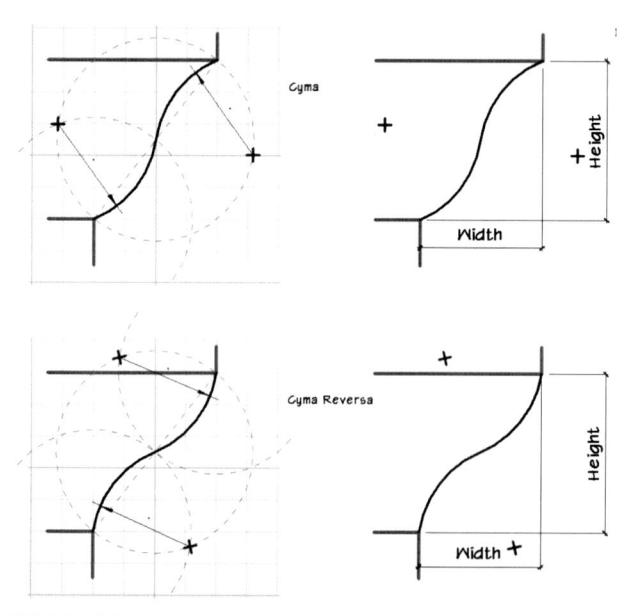

FIGURE 4.37

Constructing Cyma and Cyma Reversa profiles

Constraining Curves | 89

It just so happens that this construct also creates a regular hexagon whose vertices intersect the circle at the same points. Compare the gray dashed construction arcs in Figure 4.38 with the superimposed hexagon. A regular hexagon can be divided into six equilateral triangles. The sides of these triangles are each equal to half the length of the diagonal (between the Height and Width). This distance (the side of the equilateral triangle) is the radius of the arcs used for the cyma and cyma reversa profiles.

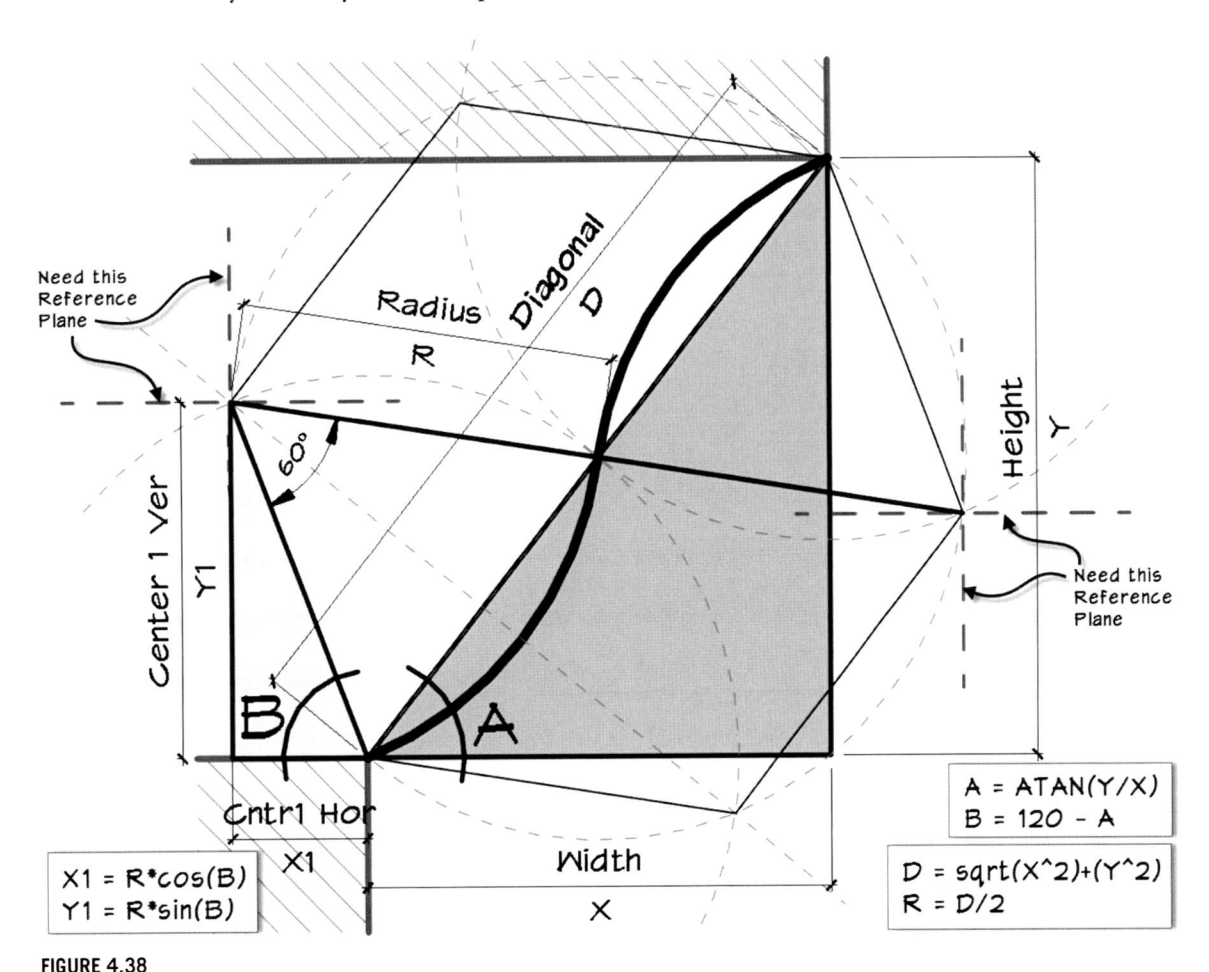

FIGURE 4.38
Applying trigonometry to locate the required Cyma reference planes

Once again, we can use trigonometry or nested detail components to construct this profile family. The trigonometric formulas are shown in the figure and in the table below.

The basic idea is that the user input is the Height (Y) and Width (X). This is used to determine the angle of the diagonal (D) which is in turn used to locate the center point of the two arcs of the compound curve and their radii. We'll start with a file based on the ovolo example above.

1. In the *Chapter04* folder, open the file: *04_Cyma Profile_Start.rfa*.
2. Save the file to the *Chapter04* folder as: **Cyma Profile**.

Some of the work has been done here already. To create this file, a copy of the Ovolo file created above was saved. This means that some of the reference planes and some of the formulas were already in place. This includes the insertion point at the lower left corner, the X Mid, X Max, Y Mid and Y Max reference planes, and the parameters X, Y, A, R and D. HD was not needed and has been removed. Additional reference planes have been added: Center Right Ver, Center Right Hor, Center Left Ver and Center Left Hor, the parameters X1 and Y1 are applied to the reference planes already (see Figure 4.39). There are also additional parameters listed in the table below.

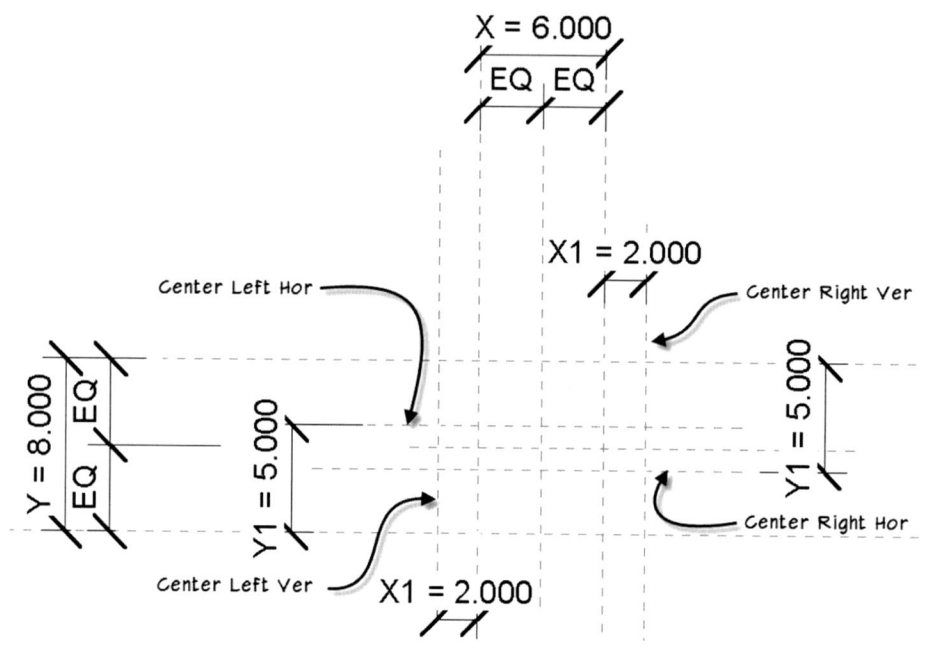

FIGURE 4.39

Starting family contains the reference planes and parameters

The formulas have not yet been added except those that came from the ovolo family. We will do this task now.

3. Open the "Family Types" dialog. Using the following table, input the formulas shown for each parameter (see Table 4.2).

TABLE 4.2

Parameter	Formula
Y1	R*sin(B)
X1	R*cos(B)
R	D/2
D	sqrt((X ^ 2) + (Y ^ 2))
B	120 – A
A	atan(Y / X)

4. Click Apply to test the values.

The reference planes should adjust slightly.

5. Try flexing with each of the types in the family already. Click OK when finished.
6. On the Create tab click the Line tool and then click the Center-Ends arc icon.
   ⇨ Snap the center of the arc to the intersection of the Center Left Hor and Center Left Ver reference planes.
7. Snap the one endpoint to the intersection of the Center (Front/Back) and Center (Left/Right) reference planes and the other to the intersection at X Mid and Y Mid (see the small dots at locations **a**, **b** and **c** on the left side of Figure 4.40).

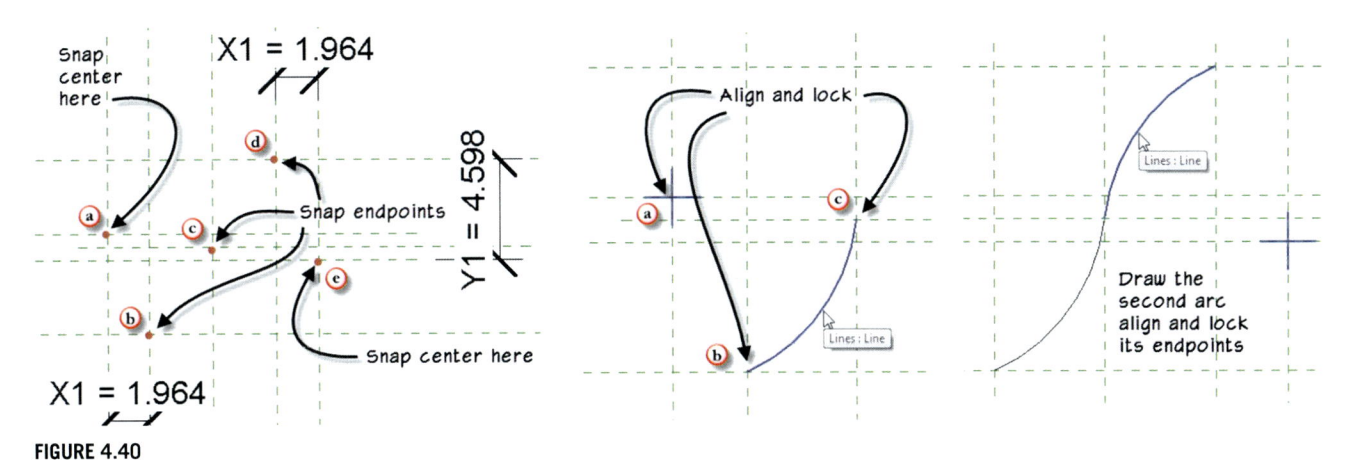

FIGURE 4.40
Draw the curves

> Select the arc and on the Properties palette, check the Center Mark Visible checkbox.

> Align and lock the center point and each arc endpoint to the reference planes in both directions (6 alignments total) (see the middle of Figure 4.40).

8. Repeat the process by drawing a second arc with center at point **e** (the intersection of the Center Right Hor and Center Right Ver reference planes) and endpoints at locations **c** and **d**.

> Turn on the center mark and align and lock all points (see the right side of Figure 4.40).

9. Open "Family Types" and flex the curve.

The curves should flex properly and remain constrained to the reference planes.

10. Draw vertical and horizontal lines locked to the reference planes for the leftmost edge and the top and bottom.

CATCH UP! You can open a file completed to this point named: *04_Cyma Profile.rfa*.

11. Flex the completed version when done.

You can load this profile into any project or family now and use it shape anything from sweeps, to wall profiles to railings. A simple family file is provided here to test it out.

12. From the *Chapter04* folder, open: *04_Cyma Sweep Flex.rfa*.

A version of the profile family is already loaded, but if you prefer, you can load your version instead.

13. Select the sweep and edit it. On the ribbon, click the Select Profile button and then from the drop-down list, choose one of the types you previously defined.

14. Finish the sweep and flex the family.

CYMA REVERSA

The Cyma Reversa is essentially the same shape just with the arcs reversed. So all we need to do to create one is save the Cyma family with a new name and redraw the arcs facing the opposite direction. However, the formulas do need adjustment due to the changed locations of the arc center points. The overall strategy and form is largely similar (see Figure 4.41). You can try your hand at one if you like, or you can simply open the example provided here.

CATCH UP! You can open a file completed to this point named: *04_Cyma Reversa Profile.rfa*.

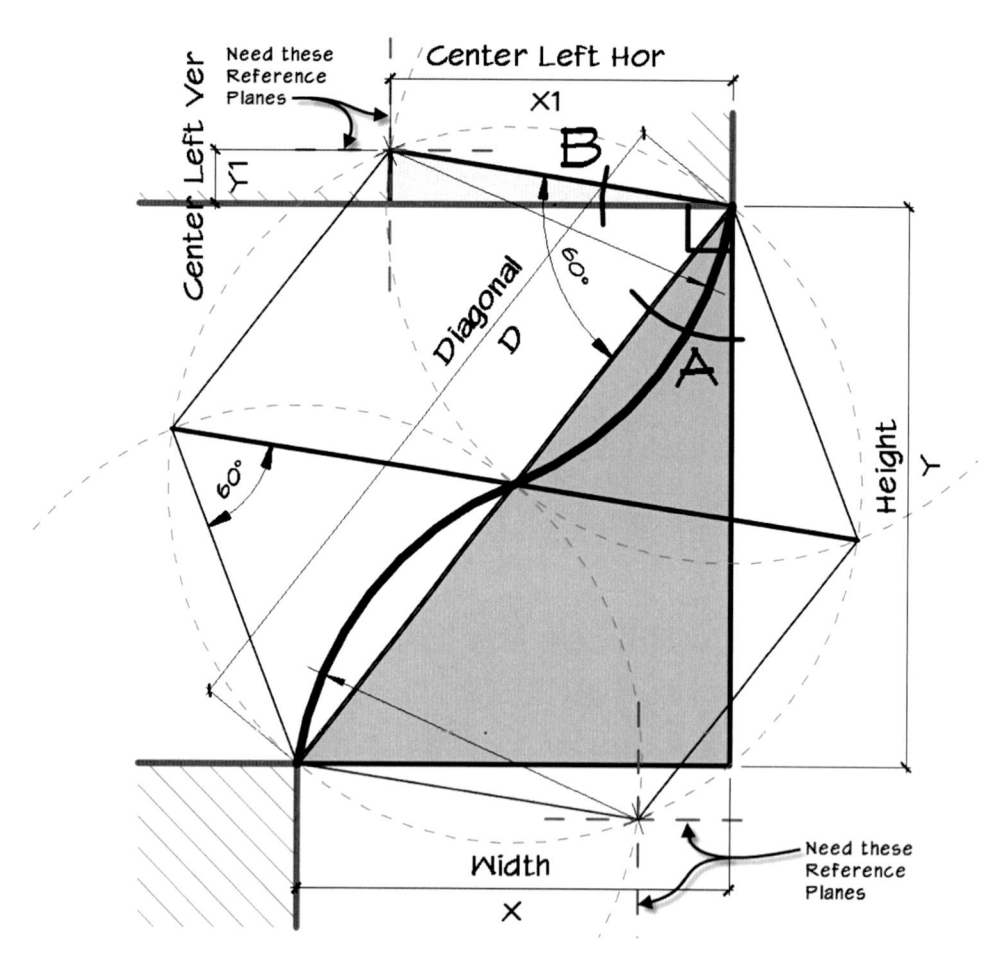

FIGURE 4.41

Cyma Reversa Construction

The critical angle is angle B. There are two known angles in its vicinity, the right angle between the reference planes X Max and Y Max and the angle between the diagonal and the top edge of the implied hexagon. The diagonal, as we saw above, is derived from the Height (Y) and Width (X) parameter inputs and the Pythagorean Theorem. As the diagrams in Figure 4.38 (above) and Figure 4.41 illustrate, the diagonal's endpoints form two vertices and becomes the bisector of an implied hexagon. The hexagon's other four vertices determine the locations of the center points of the arcs of Cyma and Cyma Reversa curves. Since a regular hexagon is easily divided into six equilateral triangles, we also know that the angle between the diagonal (bisector) and the hexagon's top edge is 60°. These known angles make it easy to calculate angle B, which in turn gives us the values X1 and Y1 and the locations of the required reference planes.

CYMA AND CYMA REVERSA RIGS

If you look on the *Families* branch in the two testing files: *04_Cyma Sweep Flex.rfa* and *04_Cyma Reversa Sweep Flex.rfa* you will find two versions of the nested profile families. The ones with the (Trig) suffix use the trigonometry formulas and the ones with (Rig) suffix use a 2D detail item family rig nested in them. Feel free to experiment with each one and open them to explore if you wish.

PROPORTIONAL SCALING STRATEGIES

Configuring curved forms so that they can be reshaped parametrically in a predictable and stable way has been the focus of all the examples in this chapter. The previous chapter focused entirely on proportion and scaling. But since proportional scaling is especially important when building classical architectural forms like Doric, Ionic or Corinthian columns, we will now look at some examples that tie the concepts from this and the previous chapters together.

Many of the examples covered so far in this chapter have allowed for flexibility in both the X and Y directions, but so far we have not discussed strategies to scale the X and Y dimensions proportionally. Naturally, you could just take great care to always make sure your inputs to X and Y match the desired proportions, but of course, this approach is hardly foolproof. With the framework we already have in place for most of the examples created so far, it is very easy to apply an additional constraint to the parameters to force them to flex proportionally. For example, if you like the proportion achieved when X = 4 and Y = 5, simply add a formula in "Family Types" for X that reads **Y * .8**. Other formats work as well, such as **Y * 5/4**, or a formula for Y instead reading: **X * 1.25**. It doesn't really matter which one you use, as they will all yield the same results. This is true because as we noted in the previous chapter, simple arithmetic formulas are bidirectional. So you can edit the value of either X or Y and the other will update accordingly automatically.

To add another level of flexibility, albeit with a touch more complexity, you can introduce a multiplier. This will enable you to establish the proportion of two or more parameters to one another, but also scale the entire family based on a single multiplier value. We did the simplest form of this approach in the previous chapter when we introduced the Base Diameter parameter. I have explored a few ways to approach this and have included a few additional profile families in the dataset that utilize some various scaling and proportional strategies. Let's have a look at them now.

CORONA

A Corona is really just a variation of the Cavetto that we considered above. It has a similar curve with a long fillet projection beneath it. I have made the projection flexible and variable. However, I have made the curve portion proportional. In addition, I have tied everything together so that a single Base Diameter parameter can scale the entire shape. So when flexing this family, you can choose different heights and depths for the rectangular portion, but when you scale, the curve always maintains its proportion (5/6 of Y in this case).

> **SAMPLE!** You can open a sample file named: *04_Corona Profile (Fixed Proportion).rfa*.

Feel free to open the file, and consider Figure 4.42. Y1 and X1 drive the size of the lower rectangular portion of the profile. Y1 and X1 are derived formulaically from user inputs to **Y Projection Mult** and **X Projection Mult**. These two parameters are formatted as Number parameters (not Length). This means that they cannot drive lengths directly. To make them drive the length parameters Y1 and X1, they are multiplied by a length parameter. Like the previous chapter, I used the parameter **Base Diameter** for this. Depending on the use of any moldings created from this profile, you can input appropriate values for the multipliers to yield a molding of the required size. In other words, if you use this molding on a pedestal, you might need a longer projection or different depth than you require when it is used on an entablature. The third numeric parameter called: **XY Mult** is used to control the size of both Y and X. It is applied directly to Y in its formula and indirectly to X since X is derived from Y.

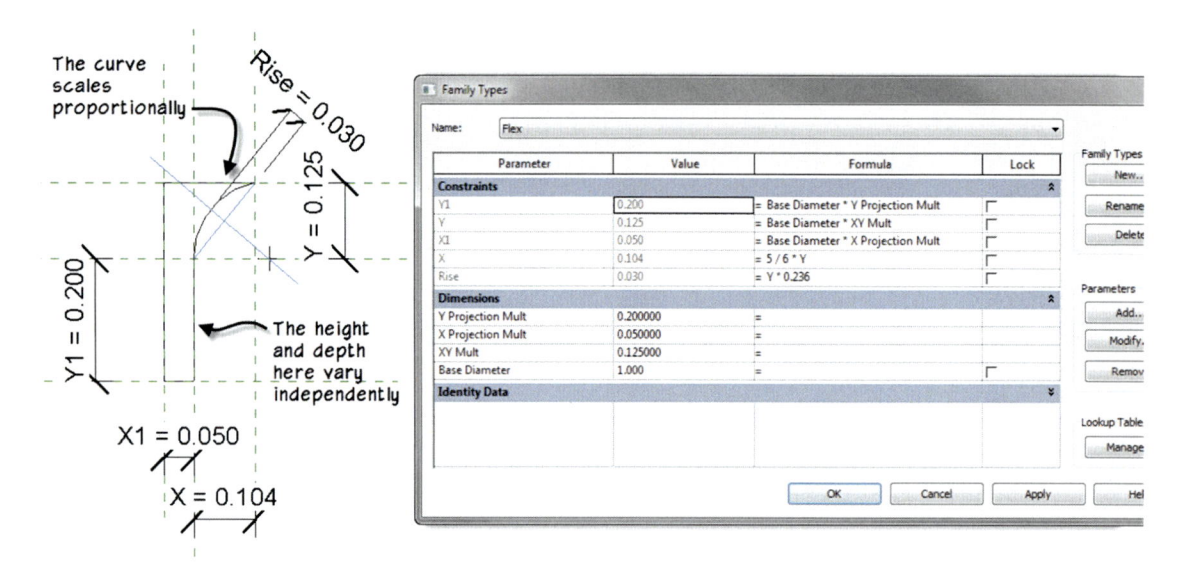

FIGURE 4.42

Construction of a Corona Profile

The additional innovation in this family is the use of a Line-based Detail Item rig. We looked at several examples of Detail Item rigs above. The rigs above were designed to allow disproportional scaling. In other words, the rig can flex differently for X and Y. These used a standard Detail Item template. The example here uses a Line Based template. A Line-based family is handy because you place it by clicking two points instead of one. This means that you can build it to scale proportionally based on the length between the two clicks. However, once the rotation is established with the two clicks, flexing it to a different proportion will often break it. So such rigs are best used in proportional scaling families like this one. Feel free to open the nested Line-based family and explore. This rig gives us a stable chord for our arc, so we can apply a parameter to the arc rise in much the same way that we did in the "Create a Parametric Segmental Arch" topic above. Here I am deriving the **Rise** parameter as a set proportion of the Y parameter. I am doing it that way to ensure that the "height" of the rise remains a constant proportion, but still scales with the Base Diameter (which is built into the formula for Y).

The Corona profile family introduces some complexity, but compensates for this by also introducing some additional flexibility. However, to make it truly flexible, it needs a few more enhancements. We'll explore a detailed example below, but let's look at one more proportional example first.

SCOTIA

The Scotia profile shown in Figure 4.43 is also fully parametric and scales proportionally. It uses some of the same techniques, but the approach is a little different and a little simpler.

> **SAMPLE!** You can open a sample file named: *04_Scotia Profile.rfa*.

A scotia is made up of a circular arc and elliptical arc. (As we noted above, a circle is really just a special case of an ellipse, so we could argue that the scotia is two elliptical arcs, one circular in form, but this is a semantic distinction). The approach shown in the dataset file and figure here uses an overall fixed proportion of 3 to 2 ½. To avoid having lots of unnecessary parameters, a grid of reference planes is used with equality dimensions to flex them. There are four reference planes set equally in both horizontal and vertical directions. A parameter called **G** is used to size one bay of the grid in each direction, which in turn sizes the entire gird. To get the ½ bay in the X direction, the last bay is subdivided again with an equality dimension and an extra reference plane. Once again the Base Diameter parameter is used to scale the overall proportions. Like the Corona, in order to make the profile flexible enough to use in varying scenarios and families, a **Multiplier** parameter is introduced which is multiplied by Base Diameter to give us **G**. G drives the size of the grid and family overall. A separate multiplier (**Projection Mult**) is used to scale the size of the Projection. The arc and ellipse are simply aligned and locked to the reference planes (both the centers and endpoints) using techniques covered previously.

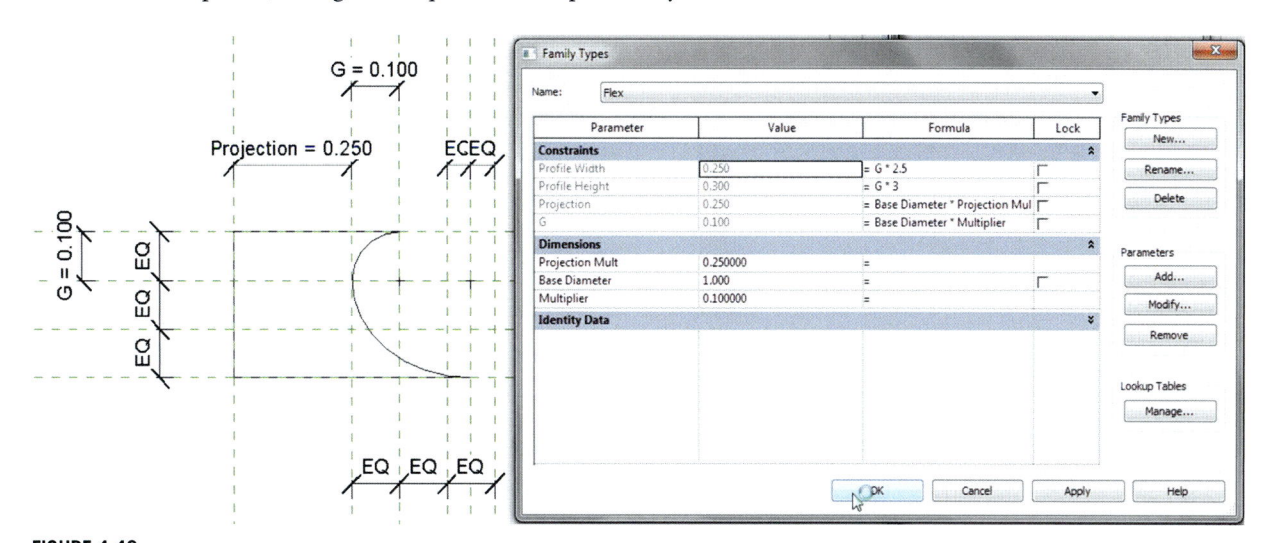

FIGURE 4.43
Construction of a Scotia Profile

No rigs or trigonometry are necessary in this family. If you keep the goals of the family fairly limited you can often avoid the more complex approaches. This makes the families easier to construct, maintain and troubleshoot. The downside is that this family only scales in the proportion built into it. If you want it to scale disproportionally, you would need to plan for Grid X and Grid Y. This might require more formulas, trigonometry or rigs. All are possible of course, but sometimes it is easier to just save the family as a new name and build two or more, each with a different proportion.

CREATE A VARIABLE CORONA PROFILE

If you look again at Figure 4.42 above, you can see that the shape of the Corona profile includes the curved portion at the top and a flat extension below. In applications where this molding is to be used directly beneath another molding or feature, this will work OK. But for many classical forms, such as the Tuscan capital we will be building in the next chapter, it will be useful to have a small fillet above the curved portion of the corona. We could build the fillet as a separate solid, but I think that in most cases, we could benefit from having the fillet as an integral part of the Corona Profile. So let's make that modification now in a copy of this family. Furthermore, at the start of this topic, we also discussed that this particular profile has the proportion of 5/6 built in. Let's also add another multiplier and make it possible to vary the X and Y relationship of the curve.

1. Open the *04_Corona Profile (Fixed Proportion)* file.
2. From the Application menu, choose **Save As > Family**.
   ⇨ For the name input: **Corona Profile (Variable Proportion)**.
3. Copy the upper horizontal reference plane up **0.030** units.
   ⇨ Add a dimension between the new reference plane and the one below it. (Be sure to dimension the reference planes, *not* the profile lines).
   ⇨ Label the dimension with a new type-based parameter named: **Y2**. Group it under Constraints (see Figure 4.44).

FIGURE 4.44

Copy the upper reference plane and label it with a new parameter

Recall from above, that the lower portion of this family is flexible based on multiplier parameters. Let's do the same for this new parameter. Instead of tying it directly to Base Diameter, we'll add another multiplier parameter.

4. Open the "Family Types" dialog.

5. Click the Add button and create a new **Number** parameter.

    ⇨ Name it: **Fillet Projection Mult**.

    ⇨ Make sure it is a Type parameter and group it under **Dimensions**.

    ⇨ Set the value of Fillet Projection Mult to **.030** (see the left side of Figure 4.45).

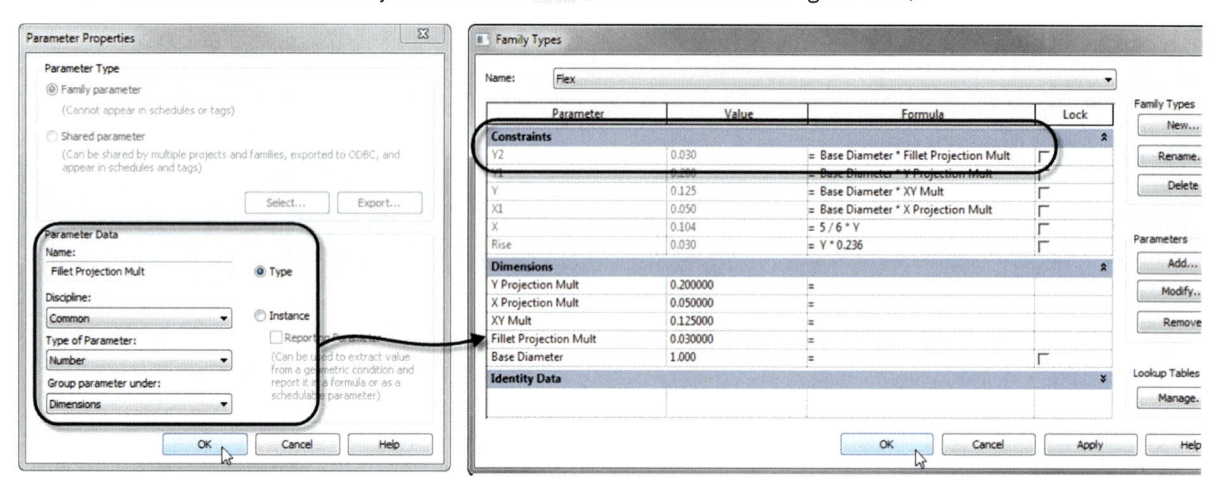

FIGURE 4.45

Create a new multiplier parameter for the fillet

6. In the Formula field next to Y2, input: **Base Diameter * Fillet Projection Mult** and then click OK (see the right side of Figure 4.45).

    ⇨ Flex the Fillet Projection Mult parameter.

    Only the top reference plane should adjust at this point. If you flex the Base Diameter however, the entire family will scale proportionally including the location of the new reference plane.

As noted above, this family uses a line based detail item rig. In my experiments, this is a novel approach, but unfortunately seems to behave badly when you scale it disproportionally. So as long as you keep the ratio between X and Y at 5/6, this family will perform nicely. However, to make this profile more flexible and useful to all the

• Renaissance Revit •

places we might need it, I think we should swap out the detail item family with the *Single Curve Rig* we used above. This also means we will need another multiplier and to adjust the formulas. Since we are still in "Family Types" let's start there.

7. Select XY Mult and on the right, click the Modify button.

    ⇨ Change the name to: **Y Mult** and then click OK.

Notice that upon renaming, it also renames this parameter in all the formulas as well.

8. Create a new **Number** parameter called **X Mult**. Group it under **Dimensions**.

    ⇨ Set the value to match X, currently **.104**.

    ⇨ Change the Formula for X to: **Base Diameter * X Mult** (see Figure 4.46).

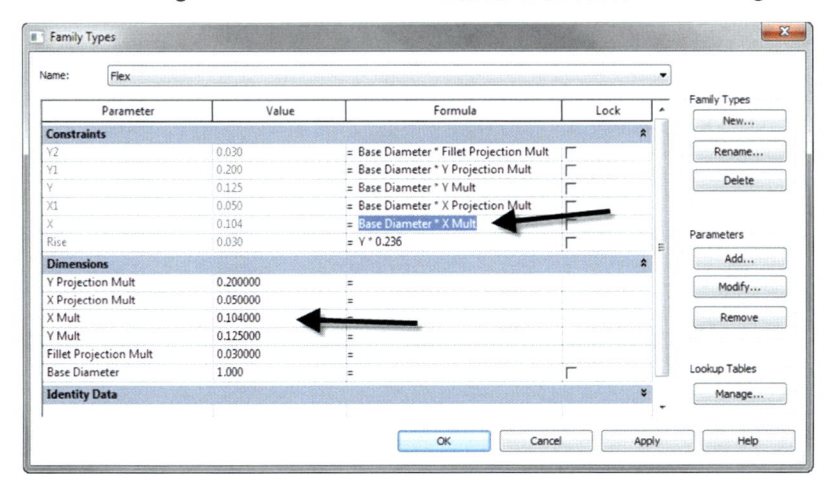

FIGURE 4.46

Create a new multiplier parameter for X

It is important that you use the same values that are here initially. If you use a different value, when you apply the formula, Revit will try to flex the curve. This does not always go so well. Even with the same values, there may be some round off in the decimals, so when we try to close the dialog, we will get a warning. This is why we need to replace the line based rig with the more stable one we built above.

9. Click OK to dismiss the dialog. Do *not* flex before closing.

    ⇨ In the warning that appears, click the Remove Constraints button.

10. Delete the top horizontal profile line, the arc and the detail item rig (see the left side of Figure 4.47).

11. On the Project Browser, expand *Families > Detail Items*.

    ⇨ Right-click the *Guide Lines* family and choose **Reload**.

    ⇨ Browse to the *Chapter04* folder and choose the *04_Single Curve Rig.rfa* file. (You can also use your version created above if you prefer).

    ⇨ When prompted that the family already exists, choose the first option: **Overwrite the existing version**.

12. Expand the family name on Project Browser, drag Flex and drop it in the view window to place it onscreen. Align and lock it on all four sides

> TIP: This family comes in very large initially. You can set the X and Y size on the Properties palette to about .25 before aligning. This will reduce the size and prevent your having to zoom out very far. Once aligned and locked, the sizes will match the context.

• *Creating Classical Architecture with Modern Software* •

For each alignment, first click one of the reference planes in the host family, and then click the nested shape handle edge in the detail item family. Use TAB if necessary to get shape handle each time (see the right side of Figure 4.47).

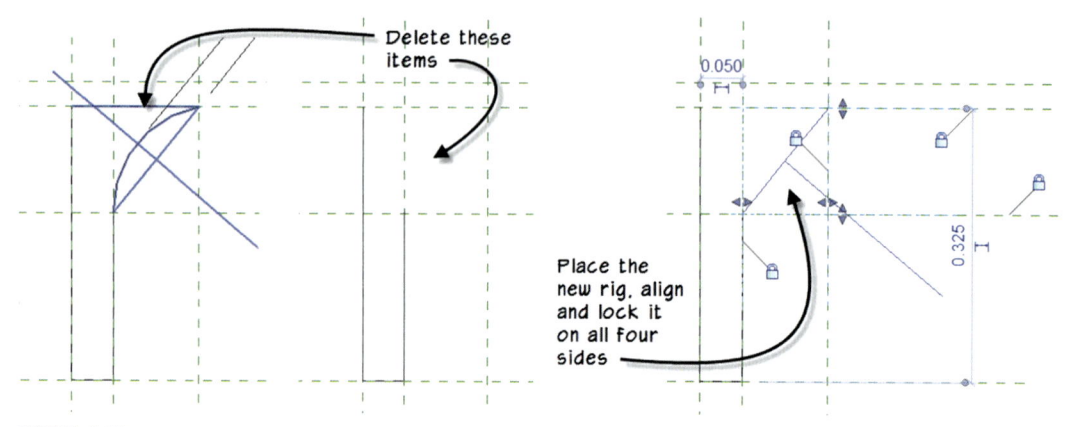

FIGURE 4.47
Delete the top portion and add the new rig

➪ Select the detail item, on the Properties palette, uncheck the Visible checkbox.

This is the same process performed above in the "Cavetto" topic.

13. Extend the vertical line on the left to the new reference plane.

➪ On the Create tab, click the Line tool and draw two new lines, one horizontal and one short vertical back down to the rig.

➪ Align and lock the two new lines to the reference planes (see the left two images in Figure 4.48).

Important: Make sure that for each alignment, you first click on a reference plane, not any other geometry or the detail item, then click the line.

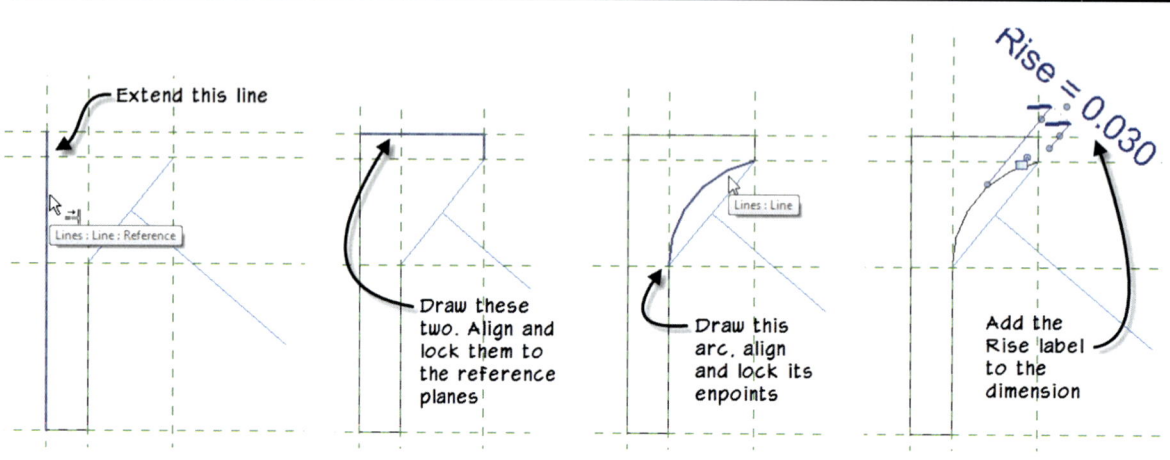

FIGURE 4.48
Adjust the shape of the profile

14. On the Create tab, click the Line tool and choose the Start-End-Radius arc.

➪ Snap the endpoints to the ends of the detail rig.

➪ Snap the radius when the arc show tangent to the other lines.

➪ Align and lock the endpoints of the arc to the reference planes (see the third image in in Figure 4.48).

• Renaissance Revit •

> **Important:** Make sure that for each alignment, you first click on a reference plane, not any other geometry or the detail item, then click the endpoint of the arc. Use TAB if necessary.

15. Finally, add a dimension between the diagonal line in the detail item rig and the arc.

   ⇨ Label the dimension with the **Rise** parameter (see the right image in Figure 4.48).

> **Note:** This procedure is the same one we followed above in the "Create a Parametric Segmental Arch" topic; see Figure 4.25 above specifically.

When you deleted the lines above, you most likely lost some dimensions too. So be sure to replace any missing dimensions. For example, the Y and Y2 dimensions. Figure 4.49 shows the completed Corona Profile with its "Family Types" showing the parameters and formulas.

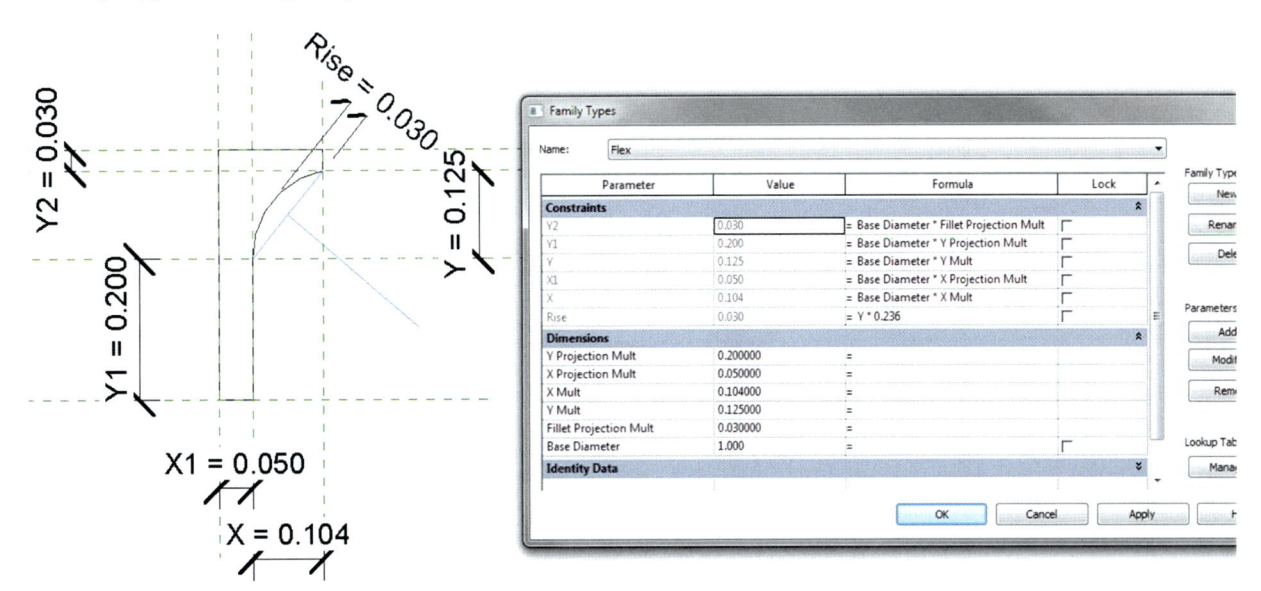

FIGURE 4.49

The completed Corona Profile and its parameters

16. Save and close the file.

> **CATCH UP!** You can open a file completed to this point named:
> *05_Corona Profile (variable Proportion).rfa*.

CONTROLLING A SPLINE

All of the examples so far have used some combination of arcs, circles and ellipses. To wrap up our inventory of curves and techniques to parametrically control curves, we'll take a brief look at splines. In the traditional family editor, the spline is the last type of curve that we have. The spline in the traditional family editor is a Bezier spline.

According to Wikipedia:

> A Bézier curve is a parametric curve frequently used in computer graphics and related fields... In vector graphics, Bézier curves are used to model smooth curves that can be scaled indefinitely.

> **SAMPLE!** You can open a sample file named: *04_Traditional Spline.rfa*.

In Revit, a spline is drawn as a series two or more control points. Splines are open curves in Revit; there is no "close" option. You can have as many intermediate points between the start and end point as required to shape the curve. With a little practice, you can create fairly complex curves from splines with little effort. When creating 3D forms from splines, the surfaces will remain smooth; no facets or edges. This can be a big advantage for certain types of forms. If you need a hard edge, consider other types of lines or create more than one spline (see the top portion of Figure 4.50).

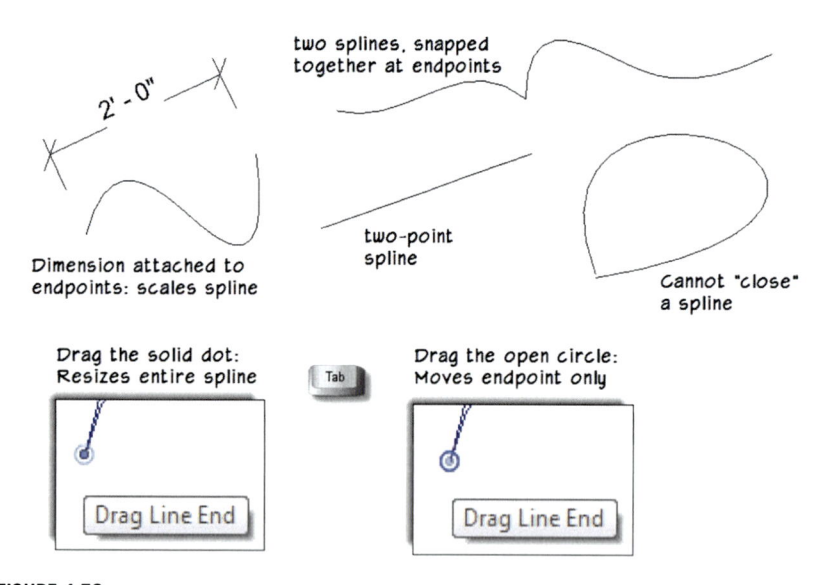

FIGURE 4.50
Working with Splines

Another interesting and useful characteristic of splines is that if you drag either endpoint, the entire spline will stretch and scale proportionally at the same time. This means that as you stretch the implied line that connects the start and end points, your spline will maintain its shape and scale proportionally as it grows larger or smaller. You do not need to do anything special to achieve this behavior. This is the built-in behavior of splines (and as the Wikipedia definition above noted, of Bezier curves in general).

If you wish to actually reshape your spline at one of its ends, make sure you press TAB to cycle the selection into the open circle at the grip point. The open circle is the control handle, while the solid dot is the endpoint. Endpoints will scale the spline. The open circles reshape it (see the bottom of Figure 4.50).

Note also in the figure that you can attach a dimension to the endpoints. This allows you to scale your spline using parameters and labeled dimensions. You can attach the dimension directly to the endpoints (TAB as necessary) or you can align and lock the endpoints to reference planes and flex them that way instead.

Given the built-in behavior of splines to scale proportionally when stretching the endpoints, it is possible to use them to shape your profiles and potentially avoid some of the techniques covered above. You can achieve a close approximation of many classical forms in this way, but it will not be completely precise. In other words, most of the moldings previously discussed use arcs: segments of circles. Splines can approximate these curves very closely, but will not be perfectly circular. If you build your splines carefully would anyone notice the difference? Perhaps not, but I much prefer to limit the use of splines to forms that do not use circles, arcs, and ellipses. For example the many organic forms in the Corinthian capital or the very subtle curvature of a column shaft's diminution. In later chapters I will show some of these examples. In the meantime, you are welcome to try to replicate some of the moldings covered here using splines in place of the arcs and decide for yourself.

COMBINING STRATEGIES

By now you should be feeling pretty comfortable with the various techniques and procedures needed to get curved forms to flex reliably in parametric Revit families. In this topic, we will perform one more exercise and use this as an opportunity to combine a few of the techniques we have learned together into a single family.

Let's create an arched doorway opening. This will be a simple example to illustrate how the pieces might fit together. We could approach this family in a few different ways, so naturally the first step should always be to do some initial planning. You can do this on a sketchpad, or directly in Revit.

What we would like here is a door family that has an arched shape. We can use any of the shapes discussed above in the "Arches" topic. In this example we will look at a new shape not covered above. This one will be a three-center arch. It combines three arcs together into a form that closely approximates an ellipse. (Feel free to use an elliptical arc like the one shown above instead if you prefer).

For this exercise, we will create the opening, a door with adjustable swing and a molding that surrounds it on both sides. This will incorporate almost everything previously discussed in this chapter in a single family! You are welcome to take it further following the completion of the tutorial that follows.

THREE CENTER ARCH

Let's start with the three center arch. A diagram of the shape is shown in Figure 4.51. The geometry is pretty simple. The two arcs on the left and right are 60° arcs with centers along the spring line. The middle arc is similar to our segmental arch above. We could use either rigs or formulas to construct this one. We'll go with a formula since the angles are fixed at 60° which makes the formula very simple.

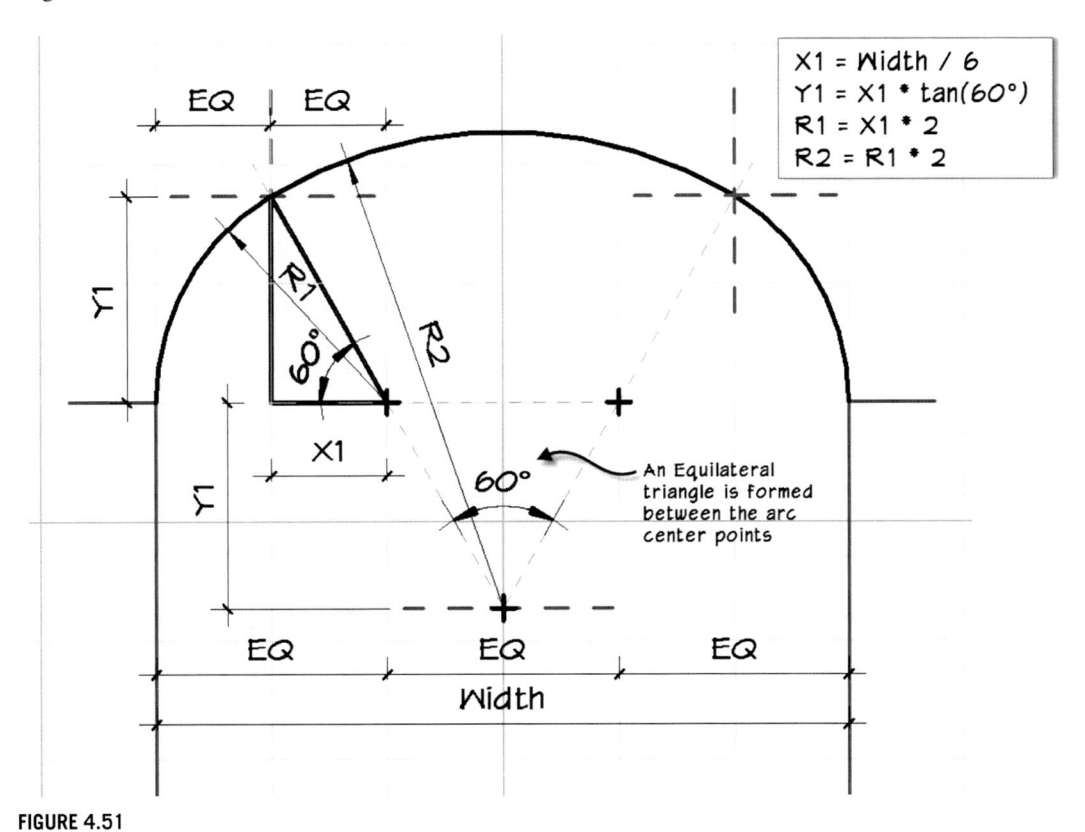

$$X1 = Width / 6$$
$$Y1 = X1 * \tan(60°)$$
$$R1 = X1 * 2$$
$$R2 = R1 * 2$$

FIGURE 4.51

Construction of a Three-Center Arch

We can create a new door family and build the sketch of this form directly in the door family. To do so, select the Opening Cut object that appears in the default *Door.rft* template and edit its sketch. However, let's build a profile family instead. You cannot use a profile family to shape the Opening Cut, so we will delete it. In its place, we'll use a Void Sweep that uses our profile. The reason for this approach, is we can reuse the same profile to create and arched shaped door panel. In this way, you will be able to edit one sweep profile and change the shape of both the opening and the door itself.

1. From the Application menu, choose **New > Family**.
   ⇨ Choose the template: *Profile.rft*.

   A copy of this file is provided in the *Template/OTB* folder with the book's dataset files.

   ⇨ Save the file as: **Three Center Arch Profile**.
2. Add a series of reference planes: four horizontal and six vertical.
   ⇨ Create the four horizontal ones above the Center (Front/Back) reference plane.
   ⇨ For the vertical ones, create three on each side.
   ⇨ Add dimensions as shown in Figure 4.52.
   ⇨ On the Properties palette, name the reference planes indicated.

Draw the vertical reference planes that have equality dimensions first. Then add the Width parameter. Add X1 after this. In the other direction, establish Height first, then R2 and its reference plane and finally Y1 and their reference planes.

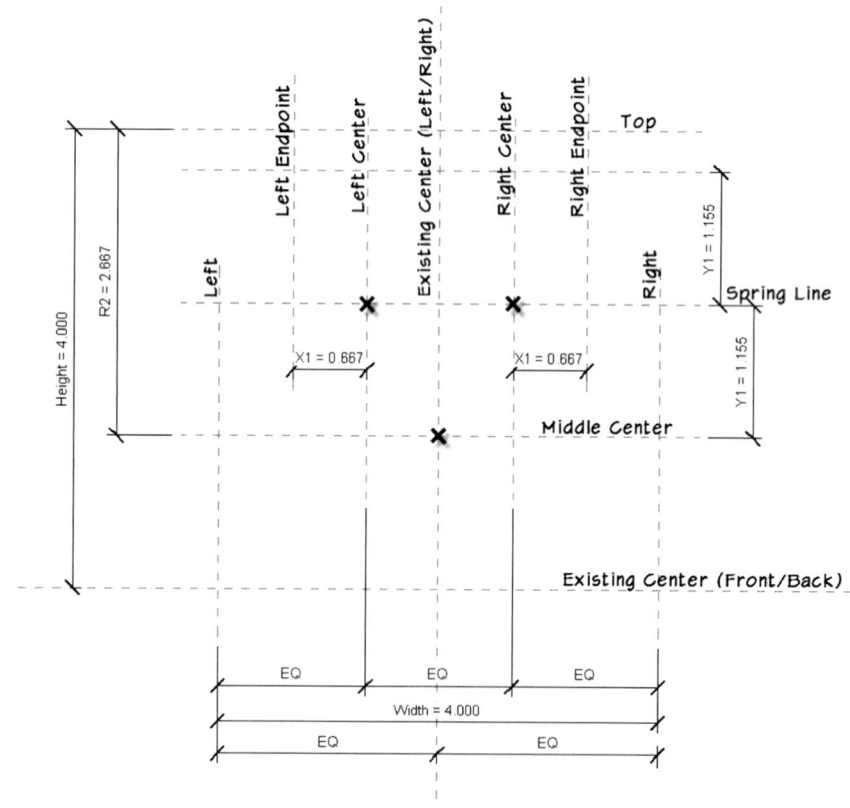

FIGURE 4.52
Create the three center arch profile family and set up reference planes and dimensions

CATCH UP! You can open a file completed to this point named: *04_Three Center Arch Profile (Ref).rfa*.

• Renaissance Revit •

3. Create the following parameters and assign them to the dimensions as shown (see Table 4.3).

TABLE 4.3

Parameter	Type	Group Under	Formula
Width	Length	Dimensions	
Height	Length	Dimensions	
X1	Length	Constraints	Width / 6
Y1	Length	Constraints	X1 * tan(60)
R1	Length	Constraints	X1 * 2
R2	Length	Constraints	R1 * 2

4. Flex everything to ensure it is working properly.

5. Using Figure 4.51 above as a guide, on the Create tab, click the Line tool and then the Center-ends Arc icon. Draw the three arcs required.

   ⇨ Draw the two arcs on the sides first. Align and lock the endpoints in both directions. (Eight total: two arcs, each with two endpoints, both X and Y).

   ⇨ Select both arcs and on the Properties palette, check Center Mark Visible.

   ⇨ Align and lock the centers in both directions.

6. Select both arcs. On the View Control Bar, click the sunglasses icon and choose Hide Element.

7. Draw the remaining arc. Turn on its center mark, align and lock the endpoints and center mark.

   If an error appears about over constraining the sketch, simply click Cancel and ignore that point.

8. Reset the Temporary Hide/Isolate and then open the "Family Types" dialog.

   ⇨ Flex the Width parameter to test the family.

   ⇨ Set it back to **4.000** when you are sure it is flexing properly.

You should get in the habit of creating a default family type for every family you create. The reason is that if you do not create one, Revit will create one for you and its name will be the same name as the family. This is not ideal[1]. You can name your default type anything you like. If the family is intended to nest into other families and will have its parameters driven by associated family parameters, as noted in the previous chapter, I like to name the default type: "**Flex.**" This name basically tells me that it is the default family and that I intend to nest it into other families and associate its parameters with parent parameters in the host family. Feel free to use a different name for your default type if you don't like the name Flex.

9. On the right, click the New button (under Family Types) and name it: **Flex**. Close the "Family Types" dialog.

10. Draw the remaining three straight lines on the Left, Right and Center (Front/Back) reference planes. Align and lock them.

11. Save the family.

---

[1] I had an interesting discussion with Aaron Maller who tech edited this book. He told me that they deliberately don't create a family type for those families that will be used with a <Family Types> parameter. When you don't have a family type, the drop-down displayed by Family Types parameters will list only the family name and not: Family Name:Type Name. This is certainly a nicer experience when using family types. So if you are building a family that will be nested into another family and used in conjunction with a Family Types parameter, then I agree with Aaron, don't create a type. As you may recall from the "Family Types Parameters" topic in the previous chapter, we will not actually be using the Family Types parameter in the lessons in this book.

104 | Chapter 4

> **CATCH UP!** You can open a file completed to this point named: *04_Three Center Arch Profile.rfa*.

COMPOUND MOLDING PROFILE

The next step is to look at the molding profile. To save some time, the family has been provided already. The molding uses both a Cyma Reversa and Ovolo as well as some straight fillet portions. Given the complexity of this shape it uses the nested detail item rigs that we have already built. This will avoid having lots of parameters and complex formulas (see Figure 4.53).

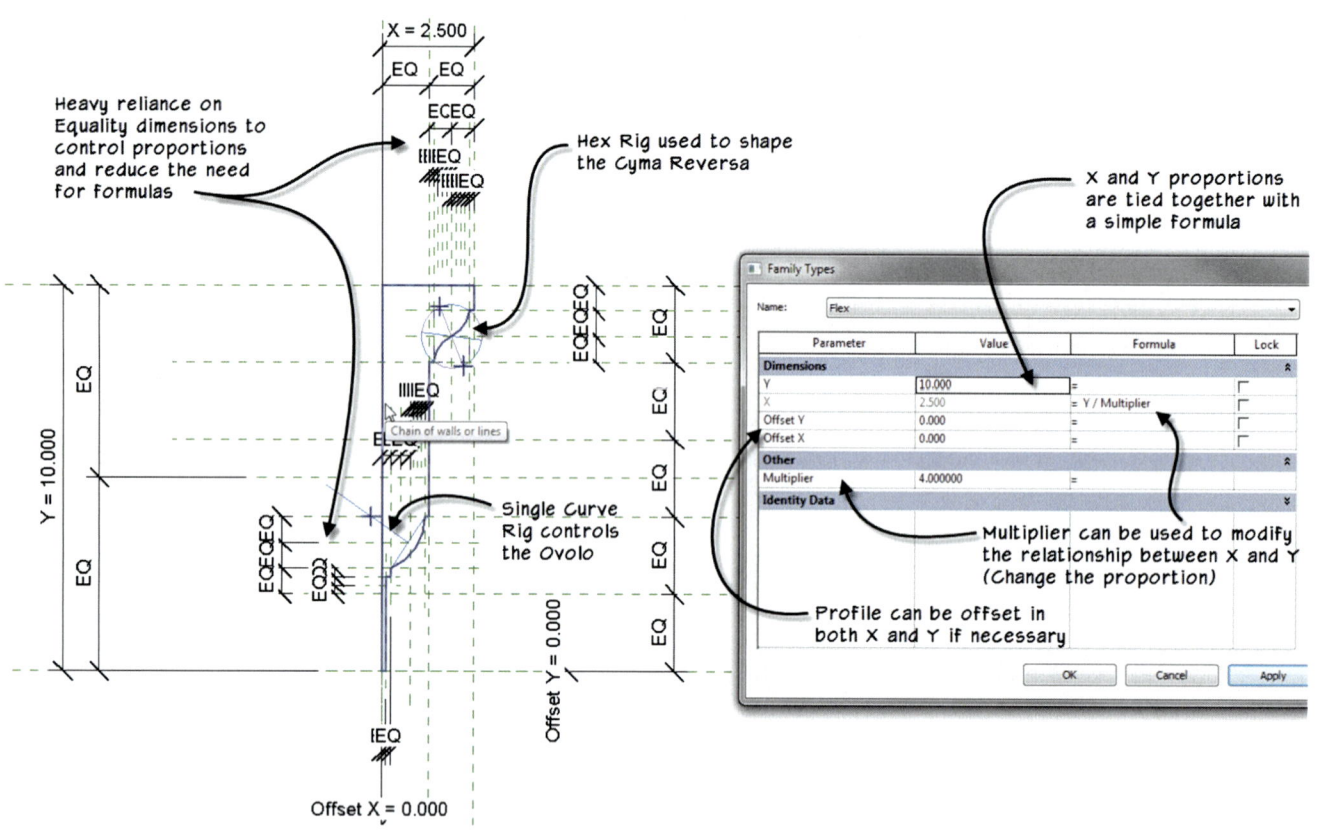

FIGURE 4.53

Understanding the Door Molding Profile Family

> **FILE PROVIDED!** Please open a sample file named: *04_Door Molding Profile (Rig).rfa*.

As you can see, this family contains MANY reference planes. When building such a family, it is recommended to approach it systematically. Have a good sketch handy and build the reference planes in small groups. Notice that they are built to varying lengths. This approach provides visual hierarchy onscreen. This is critical to helping you keep everything straight both when building and later when editing the family. Naming reference planes is also important, but you may notice that this family has few named reference planes. The reality is that coming up with meaningful names for every reference plane in an example like this provides a diminishing return when compared to the time it would take to actually select and name them. Your results may vary and you are welcome to name them if you wish.

Notice the heavy reliance on equality dimensions. Many of the reference planes in this family are used simply to leverage equality dimensions rather than parameters and formulas. For example, let's say you have a distance that should be one fifth some other distance. You can create a parameter and add a formula that calculates the correct

• Renaissance Revit •

value for you, or you can place a series of reference planes and then put an equality dimension to control them. Either approach will flex properly, but the equality approach avoids many extra parameters.

Notice the two previously discussed rigs used to shape the curved portions of this molding. The rigs were inserted, aligned and locked to the appropriate reference planes.

If you open "Family Types" notice that there is only one formula! This ties X and Y together to maintain the desired proportion. There are two additional features to note here: one is the presence of two "Offset" parameters. All of the dimensions in this family are actually associated to two reference planes that are directly on top of the default Center (Left/Right) and Center (Front/Back) ones. These two parameters are set to zero, but can be flexed to move the entire profile away from the insertion point. The reason to do this has to do with a limitation in swept forms. You can shift the profile of a sweep when inserting it, however, you cannot do so parametrically. So whatever shift you apply is fixed in the sweep. If you want to vary the offset value from one type to another or one family to another, you can use these two offset parameters instead.

Finally, there is a Multiplier parameter that allows this profile to scale disproportionately. It applies to the X value only. So it controls the relationship between X and Y. For example, the default Multiplier is set to 4. This makes the proportion between X and Y 1 to 4. Try different values if you would like to experiment.

ARCHED DOOR FAMILY

In the final step, we will utilize the two profile families in a new door family. Since we built a door family previously, we can start with that file instead of building from scratch. If you prefer, you can repeat the steps covered above in the "Create a Door Family with Variable Swing" topic instead of starting with the provided file.

1. Open the file: *04_Door w Variable Swing.rfa*.

2. Save the file as: **Door w Three Center Arch**.

The standard door family template includes an Opening Cut (which makes the hole in the wall) and some trim. We will delete both of these.

3. Delete both trim elements and the Opening Cut.

   The hole in the wall and some of the dimensions will also disappear (see Figure 4.54).

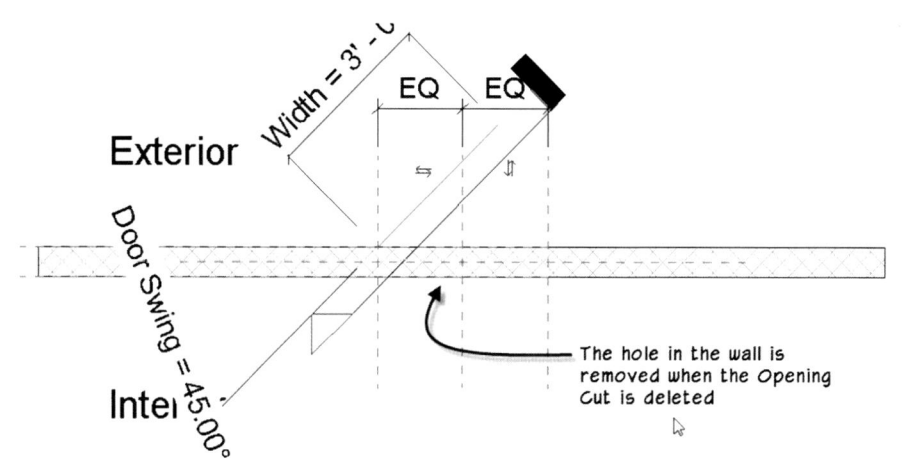

FIGURE 4.54

Delete the Opening Cut and the trim

4. On the Insert tab, click the Load Family button.

106 | Chapter 4

⇨ Load both profile families into the door family. (*04_Door Molding Profile (Rig).rfa* and *04_Three Center Arch Profile.rfa*).

> **TIP:** Use the CTRL key and select both families to load in a single step.

For the Three Center Arch Profile family, you can use your own version created above or the one provided.

> **CATCH UP!** You can open a file completed to this point named: *04_Door w Three Center Arch (01).rfa*.

Since we removed the Opening Cut, we need to create a new opening in the host wall. We will use a void form for this. Specifically a Void Sweep so we can use our profile family to shape it.

5. On the Create tab, click the Void Forms dropdown and choose **Void Sweep**.

6. Click the Sketch Path button and draw a single line segment across the thickness of the wall (draw along the Center (Left/Right) reference plane and snapping to the face of wall on each side).

> **TIP:** In this example we are making the void flush with the wall, but if you intend to build a door like this for actual projects, you might want to consider making the void extend past the faces of the wall to ensure that it will always behave as expected in projects.

⇨ Align and lock the endpoints of the line to the faces of the wall. Use the TAB key as required.

⇨ Align and lock the sketch line to the Center (Left/Right) reference plane as well (see Figure 4.55).

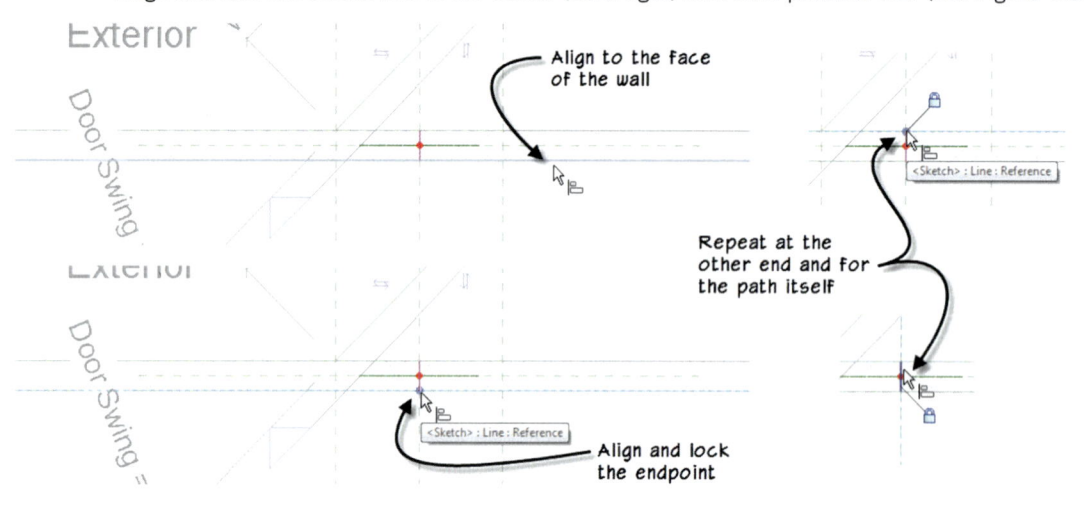

FIGURE 4.55
Sketch the path and align and lock it

7. Finish the sketch and then on the Modify | Sweep tab, click the Select Profile button.

⇨ From the Profile dropdown, choose **Three Center Arch Profile:Flex**.

⇨ Open the *Interior* elevation view.

Notice that the arch is down near the floor. Also, the shape of the profile does not have the correct height or width either. We will address those issues after we complete the sweep (see the left side of Figure 4.56).

• Renaissance Revit •

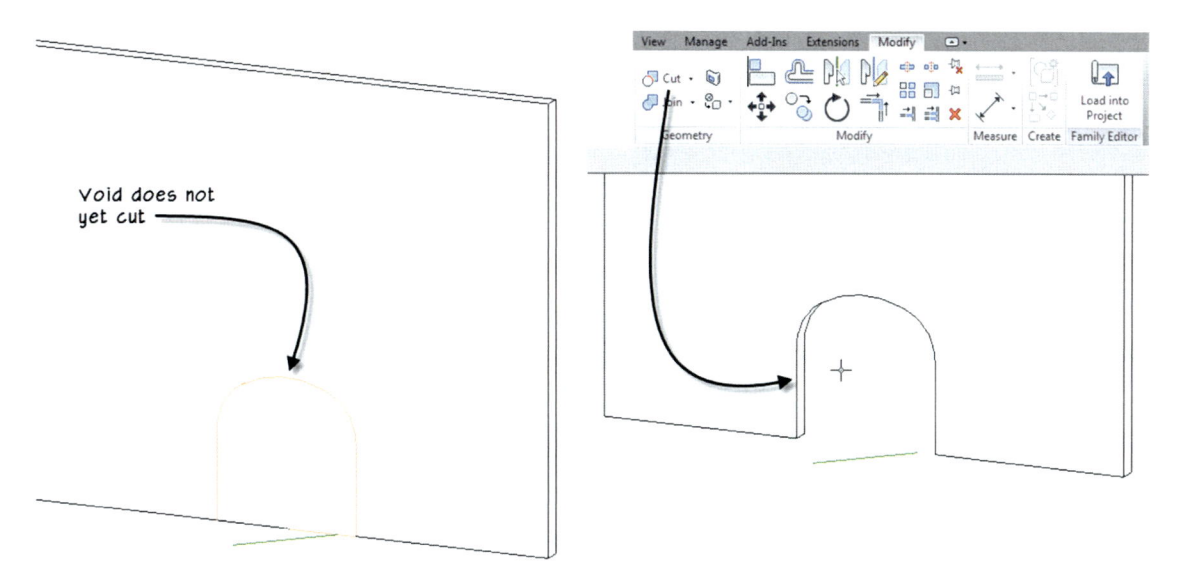

FIGURE 4.56

After completing the void it is the wrong size and unattached to the wall

8. On the ribbon, click the Finish Edit Mode button.

9. Open the 3D view. Notice that the void is not cutting anything.

   ⇨ On the Modify tab, click the Cut tool.

   ⇨ Pick the wall, then the void.

   ⇨ Click the Modify tool to complete the command (see the left side of Figure 4.56).

10. On the Project Browser, Beneath the *Families* branch, expand *Profiles*, then the *Three Center Arch Profile*.

   ⇨ Right-click on Flex and then choose **Type Properties**.

   ⇨ Next to the Width parameter, click the small Associate Family Parameter button. In the "Associate Family Parameter" dialog, choose Width and then click OK.

   ⇨ Repeat for Height and then click OK again (See Figure 4.57).

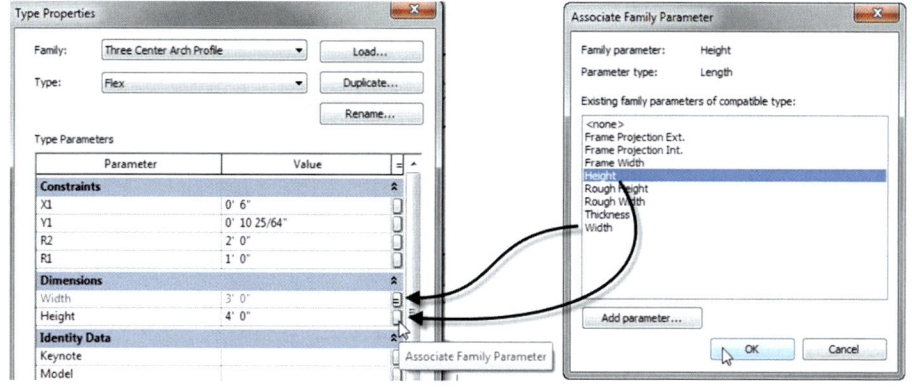

FIGURE 4.57

Associate Family Parameters to make the Profile match the door size

CATCH UP! You can open a file completed to this point named: *04_Door w Three Center Arch (02).rfa*.

You should now have a hole in your wall that matches the shape of our custom profile and the dimensions of the door family. If you flex the Width and Height, the shape of the arch will flex accordingly. Now let's build a 3D door panel from the same profile.

108 | Chapter 4

Make sure that the *Ref. Level* floor plan view is active.

11. On the Create panel, on the Work Plane panel, click the Set button.
    ⇨ In the "Work Plane" dialog, click the Pick a plane option and then click OK.
    ⇨ Click the diagonal reference line to make it the active Work Plane.
12. On the Create panel, click the Sweep button.
13. Click Sketch Path and then draw a small straight path perpendicular to and away from the midpoint of the reference line. (Draw towards the doorway at a 45°).
    ⇨ Add a dimension and label it with the **Thickness** parameter.

> TIP: It is best to draw the sketch line the same length as the parameter before you apply the label. That is 2" in this case. This way, when you apply the label, it will not also need to flex.

⇨ You can also add another dimension in the other direction from the endpoints of the reference line and toggle the equality (see Figure 4.58).

> TIP: the easiest way to get the equality dimension is to zoom in, click the first witness line on the sweep path sketch line. Then click at each of the endpoints of the reference line. If you start at the endpoints, it is much harder to get the correct points.

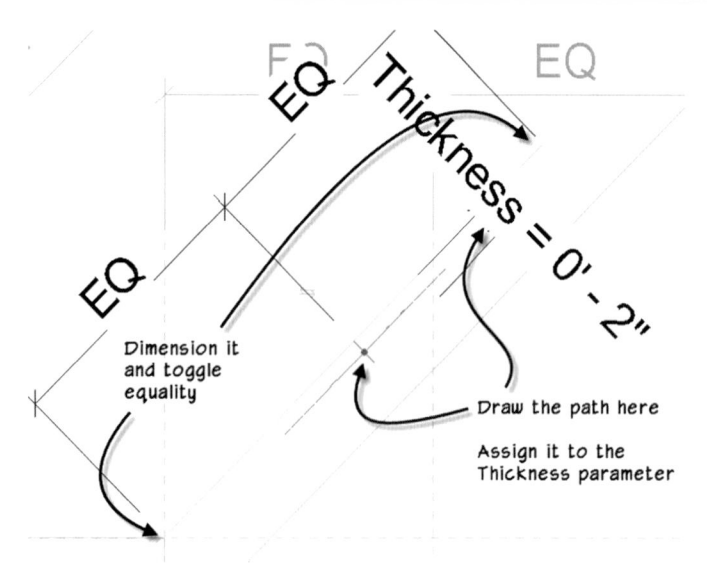

FIGURE 4.58
Sketch the path of the panel sweep, constrain and parameterize it

14. Finish the path and assign the **Three Center Arch Profile:Flex** profile to it. Finish the Sweep.
15. Open the 3D view called *View 1* and flex.

> CATCH UP! You can open a file completed to this point named: *04_Door w Three Center Arch (03).rfa*.

The final step is to add the moldings around the door opening. These will also be a sweep, but this time we will use the Pick Path option to pick the edges of the 3D door opening.

Stay in the 3D view for this step.

16. Create a new Sweep. For the path, click the Pick Path button.

• Renaissance Revit •

- Carefully click the edges around the opening on one side of the door. There will be five edges total—three arc and two lines.
- Click Finish and then select the Profile: **Door Molding Profile (Rig):Flex**.
- If necessary, rotate and flip the profile using the controls on the Options Bar.

17. Click Finish when done.
18. Repeat the entire process on the other side.

You will need to actually repeat the steps on the other side. If you mirror it, the sweep will lose its association to the 3D edges. So create a new sweep and pick new edges for the path. When you are finished, you can flex it to make sure everything works. While you are in the "Family Types" dialog, add a few family types and assign some materials to the geometry if you like. Your final result should look something like Figure 4.59.

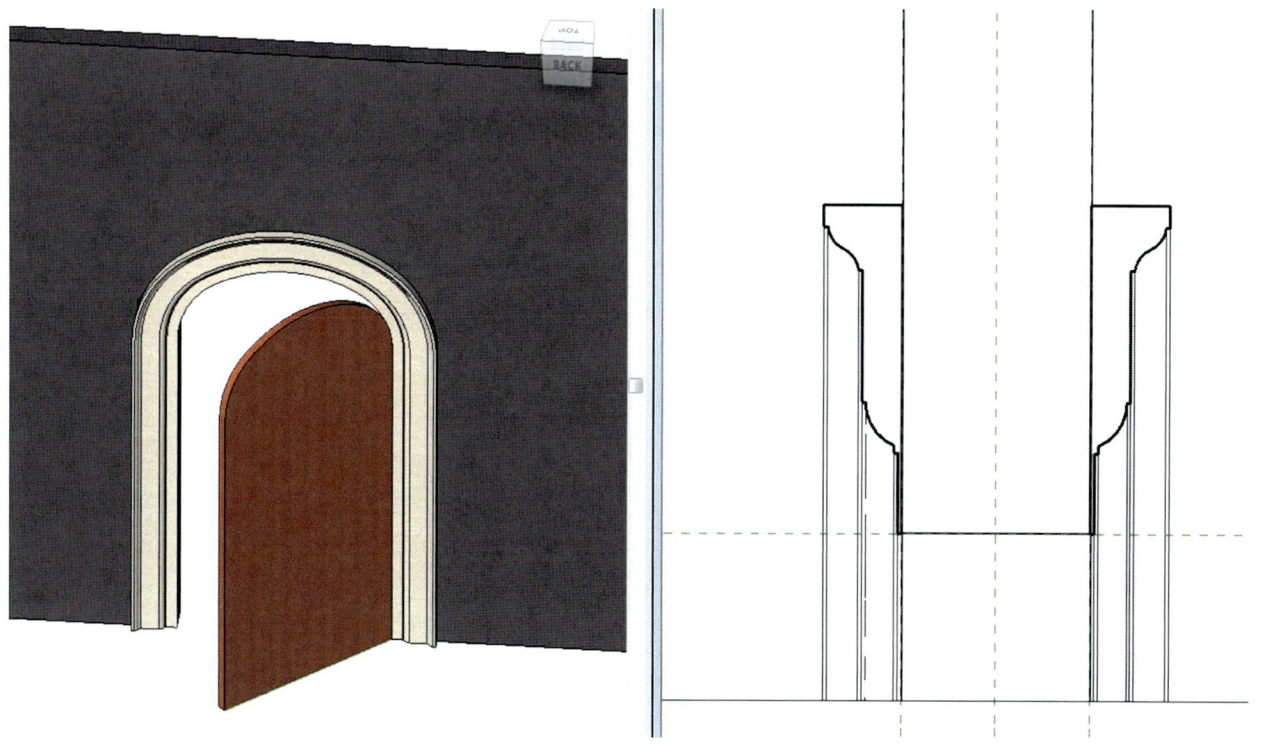

FIGURE 4.59

The finished arched door family

CATCH UP! You can open a file completed to this point named: *04_Door w Three Center Arch.rfa*.

Naturally there is much more we could do with this door family. We could add a low detail version of the molding for medium detail and turn it off completely in coarse. We could add a vision panel to the door panel. We could add 2D graphics to the elevations and plan view. We could create a closed 3D version or simply rely on the swing parameter. There are transoms, pilasters, other moldings and any number of other enhancements you could consider.

I will leave you with those suggestions and allow you to consider them as an additional exercise.

• *Creating Classical Architecture with Modern Software* •

SUMMARY

We have covered a lot of ground in last three chapters. It does take some time to digest everything, but the skills discussed here and in the previous two chapters will be the cornerstone of the lessons that follow in the coming chapters. Make sure you are comfortable with the concepts and techniques before continuing.

- ✓ Curves take a little more effort to constrain in the family editor than straight lines.
- ✓ Circles and 90° arcs usually need little more than constraining the center point.
- ✓ Angles other than 90° can be effectively constrained by aligning and locking the endpoints to reference planes in both directions.
- ✓ For ellipses and elliptical arcs, use the icon to make the temporary dimension permanent to create dimensions and label them for the axes in each direction.
- ✓ Rotation is best controlled with a reference line instead of reference planes.
- ✓ Be sure to align and lock the endpoints of the reference line to an intersection of two reference planes to fix the center of rotation. Then use an angular parameter to control rotation of the reference line.
- ✓ For segmental arches or curves where you have a chord length, you can dimension directly to the curve to control the "rise" above the chord. This allows the center point to move. Be sure to align and lock the endpoints of the arc.
- ✓ When creating complex molding shapes with arcs that do not have fixed center points, you can use trigonometry to calculate the locations of the center point reference planes. This is very stable.
- ✓ Alternatively, you can build a rig that flexes along a diagonal and use it to help shape the curve.
- ✓ Profile families are the preferred way to build your standard molding shapes.
- ✓ You can make your profile families flexible by introducing "multiplier" parameters. This will make it possible to flex them to different proportions.
- ✓ Splines offer an alternative approach to curvature. The shape of the spline is maintained when the endpoints are flexed. This allows you to create complex freeform shapes and scale them proportionally.

CUA CLASS OF '90 SKETCHING
Photo by author

Chapter 5
The Tuscan Base, Capital and Pedestal

INTRODUCTION

Over the past few chapters, I have shared with you many traditional family editor techniques. Naturally the focus has been on techniques that will be useful in creating classical columns. In this and the next few chapters, we will consider the first three orders: Tuscan, Doric and Ionic. This chapter will focus on the Tuscan order, which is admittedly the simplest of the three to construct. As noted previously, I will be deriving most of the proportions from the previously cited: *The Classical Orders of Architecture* by Robert Chitham (Chitham 1985, 2005).

OBJECTIVES

Using techniques discussed in the previous chapters, we will construct a Tuscan order from scratch. Topics in this chapter include:

- Building the Capital
- Building the Base
- Building the Shaft
- Adding a Pedestal

TUSCAN SETUP

At the end of Chapter 3, we had completed a simple schematic column. If you completed that tutorial, you may recall that the proportions we chose were based on the Tuscan. To reiterate, the base and capital are ½ the diameter tall and the overall column height is 7 diameters tall. We used three nested families to build the schematic column; one each for the capital, shaft and base. A copy of the completed family is included with the dataset for this chapter. We will use this as the seed for the creation of a more complex version of the Tuscan order. In addition, we will incorporate many of the profile families created in the previous chapter as well as the various techniques used to create them. To get started, we will perform a save as like we have done with other seed families previously.

1. From the *Chapter05* folder, open the file: *05_Column (Schematic).rfa*.
2. Save the file as: **Tuscan Column**.

As noted, this family contains three nested families. They are currently also named in a more generic fashion. So we will want to rename the nested families as well.

3. On the Project Browser, expand the *Families* branch.
⇨ Expand *Generic Models*, right-click on *03_Base (Schematic)* and choose **Rename** (see Figure 5.1).

112 | Chapter 5

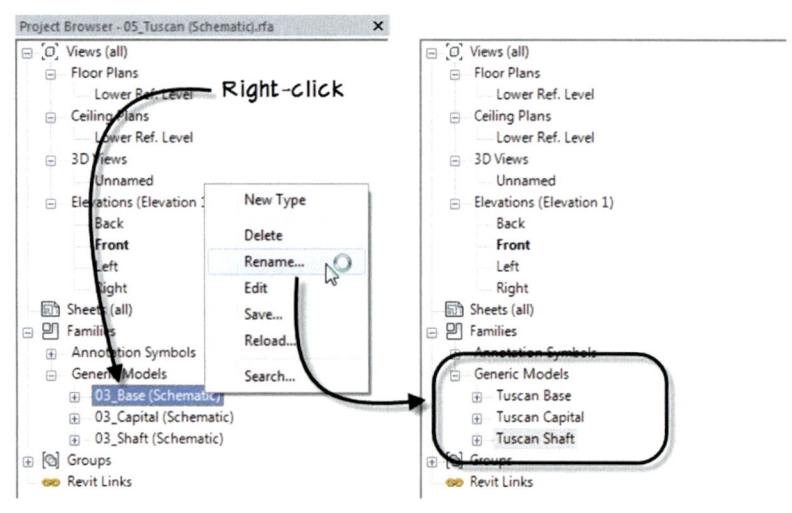

FIGURE 5.1
Rename the nested families

⇨ Name it **Tuscan Base** and then click OK.

4. Repeat the process to rename the other two families to: **Tuscan Capital** and **Tuscan Shaft**.

> TIP: a shortcut for rename is to select the item, and then press the F2 key.

5. Save the file.

If you browse the *Working* folder in Windows Explorer, you will notice that none of the nested families appear in this folder. At the moment, they are only stored inside this family. It is actually not necessary to save an RFA file for every family you create. It is often a good idea, and I usually do create separate RFA files of all of nested families I create. So in the steps that follow, we will be editing each of these nested families, making edits and saving them as separate RFA files before loading them back in to this host family.

> CATCH UP! You can open a file completed to this point named: *05_Tuscan Column.rfa*.

BUILD THE TUSCAN CAPITAL

Now that we have the column file saved and everything named properly, we'll begin working in each nested family. Let's start with the capital.

Continue in your version of the *Tuscan Column* family file or the catch-up version.

1. Minimize the two view windows for the *Tuscan Column* family.

2. On the Project Browser, right-click *Tuscan Capital* and choose **Edit**.

   This will open just the one 3D view window for the *Tuscan Capital* family.

3. On the Project Browser, double-click to open the *Ref. Level* floor plan and the *Front* elevation view.

⇨ Tile the windows.

Since we opened it from the host family and it does not currently have an RFA file, Revit will therefore perform a Save As instead and ask you where to save the family.

⇨ Save the family as: **Tuscan Capital**.

• Renaissance Revit •

Chitham details two variations for the Tuscan capital; one by Palladio and one by Gibbs. The Palladian one is a bit simpler with a simple square abacus. Gibbs adorns his abacus with a corona molding. Both use an Ovolo above a Corona molding. The proportions vary slightly with Gibbs' ovolo being nearly square in proportion and Palladio's a bit taller in the Y direction. For this example, we will use the Palladian version (see Figure 5.2). In the chapter on Doric, we will be dealing with a slightly more detailed set of moldings at the abacus. So if you prefer the capital as prescribed by Gibbs, you can follow the procedures used later for the Doric to create it.

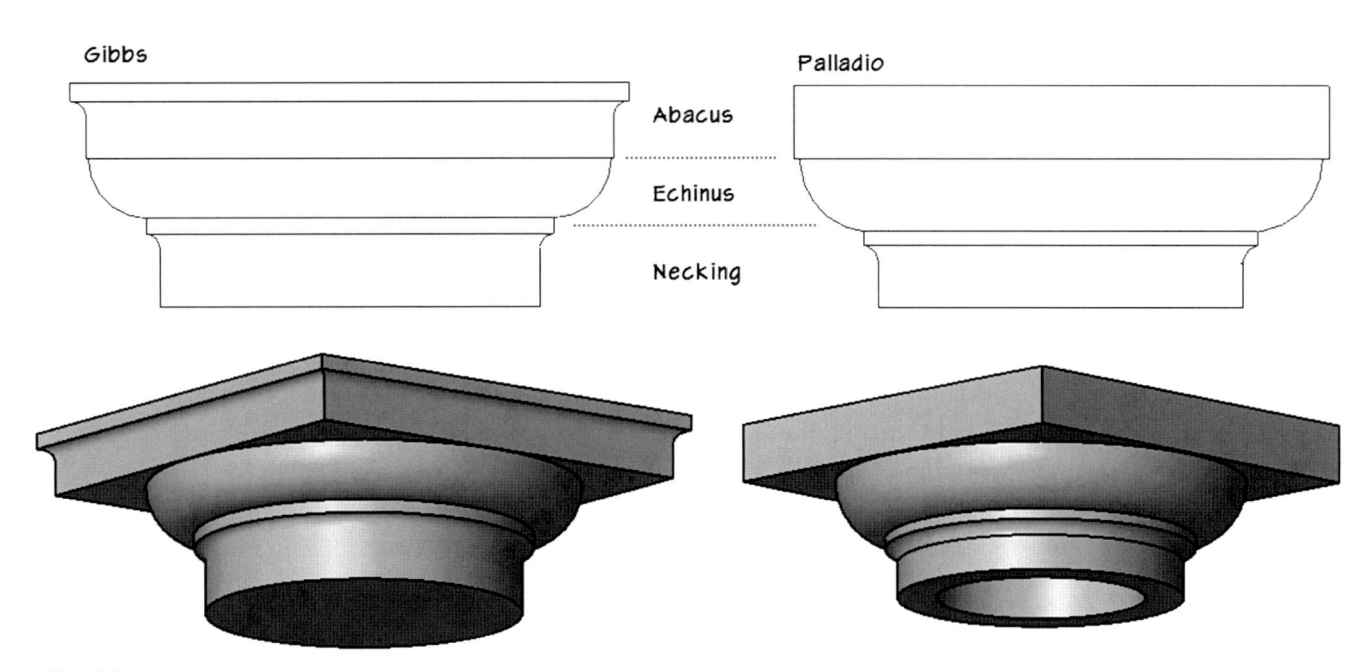

FIGURE 5.2
The Tuscan capital after Gibbs on the left and Palladio on the right

Going with the Palladian design means that we can use the form we already have in the family for the abacus. To this we will add ovolo and corona moldings; both of which we constructed profile families for in the previous chapter. So let's add reference planes and parameters, import those profiles into this family and build our solid forms.

ADD REFERENCE PLANES

The capital includes essentially three bands. So we'll start with a couple reference planes to help us locate those bands and keep their size at the correct proportion.

1. Activate the *Front* elevation view.
2. On the Create tab, on the Datum panel, click the Reference Plane button.
3. Draw two horizontal reference planes between the Ref. level and the Capital Bottom reference plane.
⇨ Draw the reference plane from right to left (see Figure 5.3).
4. Select each reference plane and on the Properties palette, name them as indicated in the figure.

• *Creating Classical Architecture with Modern Software* •

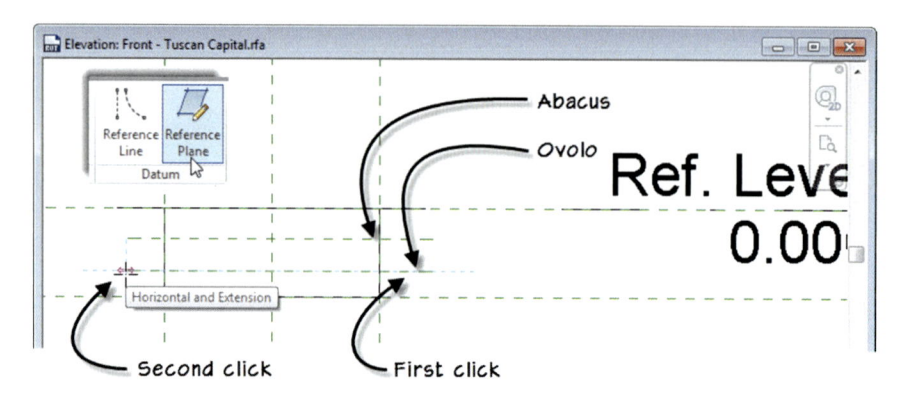

FIGURE 5.3

Add reference planes

The reason it is important to pay attention the order of click is that it helps in controlling the orientation of the reference plane. When you build forms on this reference plane, positive and negative directions and orientations will be determined by the way it was drawn. If you refer back to the "Create and Constrain a Reference Line" topic in Chapter 4, the same issue existed for reference lines. If you draw them the wrong way, it is possible to reverse the direction. Just drag one endpoint all the way past the other one to essentially reverse the reference plane.

ADD DIMENSIONS AND PARAMETERS

Now that we have our two named reference planes, let's add some dimensions and simple parameters.

> Continue in the *Front* elevation.

1. Add a dimension between the Ref. Level and the Abacus refence plane.

    ⇨ Select the Abacus reference plane and edit the value of the dimension to **.165**.

    ⇨ Label this dimension with a new type-based parameter named: **Capital Height Subdivision** (see Figure 5.4).

    ⇨ Group it under **Constraints** and then click OK.

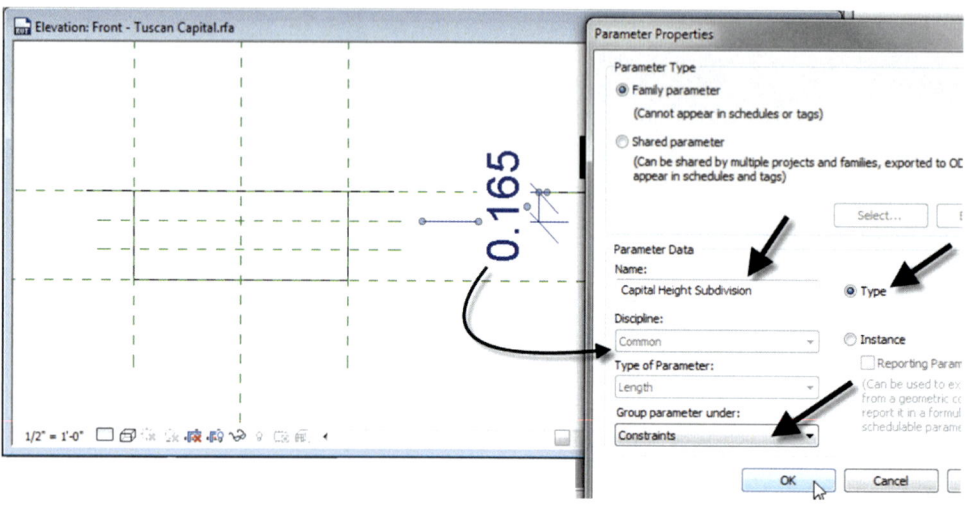

FIGURE 5.4

Create a new parameter to control the height of the abacus

2. Repeat the process to create a new dimension between the Abacus and Ovolo reference planes.

    ⇨ Label it with the same parameter.

The location of the reference plane should immediately move to match the value we assigned to the parameter above. If it does not or generates an error, undo, move the reference plane to the correct location first, and then label it again.

3. On the Create tab, click the Family Types button.

  ⇨ In the "Family Types" dialog, in the Formula column next to Capital Height Subdivision, input: **Base Diameter * 0.165** and then click OK.

Notice that we are using the same parameter for both distances here. When I built my first versions of these classical families, I tended to build many more reference planes and many parameters. I would create a unique parameter even if the value was the same. All of these parameters did tie back to the Base Diameter parameter, but with so many of them, the complexity of the family just ballooned. Furthermore, performance can become an issue. So I have continually looked for ways to simplify the families and reduce the quantity of both reference planes and the associated parameters (see Figure 5.5).

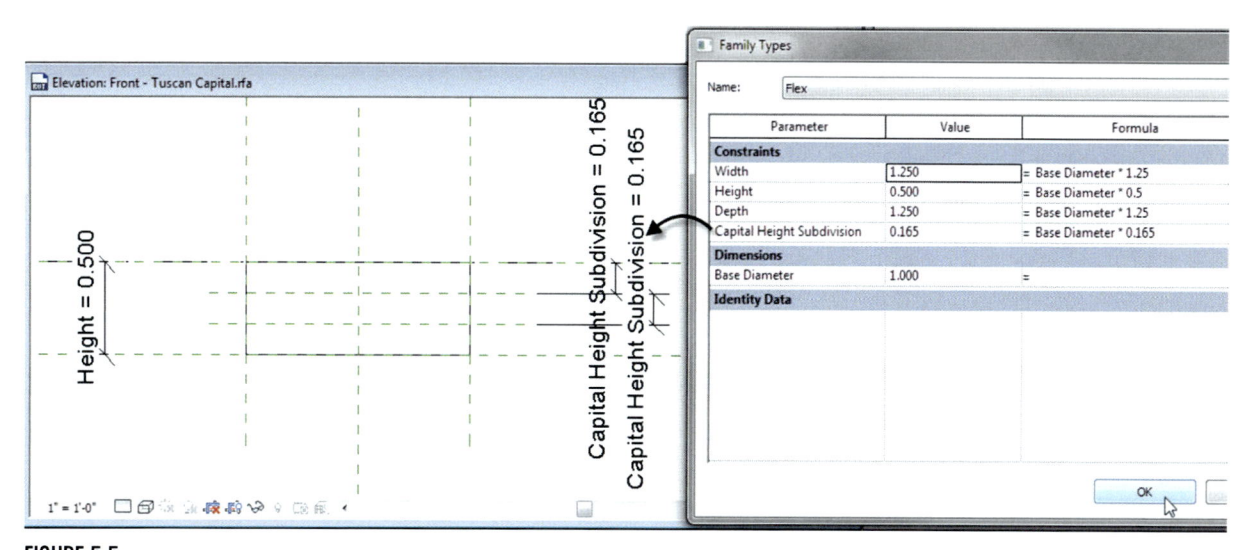

FIGURE 5.5
Apply the parameter to both dimensions

In fact, I was very tempted to simplify this one even further. The last distance here (the height between the Ovolo and Capital Bottom reference planes) is .17. This is very close the .165 value of the parameter. So why not just make them all equal and use an equality dimension instead. Well we certainly could do that. It is really a question of how closely you want to adhere to the prescribed proportions proposed by the masters and how much you want to adjust and interpret. So staying closer to the actual Palladian proportions is one reason. The other is that we will be using the profile families that we built in the previous chapter to create the moldings. This will require a numerical input for the heights anyhow. So we would still need a parameter here.

If you chose to build the curves directly into the sketches of the 3D forms, say if you chose to use a 3D revolve instead, you would probably be able to avoid the parameter and rely on an equality dimension. As I noted, it is really a matter of preference in the specifics of how you chose to interpret the classical proportions and your specific modeling techniques.

IMPORT PROFILE FAMILIES

In the previous chapter, we created many standard molding shapes. We build these as profile families and as you may recall, we can use profile families to construct sweeps. So while it might seem logical to use revolves for the turned portions of the capital, revolves cannot use profiles. So we would be forced to redraw molding shapes directly within the revolve sketch.

1. On the Insert tab, click the Load Family button.

2. Browse to the *Chapter05* folder hold down the CTRL key and load both the *Corona Profile.rfa* and the *Ovolo Profile.rfa* files.

These are copies of the final versions of each of these profiles from Chapter 4.

3. Save the file.

EXPLORE THE OVOLO PROFILE

The two profiles are copies of the ones built in Chapter 4. The Corona profile was edited extensively in the "Create a Variable Corona Profile" topic in Chapter 4, so we will use a direct copy of that version here. One of the edits we made to the Corona profile at that time was to add an adjustable fillet molding to the top. It already had an adjustable fillet at the bottom. I have made a similar modification to the Ovolo profile we are using here. When we built the Ovolo family in the previous chapter, we locked the vertical edge to the Radius reference plane. This was the most expedient thing to do at the time since our focus was on constraining the curvature. Also, the version we built did not use any multiplier parameters for the Base Diameter, but instead simply had X and Y parameters that could be edited directly.

We could use the family as is with its parameters that way, but when we link up the nested parameters, we would need to add the formulas and/or multipliers directly to the host to control proportional scaling. To save some effort, I have already added the multiplier parameters (X Mult and Y Mult) to the *Ovolo Profile* family that we just loaded. The profile also has a projection reference plane and parameter to control it. This is similar to the additional fillet we added to the Corona in the previous chapter.

1. On the Project Browser, right-click the Ovolo Profile and choose **Edit** (see Figure 5.6).

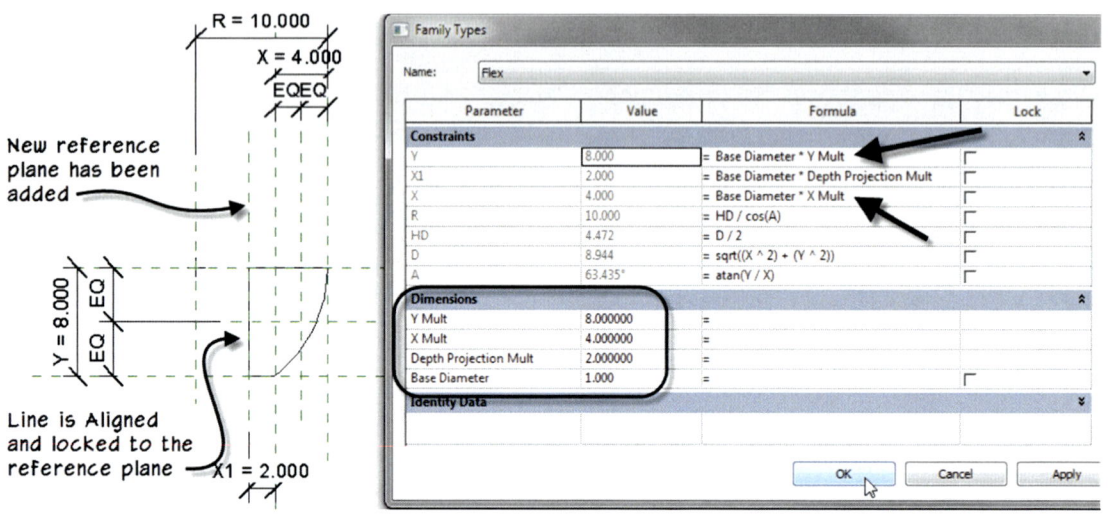

FIGURE 5.6

Explore the modifications in the Ovolo Profile

2. Open the "Family Types" dialog.

As you can see, X and Y are driven by the Base Diameter parameter and a multiplier in each direction. The X and Y multipliers allow us to change the proportion of the curve. Base Diameter changes the overall scale. I also added a projection parameter (X1) and a multiplier to drive it.

3. Close the file when you are done exploring. You do not need to save.

CREATE THE ABACUS

The geometry for our Tuscan capital will consist of an extrusion for the upper part (the abacus) and two sweeps for the moldings below it. We can start with the extrusion which is already in this file. We need to simply modify its height to make the abacus.

Work in the *Tuscan Capital* family, in the *Front* elevation view.

1. Select the extrusion already in the file.

    ⇨ Drag the grip handle at the bottom of the extrusion up.

    ⇨ Release the mouse when it snaps to the Abacus reference plane (see Figure 5.7).

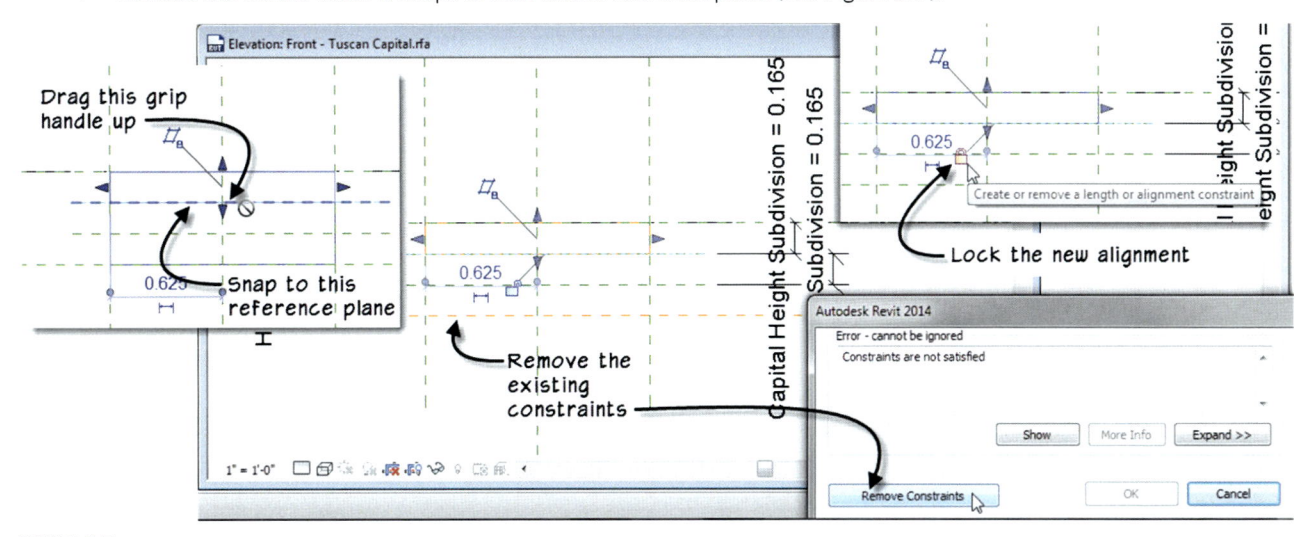

FIGURE 5.7

Adjust the height of the existing extrusion

2. In the error that appears, click the Remove Constraints button.

    ⇨ Close the lock icon.

The error displays because the bottom of the extrusion is currently locked to the Capital Bottom reference plane. So when we stretch it, we must remove this constraint. We are then applying a new constraint by clicking the lock icon. Alternatively, you can use the align command here if you prefer.

3. Save the file.

CATCH UP! You can open a file completed to this point named: *05_Tuscan Capital_A.rfa*.

CREATE THE OVOLO MOLDING

Let's build the ovolo molding next.

1. Open the *Ref. Level* floor plan view.

2. On the Create tab, on the Work Plane panel, click the Set button.

    ⇨ In the "Work Plane" dialog, from the Name drop-down list, choose **Reference Plane: Ovolo** and then click OK.

3. On the Create tab, click the Sweep button.

    ⇨ On the ribbon, click the Sketch Path button.

Chapter 5

⇨ Click the circle icon and start at the intersection of the two center reference planes.

⇨ Make the radius approximately **0.500** (see Figure 5.8).

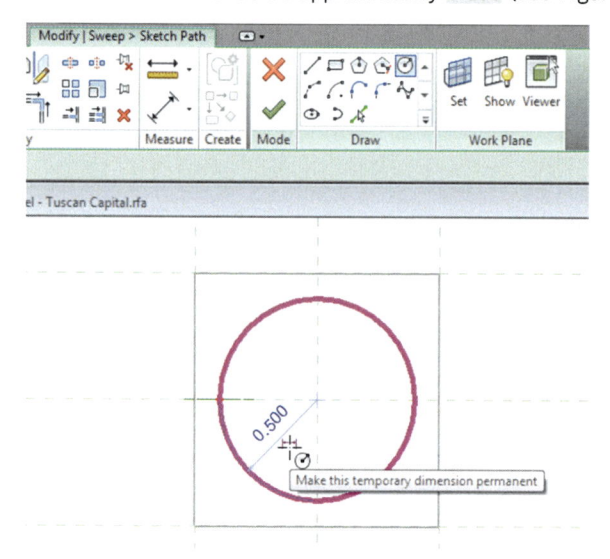

FIGURE 5.8
Sketch the path of the sweep

4. Click the small "Make this temporary dimension permanent" icon.

⇨ Click the Modify tool and then select the dimension.

⇨ Label the dimension with a new type-based parameter called **R1**. Group it under **Constraints**.

> TIP: If the dimension covers too much of the geometry, edit the "Type Properties" of the dimension and change the Text Background to Transparent.

⇨ Enable the Center Mark and align and lock the circle.

> Note: If you want more details, review the procedure outlined in the "Create a Parametric Circle" topic in Chapter 4.

⇨ Finish Edit Mode for the path.

5. On the Modify I Sweep tab, click the Select Profile button and then from the drop-down, choose **Ovolo Profile:Flex** (see Figure 5.9).

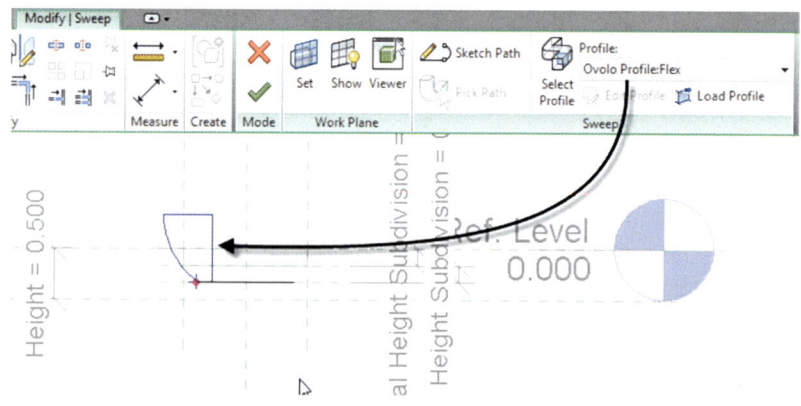

FIGURE 5.9
Choose a profile for the sweep

6. Click the Finish Edit Mode button to finish the sweep.

• Renaissance Revit •

I suspect that you are not too satisfied with the result so far. We have a nice round form using the Ovolo Profile, but its proportions are all wrong. Let's address that now.

7. On the Project Browser, expand *Families > Profiles > Ovolo Profile*.
8. Right-click on *Flex* and choose **Type Properties**.

In the "Type Properties" dialog, notice that the parameters in the Constraints grouping cannot have associated family parameters. This is because all of these are driven by formulas in the nested profile family. However, we can associate family paraemters to the ones in the Dimensions grouping. Now, here's the interesting part. The only parameter that we need to link up is Base Diameter. The others we will modify the values directly; *not* with an associated family parameter. This is because we do not need to the proportion of the molding to flex after we establish it, only the scale. And since theBase Diameter controls scale, it is the only one we need to link up.

⇨ For the Y Projection Mult, input: **0.165**.
⇨ For the X Projection Mult, input: **0.150**.
⇨ For the Depth Projection Mult, input: **0.150**.
⇨ For the Base Diameter, click the Associate Family Parameter button, select the **Base Diameter** parameter and then click OK (see Figure 5.10).

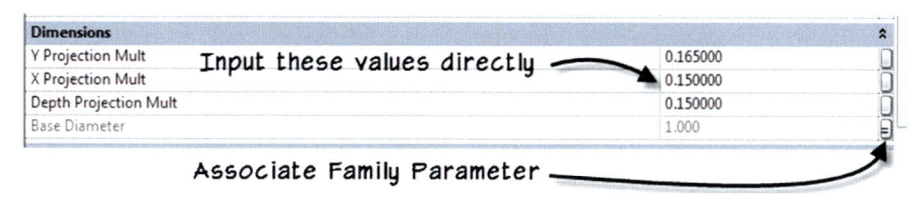

FIGURE 5.10
Edit the Type Properties of the Ovolo Profile

9. Click OK to apply the results and flex the sweep.

Much better, but notice that the Sweep's radius is still a little too large. We simply need a formula on the R1 parameter to adjust that.

10. Open the "Family Types" dialog.
⇨ In the Formula field next to R1, type: **(Base Diameter * 0.625) - Capital Height Subdivision** and then click OK.

I prefer to relate everything back to Base Diameter. So as you can see, I have done the calculation to figure out the multiplier based on Base Diameter. We could have used a formula of (Width /2) – Capital Height Subdivision. This would also work since Width (and Depth) divided by two is the same as Base Diameter times 0.625. So it is really up to you, but I find keeping all formulas related to the Base Diameter simplifies things. Also, the parentheses are important here. Remember your order of operations from math class? This formula is pretty simple arithmetic, so it would actually work with or without the parenthesis. But just the same, I always like to add them. I think it keeps everything neater and easier to understand. You will appreciate it later when you open this family in a few weeks and are trying to remember what you did.

11. Save the file.

CREATE THE CORONA MOLDING

The last piece of our capital is the Corona Molding.

1. Open the *Ref. Level* floor plan view.

120 | Chapter 5

2. On the Create tab, on the Work Plane panel, click the Set button.
    ⇨ In the "Work Plane" dialog, from the Name drop-down list, choose **Reference Plane: Capital Bottom** and then click OK.

This reference plane was part of the original file and is the lowest one.

3. On the Create tab, click the Sweep button.
    ⇨ On the ribbon, click the Sketch Path button.
    ⇨ Click the circle icon and start at the intersection of the two center reference planes.
    ⇨ Make the radius approximately **.500**.
4. Click the small "Make this temporary dimension permanent" icon.
    ⇨ Cancel the command, select the dimension and label the dimension with a new type-based parameter called **R2**. Group it under **Constraints**.
    ⇨ Enable the Center Mark and align and lock the circle.
    ⇨ Finish Edit Mode for the path.
5. On the Modify I Sweep tab, click the Select Profile button and then from the drop-down, choose **Corona Profile:Flex** (see Figure 5.11).

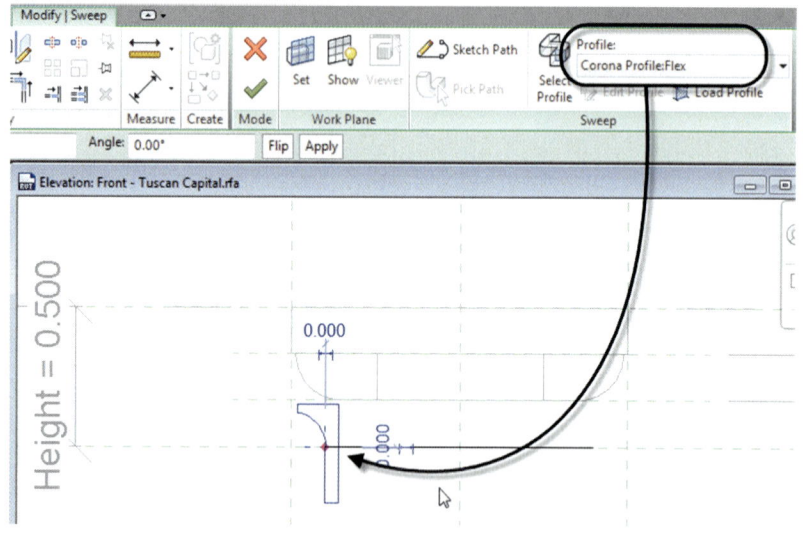

FIGURE 5.11
Build the Corona sweep

As you can see, we again need to adjust the proportions to get a size appropriate to the Tuscan capital we are building. We can do this the same way that we did above for the Ovolo profile. However, we have one additional issue here as well. The insertion point for the Corona family is at the endpoint of the curve, not the lowermost point of the profile. There are a few ways to deal with this. The exact choice you make will depend on how you plan to use this profile not only here but in other families as well. If most families would benefit from having an alternate insertion point such as the lower edge of the profile, we can edit the nested profile family and adjust the insertion point. The other option is to offset the profile with respect to its work plane.

Both approaches are easy to achieve. The one you ultimately choose is a matter of personal preference. So for the educational value, let's walk through each one. Take a look at the Properties palette and the Options Bar. Both show that the profile has a horizontal and vertical offset. There is also an angle and the ability to flip the profile if required. On the Options Bar, the offsets are listed simply as X and Y, on the Properties palette they are called

• Renaissance Revit •

Horizontal Profile Offset and Vertical Profile Offset. They are the same setting in both locations. Horizontal is X and Vertical is Y. Both can take a positive or negative number.

6. Experiment with some positive and negative numbers in the X and Y (Horizontal Profile Offset and Vertical Profile Offset) fields.

⇨ Set them back to zero when you are finished experimenting.

The problem with inputting values in either of these locations is that they are fixed numbers. In other words, we cannot link them to parameters, so later if we flex the Base Diameter, the profile will not move to the correct location.

7. Click the Finish Edit Mode button to finish the sweep.

Keep the new form selected and then take a look at the Properties palette now. Notice that in the Profile grouping there is an Associate Family Parameter button next to each offset parameter as well as the angle and the flip setting (see Figure 5.12). Let's try one out.

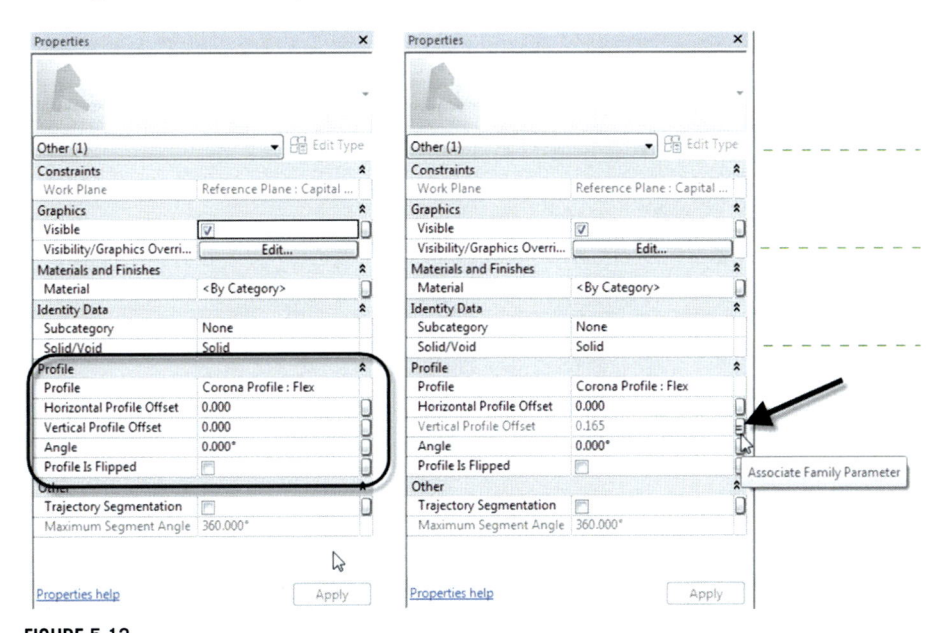

FIGURE 5.12

Profile offsets can be associated to family parameters

For this example, you can click any button and use any parameter. We will undo when we're done.

8. Next to Vertical Profile Offset, click the Associate Family Parameter button.

⇨ In the "Associate Family Parameter" dialog, choose any parameter such as **Capital Height Subdivision** and then click OK.

The location of the profile would now be controlled by the Capital Height Subdivision. Now this parameter will not actually position the corona in the correct location, so if we were going to use this approach, we would instead click the Add Parameter button in the "Associate Family Parameter" dialog and then later in "Family Types" we would add a formula to this new parameter to multiply it by Base Diameter like the others.

There is nothing wrong with this approach and you are encouraged to experiment further if you wish, but let's undo and try an alternate approach.

9. Click Undo (or press CTRL + Z) until the above associated family parameter is removed.

• *Creating Classical Architecture with Modern Software* •

122 | Chapter 5

We still want the completed corona sweep, but want the properties on the Properties palette to look like the left side of Figure 5.12 again.

The alternative approach is to edit the profile family and shift the insertion point. In this case, this will be easier to achieve, will give us the results we need and it will do so without the need for additional parameters.

10. On the Project Browser, right-click the Corona Profile and choose **Edit**.

11. Select the lowest horizontal reference plane.

   ⇨ On the Properties palette, check the Defines Origin checkbox (see Figure 5.13).

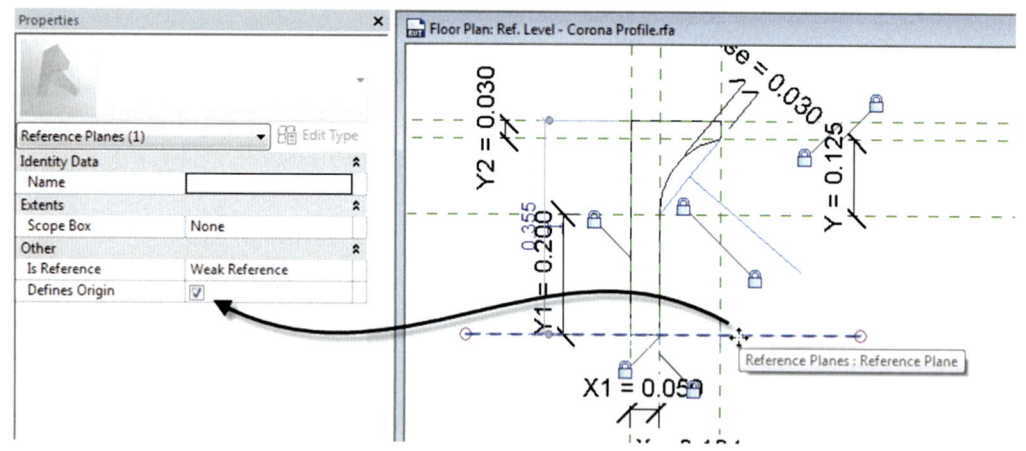

FIGURE 5.13

Change the origin point of the Corona family

12. Click the Load into Project button.

   ⇨ When prompted, choose the Overwrite the existing version (top) option.

Notice how the profile shifts up. It is now in the desired location.

> **CATCH UP!** You can open a file completed to this point named: *05_Corona Profile (Origin).rfa*.

13. On the Project Browser, expand *Families > Profiles > Corona Profile*.

14. Right-click on *Flex* and choose **Type Properties**.

As we saw for the Ovolo profile above, we only need to link up the Base Diameter as an assocaited paraemeter. But we do need to change the values of all the multipliers.

   ⇨ For the Y Projection Mult, input: **.100**.

   ⇨ For the X Projection Mult, input: **.115**.

   ⇨ For the X Mult, input: **.035**.

   ⇨ For the Y Mult, input: **.040**.

   ⇨ For the Fillet Projection Mult, input: **.030**.

   ⇨ For the Base Diameter, click the Associate Family Parameter button, select the **Base Diameter** parameter and then click OK (see Figure 5.10).

Dimensions	
Y Projection Mult	0.100000
X Projection Mult	0.115000
X Mult	0.035000
Y Mult	0.040000
Fillet Projection Mult	0.030000
Base Diameter	1.000

Input these values directly → (0.115000)

Associate Family Parameter →

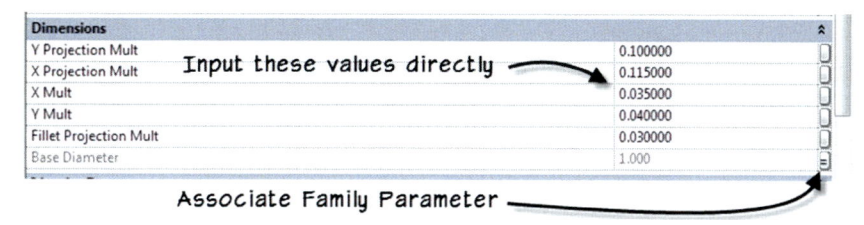

FIGURE 5.14

Edit the Type Properties of the Corona Profile

15. Click OK to apply the results and flex the sweep.

Much better, the heights and overall proportion are now correct, but notice that the Sweep's radius is still a little too large. We simply need a formula on the R2 parameter to adjust that.

16. Open the "Family Types" dialog.

⇨ In the Formula field next to R2, type: **Base Diameter * 0.425** and then click OK.

In the ovolo above, I used the Capital Height Subdivision in the formula for R1. I did this because in the traditional drafting construction steps for constructing the Tuscan capital, you would draw a 45° line from the abacus to locate the point where we added the Ovolo reference plane. The Ovolo ends up with a slightly less than 1 to 1 proportion, so there ends up being a small lip at the outside edge. Using the existing parameter just makes it easier to ensure that this relationship is maintained versus inputting the actual value of .165 in both formulas. For the formula for R2 however, I found it easier to do the math, as there was no direct relationship or existing parameter that I could easily leverage. Ultimately, as long as your math works out, you can set these parameters up any way that makes sense. Just try to be consistent in the techniques you apply.

I also calculated the value of the X Projection Mult parameter so that it would be flush on the inside of the form. You can see this best in a 3D view.

Make sure that the *View 1* 3D view is open and that it is set to shaded visual style.

17. Orbit the view to see it from all sides. (Hold down the SHIFT key and drag the wheel or use the ViewCube) (See Figure 5.15).

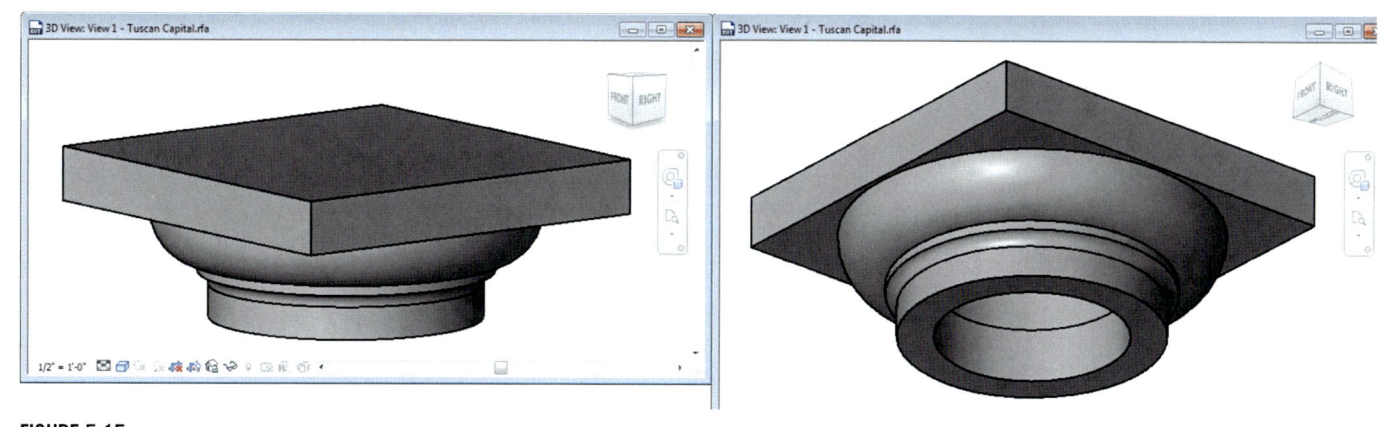

FIGURE 5.15

Study the results in 3D

If you want to fill in the hollow portion of the capital, you can build a simple extrusion with a radius that matches the size of the hollow part and then use join geometry. When using sweeps like we did here, the main advantage is the use of nested profiles and the reusing of our molding profiles. However, unlike a revolve, we could not make this solid all the way through with a sweep. It is a small inconvenience that is easily solved, but if this is not appealing to you, remember that you can use all of the techniques covered in the previous chapter to build the molding curves directly into the sketch of a revolve right in this family. You would have to create the required parameters and apply them to the sketch lines to ensure that it flexes. But is should look the same when it is done. Feel free to try this approach if you like.

The final step in this family is to flex.

18. Open the "Family Types" dialog and flex the Base Diameter parameter.

    ⇨ When you are satisfied, reset Base Diameter to **1.000** and then click OK.

19. Save the family.

> **CATCH UP!** You can open a file completed to this point named: *05_Tuscan Capital.rfa*.

BUILD THE TUSCAN BASE

The base of the Tuscan column is very simple. There is a square plinth topped with a round molding that uses a torus profile and a simple fillet above that (see Figure 6.1 in the next chapter for an illustration). Once again we can build the plinth with a simple square extrusion. The turned portions can be a revolve or a sweep. Since we ended the previous topic by suggesting that a revolve could have been used instead, and given the simplicity of the molding profile on this item, I will show the steps here as a revolve. This is mainly for the educational value so that you can see both approaches. Feel free to build a profile family for the torus and use sweeps instead.

1. Reopen your version of the *Tuscan Column* family file or open the catch-up version called *05_Tuscan Column.rfa*.

2. Minimize the two view windows for the *Tuscan Column* family.

3. On the Project Browser, right-click *Tuscan Base* and choose **Edit**.

    This will open just the one 3D view window for the *Tuscan Capital* family.

4. On the Project Browser, double-click to open the *Front* elevation view and the *Ref. Level* floor plan view.

    ⇨ Tile the windows.

Since we opened it from the host family and it does not currently have an RFA file, Revit will therefore perform a Save As instead and ask you where to save the family.

⇨ Save it as: **Tuscan Base**.

ADD REFERENCE PLANES, DIMENSIONS AND PARAMETERS

We will follow the same basic process as we did above for the capital. Let's start with the required reference planes, dimensions and parameters.

1. In the *Front* elevation view, create a horizontal reference plane parallel to the Ref. Level.

    ⇨ Draw it from right to left approximately halfway between the Ref. Level and the upper reference plane.

    ⇨ On the Properties palette, name this reference plane: **Plinth**.

2. Add a dimension from the Ref. Level and including both reference planes Plinth and Top.

    ⇨ Toggle on the equality (see Figure 5.16).

FIGURE 5.16

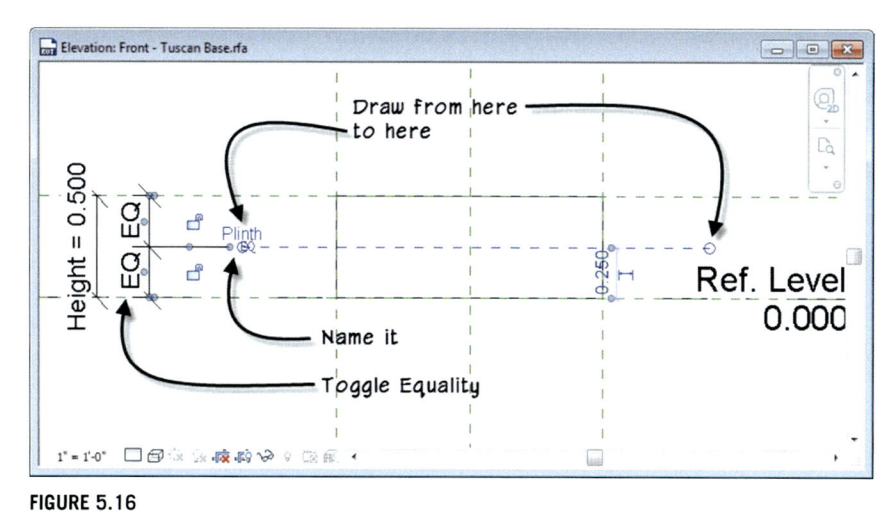

Add reference planes and an equality dimension

3. Create another reference plane above the one you just drew (but below Top). Draw it right to left again.
   ⇨ Name the new reference plane: **Fillet**.
4. Add a dimension between the Plinth and Fillet reference planes.
   ⇨ Select the Fillet reference plane and edit the value of this new dimension to move it **0.165** above Plinth.
   ⇨ Label this with a new type-based parameter named: **Torus Height** grouped under **Constraints** (see Figure 5.17).

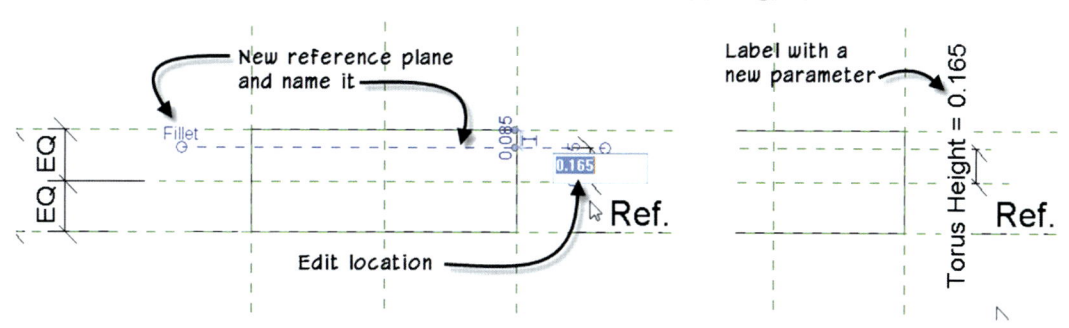

FIGURE 5.17

Add another reference plane and a new parameter

Next we need a reference plane running vertically.

5. On the left side, create a new vertical reference plane **0.085** from the Left reference plane.
   ⇨ Name it **Torus**, add a dimension between Torus and the Left reference plane.
   ⇨ Label this with a new type-based parameter called **Torus Rise** grouped under **Constraints** (see Figure 5.18).

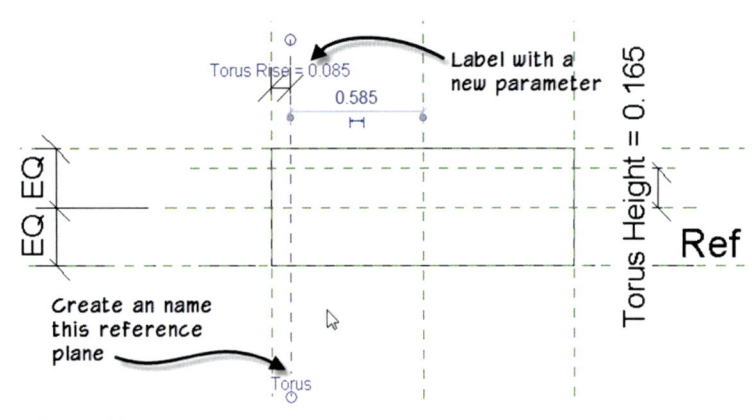

FIGURE 5.18
Add a vertical reference plane and a new parameter

Recall that a torus is a half circle. If you do the math here you will see that the proportions do not quite work for an actual torus. We would either need to flex our new Torus Rise parameter to make it half of the Torus Height, or adjust the shape of the torus molding. In the sources that I have consulted, it is not clear if this molding should be an exact half circle, or if it should be drawn along a diagonal or if the shape should be exaggerated. The only thing that is certain is that the height and width proportions of this molding are slightly different and the molding is flush to the extent of the plinth. To avoid an overly complex construct here, I am going to "cheat" a little and use an ellipse. This will allow me to create a torus shaped molding whose axes remain vertical and horizontal but satisfy the slight difference in proportion. To keep the molding a circle, we could draw a diagonal spring line and use a radius parameter. But as noted, I am trying to avoid this complexity here. Feel free to try other methods if you like.

One more reference plane will be helpful. Let's add another horizontal one with an equality dimension to locate the center of the ellipse.

6. Draw a horizontal reference plane from right to left between the Plinth and Fillet reference planes.

⇨ Add an equality dimension (see Figure 5.19).

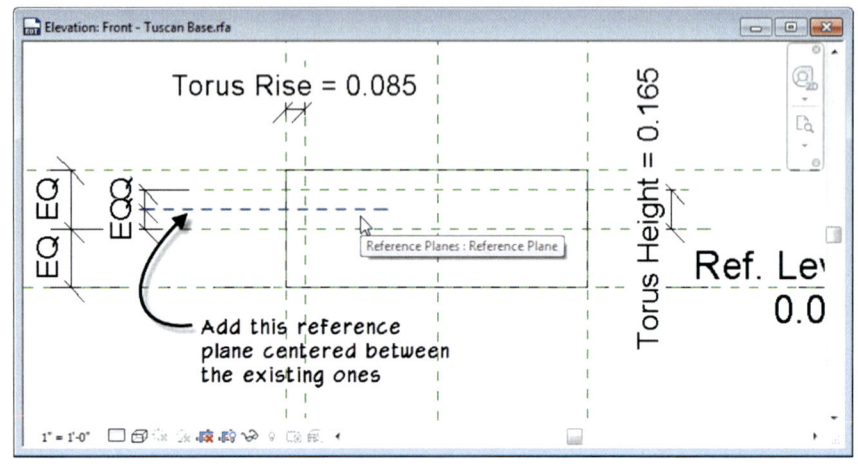

FIGURE 5.19
Add a centered reference plane for the ellipse center

> **TIP:** The scale of views in the family editor can and often should be changed. As you add many reference planes and dimensions, it can become quite cluttered. Please feel free to change the scale and/or edit the dimension types to make things more legible.

• Renaissance Revit •

The Tuscan Base, Capital and Pedestal | 127

ADD THE FORMULAS

We have all the framework in place. Now let's make sure it flexes properly. We need to add some formulas.

1. Open the "Family Types" dialog.

Formulas already exist for the Width, Height and Depth. We need only add the ones for the two new parameters we added. This is easy to do. Take their current value and use that as the multiplier times the Base Diameter parameter.

⇨ For Torus Rise, add a formula of: **Base Diameter * 0.085**. For Torus Height, add a formula of: **Base Diameter * 0.165**.

2. Flex the Base Diameter.

3. Click OK to dismiss the "Family Types" dialog and then save the file.

CREATE THE PLINTH

The geometry for our Tuscan base will consist of an extrusion for the plinth and a revolve for the molding above it. We can start with the extrusion which is already in this file. We need to simply modify its height to make the plinth.

Work in the *Tuscan Base* family, in the *Front* elevation view.

1. Select the extrusion already in the file (see Figure 5.20).

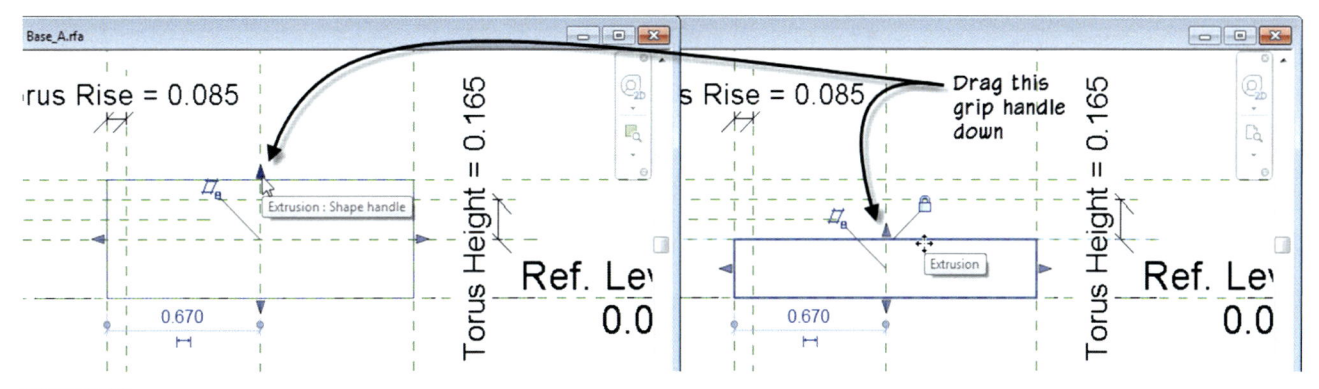

FIGURE 5.20

Adjust the height of the existing extrusion

⇨ Drag the grip handle at the top of the extrusion down.

⇨ Release the mouse when it snaps to the Plinth reference plane.

2. In the error that appears, click the Remove Constraints button.

⇨ Close the lock icon.

We saw the same error above. The error displays because the top of the extrusion is currently locked to the Top reference plane. So when we stretch it, we must remove this constraint. We are then applying a new constraint by clicking the lock icon. Alternatively, you can use the align command here if you prefer.

3. Save the file.

> **CATCH UP!** You can open a file completed to this point named: *05_Tuscan Base_A.rfa*.

CREATE THE REVOLVE MOLDING

We will build a single revolve that contains both the torus and the fillet above it.

Work in the *Tuscan Base* family, in the *Front* elevation view.

• *Creating Classical Architecture with Modern Software* •

128 | Chapter 5

1. Zoom in on the left side of the base.

2. On the Create tab, on the Work Plane panel, click the Set button.

    ⇨ In the "Work Plane" dialog, from the Name drop-down list, choose **Reference Plane: Center (Front/Back)** and then click OK.

3. On the Create tab, click the Revolve button.

    ⇨ Click the Partial Ellipse icon.

    ⇨ Snap the first point at the intersection of the Plinth and Torus reference planes (see the left side of Figure 5.21).

    ⇨ Snap the second point at the intersection of the Fillet and Torus reference planes (see the middle of Figure 5.21).

    ⇨ Click the final point at the intersection of the Left reference plane and the one centered between Fillet and Plinth (see the right side of Figure 5.21).

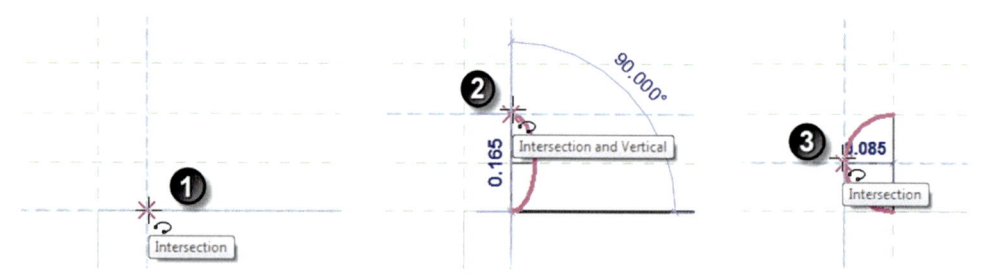

FIGURE 5.21

Draw a partial ellipse

4. Click the Modify tool to cancel.

    ⇨ Select the partial ellipse onscreen.

    ⇨ Click the icon on the horizontal temporary dimension to make it permanent.

    ⇨ Label this dimension with the Torus Rise parameter (see Figure 5.22).

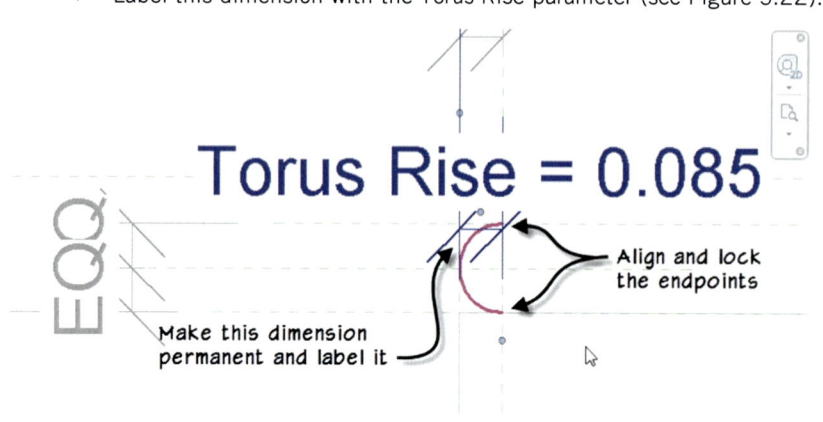

FIGURE 5.22

Make the temporary dimension permanent and label it

5. Align and lock the two endpoints in both directions.

If you want to learn more about applying parameters to an ellipse, review the "Elliptical Arches" and "Create a Parametric Ellipse" topics in Chapter 4.

6. On the Draw panel, click the Line icon.

    ⇨ Draw the lines as indicated on the left side of Figure 5.23.

    ⇨ Align and lock to the reference planes all the way around

• Renaissance Revit •

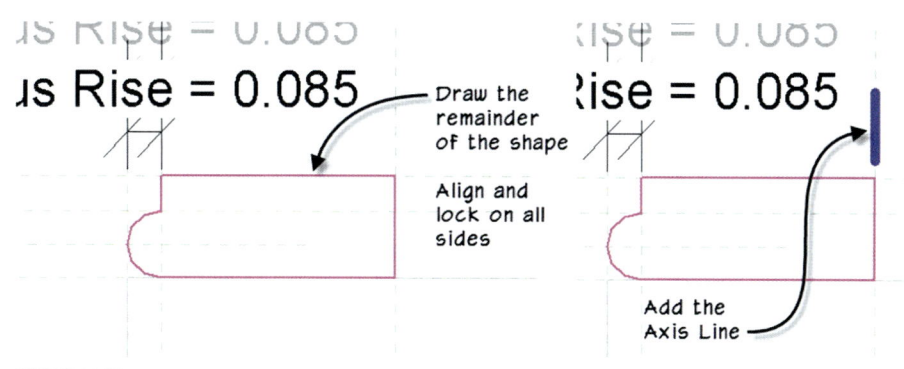

FIGURE 5.23
Draw the rest of the sketch and add the axis line

7. On the Draw panel, click the Axis Line button.
   ⇨ Draw an axis aligned with the Center (Left/Right) reference plane. It does not matter how long it is (see the right side of Figure 5.23).
8. Click the Finish Edit Mode button.

The sketch will revolve a full 360° around the axis line you drew. (See the Properties palette with the Revolve selected to control or parameterize the angle of the Revolve if you wish).

Make sure that the *View 1* 3D view is open and that it is set to shaded visual style.

9. Orbit the view to see it from all sides. (Hold down the SHIFT key and drag the wheel or use the ViewCube) (See Figure 5.24).

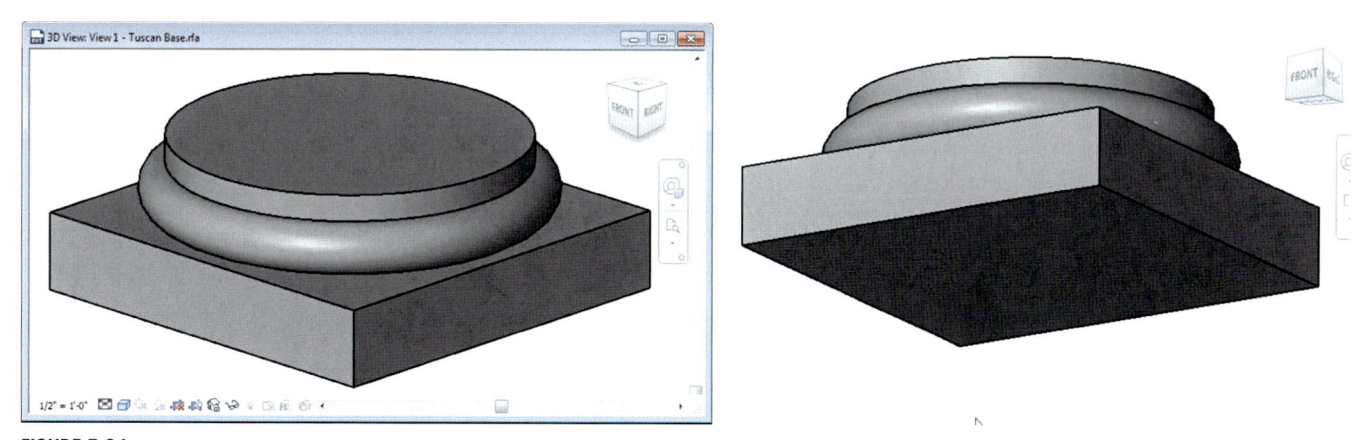

FIGURE 5.24
Study the results in 3D

Unlike the sweeps used in the capital, this form is solid all the way through. The biggest down side to the approach used here is that we cannot easily reuse this molding shape. If we have another form that needs a similar torus and fillet molding. We have to construct all of the reference planes, dimensions, parameters, lines and curves again. This is the main reason that I have been using profiles nearly exclusively in most of my more recent families.

Let's make sure we flex before we leave this family.

10. Open the "Family Types" dialog and flex the Base Diameter parameter.
    ⇨ When you are satisfied, reset Base Diameter to **1.000** and then click OK.
11. Save the family.

> **CATCH UP!** You can open a file completed to this point named: *05_Tuscan Base.rfa*.

• *Creating Classical Architecture with Modern Software* •

BUILD THE TUSCAN PEDESTAL

Each of the orders is sometimes designed with a pedestal beneath the column base. Like the other portions of the order, the proportions and specific details of the shaft vary with each order and they get progressively more complex from Tuscan through Corinthian/Composite. Like the overall column, the pedestal shares a similar structure. There is a series of base moldings, the die (a vertical portion that is sometimes paneled in the more ornate orders) and then a series of top moldings. In this heading, we will construct a Tuscan pedestal family. The easiest way to get started is to save a copy of our original Tuscan Base family.

1. Open the file named: *05_Tuscan Base_A.rfa*.

    ⇨ Tile the windows.

2. From the Application menu, choose **Save As > Family**.

    ⇨ Browse to the *Working* folder and save it as: **Tuscan Pedestal**.

PLANNING THE FAMILY

This family already has some reference planes and some of the parameters that we will need. But it is best to plan out a little of the strategy first. Figure 5.25 shows a completed version. Each molding is labeled with an explanation of how it will be constructed. Take a little time to study the figure before proceeding.

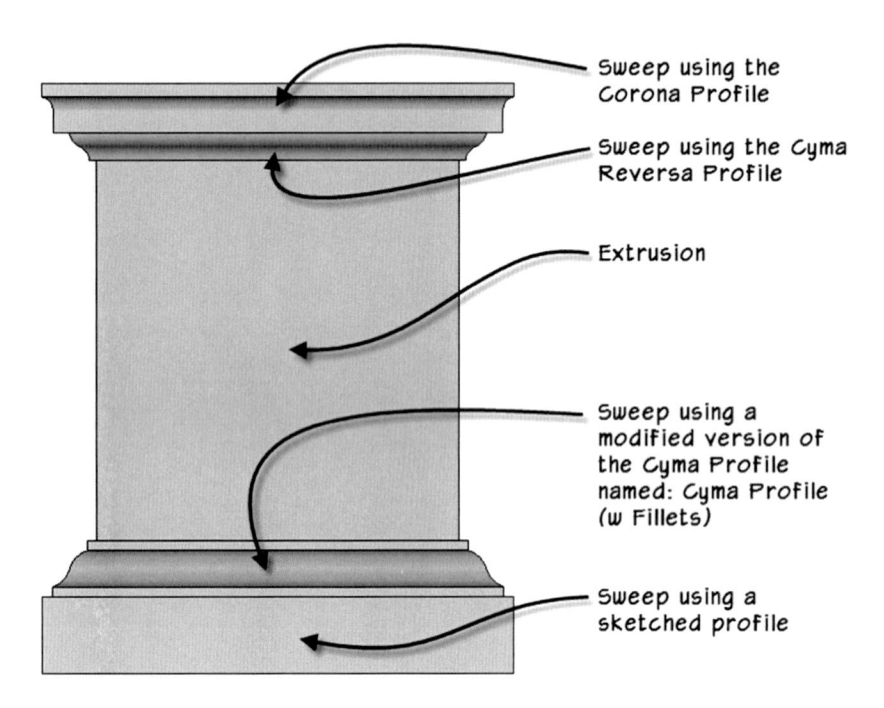

FIGURE 5.25

Planning out the Tuscan pedestal family

We will mostly use techniques already covered to construct this family. We'll adjust the reference planes to create a work plane for each sweep. We'll name these to make them easier to use as work planes and adjust or add dimensions as appropriate. The bottommost form the base platform that Cyma sits on will be a simple sweep with a sketched profile. We could also make this another extrusion, but I chose a sweep here for two reasons. The first is that as you will see we will only require one vertical reference plane to construct it. If we did an extrusion, we would need four vertical reference planes drawn as an outer square in plan. Each of those reference planes would require dimensions and parameters. So the sweep just makes things a little simpler. I also mentioned that we will sketch the profile for this sweep. We could certainly build a new profile family. This would actually eliminate the need for even the one reference plane we will add. So you might prefer to go this route. But since this a simple square shape, in this case I find it just as easy to sketch it directly.

To create the cyma molding above this, I modified the Cyma Profile family that we created in the previous chapter. The modified version is included in the *Chapter05* folder. I modified it in two ways, both of which we have already seen in the lessons earlier in this chapter and the previous chapter. First, I added two fillet moldings. To learn more about how that was accomplished, review the "Create a Variable Corona Profile" topic in Chapter 4. The other modification was to add the Base Diameter and multiplier parameters as was discussed in several previous lessons (but first discussed in the "Proportional Scaling Strategies" topic in Chapter 4). By adding the fillets directly to the molding profile, it adds some complexity to the nested profile family, but it greatly simplifies the amount of reference planes and parameters needed in this family. (I did provide a version of the original Cyma profile in the *Chapter05* folder if you prefer to build the cyma separately from the fillets).

The top two moldings use profile families as they were built in the previous chapter. There are some minor modifications. For example, we have already discussed the Corona at length earlier in this chapter. We will use it again here. I also modified the cyma reversa to add the Base Diameter and multipliers, but otherwise it is the same as the one we built in Chapter 4.

I tried to keep the parameters to a minimum, and as such, we will use a feature of sweeps that we have not yet discussed. This is the "Trajectory Segmentation" feature. With this feature, we can create a circular path as we did previously, but express the path as any regular polygon shape including a square. So we will sketch a round path, control it with a simple radius parameter, but it will end up creating a square form. Very handy indeed.

CONFIGURE REFERENCE PLANES, DIMENSIONS AND PARAMETERS

Since we saved from the base family in this example, we need to adjust the existing reference planes and parameters first.

1. Open the "Family Types" dialog.
2. Next to the Height parameter, change the Formula to: **Base Diameter * 2.1**.
3. Click the Apply button.

The family will flex and the extrusion will get a bit taller. But it is constrained to only half the total height currently. For this family, we want it to go the full height, so let's address that next.

Work in the *Front* elevation view.

4. Using the shape handle on the top of the extrusion, or the align tool, follow the procedure outlined above in the "Create the Abacus" and "Create the Plinth" topics to stretch the extrusion up to and constrain it to the Top reference plane.

As before, you'll have to remove the existing constraints and be sure to lock it.

There are two options next. We need four horizontal reference planes running between the Ref. Level and Top reference plane. We need one vertical reference plane outside of the Left one. We can move and rename the ones we already have and add a few extras, or we can delete them all and recreate them. Either approach is fine. There is one caution to note if you decide to move and rename. Be sure to delete the labeled dimensions *before* you try to move any reference planes. This is very important. If you want to give it a try to see, feel free. But be sure to undo before continuing.

132 | Chapter 5

> **Important:** If you move a reference plane that has a labeled dimension attached to it, Revit will try to flex the family based on the amount you move the reference plane. Generally, this produces poor and undesirable results so it is not recommended.

I think that it is about the same amount of work either way. So if you are very diligent about first deleting dimensions, then moving and renaming the results are fine. In this case, I am going to suggest deleting and redrawing.

5. Select the three horizontal and one vertical reference planes on the inside of the form and delete them (see Figure 5.26).

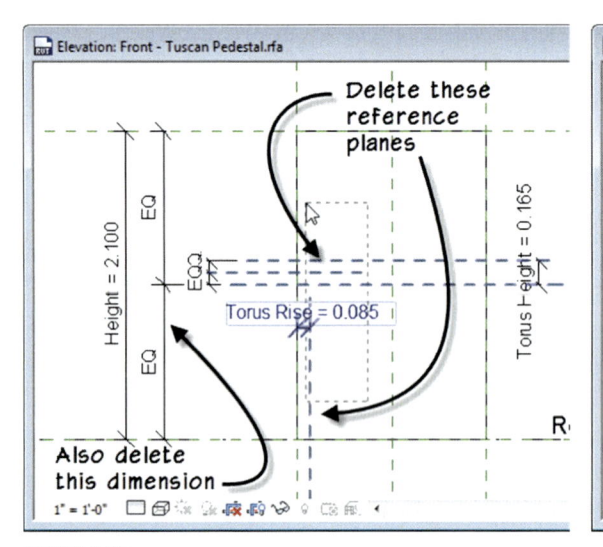

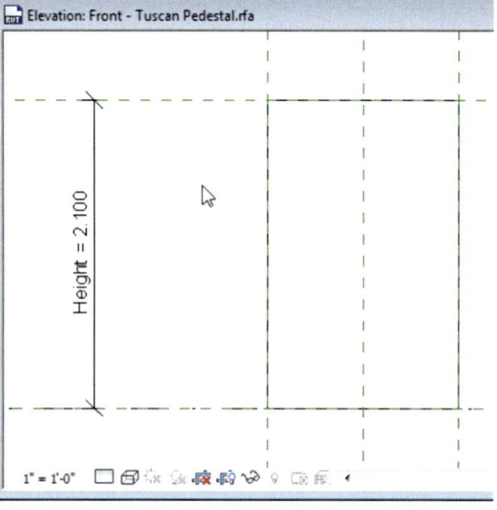

FIGURE 5.26
Delete the existing reference planes

⇨ Delete the equality dimensions too.

The two labeled dimensions (Torus Rise and Torus Height) will also be deleted.

6. Create five new reference planes.

⇨ Four horizontal drawn from right to left. Two near the bottom, two near the top.

⇨ One vertical drawn outside the form to the left.

⇨ Name each one as indicated in Figure 5.27.

7. Create dimensions for each location as shown in the figure.

⇨ Label each dimension with a new parameter named as shown. Group all parameters under **Constraints**.

• Renaissance Revit •

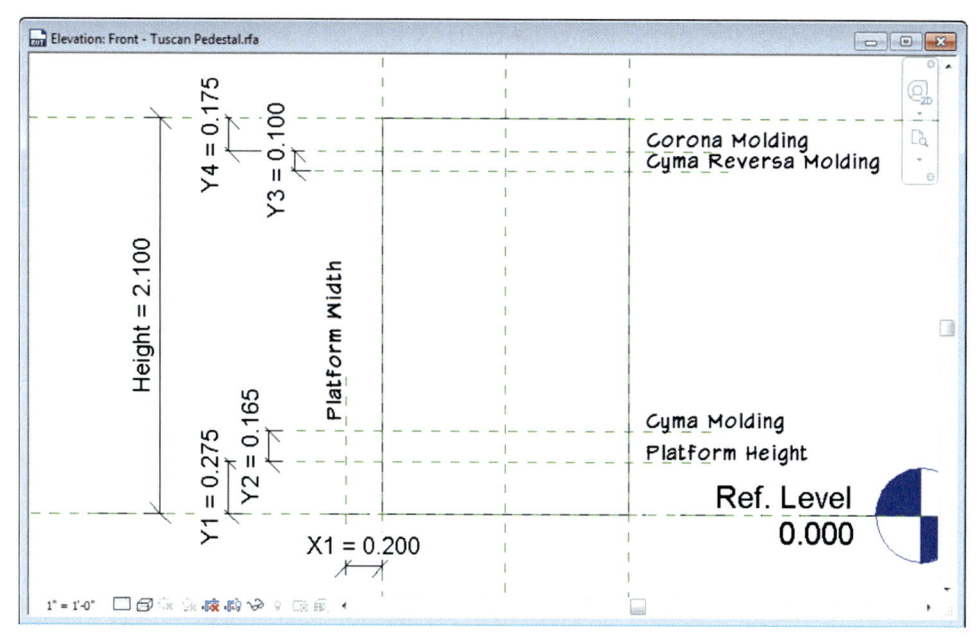

FIGURE 5.27

Create new named reference planes, dimensions and parameters

8. Add the formulas as indicated in Table 5.1 and Figure 5.28.

TABLE 5.1

Parameter	Formula
X1	Base Diameter * 0.200
Y3	Base Diameter * 0.100
Y2	Base Diameter * 0.165
Y1	Base Diameter * 0.275
R2	Base Diameter * 0.830
R1	Base Diameter * 0.695
Y4	Base Diameter * 0.175

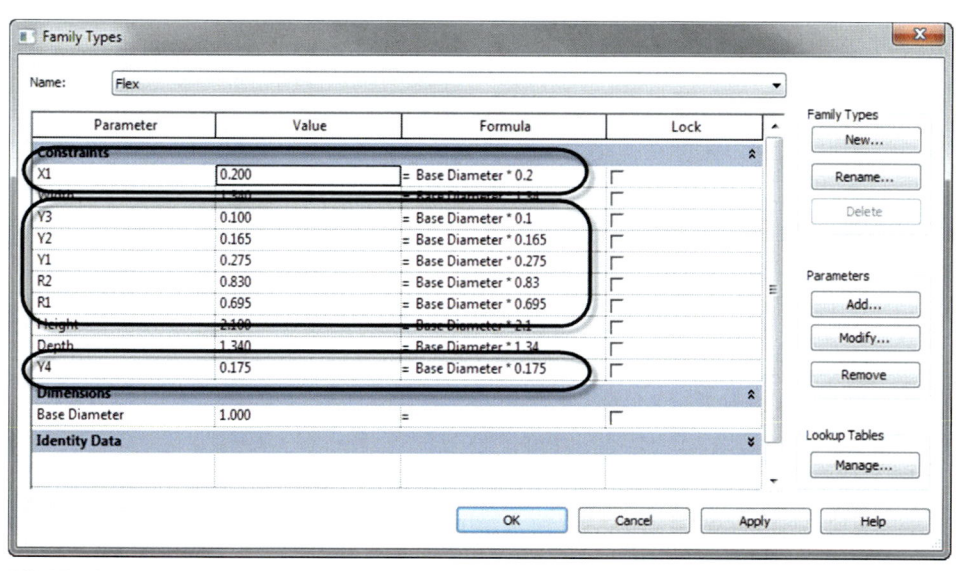

FIGURE 5.28

The "Family Types" dialog showing all of the new parameters

Notice that the figure and table shows the parameters in an odd order. There is unfortunately no way to change the order of the parameters. So pay close attention while editing. Also, notice that the figure does not show the existing Torus Rise and Torus Height parameters and instead shows R1 and R2.

9. Select Torus Rise, on the right side of the dialog, click the Modify button.

   ⇨ Rename the parameter to **R1** and click OK.

   ⇨ Change the formula of R1 to match Table 5.1 and Figure 5.28.

   ⇨ Repeat the steps to rename and reconfigure Torus Height to **R2**.

10. Save the file.

> **CATCH UP!** You can open a file completed to this point named: *05_Tuscan Pedestal_A.rfa*.

CREATE THE LOWER MOLDING GEOMETRY

We now have all the reference planes, dimensions and parameters. We are ready to begin adding the geometry. We'll start from the bottom and work our way up. The bottommost molding is the one that we will create by sketching.

1. On the Create tab, click the Sweep button.

For the other sweeps, we drew the path. For this one, let's try the Pick Path option. This option lets you use the edges of 3D geometry to create the sweep path. We'll use the bottom edges of the extrusion. The first segment of the sweep path determines where the sketch goes. So make sure you click the left edge of the extrusion first. This is so we can see it in our *Front* view which we already have open.

2. In the *View 1* 3D view, orbit the view so you can see the Left side (use the ViewCube as a guide).

3. On the ribbon, click the Pick Path button.

   ⇨ Click on the bottom edge of the extrusion's left side (see Figure 5.29).

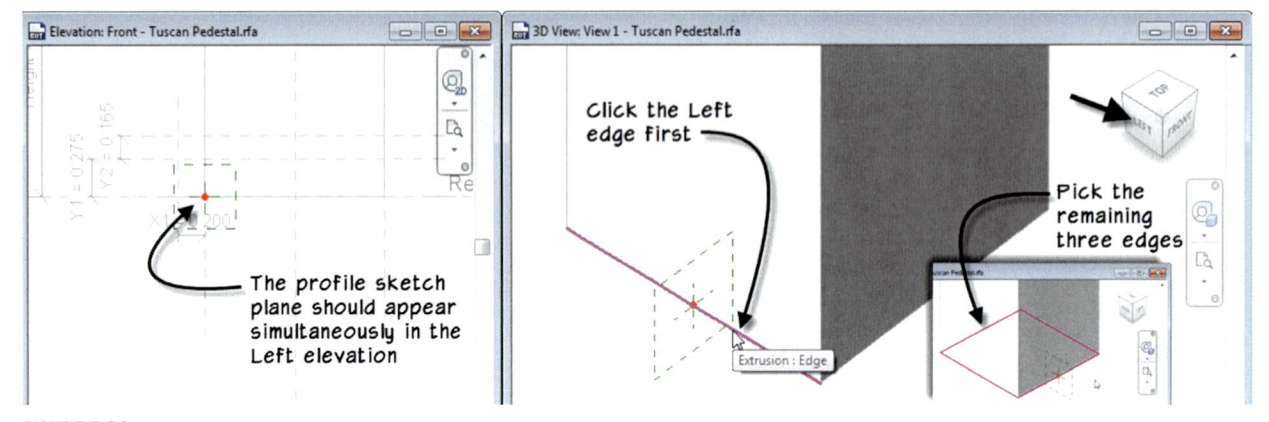

FIGURE 5.29

Use the Pick Path option to create the sweep path based on existing geometry

   ⇨ Pick the remaining three edges (four total) orbit the view as required to pick them.

   ⇨ On the ribbon, click the Finish Edit Mode button.

   Click in the *Front* elevation view to activate it.

4. On the Modify | Sweep tab, on the Sweep panel, click the Edit Profile button.

   ⇨ Click the rectangle icon and draw a rectangle snapped to the intersections of the reference planes defined by the X1 and Y1 parameters.

⇨ Lock all the locks on all four sides (see Figure 5.30).

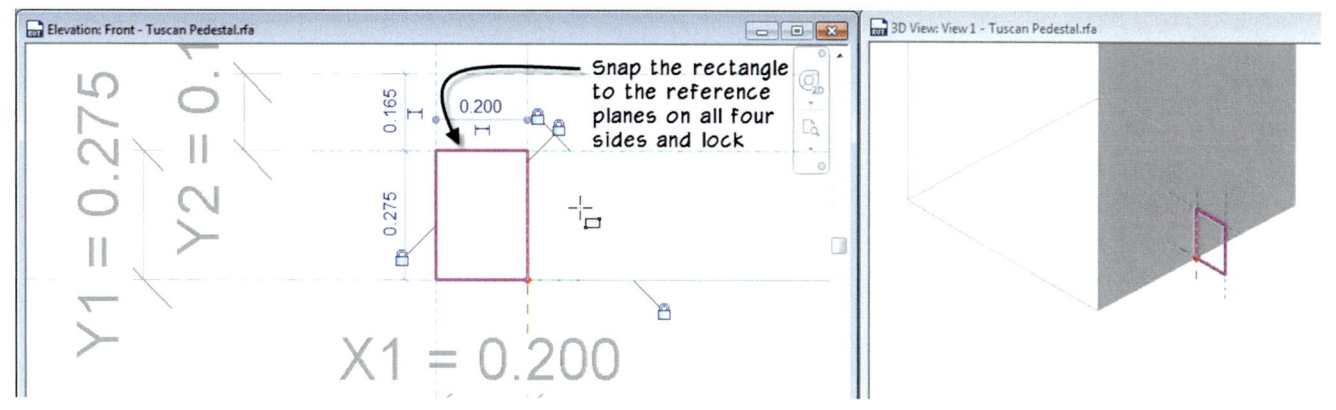

FIGURE 5.30
Sketch the profile shape

5. Click the Finish Edit Mode button for the sketch and then again to complete the sweep.

Your first molding is complete and forms a square band around the base of the existing extrusion form. Try flexing the Base Diameter parameter. I usually try a value .75, then 1.5 and sometimes 2.0. When I am satisfied that it is all working correctly, I always return the Base Diameter to 1.0.

For the next molding we move up to our cyma profile. Any edge can be picked as a sweep path including the one shared between our square molding and the extrusion form. So let's repeat the process here and use this new edge as the path for our next sweep.

Click in the *View 1* 3D view to make it active.

6. Begin a new sweep and choose the Pick Path option.

⇨ In the 3D view, be sure you are looking at the left side again, and then click the top edge of the square molding that is adjacent to the extrusion.

⇨ Click the other three edges (orbiting as necessary) and then Finish Edit Mode (see Figure 5.31).

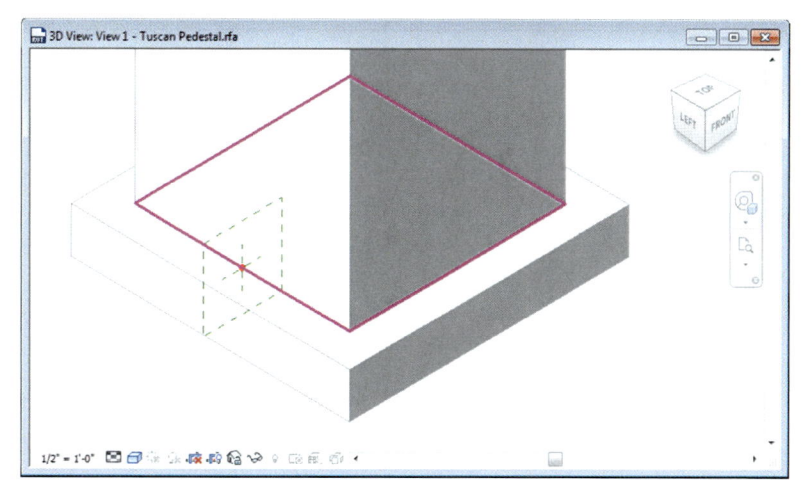

FIGURE 5.31
Pick Path for the cyma molding

This time we are using a profile family. However, we have not yet imported the family, so let's import it now.

7. On the Insert tab, click the Load Family button.

8. Browse to the *Chapter05* folder, select the *Cyma Profile (w Fillets).rfa* file and then click Open.

136 | Chapter 5

⇨ On the Modify I Sweep tab, click the Select Profile button and then from the Profile drop-down list, choose **Cyma Profile (w Fillets):Flex** (see Figure 5.32).

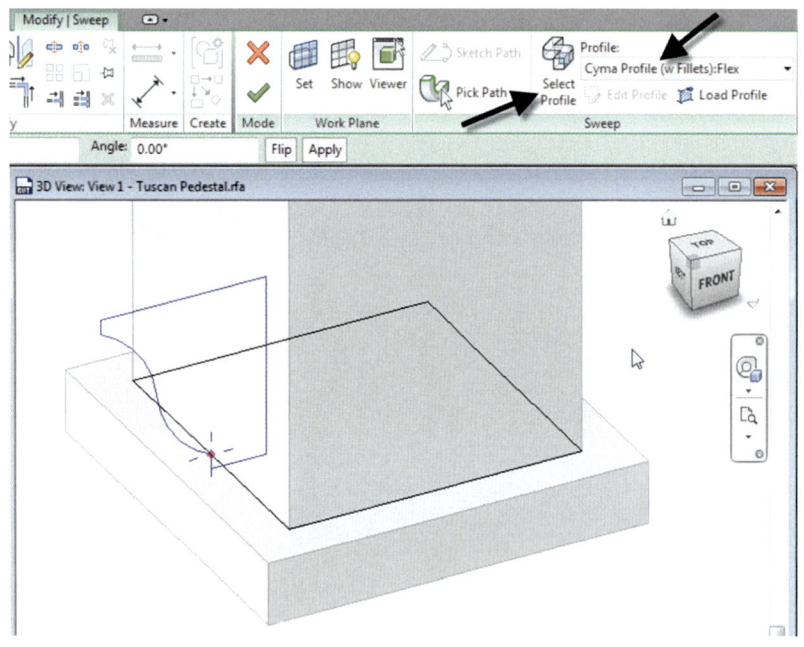

FIGURE 5.32

Import the cyma profile family and apply it

Recall from the previous exercises, that the remaining adjustments are best accomplished outside of the sweep sketch mode. So let's finish the sweep and then adjust the position and scale of the profile.

9. Click the Finish Edit Mode button.

   The sweep will remain selected. Let's therefore deal with its properties first.

10. On the Properties palette, next to Vertical Profile Offset, click the Associate Family Parameter button.

    ⇨ In the "Associate Family Parameter" dialog, choose **Y2** and then click OK.

    The form will shift up to the location of the reference plane.

    ⇨ For the Angle field, type in: **180**.

    ⇨ Check the "Profile Is Flipped" checkbox (see Figure 5.33).

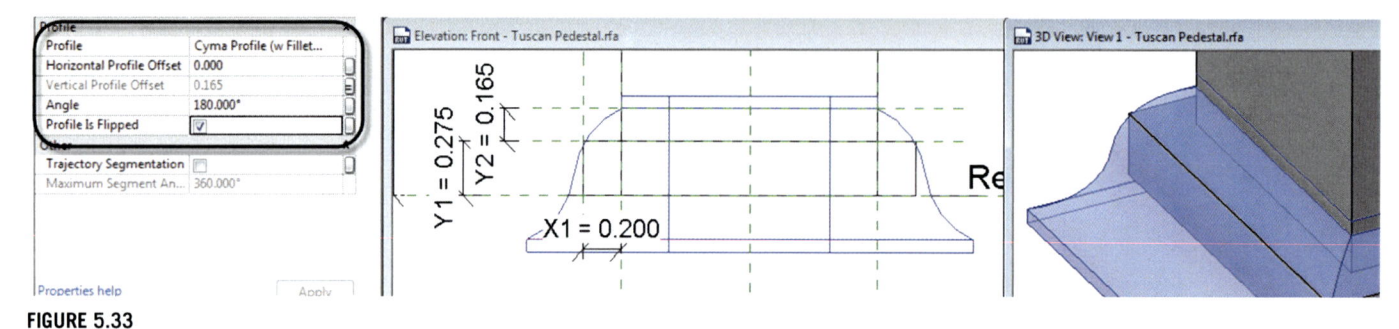

FIGURE 5.33

Adjust the profile properties

11. On the Project Browser, expand *Families > Profiles > Cyma Profile (w Fillets)*.

    ⇨ Right-click *Flex* and choose Type Properties (you can also double-click *Flex* instead).

    ⇨ For both Y Mult and X Mult, use a value of **0.130** and for Fillet Mult and Depth Projection Mult, use a value of **0.035**.

    ⇨ Associate the Base Diameter parameter (see Figure 5.34).

• Renaissance Revit •

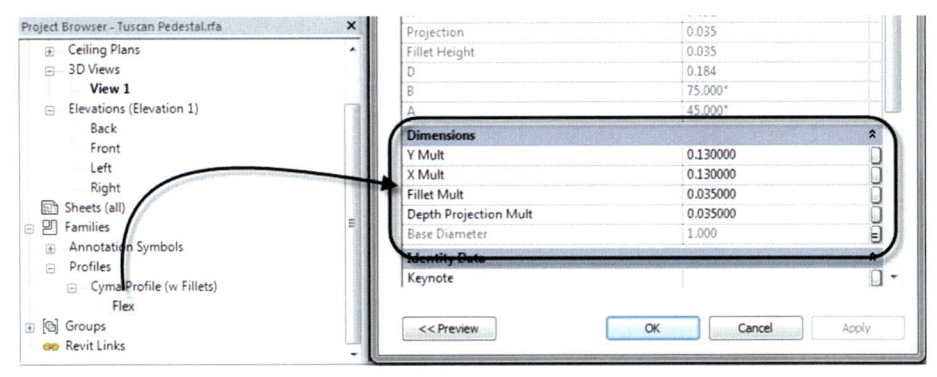

FIGURE 5.34

Edit the profile type based parameters and link up the Base Diameter

We see one small problem when we click OK. This is related once again to the insertion point of the profile family. The solution is simple, but it requires another parameter. (We could also edit the profile family and move the origin as we did in the "Create the Corona Molding" topic above, but this might limit the family's usefulness in other families). So let's just add a new parameter.

12. Select the cyma molding.

   ⇨ On the Properties palette, next to the Horizontal Profile Offset property, click the Associate Family Parameter button.

   ⇨ In the "Associate Family Parameter" dialog, click the Add Parameter button.

   ⇨ Name it **X2** and group it under **Constraints**.

13. Click OK twice and then open the "Family Types" dialog.

   ⇨ In the Formula field next to X2, input: **Base Diameter * 0.035** and then click Apply.

The molding should move out to the correct location. Now the real test:

14. Stay in "Family Types" and flex the Base Diameter parameter.

   ⇨ Reset Base Diameter to **1.000** and close the dialog when finished.

15. Save the file.

> **CATCH UP!** You can open a file completed to this point named: *05_Tuscan Pedestal_B.rfa*.

USING TRAJECTORY SEGMENTATION

For the top two moldings we will still create sweeps, but instead of Pick Path, we'll try a different approach. We'll use Trajectory Segmentation to express a circular path as a square.

   Click in the *Ref. Level* floor plan view to make it active.

1. On the Create tab, on the Work Plane panel, click the Set button.

   ⇨ From the Name list, choose **Reference Plane: Cyma Reversa Molding** and then click OK.

2. Begin a new sweep and choose the Sketch Path option.

   ⇨ Draw a circle from the intersection at the center with radius approximately **.5**.

   ⇨ Turn on the Center Mark, align and lock it in both directions.

3. Make the radius a permanent dimension and label it with the **R1** parameter created above.

   ⇨ Finish the path.

138 | Chapter 5

Once again we need to load a profile for this sweep. We will need one for the other sweep above it as well, so let's load them both now.

4. On the Modify | Sweep tab, on the Sweep panel, click the Load Profile button.

5. Browse to the *Chapter05* folder, hold down the CTRL key select the *05_Corona Profile (Origin).rfa* and the *Cyma Reversa Profile.rfa* file and then click Open.

⇨ On the Modify | Sweep tab, click the Select Profile button and then from the Profile drop-down list, choose **Cyma Reversa Profile:Flex** (see Figure 5.35).

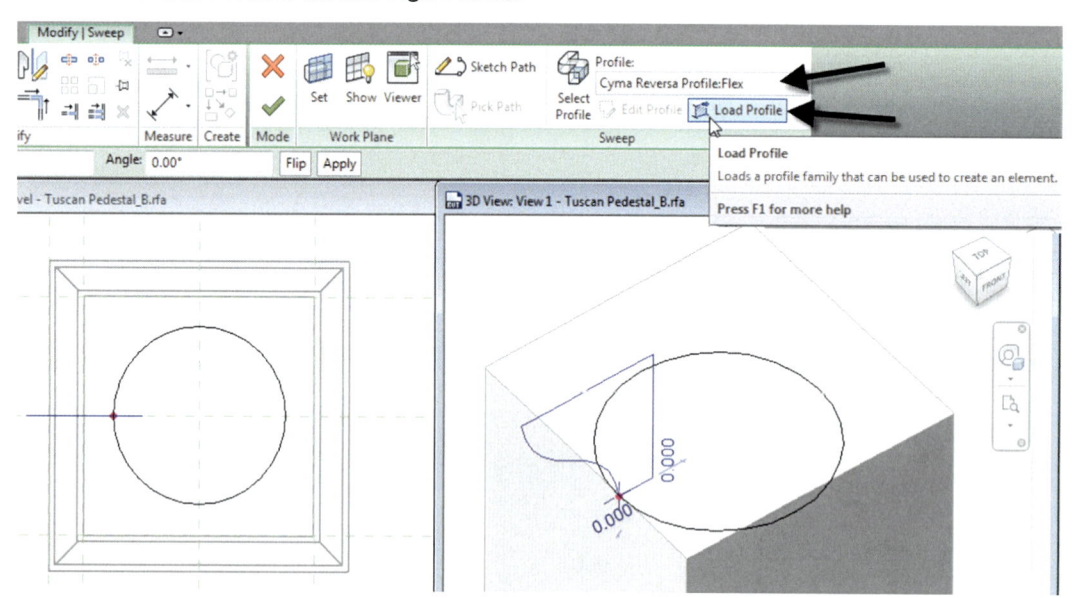

FIGURE 5.35

Draw a circular path and load in the cyma reversa profile

6. Click the Finish Edit Mode button.

As before, we need to make some adjustments.

7. On the Project Browser, expand *Families > Profiles > Cyma Reversa Profile*.

⇨ Right-click *Flex* and choose Type Properties (you can also double-click *Flex* instead).

⇨ For the Y Mult input a value of: **0.100**, for the X Mult, use a value of: **0.075**, for the Depth Projection Mult, use a value of: **0.025** and then finally, set the Base Diameter to: **1.000**.

⇨ Associate the Base Diameter parameter (see Figure 5.36). (Make sure to change Base Diameter to **1.000** before associating it).

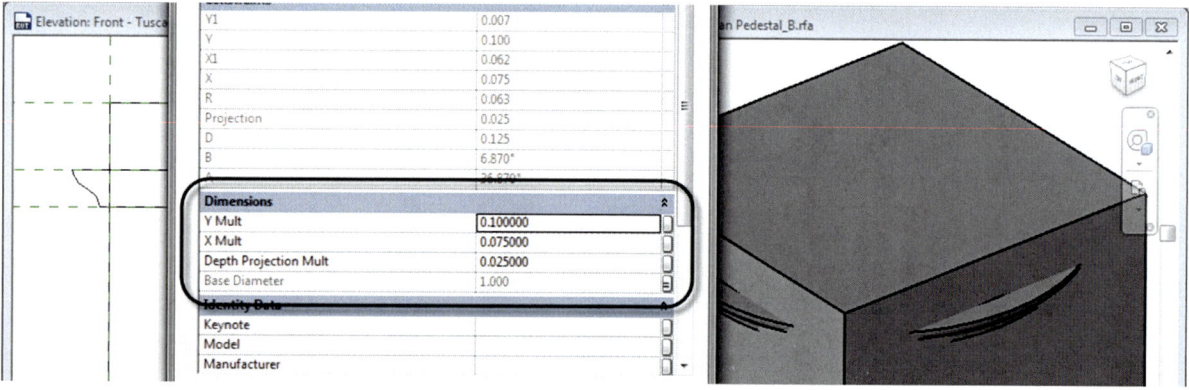

FIGURE 5.36

Edit the type properties of the cyma reversa profile

• Renaissance Revit •

This adjusts the proportions nicely as you can see in the elevation, but in the 3D view we can see that the sweep is still circular in shape. This is where Trajectory Segmentation comes in. The Trajectory Segmentation feature allows you to segment a smooth curve in the path of a sweep. When you enable this feature, a new property becomes available named Maximum Segment Angle. Use this property to determine if a curved path should be faceted instead of smooth. A setting of 0° would make a perfectly smooth path. Higher numbers begin to segment it. If you have a very low value like 1° or 2°, you will get many segments. Higher numbers begin to approximate polygons. For example, if you have a circular path with segmentation set to 60°, you will get a hexagon. Set it to 45° and you will get an octagon. But remember, the setting is "Maximum" segment angle, so the results are not always obvious. Intuition suggests that the value to get a square should be 90°. In reality simply having Trajectory Segmentation enabled for a circle will give you a square for any angle value 90° and higher. So you can actually leave it set to the default 360° and it will stay square. This would not necessary be true if the path were not a circle, so the results on different shaped path will vary.

8. Select the cyma reversa molding onscreen.

    ⇨ On the Properties palette, check the Trajectory Segmentation checkbox (see Figure 5.37).

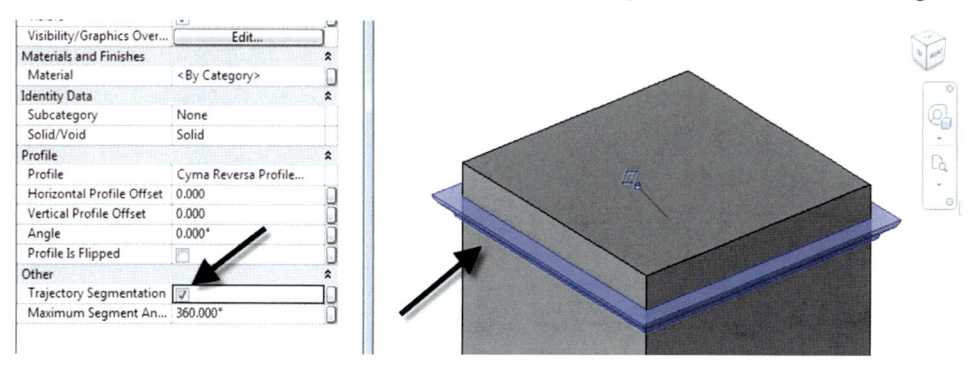

FIGURE 5.37
Turn on Trajectory Segmentation to make the round path square

9. Flex the Base Diameter parameter.

If you would like to experiment with the settings for Trajectory Segmentation, please feel free. Just be sure to set it back to at least 90° when you are done. As you can see, 360° still gives you a square. I tend to think that 90° feels more logical, but any value between 360° and 90° will work in this case.

10. Save the file.

CATCH UP! You can open a file completed to this point named: *05_Tuscan Pedestal_C.rfa*.

COPY AND MODIFY A MOLDING

The quickest way to create the last molding is to copy the one we have and modify it.

1. Select the cyma reversa molding.

    ⇨ On the Modify | Sweep tab, on the Clipboard panel, click the Copy to Clipboard button (or press CTRL + C).

    ⇨ On the Clipboard panel, click the drop-down on the Paste button and choose **Aligned to Same Place**.

    Do not use CTRL + V.

    The new copy will remain selected.

2. On the ribbon, click the Edit Work Plane button.

    ⇨ In the "Work Plane" dialog, from the Name list, choose **Reference Plane: Corona Molding** and then click OK.

140 | Chapter 5

The copied molding will move up slightly to the Corona Molding reference plane.

3. On the ribbon, click the Edit Sweep button.

    ⇨ Click the Sketch Path button. (If prompted to switch views, choose the *Ref. Level* floor plan view).

    ⇨ Select the dimension and change the label to **R2**.

    ⇨ Deselect the dimension and then click the Finish Edit Mode button.

4. On the Modify I Sweep tab, click the Select Profile button and then from the Profile drop-down list, choose **05_Corona Profile (Origin):Flex** (see Figure 5.38).

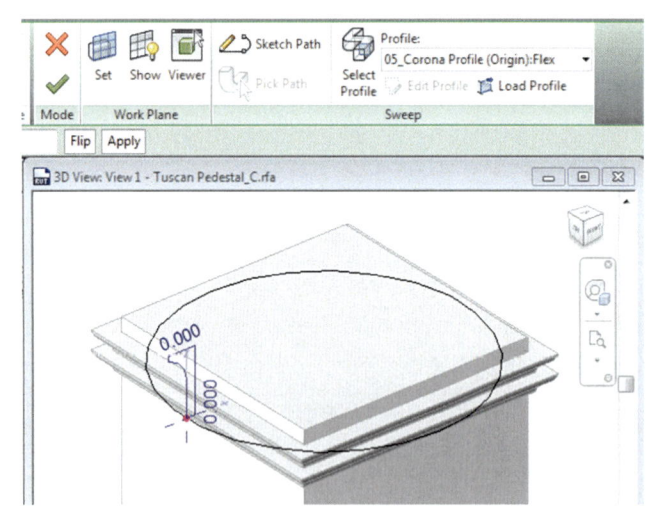

FIGURE 5.38
Change the profile for the top molding

5. Click the Finish Edit Mode button.

6. On the Project Browser, expand *Families > Profiles > 05_Corona Profile (Origin)*.

    ⇨ Right-click *Flex* and choose Type Properties (you can also double-click *Flex* instead).

    ⇨ For Y Projection Mult input a value of: **0.077** for the X Projection Mult, use a value of: **0.160**.

    ⇨ For X Mult input: **0.040,** for Y Mult input: **0.048** and the Fillet Projection Mult, use a value of: **0.050**.

    ⇨ Set the Base Diameter to: **1.000** and then Associate the Base Diameter parameter (see Figure 5.39).

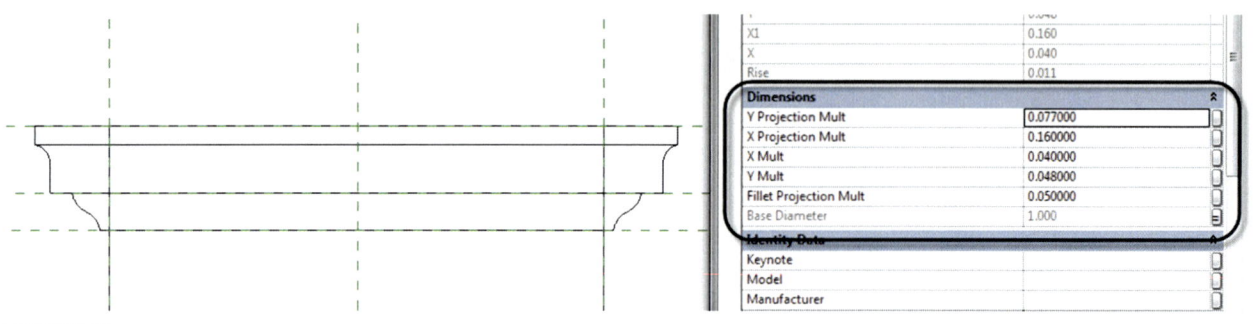

FIGURE 5.39
Edit the type properties of the corona profile

7. Flex the Base Diameter parameter.

To get rid of the seam between the molding and the overall extrusion on top of the pedestal use Join Geometry.

8. On the Modify tab, click the Join geometry tool.

• Renaissance Revit •

⇨ Click the corona molding, then click the extrusion.

You can join the other elements as well, but none of the other seams are visible, so it is not necessary. If you like, you can rename the profiles on the Project Browser to simplify the names. Orbit the model around in the 3D view to see the final result (see Figure 5.40).

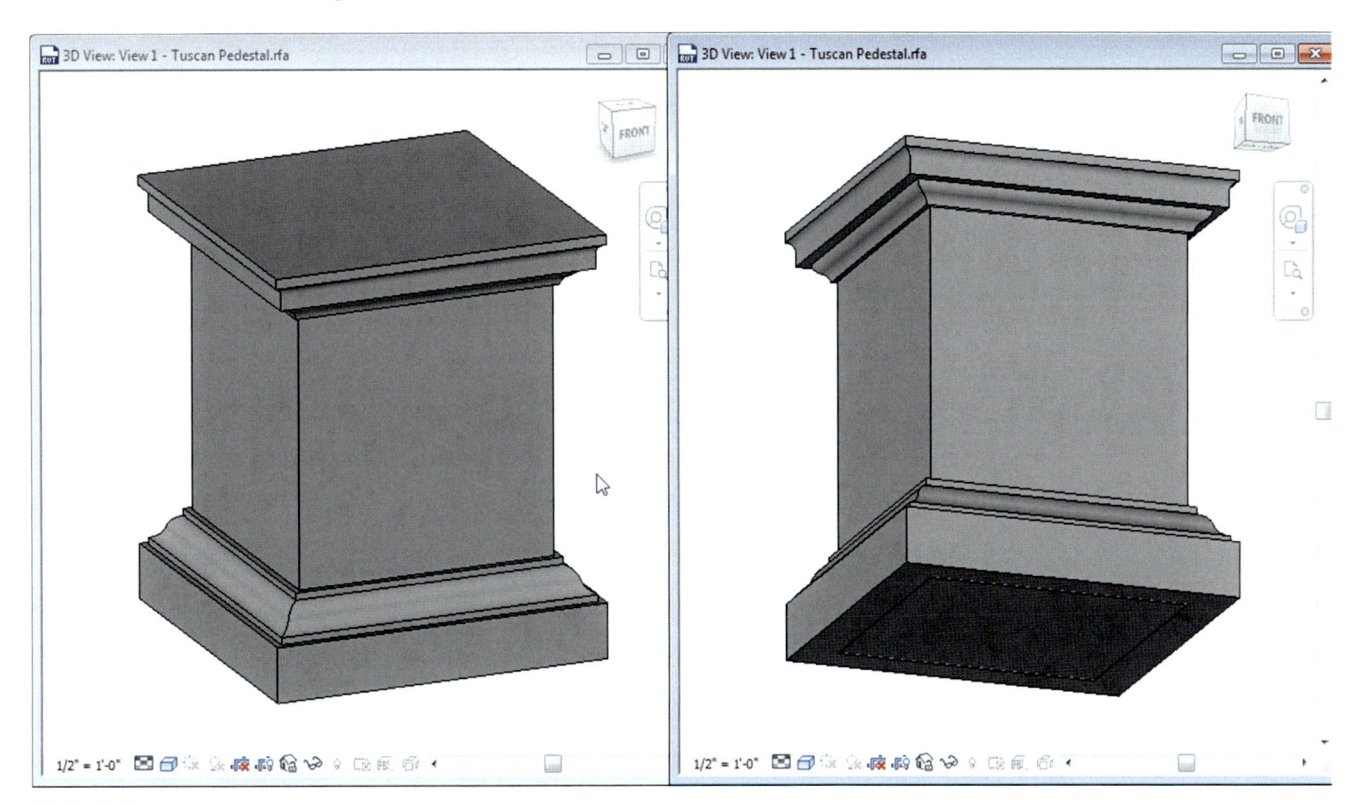

FIGURE 5.40
Study the results in 3D

9. Save the file.

CATCH UP! You can open a file completed to this point named: *05_Tuscan Pedestal.rfa*.

SUMMARY

In this chapter we have taken much of what we learned in the previous chapters and applied it toward our first order: the Tuscan order. Before we can complete the Tuscan column, we need to build the shaft. There is plenty to discuss on the shaft, so I am going to save the shaft for its own chapter. So that completes our work in this chapter. We will assemble all of the pieces we built here in the next chapter. In this chapter, we explored:

- ✓ Taking our existing schematic column family and using it as a starting point to create a more complex version.
- ✓ Creating reference planes, dimensions and parameters for the various moldings and divisions in the capital, base and pedestal of the Tuscan order.
- ✓ Strategizing how to divide the order into logical parts and take a systematic approach toward building it.
- ✓ Nesting in profile families from the library we began developing in the previous chapters.
- ✓ Making required modifications to the profile families to suit the needs of the current family.
- ✓ Adjusting the origin point of a profile family.
- ✓ Creating formulas that reference the single Base Diameter parameter to control proportional scaling.
- ✓ Consider times when using a revolve instead of a sweep can be appropriate.
- ✓ Creating a sweep from a picked 3D path.
- ✓ Creating a sweep with a sketched (instead of nested family) profile.
- ✓ How to use Trajectory Segmentation to express curved paths as polygons.
- ✓ How to copy and paste a sweep and modify its settings.
- ✓ The importance of remembering to flex between each iteration.

WASHINGTON DC
Photo by author

Chapter 6
Completing the Tuscan Order

INTRODUCTION

In this chapter we will continue where we left off in the previous chapter and complete the Tuscan order. I will walk through most of the tasks in detail as we have done in previous chapters. Specifically, we will create the Tuscan shaft, the entablature and learn how to make the pedestal optional. We'll put it all together to create the completed order.

OBJECTIVES

It takes more than just creating the nested family components to create our complete Tuscan order. There are many tasks we have yet to complete. Topics in this chapter include:

- Assembling the pieces of the Tuscan order.
- Creating choices that users can toggle on and off.
- Approaches to creating the entablature.
- Working with levels of detail.

PARTS OF THE TUSCAN ORDER

In Figure 6.1 I have created an illustration that labels each of the major parts of the Tuscan order. The source for this image comes from *The American Vignola – A Guide to the Making of Classical Architecture* by William R. Ware (Ware 1994, 1977, 1903). This is another fantastic resource that I reach for as often as I do Chitham. The figure details the column and entablature. (The pedestal was detailed already in Figure 5.25). We completed the base and capital already in the previous chapter. We'll focus on the shaft and entablature here. Looking at the figure here, we can see that an Astragal molding sits atop the shaft. Beneath the astragal is a small convex curve (conge). Using the techniques we have already covered in Chapter 4, we can stack a torus on top of a simple fillet to create the astragal and place a cavetto beneath it. At the base of the shaft, we end with a simple cavetto molding. There is also a fillet that together can be seen to make up the cincture, but in the Tuscan order, the fillet is actually part of the base. We already added this to our base family, so all we need here is the cavetto transition (see Figure 6.1).

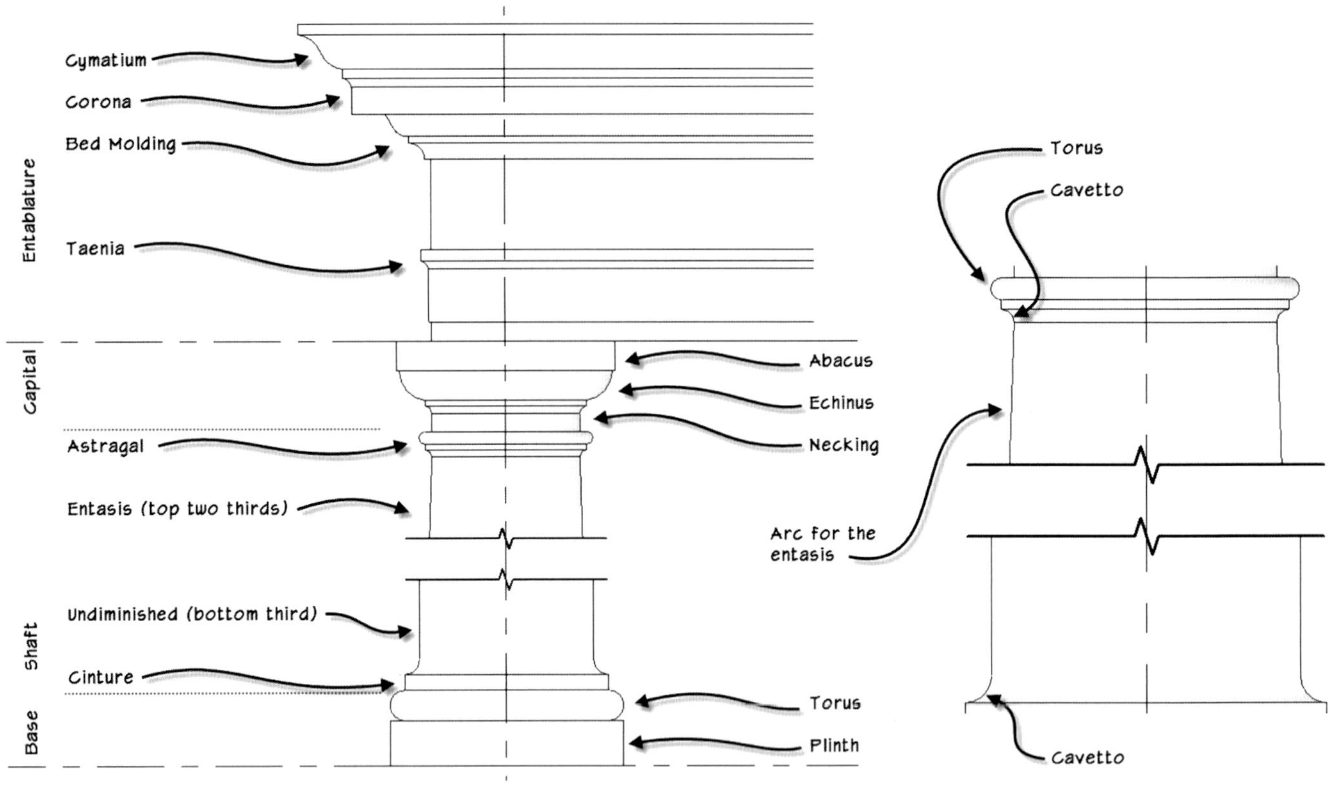

FIGURE 6.1

The parts of the Tuscan column and entablature

The major parts of the entablature are also labeled here. We will complete the entablature later on in this chapter.

THE TUSCAN SHAFT

This topic will cover the simplest approach to building a column shaft. Later in Chapter 12 we will explore the creation of the column shaft in more detail. At first blush you may be wondering why we need an entire chapter devoted to the subject of shafts. Well when you consider the shaft; and in particular a fluted shaft, you have curvature in three directions at once. This makes for some very complex construction. Fortunately for the task at hand; the completion of the Tuscan column, we do not need a fluted shaft. Fluting is never applied to Tuscan columns. So for this example, we can rely on a much simpler construction technique than some of the ones we will explore later in Chapter 12.

Smooth shafts can be used in all of the orders, and as noted are the only kind used for Tuscan columns. I have two basic techniques that I have employed for creation of a smooth shaft. The obvious approach is to use a revolve. However, as I have noted in the previous chapter, using a revolve means you have to build the sketch directly into the 3D form. This is not always undesirable, but since the essential shape of the shaft is similar between all orders, you can benefit from having it as a profile family. As you know, we cannot use a profile in a revolve, so the second approach that I often use is to create a sweep instead. This mirrors the approaches we used for the capital and base families in the previous chapter.

One other item that I am going to save for Chapter 12 is the intricacies of plotting proper entasis (or diminution). For the Tuscan column, I will be "cheating" a little and we will use a very simple curve to represent the entasis. If you are anxious to learn more about the topic now, refer to the "Entasis and Diminution" topic in Chapter 12.

CREATING THE FRAMEWORK

We will start this family the same as we have begun the others; laying out a series of reference planes. We'll begin with the files created in the previous chapter.

1. From the Application menu, choose Open.
    - Browse to the *Chapter06* folder and open the *Tuscan Column Schematic.rfa* file.

This is a copy of the file we built back in Chapter 3 and that we modified in the previous chapter.

2. Select the shaft element onscreen and then on the ribbon, click the Edit Family button.

> **TIP**: Depending on how you have your Revit Options configured, you may be able to double-click the element onscreen to open it in the family editor. You get to the "Options" dialog from the Application menu (bottom right of the menu). Click the User Interface tab, and there you will find a Customize button next to Double-click Options.

3. From the Application menu, choose **Save As > Family** and save the file in the *Chapter06* folder.

As you work in the family editor, it is easy to end up with several windows open at once. You can minimize windows you are not using at the moment to make tiling of windows easier. For now, we will be working on the shaft, so we can also close the *Tuscan Column Schematic* file for now, and then reopen it later or minimize its views. The choice is yours (see Figure 6.1).

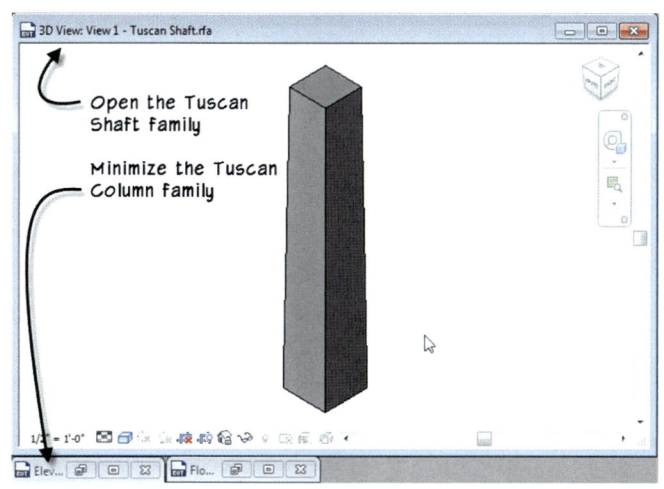

FIGURE 6.2
Open the existing Tuscan Column Schematic family and prepare your workspace

Recall that back in Chapter 3, we used a simple blend element as a stand in for the shaft. Let's delete this now and begin building the geometry for our shaft.

4. Select the blend onscreen and delete it.
    - On the Project Browser, open the *Front* elevation.
    - Tile the windows.

We have some of the reference planes we need already. We also have a few of the basic parameters. We need to locate some moldings at the top and bottom and indicate where the entasis (subtle tapering effect) should begin.

146 | Chapter 6

We'll add a few of these for the moldings here, but depending on your preference, the rest will be in a profile family or directly here as well.

5. Add two horizontal reference planes approximately equally spaced separating the height into three.

    ⇨ Add a dimension that has witness lines at the Ref. Level, these two reference planes you just added and the Top reference plane.

    ⇨ Toggle on equality.

    You should now have three equal horizontal bands.

6. Add two horizontal reference planes just below the top and very close together.

    ⇨ Dimension each of these with separate dimensions: the first one back to the Top. Set the distance to **0.070**.

    ⇨ Dimension the second reference plane to the first reference plane at a distance of **0.030** (see Figure 6.3).

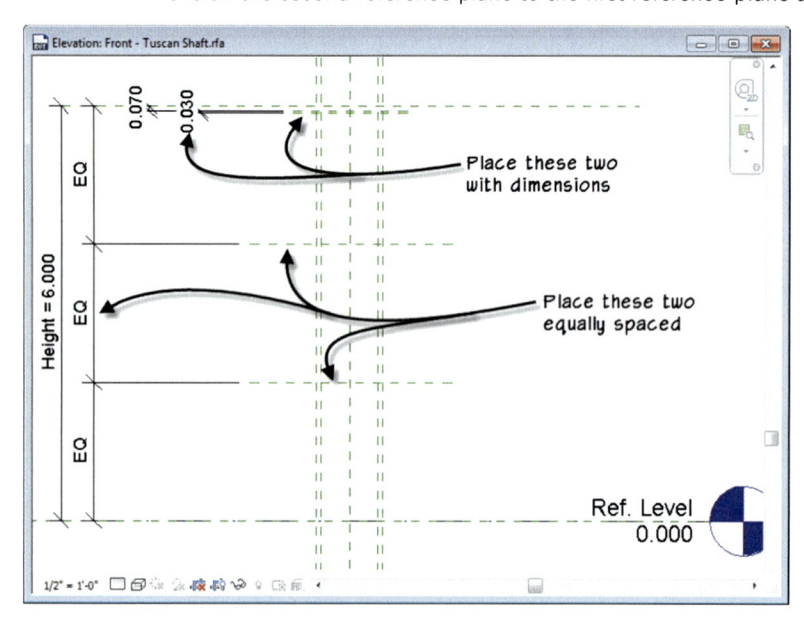

FIGURE 6.3

Place additional reference planes and dimensions

7. Label the two new dimensions with new parameters.

    ⇨ For the .070 dimension, name the parameter: **Astragal Torus**. Group it under **Constraints**.

    ⇨ For the .030 dimension, name the parameter: **Astragal Fillet**. Also group it under **Constraints**.

8. To the left side, near the top, add a vertical reference plane (it does not need to be full height).

    The vertical reference planes already in the file are named. Left and Right represent the bottom width which is equal the Base Diameter parameter. The Top Left and Top Right reference planes are narrower and represent the Top Diameter. To avoid confusion, you may want to use the grip handles at the ends and shorten Left and Right.

    ⇨ Add a dimension between the Top Left reference plane and the new one you just drew.

    ⇨ Label it with a new parameter called **Top Projection** grouped under **Constraints**.

9. Open the "Family Types" dialog.

10. Add formulas to the three new parameters:

    ⇨ For Astragal Torus: **Base Diameter * 0.070**.

    ⇨ For Astragal Fillet: **Base Diameter * 0.030**.

    ⇨ For Top Projection: **Base Diameter * 0.040**.

• Renaissance Revit •

11. Select the Height parameter, click the Modify button, rename it to: **Shaft Height** and then click OK (see Figure 6.4).

> **Note:** We are able to rename this parameter, but be aware that depending on which family template you start with, they sometimes include built-in system parameters which cannot be renamed.

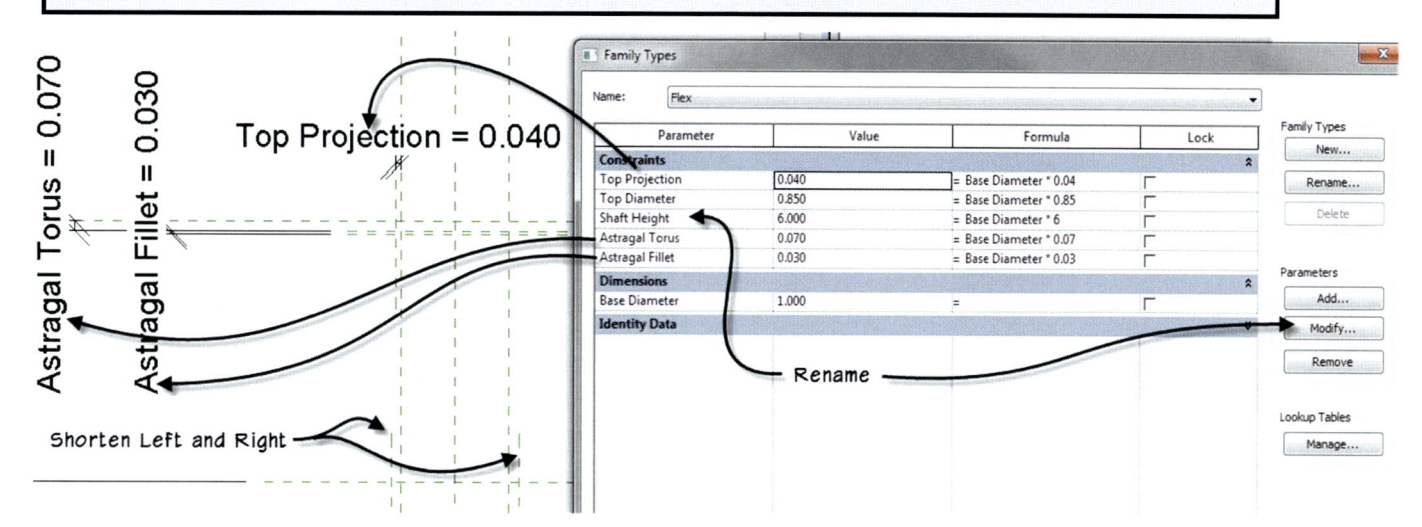

FIGURE 6.4
Add parameters and formulas

⇨ Click OK again to dismiss the "Family Types" dialog.

12. Save the file.

I am again using the dimensions from the Chitham book for this. Chitham lists two slightly different values for these dimensions that he attributes to Palladio and Gibbs. If you recall, in the previous chapter, we built the Palladian variation, so I have given the Palladian values here. If you favor the Gibbs variation (Figure 5.2 in Chapter 5), the Astragal Torus would have a value of 0.055 and Top Projection would be 0.050 instead. In some of my other source material, there seemed to be more extreme variations in the proportions here. For example, there is an excellent website (http://www.classicist.org/publications-and-bookshop/handbook/) that has drawings you can download in PDF format of each of the orders (Brandwein and Collins n.d.). In those illustrations and some of the other books, the total depth of the astragal projection is listed as 1/16th the Base Diameter, with two thirds of this given to the torus and one third to the fillet below. The decimal equivalent of 1/16th is of course 0.0625. The total of the two numbers that Chitham lists and that I have used here are for the Palladian variation: 0.100 (0.07 for the torus and 0.03 for the fillet, 0.085 total in the Gibbs version). I also checked in my copy of "The Four Books of Architecture" by Andrea Palladio. From the plates and descriptions there it is a little vague, but I come up with a value around 0.08 plus or minus. So, given the wide variations, I have opted to stick with Chitham's decimal values (Chitham 1985, 2005, 50-52). In all other texts, the dimensions are represented in fractions that are sometimes measured as a direct proportion of the base diameter and in other cases as an expression of a number of modules (parts of the overall base diameter). Ultimately this gives us one more example of where the precise proportions are left to interpretation, but all authors agree on the composition of the astragal molding including a torus above a fillet and joined to the shaft with a conge.

CREATE THE ASTRAGAL MOLDING

Now that we have the reference planes and dimensions required, let's add the astragal molding at the top of the shaft. This will be built with a simple revolve.

Continue in the *Front* elevation view.

148 | Chapter 6

1. On the Create tab, click the Revolve button.

   If you are prompted for a Work Plane, choose **Reference Plane : Center (Front/Back)** from the name list in the dialog that appears.

2. On the Modify I Create Revolve tab, accept the defaults. On the Options Bar, uncheck Chain.

When Chain is enabled, it is easier to create sketch lines in sequence, but you need to come back and align and lock the edges later. With chain off, you can lock as you go. You can also use pick lines, lock then trim. It is really a matter of personal preference however.

3. Snap to the intersection of the leftmost vertical reference plane and the Top reference plane. Snap to the intersection of Top and Center (Left/Right) (see the left side of Figure 6.5).

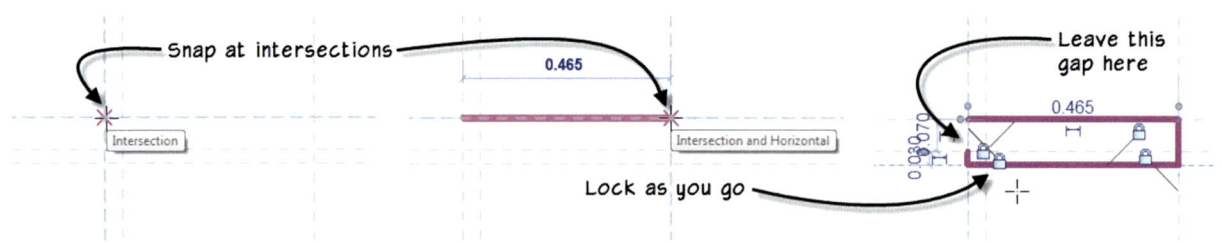

   ⇨ Close all lock icons that appear.

FIGURE 6.5
Draw the sketch lines with chain off so you can lock as you go

4. Continue drawing the shape as indicated on the right side of Figure 6.5. Lock as you go.

5. On the Draw panel, click the Start-End-Radius arc icon.

   ⇨ Snap the two endpoints to the ends of the existing sketch lines.

   ⇨ Move to the left and click when the arc snaps tangent (making a half circle) (see the left side of Figure 6.6).

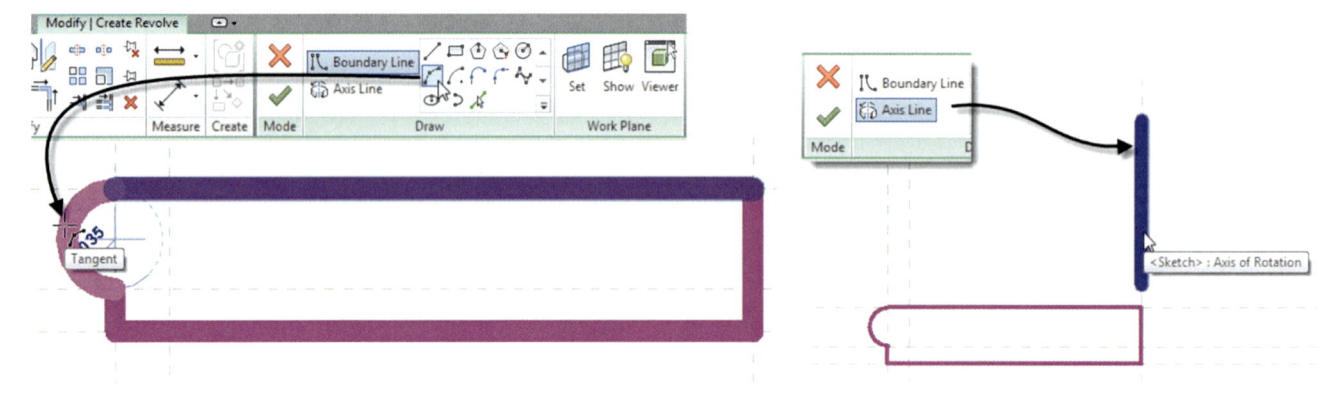

FIGURE 6.6
Add the torus curve

6. Click the Axis Line button.

   ⇨ Draw a vertical line (any length) directly on the Center (Left/Right) reference plane. Lock it) (see the right side of Figure 6.6).

7. On the ribbon, click the Finish Edit Mode button.

   ⇨ Open "Family Types" and flex the Base Diameter.

   ⇨ Reset Base Diameter to **1.000** when finished (see Figure 6.7).

• Renaissance Revit •

FIGURE 6.7

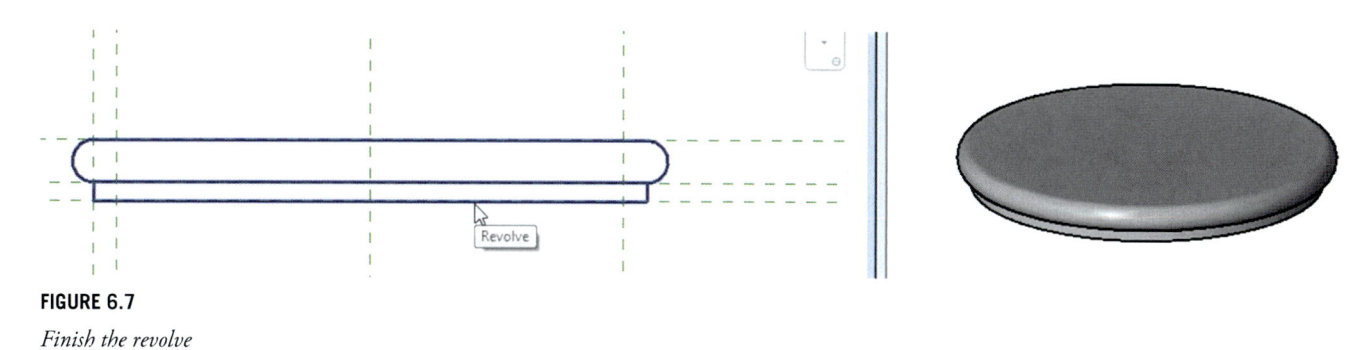

Finish the revolve

8. Save the file.

CATCH UP! You can open a file completed to this point named: *06_Tuscan Shaft_A.rfa*.

CREATE THE SHAFT AS A SWEEP

The rest of the shaft can be built as a simple revolved form as well. In fact, if you wanted to you could even build the entire shaft including the astragal molding from the previous topic all in a single revolve. I am going to demonstrate the main portion of the shaft using a profile family and sweep instead simply to showcase the other option. Furthermore, we then have the profile to optionally reuse later when building shafts for Doric, Ionic and Corinthian.

To save a little time, I have prepared a profile family for us to work with.

1. From the Application menu, choose **Open**.

⇨ Browse to the *Chapter06* folder and open the file named: *Tuscan Shaft Profile_Start.rfa*.

If you compare this file to the one we have just been working in, you can see that I have already created all of the matching reference planes with the same labeled dimensions. There are a few additional reference planes and parameters in this file as well. At the bottom, I have added a horizontal and a vertical reference plane that both use the same "Transition Bottom" parameter. These will give us the framework we need for a single arc that makes a smooth transition to the column base. It is not very clear from the sources I have read if this curve should be an equal quarter-round or more of a cavetto shape with X and Y unequal. No one seems to dimension this curve in both directions. I therefore take this to mean that it is equal in both directions. This does make constraining it a bit easier as well (see the left side of Figure 6.8). I do think there is some room for interpretation here however and if you preferred, unequal proportions, you could add the reference planes required and build the curve more like we did in the "Cavetto" topic in Chapter 4. I will leave that to you as a challenge exercise to do on your own.

You will also see a vertical reference plane and parameter named: "Profile Depth." This sets the back depth of the profile. Remember since we are sweeping along a closed circular path (in plan), we have to leave an open space in the center otherwise it will fail. This parameter is set to any convenient value for this purpose.

Looking at the top of the profile, the astragal reference planes that we built above are repeated here. Beneath them is another pair of transition reference planes and dimensions. These serve the same purpose as those at the bottom (see the right side of Figure 6.8).

150 | Chapter 6

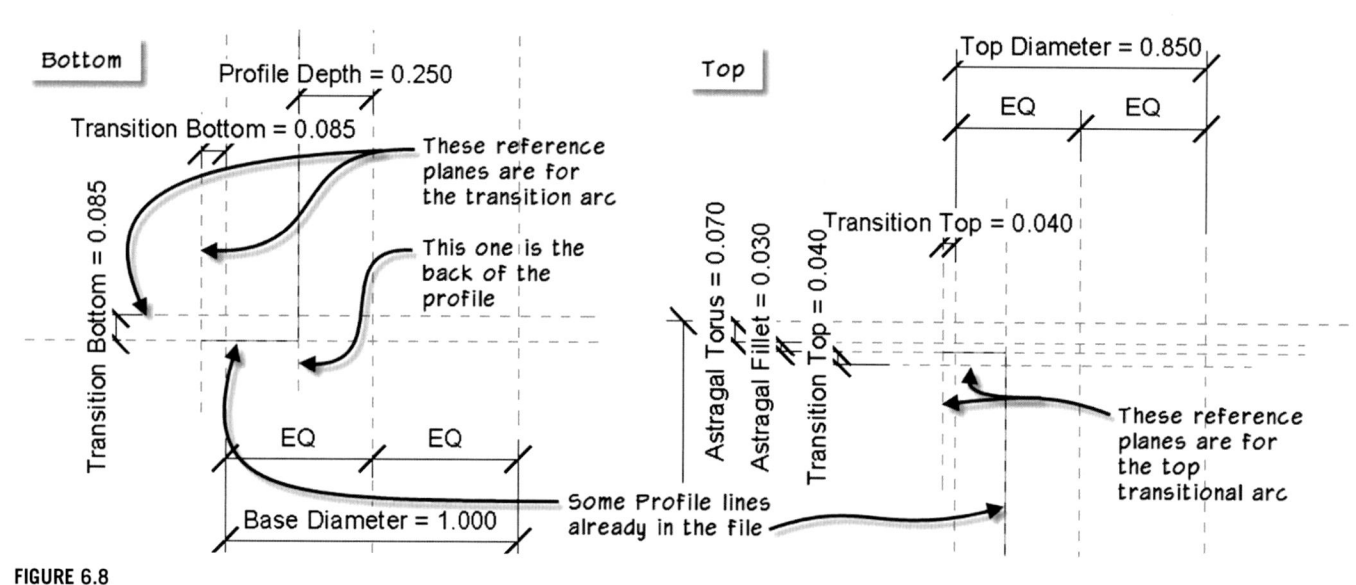

FIGURE 6.8
Explore the provided profile family

Finally to save a little more time and effort, I have already added some of the profile lines; specifically the top, bottom and back (inside) edges. Let's add the rest now.

> **Note:** if you prefer to build this profile yourself, if was begun from the *Family Seed (Profile Centered).rfa* seed file. Tile the windows of the Tuscan Shaft, *Front* elevation and the seed family and us it as a guide to build the reference planes and dimensions. Unfortunately you cannot copy and paste between a model and profile family. So you have to build everything over again.

Start at the bottom of the profile.

2. On the Create tab, click the Line tool and then click the Center-ends Arc icon.

   ⇨ Snap the center to the intersection of V1 and H1 reference planes.

   ⇨ For the first endpoint, snap to the intersection of the V1 and the Center (Front/Back) reference planes (at the left end of the line that is already there).

   ⇨ Snap the last point to the intersection of the Left and H1 reference planes.

3. Cancel the command. Select the circle, turn on the Center Mark on the Properties palette and then align and lock the center and both endpoints in both X and Y directions (see Figure 6.9).

Completing the Tuscan Order | **151**

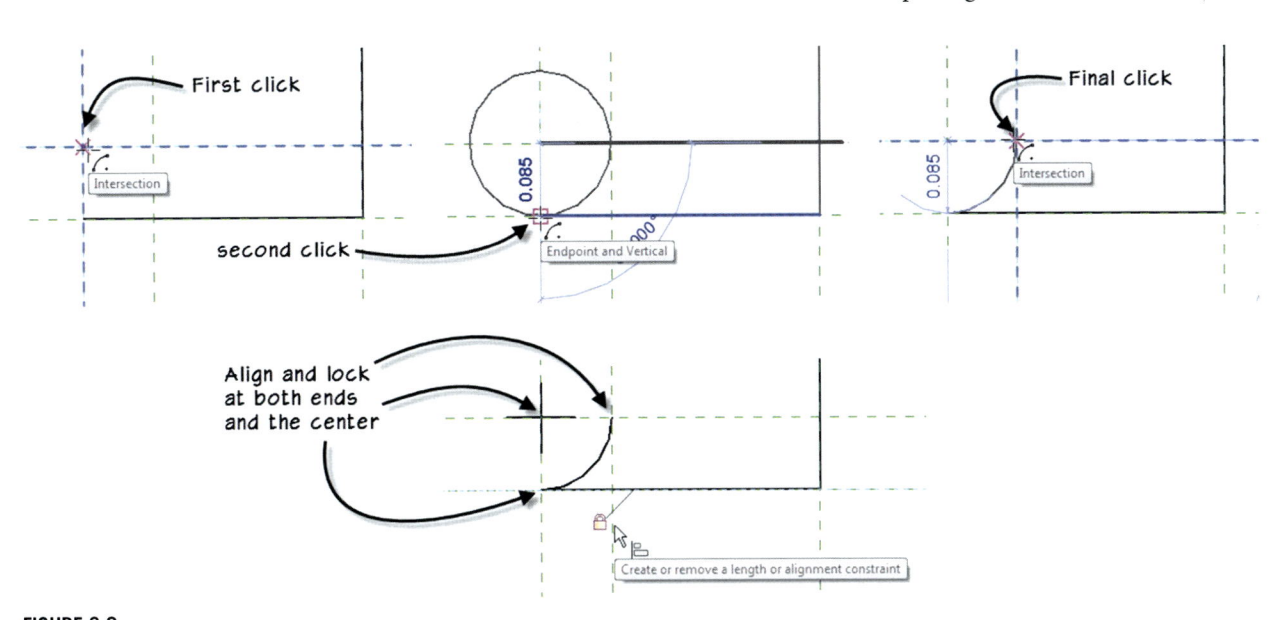

FIGURE 6.9

Add the transitional arc at the bottom

4. From the end of this arc, draw a straight line up to the intersection of the Left and First Third reference planes. Lock it.

> **Note:** If Revit informs you that locking will over constrain the sketch, simply click Cancel and keep going.

As noted above, we will take a careful look at how to accurately represent the column shaft's entasis (or diminution) which is the subtle curved tapering that occurs at the top two thirds of the shaft. The diameter of the column diminishes to 0.85 the Base Diameter along the top two thirds of its height. The tapering is not linear, but rather a subtle curve. We will postpone the discussion of how to plot this curve precisely and accurately until the "Entasis and Diminution" topic in Chapter 12. The reality is that even though the curve is not exactly a circular arc, a circular arc is almost imperceptibly similar to the actual curve. So for this example, we will simply use an arc, but specifically one of the arc tools we have not yet used.

5. On the Create tab, click the Line tool.

⇨ On the Draw panel, click the Tangent End Arc icon.

This arc allows you to start at the end of an existing line or arc and draw the arc tangent to that existing line. This is exactly the situation we have here.

6. Start the arc at the endpoint of the vertical line you just drew.

    As you move your mouse, notice how it stays tangent to the vertical line.

7. Snap the second point to the intersection of the H2 and Top Left reference planes (see Figure 6.10).

152 | Chapter 6

FIGURE 6.10
Draw a tangent arc

8. Using the Align tool, align and lock both endpoints to the reference planes in both the X and Y directions.

9. Flex the Base Diameter at this point to ensure that everything is working before you add the last curve.

⇨ Return the Base Diameter to **1.000** before continuing.

10. Using the same process as steps 2 and 3 above, add the final arc at the top using a Center-ends Arc (see Figure 6.11).

11. Align and lock everything and then flex again.

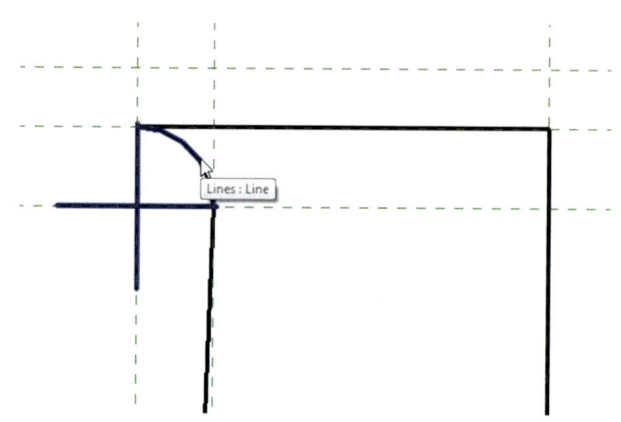

FIGURE 6.11
Add the final arc for the top transition

12. Select the reference plane called: Left.

⇨ On the Properties palette, check the Defines Origin checkbox.

13. Save the file.

> **CATCH UP!** You can open a file completed to this point named: *06_Tuscan Shaft Profile.rfa*.

LOAD THE PROFILE AND CREATE THE SWEEP

Now that we have the profile completed, we are ready to load it back into our shaft family and build the sweep.

Continue in the *Tuscan Shaft Profile* family or open the catch-up file.

1. On the ribbon, click the Load into Project button.

⇨ If the "Load into Projects" dialog appears, check the *Tuscan Shaft.rfa* file and click OK.

• Renaissance Revit •

If you only have one other family open the "Load into Projects" dialog will not appear. If you have no other files open, Revit will alert you that no other projects are open. In that case, reopen the *Tuscan Shaft.rfa* file and try again.

2. In the *Tuscan Shaft.rfa* file, open the *Ref. Level* floor plan view.

3. On the Create tab, click the Sweep button and then click on the Sketch Path button.

    ⇨ Draw a circle path from the center intersection to the outer edge (the diameter will match Base Diameter).

    ⇨ Click the Modify tool and then on the Properties palette, turn on the Center Mark and then align and lock in both directions.

4. Add a Diameter dimension to the circle and then label it with the Base Diameter parameter.

    ⇨ Deselect the dimension and then click Finish Edit Mode (see Figure 6.12).

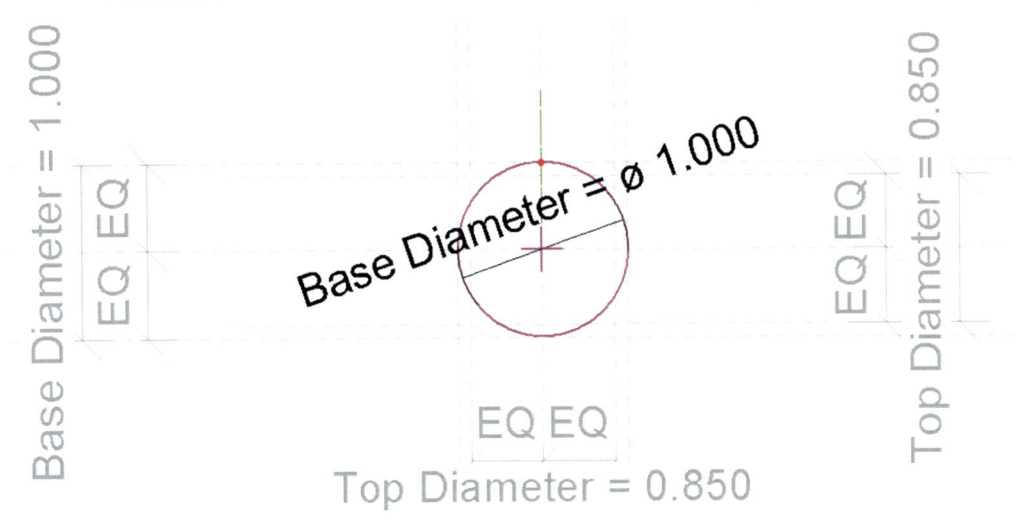

FIGURE 6.12

Draw a circular sweep path, align and lock it at the center and set the diameter to the Base Diameter parameter

5. On the Modify | Sweep tab, click the Select Profile button.

    ⇨ From the Profile drop-down, choose **Tuscan Shaft Profile:Flex**.

6. Click the Finish Edit Mode button.

It looks pretty good, but don't flex yet. We still need to link up the nested Base Diameter parameter with the host parameter. I built all of the same formulas into the starting file of the profile family, so you only need to link Base Diameter, *not* all of the others.

7. On the Project Browser, expand *Families > Profiles > Tuscan Profile Shaft*.

    ⇨ Right-click on Flex and choose **Type Properties**.

    ⇨ Associate the Base Diameter to parameter and then click OK (see Figure 6.13).

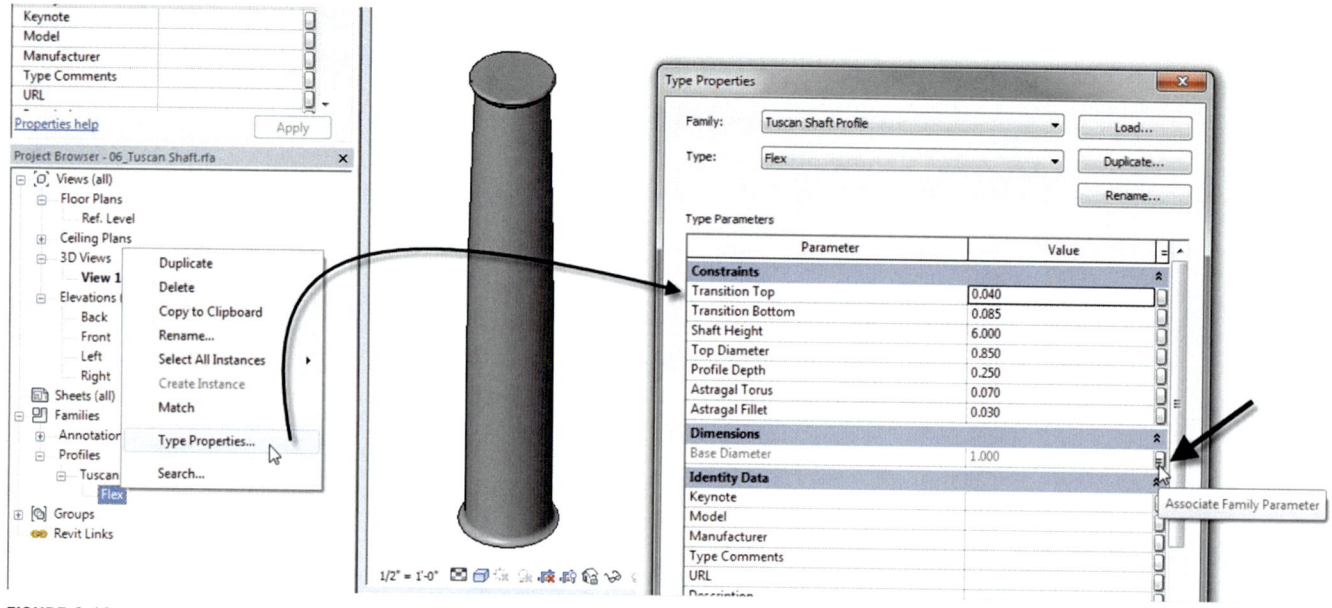

FIGURE 6.13

Associate the Base Diameter parameter to the nested profile family

8. Open "Family Types" and flex the Base Diameter.

    ⇨ Reset Base Diameter to **1.000** when finished.

9. Save the file.

> **CATCH UP!** You can open a file completed to this point named: *06_Tuscan Shaft.rfa*.

Go ahead and study the shaft from various angles. If you look at it closely in elevation, you will see that the arc we used for the entasis is convincing. In fact, if you are satisfied with this, there is really no need to do it any other way. However, I do have other methods to share with you later in Chapter 12. But for now, this one will do quite nicely.

ASSEMBLE THE TUSCAN COLUMN

With the shaft complete and the three other components completed in the previous chapter, we are ready to assemble the complete Tuscan column. For convenience I have included copies of the base, capital and pedestal in the *Chapter06* folder. We'll use these in the assembly.

RELOAD FAMILIES FROM PROJECT BROWSER

If you have not closed any files yet in this chapter, you probably have the Shaft, the Column and the Profile families all open. For the next series of steps, we only need the *Tuscan Column Schematic.rfa* file open.

1. Close all files except *Tuscan Column Schematic.rfa*. If you previously closed this file, reopen it now.

2. From the Application menu, choose Save As > Family and save the file as **Tuscan Column**.

3. On the Project Browser, expand *Families > Generic Models*.

    ⇨ Right-click on *Tuscan Base* and choose **Reload**.

    ⇨ In the "Open" dialog, browse to the *Chapter06* folder, choose *Tuscan Base.rfa* and then click Open.

4. In the "Family Already Exists" choose Overwrite the existing version (see Figure 6.14).

Completing the Tuscan Order | 155

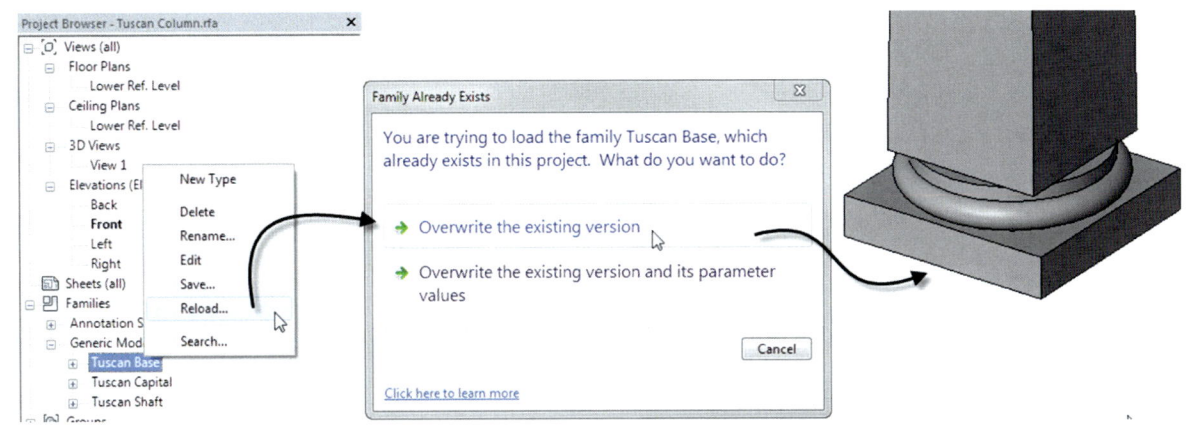

FIGURE 6.14
Replace the base family with the Chapter 6 version

5. Repeat the process twice more to replace the Shaft and Capital in the same way (see Figure 6.15).

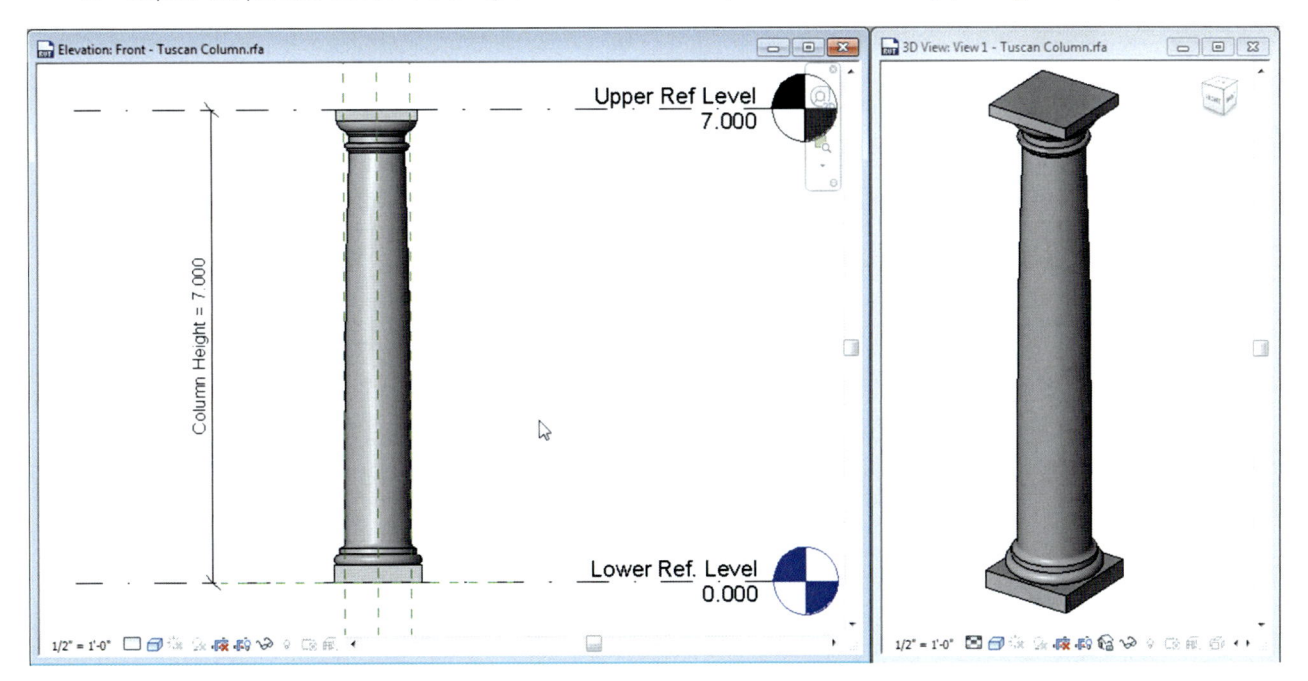

FIGURE 6.15
Replace the shaft and capital families

Recall that the way this family is set up, to flex it we change the height of the Upper Ref. Level instead of opening the "Family Types" dialog.

6. In the *Front* elevation view, select the Upper Ref. Level.

   ⇨ Input a few different values for height to flex it.

   Try values both smaller and larger than 7.000.

   ⇨ Reset the height of the Upper Ref. Level to **7.000** when finished.

7. Save the file.

CATCH UP! You can open a file completed to this point named: *06_Tuscan Column_A.rfa*.

• *Creating Classical Architecture with Modern Software* •

CREATING OPTIONAL ITEMS

So far we have focused on modeling the forms required for the various parts of the Tuscan order. In the previous exercise we swapped out the schematic versions of the parts for the more detailed versions. We still have one piece that we have not used yet, that is the pedestal. All orders use a base, shaft and capital, but pedestals are not always used. Therefore, in this topic, not only will we look at adding the pedestal to this family, but also ways to accommodate the optional items in a family. Every element in a family; both solids and nested components, has a property for visibility on the Properties palette. To create optional items, we simply need to associate a parameter to this property. This will allow us to toggle the element on or off as needed.

The first thing we need to do is load in the pedestal family and then set up some new reference planes and parameters.

LOAD THE PEDESTAL COMPONENT

A copy of the pedestal family from the previous chapter is included in this *Chapter06* folder. Let's load it into this family.

Continue in the *Tuscan Column.rfa* file.

1. On the Insert tab, click the Load Family button.

    ⇨ Browse to the *Chapter06* folder, select *Tuscan Pedestal.rfa* and then click Open.

2. Open or switch to the *Lower Ref. Level* floor plan view.

3. On the Create tab, click the Component tool.

    On the Properties palette, from the Type Selector, make sure that *Tuscan Pedestal:Flex* is chosen.

    ⇨ Click at the intersection of the Center (Right/Left) and Center (Front/Back) reference planes.

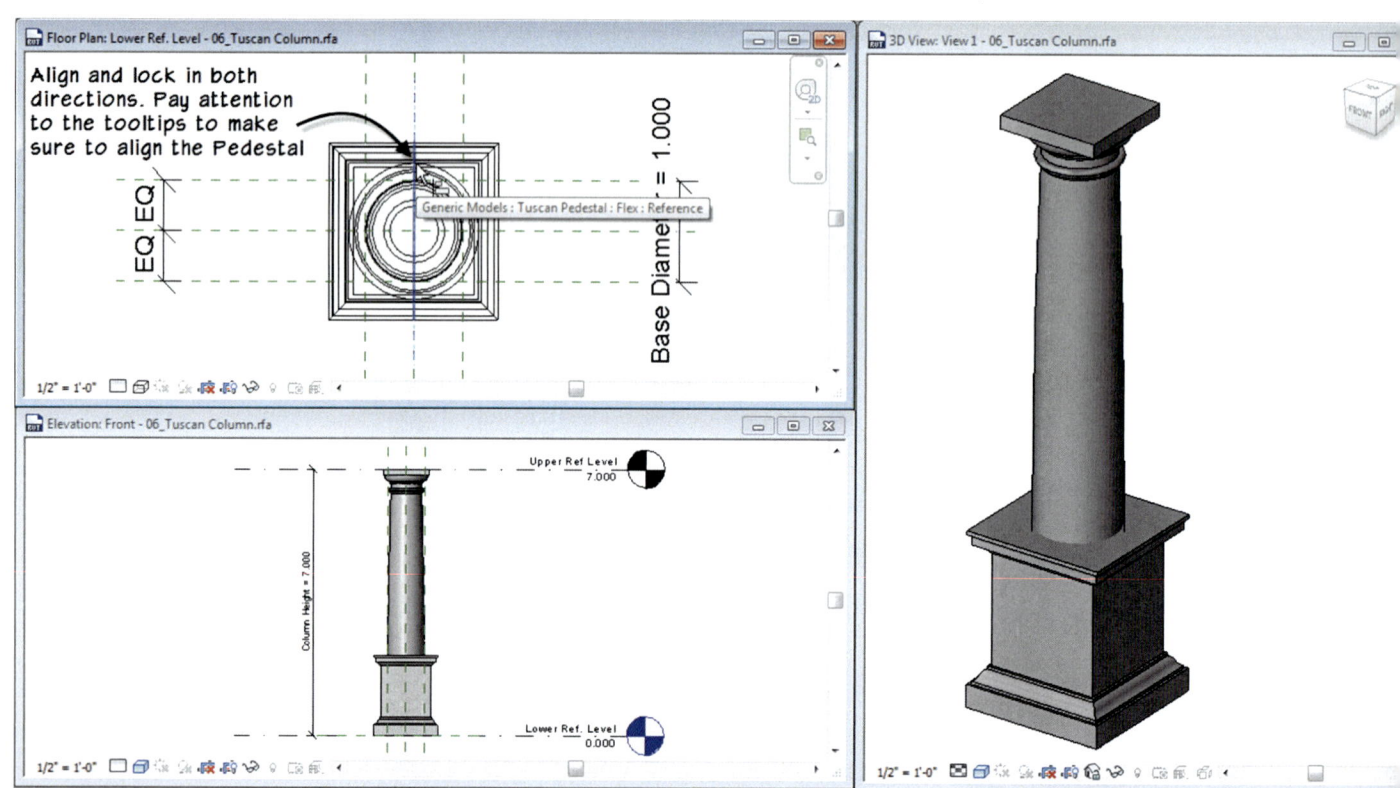

FIGURE 6.16

Place an instance of the pedestal family onscreen

4. Using the Align tool, align and lock the pedestal family to the center reference planes in both directions (see Figure 6.16).

MAKE THE PEDESTAL OPTIONAL

We clearly still have some work to do. At the moment the pedestal is completely covering the base and part of the shaft. What we need is a toggle switch to control when the pedestal displays and when it does not. When it display, we need the rest of the column to move up and sit on t top of it. When it is not displayed, it can stay where it is.

1. In the *Front* elevation view, draw a horizontal reference plane parallel to the Lower Ref. Level and near the pedestal.

2. Using the Align tool, align (*but do not lock*) the reference plane to the top of the pedestal (see the left side of Figure 6.17).

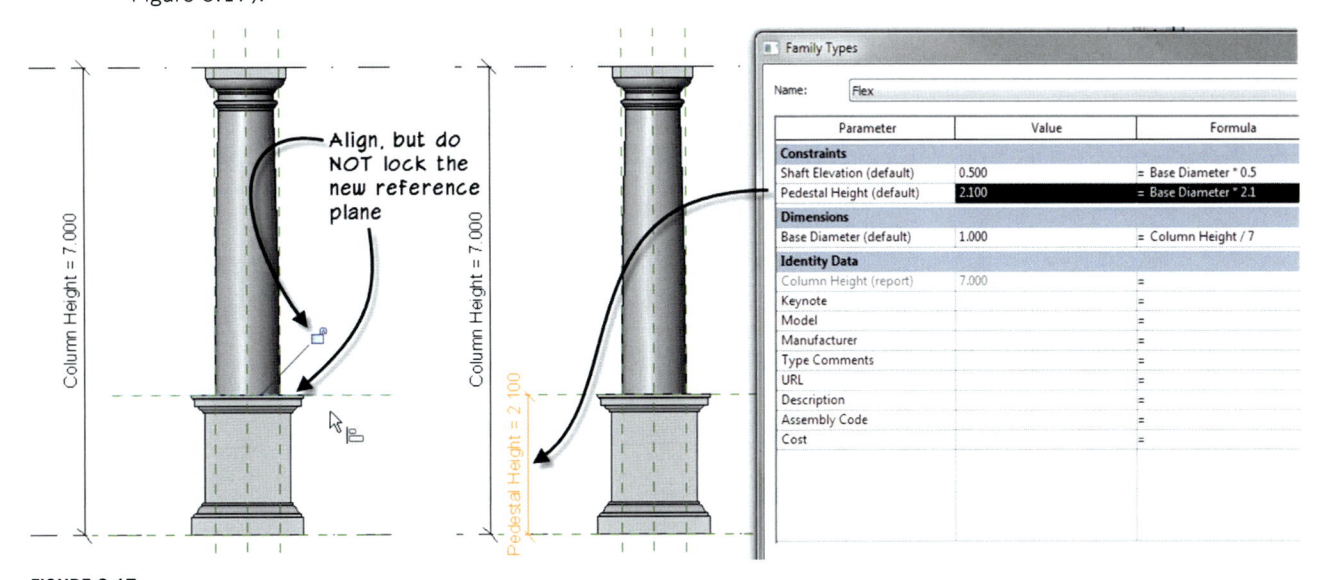

FIGURE 6.17

Add a reference plane and new parameter for the pedestal and input the formula

3. Add a dimension between Lower Ref. Level and the new reference plane.
   ⇨ Label it with a new **Instance** parameter named: **Pedestal Height**. Group it under **Constraints**.
   ⇨ Open the "Family Types" dialog and add the formula: **Base Diameter * 2.100** and then click OK (see the right side of Figure 6.17).

To understand our next step, recall that the overall height and flexing behavior of this family is being controlled by the two levels. Unlike all the individual nested pieces where we flex the Base Diameter directly, here we are driving the Base Diameter from a reporting parameter that measures the distance between the two levels. Review the "Reporting Parameters" topic in Chapter 3 for more information.

What we need to happen is that if the end user selects the option to include a pedestal, we want an additional height equal to the height of the pedestal to be added to the overall height. Furthermore, we want the base and shaft components to also move up this amount.

4. On the right side of the "Family Types" dialog, click the Add button.
   ⇨ In the "Parameter Properties" dialog, input: **Show Pedestal** for the name.
   ⇨ For the Type of Parameter, select **Yes/No**. Group it under **Graphics**, leave it as a Type parameter and then click OK (see Figure 6.18).

• *Creating Classical Architecture with Modern Software* •

158 | Chapter 6

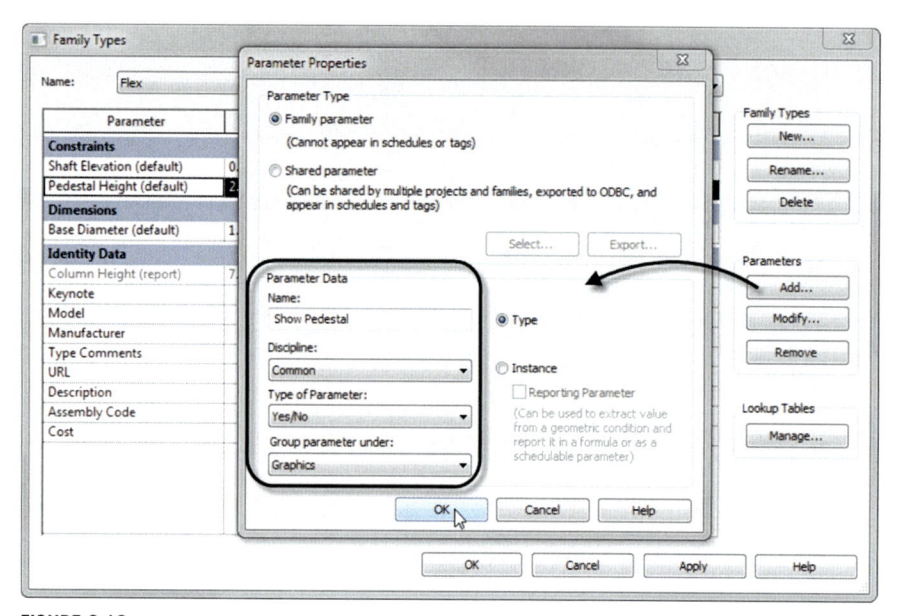

FIGURE 6.18

Create a new Yes/No parameter

5. Add another parameter.

⇨ In the "Parameter Properties" dialog, input: **Base Elevation** for the name.

⇨ For the Type of Parameter, select **Length**. Group it under **Constraints**.

⇨ Choose the Instance radio button and click OK.

ADDING AN IF STATEMENT

The yes/no parameter creates a checkbox. We now need to create a formula that contains a "conditional" statement. A conditional statement will have two possible settings. It will do one thing if the checkbox is checked and a different thing if it is no. Specifically, we want to adjust our formula values if Show Pedestal is checked, and leave them alone if unchecked.

1. In the Formula field next to each of the following parameters, input the formulas shown (see Table 6.1):

TABLE 6.1

Parameter	Formula
Base Diameter	if(Show Pedestal, Column Height / 9.1, Column Height / 7)
Shaft Elevation	if(Show Pedestal, Base Diameter * 2.6, Base Diameter * 0.5)
Base Elevation	if(Show Pedestal, Base Diameter * 2.1, 0)

With these formulas, we are giving two different measurements for each parameter which are chosen based on the value of the "Show Pedestal" parameter.

We really can't flex yet as we still need to hook up a few of these new parameters.

2. Uncheck the Show Pedestal checkbox and then click Apply.

3. Click OK to dismiss the "Family Types" dialog.

4. Select the pedestal element onscreen and then on the Properties palette, click the Edit Type button.

⇨ Associate the Base Diameter parameter as we did before and then click OK.

• Renaissance Revit •

5. With the pedestal still selected, on the Properties palette, click the Associate Family Parameter button next to Visible.

   ⇨ Select the **Show Pedestal** parameter and then click OK (see Figure 6.19).

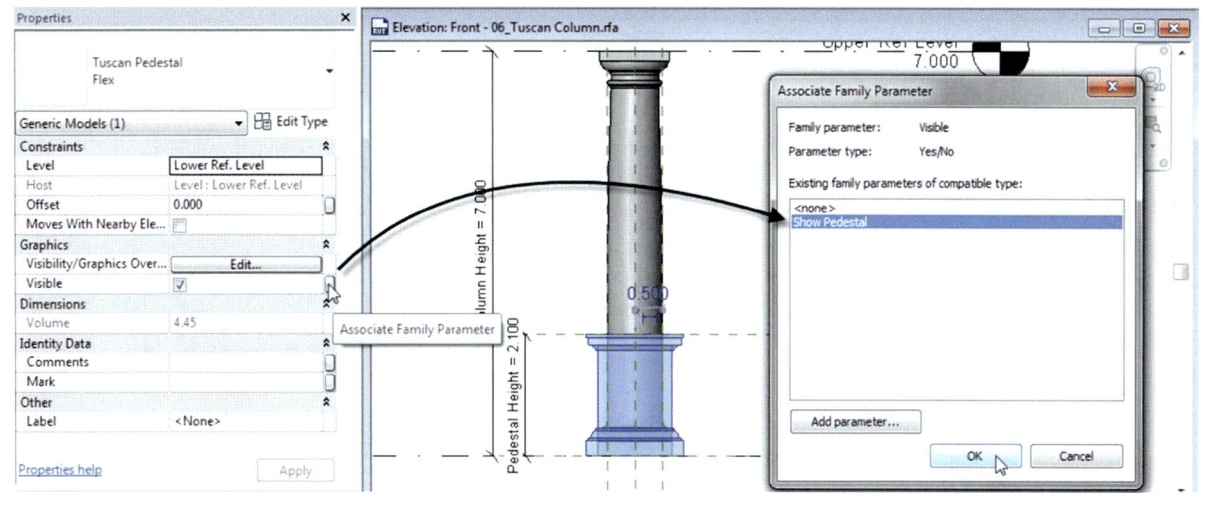

FIGURE 6.19

Associate the visibility of the Pedestal to the Show Pedestal Yes/No parameter

6. Select the Base component onscreen.

   You can make a window selection around it, or select the pedestal, use the Temporary Hide/Isolate pop-up (sunglasses) and choose **Hide Element**.

   ⇨ On the Properties palette, click the Associate Family Parameter button next to Offset.

   ⇨ In the "Associate Family Parameter" dialog, choose **Base Elevation** and then click OK.

ADD FAMILY TYPES

We are now ready to flex the family. It will be as easy as toggling the setting of Show Pedestal. If everything is working correctly, you will see the sizes and positions of all the parts adjust when Show Pedestal is enabled.

1. Open the "Family Types" dialog.

2. On the right side, click the Rename button.

   ⇨ Rename "Flex" to; **Without Pedestal** and click OK.

   ⇨ Click the New button. Name the new type: **With Pedestal** and click OK.

   ⇨ Check the Show Pedestal checkbox and then click Apply (see Figure 6.20).

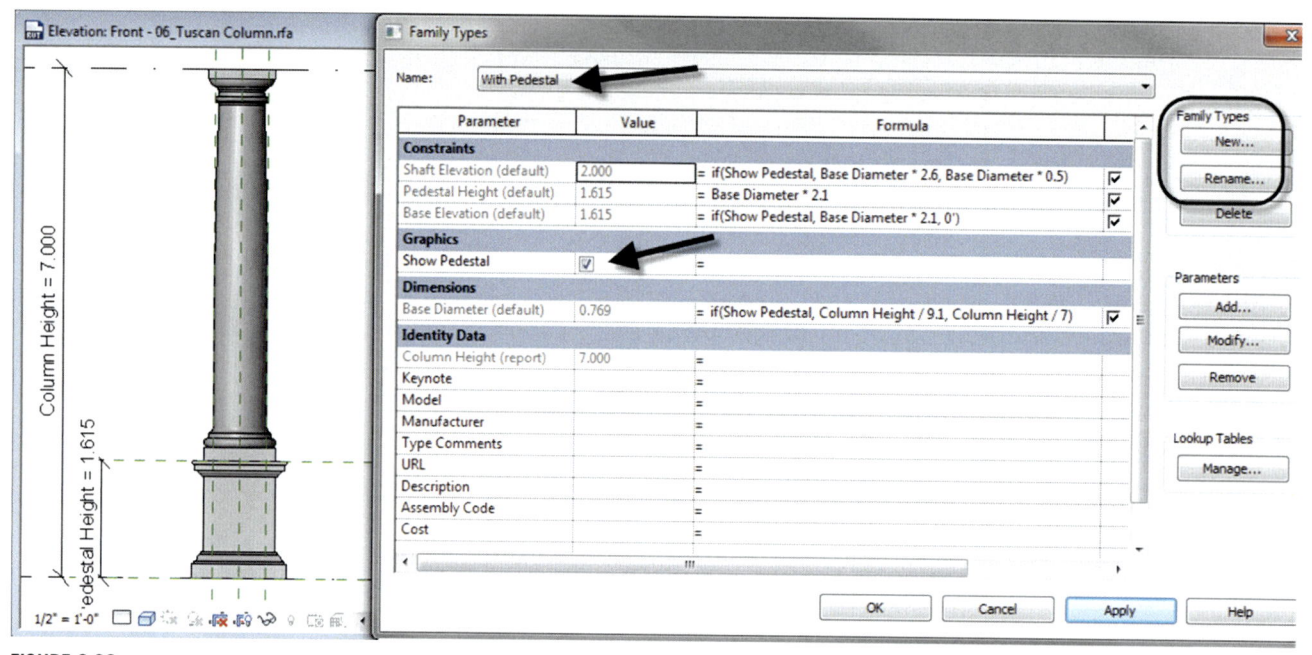

FIGURE 6.20

Edit the Family Types and flex the Show Pedestal parameter

Notice that everything is adjusting nicely. To toggle the pedestal on and off, you now simple switch between the two types and apply. To flex the rest of the family, adjust the height of the Upper Ref. Level as noted above. Try it now if you like.

You will notice that the pedestal does not actually disappear when you toggle it off in the family. The family editor will show a hidden element as gray. To see it actually disappear, you have to load the family into a project. This is of course the best way to do a final test anyhow. So let's open a project and load this family in.

3. Click OK to dismiss the "Family Types" dialog.

4. Save the family.

> **CATCH UP!** You can open a file completed to this point named: *06_Tuscan Column.rfa*.

LOAD INTO A SANDBOX FILE

A sandbox project file has been provided with the dataset files for Chapter 6.

1. Open the Revit project file named *06_Sandbox.rvt*.

2. Switch back to the *Tuscan Column* file or open the catch-up file.

> **TIP:** To switch windows, use the Switch Windows drop-down on the Quick Access toolbar, or hold down the CTRL key and then press the TAB key to cycle through the open windows. Hold CTRL + SHIFT and press TAB to cycle backwards.

3. On the ribbon, click the Load into Project button.

4. Place a few instances of the column onscreen.

⇨ On the Properties palette, adjust the Top Level of some of the instances.

⇨ On the Properties palette, from the Type Selector, choose the **With Pedestal** type (see Figure 6.21).

• Renaissance Revit •

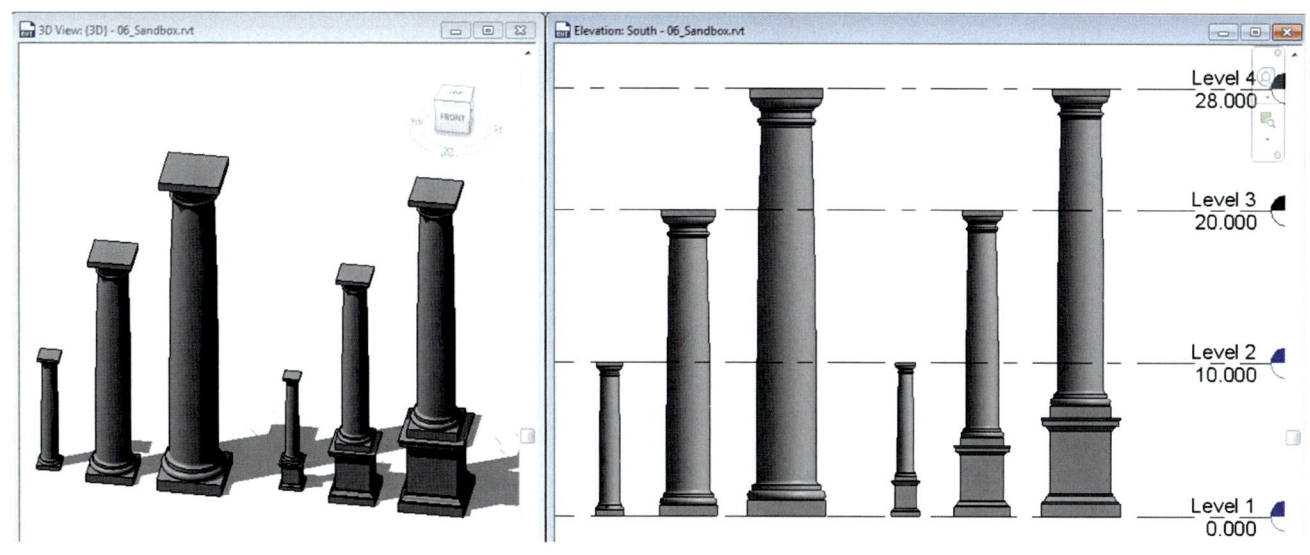

FIGURE 6.21
Place several instances in the sandbox file and adjust the properties.

5. Save and close the Sandbox file.

> **Catch Up!** You can open a file completed to this point named: *06_Sandbox_A.rvt*.

CREATING THE TUSCAN ENTABLATURE

As you might expect, to create the entablature, we have a few options that we can explore. The most obvious is perhaps using a beam. This after all is essentially what the entablature is. I explored two basic options for building this. In the first one, I built a single profile for the entire entablature cross section. This profile was based on our seed families, but turned out to be quite complex. There are many reference planes, and a variety of the techniques covered in previous chapters being used. I also tried a "built-up" approach. The built-up approach simply uses the molding profiles we have already created and adds them to the geometry of the existing beam.

If you were going to build this entablature in a real project, this is actually the way it would be done. Furthermore it is easier to construct the family this way. As you may be aware, the general Revit rule-of-thumb is to build things in your model as close to how they will really be built. In this spirit, I have showcased the "built-up" approach in the next exercise. (In Chapter 9, we will work through a detailed example of building a complex profile for the entablature of the Doric order).

LAYOUT THE ENTABLATURE EXTENTS

To build the entablature of the Tuscan order, we'll start with the family template for beams: the *Structural Framing - Beams and Braces.rft* file. Remember that each family template has some built-in super powers that relate to its specific category and purpose in the Revit model. This template is intended for structural framing members. For our entablature we are most concerned with the basic properties of beams like their ability to join with each other and miter the corners. We are not as much concerned with some of the structural characteristics, but we will nonetheless have access to those as well. Let's first consider our overall approach:

The family template contains a basic extrusion already. We will adjust the parameters, add some new reference planes and reshape this extrusion to match the required size. Then we will load in five profile families and add them as sweeps along the length of this extrusion. One of the profiles we will build as a custom shape here. The other four are standard shapes that we built in previous chapters (see Figure 6.22).

FIGURE 6.22

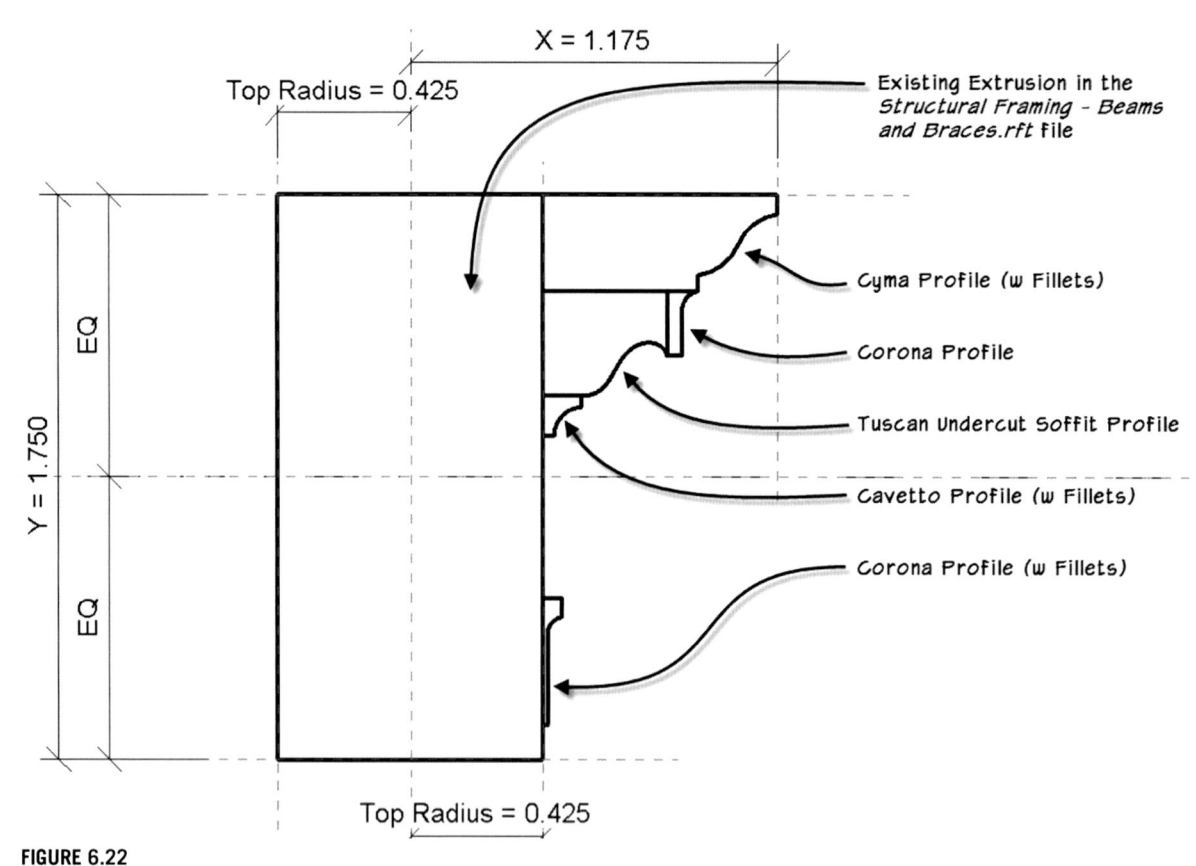

Planning the profile for the entablature

1. From the Application menu, choose **New > Family**.

    ⇨ Select the *Structural Framing - Beams and Braces.rft* file and then click Open.

    A copy of this file is provided in the *Template/OTB* folder with the book's dataset files.

Let's start by making the units match our other families

2. On the Manage tab, click the Project Units button.

3. Click the format button next to Length.

    ⇨ Choose Decimal Feet and set the Rounding to 3 decimal places.

    ⇨ Click OK twice to dismiss the dialogs.

4. From the Application menu, choose **Save As > Family**. Browse to the *Chapter06* folder and call the file: **Tuscan Entablature**.

The template opens to a plan view that includes three pairs of reference planes. Structural families use three levels of detail (coarse, medium and fine) and also display the extents of the beam differently under various circumstances. This supports a Structural Engineer in the creation of a traditional "stick" framing plan, or more detailed representations with accurate widths and sizes portrayed (Mackey 2013). As noted above, for our purposes, we will not disturb any of the items already in the plan view of this file.

5. Open the *Left* elevation view.

As always we need some reference planes. Notice that this file contains only a simple extrusion and no reference planes other than the centerline. There are some other reference planes in this family. They are actually inside the sketch of the extrusion. We'll take a look at them below. For now, we'll lay out the major divisions of the overall form of the entablature just to give ourselves a frame of reference.

6. Add two horizontal and three vertical reference planes as shown in Figure 6.23.
    ⇨ Name them as indicated.
    ⇨ Add dimensions and label them. Place all parameters under the **Constraints** grouping.
7. Open the "Family Types" dialog.
8. Add a **Base Diameter** parameter under **Dimensions**. Set the value to **1.000**.
    ⇨ For the Formula next to Y type: **Base Diameter * 1.750**.
    ⇨ For the Formula next to X type: **Base Diameter * 1.175**.
    ⇨ For the Formula next to Top Radius type: **Base Diameter * 0.425**.
9. Create a new Family Type named **Flex** and then click OK.

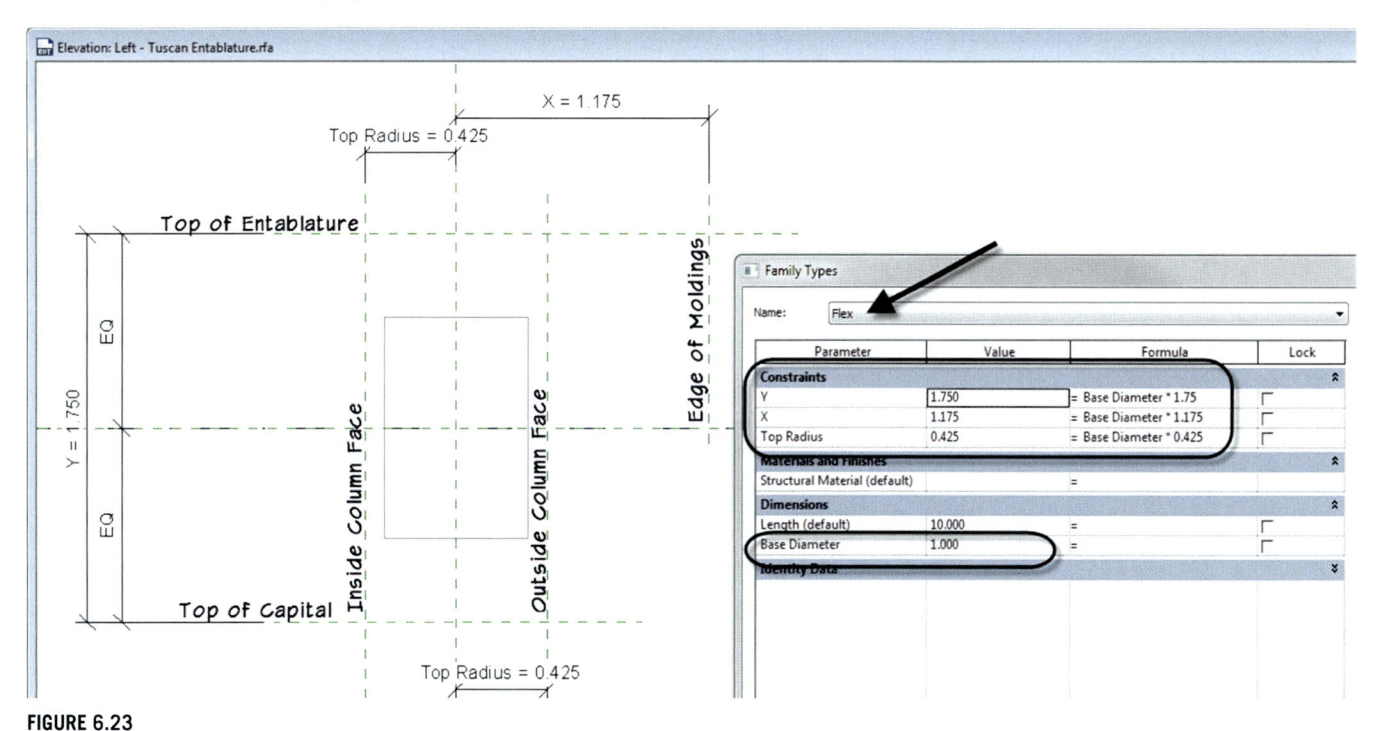

FIGURE 6.23
Add reference planes, dimensions, parameters and formulas

Notice that the beam geometry already in this file is smaller than the rectangle we just described. The next step will be to adjust the size of the extrusion to match the new reference planes.

10. Select the existing extrusion onscreen and then click the Edit Extrusion button.

Notice that there are four reference planes here inside the extrusion sketch. Let's align those to the ones we just created.

⇨ Align and lock each of the four reference planes inside the sketch to the ones we just created (see Figure 6.24).
  Be sure to align reference plane to reference plane; do *not* align the sketch lines.

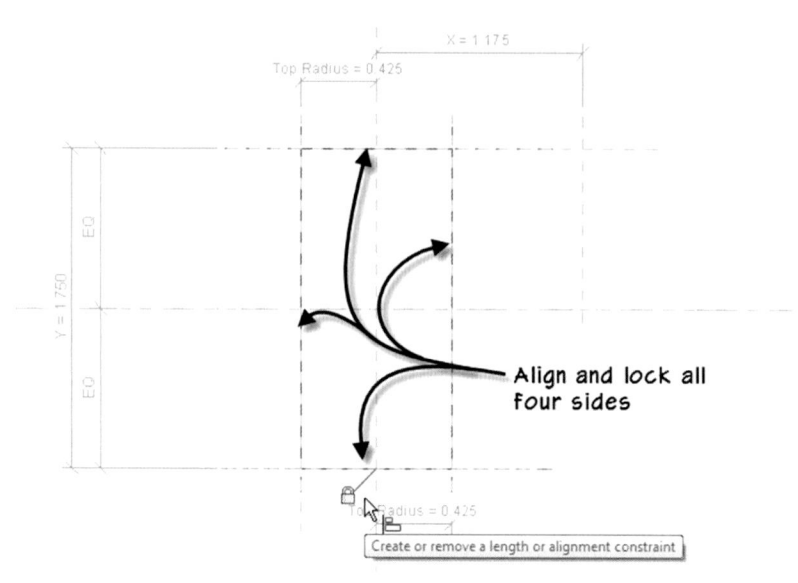

FIGURE 6.24
Adjust the shape of the extrusion to match the new reference planes

⇨ On the ribbon click the Finish Edit Mode button.

11. Flex the Base Diameter and then return to **1.000** when you are sure everything is working.

12. Save the file.

> **CATCH UP!** You can open a file completed to this point named: *06_Tuscan Entablature_A.rvt*.

IMPORT MOLDING PROFILES

The extrusion now matches the overall shape and proportion required. Next we will import the molding profile families that we need and create sweeps for each of the moldings. There will be five moldings total. I have provided finished versions of all the moldings we created back in Chapter 4 in a folder called *Moldings*. I added a couple new ones as well so that most have a version with and without integrated fillets. The first four that we need are in this folder.

Continue in your *Tuscan Entablature.rfa* file or use the catch-up file.

1. On the Insert tab, click the Load Family button.

⇨ In the book dataset folder, browse to the *Moldings* folder.

⇨ Hold down the CTRL key and select these files: *Cavetto Profile (w Fillets).rfa*, *Corona Profile (w Fillets).rfa*, *Corona Profile.rfa*, and *Cyma Profile (w Fillets).rfa*.

⇨ Click Open to load them in.

2. Repeat the process by clicking the Load Family button again.

⇨ This time browse to the *Chapter06* folder, choose *Tuscan Undercut Soffit Profile_Start.rfa* and then click Open.

3. On the Project Browser, expand the *Families* branch and then the *Profiles* item.

Each of the five profiles will be listed there. Expand each one to reveal a single type named: Flex (see the left side of Figure 6.25). The Tuscan Undercut Soffit Profile has its type named: P3. We are going to name the other ones similarly to help us keep everything organized. Remember, "Flex" is just a name I give to types when I intend for them to be flexed by their host family. But this is really just a place holder name. You can name your types anything you like, and in this case, numbering them will help us keep everything tidy.

• Renaissance Revit •

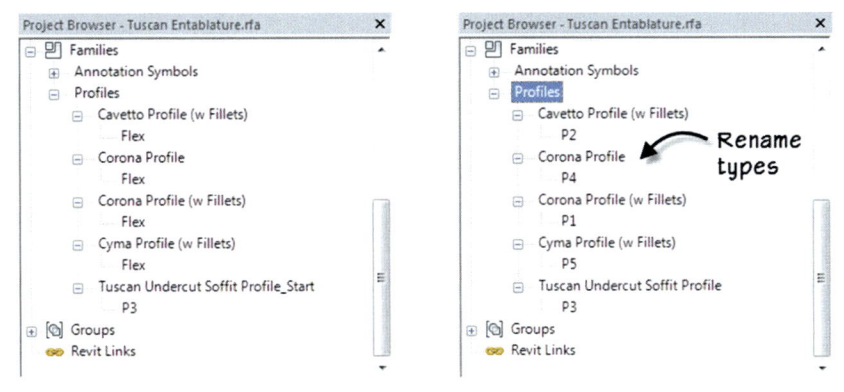

FIGURE 6.25

After loading the profiles, expand the Families branch to rename the profile types

4. Beneath the first profile; *Cavetto Profile (w Fillets)*, right-click on Flex and choose **Rename**. Name it: **P2** and then press ENTER.

⇨ Repeat for each of the others as shown on the right side of Figure 6.25. Also rename the *Tuscan Undercut Soffit Profile_Start* profile and remove the word "Start" as shown.

ADD A SWEEP PROFILE

We are now ready to add our first molding.

1. On the Project Browser, beneath *3D Views*, double-click to open the *View 1* 3D view.

⇨ On the ViewCube, click the corner between Top, Left and Front views (see Figure 6.26).

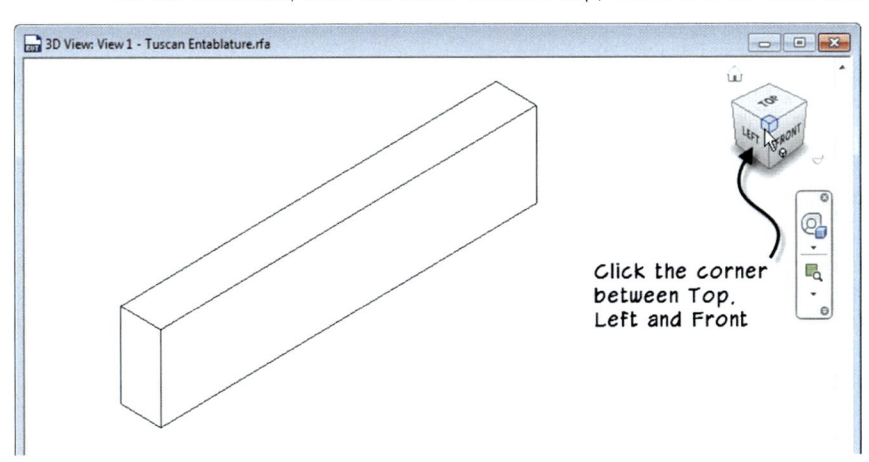

FIGURE 6.26

Change the orientation of the 3D view

This will reorient the 3D view so that it is closer to the orientation we see in the elevation.

2. Tile the windows (View tab, Tile button, or press WT).

> **Note:** Make sure that you only have the *Left* elevation and *View 1* 3D view open when you tile.

3. On the Create tab, click the Sweep button.

⇨ Click the Pick Path button.

The Pick 3D Edges button will be enabled automatically.

⇨ Click the top front edge of the beam extrusion (see Figure 6.27).

166 | Chapter 6

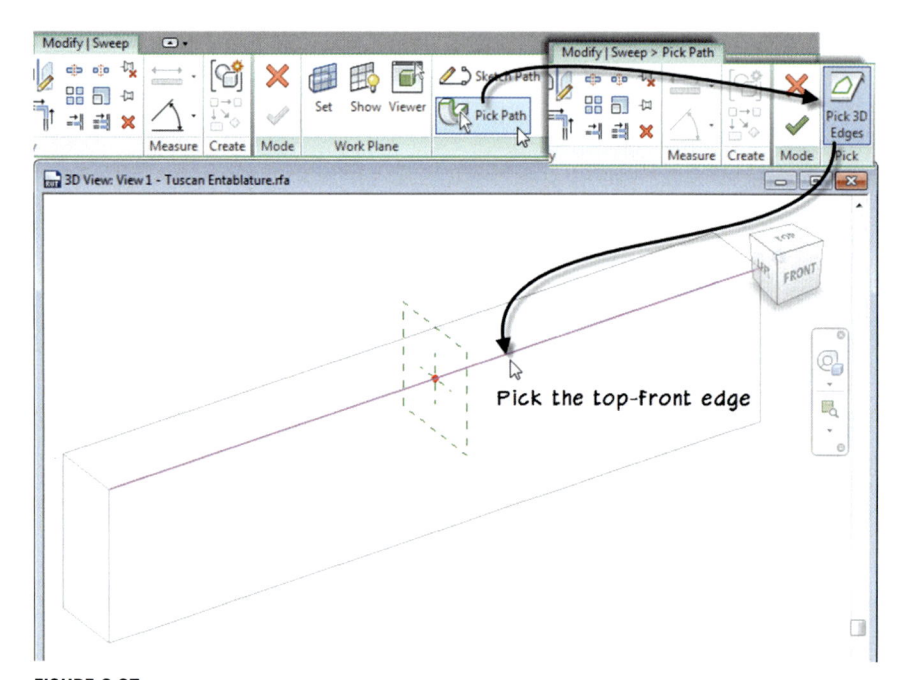

FIGURE 6.27

Pick a path for the sweep on the existing extrusion

4. Click the Finish Edit Mode button.

5. On the Modify | Sweep tab, on the Sweep panel, click the Profile drop-down and choose **Corona Profile (w Fillets):P1**.

The profile will appear disproportionally large and positioned at the top of the beam (see the left side of Figure 6.28). As we have seen with sweeps in the previous exercises and chapters, we need to adjust the type properties of the profile to adjust its size and proportion and edit its instance properties to shift it to the proper location.

⇨ Click the Finish Edit Mode button.

6. On the Project Browser, beneath *Families > Profiles > Corona (w Fillets)*, right-click P1 and choose **Type Properties**.

⇨ Edit the values of the parameters beneath Dimensions as shown in Table 6.2 and the right side of Figure 6.28:

TABLE 6.2

Parameter	Value
Y Projection Mult	0.290
X Projection Mult	0.015
X Mult	0.045
Y Mult	0.045
Fillet Projection Mult	0.060
Base Diameter	Associate Family Parameter to: **Base Diameter**

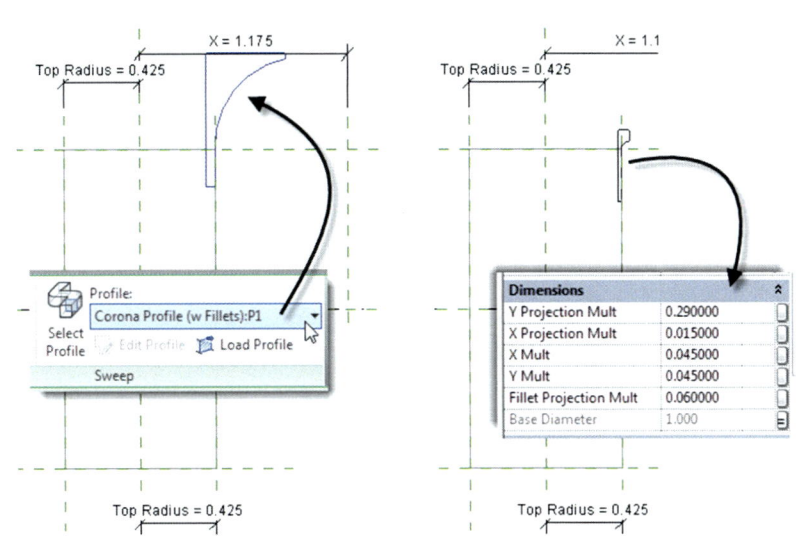

FIGURE 6.28
Place the first profile and then edit its type properties from Project Browser

7. Select the molding sweep onscreen.

    ⇨ On the Properties palette, for the Horizontal Profile Offset, input: **0.015**.

    ⇨ For the Vertical Profile Offset, input: **-1.355** (see the left side of Figure 6.29).

8. Click the Associate Family Parameter button next to Horizontal Profile Offset.

    ⇨ In the "Associate Family Parameter" dialog, click the Add Parameter button.

    ⇨ Name the new parameter: **P1 Hor**, group it under **Constraints**, leave it a Type parameter and then click OK twice

9. Repeat the process to create and associate a family parameter to the Vertical Profile Offset called **P1 Ver**. Group it under **Constraints** (see the right side of Figure 6.29).

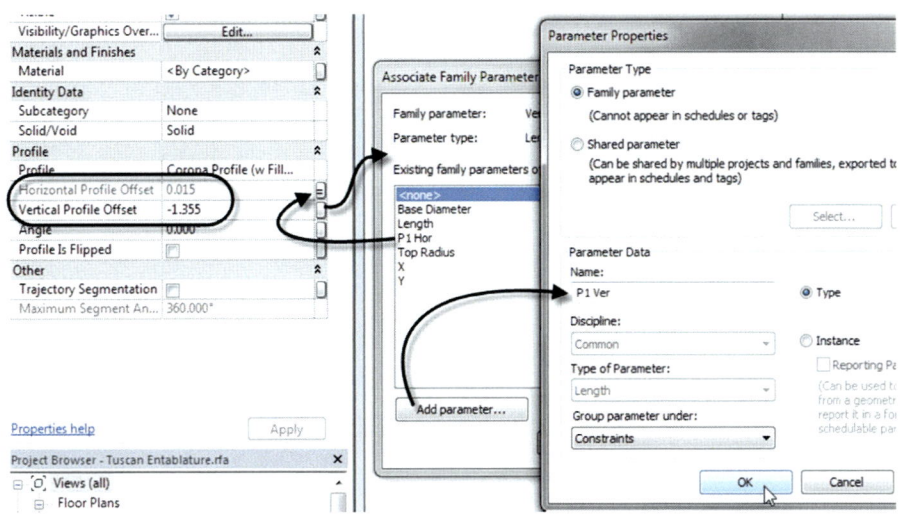

FIGURE 6.29
Edit the instance properties for the profile location and then create and associate family parameters

10. Open the "Family Types" dialog.

    ⇨ In the Formula field next to P1 Ver, type: **Base Diameter * -1.355**.

    ⇨ In the Formula field next to P1 Hor, type: **Base Diameter * 0.015**.

11. Flex the Base Diameter parameter.

• *Creating Classical Architecture with Modern Software* •

⇨ Return the value of Base Diameter to **1.000** when you are satisfied that everything is working correctly and then click OK.

12. Save the file (see Figure 6.30).

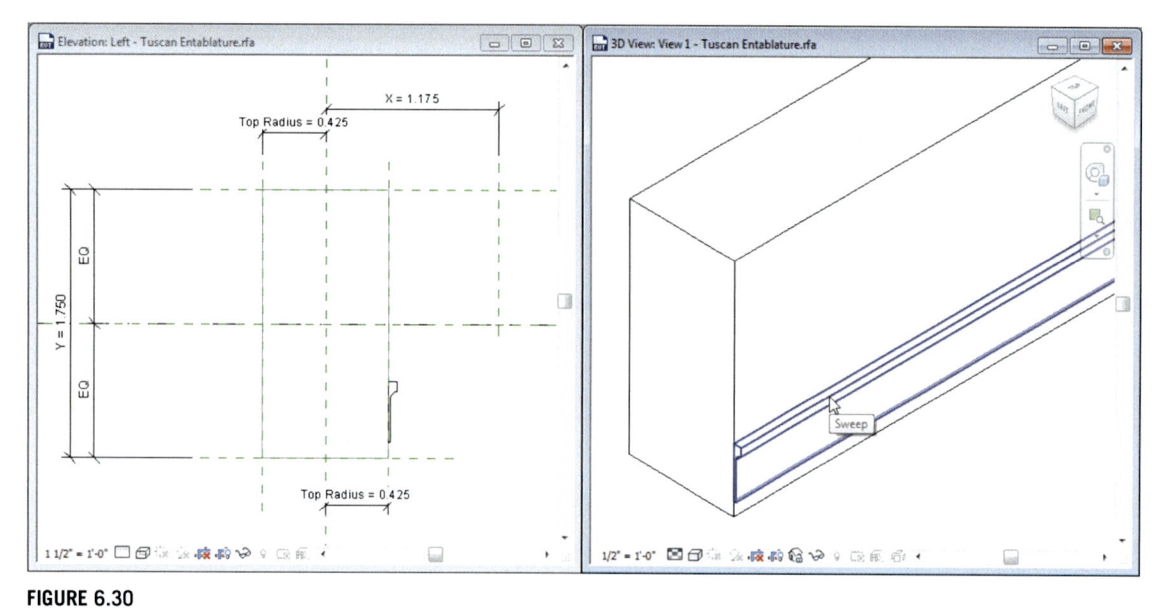

FIGURE 6.30

The first completed sweep

As you can see, there were a decent amount of steps here. I tried building this entablature a few different ways in an attempt to minimize the steps and new parameters required before settling on this approach. Regardless of the specific approach we choose, we will have to change the size and proportion of the profile in its type properties. This is straight forward and we have done this in several other examples in previous lessons.

The complexity comes in with the moving of the profile. Recall the "Create the Ovolo Molding" and "Create the Corona Molding" topics in Chapter 5. There, we discussed a few approaches we can take to moving our profile families in the sweeps. Feel free to try other options if you wish. There are essentially three approaches from which to choose for shifting the location of the profiles to the required location of the molding sweep:

Option 1—Load profiles using their default origin point. Use a common pick path for the sweep path. Add associated family parameters on the horizontal and vertical profile offsets on the Properties palette to shift their locations as required. (This is the approach shown in the previous steps).

Option 2—Add reference planes at the horizontal and vertical locations where you need the profile insertion points to end up. Create parameters for these reference planes that keep them at the proper locations when you flex. Use Set Work Plane when you draw the sweeps and draw the path on the work planes. Shifting of the horizontal and vertical profile offsets on the Properties palette not required.

Option 3—Open each profile family and save as to a new name. Adjust the origin point to match the relative location where it will need to be when loaded back into the main family. This eliminates the need for offset parameters in the host family, but requires a custom version of each profile family.

Since our goal is to reuse the profiles in multiple families, that lead me to either option 1 or 2. I tried both, and have opted for the first option in this lesson. There was about the same amount of work for either option, but I liked the flow of option 1 a little better. If you prefer you may opt for one of the other approaches instead. The specific steps will be left to you as a challenge exercise.

CATCH UP! You can open a file completed to this point named: *06_Tuscan Entablature_B.rvt*.

COPY ADDITIONAL SWEEP PROFILES

As noted, I have opted for Option 1. With this option we will need a total of eight new parameters: 4 horizontal profile offsets, and 4 vertical profile offsets. There is no quick way to make these. So let's open "Family Types" and make them now.

> **Note:** If you opted for option 2, you would require the same eight parameters. They would be driving the locations of several new reference planes instead of shifting the profiles as we will use them here. You can avoid the eight parameters in this file with option 3, but you have to edit each profile family and add offsets there instead.

Continue in your *Tuscan Entablature.rfa* file or use the catch-up file.

1. Open the "Family Types" dialog.

⇨ Create the following type-based Length parameters. Group them all under **Constraints** (see Table 6.3).

TABLE 6.3

Parameter Name	Value	Formula
P2 Ver	-0.750	Base Diameter * -0.750
P2 Hor	0.035	Base Diameter * 0.035
P3 Ver	-0.625	Base Diameter * -0.625
P3 Hor	-0.125	Base Diameter * 0.125
P4 Ver	-0.350	Base Diameter * -0.350
P4 Hor	0.450	Base Diameter * 0.450
P5 Ver	-0.250	Base Diameter * -0.250
P5 Hor	0.500	Base Diameter * 0.500

2. Click OK to dismiss the dialog and then save the file.

> **TIP:** It is always a good idea to click OK to exit and save before continuing to ensure that you preserve your work.

3. Select the existing sweep molding element onscreen.

⇨ On the Modify I Sweep tab, on the Clipboard panel, click the Copy to Clipboard button.

⇨ Click the drop-down on the Paste button and choose **Aligned to Same Place** (see the left side of Figure 6.31). You now have two copies of the molding directly on top of each other. The new copy is still selected.

4. On the Properties palette, from the Profile list, choose **Cavetto Profile (w Fillets) : P2**.

⇨ For the Horizontal Profile Offset, click the Associate Family Parameter button and link up **P2 Hor**.

⇨ Repeat for the Vertical Profile Offset and link up **P2 Ver**.

5. On the Project Browser, beneath *Families > Profiles > Cavetto (w Fillets)*, right-click P2 and choose **Type Properties**.

⇨ Set Y Mult and X Mult to **0.090**. Set Fillet Mult and Depth Mult to **0.035**.

⇨ Link up the Base Diameter parameter (see the right side of Figure 6.31).

• *Creating Classical Architecture with Modern Software* •

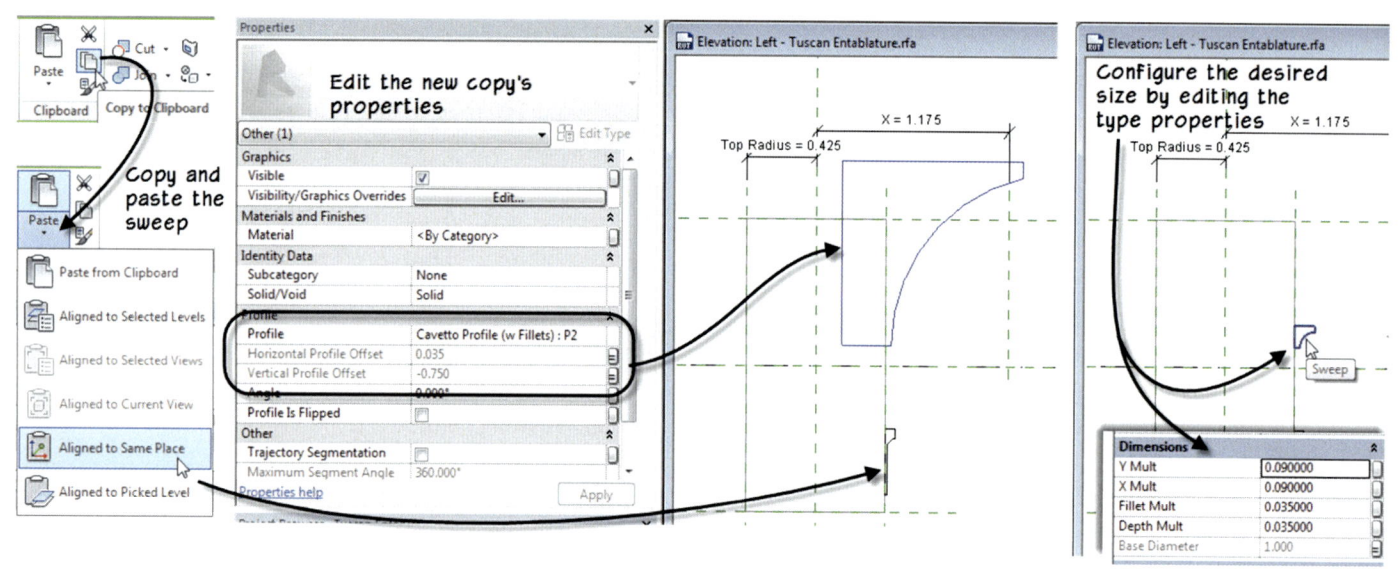

FIGURE 6.31

Paste a copy and configure its profile, offsets and type properties

The profile that I provided you for P3 is not finished yet. Therefore, we cannot build that molding yet. So let's take care of P4 and P5 and then come back to P3.

6. Repeat the entire process for profiles P4 and P5.

    ⇨ Use the parameters created above for the offsets and choose the previously renamed types.

7. For the "Type Properties" of P4, make the Y Projection Mult: **0.150**. Set the value of X Projection Mult, X Mult and Y Mult to: **0.050**. Link up Base Diameter (see the left side of Figure 6.32).

8. For the "Type Properties" of P5, make the Y Mult: **0.190**. Make X Mult: **0.250** and make Fillet Top Mult: **0.060**.

9. Set the value of both Fillet Bottom Mult to: **0.050** and Depth Projection Mult to: **0.500**. Link up Base Diameter (see the right side of Figure 6.32).

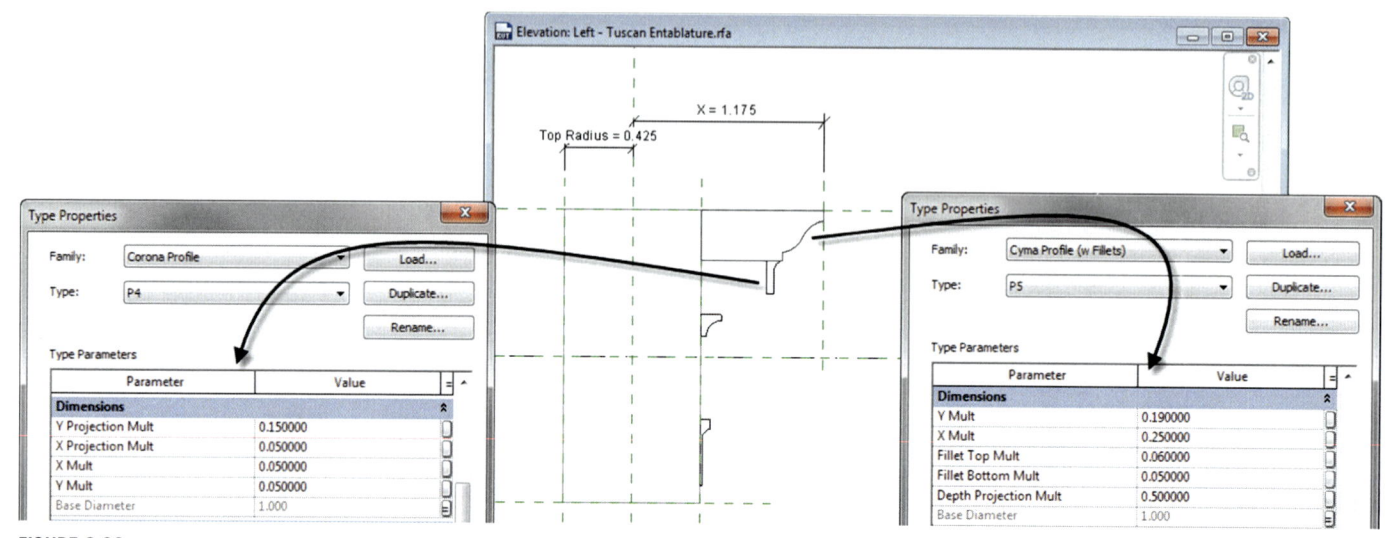

FIGURE 6.32

Configure profiles P4 and P5

We have done a quite a bit of work, so it is time to flex. We will encounter an issue when we do so.

10. Open the "Family Types" dialog, set Base Diameter to **2.000** and then click OK (see Figure 6.33).

• Renaissance Revit •

Completing the Tuscan Order | 171

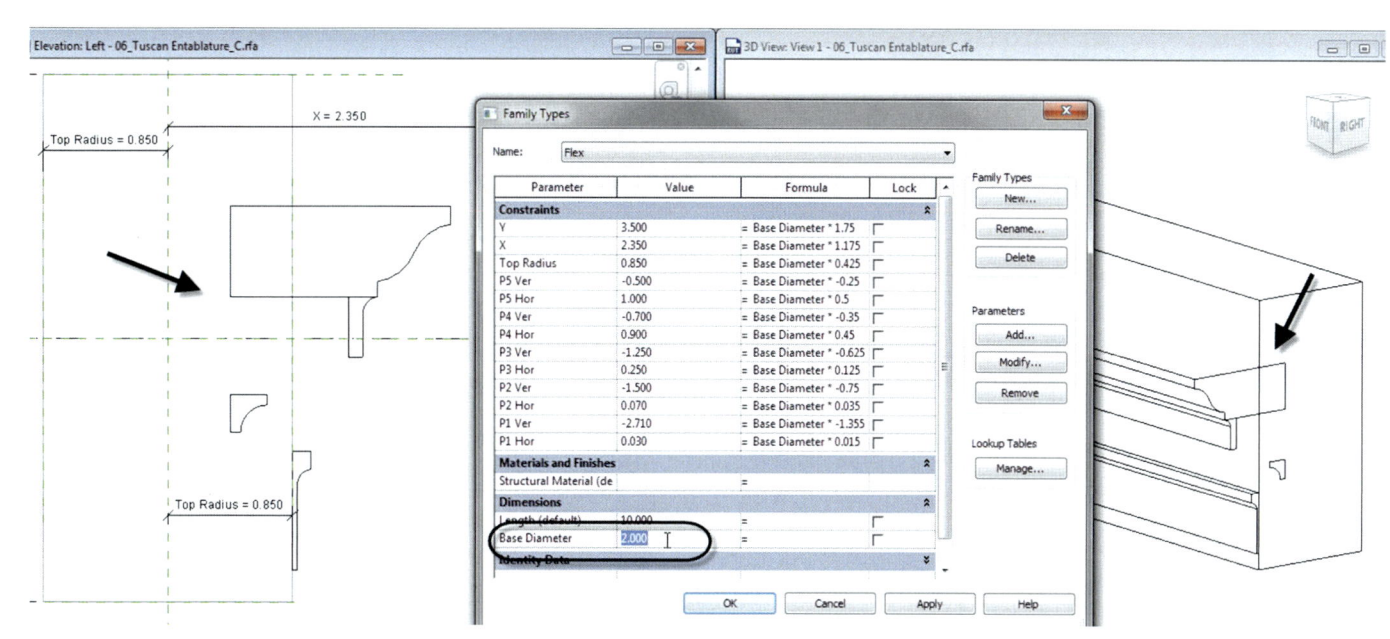

FIGURE 6.33

Flex the model and notice that the picked 3D paths are not flexing

As you can see, the profiles are not shifting properly. This is because when you paste the sweeps, the picked path is losing its association to the 3D form. Unfortunately, we have to individually edit each sweep to fix this.

11. Select one of the three sweeps that requires adjustment (the top three).

    ⇨ On the ribbon, click the Edit Sweep button and then click the Pick Path button.

    ⇨ In the 3D view, select the existing path and delete it.

12. On the Modify I Sweep > Pick Path tab, click the Pick 3D Edges button.

    ⇨ Click the top front edge of the extrusion element (the same edge we picked in the "Add a Sweep Profile" topic and shown in Figure 6.27 above).

    The ghosted out profile will disappear. This is normal and will not cause any issues.

Important: Use the TAB key as necessary to ensure that you are picking the edge of the extrusion and *not* of any of the other sweeps.

---

13. Click the Finish Edit Mode button twice to complete the operation.

The molding will now appear in the correct location.

14. Repeat the process for the remaining two moldings. Remember to use the TAB key to ensure that you are picking the edge of the extrusion each time.

Let's flex again to be sure it is working properly.

15. Open the "Family Types" dialog, set Base Diameter to **1.000** and then click OK (see Figure 6.33).

16. Save the file.

CATCH UP! You can open a file completed to this point named: *06_Tuscan Entablature_C.rvt*.

• Creating Classical Architecture with Modern Software •

ADD A SPLINE TO THE P3 PROFILE

That leaves us with Profile three. This profile has a more freeform shape. It is an undercut shape that is sort of "S" shaped. While it is possible to create a series of arcs to describe this shape, it will be much easier to approximate with a spline. Recall the "Controlling a Spline" topic in Chapter 4 where we discussed spline behavior. Given the nature of a spline, we can draw a freeform curve with as many control points as necessary to describe its curvature. As long as we lock down the endpoints on both ends, it will scale proportionally when we flex the family.

Continue in your *Tuscan Entablature.rfa* file or use the catch-up file.

1. On the Project Browser, right-click *Tuscan Undercut Soffit Profile* and choose **Edit**.

The four straight lines of this profile are already here. We need to simply add the curved line.

2. On the Create tab, click the Line button.

⇨ Draw a spline that approximates the curve shown in Figure 6.34. Be sure to snap the endpoints to the existing lines.

Eight control points were used in the example shown, but you can use more or fewer as required to approximate the curve.

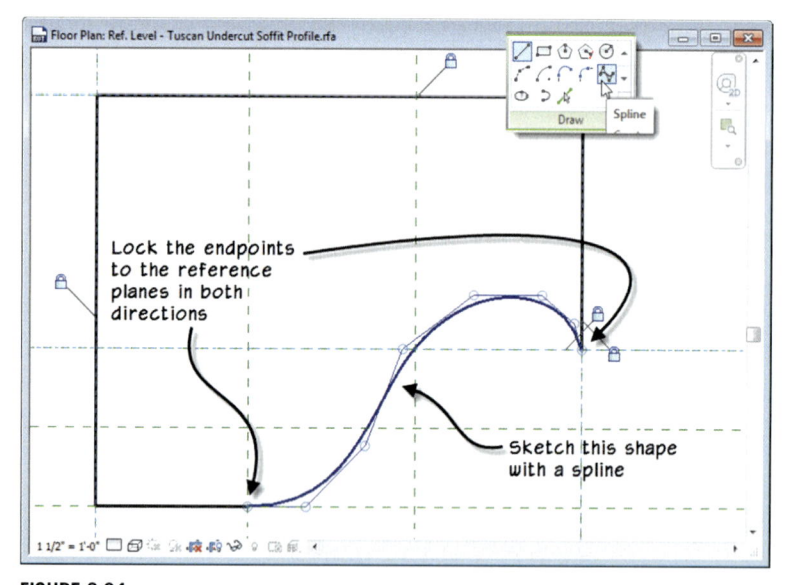

FIGURE 6.34
Add a spline curve to the profile and align and lock its endpoints

3. Align and lock the endpoint of the spline on each end to both the vertical and horizontal reference planes.

> TIP: Remember to make sure that the alignment reference is the reference plane in all cases. Use the TAB key to cycle to the endpoint of the spline to align and lock.

I have already set the multipliers in this family to match the size required. But we can flex the Base Diameter and make sure the spline scales properly.

4. Open the "Family Types" dialog.

⇨ Flex the Base Diameter. When you are satisfied it is working correctly, reset the value to **1.000** and click OK.

5. On the ribbon, click the Load into Project

⇨ In the "Family Already Exists" dialog, click the "Overwrite the existing version and its parameter values" option.

6. On the Project Browser, edit Type Properties of the *Tuscan Undercut Soffit Profile : P3*.

• Renaissance Revit •

Completing the Tuscan Order | **173**

⇨ Link up the Base Diameter and then click OK.

7. Select one of the existing sweeps. Copy and Paste Aligned to the same place.

8. On the Properties palette, choose the **P3** profile and link up the P3 Hor and P3 Ver parameters for the offsets (see Figure 6.35).

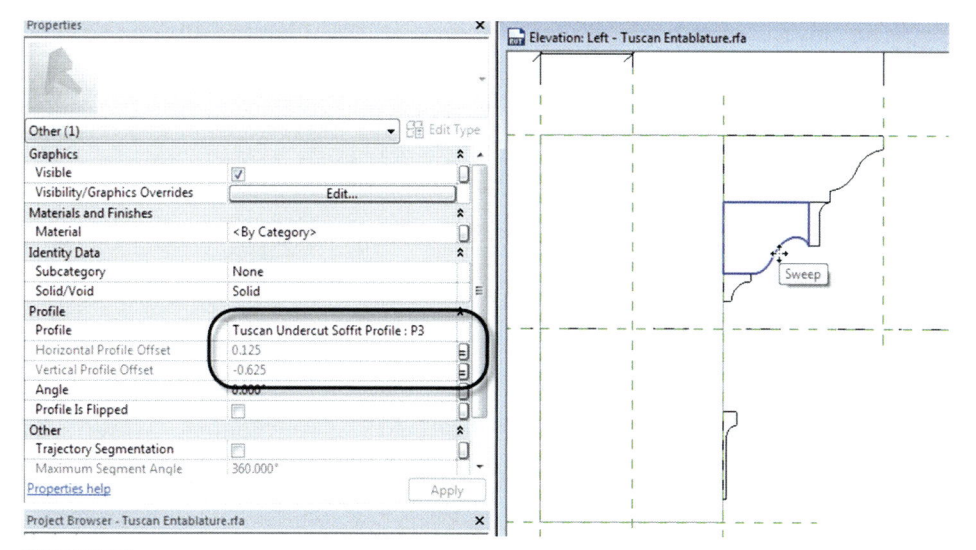

FIGURE 6.35

Paste and configure the properties of the final profile

9. Following the procedure in the "Copy Additional Sweep Profiles" topic above, edit the sweep, delete the existing path and pick a new path on the top edge of the extrusion.

10. On the Modify tab, click the Join tool.

⇨ Join all of the moldings to the beam (see Figure 6.36).

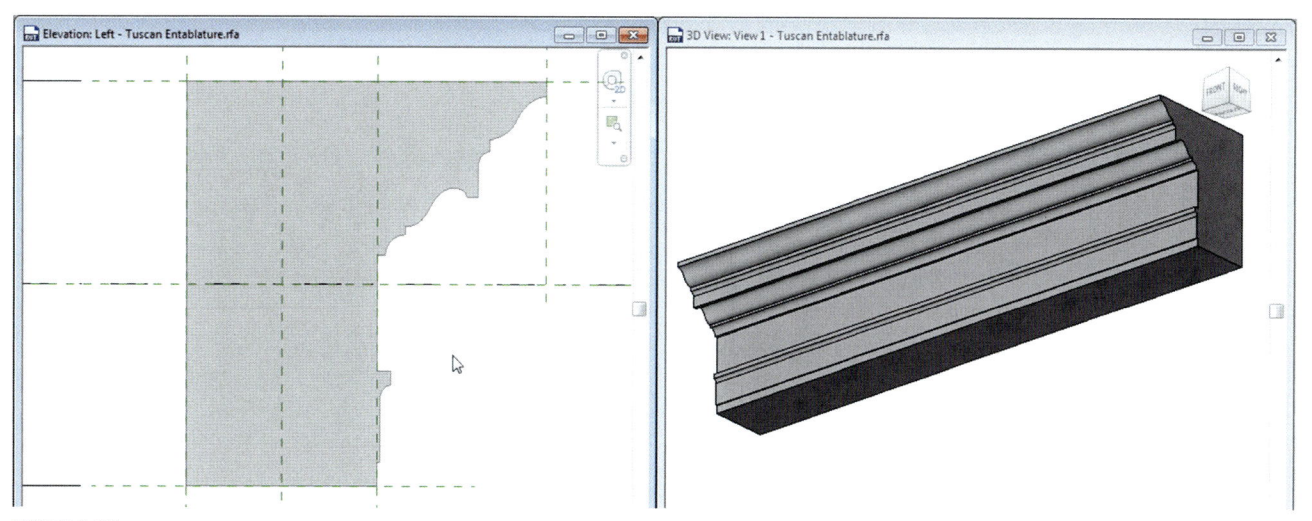

FIGURE 6.36

The completed Tuscan Entablature

11. Flex the Base Diameter parameter.

⇨ Return the value of Base Diameter to **1.000** when you are satisfied that everything is working correctly and then click OK.

12. Save the file.

• *Creating Classical Architecture with Modern Software* •

CREATE FAMILY TYPES

If you have built family content before, you have probably created some family types. Typically you would create your family and add a few common types directly in the family file. If you look at most of the out-of-the-box families like doors, windows, furniture and equipment, they are built this way. Given the special nature of the content that we have been building, we have created only a single type called Flex in most cases. As you may recall from previous discussions on the matter, this name is simply a placeholder so that when we load the family into another family, the host can flex the parameters of this nested family.

Our Tuscan Entablature family is nearly complete. But unlike the other families we have built, we are going to follow the more common procedure here and give this family some standard sizes by adding some family types. The reason for this, is that unlike our Tuscan Column family built in the previous chapters, we cannot rely on the levels in our project to flex the family for us. The entablature family did make use of the *Structural Framing - Beams and Braces.rft* family template when we started, so there is a built-in Length parameter. Theoretically, we could build a formula associated with this parameter that would apply the desired scaling. The trouble is that such an approach would tie the overall length of the entablature to its proportions, which in most applications would prove too limiting. So I will resist the urge to be too "clever" and opt instead for a more traditional approach and simply add some family types.

Continue in your *Tuscan Entablature.rfa* file.

1. Open the "Family Types" dialog.

As expected, this family has a single type named: Flex. Let's start by renaming that.

2. On the right side of the dialog, click the Rename button.

   ⇨ Change the name of Flex to **1.000** and then click OK.

3. Click the New button.

   ⇨ Name the new Type: **2.000** and then click OK.

   ⇨ Change the value of Base Diameter to **2.000** and then click Apply.

4. Create two more named: **1.500** and **0.750** editing the value of Base Diameter accordingly. Apply after each change.

5. From the drop-down list of types, try each one, clicking Apply after each. When finished, return to **1.000** and then click OK to dismiss the dialog.

6. Save the file.

CATCH UP! You can open a file completed to this point named: *Tuscan Entablature.rfa*.

ADD THE ENTABLATURE IN A SANDBOX FILE

The next thing that we should naturally do is to test the final product in a sandbox file. We will do a simple test here and save the more complete test for the next chapter. A sandbox project file has been provided with the dataset files for Chapter 6.

1. Open the Revit project file named *06_Sandbox_A.rvt*.

2. Switch back to the *Tuscan Entablature* file or open the catch-up file.

   Beams are two-pick (linear) elements. Draw next to the columns onscreen for now. Do not try to snap to them.

   ⇨ Work in the *{3D}* view. Click a point onscreen for the first endpoint. (On the Options Bar, make sure Chain is checked). Keeping it horizontal, click to place the second point. (Any length is fine).

Completing the Tuscan Order | 175

3. Turn 90° and place another point. (Again any length is fine).

⇨ Click the Modify tool or press ESC twice to cancel.

As you can see, it is very easy to draw the entablature at any length required. You will be seeing all of the moldings that you added appearing here in the 3D view. However, as you can also see, the corner did not clean up very nicely. This is simply the default behavior of beams. We can adjust this.

4. Select one of the beams onscreen.

⇨ Right-click directly on the grip handle (small dot) at the end that connects to the other beam (see the left side of Figure 6.37).

⇨ Click Edit Beam/Column Join.

There are two "Change Beam Status" shape handles at the intersection of the two beams. They look like small arrows. We can use these to change how the two beams join to one another.

⇨ Click the small arrow shown in the middle of Figure 6.37.

If you do not get a mitered result, click the same arrow again to reset, and then click the other one. I have also provided a Structural Plan view in the file. You can open this view and perform the steps there if you find it easier. The desired result is shown on the right side of Figure 6.37.

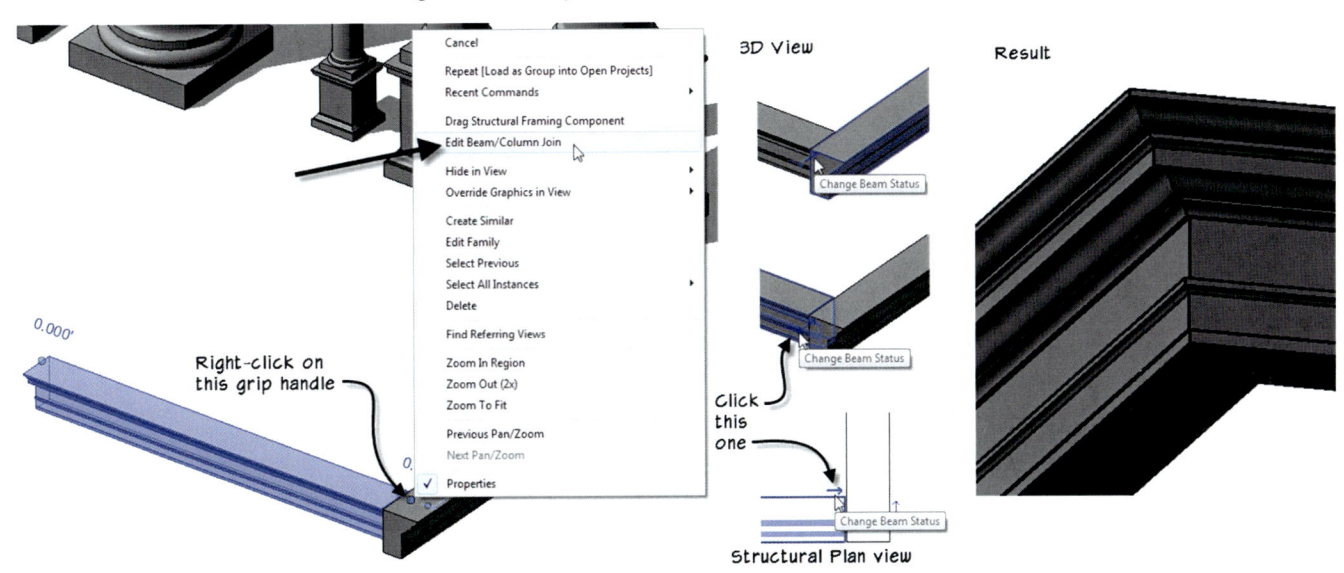

FIGURE 6.37
Using the Edit Beam command, you can miter the two beams

5. Add some additional beams or copy these.

6. On the Properties palette, on the Type Selector, you will see the four types we added in the family. Try some other sizes.

We have a few more adjustments to consider. Beams place below the level by default. Beams also contain different representation for Coarse, Medium and Fine displays by default. We have materials and other settings to consider as well. But I will save those for the next chapter.

7. Save and close the Sandbox file.

CATCH UP! You can open a file completed to this point named: *06_Sandbox_B.rvt*.

• *Creating Classical Architecture with Modern Software* •

SUMMARY

- Creating the forms for round elements like column bases, capitals and shafts can be approached using either revolved or swept forms.

- Sweeps have the advantage of being able to use a profile family for their shape, making these shapes easily reusable. Revolves must be sketched, so reusing profiles between different revolves is difficult.

- To represent entasis, there are very specific construction techniques which create a very subtle diminishing curve. The details of how to construct such a curve are reserved for Chapter 12.

- To make a simple approximation of entasis that is quite convincing for most scales and uses, a single arc with a very large radius can be used.

- To swap a nested family with a different version, right-click it on Project Browser and choose **Reload**.

- You can use visibility parameters to drive the visible parameter of family elements. When this box if unchecked, the object is removed from the family. This is an effective way to create optional items in a family such as columns with and without pedestals as we have done here.

- Using a beam family can be an effective way to create an entablature family.

- Use the existing beam extrusion and build it up with sweeps created from the nested profile families created in previous chapters.

- Alternatively, you can create a custom profile for the entire shape that contains all of the curves internally in a single profile.

- Beams have the ability to miter at the corners when used in a project. This makes them a nice option for the entablature family.

FORUM IN ROME
Photo by author

Chapter 7
Managing Graphics

INTRODUCTION

We have spent a good deal of time working on the order which Palladio quotes Vitruvius as saying: is "the most simple and plain of all the orders of architecture." (Palladio 1965, 14) But the Tuscan order—precisely because of its simplicity—has lent itself nicely as a backdrop to our exploration of many ideas critical to the mastery of the Revit Family Editor. Regardless, I am sure you are anxious to leave the Tuscan order behind and move on to the more complex orders. I assure you, we will do this very soon. But if you will indulge me as we work through this chapter, I will continue to use the Tuscan here as we explore many topics that can be thought of as finishing touches to our Tuscan order families. The sum of all skills, procedures and techniques discussed over the last several chapters will then serve as the foundation for our exploration of the Doric, Ionic and Corinthian orders in the coming chapters. So with that, let's take our final look at the Tuscan order as we explore level of detail, materials and plan vs. model graphics in this chapter.

OBJECTIVES

Several factors go into creating a fully functional and robust piece of family content. In this chapter we will add several enhancements to our families to make them accommodate more use cases in the project. We are going to look specifically how our families perform in different viewing conditions like plans, elevations and section. We'll add materials and discuss other category specific characteristics. Topics in this chapter include:

- Controlling column plan display.
- Alternatives to the entablature
- Adding Coarse, Medium and Fine level graphics.
- Adding materials and material parameters

COLUMN PLAN DISPLAY

Columns in Revit, both Architectural and Structural have a toggle setting that impacts the way they will display in plan views in your project. In most of the exercises in the previous chapters we have concerned ourselves primarily with the 3D model display. When you begin using the content in project files, you will also become concerned with 2D views like plans, sections and elevations. In this topic we'll start with plan views.

1. From the Application menu, choose Open.
   ⇨ Browse to the *Chapter07* folder and open the *07_Sandbox_Colonnade.rfa* file.

This file contains the completed versions of the families created in the previous chapter and will be the backdrop for our explorations here.

2. From the View tab, click Tile or use the keyboard shortcut WT.
3. In the Level 1 floor plan, zoom in to the left around column grid lines A1 through B4 (see Figure 7.1).

FIGURE 7.1

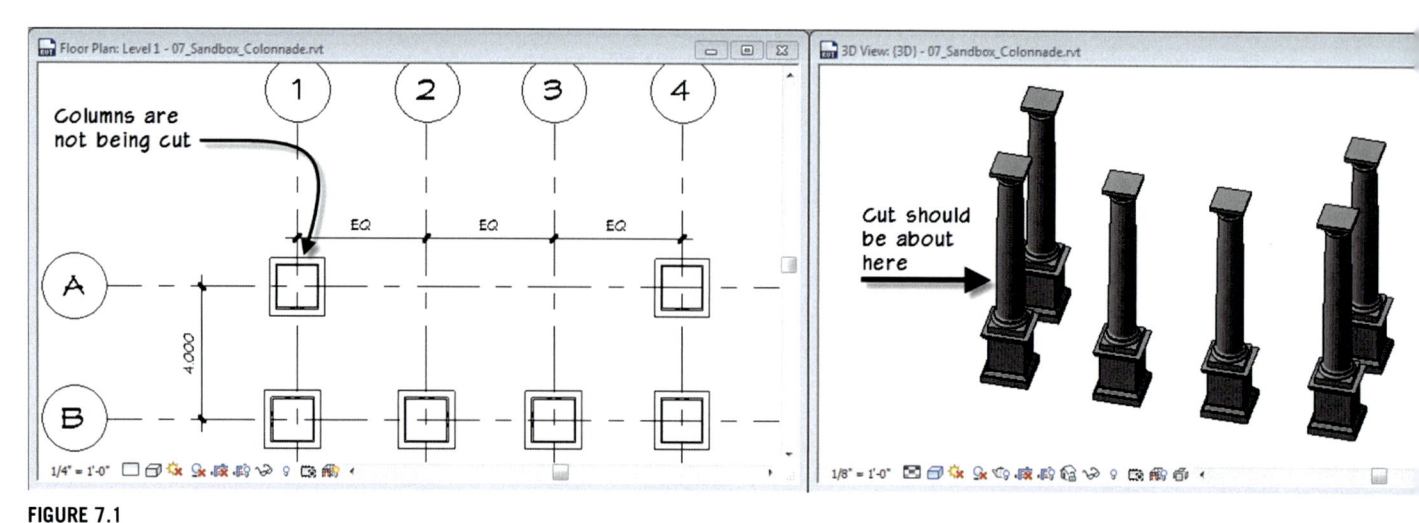

Columns are not being cut by the plan view's cut plane

This file uses the standard Revit Architectural default template file. In imperial units, the cut plane is four feet above the floor level (equivalent to about 1200mm in a metric file). This means that we should be seeing round columns as we should be cutting through the shafts of the columns in this view. There is a setting inside the column family that controls this.

4. On the Project Browser, expand *Families* and then *Columns*. Right-click *Tuscan Column* and choose **Edit**.

⇨ On the Properties palette, beneath the Other grouping, uncheck the "Show family pre-cut in plan views" checkbox.

5. From the Application menu, choose **Save As > Family**.

⇨ Save the family to the *Chapter07* folder.

6. Click the Load into Project button.

7. Choose the "Overwrite the existing version" option (see Figure 7.2).

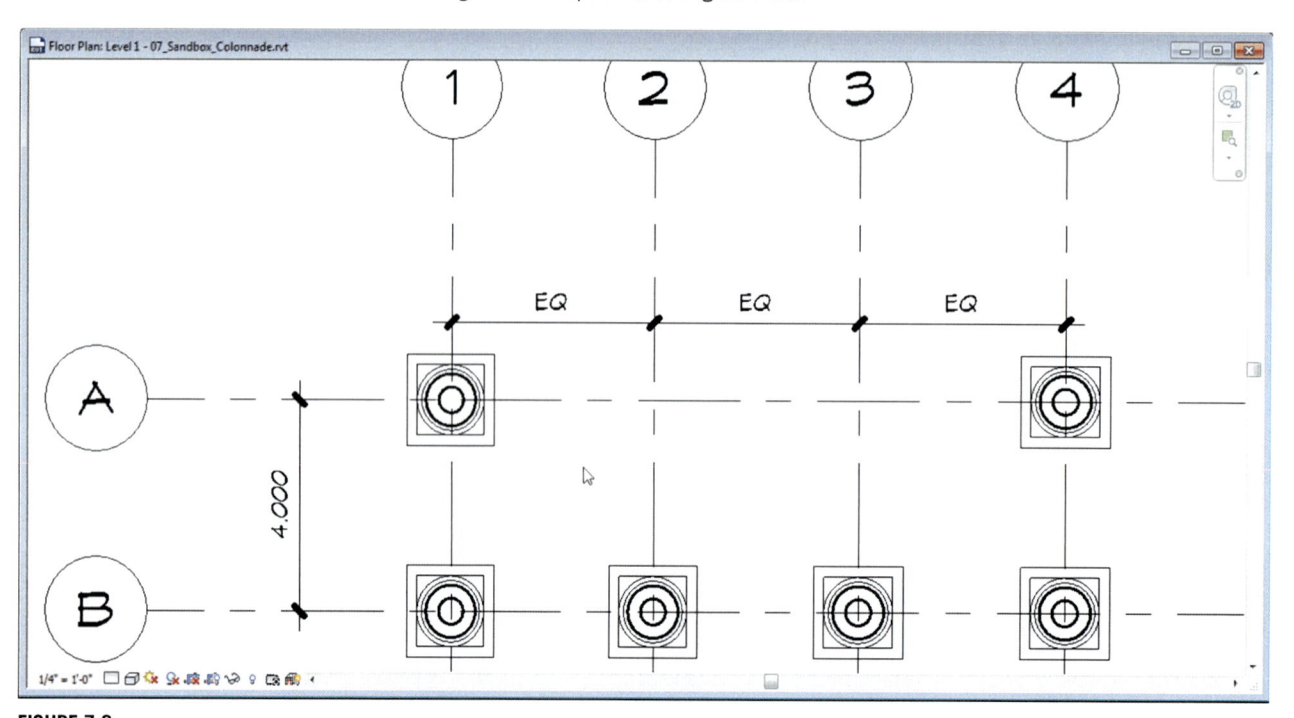

FIGURE 7.2

Turn off the "pre-cut" option and reload the family

• Renaissance Revit •

MAKE THE COLUMN SOLID

If you zoom in a bit, you can see that the family is now being cut by the cut plane of the project file. The round outline of the shaft is a nice bold lineweight where it is being cut. However, you can also now see that our column is hollow. Recall that we built the shaft with a sweep. Unlike revolves, sweeps cannot be solid all the way through, so we had to make a donut like form. There is a very simple remedy to the problem. We simply need to fill in the center of the shaft with another solid like an extrusion and then join geometry.

The Tuscan Column family should still be open.

1. Using switch windows, switch to *Tuscan Column.rfa – 3D View : View 1*. (You can also press CTRL + TAB to cycle open windows till this view appears).

2. Select the shaft onscreen.

    ⇨ On the ribbon, click the Edit Family button.

3. On the Project Browser, expand *Views (all)* and then *Floor Plans*. Double-click to open *Ref. Level*.

Notice that the Base Diameter in this file is not set to our normal default value of 1.000. This is due to eh way that we opened the file from an existing instance. There is no problem with doing it this way as long as you put the correct multiplier in the parameter formula, or flex it back to 1.000 first. I like to flex it back first. It is much easier to get the math right.

4. Open the "Family Types" dialog.

    ⇨ Set Base Diameter to **1.000** and then click OK.

5. On the Create tab, click the Extrusion button.

    ⇨ On the Modify | Create Extrusion tab, on the Draw panel, click the Circle icon.

    ⇨ Snap the center of the circle to the intersection of the two center reference planes.

    ⇨ Snap the radius to the inside edge of the hollow sweep (see Figure 7.3).

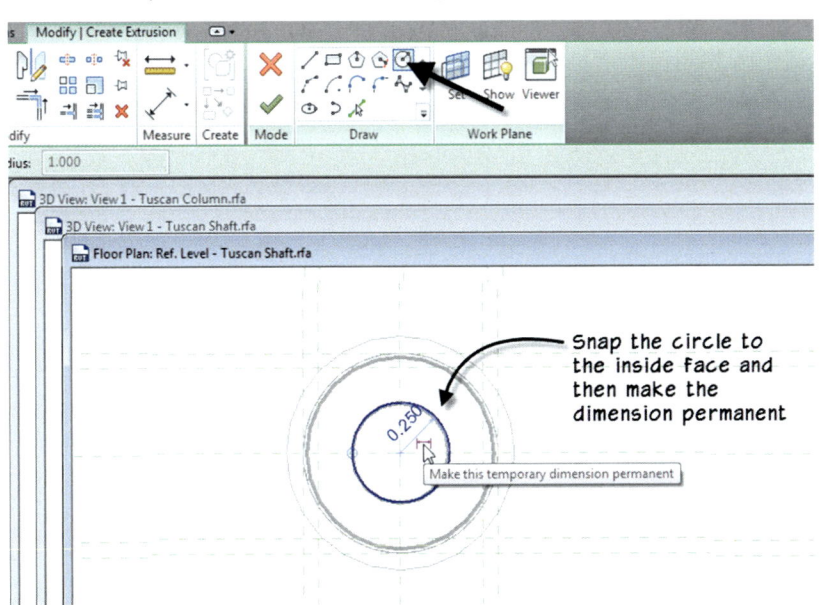

FIGURE 7.3

Create a round extrusion to fill the inside of the shaft

6. Click the icon to make the temporary dimension permanent.

⇨ Label the dimension with a new parameter called **R**. Group it under **Constraints**.

7. Finish Edit Mode.

8. Open "Family Types" again and add a Formula to R: **Base Diameter * 0.250**.

9. On the Project Browser, double-click to open the *Front* elevation view.

⇨ Using the Align tool, align the top edge of the extrusion to the reference plane just beneath the top torus molding. Lock it (see Figure 7.4).

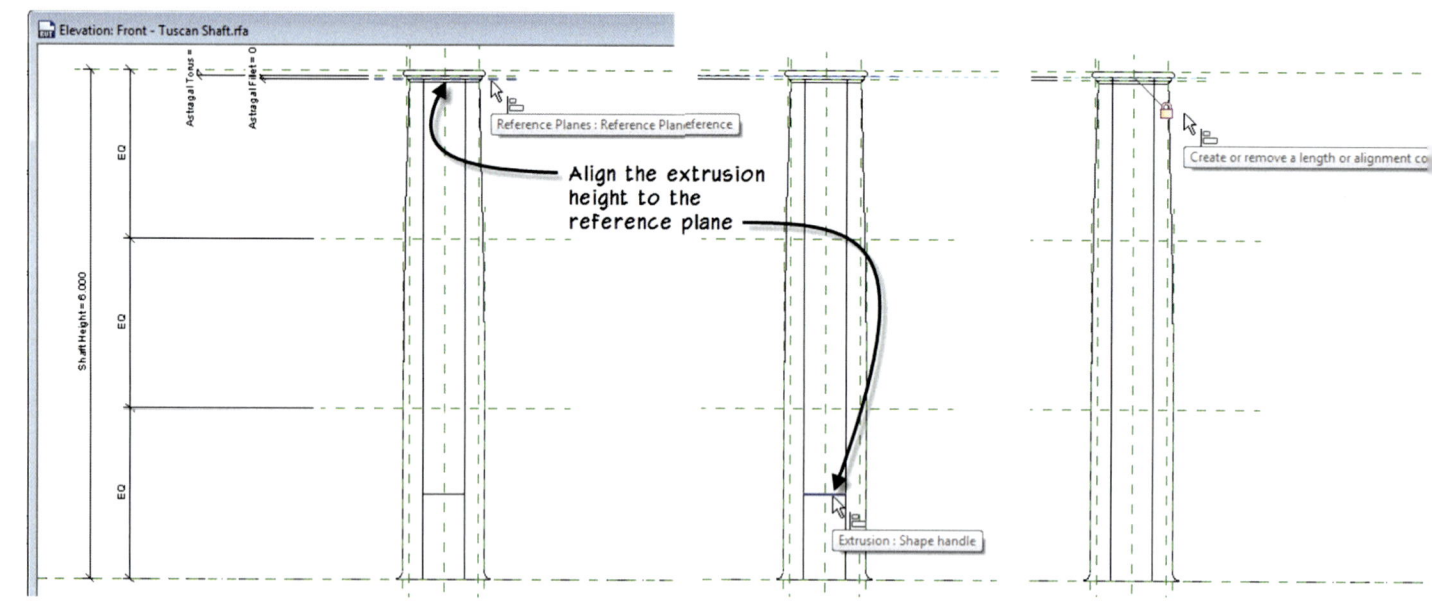

FIGURE 7.4

Using Align, match the height of the extrusion to the full height of the shaft

10. Use Join Geometry and join the extrusion to the shaft sweep.

11. Flex the Base Diameter.

If you want to save a separate copy of the shaft family, you can do so now. Save it to the *Chapter07* folder. It is not completely necessary however. If you prefer, you can simply load it into the column family without saving it separately. I will leave that choice up to you.

12. If desired, save the family to the *Chapter07* folder and then click the Load into Project button.

⇨ In the "Load into Project" dialog, check only *Tuscan Column.rfa* and then click OK.

⇨ Overwrite the existing version (choose the first option, not the second one). (The second option will fail here).

> **Note:** When you are prompted that a family already existing, you are offered two options. The first option "Overwrite the existing version" overwrites changes to the family itself only; things like geometry or other physical modifications. The second option: "Overwrite the existing version and its parameter values" also overwrites the settings in the family types. Think of it as the first option is family only, second option is family and types. In this case, it is important that we preserve the settings of the types, so we want the first option.

13. Save the family and then click Load into Project again.

⇨ This time choose only *07_Sandbox_Colonnade.rvt* and then click OK.

⇨ Once again, choose "Overwrite the existing version" (see Figure 7.5).

Managing Graphics | 181

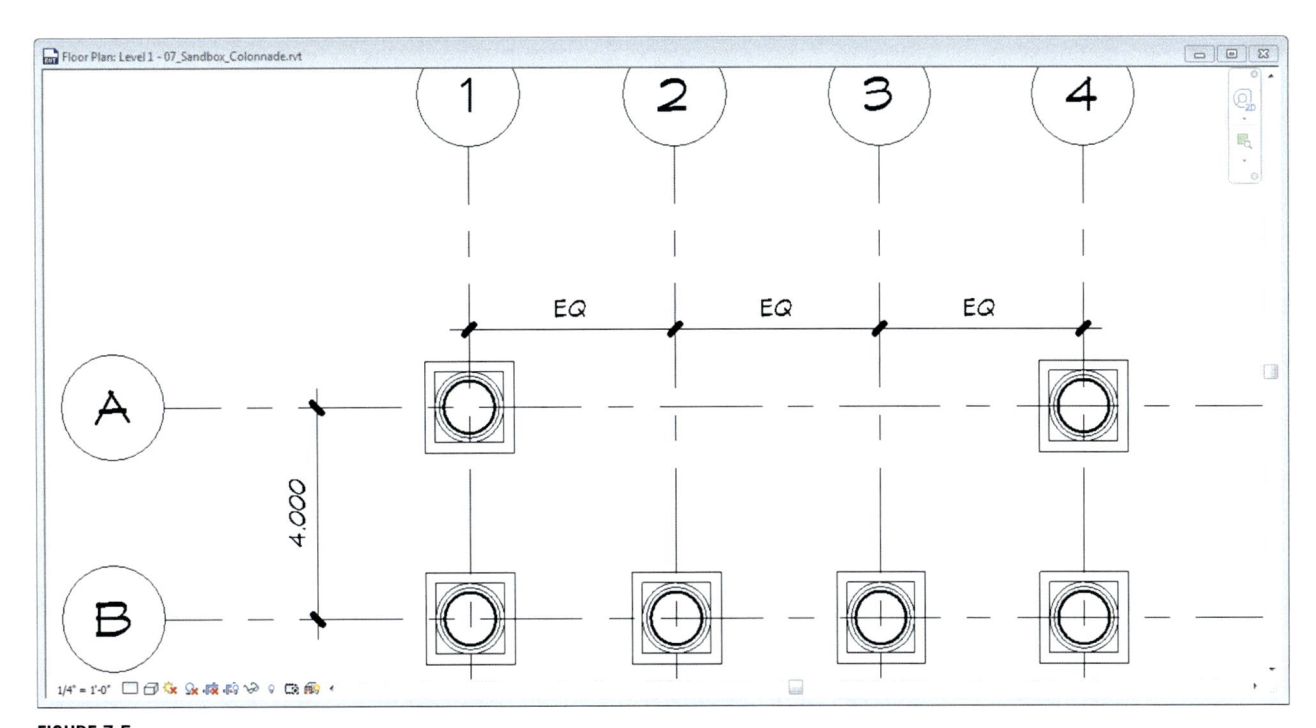

FIGURE 7.5
Load the modified shaft back into the column and then load the column back into the sandbox

You should now have nice solid columns that show the correct shape in plan view.

INTERCOLUMNIATION

In the area where we are zoomed in (around column lines A1 – B4), the columns use a Base Diameter of 1.000. Simply select one and look at the properties to see this. The columns inserted in this area use the *Tuscan Column : With Pedestal* type. Recall that this column family calculates the Base Diameter from the height between the top and base levels. In this area, I set the height of Level 2 to 9.100 to ensure we would end up with a Base Diameter of 1.000.

Next to this area is another group of column lines (A/5 – A.9/8). They use the type without the pedestal and their height is also attached to Level 2. So the total height is still 9.100, but this now makes the Base Diameter 1.300 since there is no pedestal.

Spacing of columns in classical architecture is referred to as intercolumniation. Vitruvius named each of his recommended intercolumniations with names such as pycnostyle, eustyle and araeostyle. These are 2 ½, 3 ¼ and 5 column diameters on center respectively. Vitruvius actually describes them a little differently by noting the space open between each column, but if you simply add one to each value you end up with the center to center spacing (Vitruvius 1960, 1914, 78-86).

Chitham notes that due to the lack of ornamentation on a Tuscan order, there is nothing inherent to the order to dictate its spacing (contrasted to a Doric order for example). From his research, he arrives at four recommended spacing for the Tuscan order: 3, 3 ¼, 4 and 5 diameters. Impressive as the Vitruvian names are, it is easier to simply think in terms of the desired number of diameters required. So for this reason, I have once again adopted Chitham's values here (Chitham 1985, 2005, 102-106).

The example I have in the sandbox file uses 4 diameters for the spacing. Unfortunately, unlike the Family Editor, when we are in the project environment, you cannot apply a formula to a dimension. So I had to calculate the spacing between column lines manually. I selected a column onscreen as noted above and looked on the Properties

• Creating Classical Architecture with Modern Software •

palette to find its current Base Diameter. I then multiplied this by 4 to achieve the desired spacing. To make the job a little easier, I have created an equality dimension. There are only four column lines in my example, but if you have several, you will also want to move the anchor for equality constraints. This handy little icon appears onscreen when you select one of the equality members. Drag it to the location of the member you want to stay stationary. On the left side of Figure 7.6, you can see that I dragged it to column line 5.

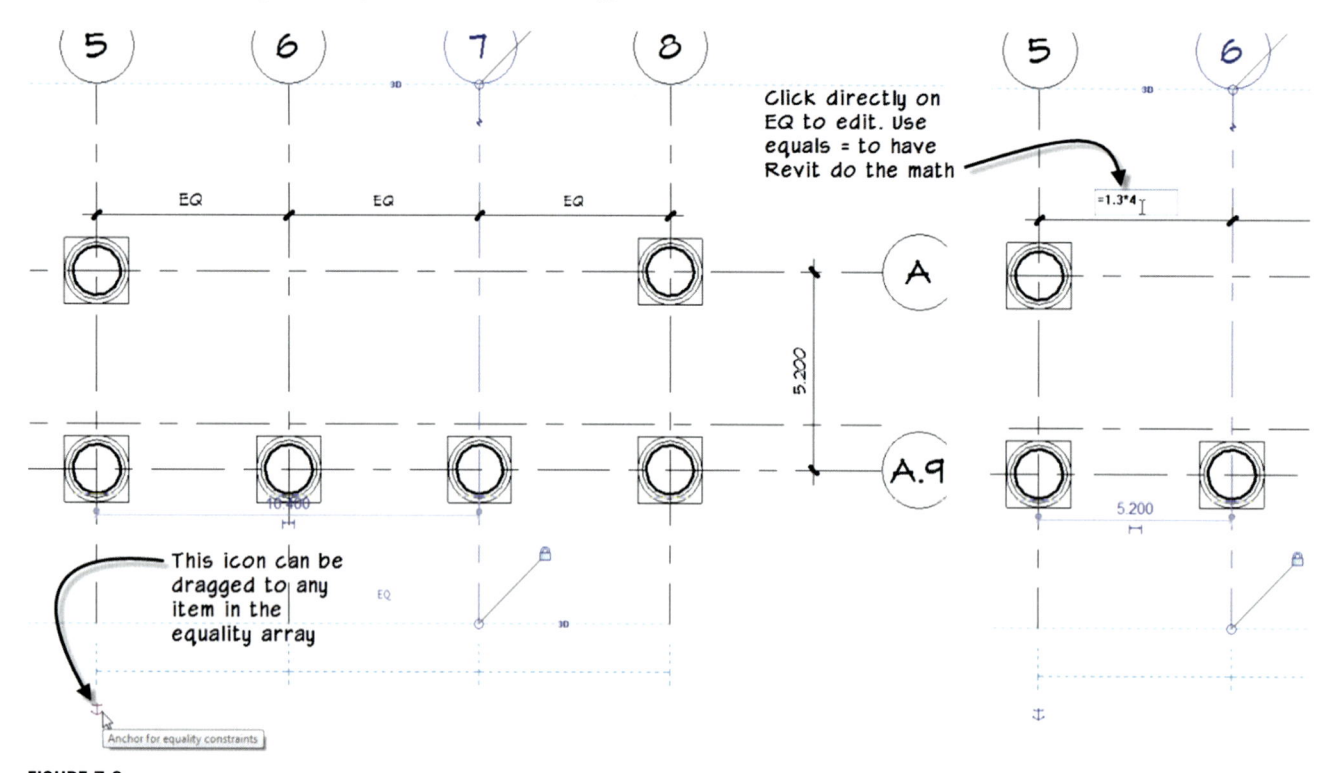

FIGURE 7.6
When using equality dimensions, you can drag the anchor to set the item in the group that should remain stationary

Once you have an equality dimension, you can edit the distance the same as any other dimension. Simply select one of the dimensioned elements (column line in this case) and then click right on the EQ dimension that activates in blue. The difference is that when you edit an EQ dimension, all elements in the array will move accordingly. On the right side of Figure 7.6, you can see that I am using an equation. Anywhere in Revit that takes numeric input, you can utilize this trick. Simply preface your equation with an equals (=) sign. Revit will do the math for you. So instead of manually figuring out what the distance of four diameters should be, I "asked" Revit to calculate it.

PLACING COLUMNS

The next two grids to the right do not yet have columns. Next to grids 9 – 13 I placed a column without a pedestal that spans to Level 3. Its Base Diameter is 2.6, so at a 4 diameter spacing, you can see that the grid lines are spaced 10.400 apart. Grids 14 – 17 are slightly closer together since the column near them does use the pedestal, has a 2.000 Base Diameter which yields an 8.000 column spacing.

> **CATCH UP!** You can open a file completed to this point named: *07_Sandbox_Colonnade_A.rvt*.

I am sure that you have placed columns on grids before, but there are a few nuances I wanted to mention here, so I left these two grids empty for you to experiment. Let's add a few columns.

　　　Continue in the *07_Sandbox_Colonnade.rvt* file or open the catch-up file.

　1.　In the *Level 1* floor plan view, zoom in on the area around column lines C9 – D13.

The sandbox file was saved with several view windows open, so you may also want to zoom in on the same area in the other views to get more feedback as you work. Be sure to place the columns in a plan view however.

2. Select the free-standing column to the right of column line 13.

   ⇨ On the Modify | Columns tab, click the Create Similar button (or press CS).

Create Similar runs the place column command and places the same type of column on the cursor. It matches all of the settings of the object we selected; except one. Notice that the column is smaller. The command will not match the height of the existing column. We have to do that manually (See Figure 7.7).

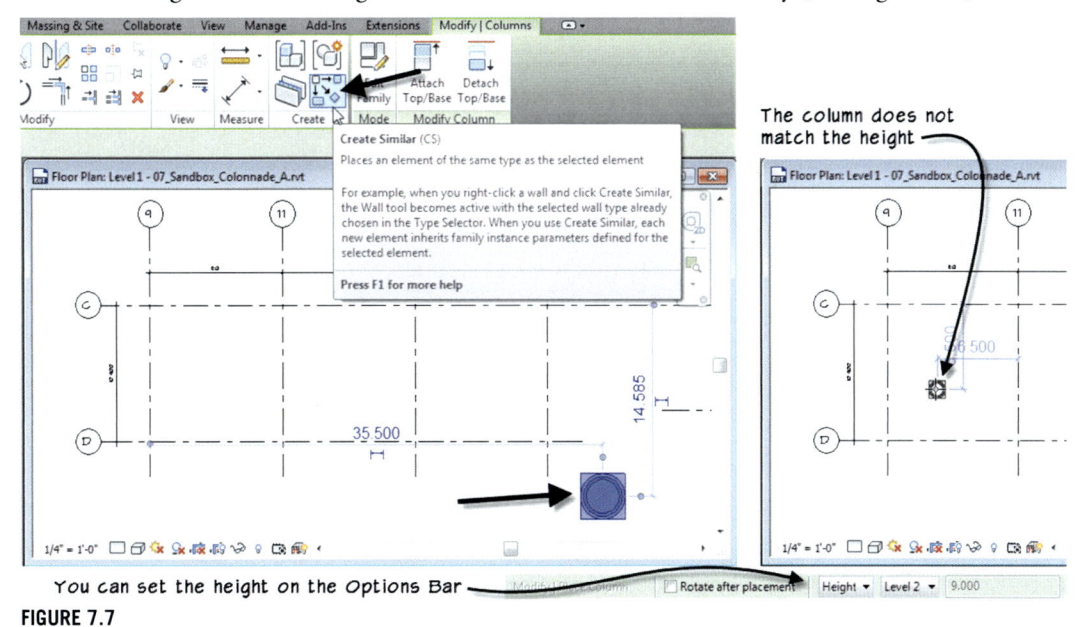

FIGURE 7.7

Create Similar will match the type of column but not the height

3. On the Options Bar, next to Height, choose **Level 3** from the drop-down.

   If you forget to do this, you can always change it later on the Properties palette.

The column will appear unchanged until you place it.

4. Click at the intersection of grid lines C and 9.

The column will automatically adjust in size. This is because of how we built the height to Base Diameter relationship back in Chapter 5.

5. Begin moving your cursor near grid lines D and 9. Click when both are highlighted (see the left side of Figure 7.8).

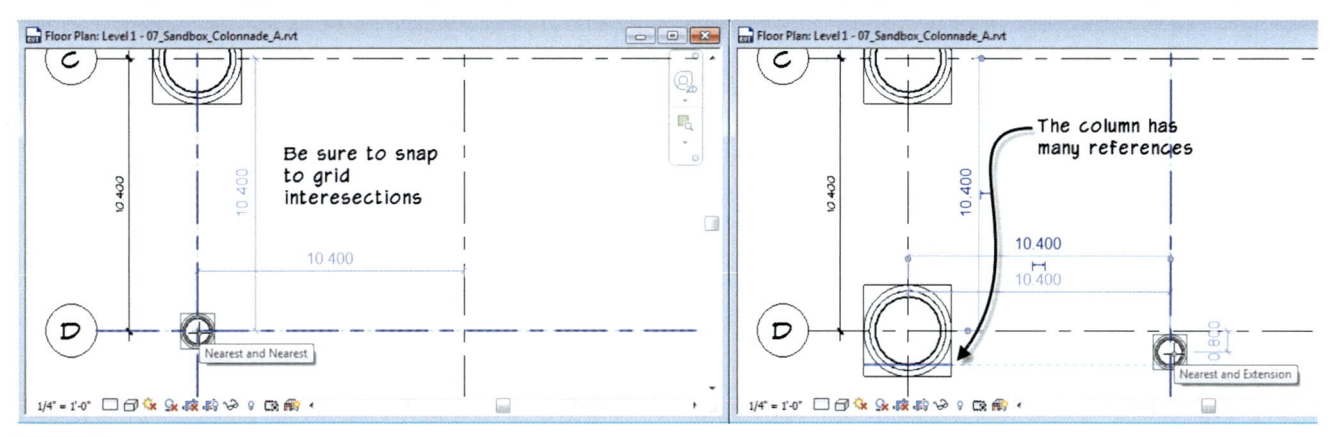

FIGURE 7.8

Load the modified shaft back into the column and then load the column back into the sandbox

• Creating Classical Architecture with Modern Software •

6. Move your cursor near the intersection of grid D and 11 (see the right side of Figure 7.8)

Notice that Revit tries to line up with various references inside the column. This is not necessarily a bad thing and you can leave them as is, but you will have to be more careful when placing columns to ensure that they center correctly. Alternatively, we can edit the column family and change the settings of these reference planes if you prefer (see the next topic). Also, please note that column 10 is missing in the dataset file.

REFERENCE PLANE "IS REFERENCE" SETTING

The "Is Reference" setting tells each reference plane in a family how to behave later in a project. There are several built in ones which help with orientation. They have names like Left, Right, Front, Back, Top and Bottom. If you imagine a box surrounding your family (bounding box), these are what Revit sees as the extreme edges. Think of the smallest box into which you could fit a basketball. That is the bounding box. If you set up two different families to (two doors for example) to have the named references like Right and Left, and then later swap one out with the other, things will swap out predictably. In other words, using the named Is Reference settings of Left, Right, Center, etc., ensures that alignments, orientations and dimensions in the project all behave predictably. So when you build family content, you should use these settings consistently if you want consistent project behavior (See Figure 7.9).

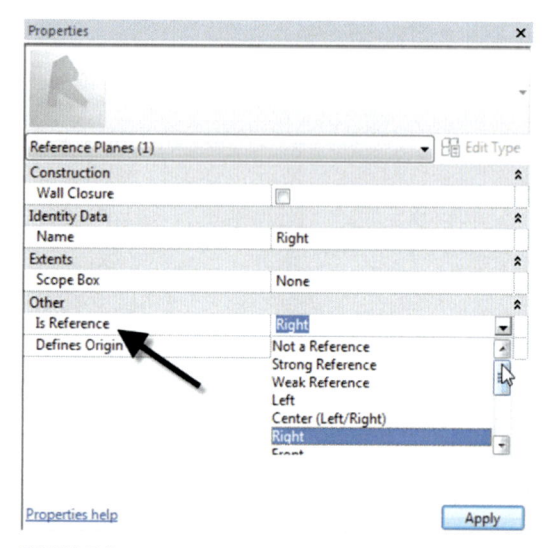

FIGURE 7.9

Consider the behavior of the Is Reference setting when building family content

The other aspect of the Is Reference setting is being able to control how "strong" a reference is. There are three settings that control this: Strong Reference, Weak Reference and Not a Reference. All of the names ones mentioned above (Right, Left, Center, Top, etc.) are also Strong References. A Strong Reference will be favored by Revit in the TAB order. Let's say you are dimensioning or using the align tool. If two reference planes are close together, and you highlight the object, the strong references will highlight first. When you press TAB, it will cycle to the weak noes next. A reference plane that is set to "Not a Reference" can still serve all of the normal functions in the family like driving geometry and attaching parameters. However, it will not be seen by dimensions or the align command in the project when the family is loaded.

The Is Reference setting for Instance Parameters also controls how the object will behave when the Align Command is used on the Reference in the family: Using the Align Command on a Reference that is set to Weak Reference with instance parameters constraining it, will move the component, to align the reference. Using the Align Command on a Reference that is set to Strong with instance parameters constraining it will try to change the values of the instance parameters themselves, to keep the family origin in the same place, while aligning the references.

You may want to consider this here. If you find it difficult to place columns with these extra strong references in the family, you can edit the family, select the reference planes on the four sides and set there Is Reference value to **Not a Reference**. When you load this back into the sandbox, you will find that it no longer tries to line up with other columns, only the grid lines.

Please consider this choice carefully however. The way that we currently have this family set up, we used the named references: Right, Left, Front and Back. This means that they are strong references and that if we swapped out another family that also used these, the orientation of the family and any attached dimensions would behave predictably when making the change. Now for a column, you might argue that most of the time it would stay square or round in shape, and so orientation is not too big a concern. You might also argue that dimensions would always be to the center line, so this is not a concern either. But remember that the align command also uses the Is Reference setting. Sometimes you might want to line something up with the face of the column. If you don't have a reference there, you will not be able to. So if you do not need the named ones (Right, Left, etc.) consider using a Weak Reference instead. In the case of our family here, we could change the four outer reference planes to weak references. These are ignored on placement, so it will be easier to snap to grid intersections when placing, and later we can still dimension and align to the weak references.

If you wish to experiment with this change, edit the Tuscan Column family. Open the plan view and select the Left, Right, Front and Back reference planes. On the Properties palette, set the Is Reference value to **Weak Reference**. Save the family and load it back into the project.

PLAN REGIONS

At the start of our explorations here in this chapter, we turned off the "Pre-cut" setting for the columns so that they would cut using the project's cut plane. This has yielded very nice graphics for all of the columns except the one on the far right. This column, (near grids C.9 and 17) uses a Base Diameter of 2.000 and a pedestal. With a Base Diameter of 2.000, the pedestal height is 4.200. The default cut plane in the Revit architectural template file is 4.000. So we are cutting through the pedestal in this location. To rectify this, we have a couple options. In some cases, you might be able to raise the cut of the plan itself (edit the View Range). But in some cases that might adversely affect other elements in the file. The other approach is to draw a plan region.

Continue in the *07_Sandbox_Colonnade.rvt* file or open the catch-up file *07_Sandbox_Colonnade_A.rvt* instead.

1. In the Level 1 floor plan view, zoom in on the area around column lines C/14 – C.9/17.
2. Select the free-standing column to the right of column line 17 and repeat the process of adding it to the grid intersections in this area (See Figure 7.10).

    Be sure that they go to Level 3.

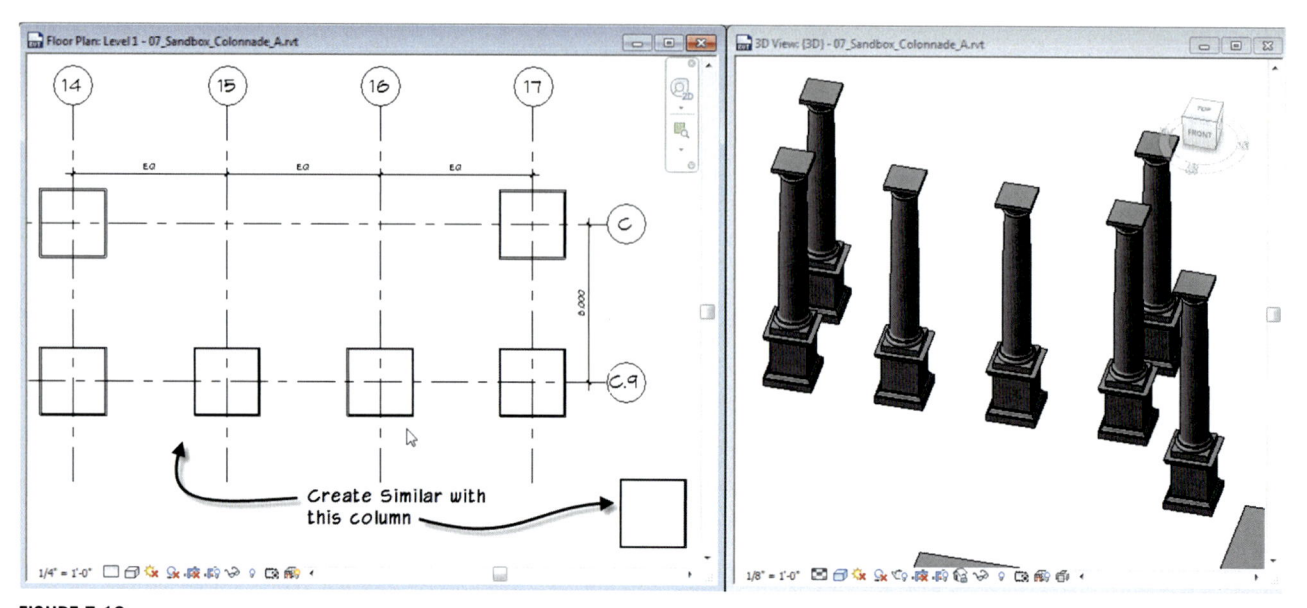

FIGURE 7.10

Add columns to the last area of grid lines

3. On the View tab, click the Plan Views drop-down and choose **Plan Region**.

   ⇨ On the Draw panel, choose the rectangle icon and then draw a rectangle big enough to surround all of the columns that you just added.

   ⇨ Click Finish Edit Model.

4. On the Modify | Plan Region tab, click the View Range button.

   ⇨ Set the Cut Plane Offset to **6.000** and then click OK (See Figure 7.11).

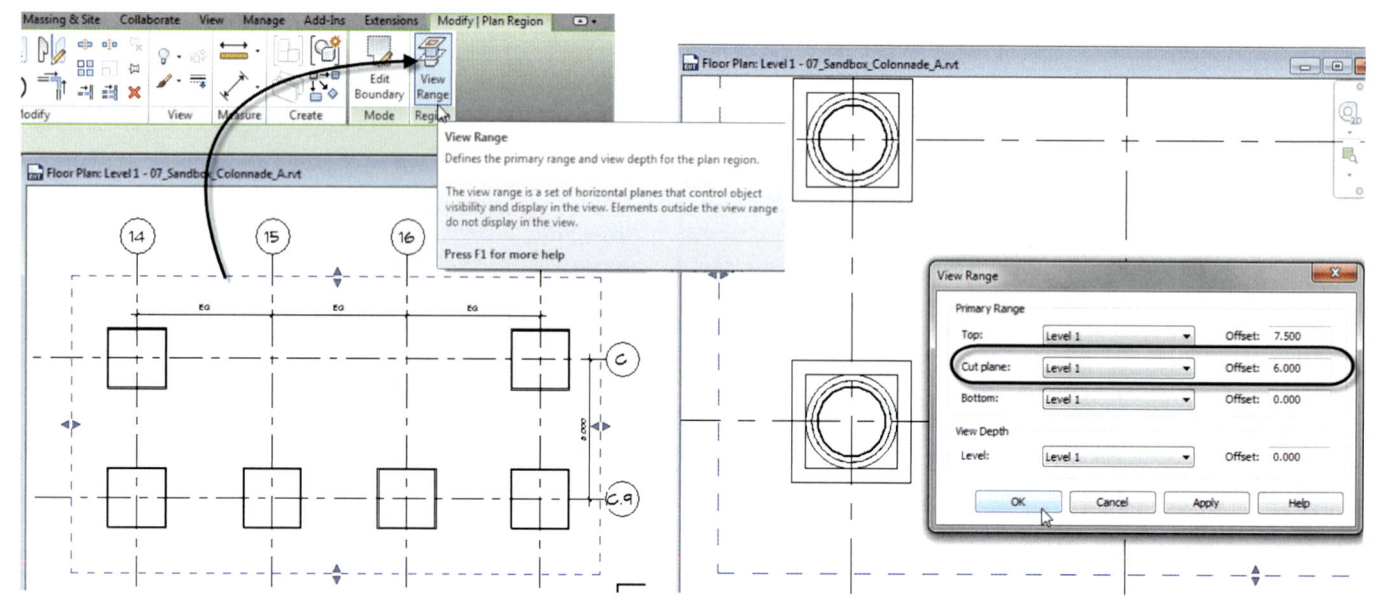

FIGURE 7.11

Create a plan region and edit its cut plane

Your columns should now be cut properly. You can actually create a plan region in any shape you like as long as it is an enclosed boundary. A single plan region can even contain more than one closed boundary. Just make sure they don't overlap each other. Not every category supports them equally, but you should be fine using them here for columns.

CATCH UP! You can open a file completed to this point named: *07_Sandbox_Colonnade_B.rvt*.

• Renaissance Revit •

PLACING BEAMS

Now that we have columns we can add the entablature above each colonnade. A copy of the custom beam family that we created in the previous chapter is already in this file. Like columns, the process to add beams is not complicated, but there are a few issues worth exploring.

Continue in the *07_Sandbox_Colonnade.rvt* file or open the catch-up file *07_Sandbox_Colonnade_B.rvt* instead.

⇨ Click the Restore Down icon at the top right corner (between minimize and close) (See Figure 7.12).

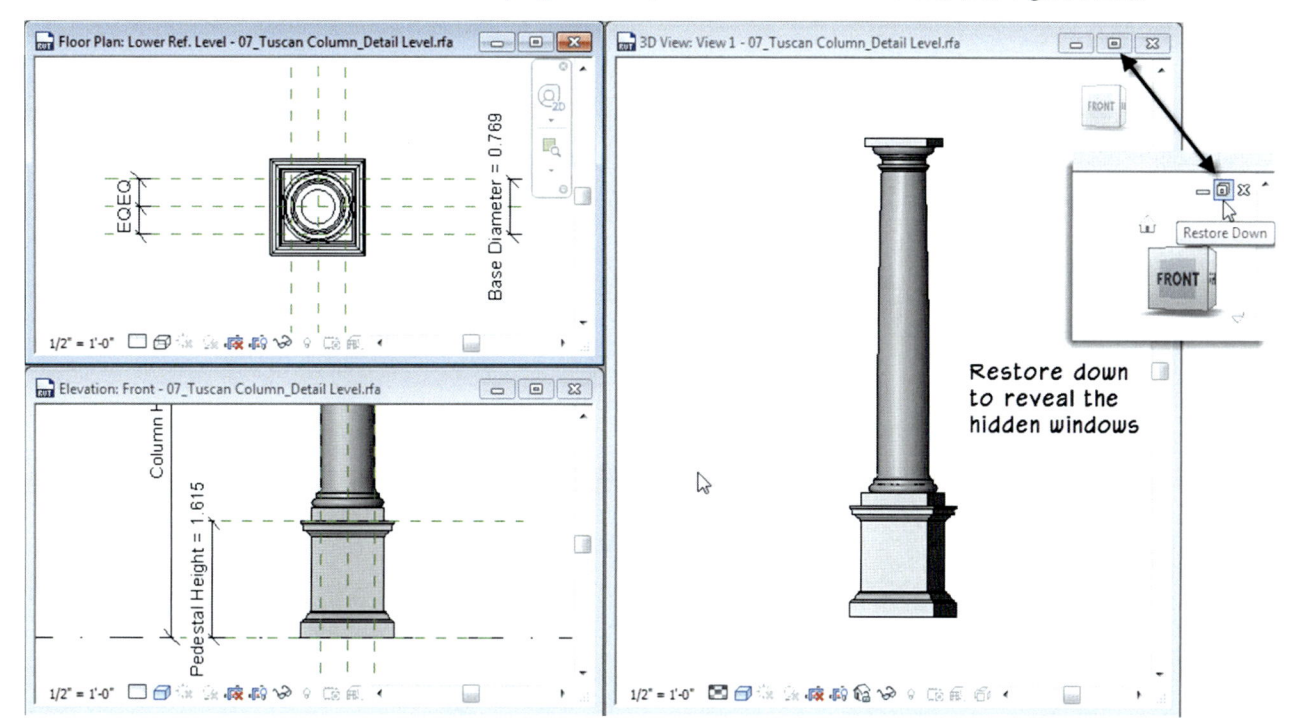

FIGURE 7.12

Restore down restores a previously saved tiled configuration

Most of the files in the dataset I have saved with more than one window open. When you first open them, they maximize the current window. If you tile the windows, it will not always restore them the same as how they were saved. Revit has some internal rules on how it tiles windows. If you want to preserve the way they were tiled when I saved them, use Restore Down instead. This will simply "un maximize" the window without retiling.

The first issue we encounter with beams is that they typically occur beneath the current level. The sandbox file has some beams in it already. However, you cannot see these in the *Level 1* floor plan view. The default view range for the architectural floor plan stops at zero. But if you look at the *Level 1* structural plan instead, you will see that the beams do display there. The default view range for the structural plan displays elements as low as -6.000. Therefore, to make our next task easier, I have provided three structural plans in the file.

1. On the Project Browser, beneath *Structural Plans*, double-click the *Level 3* view.

⇨ Zoom in on the area around column lines C/14 – C.9/17.

This is the area where we just modified the plan region above.

We built both our column and beam families to use the Base Diameter parameter to control the size and proportion. However, since they are two separate families there is no way to link these together in the project. So like the intercolumniation, we will have to do this manually. Recall that the columns in this area use a Base Diameter of 2.000. We need to make sure that we choose this size for our entablature.

2. On the Structure tab, click the Beam tool.

3. From the Type Selector on the Properties palette, choose **Tuscan Entablature : 2.000**.

   ⇨ For the first point, click the intersection of grid 14 and grid C.

   ⇨ For the next point, click the intersection of C.9 and 14, then C.9 and 17.

   ⇨ Click the final point at the intersection of C and 17 and then click the Modify tool to finish.

In the structural plan view, you will only see a single bold line. This is because the view is currently set to Coarse detail level. We will be discussing detail level below, so for now we will ignore this. If you look in the 3D view, none of the beams are mitered. We saw how to fix this in the previous chapter. Also as noted above, they are too low. There are a couple ways we can address this issue. Since we already covered it, let's fix the mitering first.

4. Following the procedure covered in the "Add the Entablature in a Sandbox File" topic in the previous chapter, miter the corners of the entablature beams (See Figure 7.13).

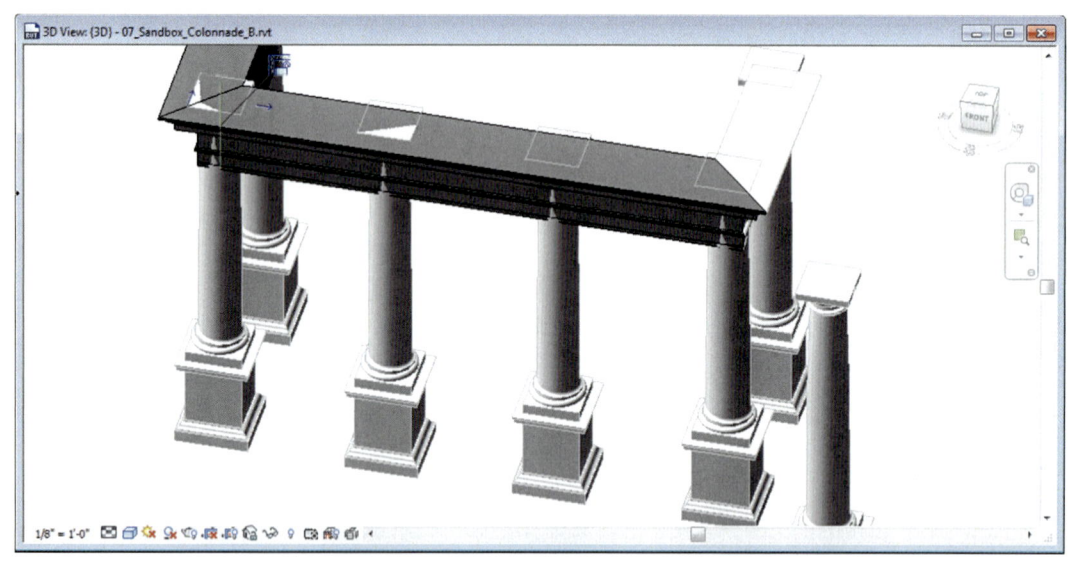

FIGURE 7.13
Miter the corners of the entablature beams

SHIFT THE Z JUSTIFICATION

Now let's address the height.

1. Select all three beams and on the Properties palette, for the z Justification, choose **Bottom** (See the left side of Figure 7.14).

FIGURE 7.14

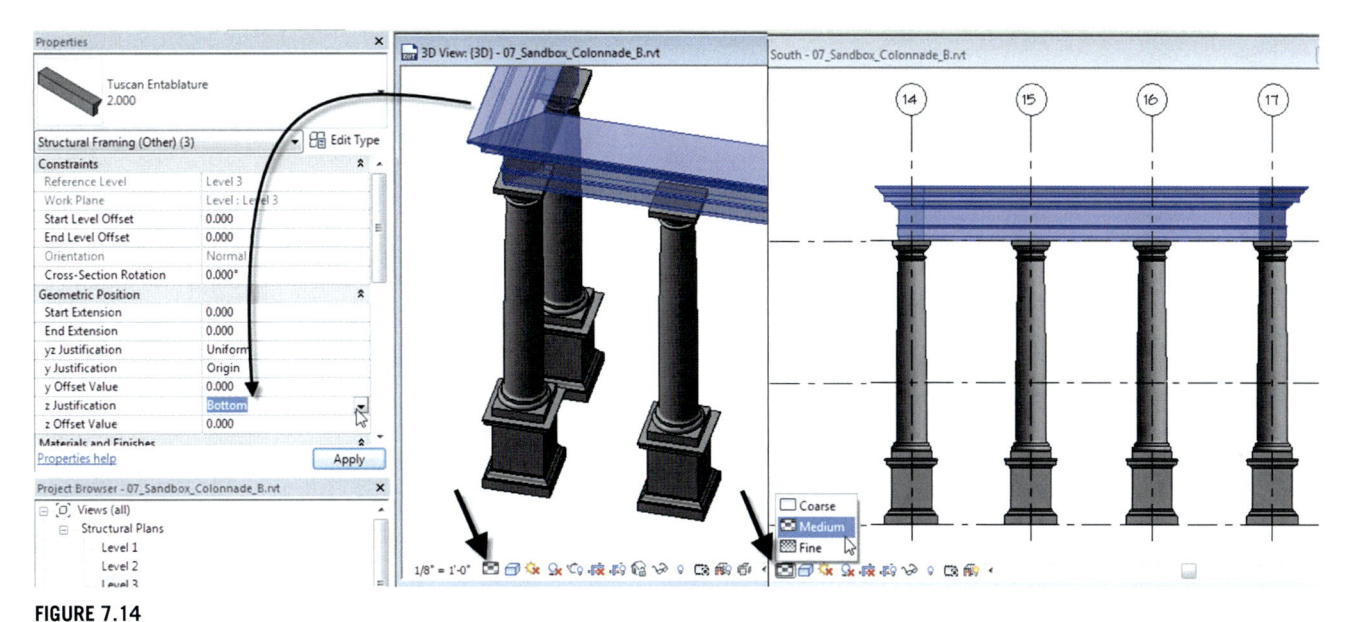

Change the z Justification to Bottom to shift the entablature up

If you are also looking at the elevation view, you will notice that like the structural plan, the elevation shows only a single thick line. This is because it is displaying Coarse level of detail. On the View Control Bar at the bottom corner of the elevation, you can click the small Detail Level pop-up and choose Medium to display the actual entablature geometry (See the right side of Figure 7.13).

Back in the structural plan view, you can adjust the ends of the entablature on the two short sides to project them past the centerlines of the columns along grid line C. Feel free to change to Medium detail in the structural plan as well.

2. Back in the *Level 3* structural plan view, place another set of beams on the next bay over to the left (grids C9 – D13).

⇨ Miter the corners.

3. Switch to the South elevation view and if you have not already done so, change the level of detail to **Medium**.

⇨ Zoom in on the area at grids 9 – 13.

4. Select one of the columns. On the Properties palette, take note of the Base Diameter (2.600 in this case) (See Figure 7.15).

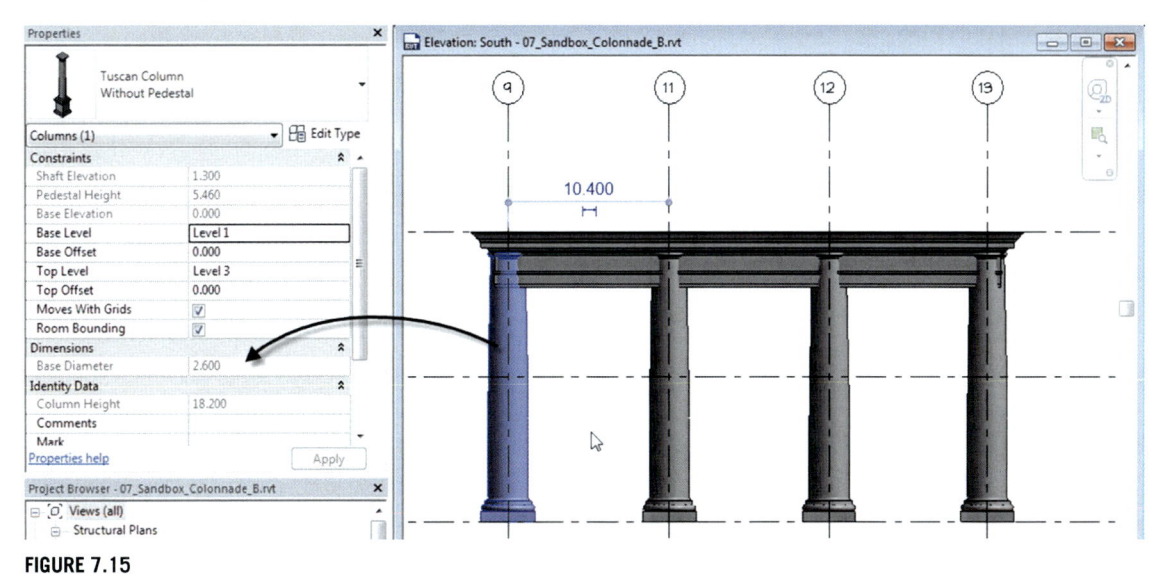

FIGURE 7.15

Use the Properties palette to query the Base Diameter

• Creating Classical Architecture with Modern Software •

5. Select the three beams in this view.

> **TIP:** Right-click one beam and choose **Select Joined Elements**. The Properties palette should report: Structural Framing (Other) (3).

6. On the Properties palette, click the Edit Type button.
   ⇨ In the "Type Properties" dialog, click the Duplicate button.
   ⇨ Name the new type: **2.600** and then click OK.
   ⇨ Change the Base Diameter to **2.600** and then click OK.
7. On the Properties palette, for the z Justification, choose **Bottom** (See Figure 7.16).

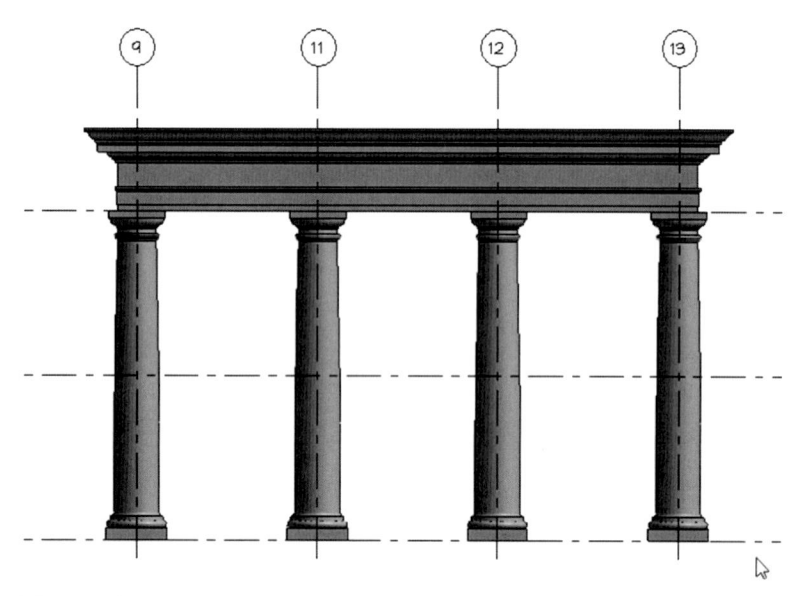

FIGURE 7.16
Create a new type for the entablature that matches the Base Diameter of the columns

If you want to add entablatures to the other two colonnades in this file, open the *Level 2* structural plan. Remember that the columns on that side are only one story tall so they do not display in Level 3.

USING COLUMN TOP OFFSET

It is possible that you may not be completely satisfied with changing the z Justification to shift the height of the entablature. There is an alternative. But it requires a little more calculation. Columns—like walls and other two-level elements—have a Base and Top Offset parameter. So as an alternative, you can calculate the required height of the entablature, subtract this from the column with the Top Offset and thereby leave the entablature justified to Top. This will place the top of the entablature at the level above which in some cases may be preferable. Let's look at a quick example.

> **CATCH UP!** You can open a file completed to this point named: *07_Sandbox_Colonnade_C.rvt*.

1. Close your version of the file. Save if prompted.
2. Open the catch-up file named: *07_Sandbox_Colonnade_C.rvt*.

This file has the Level 2 structural plan, the 3D view and the South elevation open. I added Entablatures to the colonnades on the left side by bay A1 – B4 and A5 – A.9, 8. The heights have not been adjusted yet. If you select a column on the first bay, you notice that its Base Diameter is 1.000 and they have a pedestal. The ones on the right do not have pedestals and I have attached them to a new level called Level 2.1 that I added to the file. Since the height of this level is 12.000, the columns have a Base Diameter of 1.714. I have already sized the two sets of entablature beams accordingly: on the left, a Base Diameter of 1.000 gives us an entablature height of 1.750. On the right, a Base Diameter of 1.714 yields a total entablature height of 2.999 (effectively 3.000). I included dimensions onscreen in the *South* elevation view.

3. In the *South* elevation view, select both of the columns on grid 1.

 ⇨ On the Properties palette, In the Top Offset field, type: **-1.750** and then apply it.

At first it will look as if this does the trick. The column perfectly fills the height beneath the entablature. However, on further inspection, we see that the Base Diameter is no longer 1.000. It is now smaller (See Figure 7.17).

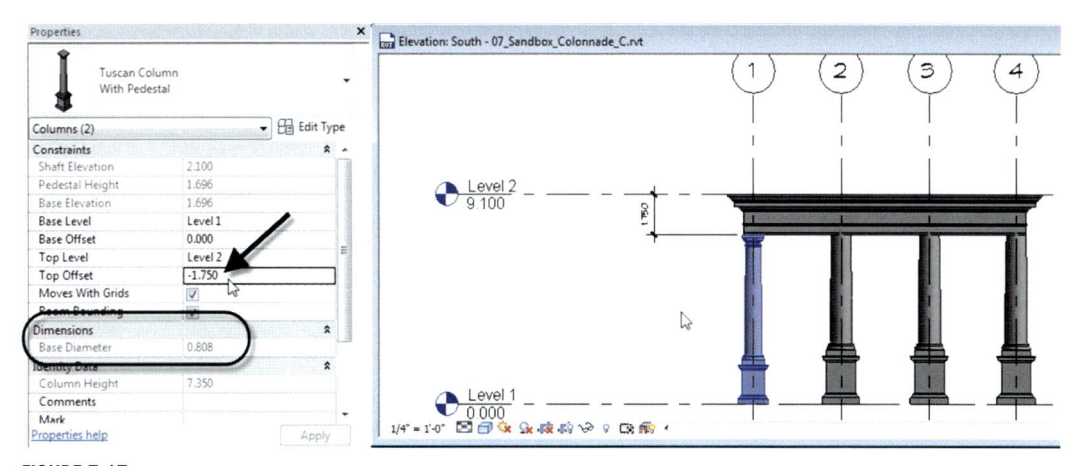

FIGURE 7.17

Adjust the Top Offset

This means that the entablature would have to get smaller and we could get stuck in a vicious circle. There are two approaches to the problem. The one you choose depends on if you know what you want your Base Diameter to be or if you know what you want the final height of the order to be instead. In both cases, we can do the math. Here are the key proportions needed (see Table 7.1):

TABLE 7.1

Component	Height
Column	7 Diameters
Pedestal	2.1 Diameters
Entablature	1.75 Diameters
Total Order w Pedestal	10.85 Diameters
Total Order w/o Pedestal	8.75 Diameters

4. Undo the previous edit (Top Offset).

Let's assume that you wanted to keep the Base Diameter at 1.000. Then according to the table, we would need the height between Level 1 and Level 2 to be 10.85.

5. Select Level 2 onscreen and change the height to: **10.85**.

6. Select all of the columns on grids 1 – 4 (6 total).

7. On the Properties palette, In the Top Offset field, type: **-1.750** and then apply it (See Figure 7.18).

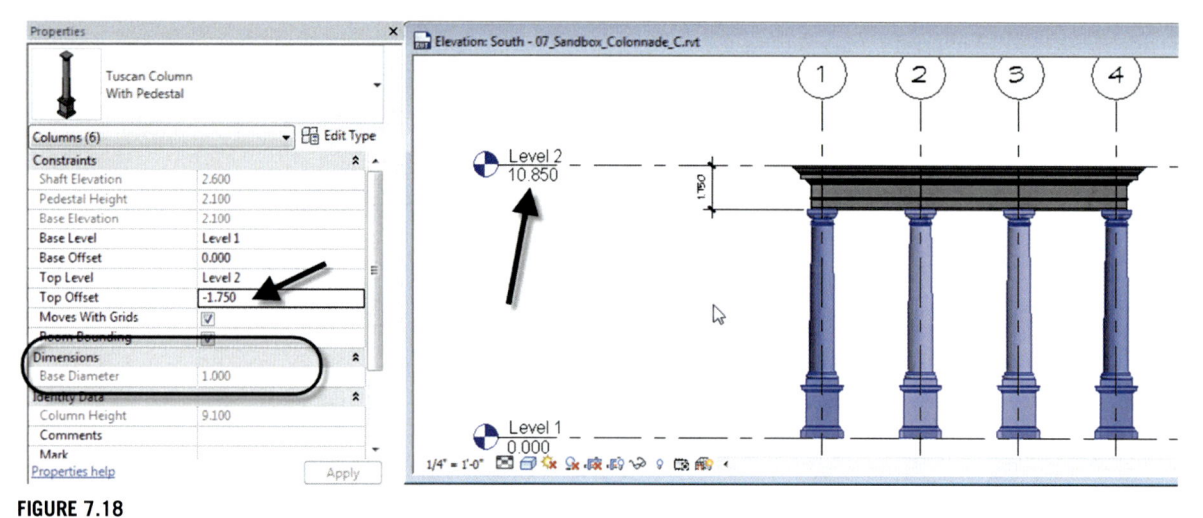

FIGURE 7.18

Change the height of Level 2 and then apply a top offset

Let's move to our final colonnade to the right at grids 5 – 8. As noted above, I have added a new level to the sandbox file here: Level 2.1. (Make sure you are in *07_Sandbox_Colonnade_C.rvt* or you won't have this level).

If you do not know the desired Base Diameter, but instead know the total height you want, you just perform slightly different calculations. In this case, let's assume we wanted to have the entire colonnade including its entablature at exactly the height of 12.000 (the height of Level 2.1).

On this example, the columns do not have pedestals. So we will use the value of 8.75 diameters multiplier from the table. Take 12.000, divide it by 8.75 which equals 1.371. This is our Base Diameter. We customize the entablature type with this value. Then we multiply this by 1.75 diameters (the height of the entablature) or 2.4. This is the Top Offset for the columns. Select a column and look at the Properties palette to verify. If the Base Diameter equals 1.371, we did the calculation correctly.

8. Right-click the entablature at grids 5 – 8 and choose **Select Joined Elements**. (It should select three elements).

   ⇨ On the Properties palette, click Edit Type. Rename the type to: **1.371** and then click OK.

   ⇨ Edit the Base Diameter to **1.371** and then click OK again.

9. Select all of the columns on grids 5 – 8 (6 total).

10. On the Properties palette, In the Top Offset field, type: **-2.400** and then apply it (See Figure 7.19).

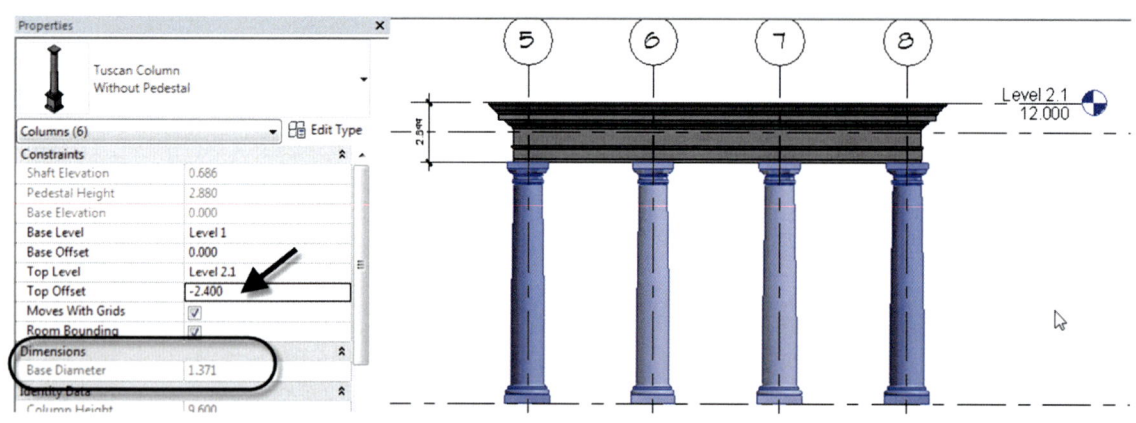

FIGURE 7.19

With a fixed height target, use the height and the entablature proportion to figure out the Base Diameter

We have looked a few approaches to using our column and beam families effectively to create a proper layout of columns and their entablatures. In both cases, some calculations are required, but most of the heavy lifting is done by the families themselves with the rules and formulas we built in over the last several chapters.

> CATCH UP! You can open a file completed to this point named: *07_Sandbox_Colonnade_D.rvt*.

ALTERNATE APPROACHES FOR ENTABLATURE

In the previous chapter, we created the entablature family as a beam. As you can see from the examples here, a beam works very effectively for this purpose. However, there are other possibilities. I am not going to do an exhaustive study of them, but I would like to share two possibilities using some provided files.

Both approaches rely on a single overall profile. When building the beam family in the previous chapter, we combined several of our previously created profile shapes; one for each molding to create the overall entablature. The other approach we could have done was to create a single profile family for the entire shape including all of its moldings. It is a much more complex profile that takes more time to construct, troubleshoot and flex. I am not going to go through the detailed steps used to create it. All of the techniques I used are covered in the previous chapters and I have provided the file in the *Chapter07* folder for you to open and study.

WALL SWEEPS

The steps that I will detail here are the use of the provided profile as both a wall sweep. Both of these objects behave much like sweeps inside the family editor. As such, they provide potential alternatives to the use of a beam family.

1. Close any files you have open. Save if prompted.
2. Open the provided sandbox file named: *07_Sandbox_Sweeps.rvt*.

This file is similar to the others. The entablature beams have been removed. Some levels have been added.

3. The *Level 2* floor plan should be open, make this the active view. (Open it if necessary).
4. On the Architecture tab, click the Wall button.
   ⇨ On the Properties palette, verify that the wall type is Generic - 8".
   ⇨ Set the Top Constraint to **Up to Level: Level 2.1**.
5. In the Level 2 floor plan, click the first point at the intersection of grids A and 1.
   ⇨ Continue to B/1, then B/4 and end at A/4. Click the Modify tool to finish (See Figure 7.20).

194 | Chapter 7

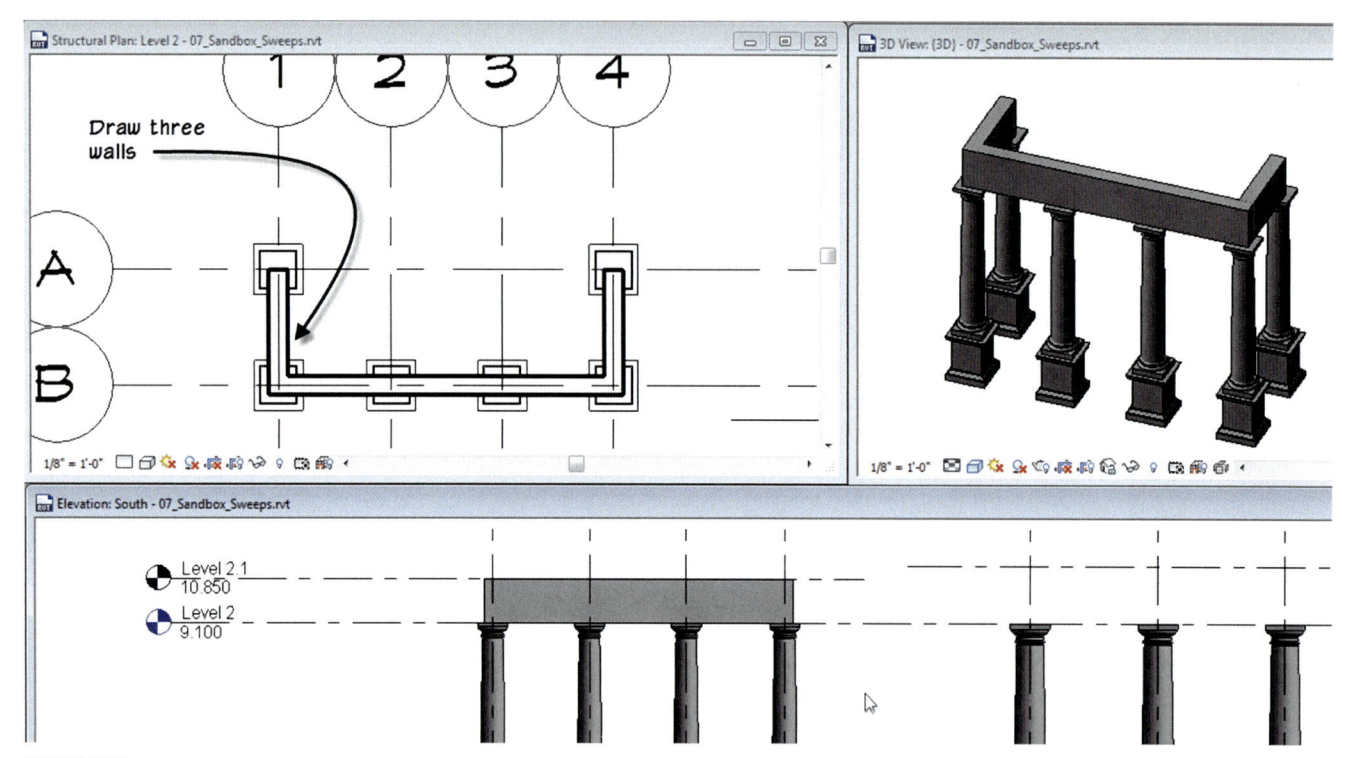

FIGURE 7.20

Add Walls where the entablature needs to go

6. On the Insert tab, click the Load Family button.

  ⇨ Browse to the Chapter07 folder, choose the *Tuscan Entablature Profile.rfa* file and then click Open.

7. Select all three walls.

8. On the Properties palette, click the Edit Type button.

  ⇨ In the "Type Properties" dialog, click the Duplicate button.

  ⇨ Name the new Type **Tuscan Entablature 1.000** and then click OK.

9. Click the Edit button next to Structure.

  ⇨ At the bottom right corner of the dialog, click the Preview button.

  ⇨ Next to the Preview button, click the drop-down next to View and choose **Section:Modify Type Attributes**.

When you turn on the preview and set it to a section view, the "Modify Vertical Structure" buttons at the bottom right become enabled. You cannot use these button unless you are looking at a section preview (See Figure 7.21).

• Renaissance Revit •

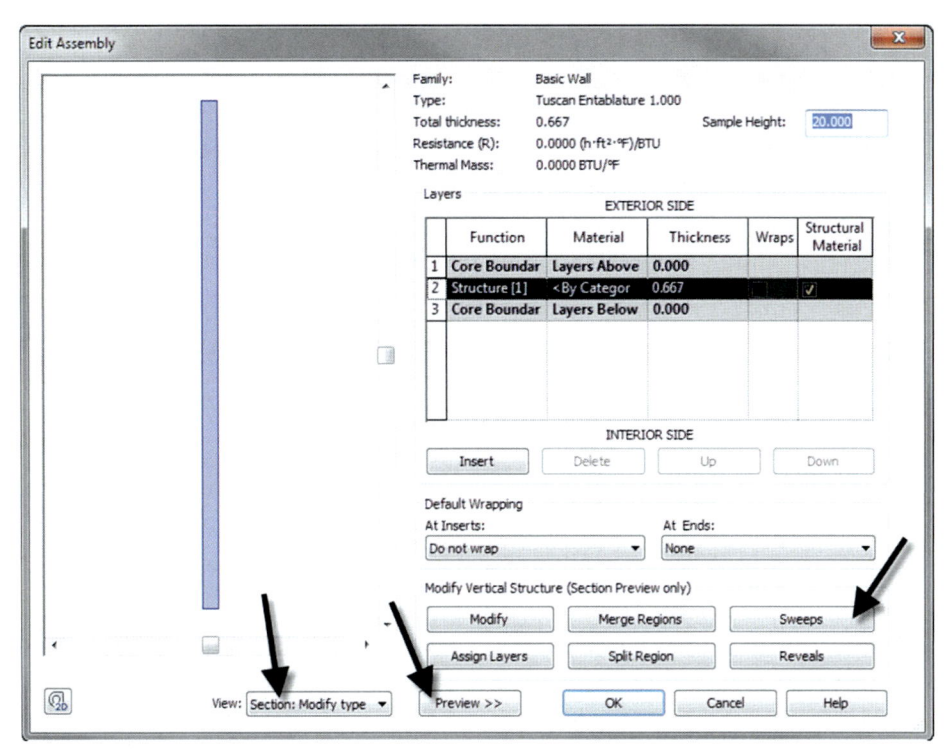

FIGURE 7.21

Edit the wall structure and turn on the preview to edit sweeps

10. Click the Sweeps button.

11. In the "Wall Sweeps" dialog, click the Add button.

⇨ For the Profile, choose **Tuscan Entablature Profile: Flex**.

⇨ For the Offset, type: **-0.250** and then click OK three times to see the result.

If your molding is on the inside, keep the walls selected and then tap the SPACEBAR to flip them.

I included this quick tutorial just to show an alternative. There are plenty of challenges to this approach. Wall sweeps require a decent amount of trial and error to get the settings correct. Even the -0.250 offset I used here is really a guess and very close but not completely correct. If you wanted to use this approach for the other colonnades with Base Diameters at different sizes, you would need to create multiple types for both the profile family, and the wall to which it is applied. Each one would need to be built at a very specific size and proportion which limits their usefulness. Building the profile is also very complex and took quite a few attempts to finally get it flexing properly.

On the up side, as you can see these moldings miter on their own since they are part of the walls. And they are categorized as walls, which in some instances might be desirable. If you like the wall sweep idea, but not the multiple wall types required if they are integral to the wall types, you can instead use the Wall :Sweep tool on the Wall drop-down button. The same profile can be used to create one of these sweeps. I like these a little better actually because they can be placed on any wall and they can have their own subcategory. This is helpful when you want to control their visibility. Furthermore, sweeps created with the Wall: Sweep tool can appear on their own schedules. It might not be critical for entablatures, but certainly helpful for other kinds of moldings like wall base, crown molding, wainscot, etc. A word of caution about wall sweeps, on large projects with lots of sweeps, performance can suffer and automatic joining fail if there are many sweeps. So this can be another factor in your decision on the approach to use.

SLAB EDGES

Another similar approach is to use a Slab Edge. Slab edges are very similar to wall sweeps. They use profiles and sweep the shape along the edges that you pick. While named "slab edge," they are not actually limited to just slabs. A very useful feature of slab edges is that you can apply them to model lines. So you can draw model lines to create the path you wish the slab edge to follow, then when building the slab edge, pick the model lines.

Some setup is required first. On the Project Browser, expand *Families > Profiles > Tuscan Entablature Profile* and then duplicate the existing type. Name it to match the size of the column you are using (for example 1.300). Edit the Base Diameter in this type to match. Beneath *Floors > Slab Edge*, do the same and duplicate the existing type. Assign it to the profile you just created. You are now ready to add the slab edge.

Start in a floor plan such as *Level 2* and draw model lines along the column grid lines. These are the path of the swept slab edge. Since they are model lines, they will also appear in 3D. From the Floor drop-down button, choose Slab Edge. Click each of the model lines (See Figure 7.22).

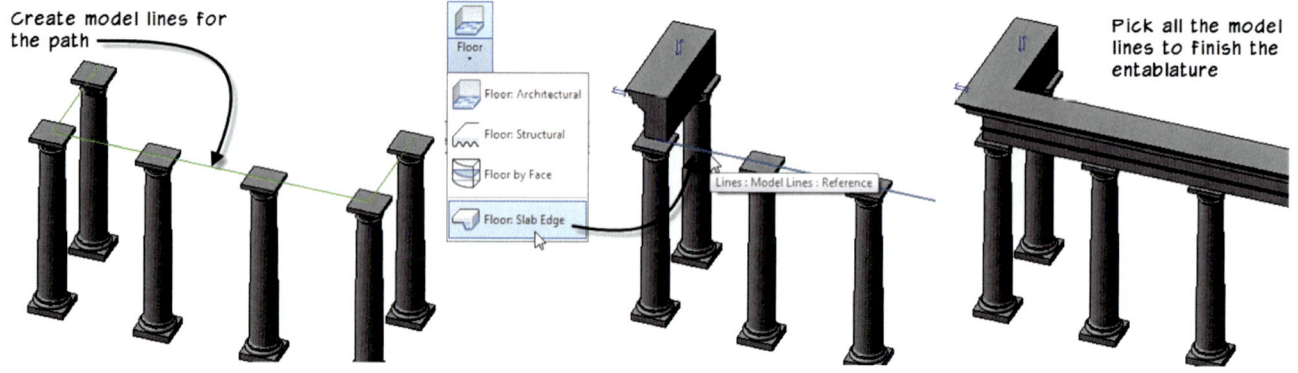

FIGURE 7.22
A slab edge can be applied to a model line, making it a compelling alternative

As you can see in the figure, the slab edges will also miter automatically. They do require a model line path, but if the path changes, the slab edge will change with it. Otherwise, they share some of the same limitations of wall sweeps, for example you need a new type for each size.

Ultimately I wanted to show you some alternatives, but I tend to prefer the beam option overall. I like that a beam is a component (loadable) family. So I get the same level of control that I do with columns. It is true that there is no relationship between the column and beam families, but this is also true with wall sweeps and slab edges, and so it is not a factor in the decision. You are encouraged to try each of the approaches we have discussed to see for yourself which you prefer.

CATCH UP! You can open a file completed to this point named: *07_Sandbox_Sweeps_A.rvt*.

WORKING WITH LEVELS OF DETAIL

In one of the earlier topics in the chapter we saw that the beams we were using for the entablature displayed as a single bold line in plans and elevations that were set to coarse level of detail. Revit has three levels of detail display built-in to the system. System families like walls, roofs, floors and ceilings use two of these detail levels. When you have a view set to course, these layered host elements show only their outline as determined by the total thickness of their layers. When you switch the view to either Medium or Fine, all of the internal layers display complete with any materials that are assigned to them. This allows the same elements to be displayed effectively at small and large scales alike.

Component families like doors, windows, fixtures, equipment and columns and beams also have this ability. The trouble is that in order to utilize it, the person building the family has to build it with level of detail in mind. In other words, if the author of a component family does not add the appropriate settings to take advantage of level of detail, the geometry in the family will display the same way regardless of which detail level; coarse, medium or fine, happens to be active. This is a shame because so many common building elements need to display at multiple scales and would surely benefit from the detail level feature. A good example provided in the out-of-the-box Revit content is the structural steel families. They utilize all three levels of detail (See Figure 7.23).

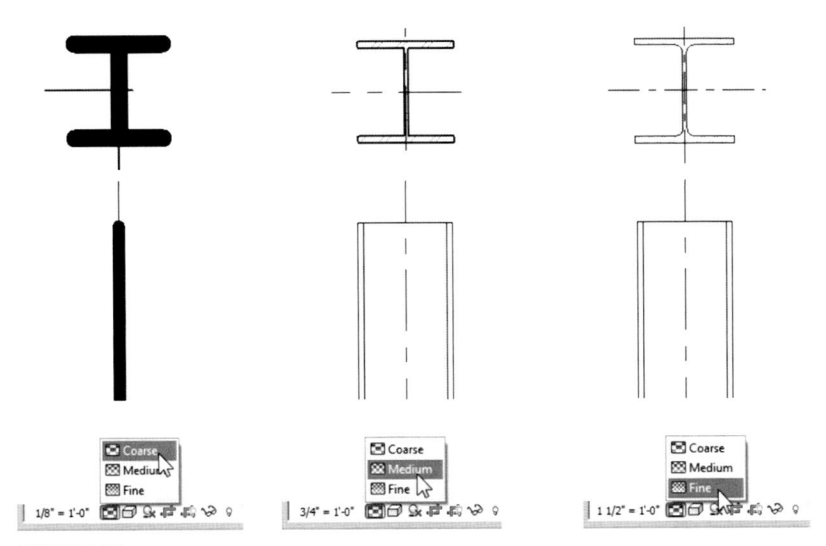

FIGURE 7.23
Out-of-the-box steel families use three levels of detail

Adding level of detail is as simple as editing the visibility settings of each element in the Family Editor and choosing among the three levels of detail, when it should display. Sometimes it is appropriate for the same element to display in all three or just two levels of detail. Sometimes it is better to create elements that only display in a single detail level. Consider a typical door family. You may want to include moldings and trim. You may also want to include hardware. It is likely that you would not want to show the hardware all of the time, so perhaps it might be configured to only display when the view is set to fine. The moldings on the other hand might display in both medium and fine, but not coarse. Sometimes, the elements themselves need to look different in each detail level. This is what we see with the steel pictured above. In small scales, when coarse is active, we see only a single thick line. In medium we see an actual solid object, but the extrusion uses only 90° corners. In fine detail, a different extrusion displays that has rounded corners.

I think that one of the most important things you can do in any family you create is contemplate how it should display differently at different scales and try to build this behavior into the family using level of detail. It does add some work to the creation process, but it is not hard to do. The benefits of doing so can make the difference sometimes between a highly effective piece of content which can be used in many circumstances to one that is mediocre and limited in its usefulness.

We have much of what we need already from the families and pieces we have been compiling throughout the last several chapters. Let's take a few minutes to assemble some of them now and implement detail levels in our column and beam families.

1. Close any files you currently have open. Save if prompted.
2. In the *Chapter07* folder, open the file named: *07_Tuscan Column_Detail Level.rfa*.

This file is a copy of the column we have been using. We can introduce level of detail here in more than one way. One approach would be to edit each of the nested families and add a coarse detail and possibly a medium detail version of the geometry to each one. For example, a box or simple cylinder in place of the more detailed moldings and forms. To keep things a bit simpler and considering that we built a nearly complete schematic version in Chapter 3, we will just nest this entire family into the current one instead.

3. Click in the Lower Ref. Level floor plan view to make it active.

4. On the Create tab, click the Component button.

⇨ On the Modify | Place Component tab, click the Load Family button.

⇨ Browse to the *Chapter07* folder and open *Tuscan Column Schematic.rfa*.

⇨ Click off to the side to place it next to the column (do not place it centered yet).

⇨ Click the Modify tool to cancel the command.

This is a copy of the schematic column that we built in Chapter 3. It is nearly identical except that I made the shaft round and have added a schematic pedestal to it. I have configured the pedestal in the same way that we did in the "Creating Optional Items" topic in Chapter 6. In other words, there are two types here: One turns on the pedestal and adjusts the position and scale of the other elements. The other that we currently have onscreen shows the column without a pedestal.

5. Select the instance of the Tuscan Column Schematic onscreen.

⇨ From the Type Selector, choose **Tuscan Column Schematic : With Pedestal** (See Figure 7.24).

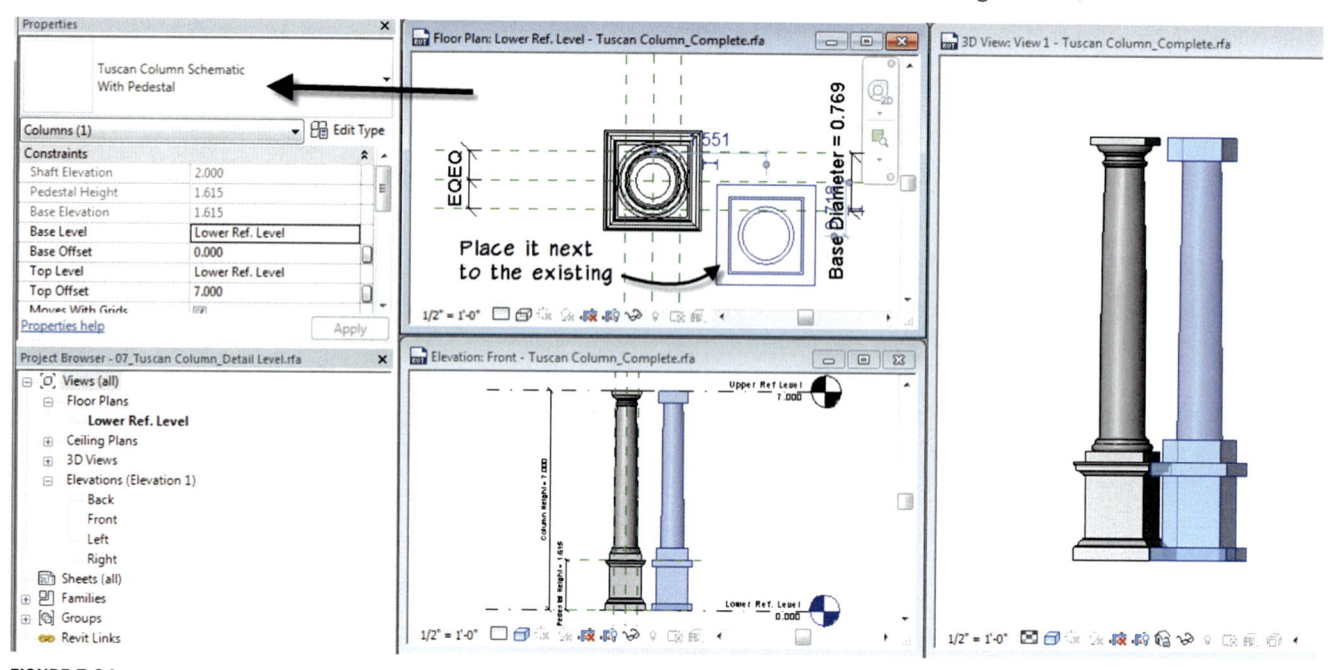

FIGURE 7.24

Place an instance of the schematic column with pedestal in the file next to the existing

Revit sometimes makes some interesting assumptions. If you still have the schematic column selected, take notice of the Base and Top Level settings. Both have been set to Lower Ref. Level. The Top Offset is set to 7.000 which is giving this instance its height. (This is visible in the figure). The way this is currently configured, the nested column will not flex its height with the host family. So we need to link up the height of the nested family with the host. We have two ways we can do this. Next to Top Offset field, there is an Associate Family Parameter button. So we could use this to associate the height of the host family and make it drive this Top Offset parameter. The other option is to change the Top Level setting and zero out the Top Offset. I like this option best, but frankly either one will work perfectly fine. So the choice is yours.

6. With the schematic column still selected, change the Top Level to Upper Ref. Level.
   ⇨ Set the Top Offset to **0** (zero).

The next thing we need to do is set the host family to drive the behavior of the pedestal. The nested family currently has two types like the host. We could actually use a <Family Types> parameter to choose between these two. We will explore <Family Types> parameters in a later chapter. For now, we will actually drive the Show Pedestal parameter directly instead.

7. On the Project Browser, expand *Families > Columns > Tuscan Column Schematic.*
   ⇨ Right-click on *Without Pedestal* and choose **Delete**.
   ⇨ Right-click on *With Pedestal* and choose **Type Properties**.
   ⇨ Click the Rename button, type **Flex** and then click OK.
   ⇨ Click the Associate Family Parameter button next to Show Pedestal and link it up with the **Show Pedestal** parameter in the host family. Click OK to dismiss the dialog.

To test that everything is working correctly, you can select the Upper Ref. Level and change its height. Both columns should resize accordingly. Open "Family Types" and switch between *With Pedestal* and *Without Pedestal* clicking Apply after each. The pedestal should disappear in the schematic version when it does in the host. (You may have to reset the value of the checkbox on these types. They sometime reset when you link up the parameter in the previous steps). Remember the one in the host will only gray out; it won't actually disappear until we use it in a project. Be sure to set the height of the levels back to 7.000 and display the *With Pedestal* type before continuing.

The last step is to assign the visibility settings. For this example, we are only going to use two variations. The schematic version will be displayed in views set to coarse and we'll use the more detailed geometry in medium and fine. This seems appropriate for the Tuscan Order. Later in the book when we build the other orders, we can consider using three levels of detail.

8. Select the schematic column.
   ⇨ On the Modify | Columns tab, click the Visibility Settings button.
   ⇨ Under Detail Levels, uncheck Medium and Fine and then click OK (See Figure 7.25).

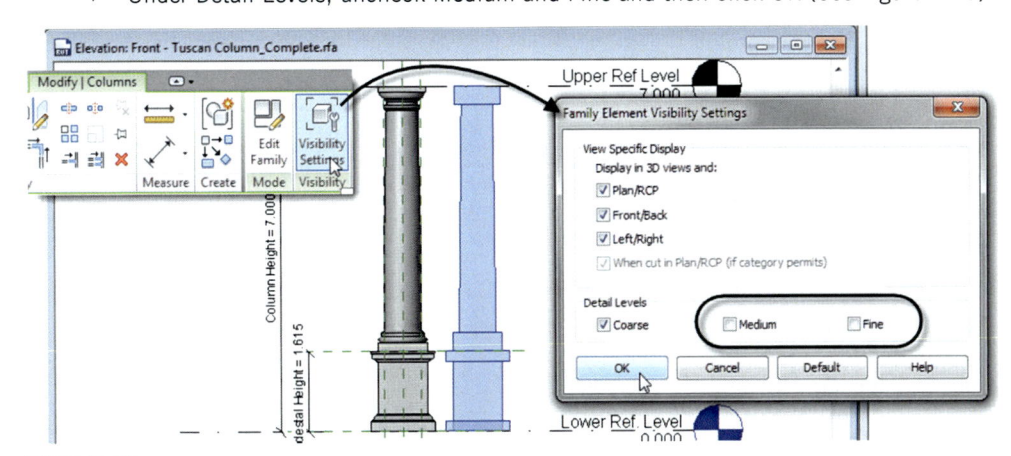

FIGURE 7.25

Turn off the display of the element in higher levels of detail

9. In the 3D view, select all elements except the schematic column.

• *Creating Classical Architecture with Modern Software* •

⇨ Click Visibility Settings again and this time uncheck only Coarse and then click OK.

When you are done making these changes, they will appear to have no effect onscreen. Changes like this are very subtle in the family editor. If you make an element invisible in the family editor, it will turn gray if it is solid geometry like an extrusion or sweep. If it is a nested component family like these items, they will not change. You will have to load it into a project to see the results. We will do this soon enough, but let's make a few more edits first.

OTHER DETAIL LEVELS AND SCHEMATIC LINES

The Tuscan Order is simple enough that we really only need two levels of detail: simple and complex. Later when we explore Ionic and Corinthian, we will have more reason to consider three levels of detail. For example, we can approach coarse detail similar to how we have done here: simple bounding box type forms. For medium detail, we might look at breaking up the form into the major bands and moldings, but keep their shapes simple, like chamfered lines instead of curves. Finally for fine detail we can do all the moldings accurately with all of their compound curves. We will see some examples of this in Chapters 11, 12 and 13.

Another common technique that is used to manage level of detail and performance is to actually hide the 3D geometry in plan views and sometimes even in certain elevation views or for certain elements in those views. For example, instead of showing a 3D form for the column that is actually cut, we can instead draw a square and circle using Symbolic Lines. The Symbolic Line tool is on the Annotate tab. Lines drawn with this tool display only in views parallel to the plan or elevation in which they were originally drawn. You can see examples of this in the out-of-the-box door and window families. The door panel and plan swing for the doors and the diagonal dashed chevron swing indication in elevation are drawn with symbolic lines. If you look at a 3D view of such families, none of these elements displays.

Using symbolic lines in place of the 3D graphics in plan view would also provide an alternative to the approach we took in the "Plan Regions" topic above. There we had to raise the cut plane in order to see the column display the way we wanted. If we had hidden the 3D forms in plan, and added symbolic lines to the family instead, we could have a static plan representation that would display in any plan view regardless of cut plane. While we will not get into the details of this technique now, but later in Chapter 14 we'll look at a technique similar to this to create a light weight 2D version of the fully detailed Corinthian capital.

MATERIALS

Before we finalize this family and load it back into our sandbox, let's add one last enhancement. If you are like me, you might find the medium gray shading a little bit dull. Let's add some materials to the family. You can add materials to both the schematic and detailed geometry if you like. To keep things simple, I will only add it to the detailed elements here. If you like, you can follow the same procedures to add materials to the schematic version too.

You can add materials directly to the solid forms. This is appropriate if the item's material is known and will not need to change. However a more flexible way to do it is to add a material parameter. This will make it possible for the materials to be changed from the project. This is how we will do it here.

1. Select the pedestal family onscreen.

    ⇨ On the ribbon, click the Edit Family button.

    The family will open to its 3D view.

2. Select all of the 3D forms onscreen.

> **Note:** If the family has voids, you cannot select everything with window select. Select with the CTRL key instead.

- On the Properties palette, click the Associate Family Parameter button next to Material.
- In the "Associate Family Parameter" dialog, click the Add parameter button.
- Name the new parameter: **Pedestal Material** and accept the remaining defaults (See Figure 7.26).

> TIP: Select the name of the parameter "Pedestal Material" and press CTRL + C to copy the name to the clipboard. We will need to create another parameter with this name in the next step and this will speed the typing. There you can press CTRL + V instead of typing again.

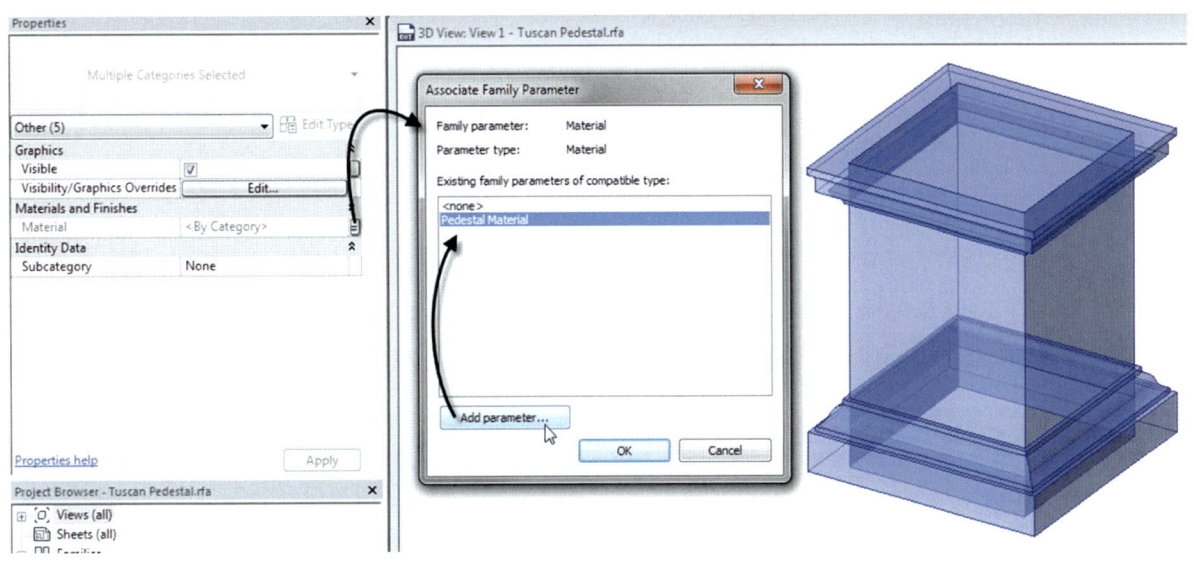

FIGURE 7.26
Add a new material parameter and associate it to the material setting for the 3D forms

Like other associated family parameters, the material field will now be grayed out and an equal sign will appear on the button. You can save the pedestal file separately if you like, or simply load it back into the host family without saving separately.

3. On the ribbon, click the Load into Project button.
   - If you have any other families open, choose only *07_Tuscan Column_Detail Level.rfa* in the dialog that appears.
   - Overwrite the existing version.
4. Select the pedestal onscreen again.
   - On the Properties palette, click the Edit Type button.
5. Next to Pedestal Material, click the Associate Family Parameter button.
   - Repeat the process above and add a new parameter also named: **Pedestal Material**. (If you followed the tip, press CTRL + V to paste the name).
   - Click OK to finish the process.
   - Switch to the Pedestal family and then from the Application menu, choose **Close**.

This process has created a material parameter in the nested family and then another one in the host family to drive it. We will now be able to change the material of the pedestal in the project using the Pedestal Material parameter. To add materials to the other components, repeat the entire process.

• *Creating Classical Architecture with Modern Software* •

6. Select the Base component next and repeat the entire process.

7. Repeat again for the Shaft and Capital. If you wish you can also repeat for the schematic family.

We now have material parameters for all four pieces of the column. Like the level of detail, we have to wait till we load into a project to properly test them. One final step and then we are ready to load it.

8. Using the align tool, align and lock the schematic column to the center reference planes in both directions.

9. Save the file and then close it.

> **CATCH UP!** You can open a file completed to this point named: *Tuscan Column_Complete.rfa*.

TEST THE COMPLETED TUSCAN COLUMN

The Tuscan Column with is new graphical properties and materials is now ready to test in a project. Let's re-open a sandbox file and try it out.

1. Open the *07_Sandbox_Colonnade_D.rvt* file.

   As before the file was saved with multiple open windows; restore down to see the tiled configuration.

2. On the Project Browser, expand *Families > Columns*.

   ⇨ Right-click on Tuscan Column and choose **Reload**.

   ⇨ Browse to the *Chapter07* folder, choose *Tuscan Column_Complete.rfa* and then click Open.

We have seen this dialog many times before. In most cases, we have been working only with geometric changes which are carried over with either choice. The second option refers specifically to type properties. If you change the values of one of the types in the family that already exists in the host, the second option replaces that type's values. We do not have that situation here. Keep in mind that new types that do not already exist in the host file are *always* brought in regardless of the choice you make in this dialog. The "parameter values" option only applies to types that already exist. In this case, either option should yield the same results this time.

3. Click Overwrite the existing version.

You should see a slight change in the *Level 1* plan view. You will not see any apparent change in the *South* elevation or 3D view. This is because the plan is the only view set to coarse, the other views are currently set to medium detail. Let's test out our coarse detail settings in elevation and 3D.

4. In each open view, click the Detail Level pop-up and choose **Coarse** (See Figure 7.27).

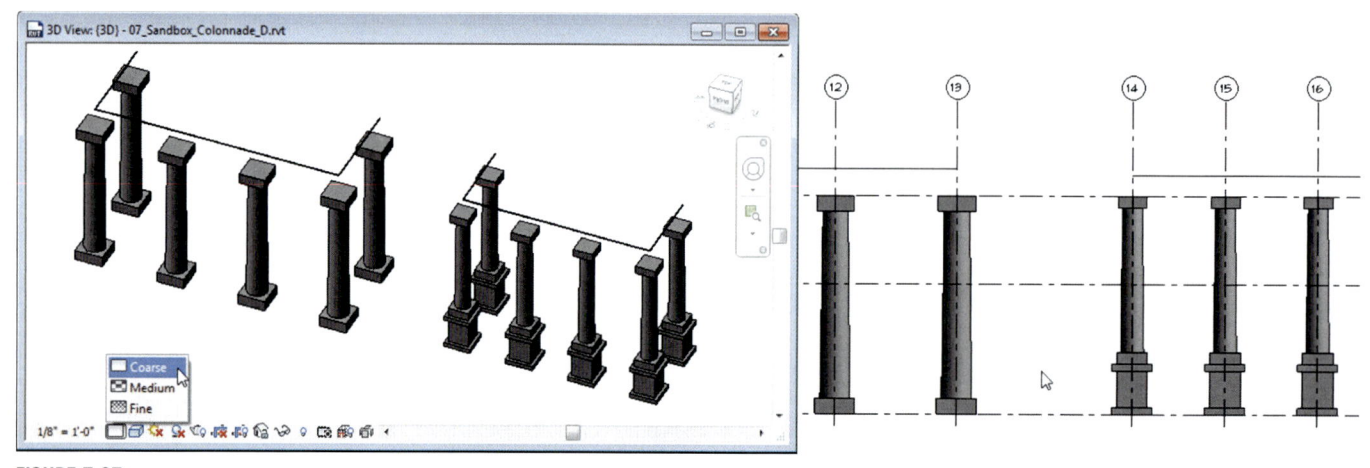

FIGURE 7.27

Set the views to coarse level of detail

• Renaissance Revit •

As you can see, the schematic version of the columns is now displaying. Notice also that the entablature has changed back to single lines. We will have to adjust that as well. This is the default way that coarse is used for structural members but we can modify it.

5. Continue to experiment with the three detail levels in all views. Reset to **Medium** in all three views when finished.

Now let's test the materials.

6. On the Manage tab, click the Materials button.

7. In the search field at the top, type: **stone**.

The material list will show only the materials that contain or are categorized as stone. The project list at the top will be empty as a consequence. But the library list at the bottom left will show several stone and concrete materials (See Figure 7.28). If you don't have access to the Autodesk materials, choose any other material you like.

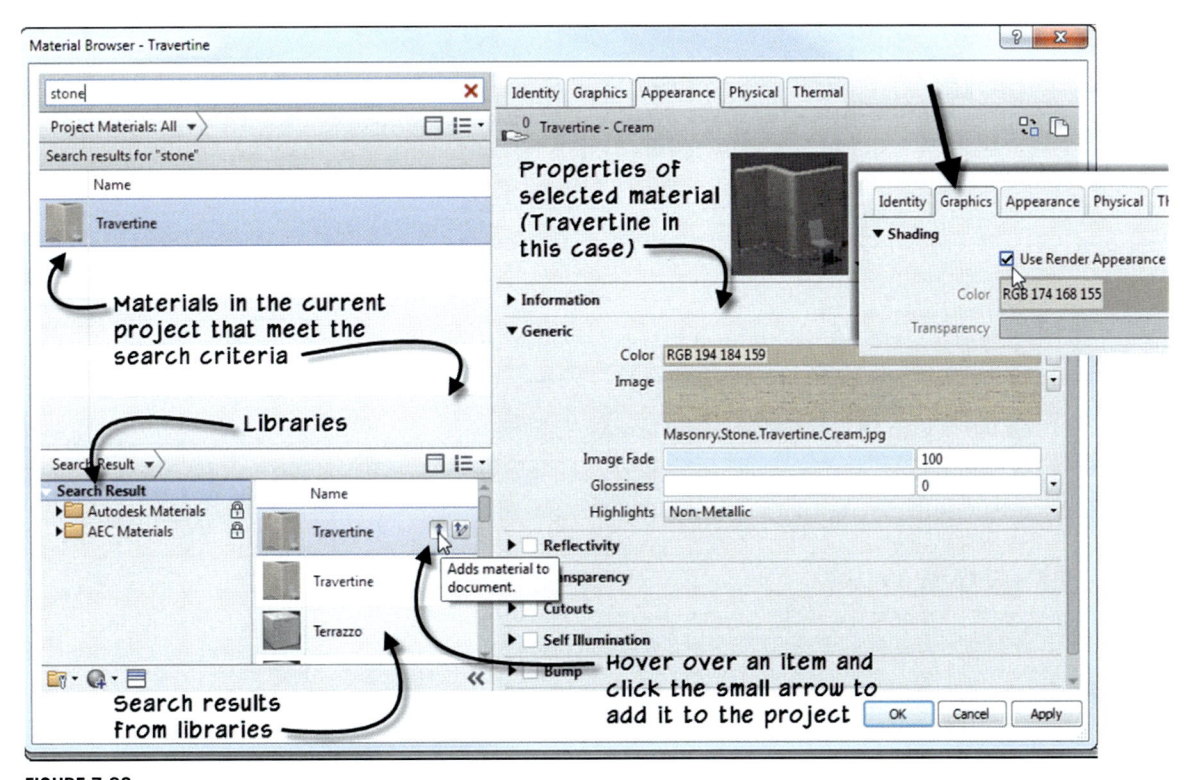

FIGURE 7.28

Search for "stone" materials to add to our project

When you hover over an item in the library list, a small "up" arrow will appear (shown in the figure). Click this arrow to add the material to the current project file.

8. Add Travertine to the current project. Add any other materials you like as well.

9. Select one of your newly imported materials on the left and then on the right side, click the Graphics tab.

   ⇨ Check the "Use Render Appearance" checkbox. Repeat for each material you imported (See the inset in Figure 7.28).

Most materials have a bitmap image used in their Appearance settings. It might be a photograph of the stone or the bricks you are using. This image file is repeated across the surface of the material when you render. The "Use Render Appearance" setting takes an average of the colors used in the bitmap and determines a matching color for material's shading properties. The color is visible when we shade the view like the elevation and 3D views in this file. So some of the stone materials will still appear as shades of gray in those views. If you choose realistic shading instead, you will see the actual bitmap image file instead of the averaged color. In that case, all of the materials should yield results more interesting than our default dull gray.

10. Click OK to dismiss the "Material Browser" dialog.

11. Select any column onscreen.

    ⇨ On the Properties palette, click the Edit Type button.

    ⇨ Choose a material for the Shaft Material parameter and then click OK (See Figure 7.29).

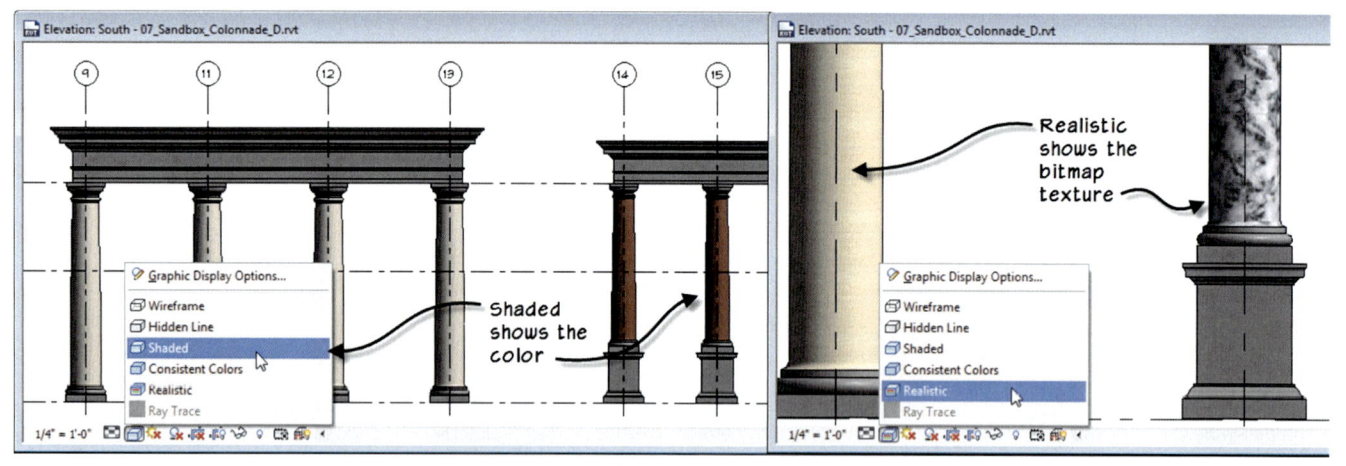

FIGURE 7.29

After applying a material study in shaded and realistic views

12. Using the Visual Style pop-up, choose either Shaded or Realistic to see the results.

If you like, you can add materials to the other components as well. Remember, these are type properties, so you will have to set materials for both the "With Pedestal" and "Without Pedestal" types. If you want to have two versions of either type that use different materials, create another type.

CUSTOMIZE THE ENTABLATURE

Our Tuscan Order is nearly complete. We only need to add a coarse detail version of the geometry and apply a material parameter.

Continue in the sandbox file.

1. Select the entablature beam near grid 1.

2. On the ribbon, click Edit Family.

   The *View 1* 3D view will open.

3. Select the Extrusion (the box) onscreen.

   ⇨ On the Modify I Extrusion tab, click the Copy to Clipboard button (or press CTRL + C).

4. On the Project Browser, expand *Floor Plans* and then double-click to open *Ref. Level*.

   ⇨ On the Modify tab, click the drop-down on the Paste button and choose **Aligned to Same Place**.

The item will remain selected displaying it shape handle grips at the ends. Take note of the two reference planes at these locations. The original is locked to these reference planes. We need this copy to also be locked to these reference planes. You can use align for this or drag these grips. To make sure we don't lose this selection let's isolate it.

5. Hold down the CTRL key and then click the two reference planes at the ends of the selected extrusion.

The Properties palette should say Common (3).

⇨ On the View Control Bar, click the Temporary Hide/Isolate pop-up (sunglasses) and choose **Isolate Element** (See Figure 7.30).

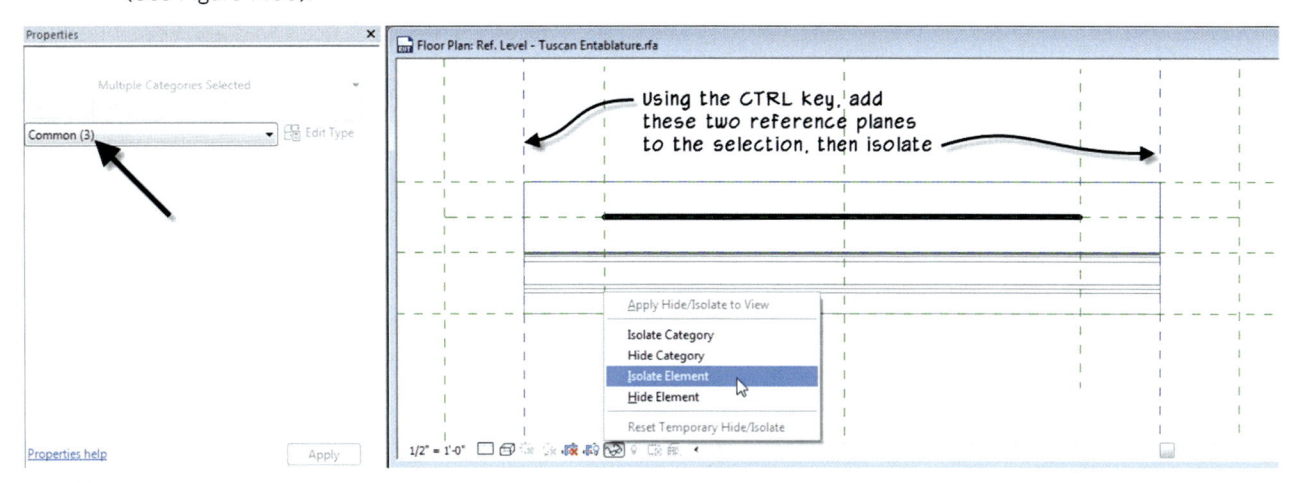

FIGURE 7.30

Isolate the 3 selected elements

6. Using the align tool, align and lock the ends of the extrusion to the reference planes at each end. Click the Modify tool when finished.

7. Select the extrusion again.

⇨ On the ribbon, click the Visibility Settings button.

⇨ For Detail Levels, check Coarse, then uncheck Medium and Fine.

8. On the ribbon, click the Edit Extrusion button.

⇨ In the "Go To View" dialog that appears, choose **Elevation : Left** and then click Open View.

9. Draw a 45° line from the upper right corner back to the sketch (See the left side of Figure 7.31).

⇨ On the angular dimension that appears, click the Make this dimension permanent icon and then lock it (See the middle of Figure 7.31).

You have to first deselect the sketch line, then click the dimension to lock it. The lock may be some distance away, so zoom if necessary.

⇨ Use the Trim/Extend to Corner tool to clean up the sketch (See the right side of Figure 7.31).

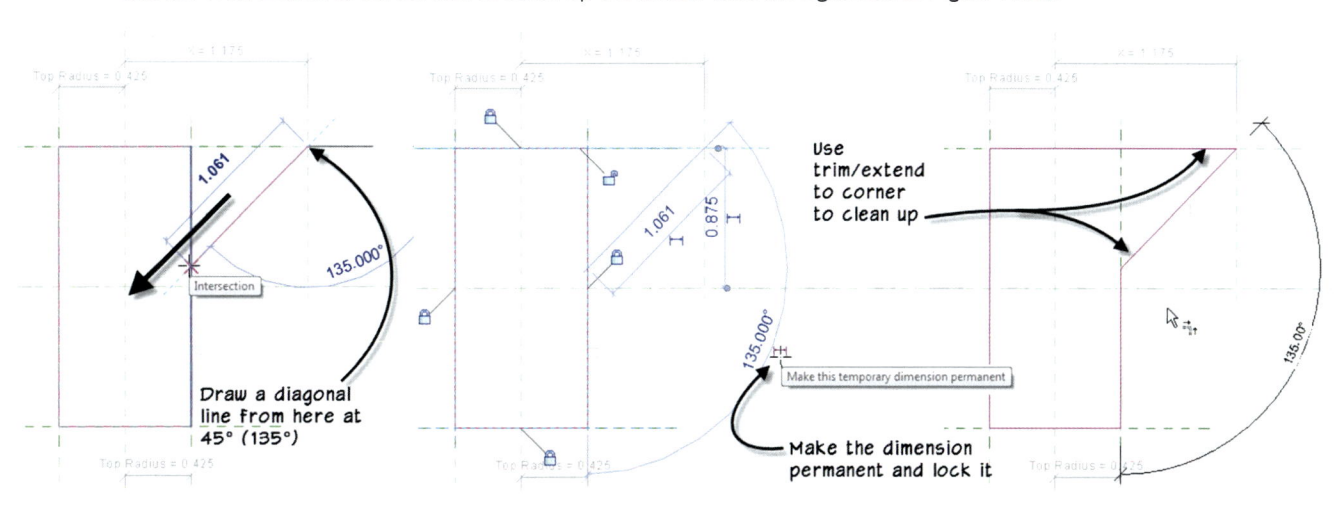

FIGURE 7.31

Modify the sketch to add a 45° extension on the front as a coarse detail representation of the moldings

I am keeping the coarse scale version very simple. If you want to modify the sketch further to more closely approximate the major features of the entablature, you can add more sketch lines. Just be careful not to make it too detailed, as it will no longer serve the purpose of being a coarse scale representation. The other issue is to be careful not to sketch something that requires many new reference planes and dimensions to flex properly. The one I have drawn here relies on the existing reference planes and should flex properly. Let's find out. We don't even have to leave the sketch to see.

10. Open the "Family Types" dialog.

    ⇨ Flex the Base Diameter parameter.

It appears that I spoke too soon. Notice that the sketch is not adjusting. The issue it turns out is that this extrusion, which we inherited from the *Structural Framing - Beams and Braces.rft* family template back in the previous chapter, has its own reference planes internal to the sketch. Recall in the "Layout the Entablature Extents" topic in Chapter 6 we aligned and locked these internal reference planes to the ones we created. Like the length of the extrusion above, when you copy and paste, you lose these alignments. Therefore, we have to repeat that process here.

11. Align and lock each of the four reference planes inside the sketch to the ones outside the sketch.

    You have to do this carefully. The ones outside the sketch are slightly grayed out. These should be picked first as the alignment reference. The ones in the sketch are not grayed out. They should be clicked second. Use the TAB key as necessary to select the correct item each time. Be sure to align reference plane to reference plane; no *not* align the sketch lines.

12. Also align and lock the endpoints of the 45° corner to the reference planes.

13. Open "Family Types" and flex again.

    Everything should be working correctly now. Return the Base Diameter to **1.000** before exiting.

14. Click the Finish Edit Mode button.

15. In the 3D view, use the TAB key and cycle the selection until you see Joined Solid Geometry on the tooltip and Status Bar.

    ⇨ Click to select the Joined Solid Geometry.

16. Repeat the process above in the "Materials" topic to create a new **Entablature Material**.

17. Load the file into the project and overwrite the existing.

18. Edit the Type Properties of the Entablature items and add materials.

19. Change the Detail Level to coarse and study the results (see Figure 7.32).

Feel free to experiment further. After several chapters of exploration, we are finished with the Tuscan Order. In the next chapter we move on to the Doric Order.

> **CATCH UP!** You can open a file completed to this point named: *Tuscan Order_Complete.rvt*.

Managing Graphics | 207

FIGURE 7.32

Test out the modified entablature in the project file

• *Creating Classical Architecture with Modern Software* •

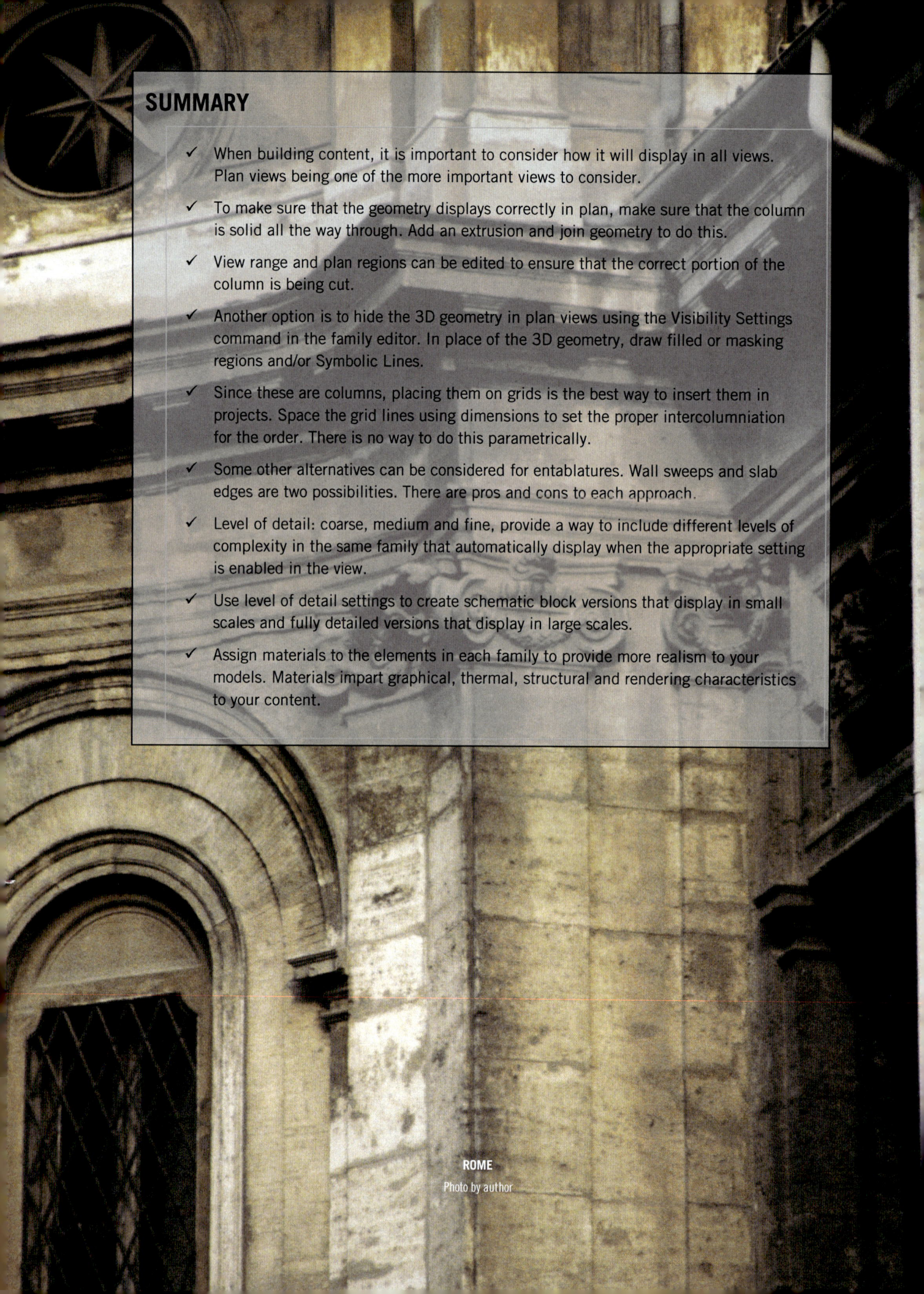

SUMMARY

- ✓ When building content, it is important to consider how it will display in all views. Plan views being one of the more important views to consider.

- ✓ To make sure that the geometry displays correctly in plan, make sure that the column is solid all the way through. Add an extrusion and join geometry to do this.

- ✓ View range and plan regions can be edited to ensure that the correct portion of the column is being cut.

- ✓ Another option is to hide the 3D geometry in plan views using the Visibility Settings command in the family editor. In place of the 3D geometry, draw filled or masking regions and/or Symbolic Lines.

- ✓ Since these are columns, placing them on grids is the best way to insert them in projects. Space the grid lines using dimensions to set the proper intercolumniation for the order. There is no way to do this parametrically.

- ✓ Some other alternatives can be considered for entablatures. Wall sweeps and slab edges are two possibilities. There are pros and cons to each approach.

- ✓ Level of detail: coarse, medium and fine, provide a way to include different levels of complexity in the same family that automatically display when the appropriate setting is enabled in the view.

- ✓ Use level of detail settings to create schematic block versions that display in small scales and fully detailed versions that display in large scales.

- ✓ Assign materials to the elements in each family to provide more realism to your models. Materials impart graphical, thermal, structural and rendering characteristics to your content.

ROME
Photo by author

Chapter 8
The Doric Column

INTRODUCTION

In this and the next chapter, we will consider the Doric Order. The Doric is quite beautiful and one of my favorites. I love the proportions of this order, and its understated complexity masked in what at first appears to be a very simple order. Particularly when expressed with a non-fluted shaft like the ones used in one of my favorite renaissance buildings: Bramante's Tempietto. If one considers only the column, it is only slightly more complex than the Tuscan. In fact, the Tuscan Order that we have spent the last several chapters building will become the seed for our Doric Order. This is fitting as the Tuscan is in many ways just a simplified version of the Doric. But the real complexity of the Doric is in its entablature and it's very tightly regulated proportions. Small details like the triglyphs and metopes must adhere to very specific proportions or it throws off the look of the entire order.

OBJECTIVES

Beginning with copies of our Tuscan Order families, we will construct an idealized Doric Order complete with column and entablature. Topics in this chapter include:

- Creation of the Schematic version of the Doric Order.
- Creation of the components of the column family.
- Building the entablature of the Doric Order.
- Explore an alternative approach to intercolumniation for the Doric Order.

INTRODUCTION TO THE DORIC ORDER

The Doric column is traditionally eight diameters tall. Like the Tuscan, the capital and base are each half a diameter leaving seven diameters for the shaft. The pedestal (when used) is slightly less than one third the height of the column at 2.4 diameters according to Chitham (Chitham 1985, 2005, 62). Palladio has it closer to 2.35 (Palladio 1965, 17-18), but I have gone with Chitham's dimensions for the most part. The entablature is one fourth the height of the column at 2 diameters. Despite these proportions, what actually controls the look and overall proportion of the Doric order is the triglyphs and metopes. Triglyphs are carved protrusions that have a series of chamfered channels. They are oriented vertically and repeat at a regular interval along the frieze of the entablature. They must line up with the centerlines of the columns. In between each triglyph is a metope. A metope is the space between triglyphs and can be left unadorned or embellished with carvings or relief. The proper shape of a metope is square. So the appearance is a vertically oriented rectangle, square, rectangle, etc. These repeat along the length of the frieze. This tightly controlled proportion means that only certain intercolumniations will work for the Doric Order. While the upcoming Ionic and Corinthian provide the most challenging modeling exercises, mastering the Doric proportions is something that is ideally suited to the parametric toolset available to us in Revit.

CREATE THE SCHEMATIC DORIC

Let's begin the Doric similarly to how we began the Tuscan: with a schematic version. We could certainly build the entire order from scratch, but so much of the work we did in the Tuscan order can be reused here, that it makes the most sense to start with the Tuscan files and resave them.

1. From the Application menu, choose **Open > Project**.
    - Browse to the *Chapter07* folder, select the *Tuscan Order_Complete.rvt* file and then click Open.

    We are starting with the file from last chapter.

2. From the Application menu, choose **Save As > Project**.
    - Browse to the *Chapter08* folder and name it **Doric Order Sandbox**.
    - Tile the windows (or simply click the Restore Down button).

RENAME ALL NESTED FAMILIES

Let's start be renaming the two families in this file.

1. On the Project Browser, expand *Families > Columns*.
    - Right-click *Tuscan Column_Complete*, and choose **Rename** (or select it and press F2).
    - Change the name to: **Doric Column**.
2. Beneath *Structural Framing*, rename *Tuscan Entablature* to **Doric Entablature**.

For the columns, the type names of "With Pedestal" and "Without Pedestal" will remain appropriate. For the entablature, we will likely need to rename the types. However, since the names are based on the sizes, we will postpone this till we have a gone further with the modifications.

3. On the Project Browser, right-click *Doric Column* and choose **Edit**.
4. Expand the *Families* branch of the Project Browser.
    - Rename all "Tuscan" families to **Doric**. (Five total, one Column, four Generic Models).

> **TIP:** to speed renaming, select the family to rename, press F2. Double-click on the word Tuscan; this will select it. Type **Doric**. Double-click on Doric, press CTRL + C to copy it to the clipboard. Move to the next item, F2, then double-click Tuscan, press CTRL + V. Repeat.

5. On the Project Browser, right-click *Doric Column Schematic* and choose **Edit**.
    - Rename all "Tuscan" families to **Doric** (Four Generic Models total) (see Figure 8.1).

• Renaissance Revit •

FIGURE 8.1

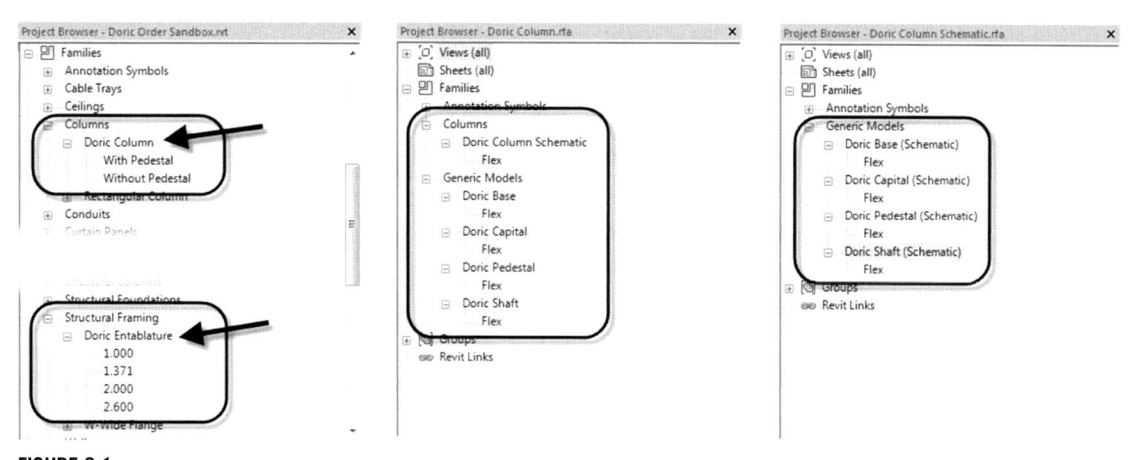

Rename all of the Tuscan families to Doric

ADJUST THE PROPORTIONS OF THE NESTED FAMILIES

The schematic family that we have onscreen is very close to what we need for the Doric, but a few of the proportions require adjustment. So we'll have to go one level deeper into the nested families. Let's start with the capital and work down.

1. On the Project Browser, right-click *Doric Capital (Schematic)* and choose **Edit**.

2. Open the "Family Types" dialog.

3. Change the Formula for both Width and Depth to: **Base Diameter * 1.300** and then click OK.

   The box will grow slightly.

> **Note:** I often like to save copies of all the sub-families as separate RFA files. This is considered best practice by many, but is technically not required. We could simply load into project, overwrite the existing and then come back and close the file without saving. In the steps that follow, I am only going to list the "Load into Project" step. If you wish to save a copy of the RFA file, then at each such step, also go to the Application menu, choose **Save As > Family** and save a copy in the current folder preserving the original name. If you prefer to omit this step, you can simply switch windows back to the family file after loading and close it without saving. The choice is up to you.

4. On the ribbon, click Load into Project.

   ⇨ In the "Load Into Projects" dialog, choose only the *Doric Column Schematic* file and then click OK.

   ⇨ Overwrite the existing version.

> **CATCH UP!** The completed file is in the *Chapter08* folder named: *Doric Capital (Schematic).rfa*.

   Remember to switch windows back to the capital file and close it before continuing.

5. On the Project Browser, right-click *Doric Shaft (Schematic)* and choose **Edit**.

6. Open the "Family Types" dialog.

7. Change the Formula for Height to: **Base Diameter * 7.000** and then click OK.

   The cylinder will grow slightly taller.

8. On the ribbon, click Load into Project.

   ⇨ In the "Load Into Projects" dialog, choose only the *Doric Column Schematic* file and then click OK.

• Creating Classical Architecture with Modern Software •

212 | Chapter 8

> ⇨ Overwrite the existing version.

The capital is currently too low and the shaft is penetrating through it. We'll adjust this shortly.

> **CATCH UP!** The completed file is in the *Chapter08* folder named: *Doric Shaft (Schematic).rfa*.

The Doric Base (Schematic) is next. However, it requires no adjustment. The base of all the orders occupies the same bounding box. So we can leave this family as is. We'll adjust its location below. That leaves the pedestal.

> Remember to switch windows back to the *Shaft* file and close it before continuing.

9. On the Project Browser, right-click *Doric Pedestal (Schematic)* and choose **Edit**.

10. Open the "Family Types" dialog.

11. Change the Formula for Height to: **Base Diameter * 2.400** and then click Apply.

> The Die will grow slightly taller.

12. Change the Formula for Y1 to: **Base Diameter * 0.710**.

13. Change the Formula for Y2 to: **Base Diameter * 0.300** and then click OK.

When we develop the detailed version of the pedestal, you will see that there is an attic base that is half a diameter in height. Atop this is a cyma reversa and cavetto molding forming roughly a 45° taper back to the pedestal die. The die on the Doric is a square in elevation. So I struggled a little in deciding what to do here. I have ultimately decided to add together the height of the cyma reversa molding and the attic base at 0.710. I also considered adding another sweep at a 45° chamfer instead to more closely represent the form. Feel free to experiment if you wish.

14. On the ribbon, click Load into Project.

> ⇨ In the "Load Into Projects" dialog, choose only the *Doric Column Schematic* file and then click OK.

> ⇨ Overwrite the existing version.

> **CATCH UP!** The completed file is in the *Chapter08* folder named: *Doric Pedestal (Schematic).rfa*.

The pedestal increases in height, but the other components did not adjust (see Figure 8.2).

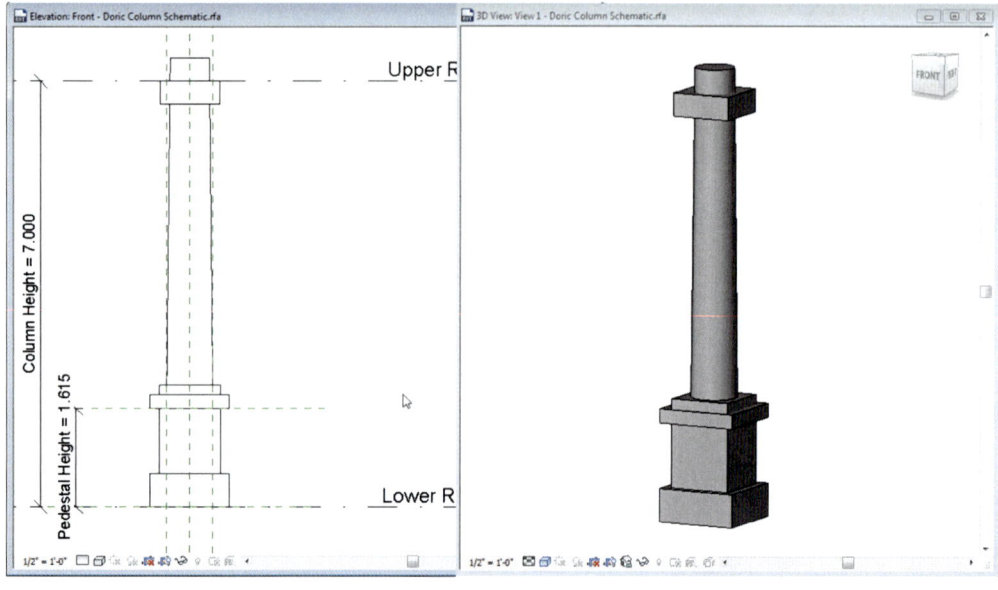

FIGURE 8.2

After updating all of the nested family's proportions, we are ready to adjust the heights

ADJUST THE HEIGHTS AND RELOAD

To adjust the heights and/or vertical locations, we need to return to Family Types in the schematic column family.

> **CATCH UP!** You can open a file completed to this point named: *Doric Column Schematic_A.rfa*.

Continue in the *Doric Column Schematic* file, or open the catch-up file.

1. Open the "Family Types" dialog.

⇨ Edit each of the formulas as shown in Table 8.1:

You might want to click Apply after each edit to see the family adjust as you work. Notice that the formulas are mostly the same, just change the numerical values where indicated (see Figure 8.3).

TABLE 8.1

Parameter	Formula
Shaft Elevation	if(Show Pedestal, Base Diameter * 2.9, Base Diameter * 0.5)
Pedestal Height	Base Diameter * 2.4
Base Elevation	if(Show Pedestal, Base Diameter * 2.4, 0)
Base Diameter	if(Show Pedestal, Column Height / 10.4, Column Height / 8)

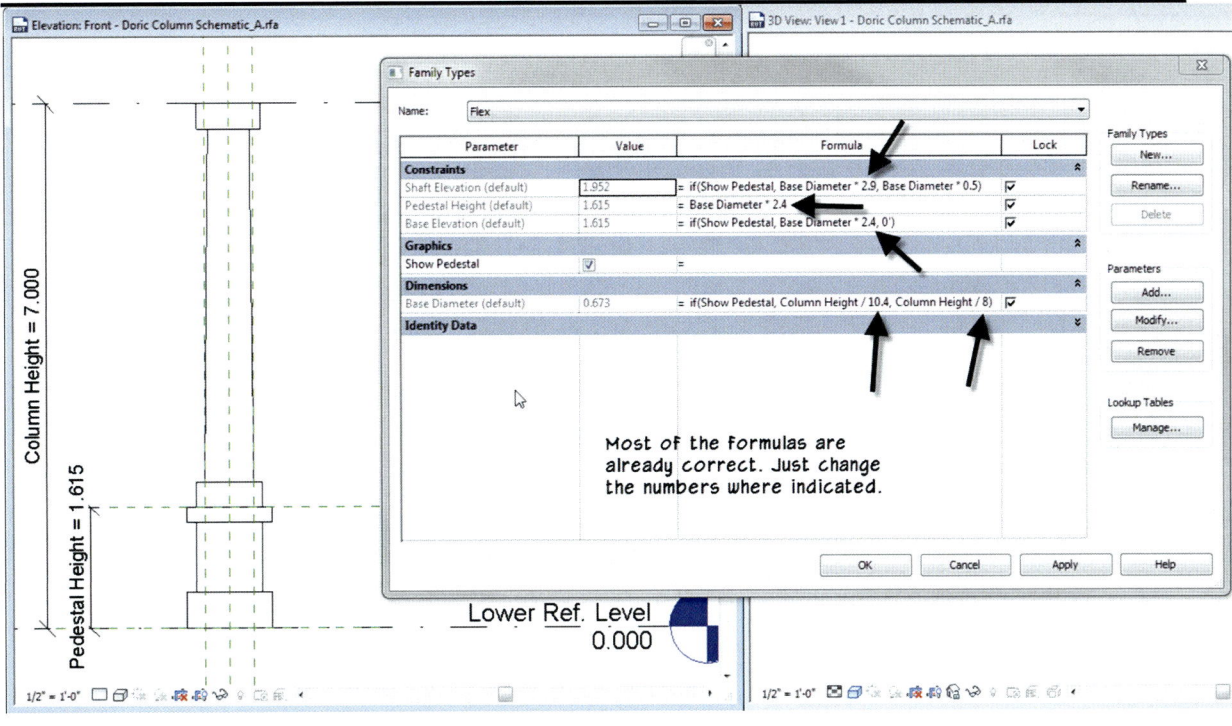

FIGURE 8.3

Finish up the schematic Doric by adjusting the formulas that control the heights

2. Click OK, to dismiss "Family Types" and then save.

> **CATCH UP!** The completed file is in the *Chapter08* folder named: *Doric Column Schematic.rfa*.

That completes the schematic version. Let's load it back into our newly renamed Doric Column family. You should still have the *Doric Column.rfa* family file open from above, but if you closed it, I have provided a catch-up file.

> **CATCH UP!** You can open a file completed to this point named: *Doric Column_A.rfa*.

• *Creating Classical Architecture with Modern Software* •

Make sure you have the *Doric Column Schematic* file open and in the background that you also have the *Doric Column* file open. Use yours or the catch-up files.

3. From the *Doric Column Schematic* family file, click the Load into Project button.

    ⇨ In the "Load into Projects" dialog, check only the *Doric Column.rfa* file and then click OK.

    ⇨ Overwrite the existing version.

The change onscreen will be very slight and nearly imperceptible. We are ready to modify each of the nested component families now.

4. Switch windows back to the schematic family and close it. If prompted to save, choose Yes.

5. Back in the *Doric Column* family, save the file.

CREATE THE DORIC CAPITAL

We'll work our way down from the capital again. This time we will be editing each of the nested components and adjusting the actual geometry. We can reuse the extrusion at the abacus and add a void to carve away the shape of the molding. We will also keep the Ovolo at the echinus and adjust its settings. For the sweep at the necking, we can reuse it by changing its profile to a cavetto (see Figure 8.4).

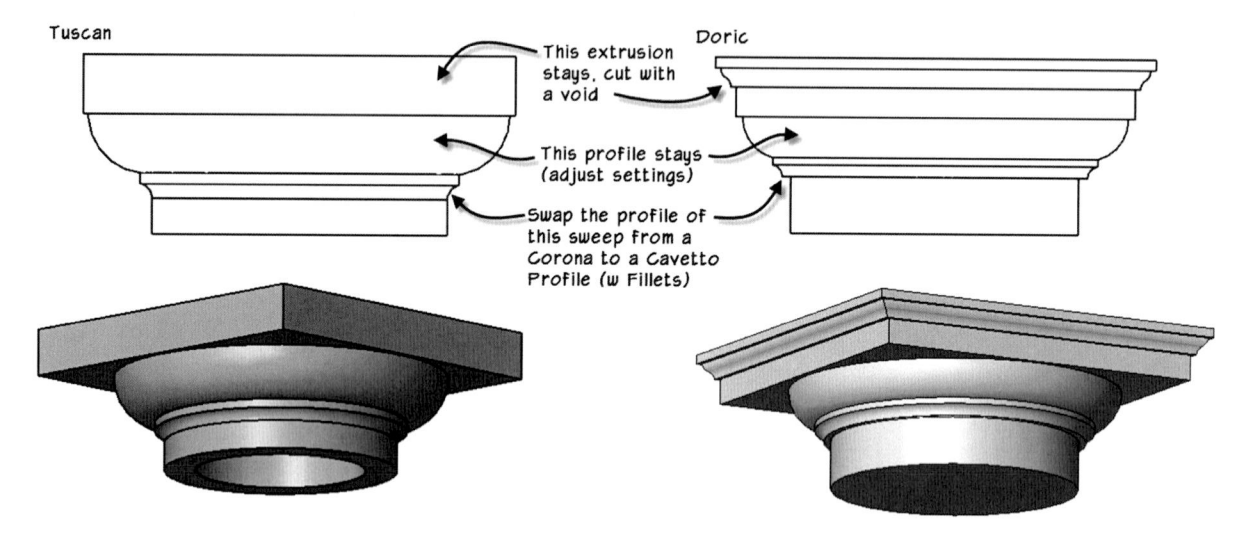

FIGURE 8.4
Comparing the Tuscan and Doric capital and planning the components

Continue in the *Doric Column* family. Close and save any other files you have open.

1. On the Project Browser right-click the *Doric Capital* family and choose **Edit**.

2. Minimize any windows that you have open for the *Doric Column* family but leave the file open.

3. On the Project Browser, double-click to open the *Ref. Level* floor plan and the *Front* elevation views.

    ⇨ Tile the windows (View tab of the ribbon, or press WT). Adjust the zoom in each window (see Figure 8.5).

FIGURE 8.5

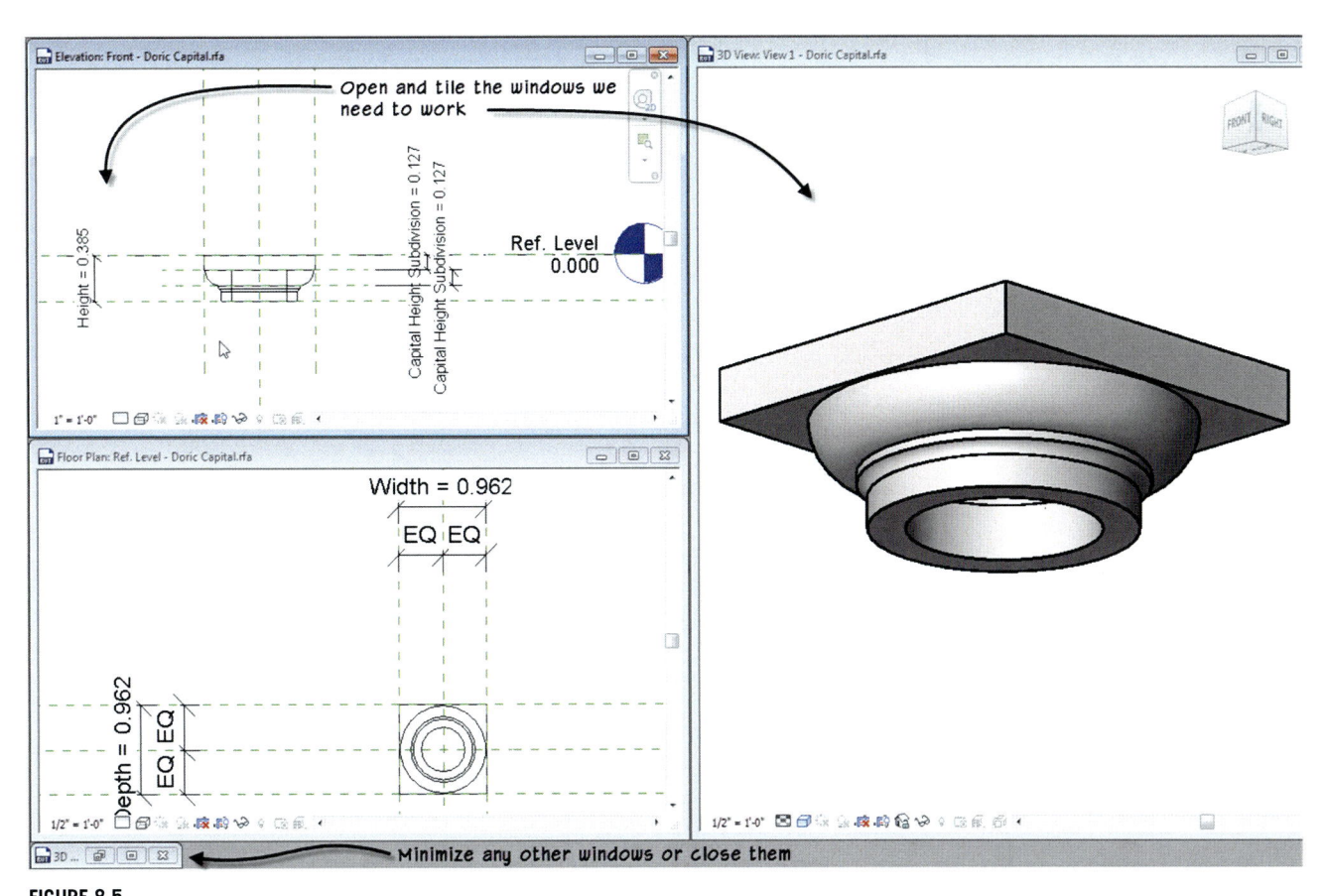

Prepare your workspace by closing or minimizing files and opening and tiling windows

The first thing I'd like to do is set the Base Diameter back to 1.000. I find it easier to manage the numerical values when starting from 1.

4. Open the "Family Types" dialog, set the Base Diameter to **1.000** and then click OK.

Next, let's adjust the formulas for the three major parts of the capital. Like the Tuscan, the Doric has the square abacus, the echinus (the ovolo portion) and the cylindrical necking. The proportions are just slightly different. Notice that currently, the same dimension is being used twice to make the top two subdivisions equal. We need them unequal, so let's make a new parameter.

5. Select the lower of the two Capital Height Subdivision dimensions (the one applied to the middle band).
- Click the Label drop-down on the Options Bar and choose **Add Parameter**.
- For the name, type: **Echinus** make it a Type parameter and group it under **Constraints**.
6. Reopen the "Family Types" dialog.
7. Select the Capital Height Subdivision parameter and then click the Modify button.
- Rename it to **Abacus** and click OK.
8. Add a Formula to the Echinus: **Base Diameter * 0.115**.
- Change the Formula of the Abacus to: **Base Diameter * 0.170**.
- Change the Formula for both Width and Depth to: **Base Diameter * 0.130** and then click OK (see Figure 8.6).

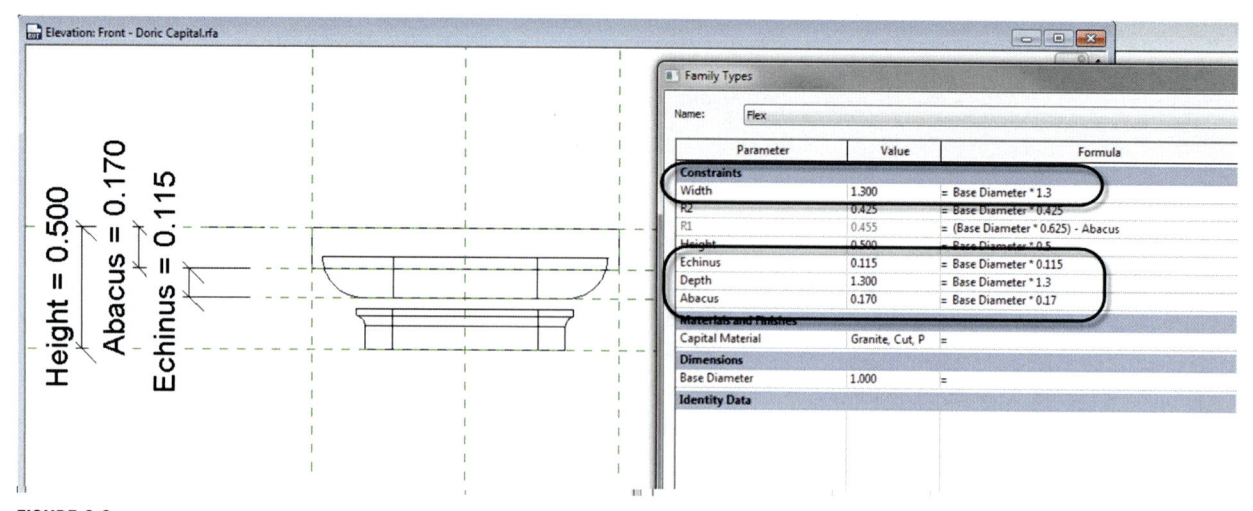

FIGURE 8.6

Rename and edit the parameters and their formulas

That takes care of the overall proportions, now let's adjust the individual moldings, starting with the ones already here.

CONFIGURE THE EXISTING MOLDINGS

There are two sweeps already here. Let's adjust their profiles.

1. On the Project Browser, expand *Profiles > Ovolo Profile*.

   ⇨ Right-click on *Flex* and choose **Type Properties**.

2. Change the Y Mult to **0.115** and the X Mult to **0.090**.

   ⇨ Click OK to apply the change (see Figure 8.7).

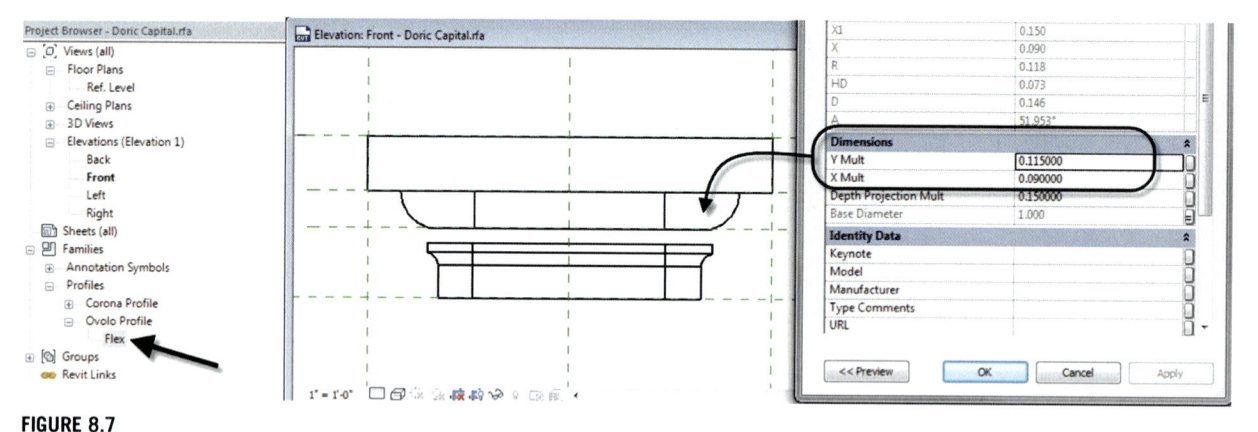

FIGURE 8.7

Adjust the ovolo molding

The proportions of the ovolo molding are now correct, but the radius of the circle that is used for its sweep path is not quite right. A return trip to Family Types will remedy that.

3. Open the "Family Types" dialog.

R1 drives the radius of this molding. Notice that currently it is using the Abacus in the Formula. This was appropriate for the Tuscan, but not for the Doric. A simple formula based on Base Diameter is all we need.

⇨ Set the formula for R1 to: **Base Diameter * 0.480** and then click OK.

• Renaissance Revit •

You should notice the ovolo increase slightly. The second sweep currently uses a corona profile. We need to replace this with a cavetto.

4. On the Insert tab, click the Load Family button.

   ⇨ Browse to the *Moldings* folder, select *Cavetto Profile (w Fillets).rfa* hold down the CTRL key and also select *Cyma Reversa Profile (w Fillets).rfa* and then click Open.

We'll use the cavetto profile now and the cyma reversa on the abacus a little later.

5. Select the corona sweep onscreen (the one for the necking).

   ⇨ On the Properties palette, for the Profile, choose **Cavetto Profile (w Fillets): Flex**.

The result is probably not quite what you were expecting. The form is huge! (See the left side of Figure 8.8). But as before, we simply need to modify the type properties of the profile.

6. On the Project Browser, expand *Profiles > Cavetto Profile (w Fillets)*.

   ⇨ Right-click on *Flex* and choose **Type Properties**.

7. Change the Y Mult to **0.035** and the X Mult to **0.030**.

   ⇨ Change the Fillet Mult to **0.020** and the Depth Mult to **0.025**.

   ⇨ For Base Diameter, associate the family parameter to the Base Diameter.

   ⇨ Click OK to apply the change (see Figure 8.8).

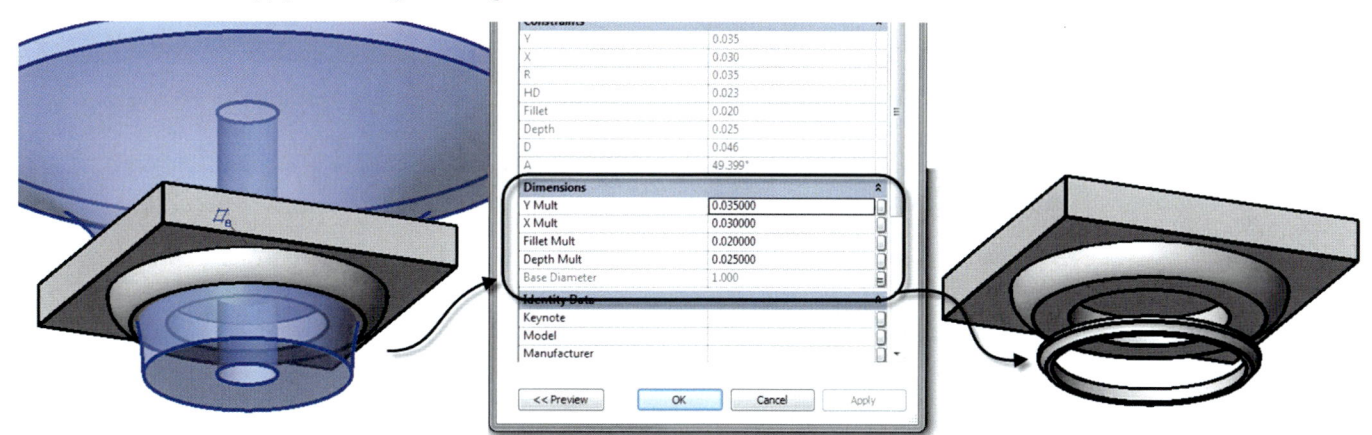

FIGURE 8.8
Adjust the type properties of the cavetto profile

We are making progress, but the new cavetto molding is in the wrong location. Previously when faced with this issue, we solved it by adding offsets to the profile on the Properties palette. The alternative is create more reference planes and parameters and edit the work plane of the sweep. I still prefer the offset approach. You can review the "Copy Additional Sweep Profiles" in Chapter 6 if you want a refresher.

8. Select the cavetto molding onscreen.

9. On the Properties palette, click the Associate Family Parameter button next to the Horizontal Profile Offset.

   ⇨ Create a new parameter called: **Cavetto X** and group it under **Constraints**.

   ⇨ Repeat to create **Cavetto Y** also under **Constraints** for the Vertical Profile Offset.

10. Open "Family Types" and add the following formulas (see Table 8.2):

TABLE 8.2

Parameter	Formula
Cavetto Y	Base Diameter * 0.160
Cavetto X	Base Diameter * 0.025

The cavetto profile will now appear snugly up against the ovolo (see Figure 8.9).

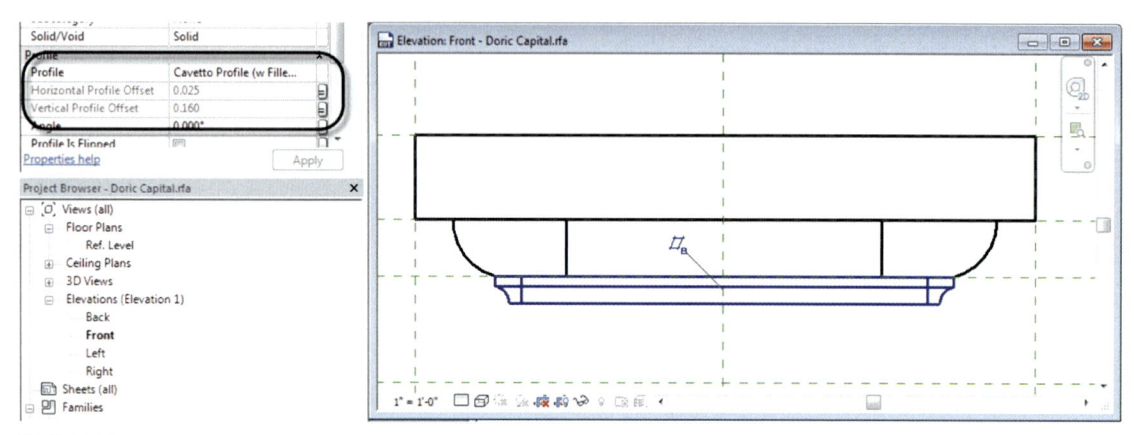

FIGURE 8.9
Adjust the offsets of the cavetto with two new parameters

> **CATCH UP!** You can open a file completed to this point named: *Doric Capital_A.rfa*.

ADD THE NECKING

For the necking which is just a cylinder, we can use another sweep with a rectangular profile or an extrusion. I'll use an extrusion here which seems a bit simpler.

1. Switch to the *Ref. Level* floor plan.

2. On the Create tab, click the Extrusion button.

    ⇨ Click the circle icon and create a circle about 0.425 in radius centered on the reference planes.

    It should snap to this value actually, but it does not have to be exact yet.

    ⇨ Make the radius dimension permanent.

3. Click the Modify tool to cancel.

    ⇨ Select the circle, make the Center Mark Visible, and then align and lock it in both directions.

    As always, be careful to use the reference planes as alignment edges.

    ⇨ Select the radius dimension and on the Options Bar, label it with the existing **R2** parameter (see Figure 8.10).

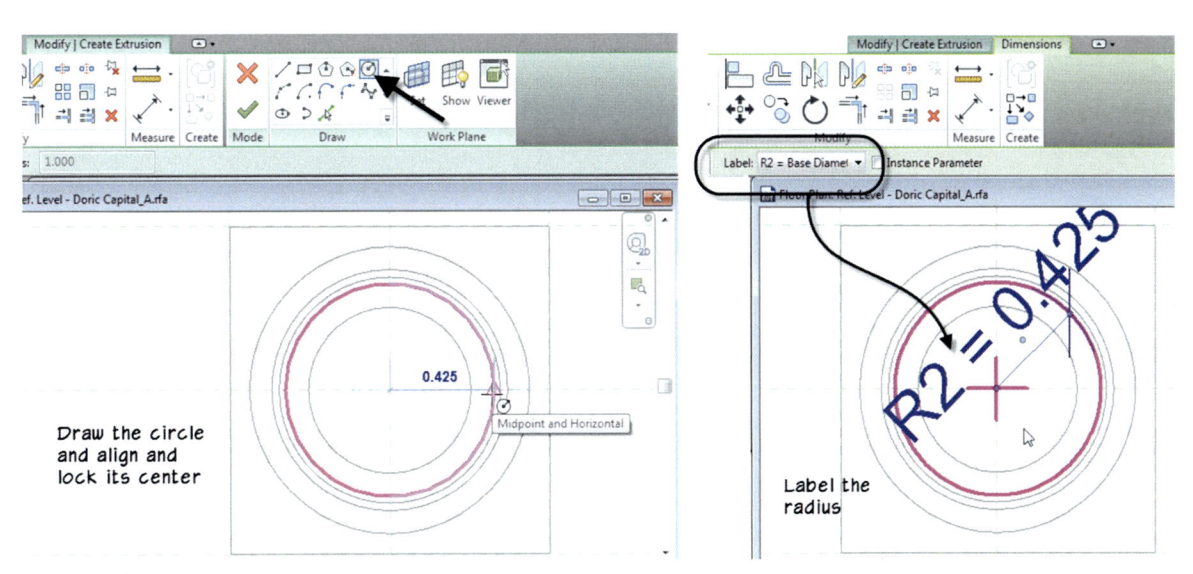

FIGURE 8.10

Create a round extrusion for the necking using the existing parameter R2

4. Click the Finish Edit Mode button.

The extrusion will appear at the default height and sitting on top of the abacus. This is because in plan view, the default work plane is the Ref. Level.

Keep the extrusion selected.

5. On the Modify I Extrusion tab, click the Edit Work Plane button.

⇨ In the "Work Plane" dialog, from the Name list, choose **Reference Plane : Capital Bottom** and then click OK.

6. Switch to the *Front* elevation view.

⇨ Using the control handle grip at the top of the cylinder, or the align tool, align and lock the top of the cylinder to the reference plane named: Ovolo (see Figure 8.11).

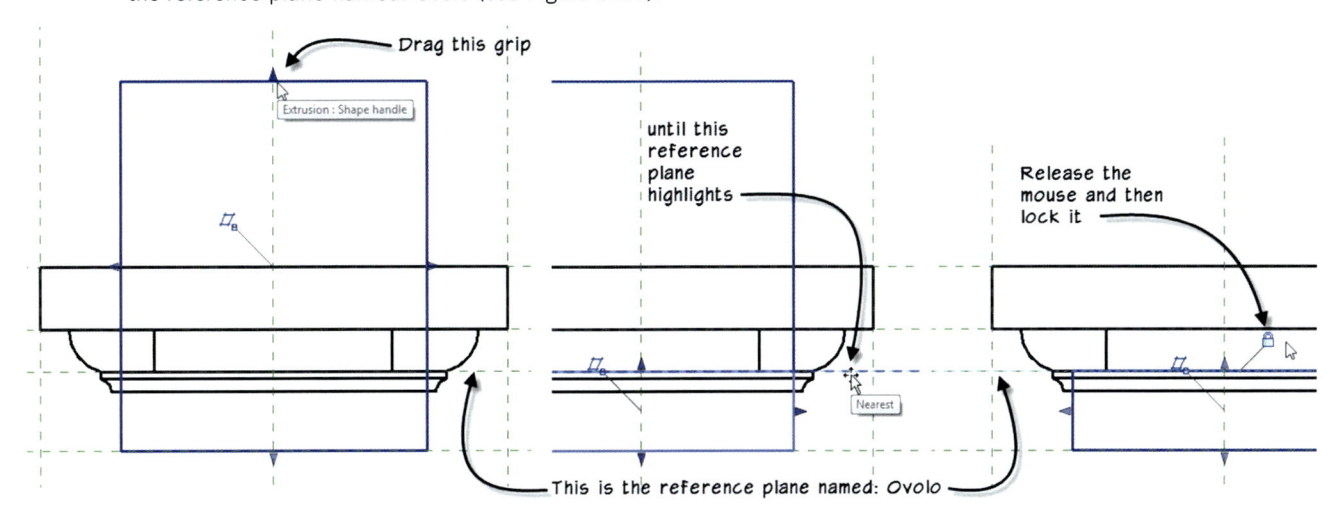

FIGURE 8.11

Adjust the height of the extrusion and lock it to the Ovolo reference plane

CREATE A VOID SWEEP

The last part of the capital is the moldings at the top of the abacus. I considered building these the same as we have before: using sweeps and a picked 3D path along the top edge of the abacus extrusion. There is nothing wrong with that approach but there is one consideration which swayed my decision against that approach. The outmost vertical reference planes (named Left and Right) are conveniently giving us the overall size of the capital. If we add sweeps to the form here, they will fall outside of the reference planes making the overall width and depth larger. We could easily compensate by adjusting the Width and Depth parameters, but I thought it would be nicer to leave our construct as is with these outer reference planes marking the extents of the element and instead use a void to carve away a portion of the extrusion to give us the desired form. In a way, this is more accurate as with both wood and stone, it is more likely that material would be carved away from the larger block of raw material. So we can think of the sweep we are about to create as a virtual "router bit."

1. Switch to the *View 1* 3D view.

    Dragging the ViewCube (or hold down the SHIFT and drag with the middle wheel button), orbit the view so that you see the Left and Front faces, the ViewCube will indicate this.

2. On the Create tab, click the Void Forms drop-down and choose **Void Sweep**.

    ⇨ On the ribbon, click the Pick Path button.

    ⇨ Click the top edge of the square extrusion on the left first. (Use the ViewCube as a guide).

    ⇨ Click the remaining three edges along the top and the click Finish Edit Mode.

If you picked the left edge first, this will be the location of the profile. Left will make it easier to see in the *Front* elevation that we have open already.

3. On the Modify | Sweep tab, click the Profile drop-down and choose **Cyma Reversa Profile (w Fillets)**.

Naturally we have a small issue with the profile. As you can see in Figure 8.12 it is huge. If you tried to finish the sweep right now, it would fail as the form would intersect itself. Fortunately, we can edit the type properties from the Project Browser without finishing the sweep.

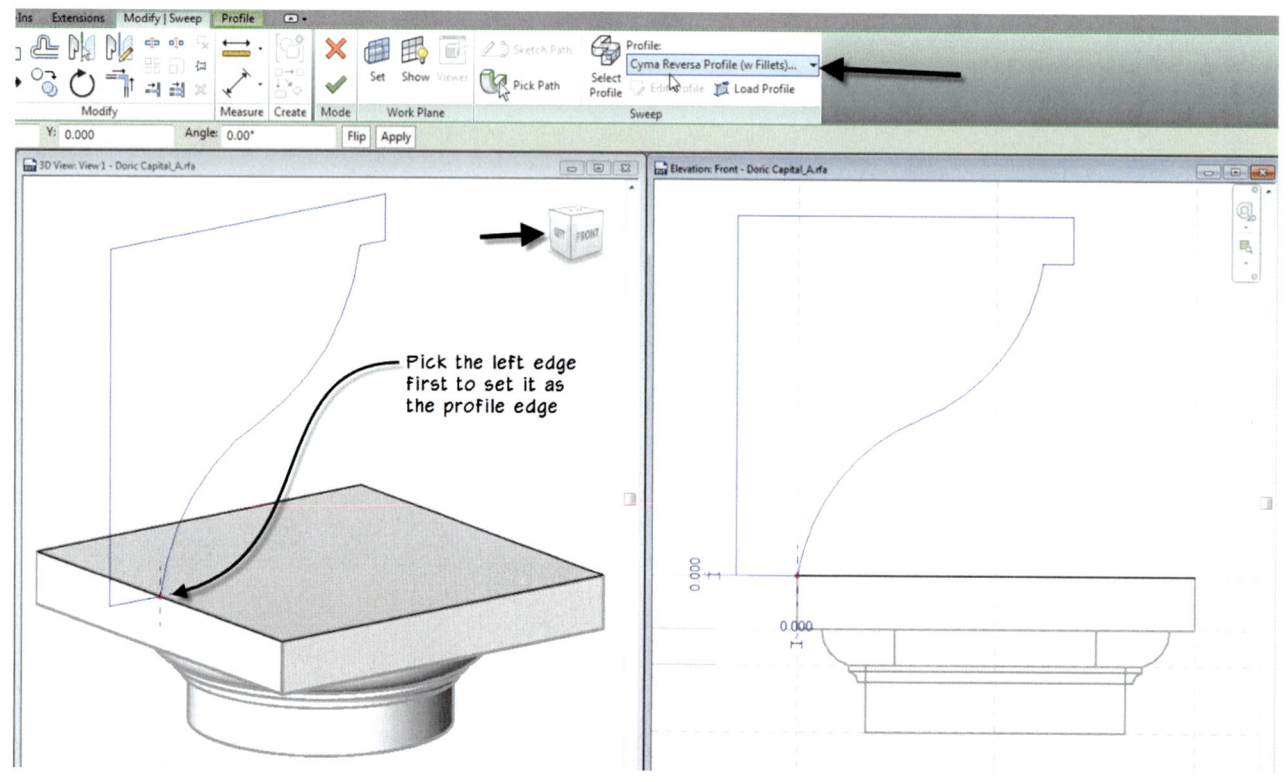

FIGURE 8.12

Set up the sweep and apply the cyma reversa profile

4. On the Project Browser, expand *Profiles > Cyma Reversa Profile (w Fillets)*.

5. Right-click on *Flex* and choose **Type Properties**.

    ⇨ Change the Y Mult to **0.055** and the X Mult to **0.030**.

    ⇨ Change the Fillet Y Mult to **0.085**.

    ⇨ Change both the Fillet X Mult and the Depth Projection Mult to **0.015**.

    ⇨ Click OK to apply the change.

I usually like to apply the changes a little at a time. So here I am applying all of the changes in proportion first to make sure that they work, then we'll go back in and link up the Base Diameter.

6. Right-click on *Flex* and choose **Type Properties** again.

    ⇨ For Base Diameter, associate the family parameter to the Base Diameter.

    ⇨ Click OK to apply the change (see Figure 8.13).

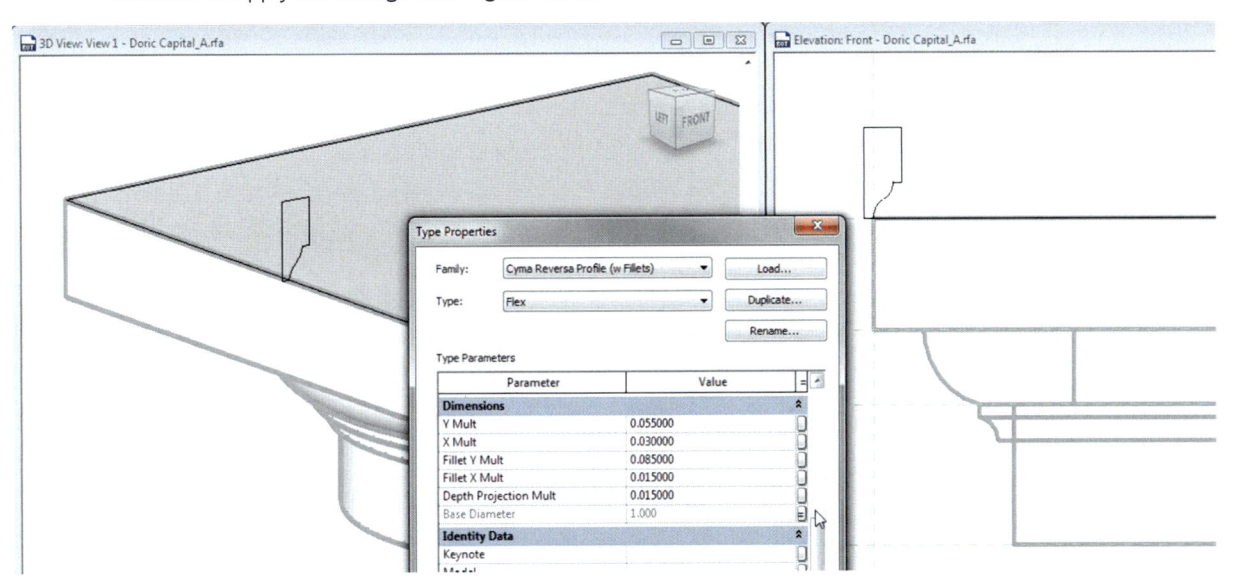

FIGURE 8.13
Adjust the size and proportion of the sweep profile in the Type Properties

We now have the profile sized correctly, but as you can see it will not cut anything in its current location. So as before, we can adjust the offsets on the Properties palette to make this profile intersect the extrusion. So if we establish the proper offsets on the Properties palette before completing the sweep, Revit will apply the cut for us, saving us a step.

However, remember the little oddity that we encountered in an earlier chapter with this. If you look at the Properties palette, while we have access to the horizontal and vertical offsets, we do not currently have access to the ability to associate family parameters to these offsets. This is not a concern. We can simply perform the action in two steps. First we'll add the offsets we need, this will prompt Revit to cut geometry for us, and then once complete, we can link up the parameters outside of the sweep sketch mode.

7. On the Properties palette, for the Horizontal Profile Offset, type: **0.015**.

    If you are not seeing these parameters, make sure to select the profile onscreen first.

    ⇨ For the Vertical Profile Offset, type: **-0.030** (negative).

    ⇨ For the Angle, input **180°** and check the Profile Is Flipped box.

• *Creating Classical Architecture with Modern Software* •

222 | Chapter 8

⇨ Click the Apply button on the Properties palette to see the results (see Figure 8.14).

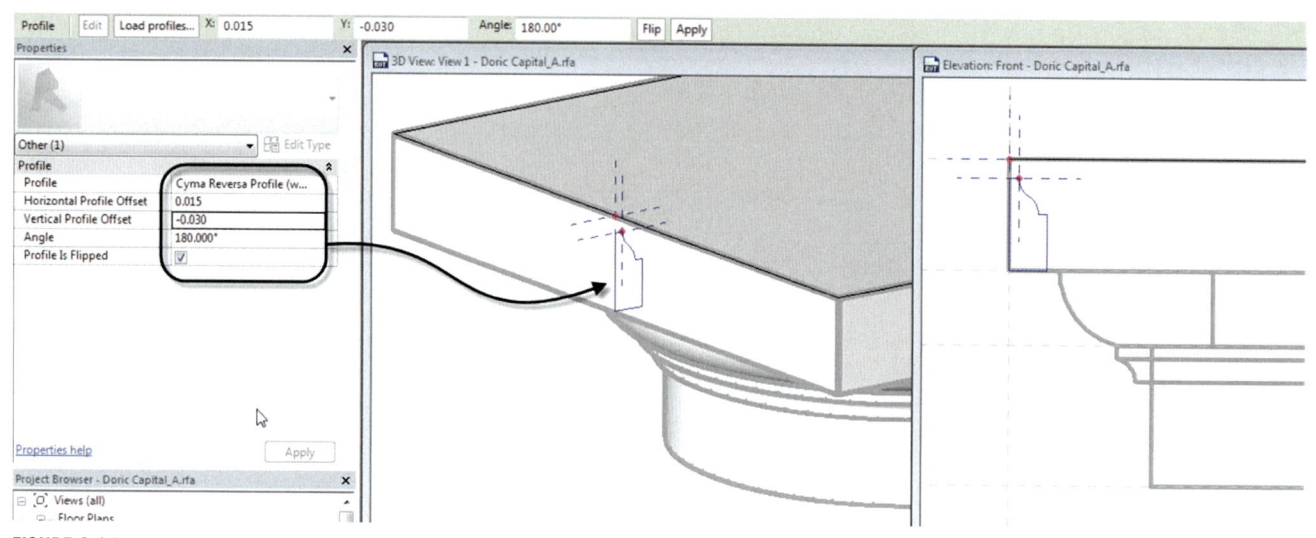

FIGURE 8.14
Adjust the location and orientation of the profile

8. On the Modify I Sweep tab, click the Finish Edit Mode button.

   Deselect the void to see the result (see Figure 8.15).

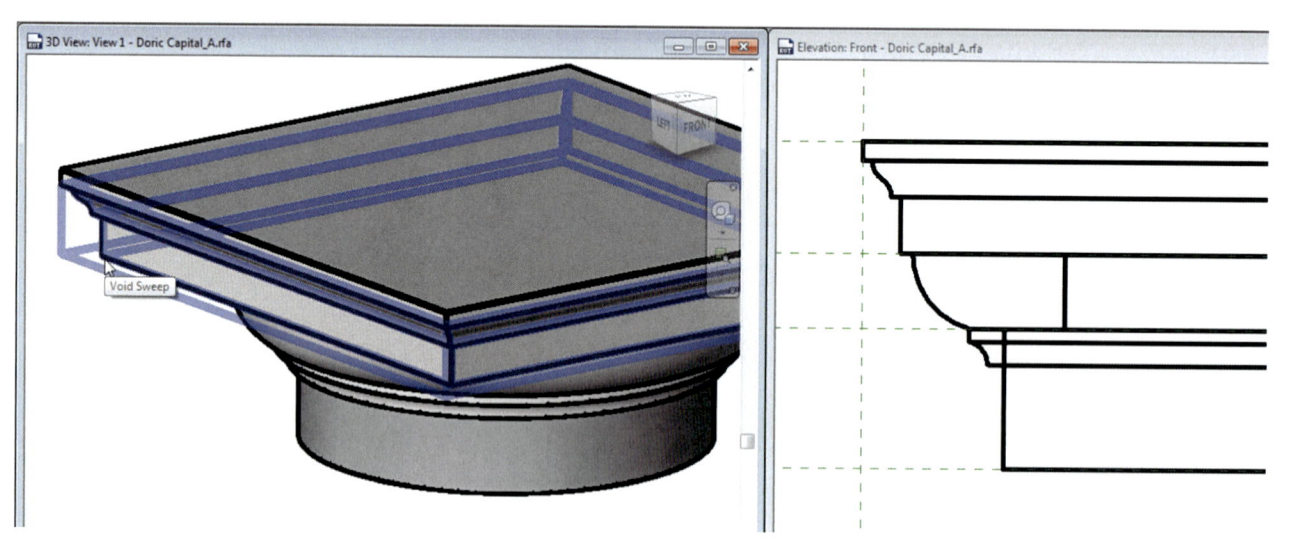

FIGURE 8.15
Deselect the void to see it cut the intersecting form

If you move your mouse near the intersection of the void and the solid, the void will highlight onscreen. When you click to select it, it will temporarily appear solid and the cut will be disabled. Do this to select the void and modify it. If you are having trouble selecting the void, move your mouse near where it ought to be and use the TAB key to assist in selection.

9. Select the void.

   On the Properties palette, you can now see that we have the Associate Family Parameter buttons we need for the horizontal and vertical offsets.

10. Next to Horizontal Profile Offset, click the Associate Family Parameter button.

    ⇨ Add a new parameter called: **Cyma Reversa X** grouped under Constraints.

    ⇨ Repeat for the Vertical Profile Offset calling it **Cyma Reversa Y**.

• Renaissance Revit •

11. Open the "Family Types" dialog and add formulas to both new parameters: **Base Diameter * -0.030** for Cyma Reversa Y and **Base Diameter * 0.015** for Cyma Reversa X.

12. Flex the Base Diameter.

13. Reset Base Diameter back to **1.000**, click OK and save the file.

> CATCH UP! You can open a file completed to this point named: *08_Doric Capital.rfa*.

You should still have the *Doric Column.rfa* family file open and minimized. If you closed it, reopen it or the catch-up file now.

14. From your *Doric Capital.rfa* file (or the catch-up file), click the Load into Project button.

15. If you have more than one file to choose from, select only *Doric Column.rfa*, and then overwrite the existing when prompted.

⇨ Switch windows back to the *Doric Capital* file; save and close it.

⇨ Back in the *Doric Column* file, save the file.

> CATCH UP! You can open a file completed to this point named: *Doric Column_B.rfa*.

We will continue following a similar process to update the other pieces in this file. Before we do though, I have a brief detour related to the cyma reversa profile.

CYMA REVERSA PROFILE ADJUSTMENTS

I'd like to take a moment to discuss the cyma reversa profile that we loaded in. We built this profile back in Chapter 4. I created the version we used here outside of the lessons in Chapter 4, but simply copied it and save it with a new name and added the fillets. However, in doing so, I discovered an issue with the profile as it was created in Chapter 4. As the ratio between the height and width drops below .6, the value of Y1 can become negative. If this happens, the profile fails. This is not because of a flaw in the math, rather it is a limitation of labeled dimensions. A labeled dimension relies on the references where its witness lines are attached. If a dimension value changes from positive to negative or vice versa, it causes the dimension to reverse, which dimensions in Revit cannot do. The solution is pretty simple: choose a witness line location that is far enough away that any reasonable value to which you expect to flex it will not cause a reversal. I have placed a copy of the original version of the *Cyma Reversa Profile* in the *Chatper08* folder. I have already addressed the problem in the *Cyma Reversa (w Fillets)* file (in the *Moldings* folder) that we used here. If you open both you can compare them. Let's open the original version and apply the same fix to it.

1. From the *Chapter08* folder, open the *08_Cyma Reversa Profile.rfa* file.

As noted, this is a copy of the file that we created back in Chapter 4. If you wish to see the problem first, hand, open "Family Types" and flex the X Mult value to **0.570**. Notice that this makes the Y1 parameter become a negative value. If you click the Apply button, you'll first get a "Constraints are not satisfied" warning. If you click Remove Constraints, another warning will appear alerting you that Y1 has an invalid value. Cancel to dismiss the warnings and the "Family Types" dialog without making changes.

If you never intend to have the ratio between Y and X less the 1 to .58, then this profile will work fine, below this ratio and it will fail. The way we fix it is to simply change where the dimension for the reference plane driven by Y1 is located.

2. Delete both dimensions that use Y1 onscreen (see the left side of Figure 8.16).

3. Create two new dimensions.

⇨ One between the reference planes named: Center (Front/Back) and Center Left Hor.

⇨ And the other between the reference planes named: Y Max and Center Right Hor.

4. Label these both with a new parameter named **Y2** and grouped beneath **Constraints** (see the middle of Figure 8.16)

5. Add a Formula to this parameter: **Y + Y1** (see the right side of Figure 8.16).

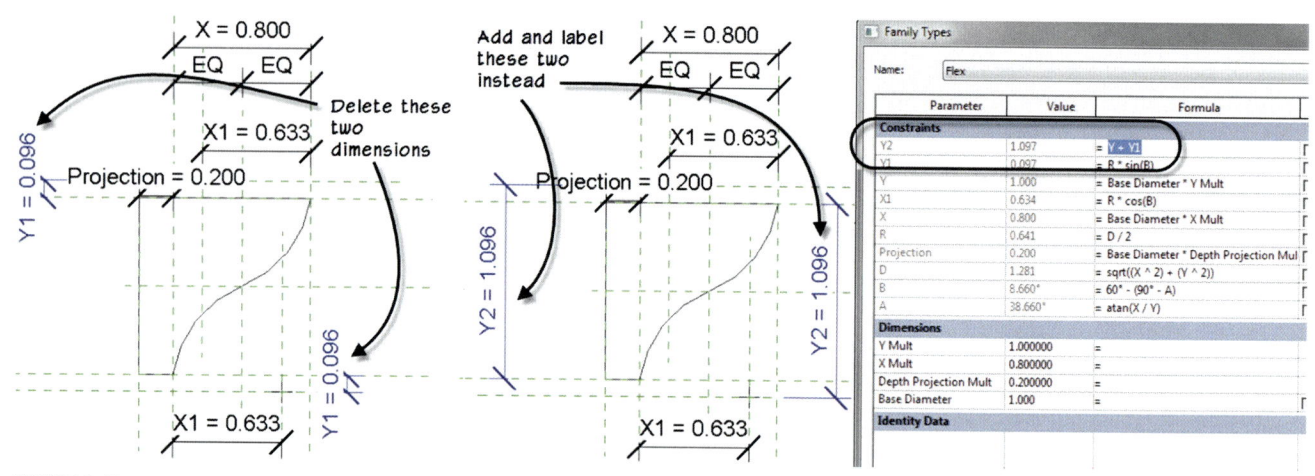

FIGURE 8.16

Reconfigure the dimensions to prevent failure when Y1 goes negative

As you can see if you flex, when Y1 goes negative, it no longer fails. This is because the driving dimension: Y2 always remains positive regardless of the value of Y1. So this configuration is much more stable and works with many more ratios.

> **CATCH UP!** You can open a file completed to this point in the *Moldings* folder named: *Cyma Reversa Profile.rfa*.

CREATE THE DORIC SHAFT

The Doric order can have a fluted or smooth shaft. Fluted versions can vary significantly depending on if they are modeled on Greek, Roman or Renaissance examples. For this chapter, I will stick to the smooth shaft. It is a much easier modeling task and later we have an entire chapter (Chapter 12) devoted just to the shaft and particularly; fluted shafts. Since we are sticking with the smooth shaft for now, the Tuscan version that we are starting from is very close to what we need. In the Tuscan order, the fillet at the foot of the column shaft (directly above the torus on the base) is included as part of the base. In the other orders including Doric, this fillet is part of the shaft. So we have two modifications to make: adjust the height proportion and add the fillet at the bottom.

Continue in your *Doric Column* file or open the *Doric Column_B.rfa* catch-up file.

1. Select the shaft element onscreen.

2. On the ribbon click Edit Family.

3. On the Project Browser, expand *Families > Profiles*.

ADJUST THE DORIC SHAFT PROFILE

Recall that the shaft uses a sweep with a profile. As you can see, that profile is still named "Tuscan".

1. Right-click on *Tuscan Shaft Profile* and choose **Rename** (or select it and press F2).

⇨ Name it: **Doric Shaft Profile**.

• Renaissance Revit •

⇨ Right-click on *Doric Shaft Profile* and choose **Edit**.

2. Open the "Family Types" dialog, set the Base Diameter to **1.000** and then click Apply.

3. Add a new Length parameter grouped under Constraints and called: **Base Fillet**.

⇨ Edit the following formulas as indicated in Table 8.3. Click Apply after each edit.

TABLE 8.3

Parameter	Formula	Comments
Transition Top	Base Diameter * 0.045	
Transition Bottom	Base Diameter * 0.055	
Shaft Height	Base Diameter * 7	Do this one last
Top Diameter	Base Diameter * 0.850	No Change
Profile Depth	Base Diameter * 0.250	No Change
Base Fillet	Base Diameter * 0.040	New Parameter
Astragal Torus	Base Diameter * 0.050	
Astragal Fillet	Base Diameter * 0.025	

4. When you are finished editing the formulas, click OK to dismiss "Family Types."

Some of the vertical reference planes will now be shorter than the extents of the profile. This is not an issue for Revit, but I personally don't like the look of it. I think it is easier to understand everything visually if there is a logical hierarchy in how the reference planes are located and sized onscreen. So while optional, I recommend stretching the lengths of the vertical reference planes past the top ones. To stretch the Center (Left/Right) reference plane, you will have to first unpin it. It is a good idea to re-pin it when you are done. Finally, it can sometimes be difficult to grab the right point to stretch these. Make sure you are dragging the small open circle at the end of the reference planes. Using the TAB key can help (see Figure 8.17).

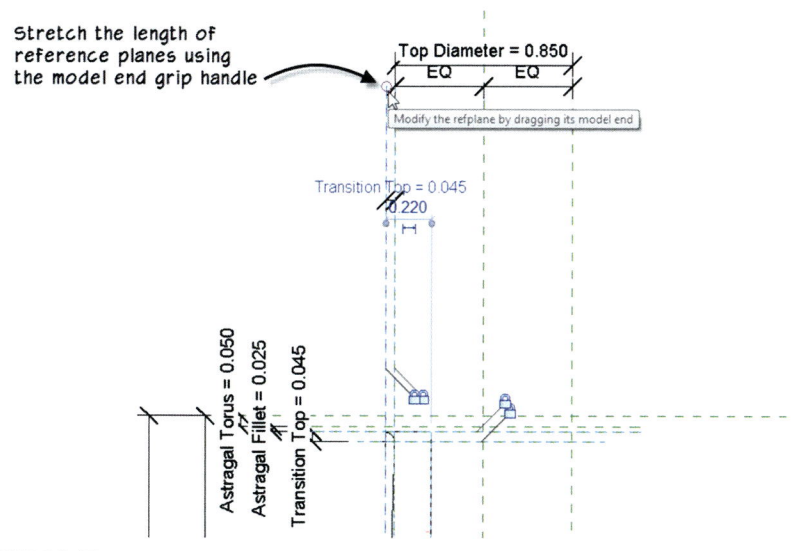

FIGURE 8.17
After editing the formulas adjust the lengths of the reference planes

Now we just need to add the fillet at the bottom.

5. Zoom in on the bottom of the profile.

6. Delete the vertically oriented Transition Bottom dimension.

226 | Chapter 8

7. Select reference plane H1 and the small arc at the bottom and move them both up slightly (the exact amount is not important, but approximately 0.050 should do).

8. A warning will appear. Click the Remove Constraints button (see Figure 8.18).

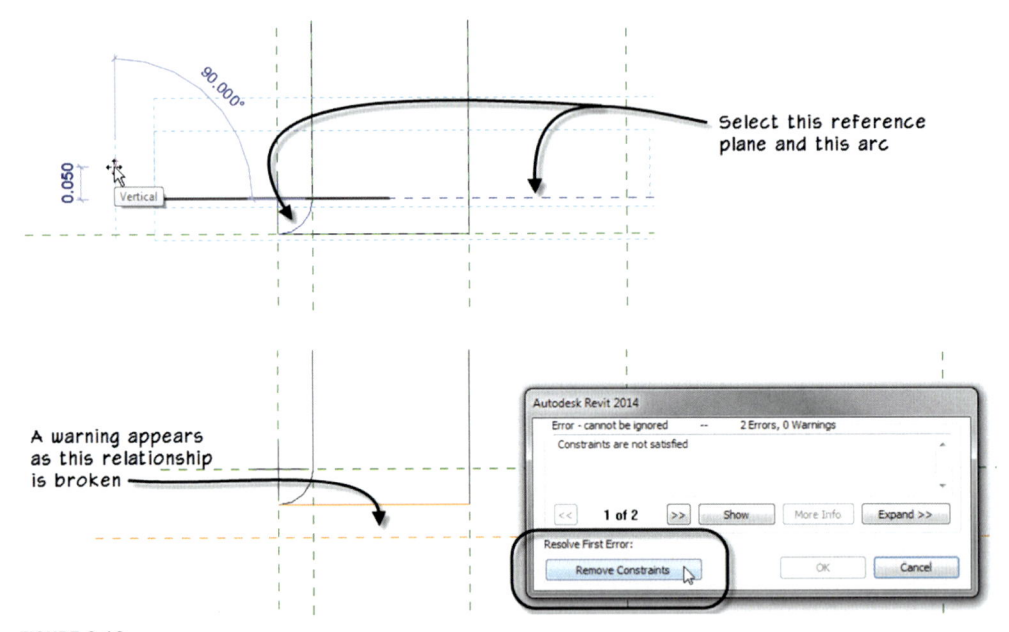

FIGURE 8.18

Moving the reference plane and arc causes a warning. Remove Constraints to resolve

Notice that the horizontal line moves as well. This is because it is currently joined to the rest of the sketch. One more example of the built-in relationships that Revit establishes for us. The line is also currently locked to the bottom reference plane. So the warning is indicating the issue we have here. The line cannot both move and remain constrained. Removing the constraints solves the issue.

9. Add a new reference plane in between the H1 and Center (Front/Back) at the same location as the horizontal line.

    Revit should line up with it automatically when the cursor is nearby.

    ⇨ On the Properties palette, name the new reference plane: **H0**.

10. Select the horizontal line, and drag the left endpoint a little to the right to disconnect it from the curve (see Figure 8.19).

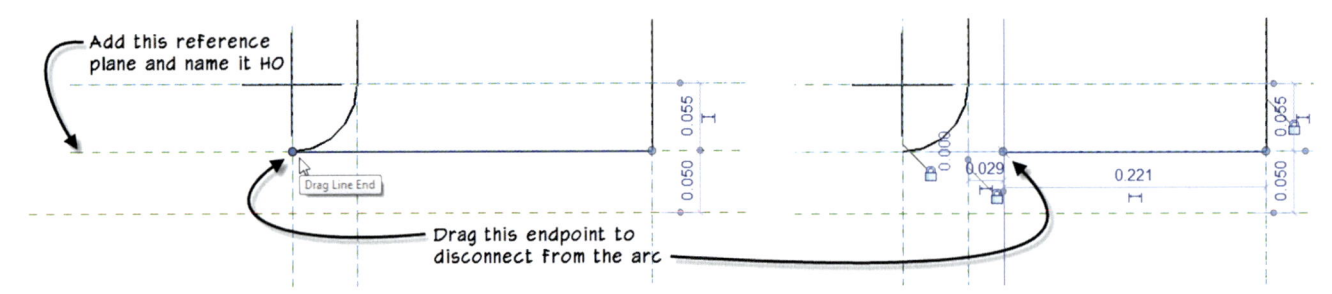

FIGURE 8.19

Add a new reference plane and disconnect the bottom line from the arc

11. Align and lock the endpoint of the open end of the arc in both directions (to the vertical reference plane; V1 and horizontal one; H0).

    If it does not let you align in the vertical direction, it means it is already locked.

    ⇨ Align the horizontal line to the Center (Front/Back) reference plane and lock it (see the left side of Figure 8.20).

• Renaissance Revit •

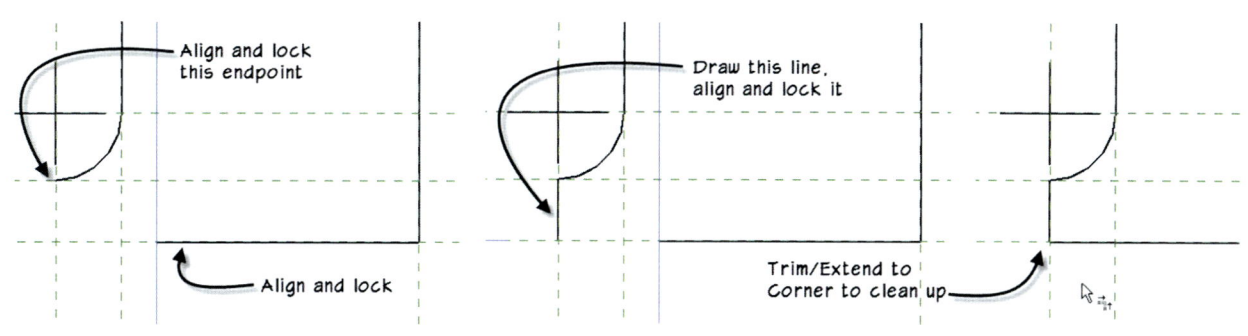

FIGURE 8.20

Adjust the profile sketch by aligning, locking and adding the missing segment

12. Draw a vertical line from the arc endpoint down to the Center (Front/Back) reference plane.
    ⇨ Align and lock it to the vertical (V1) reference plane (see the middle of Figure 8.20).
13. Use Trim/Extend to Corner to finish up the shape (see the right side of Figure 8.20).
14. Add a dimension between Center (Front/Back) and H0. Label it with the Base Fillet parameter.
    ⇨ Add another dimension between H0 and H1, label it with Transition Bottom (see Figure 8.21).

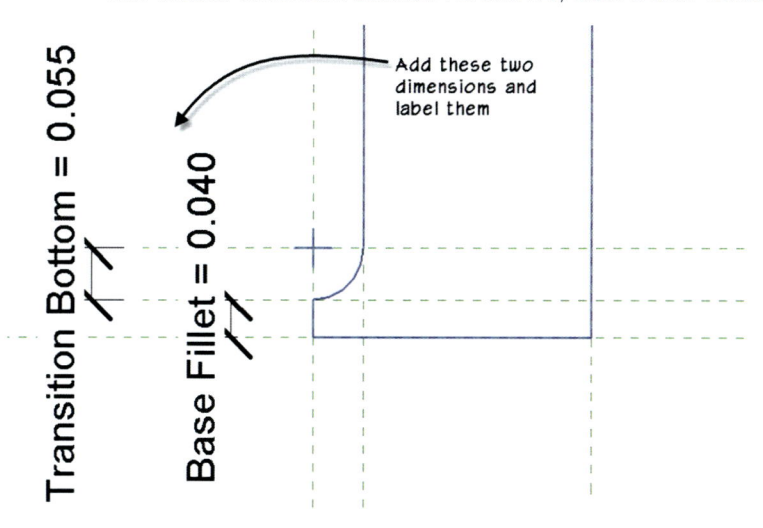

FIGURE 8.21

Add the dimensions and parameters

15. Flex the Base Diameter. When satisfied, reset to **1.000** and then save the file.

> **CATCH UP!** You can open a file completed to this point named: *08_Doric Shaft Profile.rfa*.

You should still have both the *Doric Shaft* file and the *Doric Column* file open. If you closed either one, you can reopen them now, or open the appropriate catch-up file.

16. On the Ribbon click the Load into Project button.
    ⇨ In the "Load into Projects" dialog, check only the *Doric Shaft.rfa* file and then click OK.
    ⇨ Overwrite the existing file.
17. Return to the *Doric Shaft Profile* file, from the Application menu, choose **Close** and save if prompted.

ADJUST THE SHAFT ASTRAGAL

The column shaft should immediately grow taller. Notice however that the Astragal at the top has remained unchanged. This is a separate revolved form. Let's adjust that now.

1. From the Project Browser, open the *Front* elevation view.
2. Open the "Family Types" dialog.

⇨ Set the Base Diameter to **1.000** and then click Apply.

If necessary, click OK to dismiss the dialog, zoom and pan the view to see the top portion of the shaft and then reopen Family Types. (It is easier to work with it visible in the background).

3. Edit the following formulas as indicated in Table 8.4 and shown in Figure 8.22. Click Apply after each edit.

TABLE 8.4

Parameter	Formula	Comments
Top Projection	Base Diameter * 0.045	
Top Diameter	Base Diameter * 0.850	No Change
Shaft Height	Base Diameter * 7	
R	Base Diameter * 0.250	No Change
Astragal Torus	Base Diameter * 0.050	
Astragal Fillet	Base Diameter * 0.025	

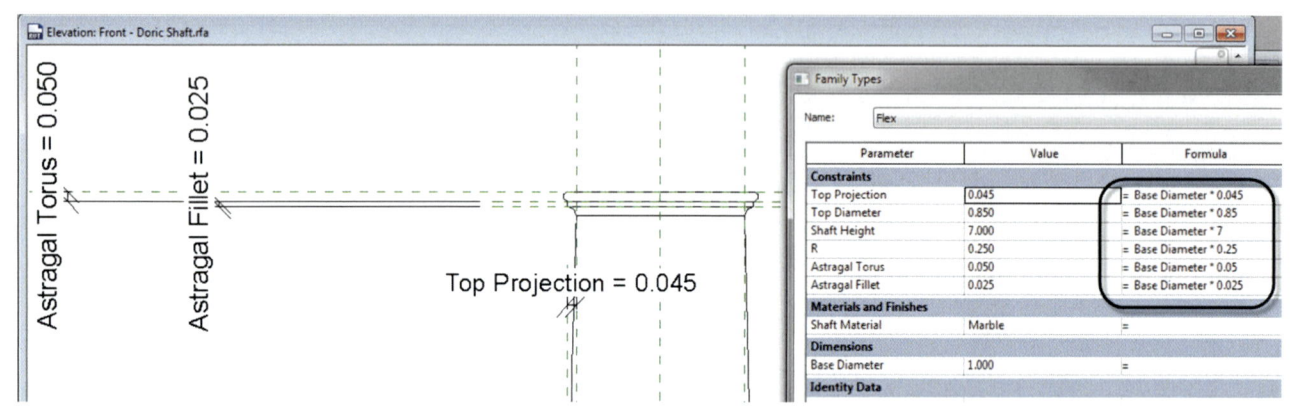

FIGURE 8.22
Adjust the parameters for the Doric shaft

4. Flex the Base Diameter. When satisfied, reset to **1.000** and then save the file.

> **CATCH UP!** You can open a file completed to this point named: *08_Doric Shaft.rfa*.

You should still have the *Doric Column* file open. If you closed it, you can reopen it now, or open the appropriate catch-up file.

5. On the Ribbon click the Load into Project button.

If the "Load into Projects" dialog appears, check only the *Doric Column.rfa* file and then click OK.

⇨ Overwrite the existing file.

The shaft should appear in the correct location, but it is too tall. We need to adjust the formulas as we did above.

6. Open "Family Types" and adjust the formulas as shown in Table 8.1 above.

> **CATCH UP!** You can open a file completed to this point named: *Doric Column_C.rfa*.

• Renaissance Revit •

CREATE THE DORIC BASE

Let's move on to the Doric base. The procedure will be much the same as what we did above for the capital. The major difference will be that we will replace the revolve that was used in the Tuscan Base family (from which this one is created) with a series of sweeps. The moldings become increasingly more complex with each order. So using the sweeps will ultimately prove more flexible.

Continue in the *Doric Column.rfa* file or open the catch-up file. Close and save any other files.

1. On the Project Browser, beneath *Generic Models*, right-click the *Doric Base* and choose **Edit**.
2. From the Project Browser, open the *Front* elevation view.
3. Open the "Family Types" dialog.
   ⇨ Set the Base Diameter to **1.000** and then click OK.
4. Delete the revolve and the equality dimension between the Ref Level, Plinth, and Top.
5. Add a new dimension between the Ref. Level and the reference plane named: Plinth.
   ⇨ Label the dimension with a new type parameter called: **Plinth**. Group it under **Constraints** (see Figure 8.23).

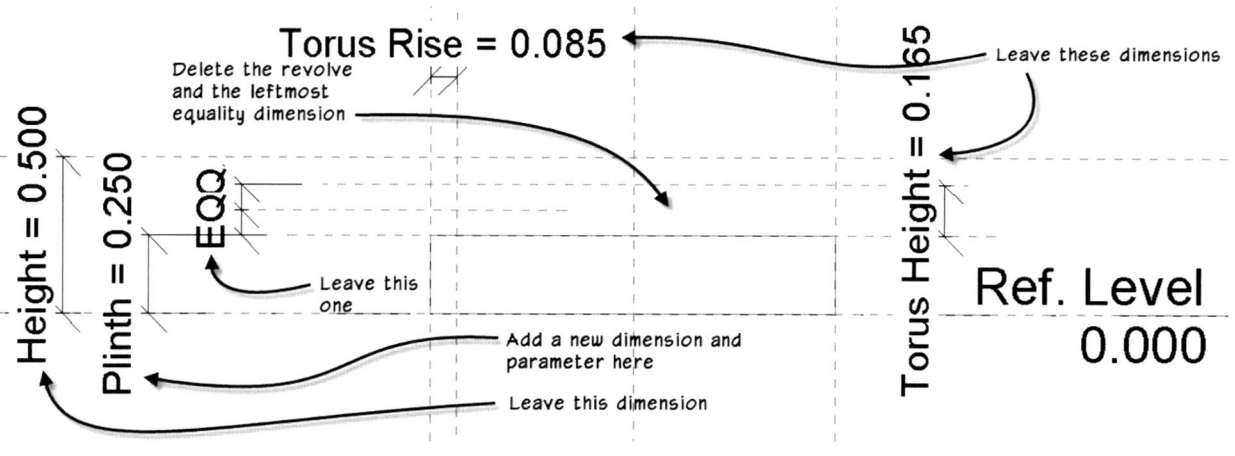

FIGURE 8.23

Delete unneeded elements and then add new dimensions and parameters

6. Open the "Family Types" dialog.
7. Select Torus Rise, click the Modify button and rename it to: **X1**. Repeat for Torus Height renaming it to **Y1**.
   ⇨ Edit the following formulas as indicated in Table 8.5 and shown in Figure 8.24. Click Apply after each edit.

TABLE 8.5

Parameter	Formula	Comments
Width	Base Diameter * 1.340	No Change
X1	Base Diameter * 0.070	
Y1	Base Diameter * 0.250	
Plinth	Base Diameter * 0.16	
Height	Base Diameter * 0.500	No Change
Depth	Base Diameter * 1.340	No Change

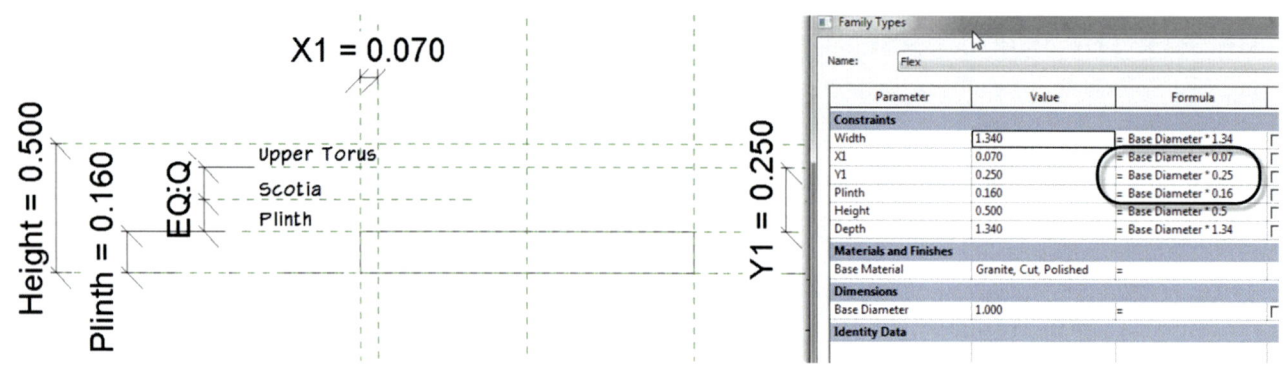

FIGURE 8.24

Update the formulas and parameters

8. Click OK to dismiss Family Types.

9. Name each of the horizontal reference planes as indicated in Figure 8.24.

ADD AN EXTRUDED CORE

Before we can construct the moldings of our Doric Base, we will actually start with an extruded cylinder. The moldings will be created from sweeps in the next topic. But recall the "Make the Column Solid" topic in Chapter 7. There we added an extrusion to the center of the shaft because when you use a sweep to create round geometry, you end up with a hollow form. The easiest way to deal with that is to fill in the hollow area with an extrusion. In this case, if we make the extrusion first, we can then use the extrusion to create the path of the sweeps.

1. From the Project Browser, open the *Ref. Level* floor plan view.

   ⇨ Set the Work Plane to the Plinth reference plane.

2. Draw a circular extrusion at the center intersection (see Figure 8.25):

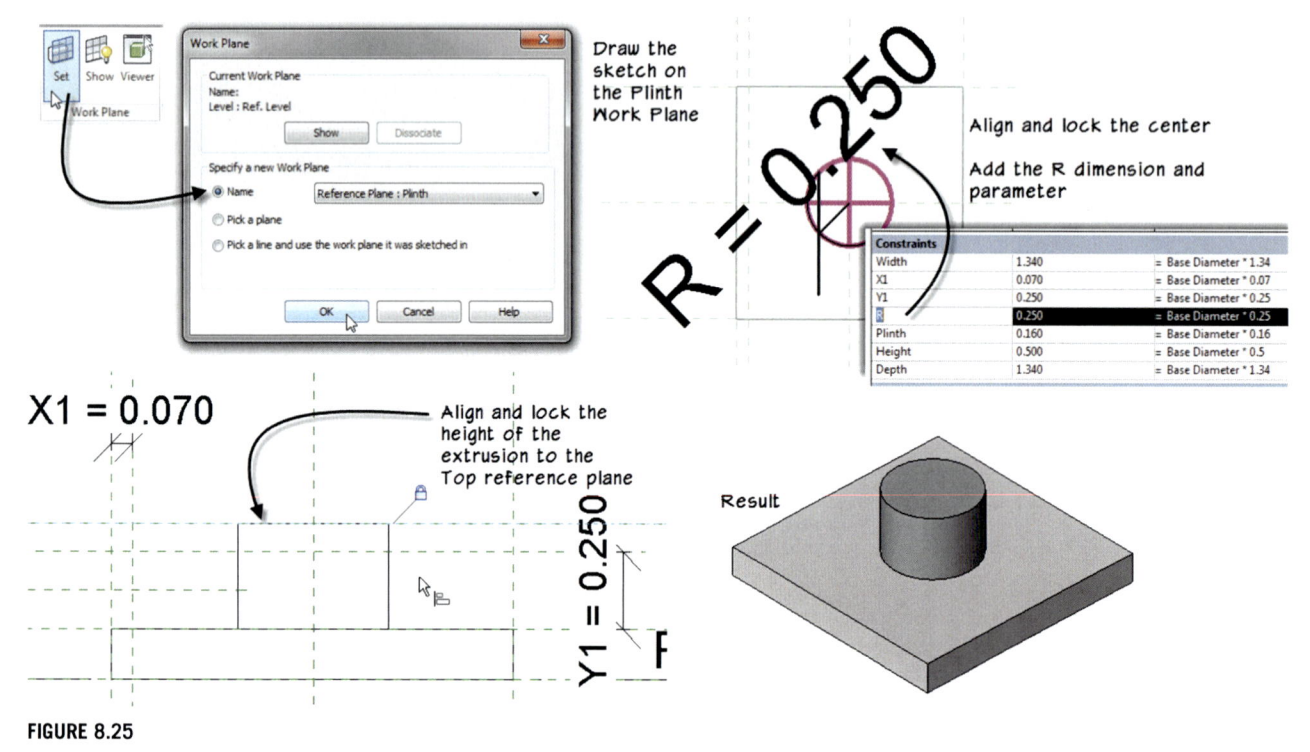

FIGURE 8.25

Add an extrusion at the center

⇨ Turn on the center mark for the circle, align and lock it the center.

• Renaissance Revit •

- Add a radius dimension with a new parameter called **R** grouped under **Constraints**. Set the Formula for this dimension to **Base Diameter * 0.250**.
- In the Front elevation, align and lock the height of the extrusion to the Top reference plane.

3. Flex Base Diameter to ensure that everything is functioning, then reset to **1.000** before continuing.

ADDING SWEEP MOLDINGS

By now we have done many sweeps in the previous lessons. So I won't give all of the details here, but instead review the overall steps required. I am going to follow the procedures we used in the "Add a Sweep Profile" and "Copy Additional Sweep Profiles" topics in Chapter 6 where we used the Pick 3D Edges option to set the sweep path and then discussed how to reuse the first sweep to create the others. As we have discussed on several occasions, there are other ways that we could build this and any of the sweeps and moldings. You are encouraged to try other techniques if you prefer and you are also encouraged to review the topics I have mentioned here if you need to review any of the techniques.

1. From the Project Browser, open the *View 1* 3D view.
2. On the Create tab, click the Sweep button. Using Pick Path, pick the bottom edges of the cylinder extrusion for the path. (Even though we drew it with a circle, there will be two edges).

   Start with the left edge so it will be the profile plane.

This file currently does not have any profiles loaded. Conveniently, there is a Load Profile button directly on the Modify | Sweep tab. The Doric base uses a scotia profile with a torus above and another below it. In previous tutorials, we have mostly drawn torus moldings directly in the sketch. This does not preclude our using a profile however. I have provided a few suitable molding profiles in the Moldings folder for this purpose. We worked with a scotia profile back in Chapter 4 and I have included that one in the Moldings folder as well.

- On the Modify | Sweep tab, click the Load Profile button.
- Browse to the *Moldings* folder, hold down the CTRL key and select both the *Scotia Profile (w Fillets).rfa* and the *Torus (Variable).rfa* and then click Open.

These two profiles represent slight variations on what we built back in Chapter 4. To the scotia, I simply added a top and bottom fillet with variable dimensions. This is exactly like the other similar molding profiles we have already seen. The torus follows the strategy we employed in the "Create the Revolve Molding" topic in Chapter 5 where we used an ellipse instead of an arc. Therefore, both a horizontal and vertical multiplier parameter is included. I also included a simple checkbox that toggles it from a circular to elliptical shape. Feel free to open these profile and explore them further on your own.

3. For the profile, choose **Torus (variable):Elliptical**.

Following the procedures we used above in the "Create a Void Sweep" topic, let's modify the parameters of the to adjust its size and proportion.

4. On the Project Browser, expand *Profiles > Torus (Variable)*.
5. Right-click on *Elliptical* and choose **Type Properties**.

Notice that in the Graphics grouping there is a checkbox labeled "Elliptical." This is the toggle parameter I noted above. When this is checked, the X Mult parameter (right above the checkbox) is used and controls the width of the profile. When this is unchecked, the Y Mult parameter (under Dimensions) controls both the height and width.

232 | Chapter 8

⇨ Under Graphics, change X Mult to: **0.070**. Under Dimensions, change the Projection Mult to: **0.350** and change the Y Mult to: **0.125**. Link up Base Diameter.

⇨ Click OK to apply the change.

While we now have the correct size and shape, as you can see, if we try to finish the sweep, it will make a self-intersecting form and fail. So continuing with the procedures we used above in the "Create a Void Sweep" topic, let's modify the instance parameters (offsets) of the profile.

6. Select the profile onscreen and adjust the offsets:

⇨ Horizontal Profile Offset: **0.350**.

⇨ Vertical Profile Offset: **-0.340**.

7. Finish the sweep (see Figure 8.26).

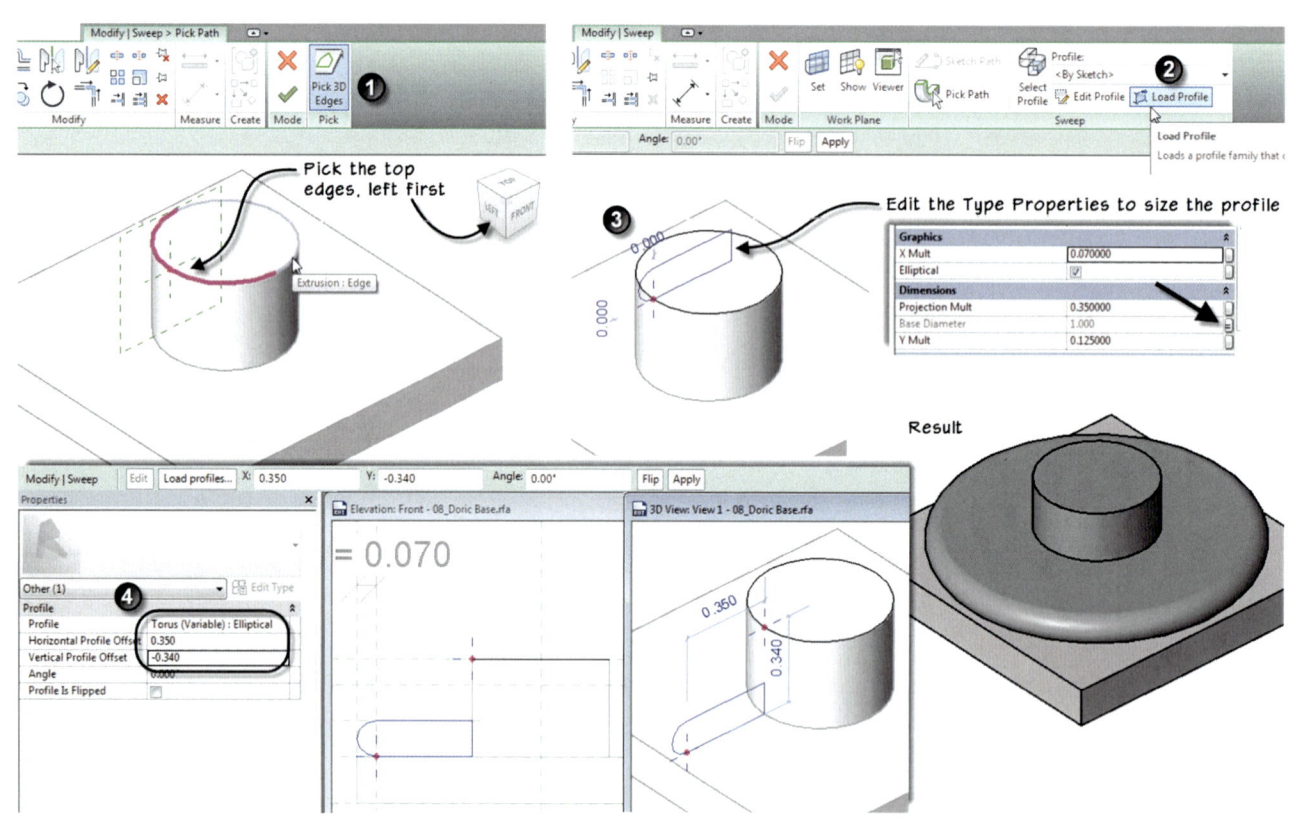

FIGURE 8.26
Create the first torus molding sweep

8. Create Assoicated Family Parameters with corresponding formulas for each offset. Flex when finished.

Now that we have the first sweep, we can use the procedure from the "Copy Additional Sweep Profiles" topic in Chapter 6 to copy and modify the molding twice more.

9. Copy and paste the molding aligned to the same place.

⇨ Edit the copy delete and re-pick its path. (Remember that this is necessary or it will not maintain the connection to the extrusion).

⇨ Change the profile to: **Scotia Profile (w Fillets):Flex**.

⇨ Edit the Type Properties of *Scotia Profile (w Fillets): Flex* as shown in Table 8.6 and shown in Figure 8.27.

TABLE 8.6

Parameter	Value	Comments
Top Fillet Mult	0.025	
Projection Mult	0.2875	
Bottom Fillet Mult	0.025	
Base Diameter	1.000	Associate Family Parameter
Multiplier	0.025	

Finish the sweep at this point without modifying the profile offsets. This is because they are currently being controlled by parameters. If you edit those offset values directly, you will end up flexing the model. To assing new parameters to the offset for this sweep, you have to finish it first.

10. Finish the sweep and then on the Properties palette, create and associate a new parameter for the Vertical Profile Offset.

    ⇨ Call it: **Scotia Y**, grouped under **Constraints** and with a formula of: **Base Diameter * -0.190**.

Since the value of Scotia X is the same as the previous Torus X, we don't need a new parameter for it.

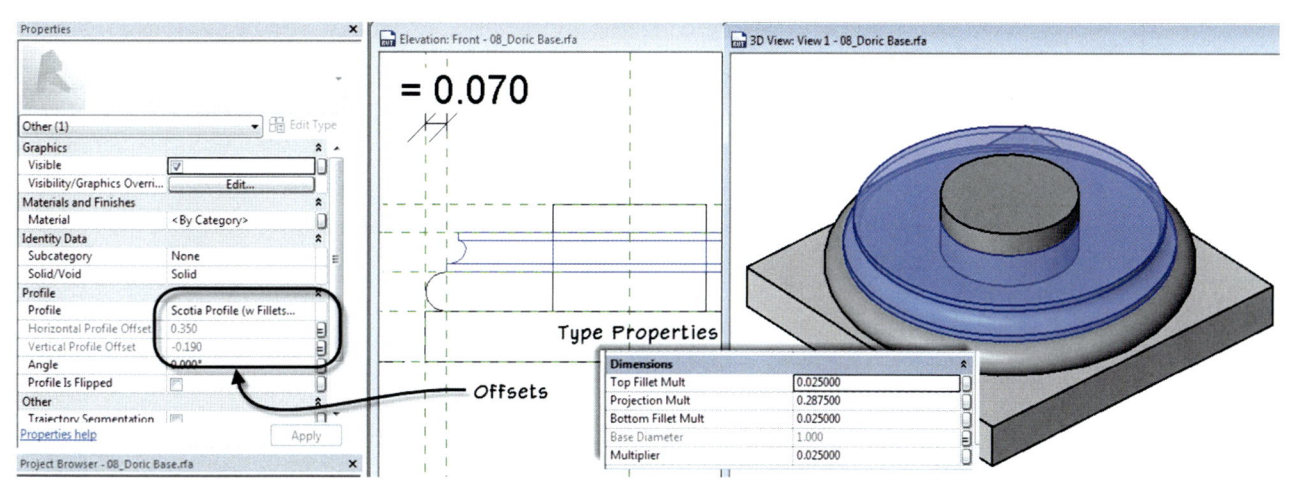

FIGURE 8.27
Copy and paste the first molding and then modify it to create the next one

11. Repeat the entire process to create the last molding.

    Again, when you paste, be sure to recreate the picked path. Choose the **Torus (Variable):Circular** profile this time and then configure the Type Properties (see Table 8.7 and Figure 8.28).

TABLE 8.7

Parameter	Value	Comments
Projection Mult	0.305	
Base Diameter	1.000	Associate Family Parameter
Y Mult	0.090	

Finish the Sweep and create and assign two new offset parameters to the offset values (see Table 8.8 and Figure 8.28).

TABLE 8.8

Parameter	Formula	Comments
Upper Torus Y	Base Diameter * -0.090	
Upper Torus X	Base Diameter * 0.305	

• *Creating Classical Architecture with Modern Software* •

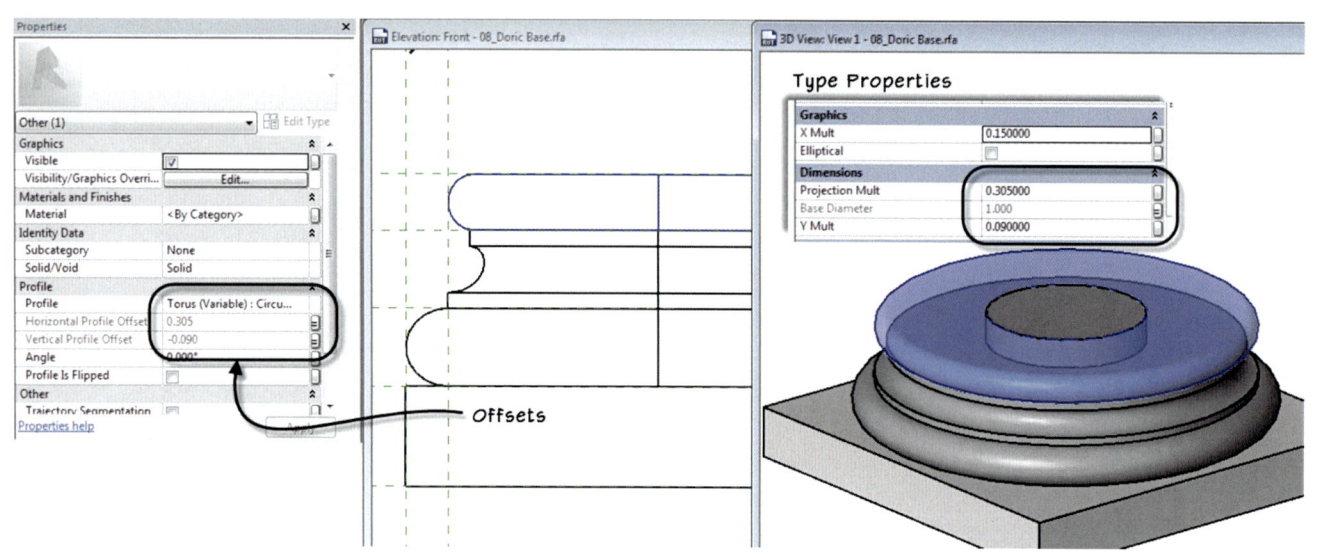

FIGURE 8.28
Paste and modify the final molding

12. Use Join Geometry to join the extrusion to the top molding (and the other forms if you wish).

This step is not really necessary as you will likely not see this family by itself too often. In other words, once it is loaded into the column, the shaft will always cover the seam between the forms. It is also not likely that you would section the column below the shaft, so there are few times if any when you will notice that the geometry is joined. I like to join it just the same, but in my tests, this sometimes caused an error when flexing. If this occurs, simply unjoin the geometry and leave it unjoined.

13. Flex the Base Diameter. When satisfied, reset to **1.000** and then save the file.
14. Select the three moldings (and optionally the cylinder) and on the Properties palette, next to Material, associate the existing **Base Material** parameter.

Optionally you can rename the two types of the Torus (Variable) profile. Do this on the Project Browser and choose names more descriptive like "Top Molding" and "Bottom Molding."

> **CATCH UP!** You can open a file completed to this point named: *08_Doric Base.rfa*.

You should still have the *Doric Column* file open. If you closed it, you can reopen it now, or open the appropriate catch-up file.

15. On the Ribbon click the Load into Project button.

    If the "Load into Projects" dialog appears, check only the *Doric Column.rfa* file and then click OK.

    ⇨ Overwrite the existing file.

The Base should now match the heights of the column perfectly.

16. Return to the *Doric Base* file, from the Application menu, choose **Close** and save if prompted.

> **CATCH UP!** You can open a file completed to this point named: *Doric Column_D.rfa*.

CREATE THE DORIC PEDESTAL

By now you should be seeing the pattern. Each family we construct builds on the previous one in logical ways. The Doric pedestal will be created from the saved and renamed Tuscan version as we did with the capital, shaft and base. The procedure is nearly identical the process we just followed for the base. So once again, I will not detail every instruction, but rather list out the overall steps required. Please refer to the previous topic, the topics noted therein and the "Build the Tuscan Pedestal" topic in Chapter 5 for further information on the techniques used here.

> Close all files except the *Doric Column_A.rfa* file. You can use your file or the catch-up file. You only need to keep open one window such as the *View 1* 3D view.

1. Minimize the Doric Column *View 1* 3D view, and then on the Project Browser, beneath *Families > Generic Models*, right-click Doric Pedstal and choose **Edit**.

This is just a slightly different way to open the file than we did before. The nice thing about minimizing first is you don't have to switch windows to minimize the other file and when you tile windows, it will not be included because it is minimized.

> ⇨ From Project Browser, open the *Front* elevation view and then tile the windows.

The Doric Pedstal is only slightly more complex than the Tuscan. So we will be able to reuse much of what we have here. The plinth is a little taller and has a similar cyma molding. We need to add a cavetto above the cyma. The die is unadorned like the Tuscan. The cap also has an extra cavetto molding and replaces the cyma reversa with an ovolo (see Figure 8.29).

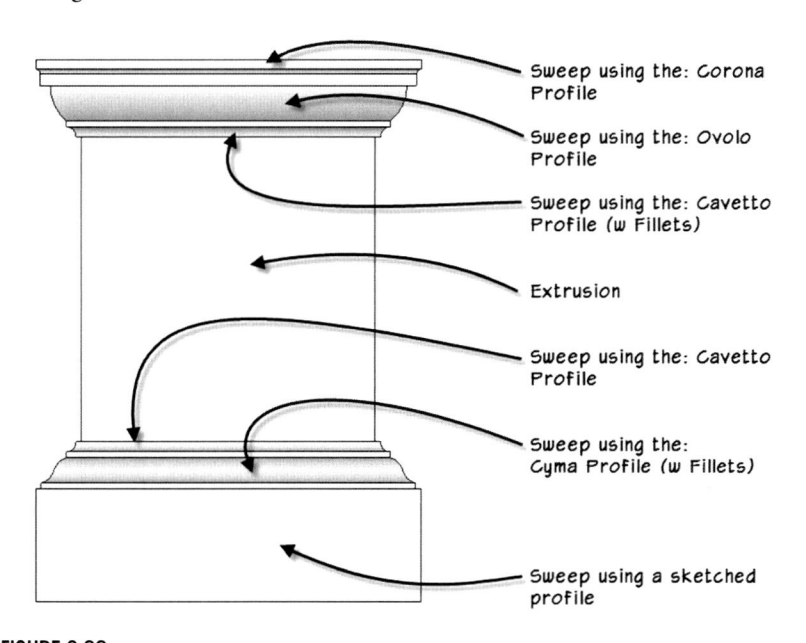

FIGURE 8.29
Understanding the Doric Pedestal

2. Open "Family Types," set Base Diameter to **1.000** and then Apply.

⇨ Make the following modifications listed in Table 8.9:

TABLE 8.9

Parameter	Formula	Comments
X2	Base Diameter * 0.070	
X1	Base Diameter * 0.210	
Width	Base Diameter * 1.340	No Change
Y3	Base Diameter * 0.225	
Y2	Base Diameter * 0.210	
Y1	Base Diameter * 0.500	
R2	Base Diameter * 0.860	
R1	Base Diameter * 0.695	No Change
Height	Base Diameter * 2.400	
Depth	Base Diameter * 1.340	No Change
Y4	Base Diameter * .115	

3. Rename X2 as **Cyma X**. Click OK to dismiss the dialog.

This adjusts the overall proportions of the family. Some of the changes are noticeable right away.

CONFIGURE THE PROFILE TYPE PARAMETERS

Next you will need to load a few additional profile families and then configure the Type Parameters of all of the profiles.

1. On the Insert tab, click the Load Family button.

⇨ Browse to the *Moldings* folder, hold down the CTRL key and select the *Cavetto Profile.rfa*, *Cavetto Profile (w Fillets).rfa* and the *Ovolo Profile.rfa* and then click Open.

2. On the Project Browser, expand *Families > Profiles*.

⇨ Table 8.10 shows the Type Properties of each of the five profile families we will need in this family. Work your way down the list editing the "Flex" type for each profile.

The Cyma Reversa Profile is not included in the table, since we will not need it for the Doric Pedestal. So you can skip this one for now. Later we will delete it from the file.

TABLE 8.10

Parameter	Value	Comments
Cavetto Profile:Flex		
Y Mult	0.045	
X Mult	0.045	
Depth Mult	0.025	
Base Diameter	1.000	Associate Family Parameter
Cavetto Profile (w Fillets):Flex		
Y Mult	0.045	
X Mult	0.045	
Fillet Mult	0.025	
Depth Mult	0.025	
Base Diameter	1.000	Associate Family Parameter
Corona Profile:Flex		
Y Projection Mult	0.055	
X Projection Mult	0.190	
X Mult	0.020	
Y Mult	0.020	
Fillet Projection Mult	0.040	
Base Diameter	1.000	Associate Family Parameter
Cyma Profile (w Fillets)		
Y Mult	0.115	
X Mult	0.115	
Fillet Mult	0.025	
Depth Mult	0.070	
Base Diameter	1.000	Associate Family Parameter
Ovolo Profile		
Y Mult	0.155	
X Mult	0.075	
Depth Projection Mult	0.070	
Base Diameter	1.000	Associate Family Parameter

I know it's a lot of parameters to configure. There are five moldings in this pedestal and each one has several parameters. So the total is a little overwhelming. Unfortunately, we are not quite done yet. We still need to adjust the offsets of the moldings as well and this will require some additional parameters. We might as well get those out of the way next.

CONFIGURE PROFILE OFFSET PARAMETERS

You may recall that when we built the Tuscan pedestal in the "Build the Tuscan Pedestal" topic in Chapter 5 that we approached the path of the sweeps in two different ways. For some of the moldings we used the pick path method and for others we drew a circular path and use trajectory segmentation to square it off. As noted in the Tuscan exercise, either approach is valid. Since both are used here, I will leave them configured as-is. For any new moldings you can use either method. This means that for the two lower moldings I will approach it as we did in the previous exercise by offsetting the profiles. For the upper three, I'll use trajectory segmentation. Both approaches will require some new parameters.

1. Open the "Family Types" dialog and use Table 8.11 to configure the following new type-based parameters.

    Group all new parameters under **Constraints**.

TABLE 8.11

Parameter	Formula	Comments
Cyma Y	Base Diameter * 0.140	
Cavetto Y	Base Diameter * 0.045	
Cavetto X	Base Diameter * 0.025	
Y5	Base Diameter * 0.070	
R3	Base Diameter * 0.740	

That finally completes all of the required parameters. Now we can use them to add and edit the sweeps.

CONFIGURE PEDESTAL MOLDINGS

We now have all of the profiles we need and all of the parameters configured. So all that remains is to perform the final assembly.

   You should still have both the *Front* elevation and the *View 1* 3D view open and tiled.

2. Select the cyma molding onscreen in the elevation view.

⇨ On the Properties palette, next to the Vertical Profile Offset, click the Associate Family Parameter button.

⇨ Choose **Cyma Y** and then click OK.

3. Keep the molding selected, copy and paste it to the same place.

4. On the Properties palette, change the Profile to **Cavetto Profile:Flex**.

⇨ Change the associated familiy parameters for both the vertical and horizontal offsets. Choose the two new parameters: **Cavetto X** and **Cavetto Y**.

5. Edit the sweep. Delete and then pick the path, again.

⇨ Pick the top edges of the cyma molding where they intersect the extrusion (see Figure 8.30).

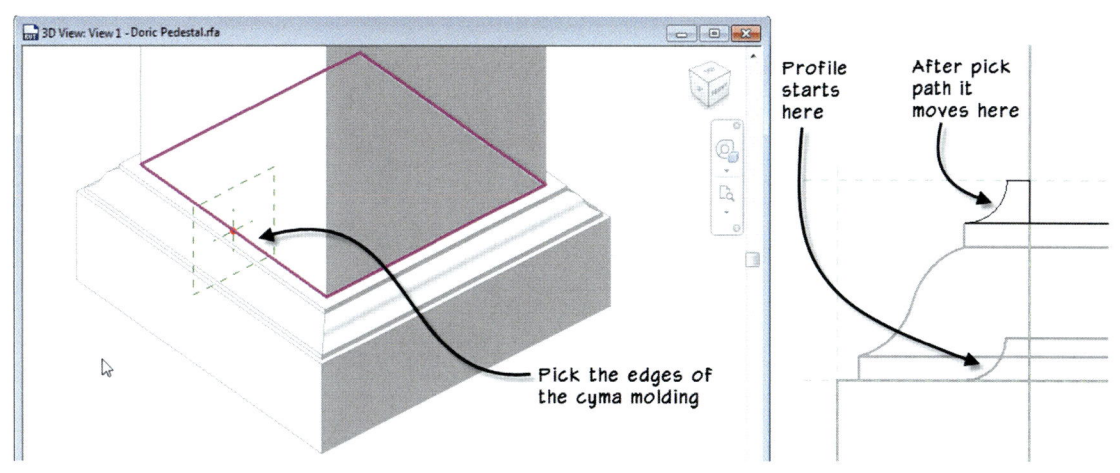

FIGURE 8.30

Edit the sweep and pick a new path

6. Finish the sweep.

For the top moldings, we'll sketch the path as noted above. We need a reference plane first.

7. In the Front elevation view, select the reference plane named: Cyma Reversa Molding. (Third one from the top).

    ⇨ On the Properties palette, rename it **Upper Cavetto**.

8. Copy it onscreen up about 0.100. (The exact amount is not important).

    ⇨ Name the new copy: **Ovolo Molding**.

    ⇨ Add a dimension between the Upper Cavetto reference plane and the new Ovolo Molding reference plane. Label it with the existing parameter: Y5 (see Figure 8.31).

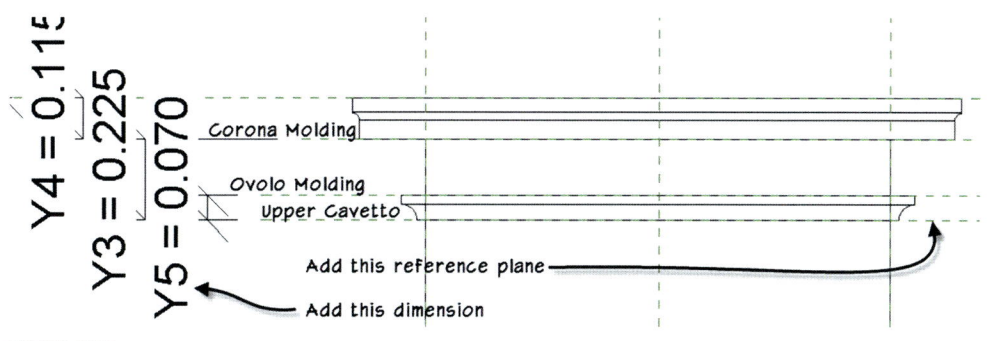

FIGURE 8.31

Add a new reference plane and dimension

9. Select the existing cyma reversa molding.

10. On the Properties palette, change the profile to: **Cavetto Profile (w Fillets):Flex**.

11. Keep this molding selected, copy and paste it to the same place.

    ⇨ On the Modify | Sweep tab, click the Edit Work Plane button.

    ⇨ From the Name list, choose **Reference Plane : Ovolo Molding** and then click OK.

    ⇨ On the Properties palette, change the profile to: **Ovolo Profile:Flex**.

12. On the Modify | Sweep tab, click the Edit Sweep button.

    ⇨ Click Sketch Path and when prompted, open Floor Plan: Ref. Level.

    ⇨ Select the dimension in the sketch (currently R1) and label it with **R3**.

• *Creating Classical Architecture with Modern Software* •

⇨ Click the Finish Edit Mode button twice to exit out (see Figure 8.32).

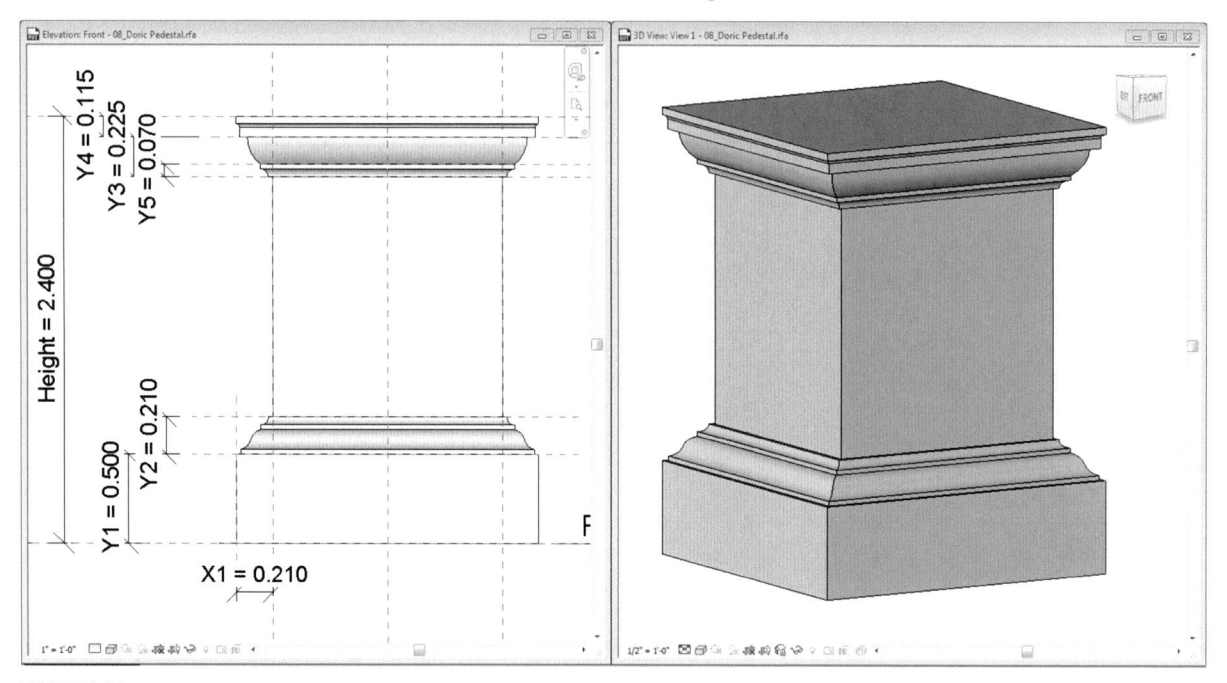

FIGURE 8.32

The completed Doric Pedestal

You can now delete the Cyma Reversa Profile from the Project Browser. This will help tidy things up a little bit.

13. Flex the Base Diameter. When satisfied, reset to **1.000** and then save the file.

CATCH UP! You can open a file completed to this point named: 08_Doric Pedestal.rfa.

You should still have the *Doric Column* file open. If you closed it, you can reopen it now, or open the appropriate catch-up file.

14. On the Ribbon click the Load into Project button.

    If the "Load into Projects" dialog appears, check only the *Doric Column.rfa* file and then click OK.

⇨ Overwrite the existing file.

The shaft should now match the heights of the column perfectly.

15. Return to the *Doric Pedestal* file, from the Application menu, choose **Close** and save if prompted.

CATCH UP! You can open a file completed to this point named: Doric Column.rfa.

LOAD INTO SANDBOX

We now have a completed Doric column. As we have done before, we will open a sandbox file and load it in there to test it out.

1. From the *Chapter08* folder, open the *08_Sandbox_Colonnade.rvt* file.

This is a simple sandbox file copied from the Tuscan version that we used in the previous chapter. At the moment I just have some simple cylindrical columns in place. They are named "Doric Column" so when you load your Doric Column in here, you will be prompted to overwrite.

2. Switch windows back to the *Doric Column.rfa* file (or open the catch-up file).

When you switch windows, Revit will often maximize the windows. If this occurred, click the Restore down button at the top right corner of the window.

> **Note:** If you use the catch-up file, be sure to either save it as *Doric Column*, or in the sandbox file, on the Project Browser, rename the *Doric Column* there to *08_Doric Column*. Either way, you want to make sure that you are prompted to overwrite the file when loading.

3. Click Load into Project.
⇨ Choose the "Overwrite the existing version and its parameter values" option.
4. Return to the *Doric Column* file, from the Application menu, choose **Close** and save if prompted (see Figure 8.33).

FIGURE 8.33
Load the Doric Column into the sandbox to test

Feel free to experiment further. Save and close the file when finished.

SUMMARY

- ✓ The fastest way to create new orders is to start with the previous order as a seed.

- ✓ Save a copy of the order, on Project Browser, rename each nested family, and then edit these renamed families and reload the edited versions when finished.

- ✓ Many of the proportions are similar from one order to the next, so simply adjusting the proportions is good first step.

- ✓ Since we built most of the nested families from sweeps with profiles, your next task is to adjust the proportions of those profiles for similar moldings and swap in different profiles for the ones that vary.

- ✓ Remember that you can create forms from both solids and voids. Creating the abacus from a void for example allows you to set the overall size of the abacus with the family's width and depth dimensions and then carve away the unwanted parts with a void sweep.

- ✓ If you want a solid shaft, add an extruded solid to fill in the hollow sweep.

- ✓ Load all pieces back into the host family, overwrite the existing ones and flex.

- ✓ Load it into a project to test everything out.

Chapter 9
The Doric Entablature

INTRODUCTION

We'll complete the Doric Order in this chapter with a look at the Doric entablature. There will be some similarities to the approach that we took with the Tuscan Entablature, but we will also be exploring some differences as well. Particular as they apply to the repetitive elements that occur along the length of the Doric entablature.

OBJECTIVES

In this chapter we are going to explore various options to create the entablature of the Doric Order. Topics in this chapter include:

- Understanding "two-pick" drawing options.
- Creating a custom Line-Based family.
- Using Railing elements to create repetitive elements.

LINE BASED OPTIONS

In some of the previous exercises, we have looked at some line-based elements. Line-based elements are those that are created with two picks onscreen such as walls, beams, datum elements and even simple stairs. In Chapter 6, we used a beam family to create the entablature of the Tuscan order to take advantage of its line-based characteristics and because "beam" seemed like a good choice of category for the entablature. As we move into more complex orders, we will find that the choice of family seed and category becomes more difficult. There are several options available and each has its pros and cons. Let's take a quick inventory of each approach that we can entertain and discuss the advantages and disadvantages of each approach.

BEAMS

I'll start the discussion with beams. We have already looked at using beams in great detail back in the "Creating the Tuscan Entablature" topic in Chapter 6. So I will just review the main pros and cons of this approach. Beams work well for a few reasons: they are the logical choice considering that the entablature is the horizontal lintel spanning across two or more columns; essentially a beam. In reality, you might find the actual beam buried inside the entablature with its moldings and other features being applied as non-structural embellishments. But this might be too fine a distinction to influence your choice in building the model.

The other very nice advantage that we gain with beams is the ability to miter them where they join one another. This does take an extra step as we saw in Chapter 6, but it is easy to do and quite effective. We also saw in the Tuscan exercise that we can very easily build up the overall form from a series of the separate sweeps using the profiles we have already built. All of these characteristics make the beam a compelling first choice for building the entablature.

There is however, one significant disadvantage: in my tests, repeating elements do not behave well. The Doric entablature is intricately ornamented with elements that repeat in very controlled patterns along the length. Depending on the specific design we can have triglyphs, metopes, mutules and dentils. All of these elements must repeat in highly controlled patterns. It is easy enough to add these repetitive elements along the length, but as soon as we miter two beams together it distorts the elements. Given the importance of repetitive elements in the Doric Order, this is unfortunately a "deal breaker" for mitered beams (see Figure 9.1).

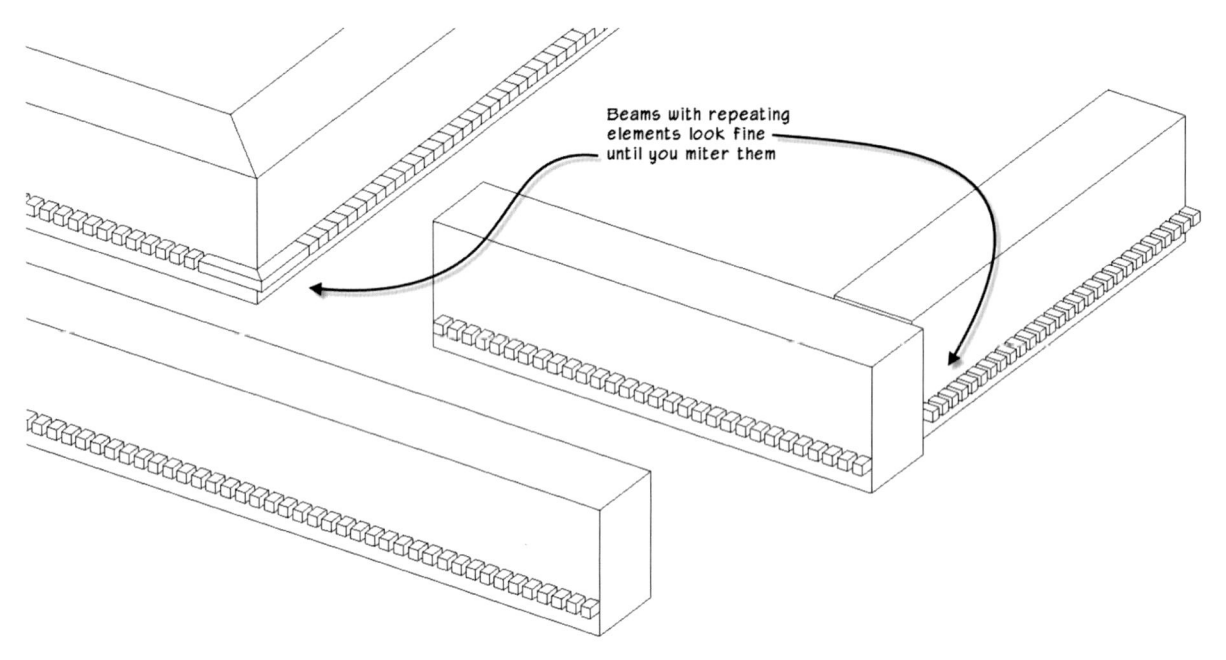

FIGURE 9.1

Repeating elements in beam families get distorted when you miter

WALLS

This is another option that we have already discussed back in the "Wall Sweeps" topic in Chapter 7. Walls can have sweeps. Sweeps in the project use the same profiles that sweeps in the family editor use. So it is possible to create a wall sweep that uses the same moldings and creates the basic geometry required for the entablature. Walls automatically join with one another, so we don't even need to miter them as a separate step. Simply drawing the walls will automatically apply miters to any integral sweeps (sweeps added in the wall "Type Properties" dialog). Being part of the wall, they are categorized as walls which may in some cases be preferable over beams. The steps for adding such a sweep were already covered in the above referenced topic, so I won't repeat them here.

There were a few items that I did not mention in Chapter 7. First, walls are a system family. So when you want to change the Base Diameter, you cannot link up the parameter as you can in a component family. You will have to duplicate the type, perform any calculations manually and then carefully apply the values to the type properties of the new type. This includes the type properties of any profiles you are using; each will have to be duplicated as well. Formulas are not able to be built into system family types like they can in component families. This was one of the main reasons why I provided a single overall profile for the entire Tuscan Entablature back in the "Wall Sweeps" topic in Chapter 7. It would certainly have been possible to add several separate sweeps to the wall; one for each individual molding, however, when we needed to change the Base Diameter, we would have had to make duplicate types of all the profiles, then a duplicate wall type and finally perform the calculations and set the values in the new type. All this because formulas cannot be added to system families. So even though the profile was considerably more complex and difficult to build, building it was the only practical way to use a wall sweep.

Another item I did not mention was that sweeps can also be added as separate elements that are not automatically part of the wall type. These are sometimes referred to as "Host Sweeps" or just Wall Sweeps. To add one, use the Wall:Sweep command on the Wall drop-down button. Sweeps added this way differ from the ones that are applied at the type level (I like to call type-based sweeps: "integral sweep.") in a few ways. First, you can place them on just the walls you chose without having to create a new wall type to do so. Wall sweeps can appear on schedules and, my favorite feature: they be assigned to a custom subcategory. The separate subcategory give us much more control over display of our seeps. We can turn this subcategory on and off in different views to suit the needs of the specific view.

Both integral wall sweeps and individual host wall sweeps have some compelling advantages. However as you might expect, there are some downsides as well. Of minor concern is the height of the wall. You have to plan the wall height start and end a little more carefully if using it strictly as an entablature. This is not hard to do, but you do have to be aware of and plan for it. Category is again a concern (more so with integral sweeps) so in some cases having the sweeps part of the walls category might make managing display or scheduling in your model a bit more challenging. This is again not insurmountable, but could pose a concern. Perhaps the biggest limitation with using walls for the entablature is the same issue we have with beams: they cannot have elements natively repeating along the length.

To be clear, I am talking about building in an automated repetitive element. Walls have settings for the layers and linear elements along its length, but not for elements that repeat *along* the length. This would have to occur manually on a wall. So, if you like, you can certainly add items such as the triglyphs and mutules to the wall after placement. This is certainly possible, but requires more manual configuration and ongoing maintenance in the model as the design changes. Incidentally, I should note that the same is true for beams. If you chose, you can create separate families for elements you wish to repeat along the length and apply them to the beams after they are drawn. You could even do a line-based repeating family containing just these items (see Figure 9.2).

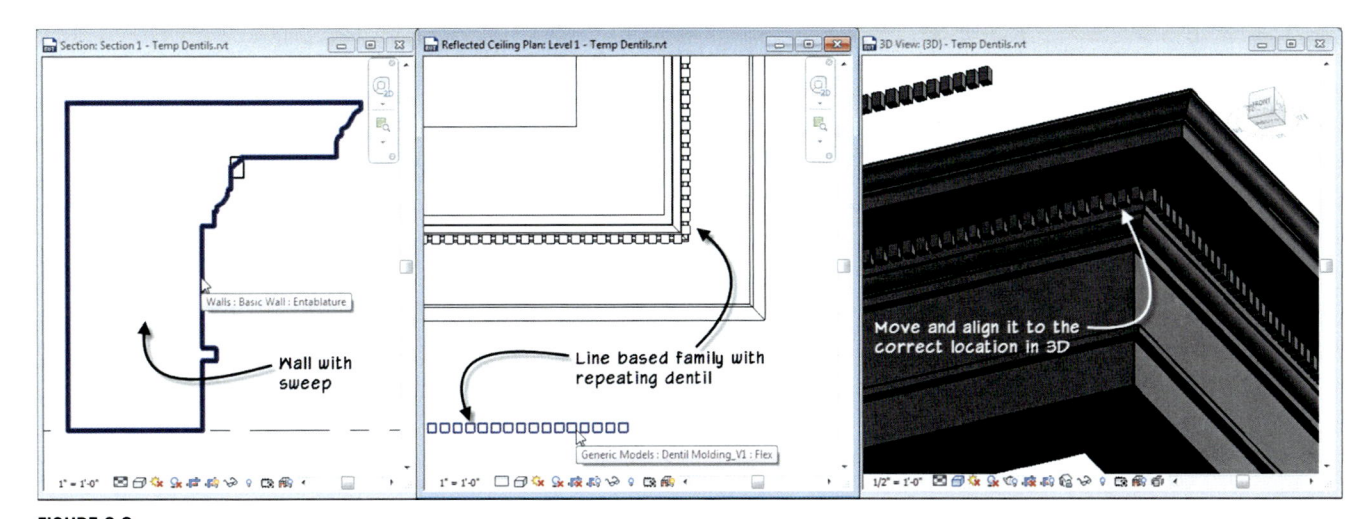

FIGURE 9.2
Walls with sweeps used as the main form of the entablature with a line-based family used for the repeating parts

Even though I am not providing a tutorial to create the file pictured in the figure, I have provided the file with the other Chapter 9 files for you to open and explore. The name of the file is: *09_Sandbox_Walls and Beams with Dentils.rvt* and is in the *Chapter09* folder.

SLAB EDGES

This option was also discussed in the "Wall Sweeps" topic in Chapter 7. By now I think you might be seeing a pattern. This option has many of the same advantages and disadvantages as the previous two. Once again, the big limitation is there is no automatic way to add repetitive elements along the length of a slab edge.

CURTAIN WALLS

I have not mentioned curtain walls previously. I do not think they offer a good alternative here, but I will mention them briefly to explain why. Curtain walls are compelling at first because unlike walls, they *can* have repetition along their length. We can define this repetition at the type or instance level. To make it more automated, type-based would seem preferable.

There would be several challenges to trying to use curtain walls for an element like the entablature. With curtain walls, you can use profile families (including the ones we have built in this book) for mullions. However, it is very difficult and in some cases not possible to get a curtain wall to put more than one mullion adjacent to each other, so the "built-up" approach wouldn't work. This means that like the wall sweep approach, you will be forced to build a single profile family for the entire entablature. Mitering at corners can sometimes be tricky but it is manageable.

These are not the real issues however. More concerning is that even though you can divide the curtain wall along its length, when you do so, it breaks the entire curtain wall including the mullions. So your overall sweep for the moldings will be broken into several segments. This is not too bad if the spacing is reasonable, but I would not want to try this to do a dentil molding. You would have dozens or maybe hundreds of tiny mullion segments touching end to end if it actually works. In my tests, it fails to draw the entablature when you make the spacing too small. But the real issue is that you can only define one pattern in each direction: one horizontal and one vertical. Given the complexity of the Doric frieze alone, these issues make a curtain wall highly impractical (see Figure 9.3).

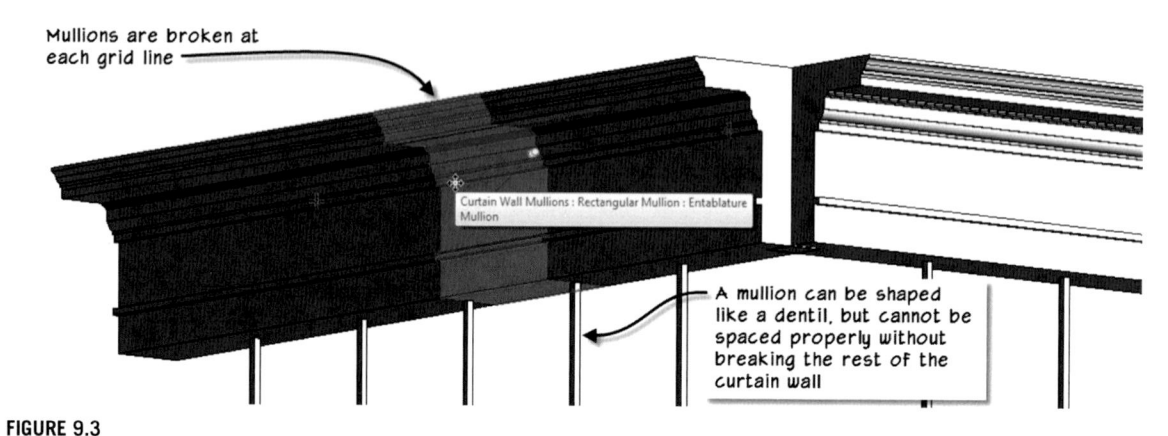

FIGURE 9.3
Curtain walls have too many issues to be practical for the entablature

LINE BASED FAMILIES

By now you are probably noticing that most of the options offer compelling advantages but all seem to have at least one fatal flaw. So what about just building our own family? Can we just create an entablature family maybe even starting with a generic model? Certainly we can. It's just that we are trying to eliminate as much repetitive manual effort along the way as we can. Furthermore, with the intricate nature of the Doric frieze, it is really easy to make errors the more we rely on manual calculations and placement.

There is however a useful family template that we have not used so far. The *Generic Model line based.rft* template incorporates a reference line that becomes the family's backbone and is placed in a project using two picks like a beam or a wall. We can even toggle on "chain" and draw line-based families end to end. Combine this with standard techniques like parametrically driven arrays and we can build in all of the repetitive elements that our Doric entablature's frieze requires and have them automatically repeat along the length of the family as we pick two points to place it in the project. Furthermore, being a component family, we can use all of the techniques that we already explored when building the Tuscan beam family, use the Base Diameter, apply formulas, etc.

There is only one significant disadvantage. Line-based families do not miter. While disappointing, this is not insurmountable. It turns out that with a little bit of extra effort, we can create the mitering we require manually. Learning how to do this will be the subject of the first tutorial that we will explore here in this chapter (see Figure 9.4).

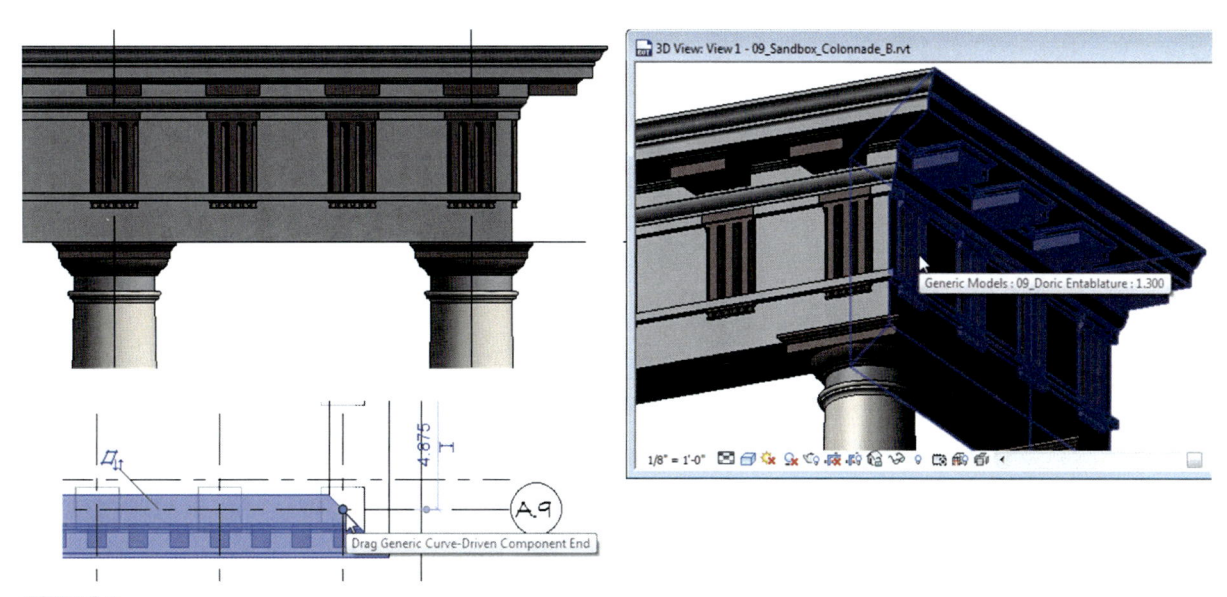

FIGURE 9.4
Using a line based family is one of our best alternatives

RAILINGS

The use of a railing for your entablature may be the most unusual option of them all. In the previous items, I began with the advantages and then discussed the disadvantages. In this case, let me reverse that and start right in with the major disadvantage to using a railing. The category is wrong. In a program like Revit deliberately using an improper category to model something could be argued as breaking the first rule of building information modeling. In most cases, I would be inclined to agree. But the railing element offers some compelling features that are simply not available in any other element. So while choosing this approach breaks the rules, sometimes breaking or bending the rules is justified. Let's look at some of the advantages of using railings to create classical entablatures.

They are very easy to draw. When you click the railing tool, you are placed in sketch mode and you can draw any path you like for the railing. It can be closed or open. It can be one segment or several. When you finish the sketch, all corners will be mitered and the railing will be a single element. None of the other solutions above that have mitering capability (beams, walls and line-based families) have this feature. With all of the others, each segment remains a separate element.

Railings can have complex form. Very detailed patterns can be configured directly in the "Type Properties" dialog. Unlike curtain walls for example, you are not limited to a single pattern in each direction. Railings are made up of rails and balusters. Rails run the length of the railing sketch. Balusters are repeated in the pattern you designate along the length. Special rules are available for the ends and corners. You can use more than one kind of baluster in a given railing type. Balusters are fully customizable component families (see Figure 9.5).

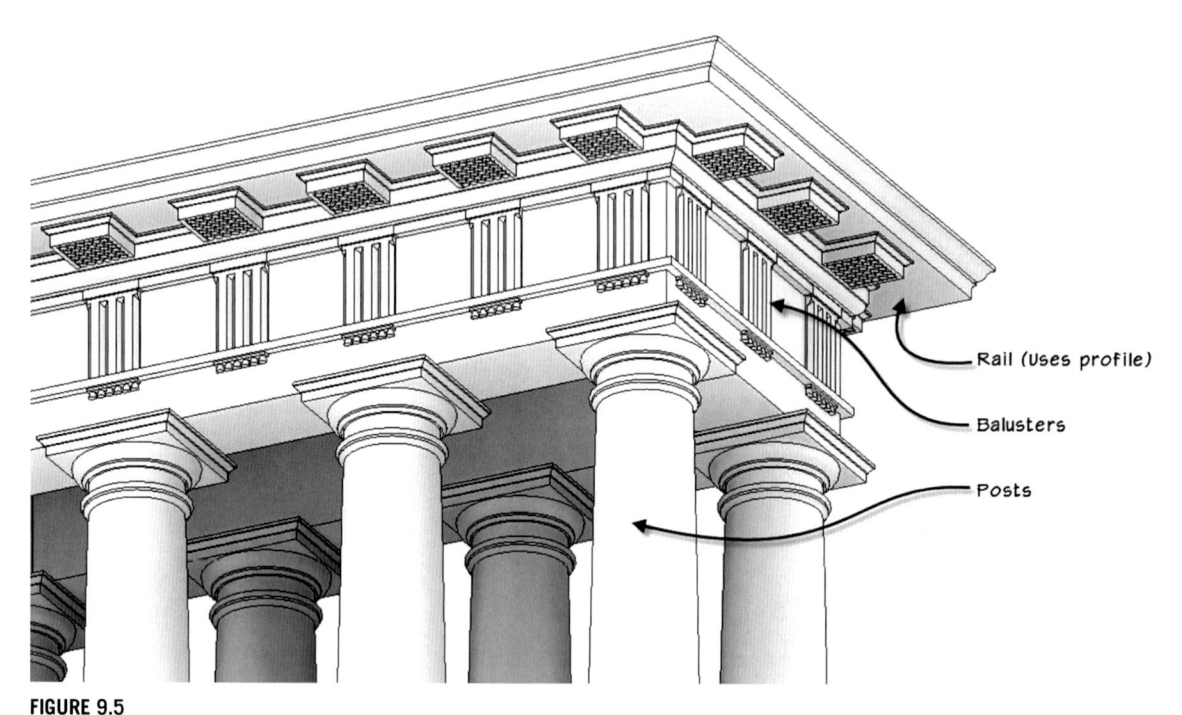

FIGURE 9.5

Railings have all the features we need, the only downside is that they are railings

You can have one or several rails. Rails can use profiles for their shape. You can define a single rail with one complex profile family, or do the built-up approach and leverage the profiles that we have already built. We can even use another kind of component family called a railing support. These are designed specifically for use in railings in their intended use, so I find these harder to work with than balusters for elements like triglyphs and mutules.

Finally, there are two additional features of railings which make them well worth considering. One is that you don't have to stop with just the entablature. It is actually possible to embed your column family into a baluster family and create a single railing type that draws the columns and entablature all in one shot. This may not always be desirable, but it is a compelling option nonetheless. The other very interesting feature of railings is that their paths do not have to be straight lines. You can draw curved paths. Most importantly is that the pattern you devise for your railing entablature will wrap itself around the curve accordingly! (See Figure 9.6).

FIGURE 9.6
The same railing type can follow a curved path

I can understand if you may still be uncomfortable with the idea of using a category for something unintended. I am not completely satisfied with the approach either. But we will go through an exercise below to explore the technique in more detail so you can make a more informed decision. If you decide to implement this technique in real projects, there are measures you can employ to overcome some of the disadvantages of using the wrong category. One of the arguments against using the incorrect category is what happens in schedules and visibility/graphics. Unless you tell them otherwise, a schedules and view visibility have no way of knowing that an entablature railing is not a "real" railing. All we have to do is add a subcategory and/or custom parameter to mitigate this.

> **Note:** to get the shaded effect I have used in the last two figures, open the "Graphic Display Options" dialog and turn on Show Ambient Shadows. You can get to Graphic Display Options from the View Control Bar at the bottom of the view window, from the dialog launcher icon on the Graphics panel of the View tab, or type the keyboard shortcut GD.

ADAPTIVE COMPONENT

With all the pros and cons of the various techniques that have been outlined above, you may be wondering why I have not mentioned adaptive components. Mainly it is because I have been saving them for later. Starting with Chapter 11 we will begin looking at the massing environment in general and specifically at adaptive components.

Adaptive components are a special kind of Revit family that can have behaviors not available in families created in the traditional family editor with which we have been working so far. Three features in particular set adaptive components apart from traditional families: they can have one or more "insertion" points. When you place the family, you click the locations of each of these insertion points (called placement points) and the family "adapts" its form to the locations you click. This is how the adaptive component gets its name. Form making in adaptive components occurs in three-dimensional space; it is not limited to 2D sketch mode. As such, very complex three-dimensional forms can be achieved, many of which would be extremely difficult or impossible in the traditional family editor. And finally, Adaptive components have a very handy "divide and repeat" feature. This feature can be applied to surfaces or lines and allows you to quickly set up a series of repetitive elements that adjusts dynamically as the family flexes. To see some examples, look at Figure 11.24 and Figure 11.27 in Chapter 11.

For all of these reasons, adaptive components are a viable option, not only for the Doric entablature, but for many of the classical forms we will be creating. That being said, I will save detailed discussion of adaptive components for later chapters. Adaptive families are more powerful, but also more complex. There is a significant learning curve to them if you have never worked in the massing environment and adaptive families can become quite large. Furthermore, you must choose carefully. While it is possible to nest component families into adaptive families, you cannot nest adaptive families in traditional families. Also, traditional profile families cannot be used in adaptive families. So there are certainly some issues to consider. But as I said, we will save those for future chapters and for now focus on the line-based and railing options noted here.

CREATING A COMPLEX PROFILE

Back in the "Alternate Approaches for Entablature" topic in Chapter 7, I discussed a few alternate techniques to build the entablature, each of which required a profile family that incorporated all of the moldings in a single file, rather than a built-up approach using several separate sweeps each with their own profile family. At the time I provided the complex molding profile for you to use in the exercise. In this exercise, I thought we would take a look at how you would approach the creation of a profile like this. In this exercise, we will create a single profile for the entire Doric entablature. I must warn you however, that this will be a very complex shape and one of the more advanced exercises we have attempted so far. If you get behind, I have provided catch-up files later in the exercise.

1. From the Application menu, choose **Open**.
   - Browse to the *Seed Families* folder, select the *Family Seed (Profile Proportional).rfa* file and then click Open.
2. Save the file in the *Chapter09* folder as: **Doric Entablature Profile**.

   For the next several steps, refer to: Table 9.1 and Figure 9.7.

3. Delete the two horizontal dimensions (X and Equality).
   - Rename the vertical reference plane in the middle (currently X Mid) to **Face of Column**.
   - Mirror this reference plane to the other side of the Center (Left/Right) one. Name the new copy: **Back of Column**.
4. Add a new equality dimension that includes Back of Column, Center (Left/Rigth) and Face of Column.
5. Add a dimension between Face of Column and Back of Column.
   - Label this with a new type-based parameter called: **Column Top Diameter** and group it under **Constraints**.
6. Add a dimension between Face of Column and X Max (rightmost vertical reference plane).
   - Label this dimension with the existing **X** parameter.

   It will flex to the right.

7. Delete the vertical equality dimension on the left.
   - Copy the horizontal (Y Mid) reference plane up, (but not past Y Max). Name the new copy: **Cornice**.
   - Rename Y Mid to: **Frieze**. Rename Center (Front/Back) to: **Architrave**.

8. Add two dimensions, one between Cornice and Y Max, labeled: **Cornice Height**. The other between Architrave and Frieze, labeled: **Architrave Height**. Group both under **Constraints**.

9. Open the "Family Types" dialog rename the Y and X parameters and edit or add the formulas (see Table 9.1 and Figure 9.7).

TABLE 9.1

Parameter	Formula	Comments
Profile Height	Base Diameter * 2.000	Renamed from Y
Profile Width	Base Diameter	Renamed from X
Cornice Height	Base Diameter * 0.750	
Column Top Diameter	Base Diameter * 0.850	
Architrave Height	Base Diameter * 0.500	

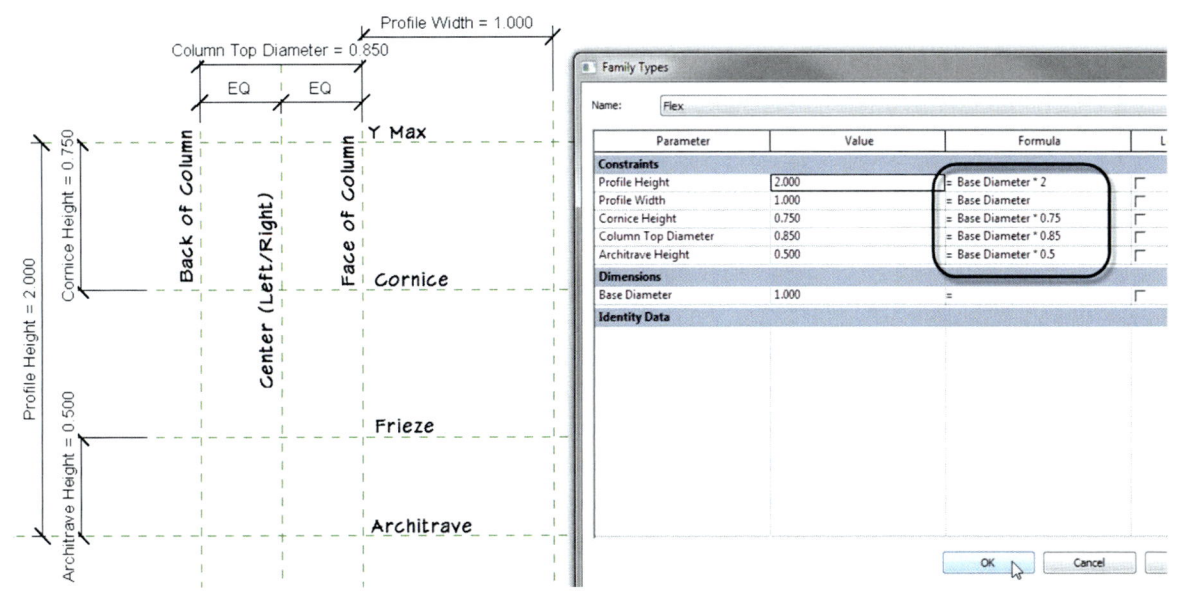

FIGURE 9.7

Adjust the existing reference planes, make new dimensions and flex the model

10. Delete the three profile lines onscreen.

CREATE THE CORNICE CYMA

The first molding is at the very top on the right side. We need a cyma here. The overall X and Y dimensions of this profile are both 0.125. We can use the same basic procedure we used back in Chapter 4. To construct it.

1. In the top right corner, create three reference planes:

⇨ One horizontal at .165 below the Y Max reference plane. Name it: **Cornice Cyma Bottom**.

⇨ Another horizontal at 0.040 below Y Max called: **Fillet A**.

⇨ One Vertical at 0.125 left of X Max reference plane. Name it: **Cornice Cyma Left**.

2. Add labeled dimensions with corresponding formulas for each of these reference planes.

3. Draw the horizontal and vertical lines for the topmost edge and the small vertical of the fillet (see Figure 9.8).

FIGURE 9.8

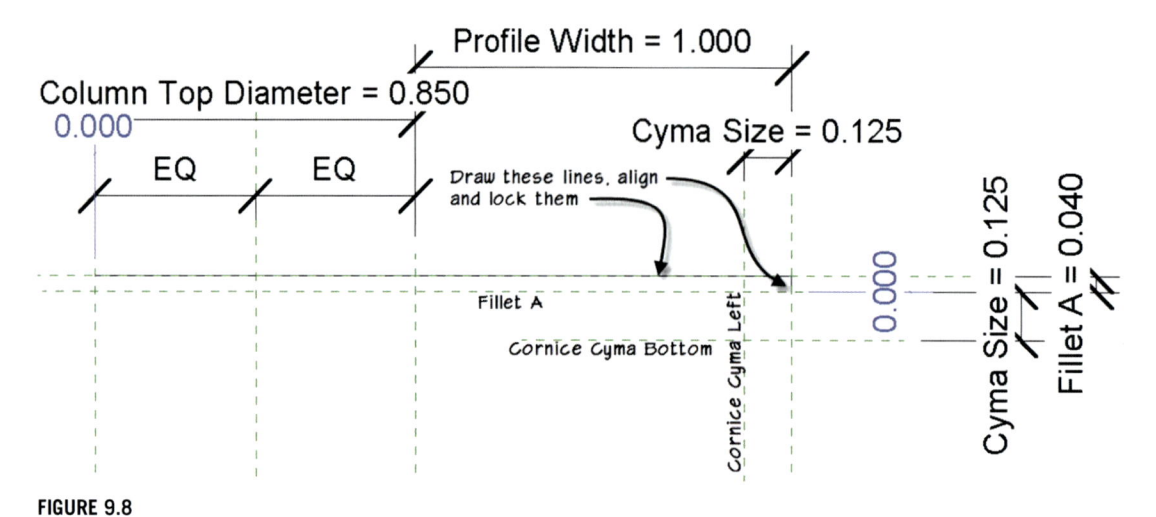

Block out the area for the cyma molding at the top of the cornice

In the small square are that we have defined with these new reference planes, we need a cyma molding. I tried copying and pasting from the cyma family that we built, but it was not too successful. So unfortunately we will have to construct the required armature again. The process is identical to the steps followed in the "Cyma" topic of Chapter 4.

4. Following the procedure outlined in the "Cyma" topic of Chapter 4, create the required reference planes and labeled dimensions.

> **Note:** The next few figures are provided in a PDF in the *Chapter09* folder so you can print them larger.

We'll make a few adjustments to the formulas, so just build the reference planes and dimensions first (see Figure 9.9).

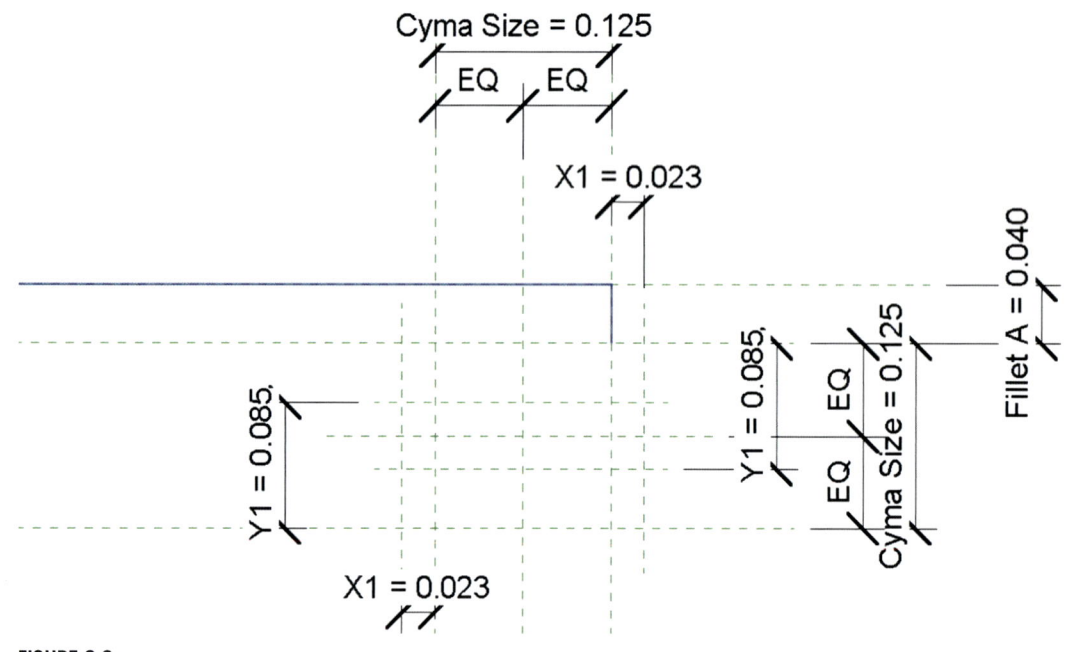

FIGURE 9.9

Create the armature required for the cyma curve

I kept the parameters labeled as Y1 and X1 for this molding, but as we work our way down, we'll have to adjust some names. For example, the "R" parameter used in Chapter 4 I have called "R1" here instead. I have also taken the opportunity to simplify things a bit. We will end up with four curved moldings and several fillets before we are finished with this profile. Therefore, we are going to end up with lots of parameters. "R1" therefore incorporates the formulas from both "R" and "D" in the original, saving us one parameter.

5. Open "Family Types" and create a parameter called **R1**, group it under **Constraints** and for the Formula input: **(sqrt((Cyma Size ^ 2) + (Cyma Size ^ 2))) / 2**

    Be careful to get all the parenthesis right. Try working out the formula in Notepad or Notepad ++ first, then copy and paste it into Revit.

The profiles we built in Chapter 4 were more general purpose. So they needed to be flexible to accommodate different proportions. Here, we already know the proportion. The cyma we are now building fits in a square, so it has a 45° diagonal. This eliminates the need for parameter "A." We also had a second parameter called "B" that subtracted the calculated angle from 120°. With "A" no longer a variable, we can do the math ahead of time: 120 minus 45, giving us 75°. This is the angle we need in the cosine and sine functions used to calculate "Y1" and "X1."

6. Remain in "Family Types" and add Formulas to Y1: **R1 * sin(75°)** and X1: **R1 * cos(75°)**.

7. Continue the process from Chapter 4, using Figure 4.40 as a guide, draw the two arcs, align and lock their centers and endpoints.

COMPLETING THE PROFILE

Right below the cyma is another fillet, then a corona. Beneath that will be a soffit area with a rather long projection. A small cyma reversa comes next, with a broad fillet beneath it and then an ovolo. There are a few more fillets beneath that.

1. Add more reference planes named and dimensioned as indicated in Figure 9.10.

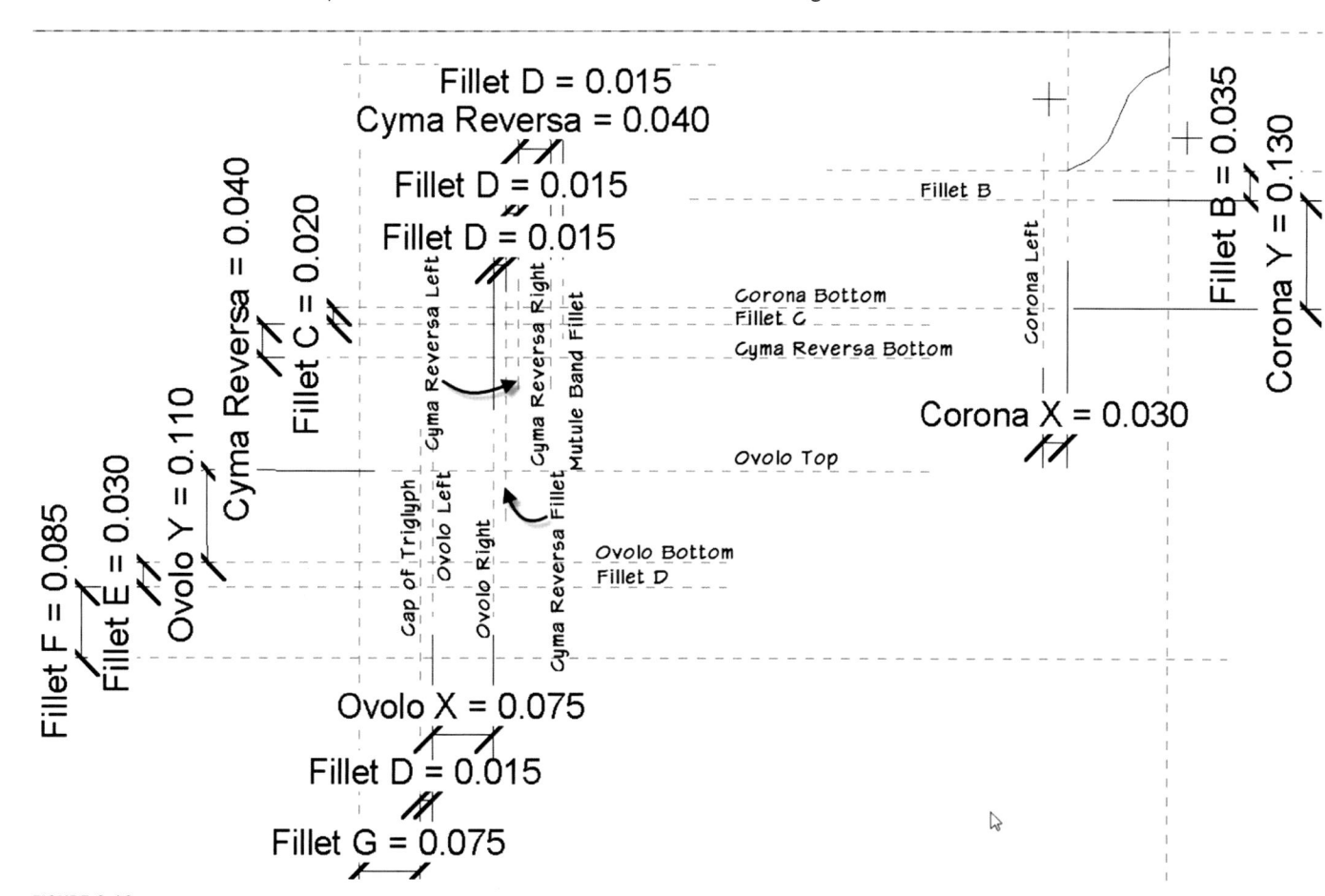

FIGURE 9.10

Adding the overall reference planes for each molding

➪ Open "Family Types" and add a formula for each new parameter: **Base Diameter * "value"**.

This is an intense image, I realize. This is one of the most advanced profiles we will build in this book. So there is a lot information here. As before, I have provided catch-up files to help you if you get behind. There is also a PDF that has a larger version of this image that you can print out.

> **CATCH UP!** You can open a file completed to this point named: *09_Doric Entablature Profile_A.rfa*.

It might be easier to understand what we need to do next if get some of the lines drawn in. Let's add all of the straight lines for the various fillets.

2. Using Figure 9.11 as a guide, draw in all of the straight profile line segments. Align and lock each one to the various reference planes.

As you align and lock, automatic sketch dimensions will disappear. Continue aligning and locking until all automatic sketch dimensions are gone. In some cases, you may need to lock endpoints, but mostly you should be able to align just the edges.

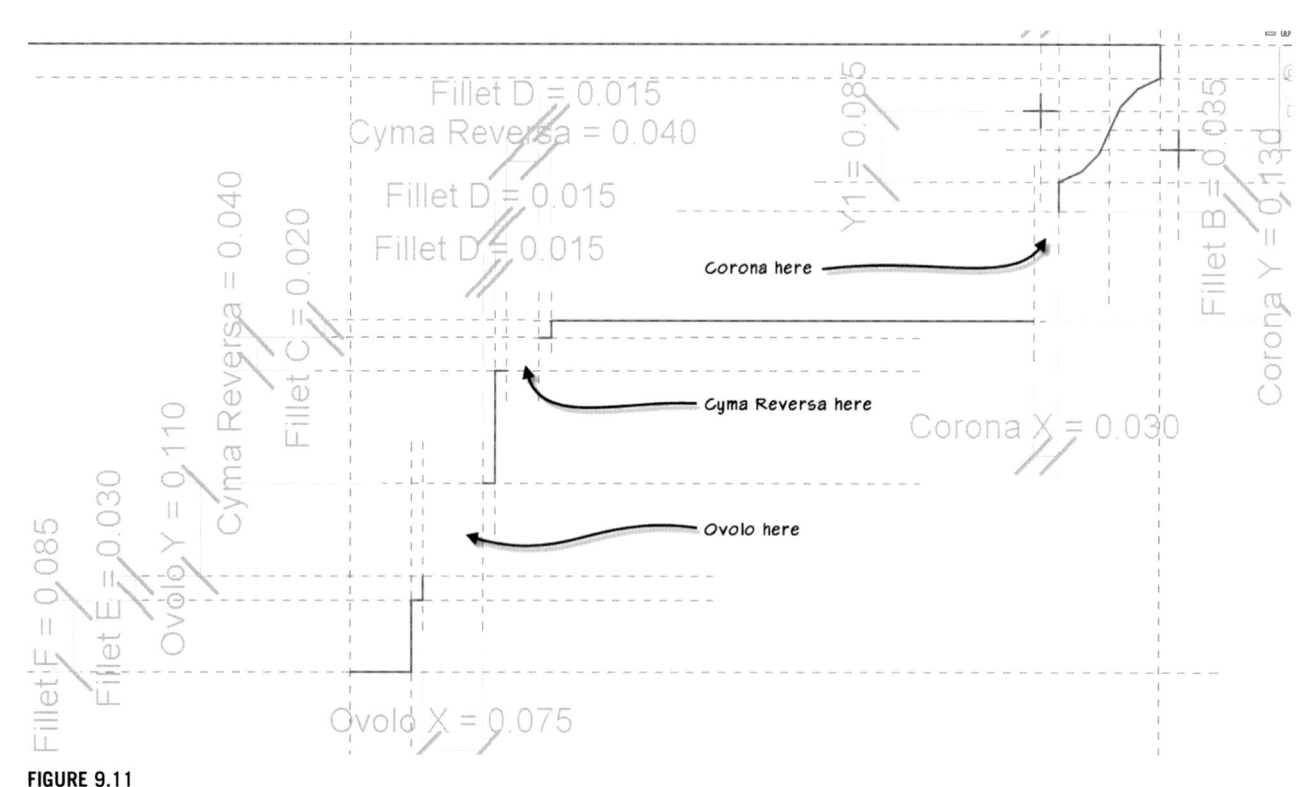

FIGURE 9.11
Add the straight line segments, align and lock them to reference planes (lines enhanced in the image for clarity)

You will need some additional reference planes and parameters to create the remaining three curves. You can approach the corona and ovolo similar to each other. While we presented them using two different strategies back in Chapter 4, you can use either technique (trigonometry or detail component rig) to create either curve. Refer to the "Ovolo" and "Corona" topics in Chapter 4 for more information. I went with trigonometry in my version provided here, but you can use whichever technique you prefer.

3. Create a horizontal reference plane 0.035 below the Fillet B reference plane.

➪ Dimension and label it with a new parameter called **Y2**.

4. Create a vertical reference plane to the right of the Cornice Cyma Left reference plane.

⇨ Dimension it to the Corona Left reference plane, label with a new parameter called **R2**.

5. In "Family Types" create the additional parameters and add formulas as shown in Table 9.2:

TABLE 9.2

Parameter	Formula	Type of Parameter
Y2	Base Diameter * 0.035	Length
D1	(sqrt((Corona X ^ 2) + (Y2 ^ 2))) / 2	Length
A1	atan(Y2 / Corona X)	Angle
R2	D1 / cos(A1)	Length

6. Add the arc with center point at the intersection of the two new reference planes.

⇨ Align and lock the center point and the endpoints to the reference planes (see Figure 9.12).

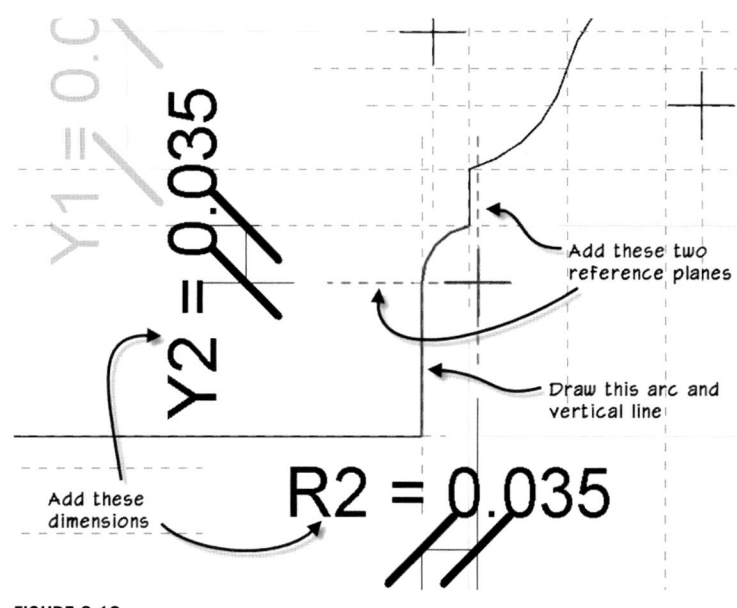

FIGURE 9.12
Add the corona molding

Build the Ovolo similarly.

7. Add a new vertical reference plane to the left of Cap of Triglyph. Dimension it to Ovolo Right and label with a new parameter. Name this **R3**.

⇨ In "Family Types" create additional parameters and configure formulas as indicated in Table 9.3

TABLE 9.3

Parameter	Formula	Type of Parameter
D2	(sqrt((Ovolo X ^ 2) + (Ovolo Y ^ 2))) / 2	Length
A2	atan(Ovolo Y/Ovolo X)	Angle
R3	D2 / cos(A2)	Length

8. Add the arc using the center point at the intersection of the new reference plane and the existing Ovolo Top reference plane (see Figure 9.13).

⇨ Align and lock the center point and endpoints.

Tip: If you get any errors while you try to add the arc, try deleting the adjacent straight lines, create the arc, align and lock it and then redraw the straight lines.

FIGURE 9.13
Create the ovolo

9. Create the remaining cyma reversa in the small square space that remains using a process similar to what we used for the other cyma above.

It's a tight space, so you might want to change the scale of the view to reduce the size of the dimensions and make it easier to work.

10. Add the required reference planes; two in each direction to mark the center point of each arc (four total as above).

⇨ Label with new parameters **Y3** and **X2**.

These are oriented slightly differently than the cyma. You can review the "Cyma Reversa" topic in Chapter 4 for more details. Like the cyma above, we know the angle of the diagonal is 45° based on the fact that the profile is square. This means that the formula used in Chapter 4 can be simplified here too. Plugging 45° into the formulas used there yields a value of 15°.

11. Open "Family Types" and create a parameter called **R4**, group it under **Constraints** and for the Formula input: **(sqrt((Cyma Reversa ^ 2) + (Cyma Reversa ^ 2))) / 2**

12. Remain in "Family Types" and add Formulas to Y3: **(R4 * sin(15°)) + Cyma Reversa** and X2: **R4 * cos(15°)**.

13. Add the two arcs using the new center points. Align and lock the centers and endpoints (see Figure 9.14).

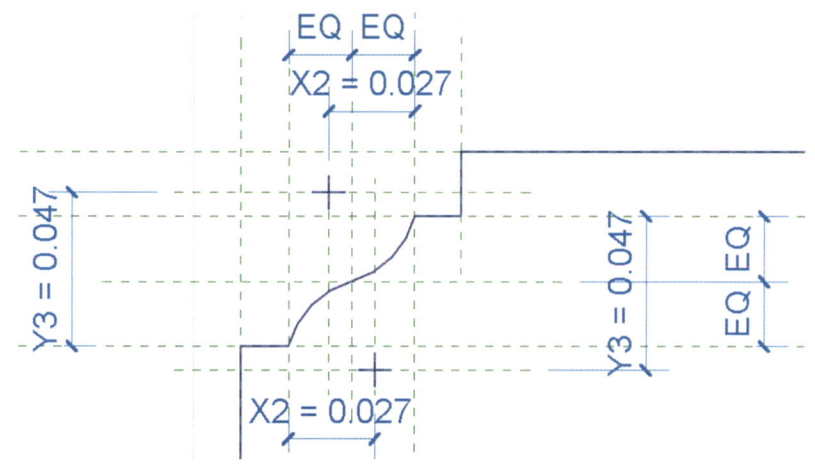

FIGURE 9.14
Add the remaining cyma reversa

There is one additional fillet down near the Frieze reference plane.

14. Add a 0.085 x 0.075 fillet at the frieze line, draw the remaining lines and be sure to align and lock everything (see Figure 9.15).

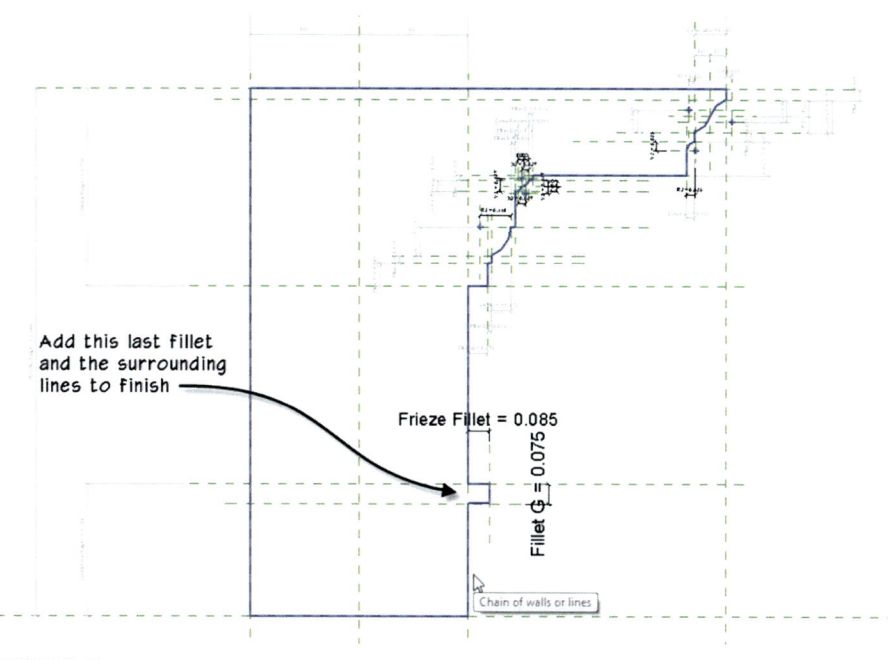

FIGURE 9.15
The completed profile

15. Flex the Base Diameter to make sure everything is working correctly. Be sure to rest to **1.00** before continuing.

16. Save and close the file.

> **CATCH UP!** You can open a file completed to this point named: *09_Doric Entablature Profile.rfa*.

If you open this catch-up file, you will see that I have color-coded the dimensions to make it easier to understand. As noted above, this is one of the most complex families we have built so far and with so many parameters, the colors help to tell them apart.

CREATE A LINE-BASED FAMILY

As noted in our inventory of two-pick options above, we will look at a line based family and a railing example in detail. In this topic we will start with the line based family. We did not create a seed family for this back in Chapter 2, so I have provided one for our use here. All I have done is change the units to match our other files and add the Base Diameter parameter. Otherwise, the file we will use is a copy of the out-of-the-box *Generic Model line based.rft* version.

1. From the *Seed Families* folder, open the *Family Seed (Line Based).rfa* file.

2. Save the file to the *Chapter09* folder and call it: **Doric Entablature**.

3. On the Insert tab, click the Load Family button. Browse to the *Chapter09* folder and load the *Doric Entablature Profile.rfa* file.

   You can load your own version completed in the previous exercise, or the catch-up file.

A line based family is actually very similar to the beam family that we worked with for the Tuscan entablature. When you load this family into a project, you will be prompted to click two points onscreen. The length parameter that you see here is tied to these two clicks, so the two clicks dynamically determines the length. So all we have to do is build our geometry so that it is associated to the references that you see here onscreen. So we will create a

• *Creating Classical Architecture with Modern Software* •

sweep that uses the profile family we just loaded and associate its path to the reference line here onscreen. We will treat the reference line as the centerline of our columns, so if you recall the shape of our profile, the soffit will overhang to one side.

If all we needed was a straight extrusion along the length, our task would be quite simple. But earlier when we were discussing the pros and cons of each line-based approach, we discussed the need for mitering when two segments come together. To achieve this, we will make the sweep longer than the built in reference line and then use a flexible void at each end to trim the sweep at the desired miter.

BUILD A ROTATION RIG

We have already explored all we need to create the voids we need. Since we want flexible mitering, we need to be able to input the miter angle and have the void adjust accordingly. This is easily achieved using a rotation rig like the ones we discussed in the "Controlling Rotation" topic in Chapter 4.

1. On the Create tab, on the Work Plane panel, click the Set button.
    - In the "Work Plane" dialog, click the Pick a Plane option and then click OK.
    - Click on the reference line onscreen (see Figure 9.16).

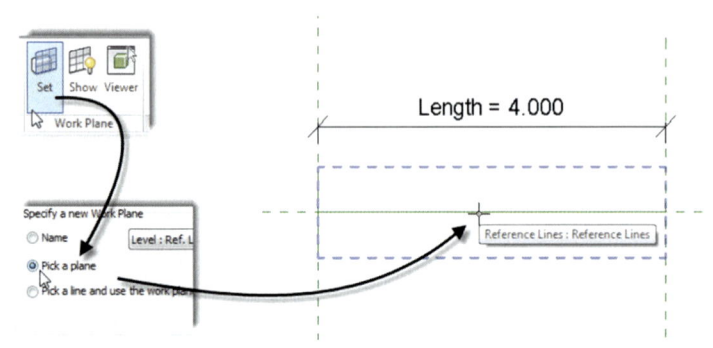

FIGURE 9.16
Set the reference line as the work plane

2. On the Create tab, on the Datum panel click the Reference Line tool.
    - Draw a reference line starting at the right endpoint of the existing one and going up and to the left at 135°. Make it 1.000 long.
    - Repeat at the other end drawing this one at 45° (up and to the right).

I turned on Automatic Sketch Dimensions in the seed family, so you should see some appear now. These are assuming that we want the new reference lines to stay at the ends of the existing one. This is exactly what we want, but remember that automatic dimensions can sometimes shift. So I always prefer to lock in my intent.

3. Align and lock the endpoints in both directions. (Some of the Automatic Dimensions should disappear).
4. Select one of the new reference lines and click the "Make this temporary dimension permanent" icon. Repeat for the other side.
    - Select both dimension and label them with a new parameter called: **Extension** grouped under **Constraints** (see Figure 9.17).

The Doric Entablature | 259

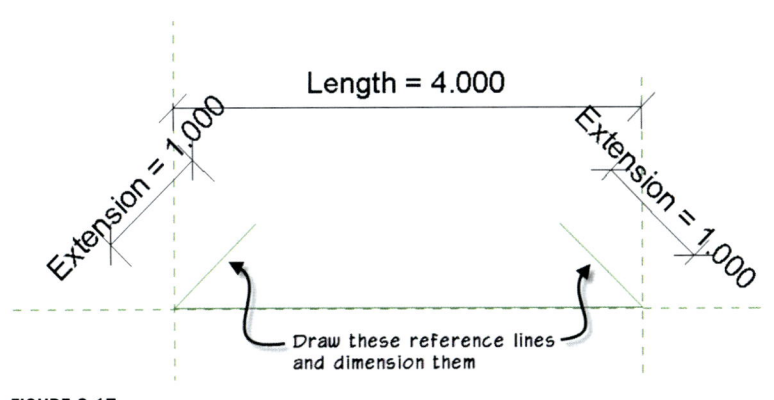

FIGURE 9.17
Add reference lines with labeled dimensions

5. Add an Angular dimension to each side. Be sure to click the original horizontal reference line first, then the angled one. Place the dimensions in the middle.

6. Label the angle on the left as: **Start Miter**. Label the one on the right as: **End Miter**.

   ⇨ Leave them grouped under **Dimensions** this time. Make them both **Instance** parameters (see Figure 9.18).

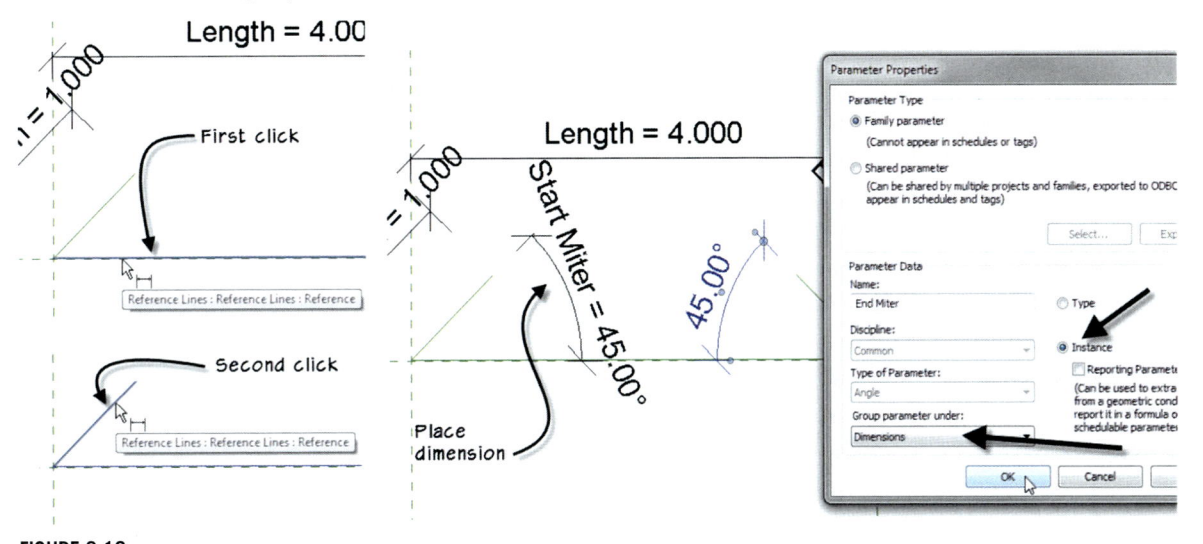

FIGURE 9.18
Add angular dimensions

7. Open the "Family Types" dialog.

   ⇨ Add a Formula to the Extension parameter: **Base Diameter**.

   ⇨ Flex the angles. Try several variations before resetting them both back to 45°.

8. Add four new reference planes (reference planes this time, not reference lines).

   ⇨ Draw two horizontal; one 0.500 above and one 0.0500 below the existing horizontal.

   ⇨ Draw two vertical; one at 1.000 to the right and the other 1.000 to the left.

9. Add dimensions and label them as indicated in Figure 9.19.

• *Creating Classical Architecture with Modern Software* •

260 | Chapter 9

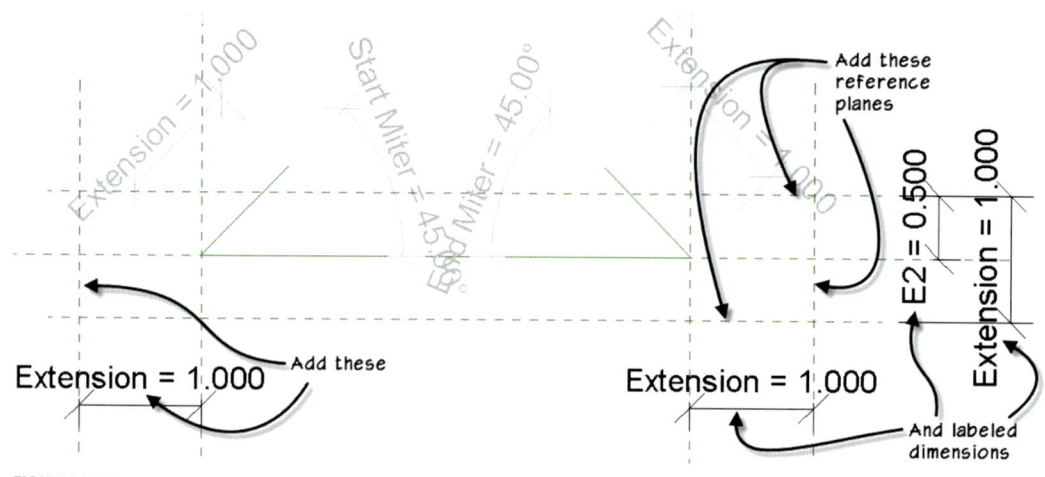

FIGURE 9.19
Add reference planes and dimensions

⇨ Add a formula for E2 of: **Extension * 0.500**.

The Extension distance is somewhat arbitrary as you will see. We just need the distance large enough to ensure that the void cuts all the way through the geometry. Speaking of geometry, let's add some.

> **CATCH UP!** You can open a file completed to this point named: *09_Doric Entablature_A.rfa*.

ADDING GEOMETRY

We'll start with two simple forms. The sweep that uses our custom profile and an extrusion void to miter the ends.

Continue in the *Doric Entablature* file or open the catch-up file.

1. On the Create tab, click the Sweep button and then click Sketch Path.

⇨ Draw a straight horizontal path starting at the intersection of the rightmost vertical and Center (Front/Back) reference planes and ending at the intersection with the leftmost vertical reference plane.

The direction you draw *does* matter, so be sure to draw right to left (see Figure 9.20).

2. Click the Modify tool and then align and lock. Align the line itself to the reference line. Use the TAB key to select the reference line underneath the line.

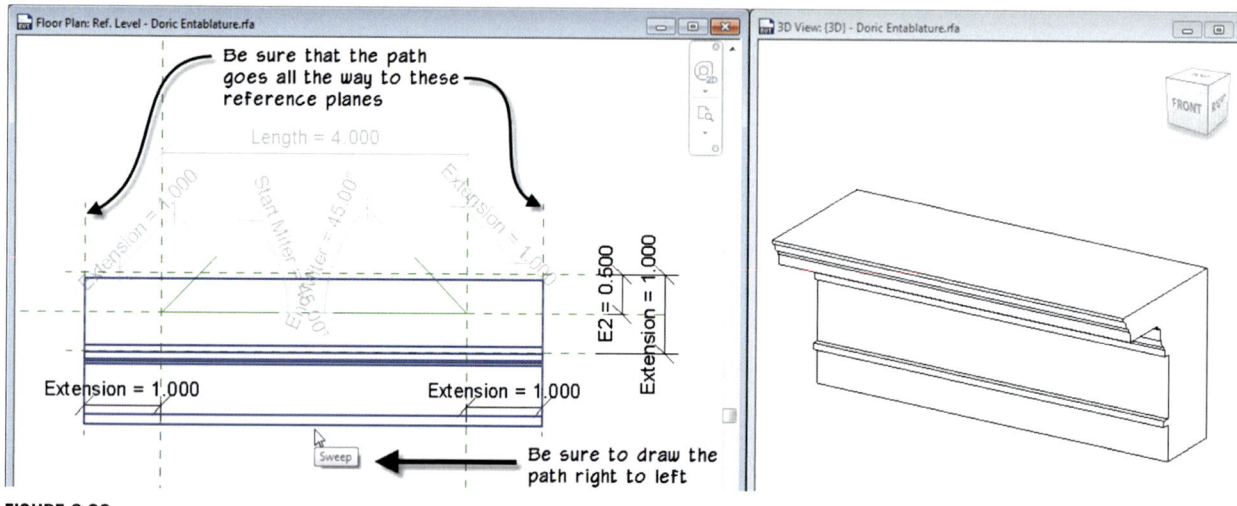

FIGURE 9.20
Create the sweep

• Renaissance Revit •

➪ Align each endpoint to the vertical reference planes.

3. Finish the path.

➪ From the Profile list, choose **Doric Entablature Profile:Flex**.

➪ Finish Edit Model.

4. On the Project Browser, expand *Families > Profiles > Doric Entablature Profile*.

➪ Edit the Type Properties of Flex and link up the Base Diameter parameter.

5. Open "Family Types" and flex Base Diameter. When you are satisfied that everything is working, return Base Diameter to **1.000** and then click OK.

Now let's create the void. This will be a simple extrusion. Before we begin, if you take a close look at the reference planes that we created to define the void, they do not currently define a space big enough to completely cut the end of the beam. Given the way that we set up the parameters, this is easy to remedy.

Switch to the Ref. Level floor plan view. (This is important or the work plane for the extrusion will not be correct).

6. Open the "Family Types" dialog.

➪ Edit the formula for Extension to: **Base Diameter * 2**.

➪ Edit the formula for E2 to: **Extension * 0.250** and then click OK (see Figure 9.21).

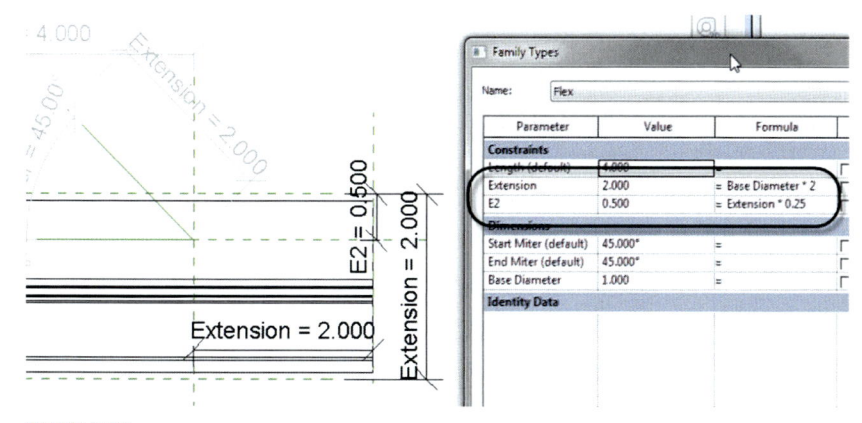

FIGURE 9.21

Adjust the position of the reference line outlines by adjusting the extension formulas

7. On the Create tab, click the Void Forms drop-down and then choose **Void Extrusion**.

8. Trace the reference planes and angled reference line to create a wedge shapes on each end.

9. Align and lock the edges to the reference planes and reference lines (see Figure 9.22).

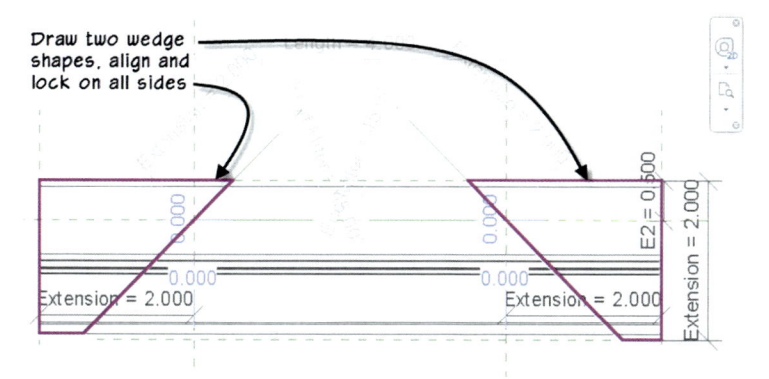

FIGURE 9.22

Create sketch lines along the extension reference planes and angled reference lines

10. On the Properties palette, next to Extrusion End, click the Associate Family Parameter button, choose **Extension** and then click OK.

11. Finish Edit Mode.

If you have the 3D view open, you will notice that even though the parameter we just applied is a positive value, the extrusion went down. If you recall the "Create and Constrain a Reference Line" topic back in Chapter 4, you may remember that reference lines and reference planes have "normal" or positive directions. Since we set the reference line as the active work plane earlier, this extrusion is using that work plane and it appears that its normal points down. We could create a new parameter that multiplies the Extrusion parameter by negative one, but I am not a big fan of negative extrusions if it can be avoided. Instead, let's change the work plane of the extrusion to the Ref. Level.

12. With the extrusion still selected, click the Edit Work Plane button.

    ⇨ From the Name list, choose **Level : Ref. Level** and then click OK.

The extrusion will reverse direction and now overlap the ends of the sweep. When you deselect the extrusion, it will apply the void to the sweep and chamfer the ends. If for some reason it does not automatically apply the void, you can use the Cut Geometry tool on the Modify tab to cut it manually.

13. Open "Family Types" and flex the family. Flex both angles, the Length and Base Diameter parameters. Return all values to their starting points before closing the dialog.

Depending on the values you chose, you may get an error message. If you do, simply click Cancel. I had success with any value for Length 1.100 and higher. Below this, it failed. With the angles, I had success with angles in the range between 37° – 159°. Angles outside of this range also generated an error. If you really wanted to, we could construct this family differently to make it more error tolerant. However, consider the range of realistic values that a user of the family is likely to choose. Given that the minimum intercolumniation allowable for Doric is 1.25 diameters, we should never run into the minimum identified here. Likewise, when considering all of the classical precedents, it is unlikely that you will require miter angles outside the allowable range. In fact, in most cases you will select either 90° or 45° for your miter, both of which work perfectly fine. So I consider the flexibility of this family within acceptable limits. Also be careful when flexing off of 90° in the family editor. This can fail in the family editor, but generally works fine in the project environment.

CATCH UP! You can open a file completed to this point named: *09_Doric Entablature_B.rfa*.

PRELIMINARY SANDBOX TEST

I have provided a copy of the sandbox file in this chapter's folder. Let's test what we have so far.

1. From the *Chapter09* folder, open the file named: *09_Sandbox_Colonnade.rvt*.

Three windows will open in a tile configuration. If yours open maximized, click the restore down icon in the top right corner of the active window to see the tile configuration. I saved the file with the second floor plan active. This is because our entablature family is built on its Ref. Level. That means it will come in on the floor of whatever plan is active. Drawing in the second floor plan ensures that it will come in at the tops of the columns.

2. Switch windows back to the Doric Entablature family (or open the catch-up file).

    ⇨ Click Load into Project.

    In the sandbox, on the Options Bar, make sure that the Chain checkbox is checked.

    On the Modify I Place Component tab, on the Placement panel, click the Place on Work Plane button.

3. In the *Level 2* floor plan, click the first point at the intersection of grid A1.
⇨ Click B1 next, then B4 and end at A4.

> **TIP:** If you have any difficulty snapping to the grid intersections, type SI; the keyboard shortcut for Snap Intersection.

4. Select the short segment on grid 1 and on the Properties palette, change the start miter to **90**.
5. Repeat for the other short segment changing the End Miter this time (see Figure 9.23).

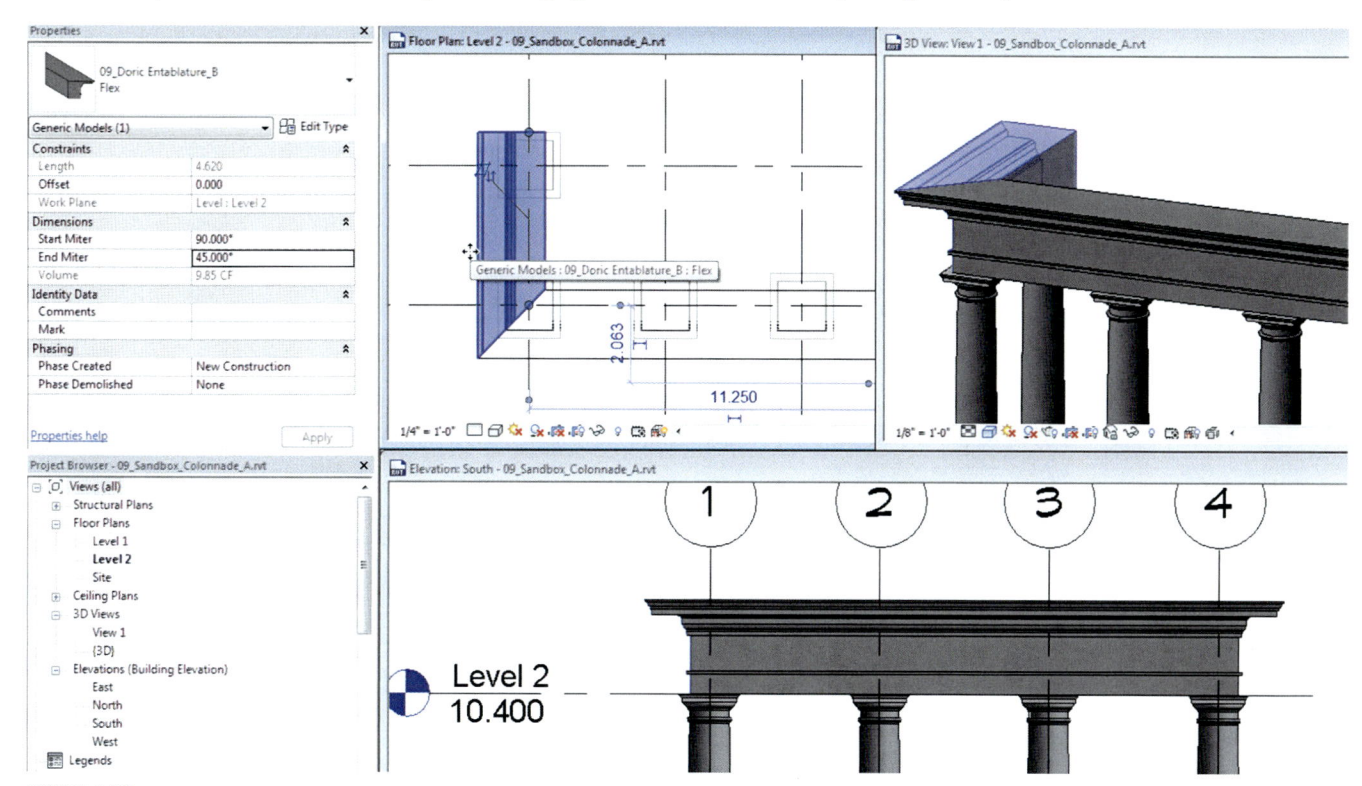

FIGURE 9.23
Add three segments of entablature, adjust the miters and ends as required

> **CATCH UP!** You can open a file completed to this point named: *09_Sandbox Colonnade_A.rvt*.

MUTULES, TRIGLYPHS AND METOPES

The most characteristic feature of the Doric order is its triglyphs and metopes. A triglyph is an adornment that is meant to represent the ends of a beam as they would appear projecting through the frieze of the entablature. A metope is the portion of the frieze between each triglyph. Metopes are precisely square in shape at 0.750 diameters per side. A triglyph is 0.750 diameters high by 0.500 diameters wide. Directly above each triglyph is a mutule. Like the triglyph, the mutule is meant to evoke the framing members; in this case the rafters above (Chitham 1985, 2005, 64-66) (Ware 1994, 1977, 1903, 15-17).

The precise shape and proportion of these members gives the Doric Order its characteristic appearance and also dictates a rather rigid set of possible intercolumniations. In the *Chapter09* folder, I have provided some prebuilt families for the triglyphs and mutules. We will use these in the next sequence.

1. From the *Chapter09* folder, open the file named *Mutule.rfa*.

264 | Chapter 9

The file should open with four tile views. If it opens maximized, click the restore down icon in the corner.

2. In the 3D view, highlight near the edge and find the overall gray box and select it.

You will know you have the right one if you click the Visibility Settings button on the ribbon and under Detail Levels, only Coarse is checked. Using Temporary Hide/Isolate (the sunglasses), hide this element. The family is comprised of two extrusions for the main box form, one thin one across the top behind the sweep and another "U" shaped one surrounding the pegs. The pegs are a single extrusion containing multiple circles in its sketch. All of these elements display in medium and fine only. The box that we just hid displays in coarse only (See the left side of Figure 9.24).

3. From the *Chapter09* folder, open the file named *Triglyph.rfa*.

Again there is a coarse detail extrusion concealing the medium and fine detail elements. Hide this element to see the remaining forms. There are several reference planes to shape the channels of the triglyph. Most of them use equality dimensions to maintain their proportions rather than excessive formulas. To create the chamfer at the top of the channels, an extrusion drawn in elevation is joined to one drawn in plan. The guttae (small conical shaped peg forms) are created from blends (See the right side of Figure 9.24).

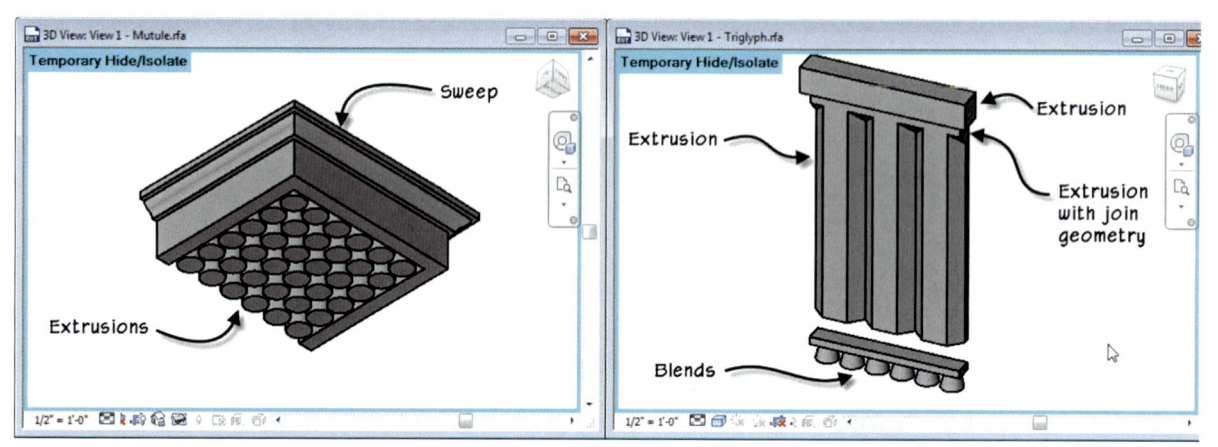

FIGURE 9.24
Open and explore the provided mutule and triglyph files

4. Load both the *Mutule.rfa* and *Triglyph.rfa* files into the *Doric Entablature.rfa* file (or the catch-up version). But don't place them onscreen yet.

5. Close both the *Mutule.rfa* and *Triglyph.rfa* files. It is not necessary to save these files.

    If you still have the sandbox open, close it too, if prompted to save, choose Yes. You should only have the *Doric Entablature* file open at this time.

6. On the Project Browser, expand *Families > Generic Models* and then edit the Type Properties of the type named: Flex for both *Mutule.rfa* and *Triglyph.rfa*.

    ⇨ Link up the Base Diameter in both files.

    ⇨ Also link up and create a new Material parameter called: **Entablature Material**.

PLACE AND POSITION THE FIRST COMPONENTS

In this sequence, we'll add the two families we just loaded to the entablature, configure their spacing and make the quantity parameteric so that it adjusts with the length.

Continue in the *Doric Entablature* file. Close any other open files.

1. Open the *Ref. Level* ceiling plan, the *Front* elevation, the *Left* elevation, and the *View 1* 3D view.

• Renaissance Revit •

⇨   Close the *Ref. Level* floor plan (we will use the ceiling plan instead). Tile the windows.

In the family editor most views default to wireframe and coarse level display. For this exercise, given the amount of lines and edges our moldings have in some views (particularly the floor plan) the ceiling plan displayed in hidden line should give better feedback. The trouble is, the ceiling plan currently appears empty. This is simply because the cut plane is too high. To access view properties in the family editor however, you have to select the view on the Project Browser or use the Properties Filter drop-down on the Properties palette.

2. On the Project Browser, select the *Ref. Level* ceiling plan view.

    ⇨   On the Properties palette, click the View Range button.

    ⇨   Set the Cut Plane to **0** (zero) and then click OK.

3. Zoom, pan and orbit all open views to get in closer.

4. Set all four views to **Medium** detail level and **Hidden Line** visual style.

    Make the ceiling plan view active.

5. On the create tab, click the Component tool.

    ⇨   Place a single instance of the Mutule and the Triglyph below the entablature in plan. The exact location is unimportant, but do not snap to any reference planes.

    ⇨   Cancel the command (See Figure 9.25).

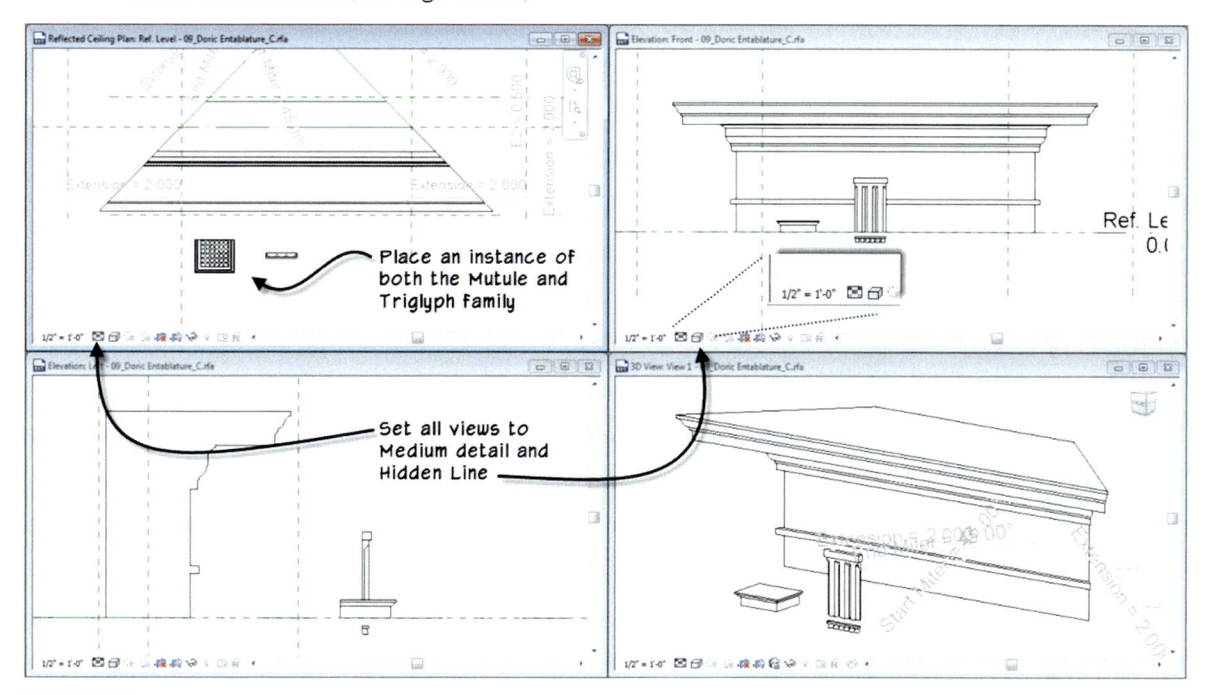

FIGURE 9.25

Arrange all of the view windows and insert and instance of each family

Naturally we will have to adjust the placement of the two families. Let's do the height first.

6. Select the Triglyph element. On the Properites palette, next to Offset, click the Assocaite Family Paraemter button.

    ⇨   Add a new type-based parameter called: **Triglyph Z**, grouped under **Constraints**.

    ⇨   Repeat for the Mutule. Name the new parameter **Mutule Z** also grouped under **Constraints**.

7. Open "Family Types" and add formulas to these two parameters (see Table 9.4):

TABLE 9.4

Parameter	Formula	Comments
Triglyph Z	Base Diameter * 0.500	
Mutule Z	Base Diameter * 1.500	

As you can see, I have relied on the Offset parameter here. We could have created reference planes and dimensions, but this is simpler, reduces extra clutter and will function better in the array below.

For the location along the length, (the X direction), my first instinct was to lock them to the left reference plane. The intersection of Left and Right reference planes and the Length reference line and end up exactly at the centers of the columns when we use this family in a project. This is precisely what we want and works quite well when we have a mitered entablature. However, in situations where the entablature ends at 90°, it would stop right in the middle of a column which would not be desirable. So we would want to extend the entabalture in such a case. If we lock our triglyphs and mutules to this endpoint they would shift when we make such an extension thereby throwing off the required spacing. Triglyphs must be centered on the column. So, we will create another reference plane for this purpose and control it with an instance parameter that can be adjusted when the end is set to 90°.

8. Draw a vertical reference plane on the right side and parallel to the existing Left reference plane. The exact distance between is not important yet.

   ⇨ Name it: **Triglyph Start**.

9. In the *Front* view, align and lock the triglyph and the mutule to this reference plane. Align each family's center to the reference plane (See the left side of Figure 9.26).

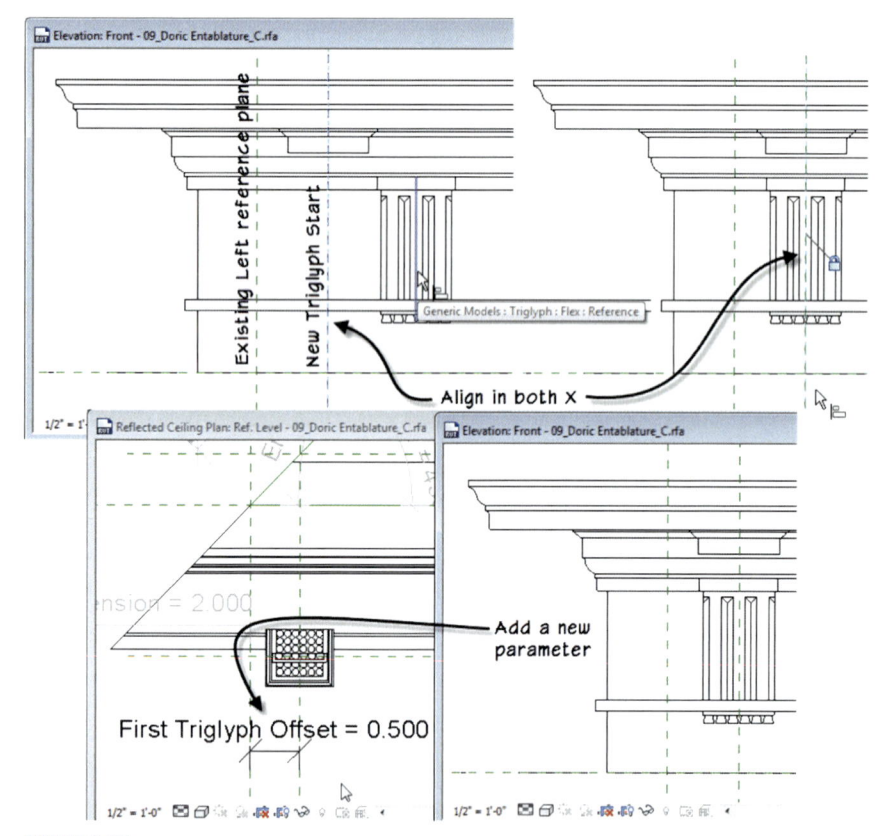

FIGURE 9.26

Align and lock the Triglyph and Mutules in the X direction and add a new parameter

10. Back in the ceiling plan view, add a dimension between the Left and Triglyph Start reference planes.

    ⇨ Label the dimension with a new **Instance** parameter called: **First Triglyph Offset**. Leave it under **Dimensions**.

• Renaissance Revit •

⇨ Flex the value of this new parameter to **0.500** for now (See the right side of Figure 9.26).

> **Note:** If you open the Triglyph and Mutule families, you will notice that there are many reference planes within them. When I added these reference planes, for most of them I set the "Is Reference" parameter to "Not a Reference." This makes it much easier to align and lock to meaningful points in the family. For example, I needed reference planes to locate each guttae (drip) but it is unlikely that you would want to align or dimension to these references. If you want to study this further, open the families, select a reference plane and take a look at how the Is Reference parameter is configured for each one.

> **CATCH UP!** You can open a file completed to this point named: *09_Doric Entablature_C.rfa*.

We still need to position the elements in the Y direction, but we will move on and build the array first. It will be easier to ensure the everything flexes properly this way.

CREATE A PARAMETRIC ARRAY

The next step is to create an array to repeat the mutules and triglyphs.

1. Select the Triglyph element onscreen.

2. On the Modify I Generic Models tab, click the Array button.

3. On the Options Bar, work from left to right.

⇨ Make sure Linear is selected.

⇨ Make sure that "Group and Associate" is checked.

⇨ Leave the quantity set to **2** and the "Move To" option set to 2nd.

⇨ Check the Constrain checkbox.

If you have used the array tool before, then these should be familiar, but I'll give a brief review of the settings. Arrays can be linear or radial. Naturally we need linear in this case. The "Group and Associate" feature is required to make the array parametric. This setting will create an array whose quantity and spacing can be adjusted dynamically; even with parameters! Since we will be adjusting it parametrically, I always start with a quantity of 2 and then flex it later to make sure it is working. It is usually easier this way. Finally the choice of 2nd or Last determines how elements will be added and removed from the array when you later flex the quantity. With "2nd," they will get added and removed from the end and the spacing remains constant. With "Last," they first and last will stay stationary and the quantity and spacing will adjust in the middle.

4. Click a point near the selected items, move directly to the right and then type: **1.250** (See Figure 9.27).

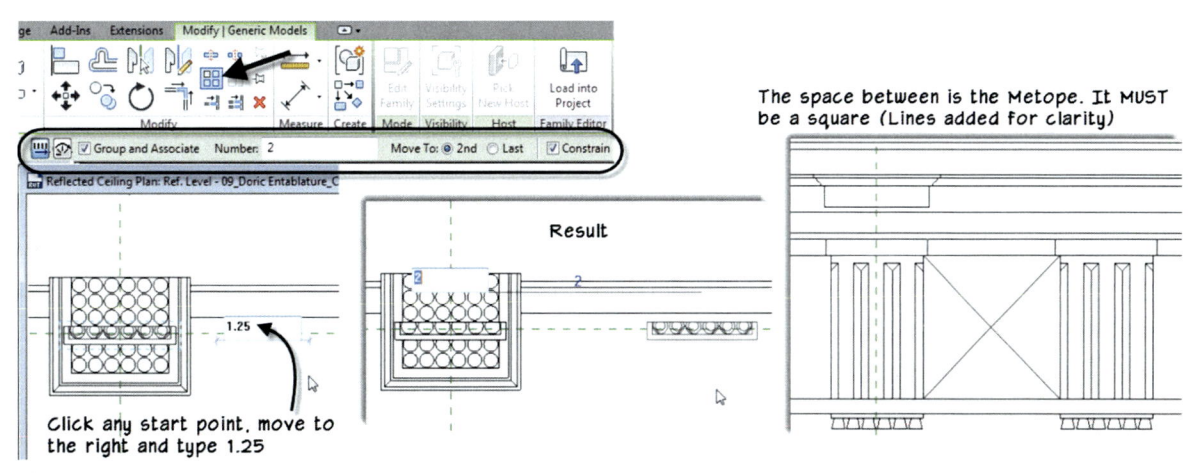

FIGURE 9.27

Create a 2 element array at a specified distance

268 | Chapter 9

> With the Constrain checkbox on, the cursor should only move horizontally. The typed distance sets the second point of the linear array.

I added two diagonal lines in the figure to illustrate the importance of the typed distance. The distance between the two triglyphs must be 1.25 in order to make a perfectly square metope. So let's make this a parameter. We also need a parameter for the array quantity.

    5. Add a dimension between the centers of the two triglyphs.

    ⇨ Create a type-based parameter named: **Triglyph Spacing** and group it under **Constraints**. Add a formula: **Base Diameter * 1.250**.

    6. Select one of the array items (notice that it is a group as indicated by the dashed box surrounding it) (See the left side of Figure 9.28).

A number 2 will appear breifly onscreen when you select the array element. You need to move your cursor around in proximity to this number. Hidden there you will find the Array element.

    7. Click to select the Array element. On the Options Bar, click the Label drop-down and choose **Add Parameter** (See the right side of Figure 9.28).

    ⇨ Name the new parameter: **Number of Triglyphs**, make it an **Instance** parameter and group it under **Graphics**.

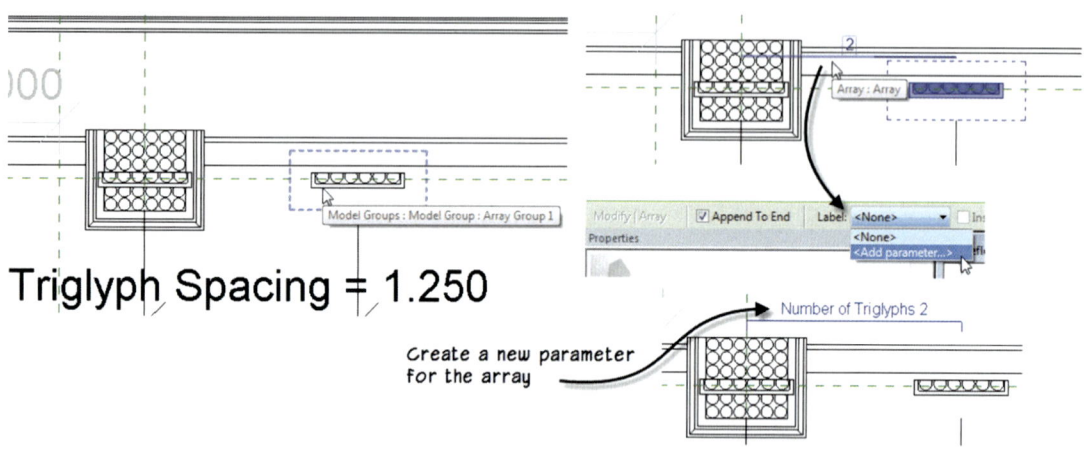

FIGURE 9.28

Select the Array element onscreen and label it

Notice that the label now appears next to the array quantity like it would for other labeled dimensions. Now with a formula, we can tie the quantity to the Length of the family. If you recall our strategy above, we added an offset reference plane and corresponding parameter. This gives us flexibility when modeling needs dictate. Likewise, the overall calculation of required number of triglyphs is simple arithmetic. But in cases where we do not have mitered end, or have to do a manual extension, it could throw off our count. Remember, the most important aspect of the Doric frieze is that the triglyphs are centered on the columns and that the metopes are square. This cannot be compromised. So we have a choice to make: do some complex formulas to calculate the required quantity very precisely and incorporate error trapping for all the possible special outcomes or simply incorporate another manual instance parameter to allow us flexibility to adjust the quantity. I have decided that option 2 makes much more sense and so we will do a simple Integer parameter that can be added or subtracted from our calculated quantity.

    8. Open the "Family Types" dialog.

    9. On the right, click the Add parameter button.

    ⇨ Name the new parameter: **Extra Triglyphs**, set the Type of Parameter to: **Integer**, make it and **Instance** parameter and group it under **Graphics**.

• Renaissance Revit •

> **Note:** remember that the group under is really a matter of preference. It is common best practice to place things that are driven by formulas under "Other." I like this one under graphics because I think that it is changing the way this object displays but you could easily make an argument for other groupings like Other or even Construction.

10. For the Number of Triglyphs parameter add a Formula: **(Length / Triglyph Spacing) + Extra Triglyphs** (See Figure 9.29).

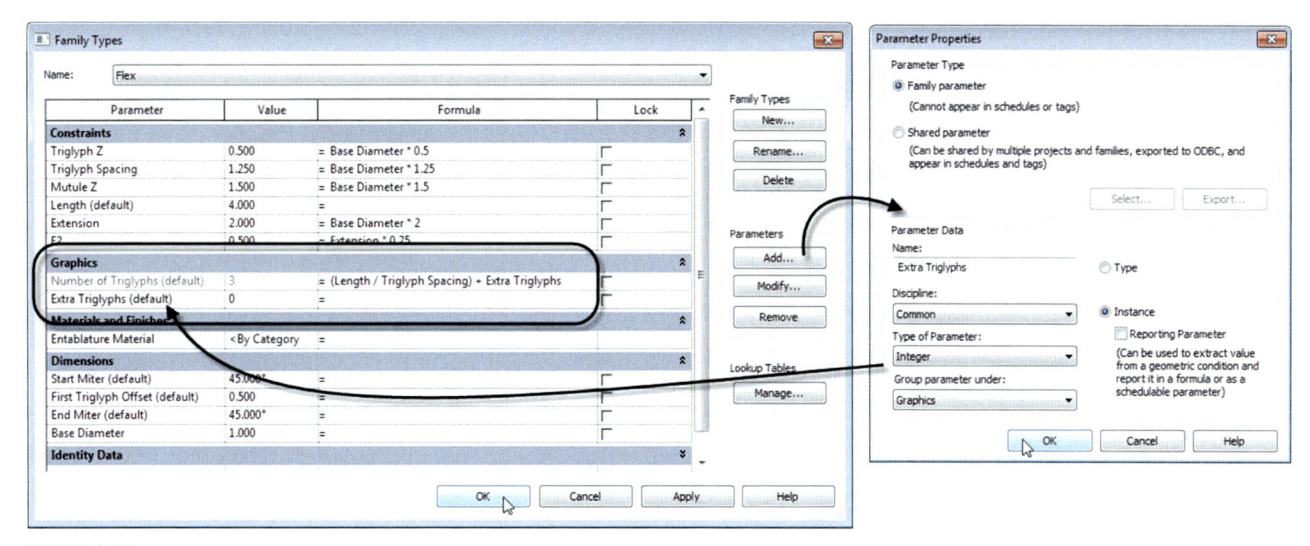

FIGURE 9.29
Add a formula to control the number of triglyphs

Let's flex the model. For now we will just focus on these new quantity parameters.

11. Zoom out in the ceiling plan and/or elevation views and then return to "Family Types."

   ⇨ Change the Length to **2.000** and then click Apply. Try **6.000**, then **8.000**, then **10.000**. Apply after each change.

   ⇨ For Extra Triglyphs, try values of **1** and **-1**. Apply after each.

As you can see this parameter offers an easy way to adjust the quantity. Avoid using any combination of values that would make the Number of Triglyphs less than 2. 2 is the minimum allowable array quantity. If you go lower than this, the family will break. You could error trap for this, but our entablature will always be long enough to allow for at least 2 triglyphs. So while I would normally recommend including a formula (see the tip), in this case I will leave it out.

> **TIP:** If you want to prevent an array parameter from breaking, you can use an IF statement to check it for errors. Create two Integer parameters: one that drives the array, and one that records the desired quantity. The Formula for the Array parameter would look like this: **if(Quantity < 2, 2, Quantity)**. The formula checks the input in the "Quantity" parameter and if it is less than 2 it uses 2 instead. If it is 2 or greater, it uses the Quantity value as input. If you have a situation where you need to see just one item, you can use the same formula to drive a Yes/No parameter that hides and shows a single instance that it not part of the array. So if the array value is 1, the array stays at 2 but gets hidden and the single instance turns on instead.

12. Reset Length to **4.000** and Extra Triglyphs to **0**. Click OK.

> **CATCH UP!** You can open a file completed to this point named: *09_Doric Entablature_D.rfa*.

ADJUST THE Y POSITION

We are nearly finished now. All that remains are some finishing touches. For one, the triglyphs and mutules are still floating out away from the rest of the form. Let's address that now. When I first began designing this family, I adjusted the Y position before building the array. I amended that approach here because arrays can be fickle. If they are perfectly positioned, it can sometimes be difficult to fine-tune the array parameters without inadvertently disrupting some other relationship or part of the array. So by leaving them free floating it becomes much more obvious that you are aligning the correct elements to one another when the time comes. This approach is similar to why I always recommend building rotational parameters on a 45° angle and then flexing into position. It is just much easier to tell when things go wrong and more importantly understand *what* went wrong.

> Continue in the same file with the same tiled windows or open the catch-up file.

1. In the *Left* elevation view, click the Align tool.

    ⇨ For the aligment edge, click the face of the frieze on the sweep (See the left side of Figure 9.30).

    ⇨ For the object to align, click the back face of the triglyph element (See the middle of Figure 9.30).

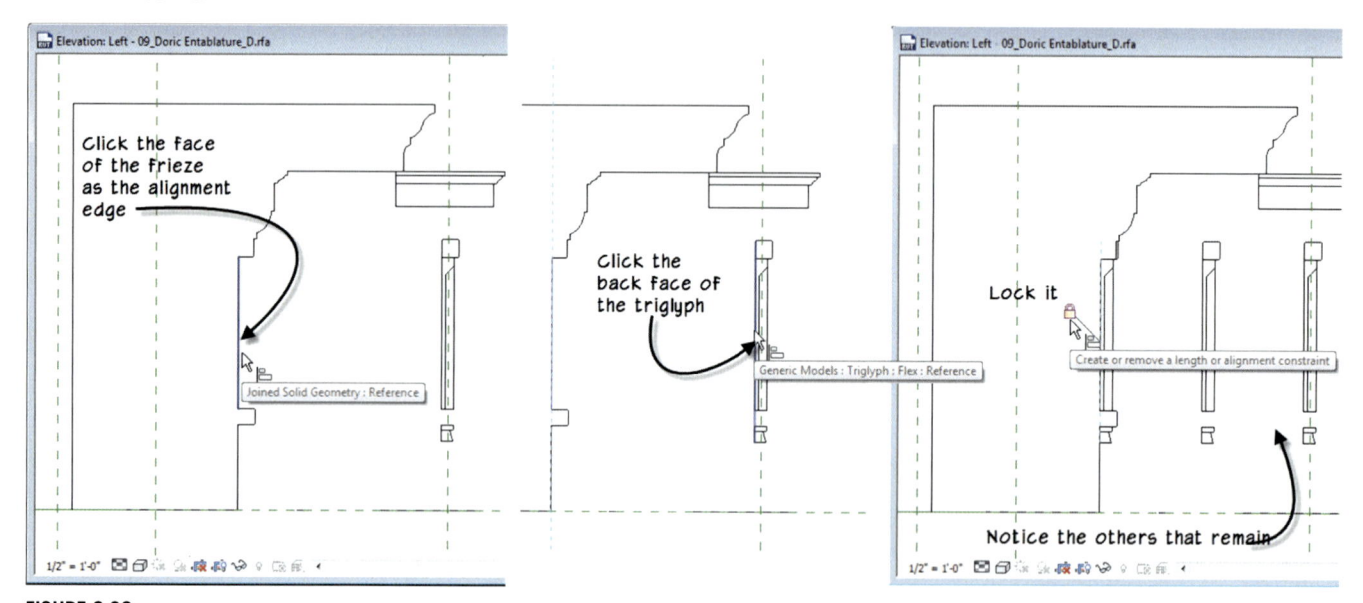

    ⇨ Lock it.

FIGURE 9.30
Add an offset parameter to the start

Notice on the right side of the figure, that the other two triglyphs did not follow the aligned one. If you look at what has occurred in plan, you will notice that the array now follows a diagonal path. A linear array can go at any angle. The trick is to remember that to create a line you need two points. So to control a linear array, you must align and lock two of its elements. You will get best results if you align and lock the first and second one, or the first and last one depending on whether you chose 2nd or last on the Options Bar when building the array. So since we chose 2nd, that is the one we'll align.

> Remain in the *Left* elevation view.

We want to be sure to align the proper edges.

2. Select the first element (the one you just aligned) and on the View Control Bar, click the Temporary Hide/Isolate pop-up and choose **Hide Element**.

3. Repeat the align command. For the alignment edge, click the same face of the sweep again.

⇨ For the element to align, click the back edge of the second triglyph this time. Lock it.

⇨ Reset the Temporary Hide/Isolate mode.

Notice that all of the elements now align with the plane of the frieze. Again, we only need two points. Flex the model to make sure everything is working as expected. Be sure to reset default values before continuing.

The last step is to align the mutules.

4. Starting at the "Create a Parametric Array" topic above, repeat the entire process.

⇨ Select the Mutule family this time. Array it using the same settings as above.

⇨ Add a dimension between the centers of the 1st and 2nd elements and apply the **Triglyph Spacing** parameter.

⇨ Select the Array dimension and label it with the same **Number of Triglyphs** parameter.

5. In the Left elevation, repeat the align and lock procedure to align both the 1st and 2nd mutule to the face of the Mutule Band on the sweep (See Figure 9.31).

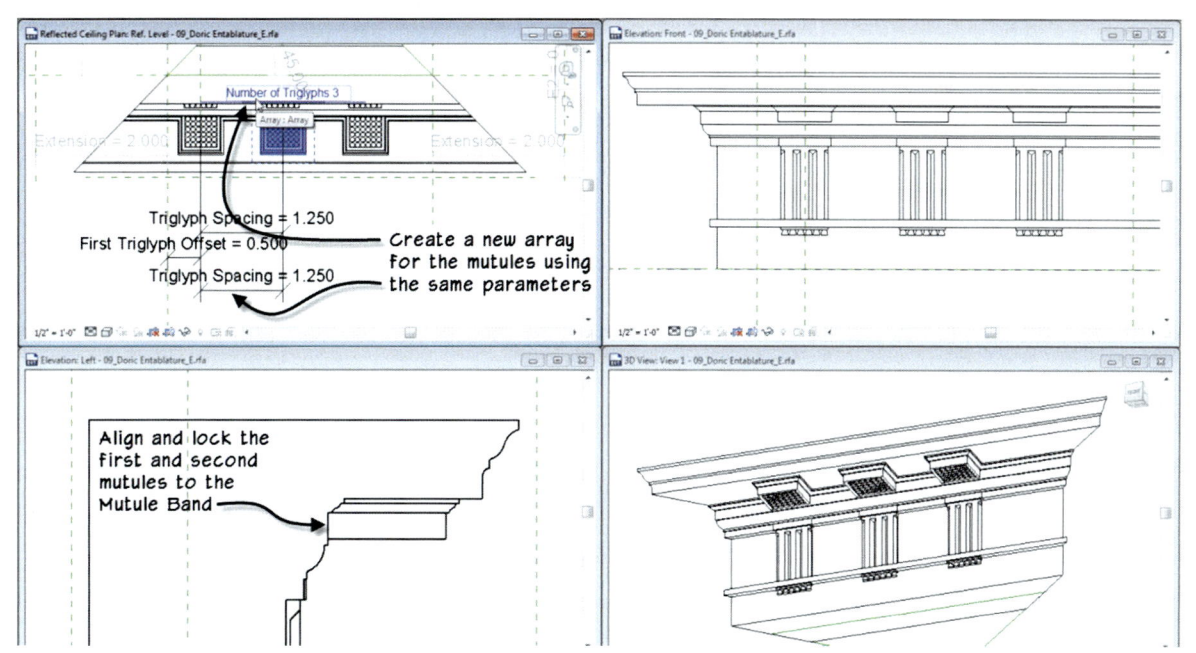

FIGURE 9.31
Add three segments of entablature, adjust the miters and ends as required

6. Thoroughly flex the family.

This family takes a little more effort to properly flex. All of the parameters under Dimensions are independent. Additionally, the built-in Length parameter is also independent. So to fully flex this family, you have try variations on all of these. Remember to stay within acceptable ranges for values we have previously flexed like the angles and Length. Also be careful not to inadvertently choose a combination that makes the Number of Triglyphs less than 2.

7. When you are satisfied, reset the Length to **4.000**, the Base Diameter to **1.000** and each of the miter angles to **45**. Set the First Triglyph value to **0** (zero).

8. Save the file.

> **CATCH UP!** You can open a file completed to this point named: *09_Doric Entablature.rfa*.

LOAD INTO SANDBOX

Let's perform the final test by loading the family into a sandbox file.

1. From the *Chapter09* folder, open the file named: *09_Sandbox_Colonnade_A.rvt*.

Three windows will open in a tile configuration. If yours open maximized, click the restore down icon in the top right corner of the active window to see the tile configuration. This is a copy of the file we used earlier in the chapter and I have renamed the existing entablature in here to avoid conflict.

2. Switch windows back to the Doric Entablature family (or open the catch-up file).

    ⇨ Click Load into Project.

    In the sandbox, on the Options Bar, make sure that the Chain checkbox is checked.

    ⇨ On the Modify I Place Component tab, on the Placement panel, click the Place on Work Plane button.

3. In the *Level 2* floor plan, click the first point at the intersection of grid A/5.

    ⇨ Click B/5 next, then B/8 and end at A/8.

> TIP: If you have any difficulty snapping to the grid intersections, type SI; the keyboard shortcut for Snap Intersection.

4. Select the short segment on grid 5 and on the Properties palette, change the start miter to **90**.
5. Repeat for the other short segment changing the End Miter this time.
6. Select all three segments. On the Properties palette, click the Edit Type button.

    ⇨ Click the Duplicate button and name the copy: **1.300** and then click OK.

    ⇨ Edit the Base Diameter to **1.300** as well. Assign a material if you like and then click OK.

7. Zoom in on the South elevation (See Figure 9.32).

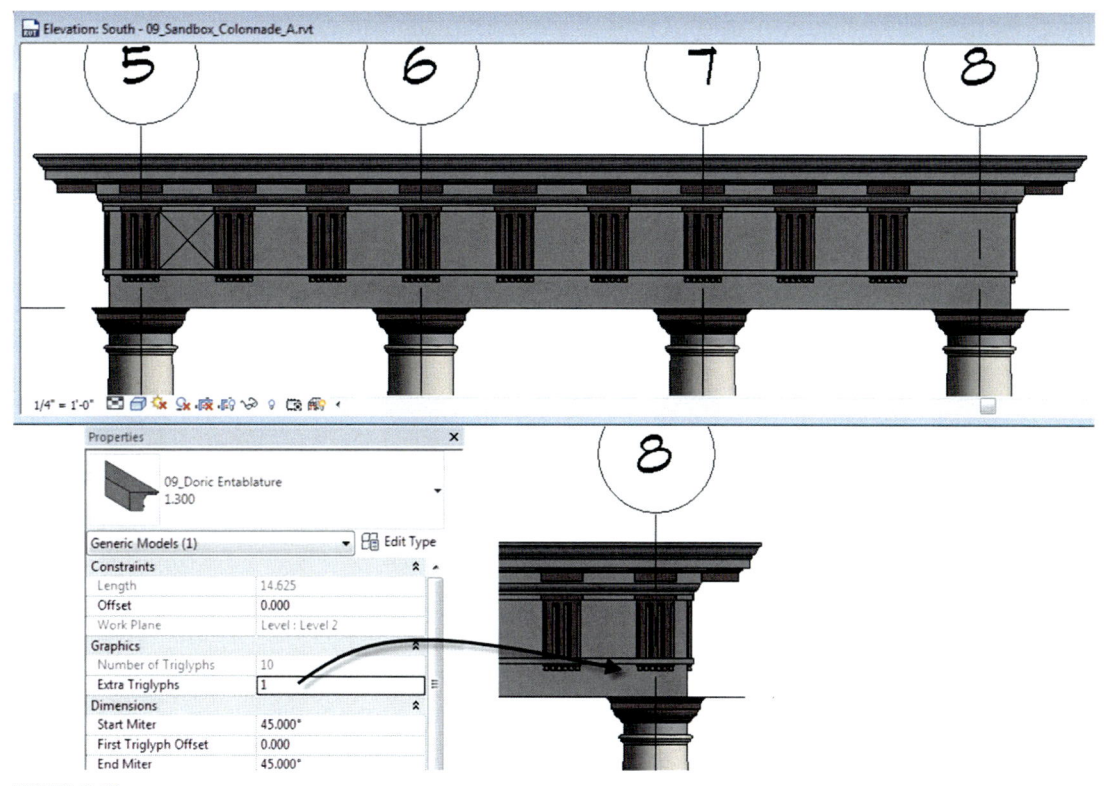

FIGURE 9.32

After loading into project, draw some entablature elements and study the results

Notice that the triglyph on the left side is perfect. It aligns directly over the center of the column on grid 5 as it should. Notice that the metopes are also perfect squares (once again, I added the diagonal lines for clarity in the figure). The only adjustment we need is on the right. We are short one triglyph.

8. Select the entablature element facing us in view. On the Properties palette, Set Extra Triglyphs to **1**.

9. Continue adding other entablature elements if you like and save and close the file when finished.

Don't forget to toggle to coarse level of detail as well. You will see the simpler versions of the mutules and triglyphs in that display. The two-toned coloring you see in the figure was actually unintentional. I forgot to have you assign a material to the sweep in the entablature family. But once I saw the effect, I kind of liked it, so I left it. Naturally if you want control over the material, you can return to the entablature family, select the sweep and add a material parameter. It can be the same one if you want the material uniform or a new one if you like the two material effect.

If you view one of the short sides in an elevation (creating a quick section is easiest) you can experiment with the First Triglyph Offset parameter. I have completed a few in the catch-up file.

> **CATCH UP!** You can open a file completed to this point named: *09_Sandbox Colonnade_B.rvt.*

USING RAILINGS

In our inventory of two pick options at the start of this chapter we discussed the use of a custom railing type to represent your entablature. In this topic I have provided some completed examples for us to open and explore.

Railings have a few interesting characteristics. First, they have rails which can be placed at any height, follow the sketched path of the railing and can be customized with profile families. So our entablature profile that we built at the beginning of this chapter can be used directly in a custom railing type as a rail. Second, you can have more than one rail. While we won't require that feature in this example, it is compelling nonetheless for use in other examples. Third, you can repeat one or more elements along the length of the railing in a user-defined pattern and spacing. Fourth, the elements that you use in the pattern are all customizable baluster families. Apart from a few behaviors unique the baluster category, these families are not unlike other custom model families we can create. Finally, not only can you use more than one baluster family in your repeating pattern, you can also use other ones at the corners and ends of the railing.

All of these features make the use of a railing pretty compelling indeed. The only real downsides are that a railing is a system family which means that we have to rely more heavily on duplicating types to make variations and it is the wrong category.

I have provided a sandbox file. Let's open it up and take a look around.

1. From the *Railing* folder in the *Chapter09* folder, open the file named: *09_Sandbox_Railing.rvt*.
⇨ Click the restore down icon to see the open windows.
2. Zoom and pan in each of the views to take a quick look.
3. In the plan view, click on the railing at grid A1.

Notice that all eight columns in this area highlight. The entire collonade is a single railing object that includes the columns and entablature. Each one of the railings in this file is configured this way. Each one simply uses different spacings and in some cases different Base Diameter sizes.

I have indicated in the type names how each one is configured. So the one we have selected uses a Base Diameter of 1.000 and a column spacing of 3.750 diameters (See Figure 9.33).

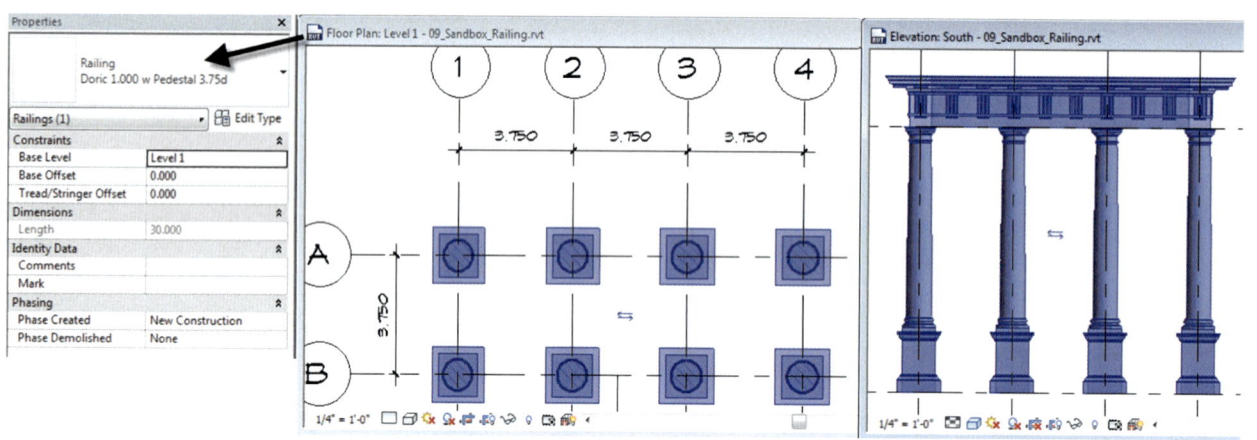

FIGURE 9.33
The railing types in this file contain the columns and entablature

The general structure is simple. The entablature is a "rail" that uses our custom entablature profile. The columns are balusters that have our Doric Order family nested within them. The triglyphs and mutules are also balusters.

You can see these items on the Project Browser beneath the *Families* branch. Beneath *Profiles*, you will see the *Doric Entablature Profile* which contains two types: *1.000* and *1.300* (See the left side of Figure 9.34).

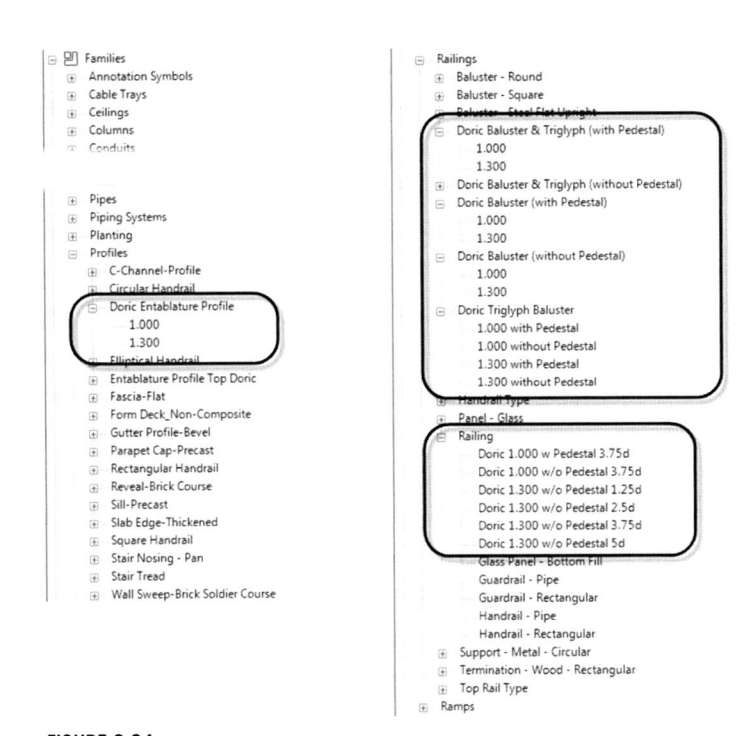

FIGURE 9.34

All of the custom elements can be seen on Project Browser

Beneath Railings you will see the baluster families and the actual railing types. Notice that I have had to create two types for nearly every item: 1.000 and 1.300. Unfortunately this illustrates one of the disadvantages to the railing approach. Railings are system families, which means that you can only customize their types and this can only occur in a project. In other words, you cannot create railing types in the family editor, so to flex the Base Diameter for a single railing type, might require the duplication of several elements that are referenced by the railing type. Each one has to have its Base Diameter adjusted.

4. Edit the Type Properties of the *Doric Entablature Profile: 1.000* type.

Notice that under Dimensions, the Base Diameter is 1.000. Close this dialog and then edit the 1.300 type. Its Base Diameter is 1.300. If you wanted to use your Doric Order in a sitaution that required a 2.000 diamter, you would have to duplicate one of these types and modify the Base Diameter accordingly. Then you would have to repeat that process for each of the baluster families as well. There are five of them total.

Originally I had only three. But unfortunatley, the technique that we used in previous chapters to hide the pedestal was unsuccessful when embedding it in a railing. So I was forced to edit the families and create two separate families instead; one with a pedestal, and one without.

If you wish, you can edit any of these baluster families to see them in the family editor. You will find them very simple. I basically created a new baluster family from the out-of-the-box baluster template (*Baluster.rft*). Then I loaded our Doric Order family and placed in in the file centered on the reference planes. Link up a few parameters and it is ready to go. I made two copies, one with and one without the pedestal. I used the same process for the triglyphs by creating another baluster family and nesting in both the triglyph and the mutule, setting them to the correct height and relative offsets, link up the parameters and save the file. The final family incorporated both the column and the triglyphs in a single baluster family. This one is used at the corners. The reason I did it this way is that unlike the main pattern in the railing type, only one corner post is allowed. So in the main pattern, I am placing two balusters (the column and the triglyph) in essentially the same location (stacked vertically). But I can't do this

276 | Chapter 9

at the corners since only one "post" is allowed. So the solution was to make a post family that contained the column and the triglyph elements on each side of the corner.

Let's take a look at the railing type dialog and see how it all fits together (See Figure 9.35).

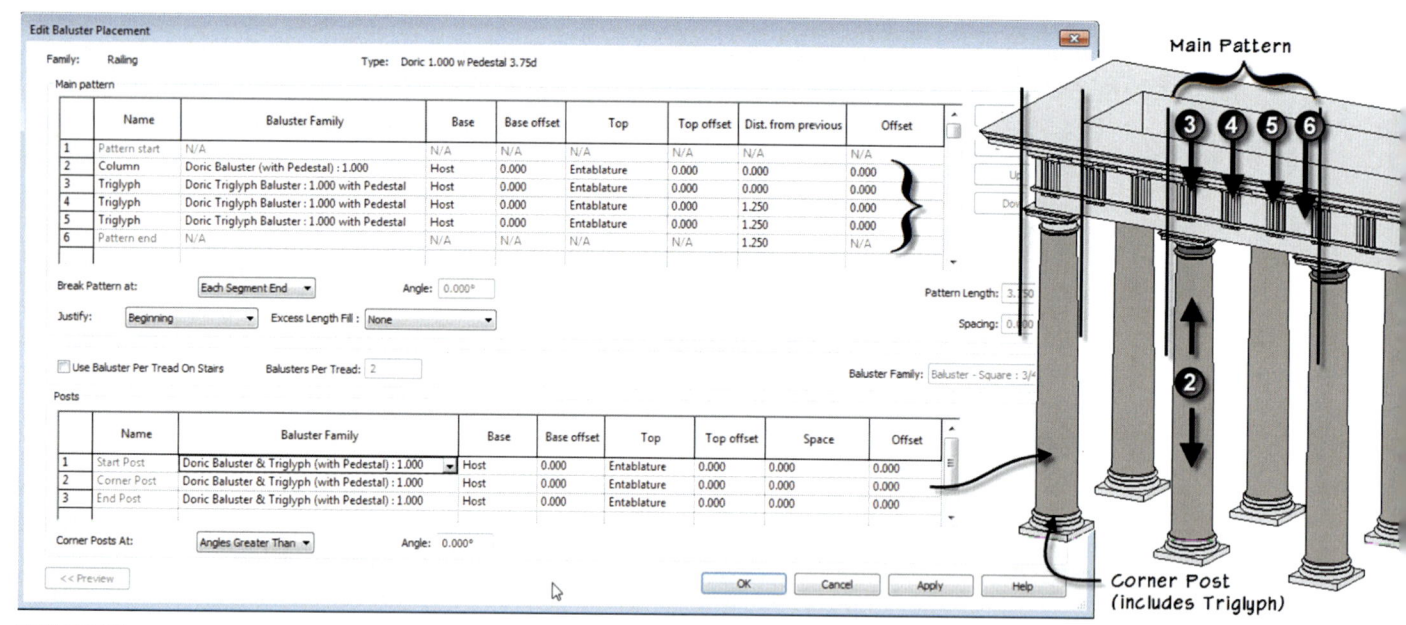

FIGURE 9.35

Explore the type properties of the custom railing

5. Select the railing onscreen.

⇨ On the Properties palette, click the Edit Type button.

⇨ In the "Type Properties" dialog, click the Edit button next to Baluster Placement.

At the top of the dialog is the main pattern. Items in the main pattern are numbered on the far left. I have added the corresponding numbers to the illustration on the right of the figure. So as you can see, component 2 is the column. Directly above it is component 3. The "Dist. from previous" column shows spacing between each component. As you can see, component 2 and 3 have this setting at zero, so they directly line up. It is possible to use the "Base" and "Base offset" settings to shift items vertically. I chose to place them in the baluster family at the desired height instead and leave these values constant at zero. Notice that components 4 and 5 come next and are at a distance of 1.25. Recall from above that this is the required spacing to ensure that we end up with perfectly square metopes. Finally, item 6 is not another component but rather a spacing before the pattern repeats. In this case, the same value achieves the result we need.

At the bottom of the dialog are settings for the start, end and corner posts. If you draw an open path railing, the start and end posts would come into play. In this example, we only see the corner post. These all use the special baluster family that I created containing both column and triglyphs. Since I built it centered and at the correct height, all of the numberical values can stay zero.

The entablature profile is loaded in the Rail Structure dialog. Click the Edit button to see the settings. These are very simple and include the profile, height and material. You could add other rails, but in this case it is not necessary. I left the offset at zero since we already built the profile to align perfectly with the column centerline. This means that when you draw a new collonade with this railing, your sketch lines will be the column centerlines. This makes

• Renaissance Revit •

it very easy to snap to grids for placement. You can see several examples of this here. I even locked the sketch lines to the grid lines in many cases, just select a railing and click Edit Path on the ribbon to see this.

I chose non-continuous rails for most of the railing types in this file. For this use case, I did not see much avantage to the newer continuous top or handrail types. However, I did create one version that uses a Top Rail in the sandbox file. You can it in the default *{3D}* view and in a section called *Section at Continuous Top Rail Type*. One small advantage that continuous rails have over their non-continuous counterparts is that they can be selected independently from the railing using the TAB key. Again for this use case, I don't see a lot of advantage to this. This is a very handy feature when using railings as actual railings, but when using them as collonades, not as much.

I did not include an example that uses supports in place of balusters. Railing supports are another kind of component family that can be repeated along the length of a railing. Specifically along the length of Handrails. We also have Termination families that can be applied to the ends of Top or Handrails. If you think of a railing used in its intended context, these two make perfect sense: the terminiations are useful if you return the handrail to the wall and want to show an escutcheon plate. Supports repeat along the length of the handrail and can represent the mouting brackets that attach the rail back to the main railing or the wall. A nice advantage of supports is that you can selecte them individually with the TAB key and even move them manually. While very handy for a proper railing, I saw no real advantage in this for a Doric collonade. The big limitation is that you can only assign one support type per rail. So in this case, we would run into trouble since the triglyphs repeat at different intervals than the columns. If you break the entablature into separate rails, you could vary the support type assigned to each one, but this seems pretty convoluted to me. Another option is to build a railing type that only includes the entablature. This might be more successful as you would only need to repeat the triglyphs and then you just place the columns manually as we did in the previous chapter. Definitely worth some experimentation if you are up to it.

SUMMARY

- ✓ In order to achieve the carefully defined proportions of Classical orders when placing columns and other elements, it is desirable to try to build the intercolumniation and other spacing rules directly into the families.
- ✓ Several line-based options exist that offer potential to this endeavor.
- ✓ While options include walls, sweeps, beams and slab edges, line-based families and railings offer the best combination of features and benefits when weighed against their corresponding disadvantages.
- ✓ Most methods will work best if creating a single complex profile for the overall section of the entablature. This profile will take time and effort to create, but typically yields the best results.
- ✓ Line-based families cannot automatically miter, but this is easily overcome by building void elements into the family at each end.
- ✓ Use a rotational rig to set the miter angle of the void form at the ends of the family.
- ✓ Use parametrically driven arrays to repeat elements like triglyphs and mutules along the length of the entablature at the proper spacing.
- ✓ Railings offer a compelling alternative. Use the same profile as a rail for the main extruded form of the entablature. Use custom baluster families for repeating elements including the columns themselves.
- ✓ Baluster families can be customized by nesting in existing column, triglyph and mutule families. These elements can be repeated at the proper spacing in the railing type settings.
- ✓ The best part of a railing is that once the type is devised, it is a simple sketch-based element and follow any shape path: linear, curved, open or closed in shape.

Chapter 10

The Ionic Order

INTRODUCTION

In this chapter we will explore the Ionic order. Once again we will reuse components from previous chapters to get us started. We can easily follow the same procedure as the Doric order and save a copy of the Doric or Tuscan, rename the components and then edit each one. Since we have already covered these steps in detail in the previous chapter, we will focus the most attention here in this chapter on what makes the Ionic column so unique: the capital with its distinctive volutes.

OBJECTIVES

The main goal of this chapter is to build an Ionic column capital. We are still working in the traditional family editor in this chapter, so making sure we can model the complex forms required by the Ionic order will be paramount. Topics in this chapter include:

- Constructing the Ionic volute
- Creating the Ionic capital using the volute profile
- Building the scrolls and completing the capital geometry

THE IONIC CAPITAL

In this chapter I will focus much of our discussion on the Ionic capital. I have two reasons for this. The first one is that much of what we have already discussed for the Tuscan and Doric Orders is fully applicable here. But perhaps the more important reason is that the Ionic capital is the most interesting part of the order.

To build the complete order we can start in the same fashion as we did at the beginning of Chapter 8, open the previous order (Doric in this case), save as and rename everything. This is in fact exactly what I have done with the provided files. I had to make slight variations to the shaft to add an extra astragal at the bottom and to adjust the height formulas. Also, the Ionic shaft overlaps the capital, so the height formula takes this into account. I did not embellish the shaft any further at this time. As noted previously, we have an entire upcoming chapter devoted to modeling the shaft. The base is actually identical to the Doric. Finally if you look at the schematic version, I added some cylinders to represent the volutes. Let's start with a quick look at this file.

> **Note:** I have removed the pedestal in the provided files to simplify things a bit. You are welcome to try your hand at a variation with the pedestal if you wish. It is very similar to the Doric, but taller (2.700 diameters compared to 2.400). There is an astragal molding added above and below the cavetto moldings. I'll post an image on my website that you can use for reference.

THE IONIC SCHEMATIC CAPITAL

The schematic versions used for the Ionic order are just copies of the Doric and Tuscan that we used before with a small addition in the capital. Let's open up the schematic Ionic capital and explore the changes.

1. From the *Chapter10\Schematic* folder, open the file named: *Ionic Capital (Schematic).rfa*.
2. On the Project Browser, open the *View 1* 3D view and then tile the windows.

    Orbit the view from different angles to study the form.

Remember that the easiest way to orbit is to hold down the SHIFT key and then drag with the middle wheel button depresed (just like panning, only with SHIFT held down). The Ionic order has a very iconic look. So I think that it is important to convey this even in schematic. The cynliders here are both contained in a single simple extrusion. Its sketch is just two circles.

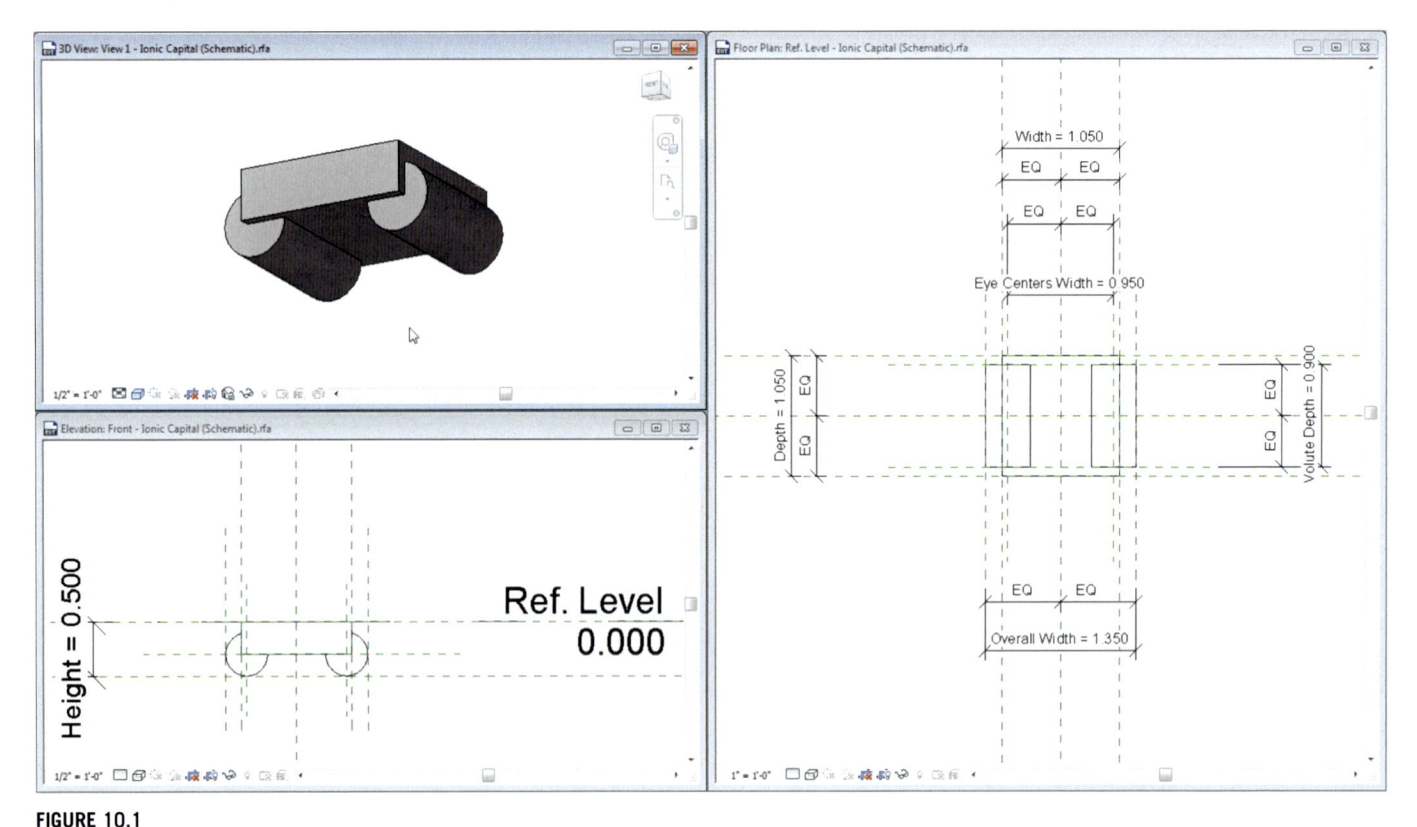

FIGURE 10.1

The schematic Ionic capital has a simple extruded form to represent the volutes

Feel free to edit the extrusion and take a look. Use the big red "X" button on the ribbon to cancel the sketch mode when you are done without making any changes. I went with circles here, but some of the books I have use rectangles in their schematic or block orders instead. It is not important the specific form you choose, just that you suggest the overall form of the Order.

You'll also notice that there are more reference planes and dimensions in this capital than our other schematic orders. Given the extra complexity of the Ionic capital, this was unavoidable. We will be able to reuse these references and parameters in our medium/fine version.

3. When you are finished exploring you can close the file without saving.

THE IONIC VOLUTE

To properly construct the volute of the Ionic Order, it takes no less than 24 separate arcs. Talk about putting our curve constraining strategies to the test! The volute is a spiral form made from progressively smaller arc segments. Each is 90° and reduces in radius until they converge on the "eye" (a round protrusion) in the middle region (but not exactly in the center) of the volute. If you want to learn how to construct this form, there are dozens of authorities on the subject. As I write this I have approximately seven of them spread out across my desk. Vignola uses a method of dividing an arc with diagonals and plotting these on a straight line; almost as if the line were peeled away from the arc like the arc was "unrolled" to become straight (Vignola 2011, 1669, 19). Palladio's method uses concentric squares bisected by diagonals (Palladio 1965, 19-20). I have seen this method in several other resources as well such as Gibbs (Gibbs 1732, 15-16). As I have noted in the previous chapters, I tend to rely heavily on Chitham due to his being a more contemporary source and for his use of decimal measurements which are easy to transfer to "Family Types." I have continued that practice here and have used Chitham's method to construct the volute (Chitham 1985, 2005, 72-73). Chitham credits the method to Chambers. Chambers in turn credits his method to Goldman and gives comparison and comentary on several other masters (Chambers 2003, 1791, 52-55). So you choice of source material is vast.

Chitham has this to say about the Ionic volute (Chitham 1985, 2005, 148):

> "The volute is the most difficult single element in the orders to draw, because the dimensional tolerances are so fine."

I would be hard pressed to disagree with this statement. I have had many failed attempts before arriving at a success for this tutorial. Actually, if we were only concerened with drawing a single static representation of the volute, then it is fairly easy to acomplish using a computer program like Revit. There are many steps to be sure, but the form creation is mostly repeditive; not difficult. However, to not only draw the form, but make it fully parametric is another matter entirely. This has proved quite challenging. If you completed the earlier chapters, particularly exercises like the "Ovolo," "Cyma" and "Cyma Reversa" topics in Chapter 4, then I am sure you can imagine the challenge that we are up against. As before, I have provided progress files along the way, so if you get stuck feel free to open a catch-up file to continue.

UNDERSTANDING THE APPROACH

Back in Chapter 4 we looked at several strategies for constraining curves. Several options from that chapter would work here. However, the sheer quantity of arcs presents a practical limitation. Typically, we would want to create intersecting reference planes for each center point and each endpoint. With 24 arcs required, that would be quite a few reference planes indeed! And most of them in a very tight space. For this reason, I am going to use the nested detail component rig approach coupled with equality dimensions instead. We will still have several reference planes to deal with; we will just hide many of them inside the nested family to make it easier to work with. The good news on this approach is that we will have virtually no parameters to create! Instead, we will leverage the fact that everything is based off of proportions and rely on equality dimensions to subdivide each part into smaller and smaller parts. There will still be plenty of detailed and meticulous work requiring patience to complete, so consider yourself forewarned.

Let's start with a look at the rig. I have provided this as a detail component family in the *Chapter10* folder. I have an illustration of the family in Figure 10.2. It is a bit intense, but remember, we have to locate 24 center points! Study the figure and open the file if you like. It is in the *Chapter10* folder and is named: *Volute Eye Rig.rfa*.

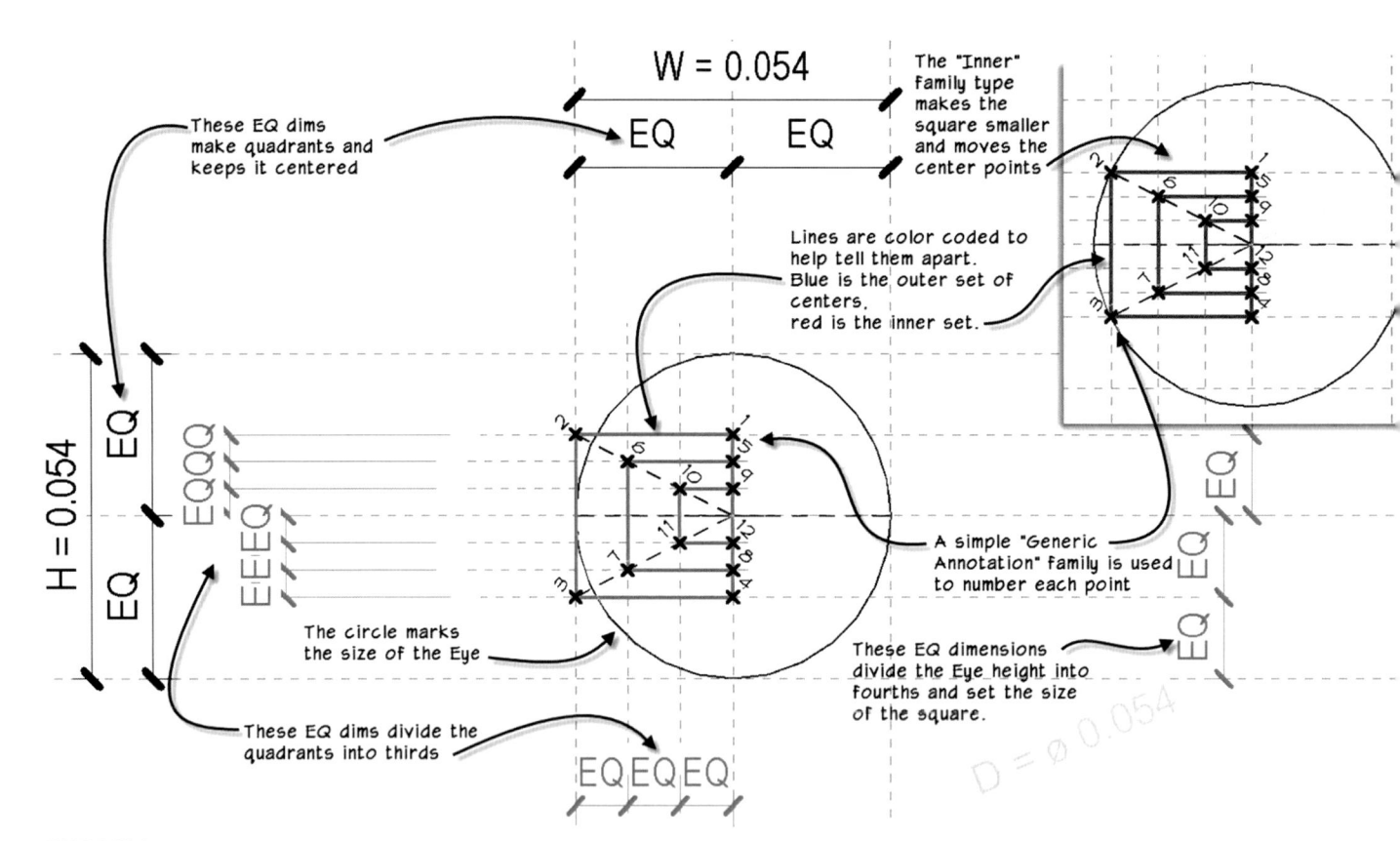

FIGURE 10.2

A Detail Component family will be used as a rig to locate the centers in the Ionic volute

The layout technique starts with a circle for the eye of the volute. A square with the side equal to the radius of this circle is constructed to one side of the circle and centered vertically. The outermost reference planes describe a square shape. These have parameters H and W applied to control the width and height. In reality I could have used the same parameter for both, but just left these two in here from the seed family. The square has two diagonals from the center of the circle to the outside corners. The vertical edge of the square passing through the center is divided into six parts. I did this with reference planes and equality dimensions. Finally, the intersections of each diagonal and the dividing reference planes gives us the 12 points we need for the outside edge of the fillet. I created some subcategories in the "Object Styles" dialog (Manage tab). I assigned them to colors to make it easier to read everything. I drew lines connecting the points and used a blue colored line to help identify the outer edge.

For the inner edge of the fillet, Chitham describes a method using a small triangle to determine the proportion of reduction for the inside edge. I contemplated another rig for this, but instead opted to handle it with formulas. The trigonometry for this was fairly simple. So if you open "Family Types" you can see the formulas and how they are applied. Basically when you choose between the "Inner" and "Outer" types, it adjusts the scale of the family and turns on and off the correct set of colored lines.

To keep track of the center points, I created a simple annotation family to number each point. To create this family, I used the *Generic Annotation.rft* template. I drew a small "X" using two small lines. Then you click the Label button on the ribbon. A Label is a piece of text that reports a parameter. This is what tag families use. The "Edit Label" dialog will appear empty at first, but you can click the Add Parameter icon at the bottom to create a new parameter (see Figure 10.3). In this case, I made it an instance parameter. It can be a text parameter, but I went with type: Integer. (If you want to also be able to "letter" your points, use Text instead). This family is provided in the *Chapter10* folder as well named: *Point Label.rfa*.

• Renaissance Revit •

FIGURE 10.3

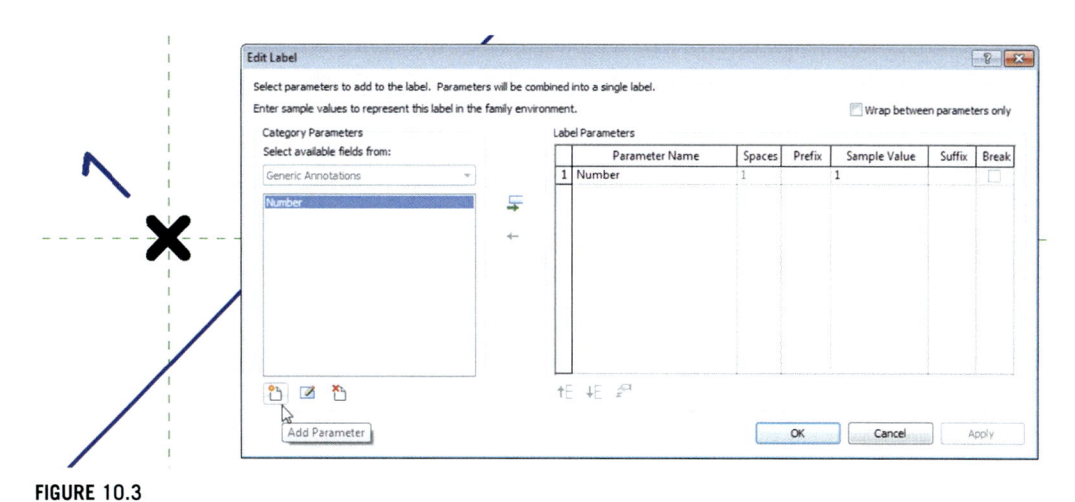

Creating a custom parameter for the label in a generic annotation family

Chitham has the eye diamter at 0.050. He also has the distance from the top edge of the volute to the center of the eye at 0.225 (Chitham 1985, 2005, 72). I found it necessary to adjust both of these values slightly. When using these numbers direclty, many of the arcs generated radii with repeating decimals like .33333 or .66666. The trouble with this is that as noted in the Chitham quote above, when dealing with such tight tolerances, if Revit rounds off the value in your formula, it can cause the family to fail when you flex. This can be quite frustrating particularly when dealing with 5 or more decimal places and dozens of arcs. So instead, if you consider the figure again, all of the equality dimensions are dividing the spaces into thirds. So I went with a numer that was cleanly divisble by three (0.054) and achieved much cleaner results.

You are welcome to recreate these families if you wish, but they have already been provided in the dataset. In fact, we will start with a profile family that I created from one of the seed families we built back in Chapter 2. Some basic reference planes are already in place as well as some of the parameters we will need. The detail component rig is already in the file. We'll finish a few setup items and then begin drawing the volute spiral. Once complete, we will use it to create a sweep in the Ionic capital family. To that we will add other geometry as required. The Ionic capital offers some complex modeling challenges, but it is also one of the most beautiful of the orders. So let's get started.

CREATE THE VOLUTE PROFILE FAMILY

As noted in the previous passage, you can build everything from scratch with the guidance above or you can start with the provided file which has the basics already begun.

1. From the *Chapter10* folder, open the file named: *Ionic Volute Profile_Start.rfa*.

    ⇨ From the Application menu, choose **Save As > Family** and name the new file: **Ionic Volute Profile**.

Everything will appear very small. I have set the scale to full scale given the small size of the volute eye rig. If you set the scale much larger, the numbers become illegible. So we'll have to rely on zooming for the time being.

2. Zoom in on the Volute Eye Rig detail component.

3. Select the detail rig onscreen. On the Properties palette, click the Edit Type button.

    ⇨ In the "Type Properties" dialog, click the Associate Family Parameter button next to Base Diameter, choose Base Diameter and then click OK twice.

4. Align the detail component rig onscreen to the intersection of the Center (Left/Right) and Center (Vertical) reference planes. Lock in both directions.

284 | Chapter 10

Align so the circle is centered—the square will appear off to the left (see Figure 10.4).

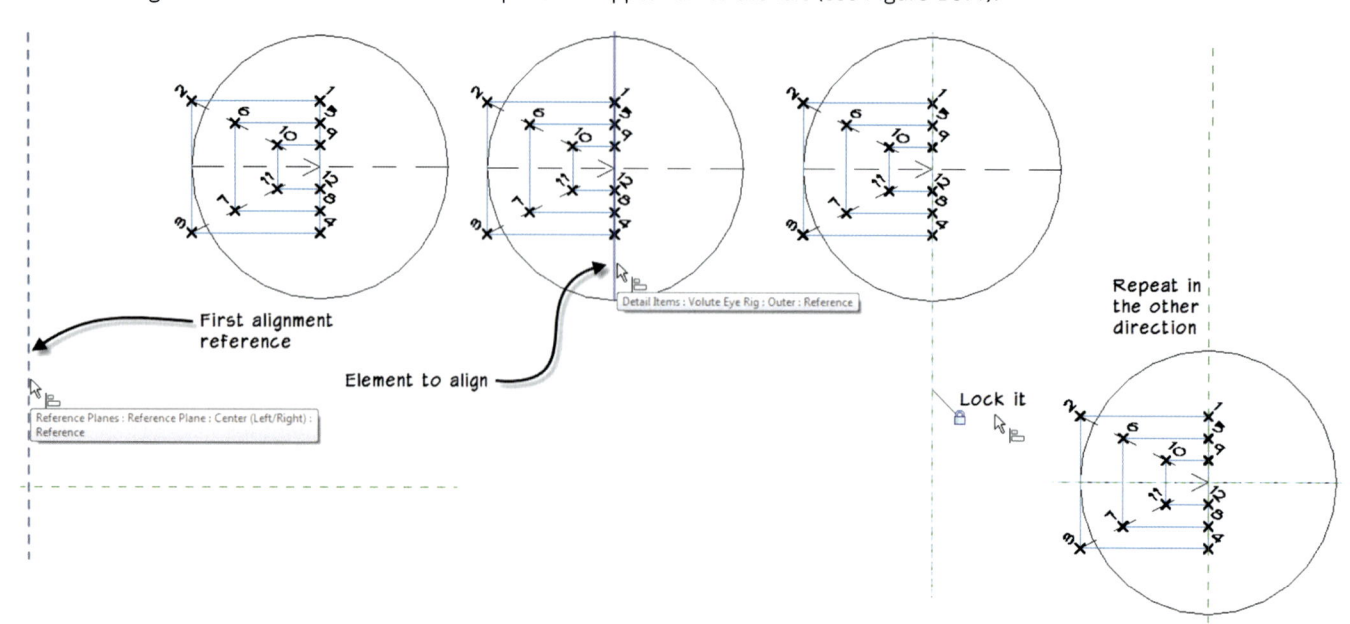

FIGURE 10.4
Align and lock the Detail Component to the centers

Zoom in closely on the detail rig.

5. On the Create tab, click the Line button and then click the Center-ends Arc.

   ⇨ Snap the center point to the intersection at point 1 on the rig.

   ⇨ Pull straight up 90° and snap to the topmost reference plane. (Make sure it is exactly 90° before you click).

   ⇨ Pull straight to the left at 90° again and then click (see Figure 10.5).

You should have a quarter circle centered on point 1.

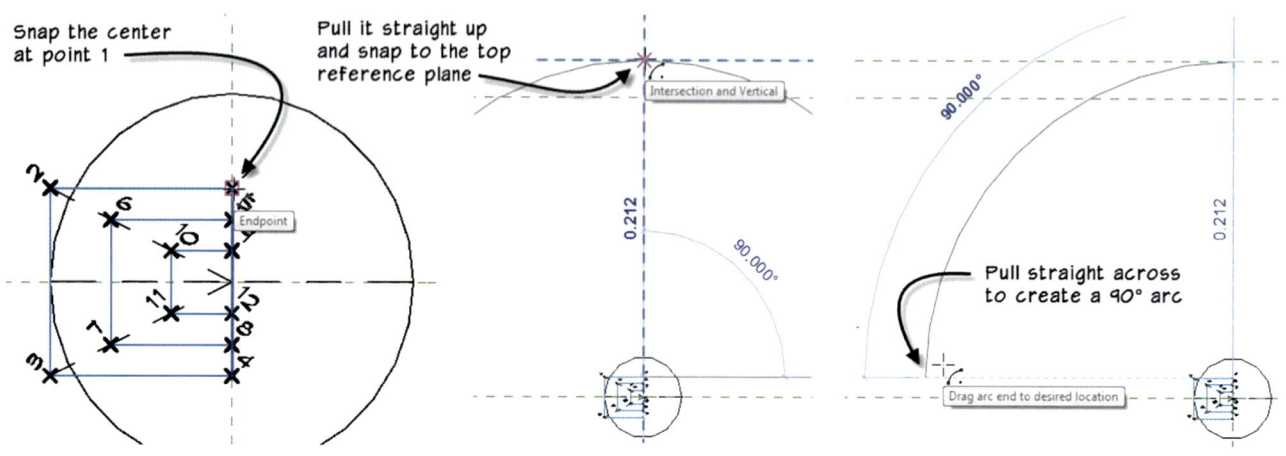

FIGURE 10.5
Draw the first arc centered on point 1 and 90°

6. Cancel the command, select the arc and on the Properties palette, turn on the center mark.

7. Zoom in on the detail rig. Align and lock the center mark to the detail rig in two directions.

   Use the vertical line in the center of the rig for the first reference. Lock it to the center mark.

   Use the blue horizontal line at the top of the square for the second reference. Lock it to the center mark.

• Renaissance Revit •

Notice that the Automatic Sketch Dimensions disappear when you lock. Be very careful about which edges you select. For the first twelve points, we only want to align and lock to the **blue** lines in the rig.

8. Zoom back out. Align and lock the endpoint at the top of the arc to the horizontal reference plane (see Figure 10.6). (One direction; horizontal reference plane only this time).

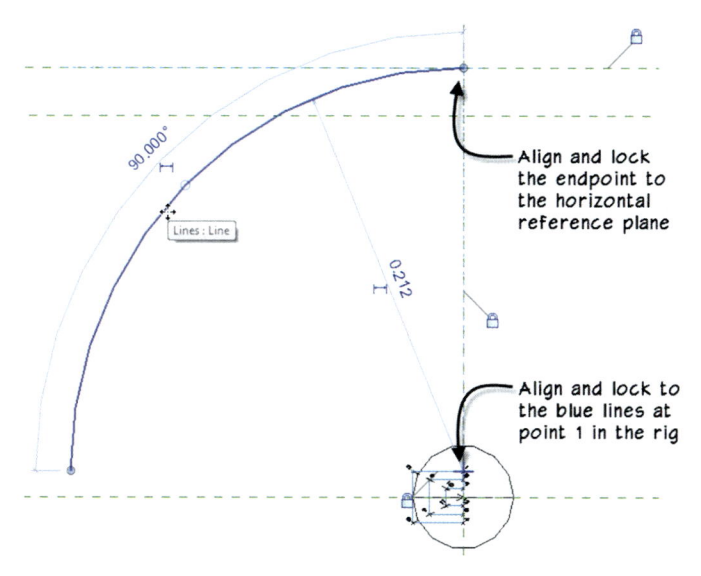

FIGURE 10.6
Align and lock the arc at the center point and the first endpoint

9. Open "Family Types" and flex the Base Diameter to **2.000** and then click OK.

Notice that the arc adjusts as expected. The center is constrained to the detail rig. The detail rig has its internal Base Diameter parameter linked to the Base Diameter in this file so it is flexing as well. And with the endpoint locked to the reference plane, the radius is established as well.

10. Reset the Base Diameter back to **1.000** to continue.

11. Save the file.

CATCH UP! You can open a file completed to this point named: *10_Ionic Volute Profile_A.rvt.*

12. Return to the Line command, select the Center-ends Arc again and snap the center point to point 2 this time.
    ⇨ Move to the left and snap to the endpoint of the existing arc.
    ⇨ Move straight down at 90° and then click.
13. Once again, cancel, turn on the center mark, align and lock (both directions to the blue lines of the rig, and just the horizontal reference plane down below).
    ⇨ Flex again.

Now here's the really tedious part: we have to repeat this process 10 more times for the outer edge of the fillet and then 12 more times for the inner edge. Yes, 22 more arcs, alignments and locks. So these two were some of the easy ones. Unfortunately there is no shortcut. So just be patient and methodical and be sure not to miss any steps along the way or things might misbehave when you flex. I recommend **frequent** flexing as well. This way if one of the arcs is misbehaving, you will find out which one right away.

14. Repeat the process to add arcs 3 through 5.

Add each arc one at a time and stop and turn on the center mark and align and lock as you go. Align and lock any time you see an Automatic Sketch Dimension appear. Arcs 2 and 3 can be aligned to the horizontal reference plane at the bottom of the screen. Arcs 4 and 5 will sense a reference plane off screen to the left. You can align and lock to this reference plane even though it is off to the side. This helps a lot to keep the onscreen clutter in check (see Figure 10.7).

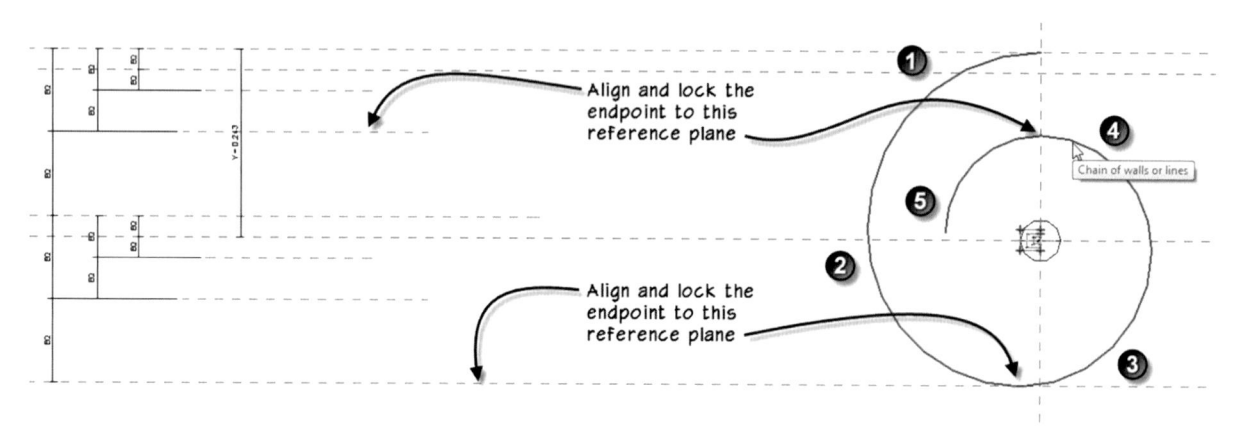

FIGURE 10.7
Create the first five arcs of the outer shape of the volute fillet

15. Save the file.

CATCH UP! You can open a file completed to this point named: *10_Ionic Volute Profile_B.rvt*.

ADD REFERENCE PLANES WITH EQUALITY DIMENSIONS

The collection of reference planes off to the left side at first looks somewhat chaotic. However, there is a strategy to how I have laid them out. Zoom the screen so you can see all of the reference plans at the left. In Figure 10.8 I have added a graphic scale to the left to help illustrate the relationships of the reference planes. Note first that everything is slightly off center. The overall distance between Top and Bottom reference planes is the height of the volute. The Y parameter controls the distance from the Center (Vertical) reference plane (which is the origin of this family) and the Top reference plane. The Center (Vertical) reference plane is also the location of the volute eye. Everything else is driven by a series of nested equality dimensions.

As you study the groupings of reference planes, notice that I have varied the lengths of each set to help make them easier to understand. I also stagger the dimensions. So first we divide the total height into four. Then we subdivide the top quarter in half to make each an eighth of the total. Then subdivide it in half again to give us the size of the fillet at the top. I carried this reference plane all the way across since we start our arcs at the top. A similar subdivision occurs to locate the eye at the Center (Vertical) reference plane.

FIGURE 10.8

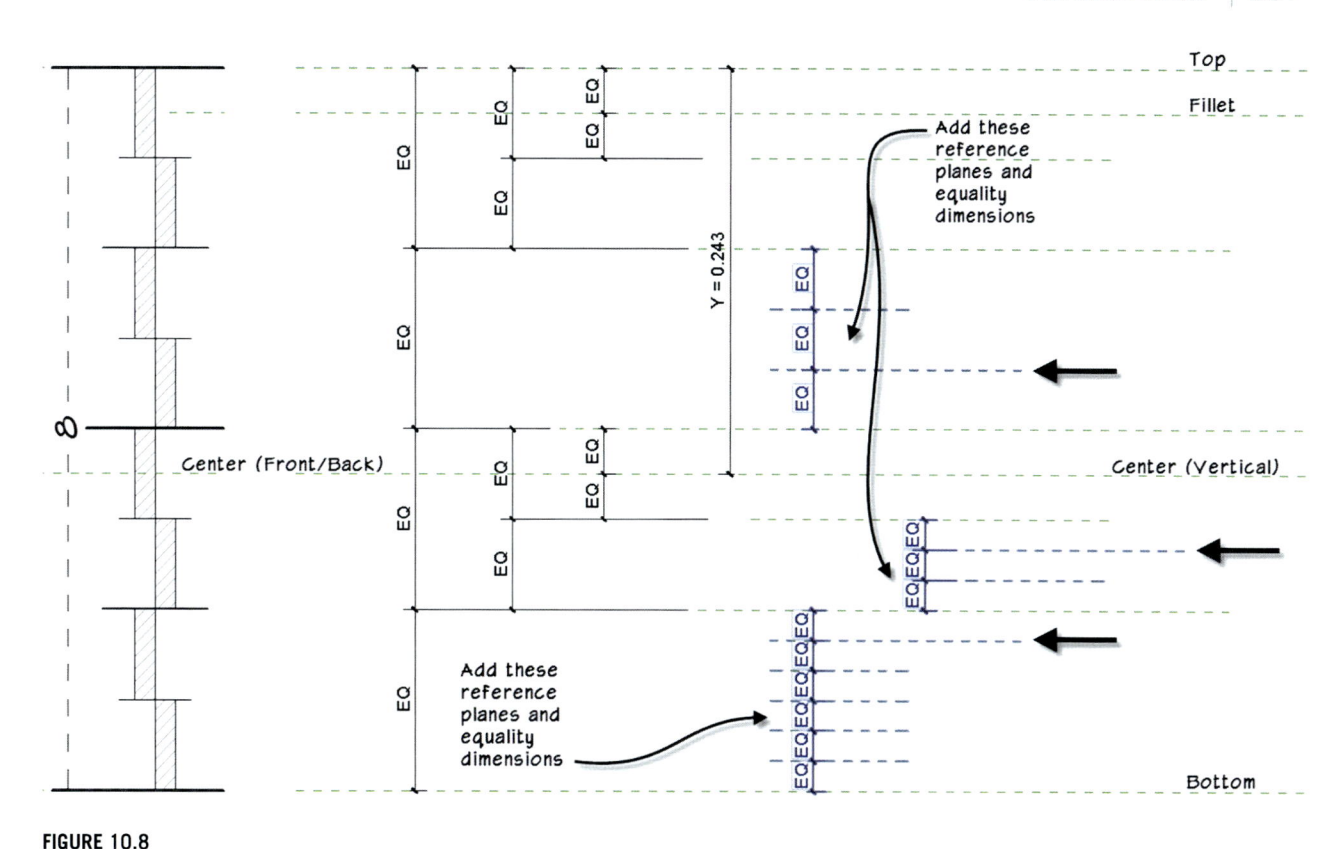

Analyze the reference planes and equality dimensions existing in the file and add additional ones

As you saw when creating arcs 4 and 5, even if the reference plane is off screen, you can still snap to it and lock to it. So, let's create a few more groups of equally spaced reference planes. We really only need three for the purposes of snapping geometry. These are the ones indicated with the bold arrows in Figure 10.8. However, in order to use the equality dimensions you have to add additional ones as well. I like to vary the length make the important ones stand out. So when creating the reference planes indicated in the figure, make the ones with the arrows a little longer.

1. Using Figure 10.8 as a guide, create three groups of reference planes and equality dimensions as indicated.
    ⇨ At the bottom, create five total (for six equal spaces) with the top one longer. Add the equality dimension.
    ⇨ In the other two areas, add two reference planes (for three equal spaces).
2. Continue the procedure outlined above to add arcs 6 through 12.

Remember, it is best to add each arc one at a time and stop and turn on the center mark and align and lock as you go. Align and lock any time you see an Automatic Sketch Dimension appear.

   Be sure to flex often as you work.

3. When you complete arc 12, flex again trying several different values like: **0.500**, **0.750**, **1.250**, **1.500** and **2.000**. Return to **1.000** before continuing (see Figure 10.9).

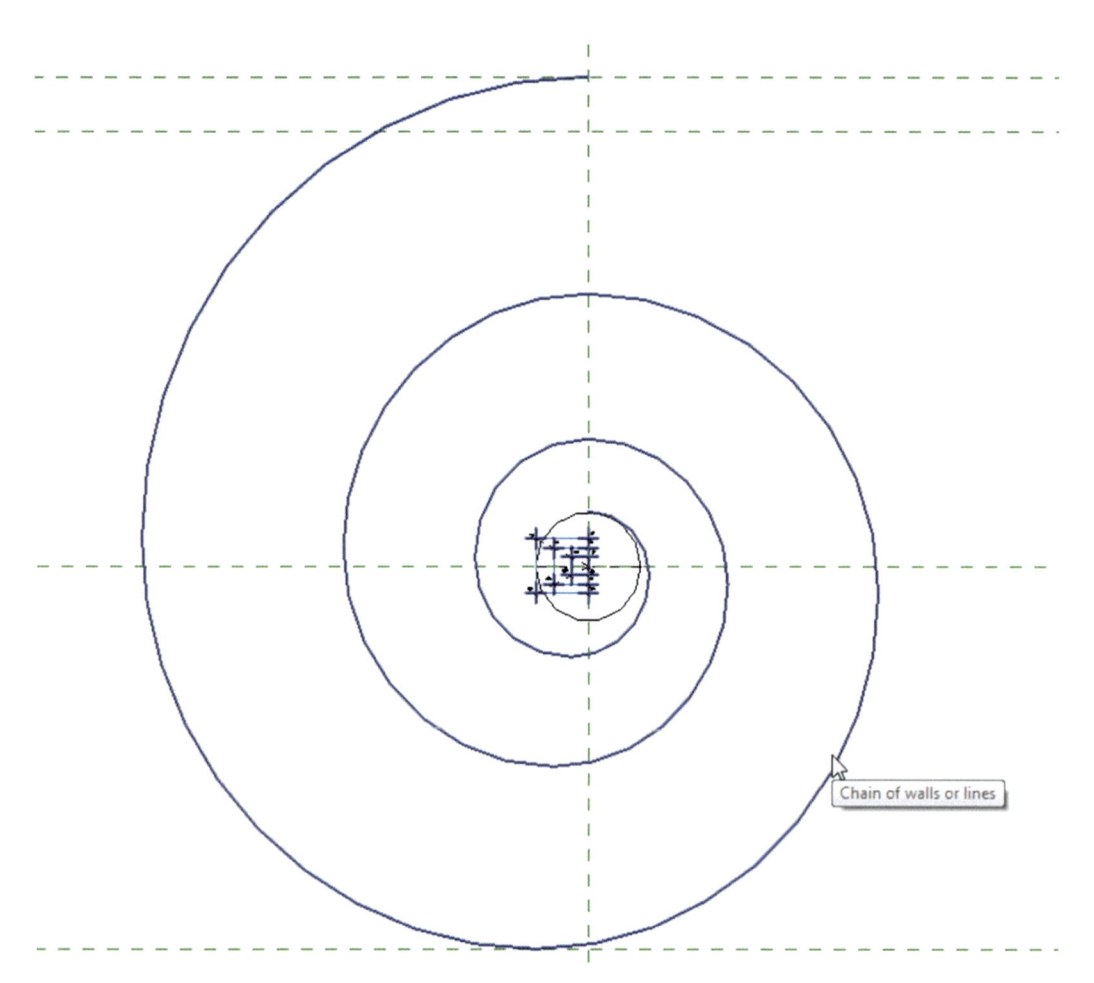

FIGURE 10.9

Add the remainder of the 12 arcs and flex to ensure everything is working

4. Save the file.

CATCH UP! You can open a file completed to this point named: *10_Ionic Volute Profile_C.rvt*.

CREATE THE INNER FILLET EDGE

We are half way there! The twelve arcs we have here are the outside edge of the volute fillet. We need to create a second spiral inside of the first one that will be the inside edge of the fillet. The process is nearly the same. But this time, I'll save you some effort. I built another rig to help us along.

Continue in the same file or open the catch-up file.

1. Select the Volute Eye Rig onscreen.

⇨ On the View Control Bar, click the Temporary Hide/Isolate pop-up (sunglasses) and choose **Hide Element**.

2. Highlight one of the arcs, press TAB (they will all highlight) and then click to select the chain.

⇨ From the Temporary Hide/Isolate pop-up choose **Hide Element** again.

3. On the Create tab, click the Detail Component button.

4. From the Type Selector, choose **Inner** and then click at the intersection of the two center reference planes to place it (see Figure 10.10).

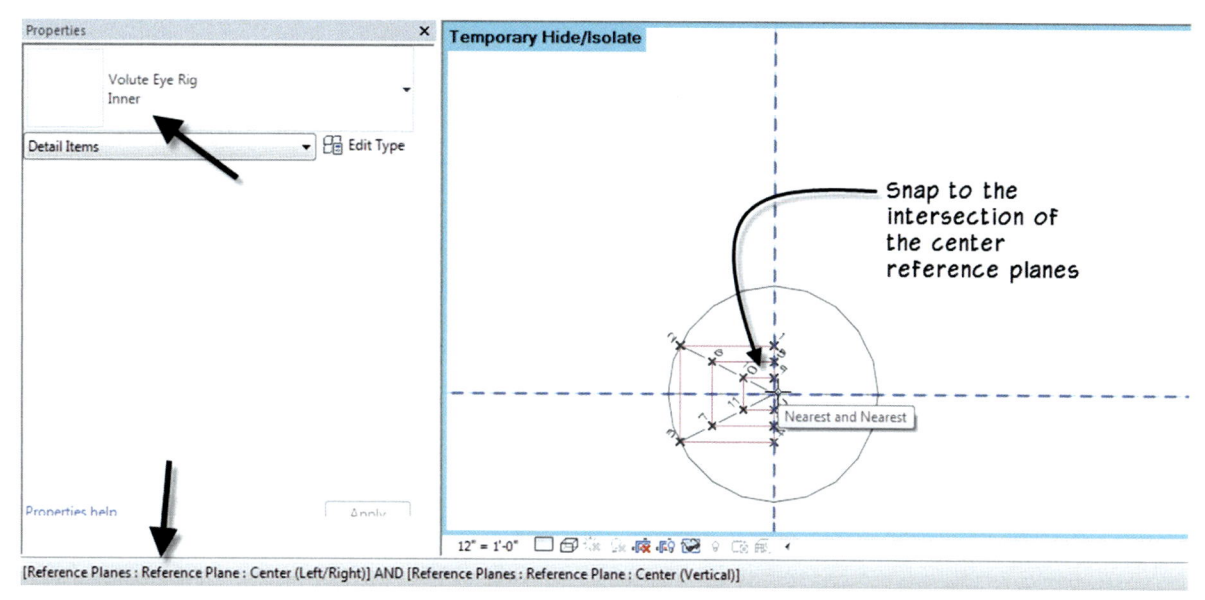

FIGURE 10.10

Place another rig for the inner points

5. Align and lock this rig in both directions.

   ⇨ Select the element onscreen, on the Properties palette, click the Edit Type button and link up the Base Diameter parameter.

We'll also need another collection of reference planes like the ones on the left in the same proportions but slightly closer together. We could simply layout more reference planes, carefully place them in groups, add dimensions, toggle on equality, etc. But I have created another detail item family for this instead. The family contains a copy of all the reference planes and equality dimensions on the left. In fact, I have set up two types in this family like the Volute Eye Rig, so if you wanted to, you could use it for both the inner and outer fillet arcs. But since we already built the outer ones I would suggest leaving them as is. You can use this rig for any future volutes you might need to create however.

6. On the Create tab, click the Detail Component button again.

   ⇨ On the Modify | Place Detail Component tab, click the Load Family button.

   ⇨ Browse to the *Chapter10* folder, select the *Reference Rig.rfa* file and then click Open.

7. On the Type Selector, make sure that **Inner** is chosen and then place an instance at the intersection of the two center reference planes.

   ⇨ Align and lock in both directions. (Pay close attention to the Status Bar to make sure you are selecting the correct alignment edges).

   ⇨ Select the element onscreen, and then on the Properties palette, click the Edit Type button and link up the Base Diameter parameter (see Figure 10.11).

8. Flex the family. Reset to **1.000** before continuing.

• *Creating Classical Architecture with Modern Software* •

290 | Chapter 10

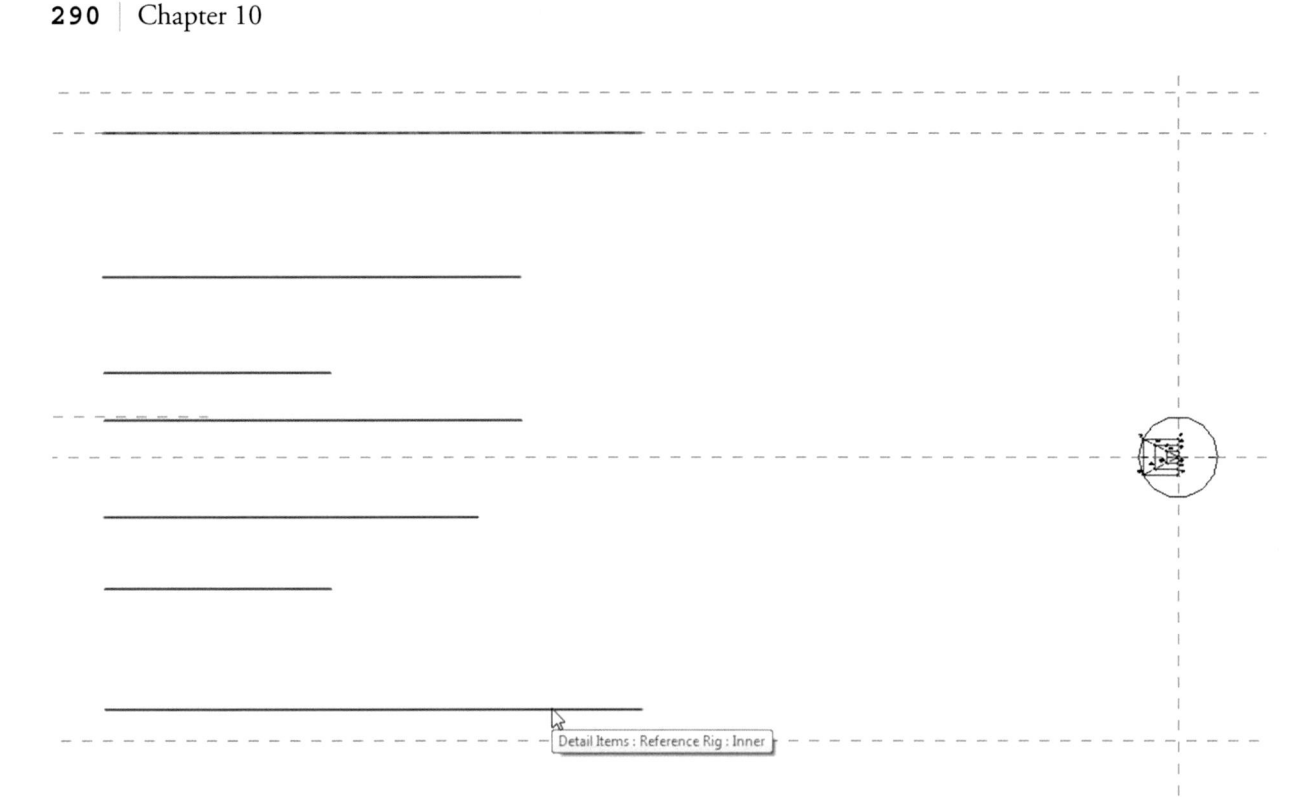

FIGURE 10.11
Insert the Reference Rig to control the radii of the inner fillet arcs

Following the procedure above, create all of the arcs.

> Zoom in closely on the detail rig.

9. On the Create tab, click the Line button and then click the Center-ends Arc.

   ⇨ Snap the center point to the intersection at point 1 on the rig.

   ⇨ Pull straight up 90° and snap to the topmost reference plane. (Make sure it is exactly 90° before you click).

   ⇨ Pull straight to the left at 90° again and then click (similar to Figure 10.5 above).

   ⇨ Enable the center mark and then align and lock the endpoints at each end in both X and Y directions.

You should have a quarter circle centered on point 1.

10. Repeat the process to add arcs 2 through 12.

Remember, take your time. Align everything carefully. Try to eliminate all Automatic Sketch Dimensions as you go. It is possible to draw all the arcs and then align and lock everything, but if you are not extra diligent in doing so, you can easily miss some. So even though it is more tedious, I recommend doing one arc at a time. Save and flex regularly.

11. On the View Control Bar, from the Temporary Hide/Isolate pop-up, choose **Reset** (see Figure 10.12).

• Renaissance Revit •

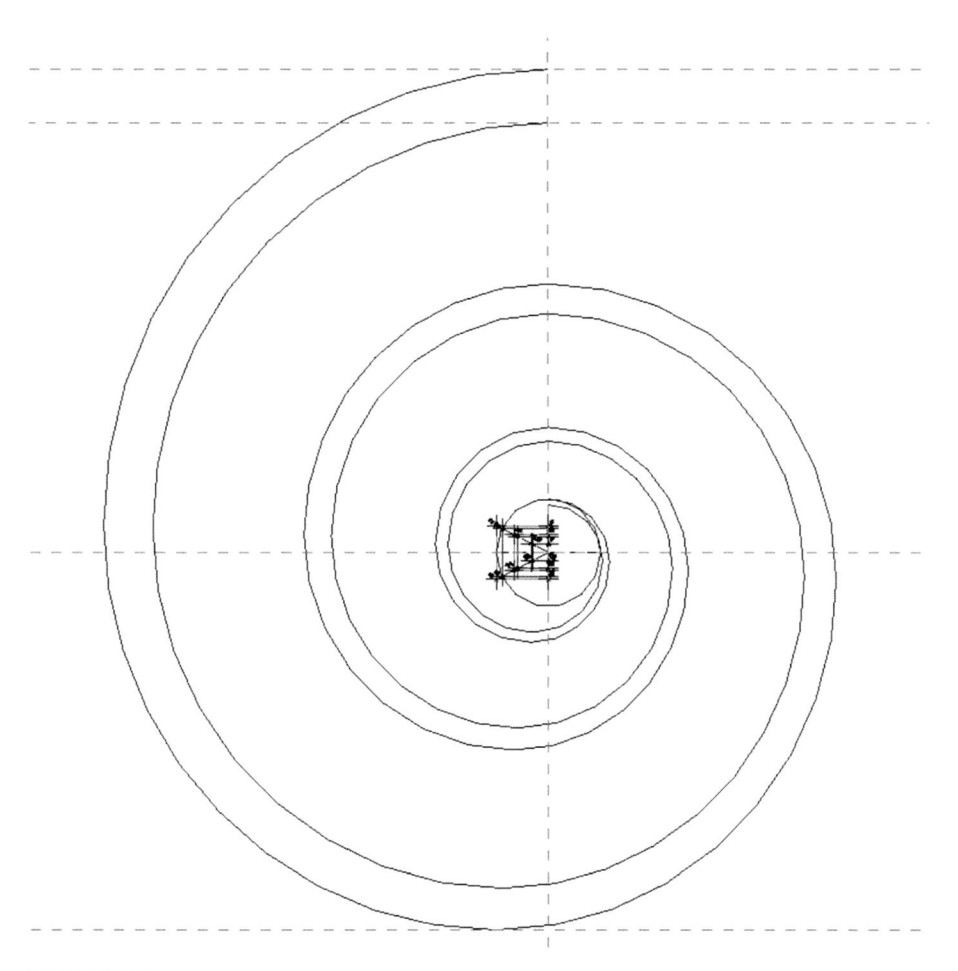

FIGURE 10.12
All of the arcs complete

    12. Save the file.

> **CATCH UP!** You can open a file completed to this point named: *10_Ionic Volute Profile_D.rvt*.

COMPLETE THE PROFILE

We've completed the hard part. All that remains is to add a few additional line segments to close off the profile. Off to the right in this file is a vertical reference plane named: "Centerline of Column." There is a labeled dimension (X1) connecting this to the Center (Left/Right) reference plane. Some authorities put the centerline of the eye directly over the outside edge of the column at the base, others have the edge of the eye lined up with the column edge or even the center of the eye lined up with the edge of the entablature. Since these variances exist, I have added a multiplier to the formula for the X1 parameter. You can open "Family Types" to see this.

Another consideration is the type of capital you are creating. The Ionic capital can be four sided (with the volutes at 45° angles) or two sided (where the volutes are flat to the viewing plane and parallel to one another). There are even some variations that combine the two for corner conditions. (One corner will project out at a 45° angle and the other faces will be flat). I am demonstrating the flat or 2-sided version here. However, it is possible to reuse this volute profile in the other contexts as well. So this is another reason why the multiplier on X1 is important. As you might expect, the distance of the projection along X1 would vary in each type of capital.

Let's add the remaining lines needed to enclose this profile.

    Continue in the Ionic Volute Profile file or open the catch-up file.

• Creating Classical Architecture with Modern Software •

1. Zoom in close on the eye.

2. Draw a small straight line to connect the endpoints of the inner and outer arc 12.

    ⇨ Align and lock it to the vertical reference plane (see the left side of Figure 10.13).

TIP: If you have trouble selecting the vertical reference plane to align, use Temporary Hide/Isolate to hide the rig detail families.

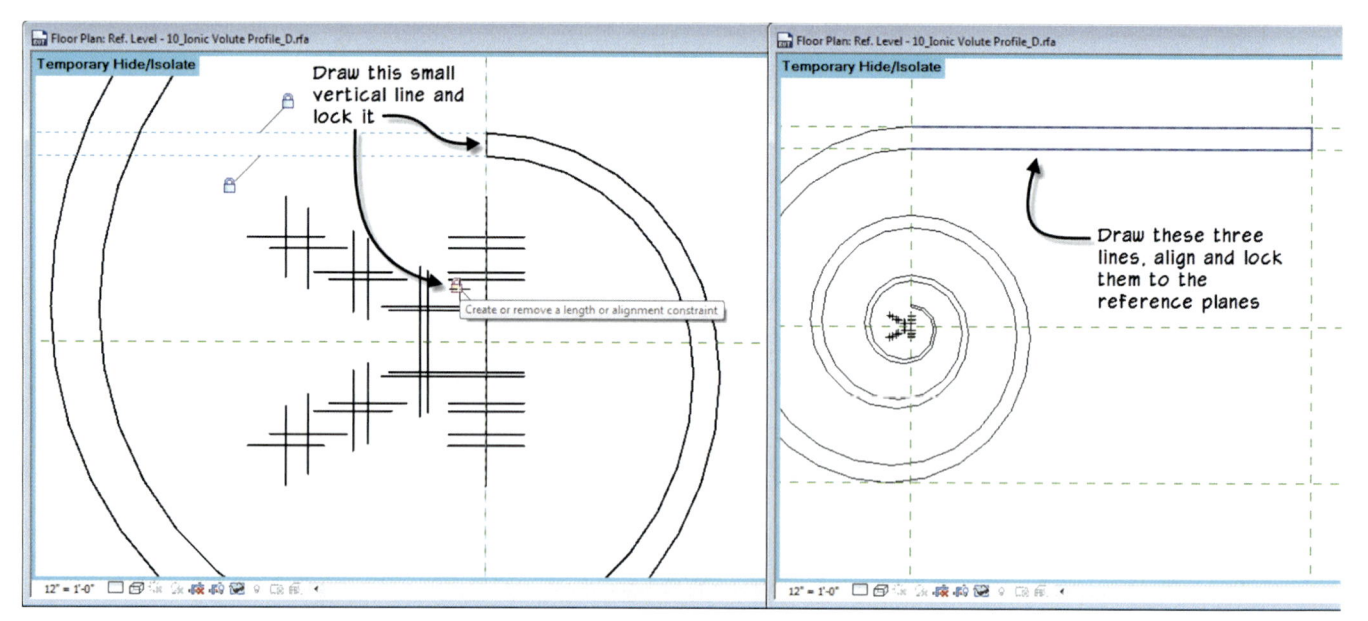

FIGURE 10.13
Add a vertical line to close the ends of inner and outer arc 12. Complete the horizontal portion at the right

3. Add three straight lines at the right:

    ⇨ One aligned and locked with the Top reference plane.

    ⇨ One aligned and locked to the Centerline of Column reference plane.

    ⇨ The last one aligned and locked to the Fillet reference plane.

4. Open "Family Types" and flex the Distance Center to Eye parameter. Reset to **0.500** before continuing.

5. Reset the Temporary Hide/Isolate and then save the file.

Congratulations! That was the toughest profile to create in the whole book. (Although it could be argued that the Doric entablature profile in the previous chapter was harder). We'll have plenty more exercises that come close, but this one was certainly a challenge.

CATCH UP! You can open a file completed to this point named: *10_Ionic Volute Profile.rvt*.

CREATE THE SECOND VOLUTE PROFILE

I know what you're thinking, "second profile?" Don't worry, this one is much simpler than the first. The volute we will be creating is actually made up of two pieces. The profile we just built is for the fillet that spirals around the edge of the volute. This new profile is the backup material from which the fillet will rise. Here's the best part; we only need to save the current file with a new name and delete what we don't need. So it will be much simpler indeed.

Continue in the Ionic Volute Profile file or open the catch-up file.

• Renaissance Revit •

The Ionic Order | 293

1. From the Application menu, choose **Save As > Family** and name the new file: **Ionic Volute Back Profile**.
2. Zoom in on the eye and delete the small vertical segment that we drew in the previous exercise.
   ⇨ Zoom back out and delete arc 1 for the inner edge (see the left side of Figure 10.14).

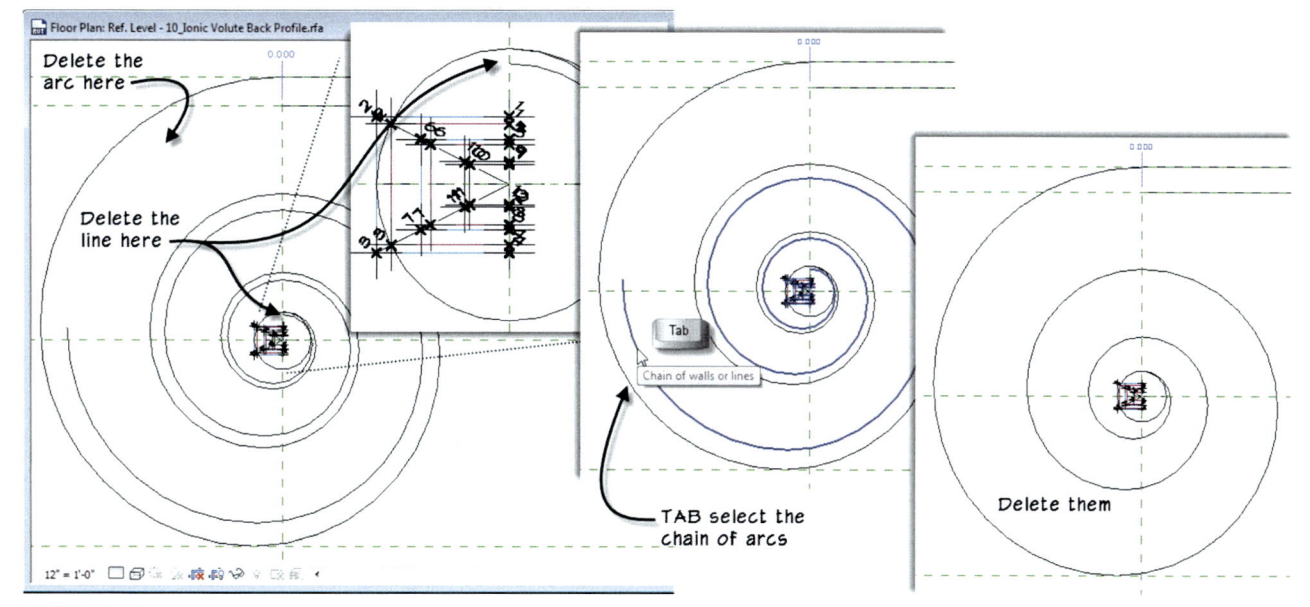

FIGURE 10.14
Delete the unneeded lines

3. Highlight arc 2, press TAB to highlight all of the inner arcs and then click to select the chain.
   ⇨ Delete this chain of arcs (see the right side of Figure 10.14).
4. Delete arc 5.
   ⇨ Chain select arcs 6 through 12 and delete these as well.
   ⇨ Delete the Reference Rig onscreen. (The one with the horizontal red lines).
   ⇨ Zoom in close on the eye. Delete *only* the Inner Volute Eye Rig.

Important: Do *not* delete the Outer one.

5. Zoom out. On the Modify tab, click the Align tool.
   ⇨ For the reference line, click the horizontal reference plane that lines up with the endpoint of arc 4 (this is the fourth horizontal reference plane from the top).
   ⇨ For the entity to align, click the horizontal line on the Fillet reference plane.
   ⇨ In the warning that appears, click the Remove Constraints button.

   The element is currently locked to the Fillet reference plane. So we must unconstrain it before we can lock it to a different reference plane.

6. Lock the alignment (see Figure 10.15).

• *Creating Classical Architecture with Modern Software* •

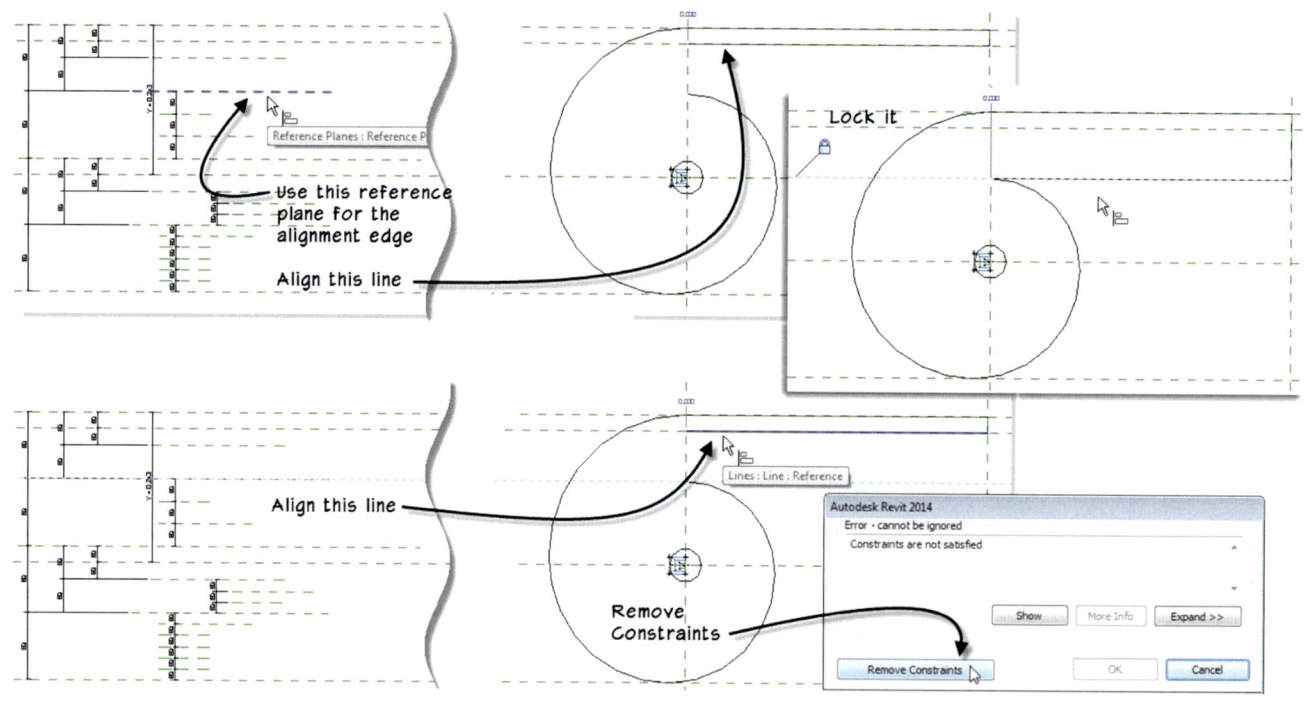

FIGURE 10.15

Adjust the shape of the profile

7. You will notice one Automatic Sketch Dimension remains. Align and lock the endpoint of the horizontal line to eliminate this.

8. Open "Family Types" and flex. Reset all values before continuing.

9. Save the file.

If you like, you can clean up the file a little by deleting the reference planes that are no longer needed. But this is not necessary.

CATCH UP! You can open a file completed to this point named: *10_Ionic Volute Back Profile.rvt*.

CREATE THE IONIC CAPITAL

Much of the basic structure we need for the Ionic capital (minus the volutes) is already contained in the Doric capital. The abacus is square in plan with a cyma reversa molding and there is an ovolo molding below that. The moldings below that are not needed. Like we have done in previous chapters, all we need to do it open our Doric capital file, save it to a new name and then delete what we don't need and modify what is already there.

I have provided another starting file for this part. I have deleted the unneeded moldings and adjusted the type properties of the profiles we are keeping. In Figure 10.16 I have included an image of the Doric capital side by side for comparison. I have also included the "Type Properties" dialogs for both moldings that remain in the file. If you would like to learn more about how we constructed the Doric capital, refer back to Chapter 8.

The Ionic Order | 295

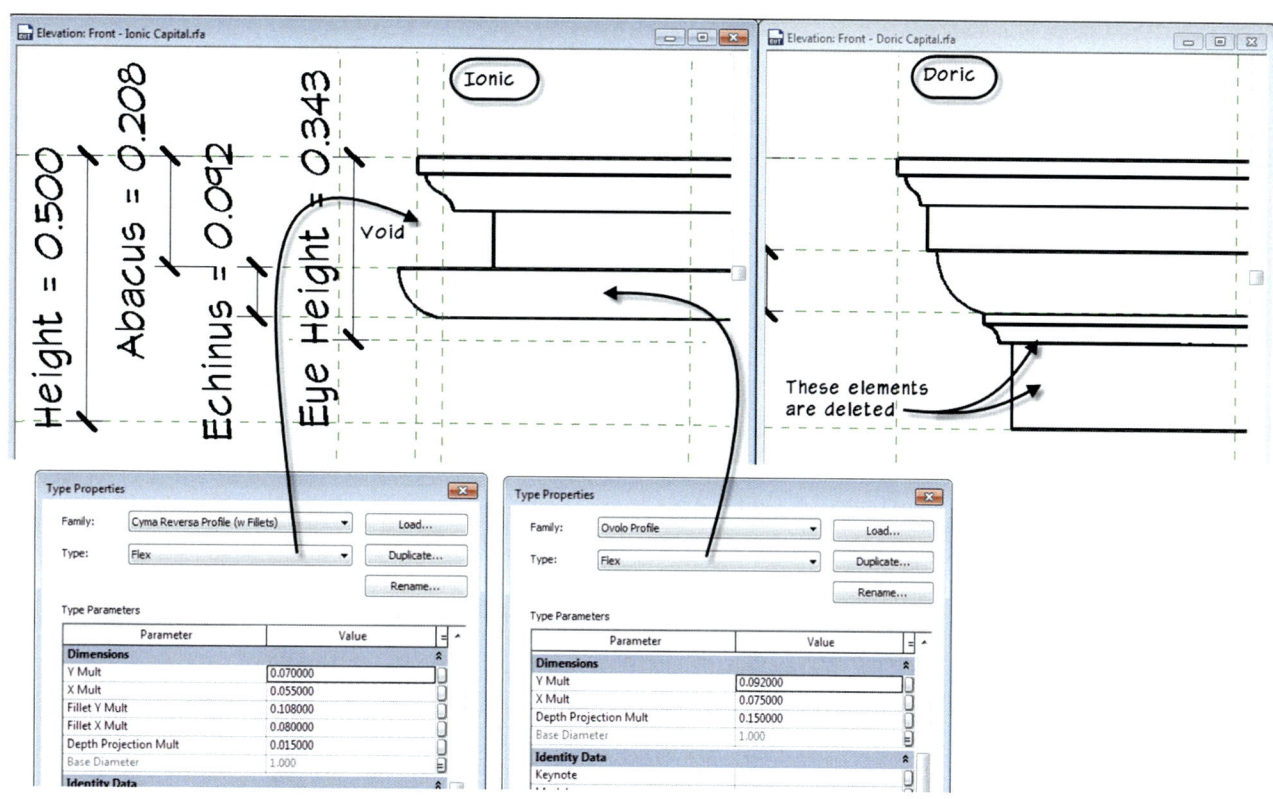

FIGURE 10.16

A comparison of the moldings in the Ionic capital start file and the Doric capitals

ADJUST THE ABACUS

We still need to make one adjustment to the abacus. Look carefully at the left side of the figure and you will see that we have quite a deep recess above the ovolo. This is controlled by the Fillet X Mult parameter in the Type Properties of the Cyma Reversa Profile. I chose this depth because it is what is needed on the front and back of the capital to accommodate the depth of the volutes. However, as you can see, this might be too deep on the sides. So let's rework the void at the abacus.

1. Close any open files and then open the file named: *Ionic Capital_Start.rfa*.
2. Save the file as: **Ionic Capital**.

Feel free to explore the file a bit before continuing.

3. On the Project Browser, expand *Families > Profiles > Cyma Reversa Profile (w Fillets)*.
   - Right-click Flex and choose **Duplicate**. Name it: **Sides**.
   - Right-click Flex again and choose **Rename**. Name it: **Front and Back**.
4. Right-click *Sides* and choose **Type Properties**.
   - Change the Fillet X Mult to: **0.005**, link up the Base Diameter parameter and then click OK.
5. In the 3D view, select the void form. (Use TAB if necessary).
   - On the Modify I Void Sweep tab, click Edit Sweep. Click Pick Path and delete the left, back and right sides leaving a single line along the front edge. (Use the ViewCube to assist you in orientation).
   - Click the Finish Edit Mode twice.

   The void now only cuts the front edge. We now need to make three copies and modify each one.

• *Creating Classical Architecture with Modern Software* •

6. Keep the void sweep selected. On the Modify | Void Sweep tab, on the Clipboard panel, choose Copy to Clipboard and the from the Paste drop-down, choose **Aligned to Same Place**.

- Click Edit Sweep and then Pick Path again. Delete the existing path line and then click the Pick 3D Edges button.
- Click only the right edge at the top of the extrusion. (Use the ViewCube to assist you in orientation).

7. Click the Finish Edit mode button once.

- Click the Select Profile button, and then on the Modify | Sweep tab, choose **Cyma Reversa Profile (w Fillets):Sides** from the Profile list.
- Click the Finish Edit Mode button.

We now have two different voids cutting the extrusion at the top. They each cut at a different depth (see Figure 10.17).

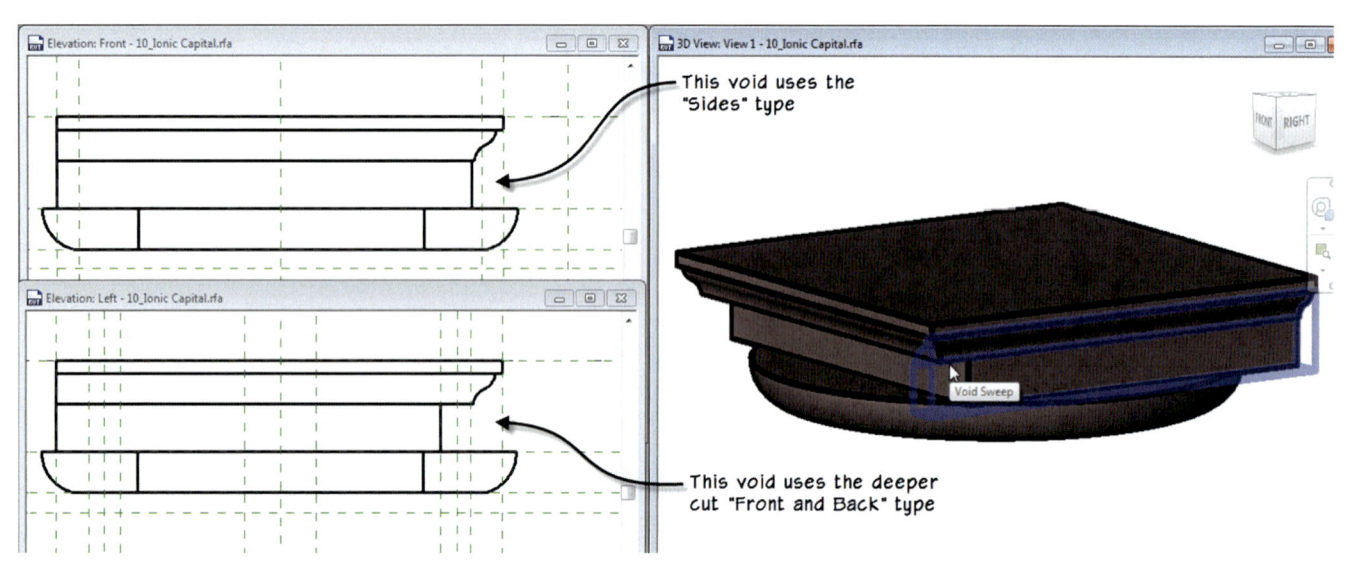

FIGURE 10.17
Modify the first sweep, copy and paste it to make a variation

8. Repeat the process twice more.

- Copy and paste the one on the right. Edit the path, delete the existing and pick the left side instead. Finish Edit Mode.
- Copy and paste the one on the front. Edit the path, delete the existing and pick the back side instead. Use the technique above to switch the profile back to "Front and Back."
- Finish Edit Mode.

9. Flex Base Diameter to be sure everything is working. Return the value to **1.000** before continuing. Save the file.

While not completely necessary, these modifications will give a much nicer final result when we are done adding the volutes and scrolls.

CREATE THE VOLUTE SWEEPS

If you completed the previous exercise, you are probably anxious to create some geometry from the scrolling profile that we built. So let's get to work.

Continue in the *Ionic Capital* file.

1. Open the *Ref. Level* floor plan view.

As you can see, I have transferred the extra reference planes and parameters from the schematic capital that we discussed at the start of the chapter. I have also added a couple additional ones that we will use for creating the volutes.

2. On the left side, near the bottom of the screen, select each reference plane in turn to familiarize yourself with their names.

   The first sweep will be drawn from Volute Scroll Front to Volute Fillet Front.

3. On the Create tab, click the Sweep button. Then click the Sketch Path button.

   ⇨ On the Work Plane panel, click the Set button.

   ⇨ In the "Work Plane" dialog, from the Name list, choose: **Reference Plane : Eye Height** and then click OK.

   ⇨ Draw a single short line segment running vertically along the "Volute Eye Center Left" reference plane.

   Snap its length between the intersection of "Volute Scroll Front" and "Volute Eye Center Left" to the intersection of "Volute Fillet Front" and "Volute Eye Center Left" (see Figure 10.18).

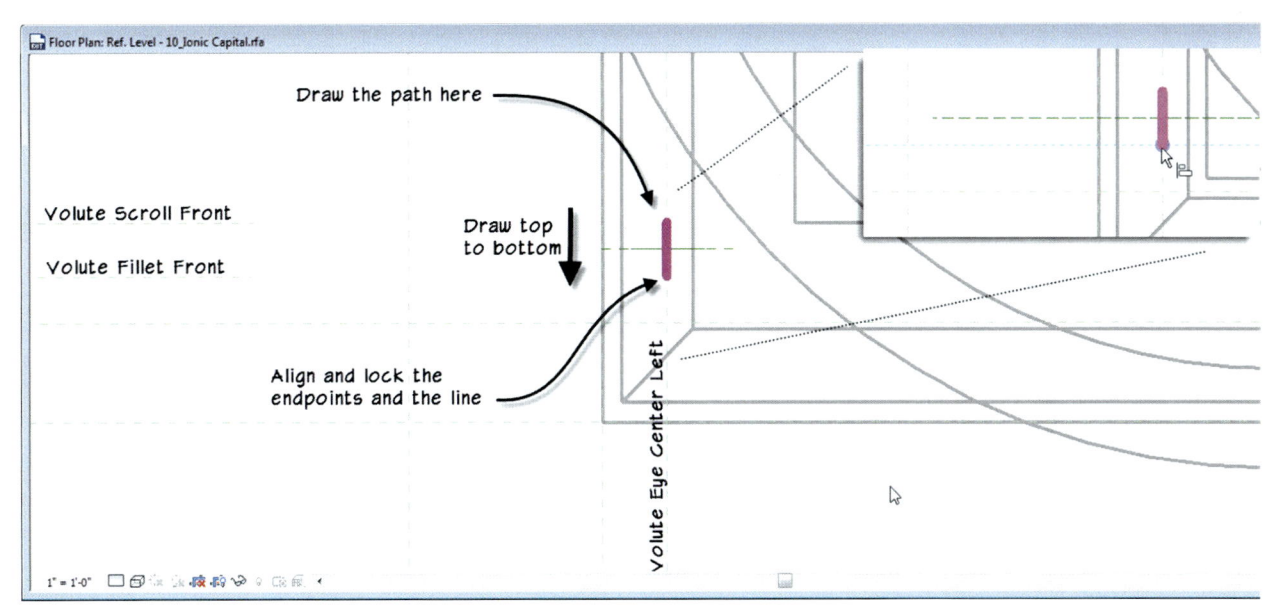

FIGURE 10.18
Sketch the sweep path and lock it to the reference planes

4. Align and lock the sketch line to the "Volute Eye Center Left" reference plane.

   ⇨ Align and lock each endpoint to the horizontal reference planes as well.

5. Click the Finish Edit Mode button.

6. On the Modify | Sweep tab, click the Load Profile button.

   ⇨ Browse to the *Chapter10* folder and load your *Ionic Volute Back Profile.rfa* file (or use the catch-up file).

   ⇨ From the Profile drop-down, choose the **Ionic Volute Back Profile:Flex** profile.

7. Finish Edit Mode.

   Take a look at the results in elevation and 3D.

8. Back in plan view, repeat the process to create the scroll in front of the backing sweep.

   ⇨ Draw the path on the same line, but this time snap it between the intersection of "Volute Fillet Front" and "Volute Eye Center Left" to the intersection of "Volute Front" and "Volute Eye Center Left."

   ⇨ Be sure to lock the edge and both end points.

• *Creating Classical Architecture with Modern Software* •

- Load the *Ionic Volute Profile.rfa* file (or use the catch-up file) for the profile.

9. Add a small cylinder at the eye location.

The eye cylinder has a radius of 0.027 times the Base Diameter. I have already included a parameter in the file for this named: **Eye R**. You can either switch to *Front* view, and draw a cylindrical extrusion, or you can stay in plan and do another sweep. The cylinder should protrude slightly beyond the front of the scrolls. I reused the **Scroll Backing** parameter for this which achieves the result. If you prefer, you can define new reference planes and parameters (see Figure 10.19).

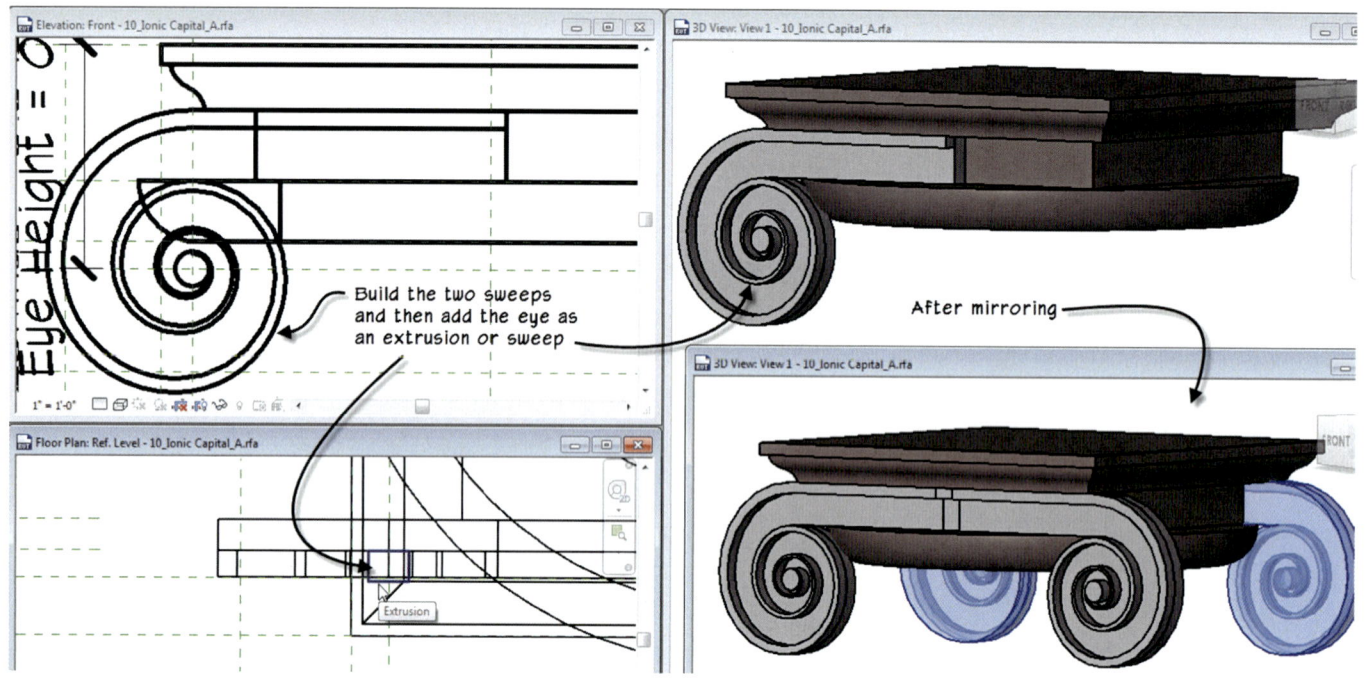

FIGURE 10.19
Create sweeps for the volute, an extrusion for the eye and then mirror them

10. Select both sweeps and the eye (extrusion or sweep).
- Mirror them to the right.
- Select the originals and the copies (6 elements) and mirror to the back.

Now we have something that looks like an Ionic capital! All that hard work begins to pay off. There are a few finishing touches.

11. On the Project Browser, edit the Type Properties of both volute profiles.
- Link up the Base Diameter parameter and change the value of Distance Center to Eye to: **0.475**.

12. Use Join Geometry and join all parts of the volute together.

13. Select the volutes and link up their Material to the **Capital Material**.

TIP: Use the TAB key to highlight and select Solid Joined Geometry before linking up the material parameter.

14. Flex Base Diameter to be sure everything is working. Return the value to **1.000** before continuing. Save the file.

CATCH UP! You can open a file completed to this point named: *10_Ionic Capital_A.rvt*.

• Renaissance Revit •

CREATE THE SCROLLS

The last piece we need is the model is the scrolls that span across the depth connecting the two volutes together. The form of these is somewhat challenging. In plan, they follow the curvature of the column shaft on the inside. The outside shape is a little more flattened but still freeform. The same is true in elevation. I tried a lot of variations for this form. Ultimately I settled on a swept blend. Swept blends can use two profiles and blends between them along a single segment path. We saw an example back in the "Create a Swept Blend using Profiles" topic in Chapter 2. While the path of a swept blend can only be a single segment, it can be nearly any shape. I experimented with an arc, an ellipse and spline path shapes. I settled on the picked path because it proved a nice compromise between the other options and it stays constrained to the picked form which is a big help. We'll need to do a little setup; a few reference planes and dimensions.

IMPORT THE PROFILE FAMILIES

To save some steps, I have created the profiles already and provided them in the dataset.

Continue in the *Ionic Capital* file or open the catch-up file.

1. Open the *Ref. Level* floor plan view.
2. Draw a section from right to left along the center line. (It will cut right through the capital and look down).

Adjust the crop region to crop a little closer. Set the scale as desired and zoom in (see Figure 10.20).

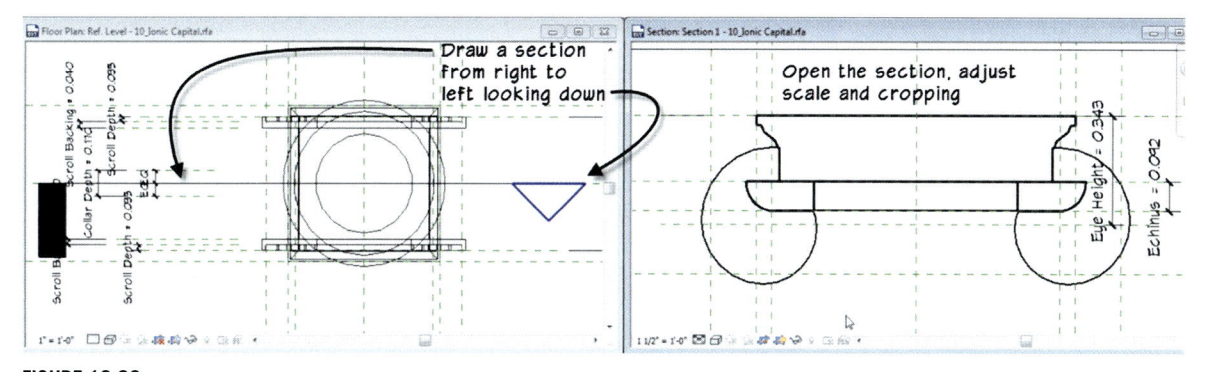

FIGURE 10.20
Create a section view

I have created three profiles for this task. Let's load them now.

3. On the Insert tab, click the Load Family button.

⇨ Browse to the *Chapter10* folder hold down the CTRL key, select the *Ionic Collar.rfa*, *Ionic Scroll Inside.rfa* and *Ionic Scroll Outside.rfa* files and then click Open.

On Project Browser these three files will now be listed with the other Profiles.

4. Edit the Type Properties of each of these three loaded profiles and link up their Base Diameter parameters.

If you like, you can right-click any of these files and choose **Edit** to open the files and explore them. The parameters are very basic; mostly X and Y offsets and widths. Each of these files uses a spline for the freeform part of the curve. If you recall our discussion about splines in the "Controlling a Spline" topic in Chapter 4, we saw that you only need to lock the endpoints of the spline in both directions. With it constrained this way, it will scale proportionally and maintain its shape (see Figure 10.21).

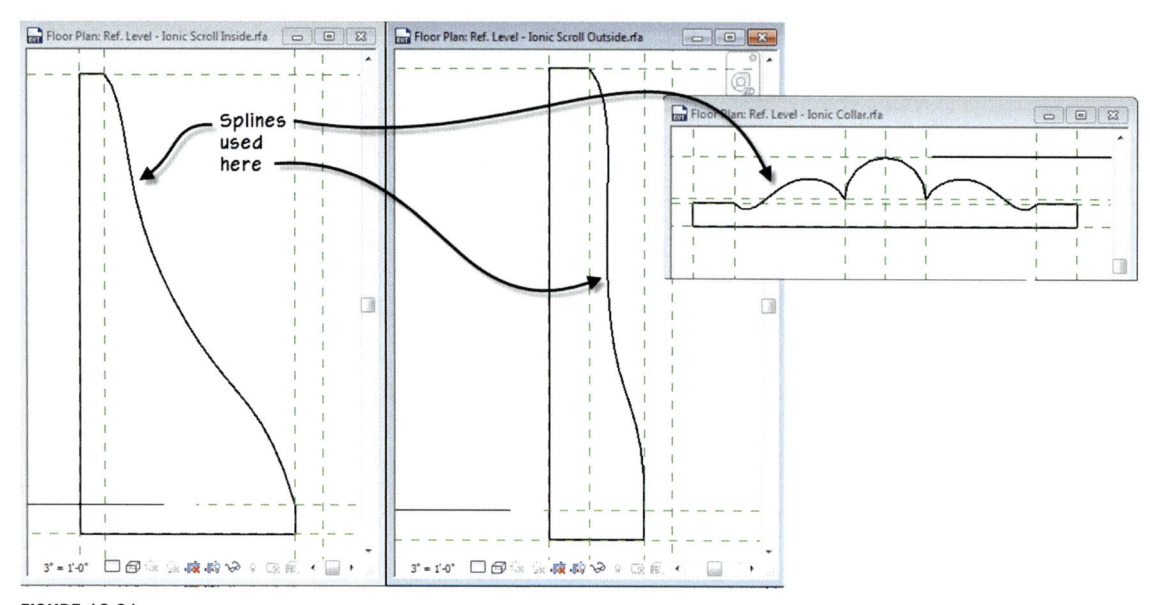

FIGURE 10.21

Open the profiles and study them if you like. They use splines for the freeform edges

CREATE THE SCROLL FORMS

The scroll form will be constructed from the loaded profiles using a sweep and a swept blend.

1. In the *Section 1* view, create a new Sweep.
   - Click the Pick Path button. On the left side of the screen, click the inside bottom edge. (This was arc 3 above). An arc will be created along the picked edge.

2. Click Finish Edit Mode, and then from the Profile drop-down choose **Ionic Scroll Inside:Flex**.
   - Click Finish Edit Mode (see Figure 10.22).

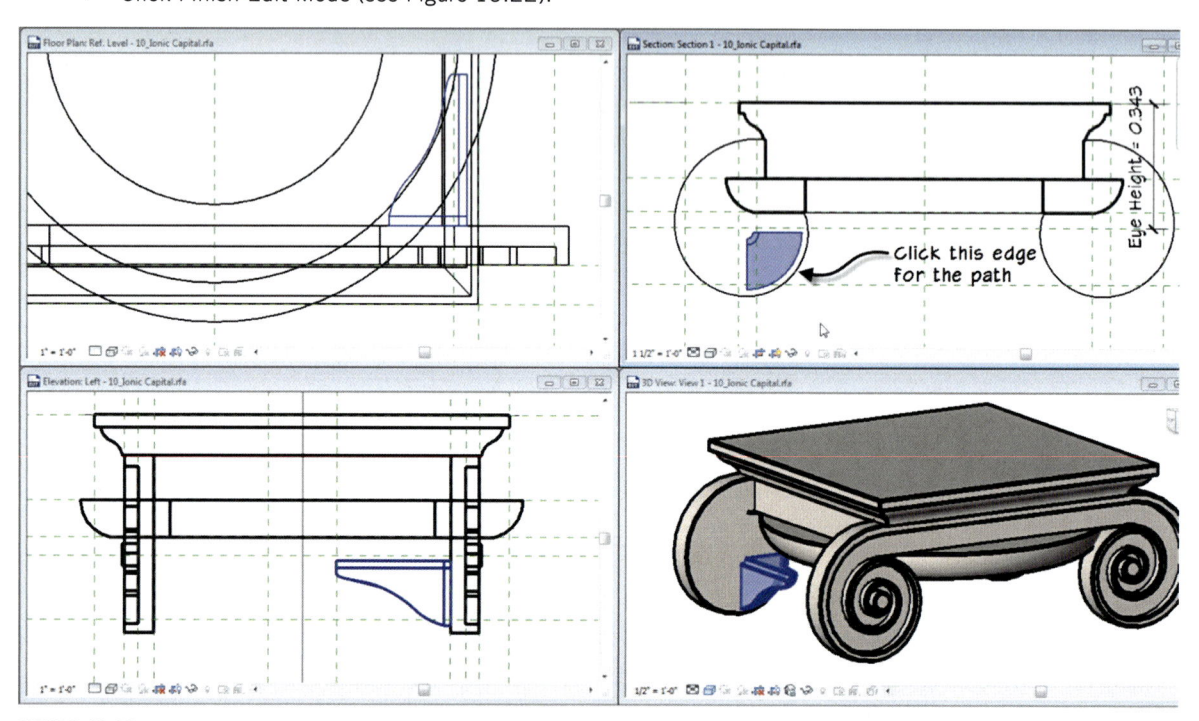

FIGURE 10.22

Create a sweep using the Pick Path option

• Renaissance Revit •

Next to this form, we'll create a swept blend.

3. On the Create tab, click Swept Blend.
    - Click the Pick Path button. On the left side of the screen, click the outside bottom edge. (This was arc 2 above). An arc will be created along the picked edge.
4. Click Finish Edit Mode, and then from the Profile drop-down choose **Ionic Scroll Inside:Flex**.
    - Click the Select Profile 2 button, and then from the Profile drop-down choose **Ionic Scroll Outside:Flex**.
    - Click Finish Edit Mode (see Figure 10.23).

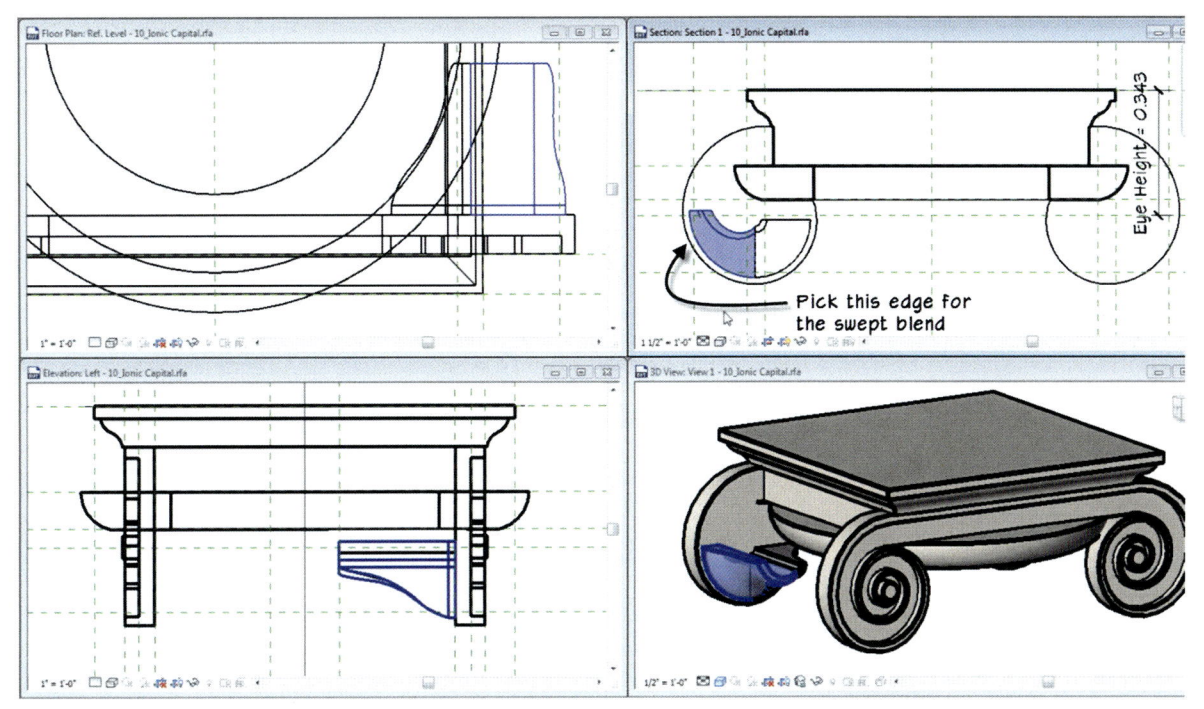

FIGURE 10.23
Create a sweep using the Pick Path option

Obviously this form needs a little work. But let's flex everything first before we continue.

5. Flex Base Diameter to: **2.000** to be sure everything is working. Return the value to **1.000** before continuing. Save the file.

> **Note:** If you try to flex below a value of 0.900, the volute profile will fail. The tolerances at that size become a little too small. But if we consider that a base diameter of 0.900 would yield a column that is about 8 feet tall (2,400 mm), this seems an acceptable lower limit size for most practical applications.

EDITING SWEEP AND SWEPT BLEND PATHS

Here's the really interesting thing about Pick Path; we can adjust the length of these lines. This means that we can take these two forms and adjust them directly by adjusting the path. Remember, sweeps can have more than one segment in their path. Swept blends cannot. But in both cases, I opted for a single segment picked path and then manual adjustments because in my experiments this yielded the best results.

1. In the *Section 1* view, select the swept blend. On the ribbon click the Edit Swept Blend button.
    - Click the Pick Path button.

• *Creating Classical Architecture with Modern Software* •

302 | Chapter 10

Make sure that on the ribbon, the Pick 3D Edges button in *not* activated.

2. Click on the existing path sketch line onscreen.

⇨ Grips will appear at both ends. Drag the grip handle at the top until it curves around and snaps to the abacus above (see the left side of Figure 10.24).

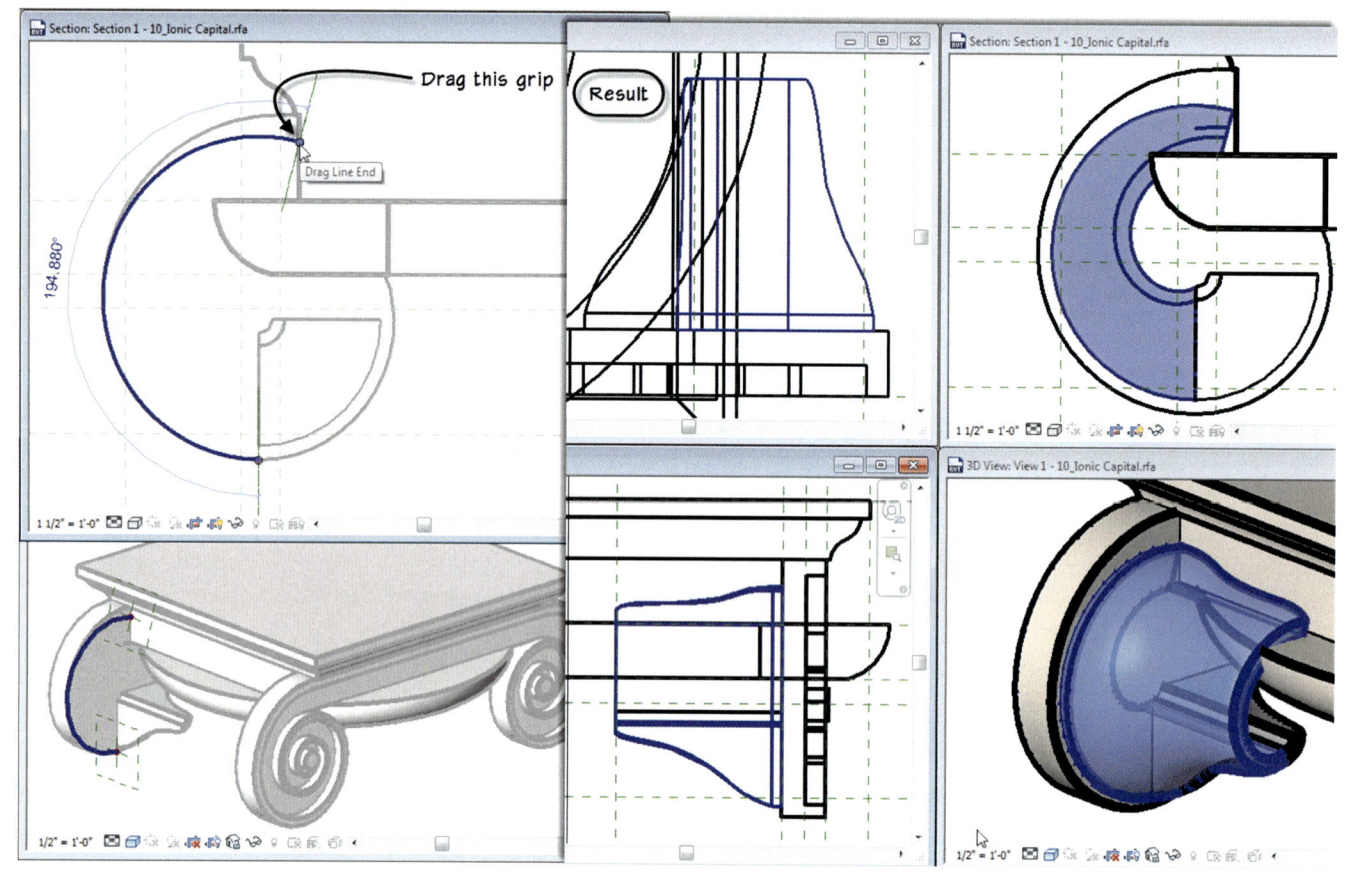

FIGURE 10.24
Adjust the picked path of the swept blend

⇨ Click the Finish Edit Mode button twice (see the right side of Figure 10.24).

I especially like the way it looks in the plan view. In my experiments with these forms, I found that one view was always nicer than the others. I think that the plan view currently looks best and closest to the source materials I am trying to emulate. The elevation view is also very close. In the section view the compromise is obvious; we are using a single arc for the path, but the volute form that it sits against uses a compound curve made of more than one arc. I tried other variations as well. I tried sketching the path instead of picking it. When sketching, you have to set your path work plane. I used the "Volute Scroll Front" work plane. Remember that with a swept blend you must use a single curve for the path. A spline is an obvious choice. You can get the spline shape very close to the existing curve. An elliptical arc actually produced better results in my test. But ultimately I decided that the tradeoff here with the picked arc curve was acceptable. You are welcome to experiment with other paths if you wish. Just keep in mind that if you sketch the path, you will have to constrain the sketch in order to be able to flex the model. This will likely require some additional reference planes, dimensions and parameters.

Let's adjust the sweep path the same way. This one we are going to stretch around to make a half circle.

3. Select the sweep. Edit it and the click Edit Path.

⇨ Like we did for the swept blend, drag the top end point up until the angle of the arc is 180° and then click Finish Edit Mode twice.

The inner curve looks a bit odd, but except for the small kink where the two curves come together it matches the source material very closely. The outer form is shaping up quite nicely. Despite the very detailed descriptions, images and proportions that all of the sources have for the orders, there are only illustrations and some overall dimensions for the scroll form. You will also find a great deal of variation from one Ionic column to the next. So basically just choose one that you wish to emulate and build your profiles to match. As noted previously, Chitham is my primary source, but Chitham does not provide a section cut through the scroll. J. M. Mauch's "The Architectural Orders of the Greeks and Romans" is a treasure trove of intricately detailed plates and provides many examples of actual Ionic orders complete with section cuts through the scrolls and other key parts of the order (Mauch 1910, 1845, 51-52). In this absolutely stunning work, the author has meticulously documented some of the most famous works of the ancients in 100 plates. You can find the work as a digital reprint, but the scanning does not do the original illustrations justice. If you have the means, I highly recommend searching out an original or non-scanned reprint from a second hand book reseller.

4. Save the file.

CATCH UP! You can open a file completed to this point named: *10_Ionic Capital_B.rvt*.

ADDING THE COLLAR

If you look at the Left elevation view, you will notice that if we mirror these two forms, there will still be a sizable gap between them. (Don't actually mirror them now; we'll discuss mirroring and copying them in the next topic). In this space is another form that is like a band or a cord that wraps around the form like a belt or cincture. You could almost image that the scrolls started off as more cylindrical form and then someone tied a cord around the middle and tightened it, which scrunched the middle.

To add this band or collar, we'll do another sweep. In my first attempt, I tried to use pick lines again and build the sweep from the scroll forms. The trouble is that given the irregular shape of the curve at this point, we are unable to stretch the endpoints of the path like we did for the other two above. Furthermore, even though it is a sweep, the complex curve again presents a limitation and Revit will not let us pick more than one edge for the path. So if you use pick path, you will end up with the collar ending in a sort of unnatural way. It would look OK from elevation, but not from other views. So for this last sweep, we will instead sketch the path with a spline to follow the curve as closely as possible.

However, since there might be some trial and error involved, it is sometimes easier to draw the path first as a model line. This way you can focus on perfecting the shape without having to worry about actually finishing the sweep to test it out. Once you have the shape of the curve to your liking, you can then use it as the source for pick path. In this way we achieve the best of both approaches: sketching and picking the path.

Remember that all we need to constrain a spline and have it scale proportionally is to lock down its endpoints. To do this, we'll add a few reference planes. It turns out we can get away with a single parameter to lock down the new reference planes. I have already included the parameter in the file. It is called "Spline Offset" and is set to a value of Base Diameter * 0.030. We'll work in the section view.

Continue in the *Ionic Capital* file or open the catch-up file.

1. Open the *Section 1* view.
2. Add three reference planes in the locations indicated in Figure 10.25.

304 | Chapter 10

⇨ Add a dimension to each one and label all three dimensions with the Spline Offset parameter.

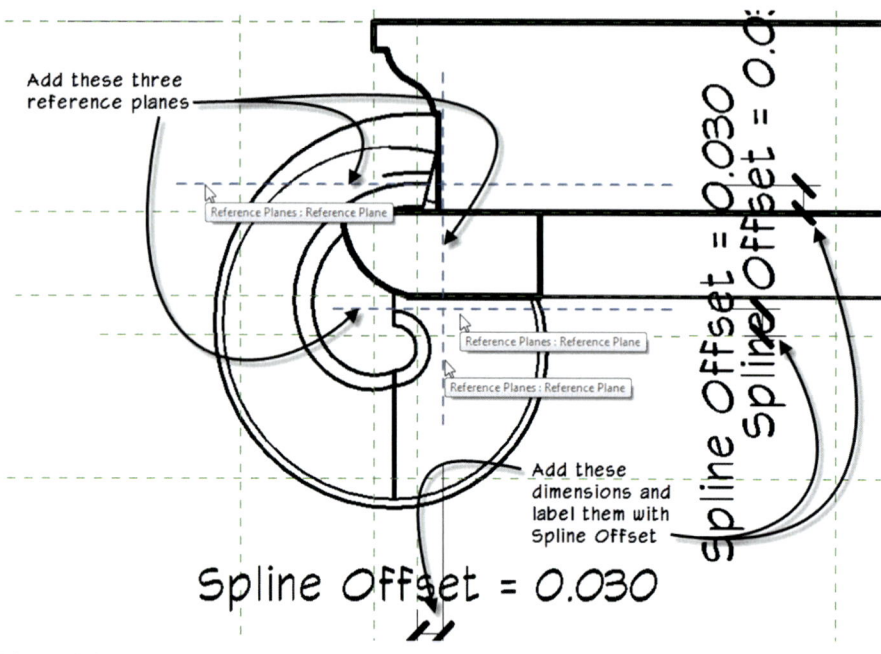

FIGURE 10.25

Add new reference planes and dimensions

3. On the Create tab, on the Work Plane panel, click the Set button.

⇨ In the "Work Plane" dialog from the Name list, choose: **Reference Plane : Center (Front/Back)** and then click OK.

4. On the Create tab, click the Model Line tool and then click the Spline icon.

⇨ Snap the first point of the spline to the intersection of the two new reference planes above the ovolo.

⇨ Snap the last point to the intersection of the existing reference plane named: "Right" and the other new one.

⇨ Add as many control points as needed to closely match the curved shape of the scroll forms (see Figure 10.26).

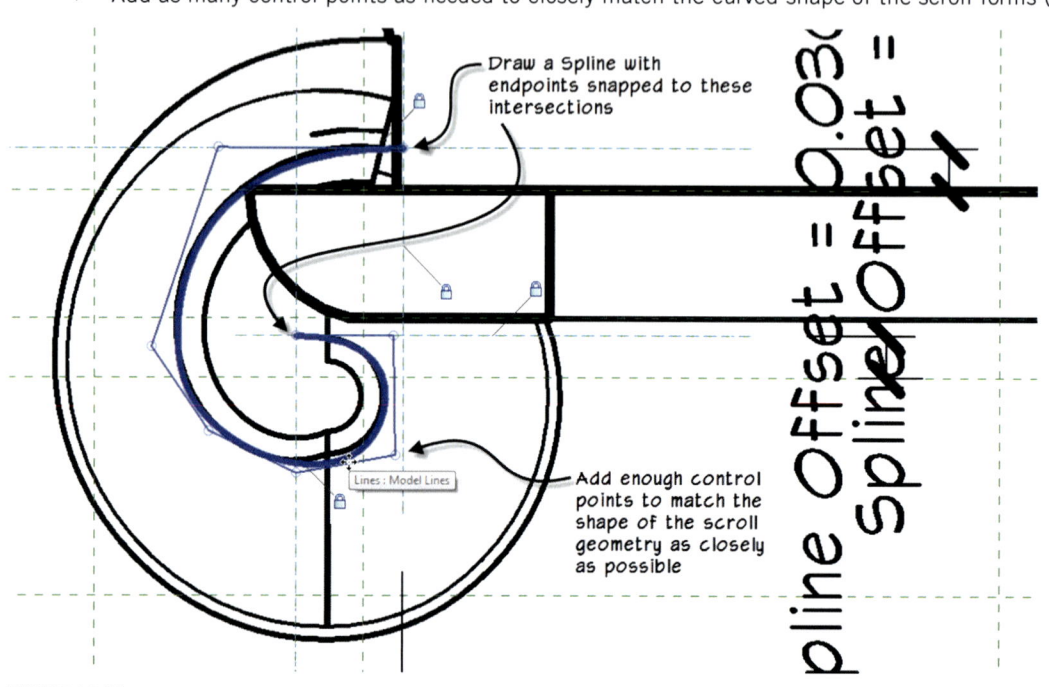

FIGURE 10.26

Create a spline model line matching the shape at the end of the scroll forms

• Renaissance Revit •

It is best to rough out the shape with several points first, (I used six control points) and then come back and fine-tune their placement. If you need to move the endpoint and do not want the whole spline to stretch, be sure to TAB before selecting it. You do not need to TAB for the other control points. Only the endpoints. Take your time to get the curve to match, but keep it as smooth as possible. Notice that I did not replicate the small kink at the bottom but instead kept the curve smooth.

5. Align and lock the two endpoints in both directions to the reference planes. Use TAB if necessary.

6. Flex Base Diameter to: **2.000** to be sure everything is working. Return the value to **1.000** before continuing. Save the file.

The curve should flex and maintain its shape. If it did not, go back and make adjustments and make sure the two endpoints are locked to the reference planes in both directions.

7. On the Create tab, click the Sweep button.

⇨ Click the Pick Path button, click the model line spline we just drew and then click Finish Edit Mode.

⇨ For the Profile, choose **Ionic Collar:Flex**.

⇨ On the Options Bar, for the Angle, type: **-90** (negative) and then click Finish Edit Mode (see Figure 10.27).

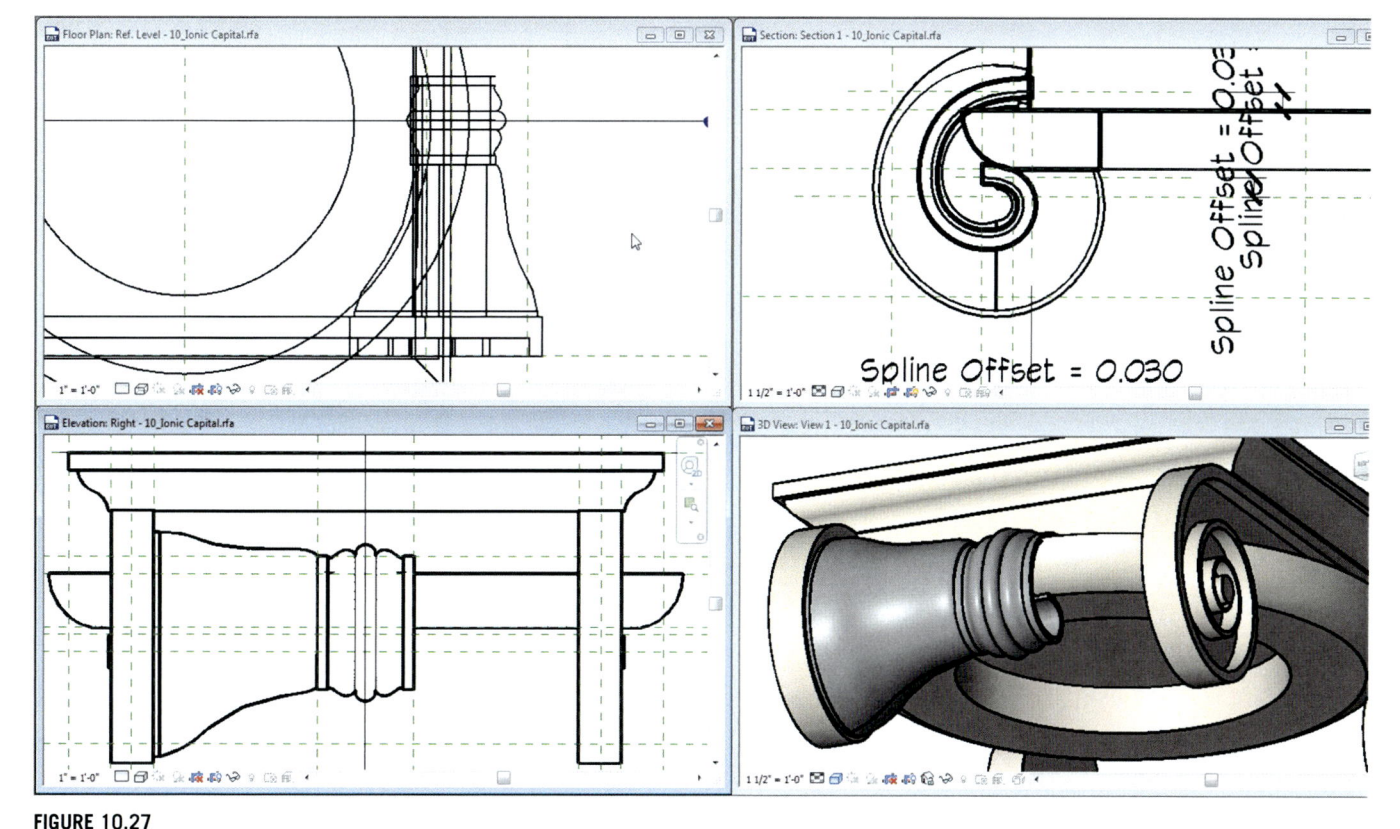

FIGURE 10.27
Add the collar sweep

8. Flex Base Diameter to: **2.000** to be sure everything is working. Return the value to **1.000** before continuing. Save the file.

COPY AND ADJUST

You will need to repeat the steps to create the remaining three pieces for the scrolls and the other collar. You can mirror the forms, but you will need to make adjustments to each one when you do. For example, remember that when copying forms that rely on Pick Path, you have to reestablish the path manually or they will not flex properly.

• *Creating Classical Architecture with Modern Software* •

So, mirror the forms, then edit each one, erase the existing path, and then pick it again. You will have manually stretch the endpoints again as we did above after picking the new path. Also, sometimes the profiles will flip when you mirror. Be sure to pick the new path first, as most of the time this will correct the flipped profiles as well. However, is cases where they are still flipped, it is easy to fix. Select the form, and then on the Properties palette, check or uncheck the "Profile is Flipped" checkbox. The swept blend might also reverse the profiles. So they will appear on the wrong ends. You can easily fix this on the Properties palette as well.

When adjusting the paths, finding a good view can be tricky. Tile a few windows like the section the 3D and the *Front* elevation. If necessary, you can use Temporary Hide/Isolate to hide elements while you work. It might also be easier to pick the basic path first, finish the form and let it update. Then go back in to adjust the endpoint.

Before mirroring the collar, be sure you have all the reference planes you require. The two horizontal ones are all set. You can extend them across if you want, but they can be snapped and locked to even without lengthening them. This means you should only need to mirror the vertical one we added above. Be sure to add the dimension labeled with the Collar Offset parameter. Don't forget to lock the endpoints of the mirrored spline to the reference planes in its new location. Also, you will need to adjust the Angle of the profile for the collar sweep after mirroring. Like the other settings, you can do this on the Properties palette. Simply set the Angle to 90° (positive) instead of negative 90°.

9. Select all of the sweeps and apply the Capital Material property to them (see Figure 10.28).
10. Flex Base Diameter to be sure everything is working. Return the value to **1.000** before continuing. Save the file.

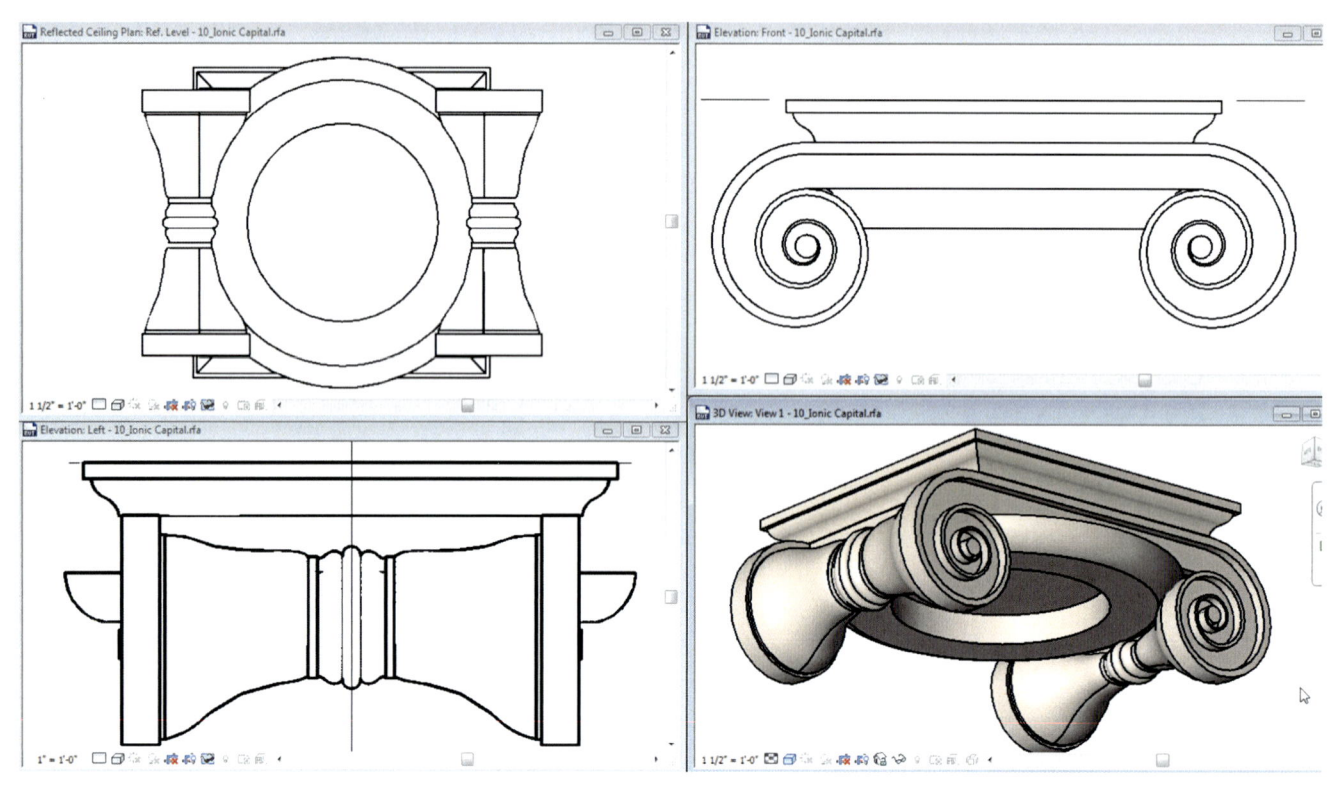

FIGURE 10.28

The completed Ionic Capital

The file should flex just fine with a Base Diameter of 0.860 or higher. The problem is in the Volute Profile that we built above. It has something to do with a minimum thickness allowable by the sweep. As the profile spirals in, it gets progressively smaller. So we are hitting the minimum thickness that Revit finds allowable. For our purposes however, the 0.860 value places the column that uses this family within an acceptable minimum. This is about 10

½ inches for the Base Diameter and would yield a column height only seven and half feet. There shouldn't be too many situations where we need a column that short.

> **CATCH UP!** You can open a file completed to this point named: *10_Ionic Capital.rvt*.

COMPLETING THE ORDER

We have already covered the steps to update the overall column file in other chapters so I won't reiterate them here. Feel free to experiment further with this file before continuing and when you are ready, you can load the capital into the provided *Ionic Column (without Pedestal).rfa* file and update the existing one. I have also provided a sandbox file: *10_Sandbox_Colonnade.rvt* into which you can load your completed column (see Figure 10.29).

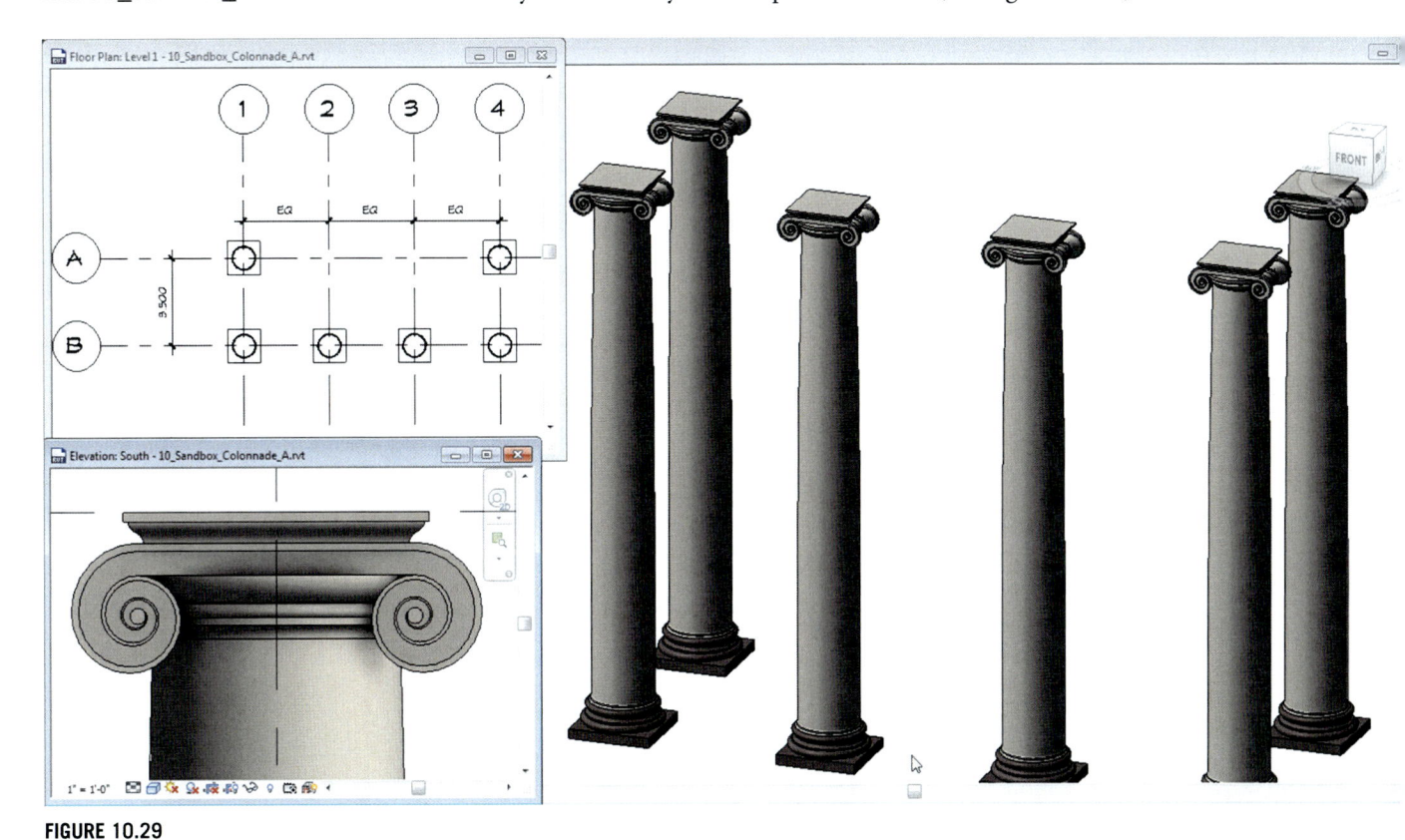

FIGURE 10.29
The Ionic sandbox file with the column loaded

11. Save and close all files.

SUMMARY

- ✓ The strategy for the Ionic order mirrors that of the previous orders; separate families for base, capital and shaft are loaded into a column family. Start with the previous order, rename the pieces and then modify it.

- ✓ The base and shaft are very similar to the Doric; only minor modifications are needed.

- ✓ To build the capital, create a slightly more complex schematic version which includes block renditions of the volutes.

- ✓ The volute is created from a profile family containing 24 arcs in a complex chain.

- ✓ To layout the arcs properly, a detail item rig is used to locate the centers. There are many authorities on the subject from which to base the rig.

- ✓ Carefully snap, align and lock each arc to the detail rig and nearby reference planes.

- ✓ Reference planes do not have to be immediately adjacent for align and lock to work.

- ✓ Organize the references in a visual hierarchy to make them easier to understand and use.

- ✓ Nesting equality constraints with groups of reference planes eliminates the need for many parameters.

- ✓ The scrolls can be created from swept blends. Use a smooth path picked from the geometry.

- ✓ The use of splines in the profiles makes for a nice smooth and organic form.

- ✓ Combine the swept blends with a sweep along a spline path to create a very pleasing yet sculptural and organic final result; all while staying in the traditional family editor!

MIT, BOSTON, MA
Photo by author

Chapter 11
The Massing Environment

INTRODUCTION

A few years ago the Factory[2] released a completely redesigned set of modeling tools optimized for performing work directly in three-dimensional space. In some ways these tools address perceived and actual deficiencies with the traditional modeling tools. In other ways it is a completely reimagined workflow that represents a somewhat radical departure from the traditional Revit workflow. I raise these point merely in the interest of introduction. I have tried to show in the last several chapters that the traditional family editor modeling environment is quite robust. If you completed the last chapter, you saw that it is capable of producing some very complex and freeform geometry. That being said, my intention is not to argue the merits and/or weaknesses of either modeling environment. Rather, as we move to more complex classical forms like the fluted column shaft and the Corinthian column capital, I will present the massing environment as an alternative. It has some unique features that offer us some very useful modeling techniques not available in the traditional space. However, if this is your first time in the massing environment, be forewarned: even basic skills like object selection and the creation of forms vary considerably in this environment. Therefore, this chapter is presented as an introduction to creating form in the Revit massing environment.

I am not attempting to give comprehensive coverage all features in the massing environment, rather I am focusing only on those features that we need to complete the tasks at hand. I do have other resources that cover the massing environment. I have included a PDF version of Chapter 16 from my book: *The Aubin Academy Master Series: Revit Architecture 2013 and beyond* (Aubin 2013, 797-848). This chapter is provided as a supplement to the content in this chapter as is provided with permission from the publisher of that volume. You can find the PDF included with the dataset files for this chapter. You can also check out my video training courses at lynda.com. My course: Advanced Modeling in Revit Architecture (Aubin 2012) covers many facets of the massing environment. You can learn more at **www.lynda.com/paulaubin**.

OBJECTIVES

The goal of this chapter is simple: it will introduce you to the core skills required to use the massing environment successfully. Discussion of the mass modeling capabilities in Revit could fill an entire book on their own. Time and space here will therefore not permit complete coverage. The goal of this chapter is to introduce you to the basic workflow and features to get you started using this exciting toolset. Topics in this chapter include:

- Accessing the Massing Environment and understanding massing categories
- Working in 3D and massing environment interface differences
- Creating traditional forms in massing
- Creating profiles for use in massing and building lofted forms

---

[2] "The Factory" is an informal name for the development team at Autodesk that is responsible to Revit. It was popularized by an Autodesk blog about Revit called "Inside the Factory." That blog has since gone on hiatus, but many in the Revit community still refer to Autodesk and specifically the folks at Autodesk responsible for Revit as "The Factory."

> - Working with reference lines and points—building rigs

ACCESSING THE MASSING ENVIRONMENT TOOLS

Revit's massing environment offers tools to explore conceptual design concepts in a free-form 3D environment. The massing environment is a variation of the family editor and, therefore, shares many of its traits with all other Revit families. The environment allows you to easily create and edit forms, create complex parametric shapes and patterned surfaces, and apply adaptable sub-components to patterned surfaces. The conceptual massing environment is meant to facilitate working/designing/creating/experimenting all while remaining in a 3D (axonometric) view. This is why, when you open up the conceptual massing environment, the default three-dimensional view {3D} is active. It is possible to make most of the shapes and forms that are available in the standard family editor as well, but the tools and workflows are different and there is an enhanced ability to edit and manipulate the forms in real-time without sketch modes. Complex interactive and parametric form modeling and design rationalization is also possible.

Since the massing environment is a family editing environment, it is accessed like other families. Simple create a new family and choose an appropriate template. If you choose one of the massing family templates provided with the software, you will be in the massing environment.

> **Note:** It is also possible to access the massing environment via an In-Place massing family. However we will not be covering that approach in this book.

To access the tools of the massing environment, you must start with one of these templates files (or their metric equivalents): *Mass.rft*, *Curtain Panel Pattern Based.rft*, *Generic Model Pattern Based.rft* and *Generic Model Adaptive.rft*. Typically, you will know that you are in the massing environment because the onscreen look will be very different. All of the templates start in the default {3D} view and have a gradient background (instead of white) displayed in the viewport (see Figure 11.1).

Choosing any one of those templates will get you into the massing family editor, but they are far from equal. So the one you choose is *very* important. There are some features which are available only in the massing environment. Furthermore, the "Mass" family category is a "closed" category and cannot be changed. So while you will get access to the massing tools in the *Mass.rft* template file, you cannot change it to a more useable category. So this template should not be used for the lessons in this book. (The Mass template is intended for building massing studies only. Not for creating component elements).

The remaining three templates can have their category changed. So they would be better choices if you plan to use the massing environment to model anything other than a building study. The two "pattern based" templates have the ability to nested into other massing families and repeated along the surfaces of mass forms. Imagine you are designing a custom metal cladding system. You can build the overall form of the building that will use the cladding in a massing family. Select the surfaces of the form, and divide them using many rationalized patterns available in the software. Then you can create a custom panel component using either the *Curtain Panel Pattern Based.rft* or *Generic Model Pattern Based.rft* template. Finally you load these into the family with the massing form and apply the custom panel to the surfaces of the form. This is one of the primary workflows for which the massing environment was designed and intended.

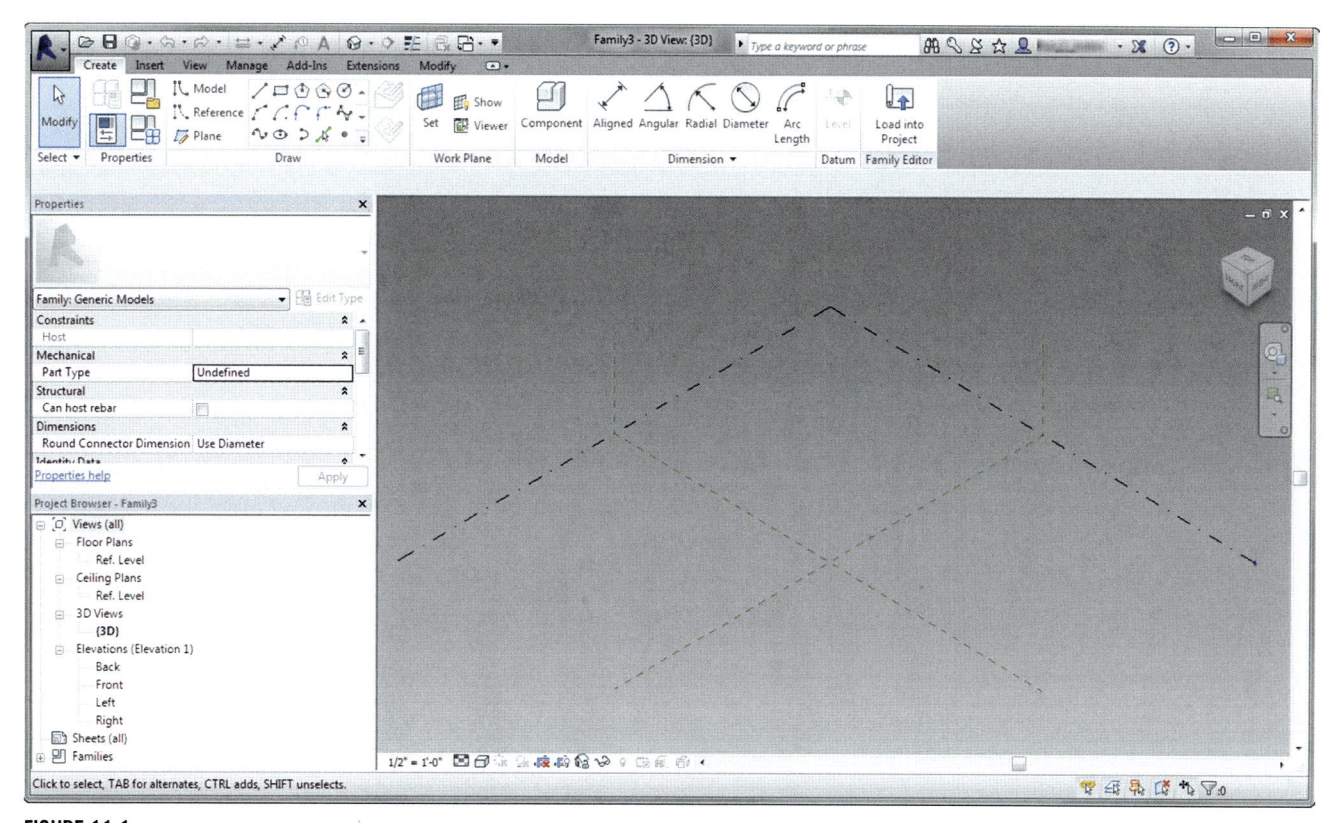

FIGURE 11.1
Opening the Massing Environment loads into a 3D view with gradient background displayed

CHANGING THE CATEGORY OF MASSING FAMILIES

Let's revisit the notion of changing categories. Even if you do not intend to follow the "massing: to divided surface rationalization" approach just described, the fact that you can change the category of a pattern-based or adaptive massing family makes their use very compelling to create geometry that would be difficult or impossible to achieve in the traditional family editor. This is where I will focus our discussion of them here in this and the remaining chapters of this book. So let's start with the procedure to access the massing environment and change the category.

1. From the Application menu, choose **New > Family**.

   ⇨ In the "New Family" dialog, choose *Generic Model Adaptive.rft* and then click Open.

The main difference between the *Curtain Panel Pattern Based.rft* and the *Generic Model Pattern Based.rft* and the *Generic Model Adaptive.rft* template is that the two pattern-based variations contain a divided surface, some reference lines and some adaptive points. We will discuss adaptive points below. But this starting infrastructure remains a permanent part of the file and cannot be deleted even if you change category. So if you are not intending to use the family with a divided surface, it may not be necessary. There are other reasons to choose the pattern-based templates, but to keep things simple for now, we will go with the non-pattern-based one.

Adaptive Components do not have the pattern or other elements in them. They are so named because of their ability to "adapt" to the shape of other geometry. They can have multiple "placement points" which means that they placed by making several clicks during insertion. Each click places a placement point and the family will flex to the shape of the placement points. When created carefully, this feature is very powerful indeed. For now, our main concern is choosing a template that gives us access to the massing tool, and can have its category changed. Since we don't need the pattern, *Generic Model Adaptive* is our best choice.

2. On the Create tab, click the Family Category and Parameters button.

⇨ In the "Family Category and Parameters" dialog, choose the category you wish, such as Column and then click OK (see Figure 11.2).

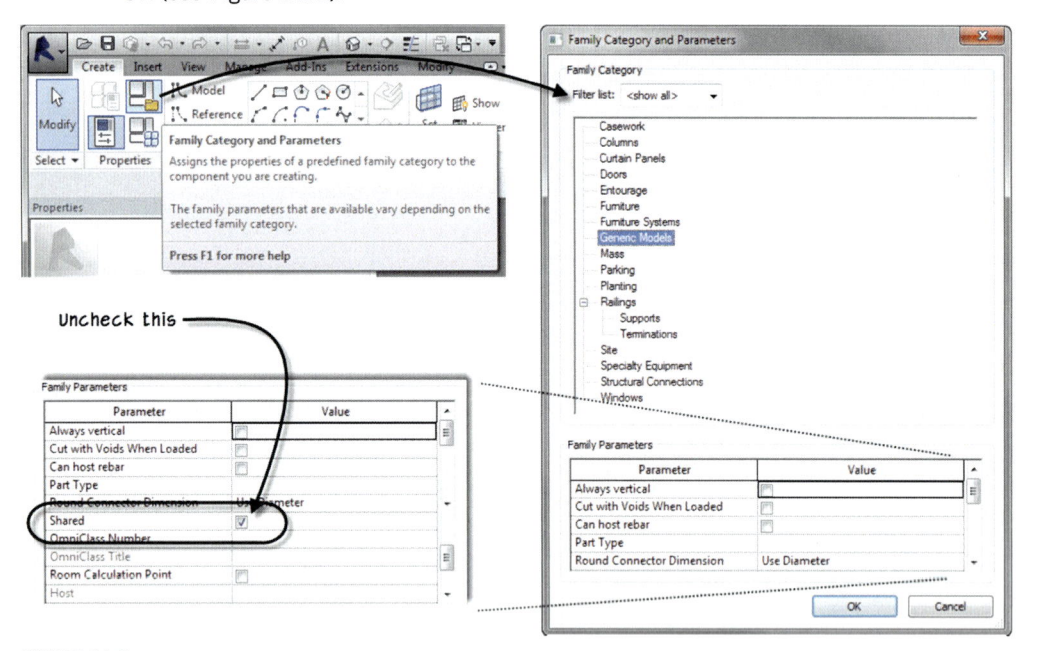

FIGURE 11.2
See and change the category of a family with the Family Category and Parameters dialog

SHARED OR NON-SHARED

Another important thing to check while in this dialog is the "Family Parameters" section at the bottom. If you scroll down a bit you will see the "Shared" setting. This is **on** by default in massing families. We are going to uncheck this for our examples. Most of the families we have built in this book rely on driving nested family type-based parameters using an associated parameter in the host. If you make the nested family shared, you will be *unable* to drive its type-based parameters. A shared family by definition exists in both the host *and* on its own. It is literally "shared" between the nested family and the project when inserted. This can be a very useful feature, but the tradeoff is you lose the ability to drive the nested type-based parameters; it would create a kind of circular reference. You *can* use shared families in conjunction with driven *instance-based* parameters. All of the families we have built (except the Profile families) can be set to shared and all of the parameters could have been instance-based. So you may be wondering why we didn't go that route. The main advantage of using shared families is the ability to schedule the nested sub-components from the project when they are inserted. If you think you will want to have the individual parts and pieces of your classical components (base, capital, shaft, etc.) appear separately on schedules in your projects, you will want to enable shared and rethink the way we built the parameters in the previous families.

I have not use the shared setting for the content in this book. I chose not to use shared families with nested instance parameters for a couple reasons. The first is that I did not think it would be that important to schedule the nested components like the individual base, capital and shaft components; or when we get to the Corinthian capital, I did not think that scheduling the leaves, volutes or other parts would be all that valuable. The second reason is that I think that with the sheer quantity of parameters that most of our families have, doing them as instance parameters might have a bit of a shock effect on the end user who selects an element in the project. Imagine the Properties palette with dozens of parameters and numbers on it. By using non-shared families and nesting the parameters in as type-based, we hide some of this complexity from the end user. Furthermore, the Project Browser only shows the top level family, not all of the nested sub-components as it would if they were all shared.

There is another potentially important consideration. If you want to use the Displace Elements tool it will work on shared families. So you could do an exploded diagram of your columns like those shown in Figure 13.2 and Figure 13.3. The nested subcomponent families have to be set to shared for this to work. In building those diagrams, I also discovered that the shared versions had file sizes considerably smaller than the non-shared versions. This makes for an interesting and potentially important criterion in your decision as well. I will discuss file size and its potential implications in the "Managing File Size" topic in Chapter 14. For now, despite the potential advantages, for the reasons I noted here, I am going to stick with non-shared.

In the end, the choice of shared or non-shared really comes down to how you intend to use the families. And there is not a "correct" way to do it. My technical editor Aaron Maller and I disagree on this point for example. I have chosen non-shared with nested type-based parameters and he would have preferred shared with nested instance-based parameters. So ultimately the choice is up to you and your team. I encourage you to try building some content each way on your own to test the differences in behavior. If you would like to experiment with that concept now, you can optionally build all parameters from now on as instance parameters and give it a try. But keep in mind that the steps as written will assume that you are using type-based and non-shared families.

3. Uncheck Shared and then click OK.

There will be other settings to adjust, but let's get a little more familiar with the environment first.

SETTING WORK PLANES IN 3D

Directing your attention to the interface in the massing environment, the most obvious difference in working in the massing environment is the ability to work and snap to elements in 3D. Even seasoned family editor experts need time to get used to the massing environment the first time they open it.

The environment includes one level and two vertical reference planes by default. Similar to other family templates, the two reference planes (shown in the standard green dashed lines) are pinned and the intersection of the two reference planes indicates the insertion point of the family when it is loaded and placed in a project (adaptive families can have more than one insertion point). Levels in this environment display in 3D and appear in the "back" of the model area; therefore, if you spin the model, you will notice that the level lines always make an upside down V-shape (shown in centerlines) at the back of the model. You can create additional levels and reference planes using the tools on the Create tab of the ribbon and you can create them directly in a 3D view.

Unique to the conceptual mas sing environment, reference planes and levels show in 3D! To set an active work plane, you simply click on the plane. This includes the surfaces of other objects. So you have to be careful where and how you select things. Let's try a little experiment.

1. Click on the centerline "V" shape onscreen.

    This selects the level and makes it the active work plane.

2. On the Modify I Levels tab, click the circle button and then draw a circle anywhere onscreen at any size.

3. Cancel the command and then click on one of the dashed green lines.

    The reference plane is now the active work plane.

4. Draw another circle.

Notice that this circle is on the reference plane and the first one is on the level. Orbit the view in 3D (hold down the SHIFT and drag with the wheel pushed in) to orbit the view and see this better (see Figure 11.3).

• *Creating Classical Architecture with Modern Software* •

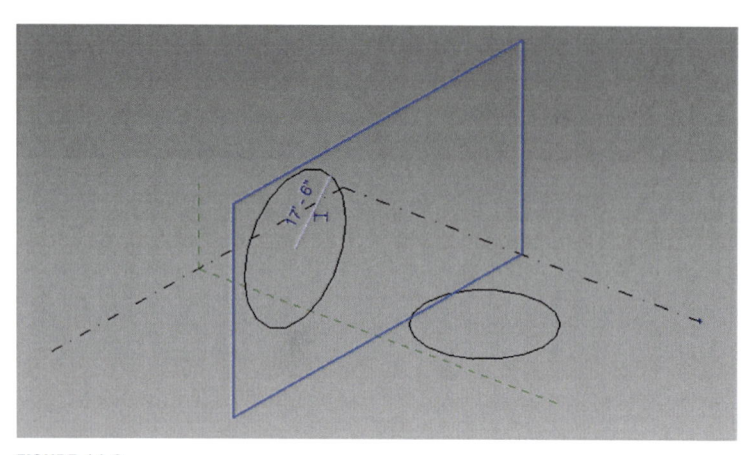

FIGURE 11.3
Simply clicking a plane make it the active work plane

The Set button is still available, but in most cases, the quickest way to set the work plane is to just click on it as we have done here. You do have to be careful though. Sometimes you will select an element and the work plane will change when you did not intend to. So always make sure that the correct work plane is active before you perform a task.

5. Click to select any one of the shapes onscreen.

If you are not sure which work plane an element belongs to, you can click on it and look on the Properties palette or Options Bar. On the Options Bar you can change it. The value is read-only on the Properties palette (see Figure 11.4).

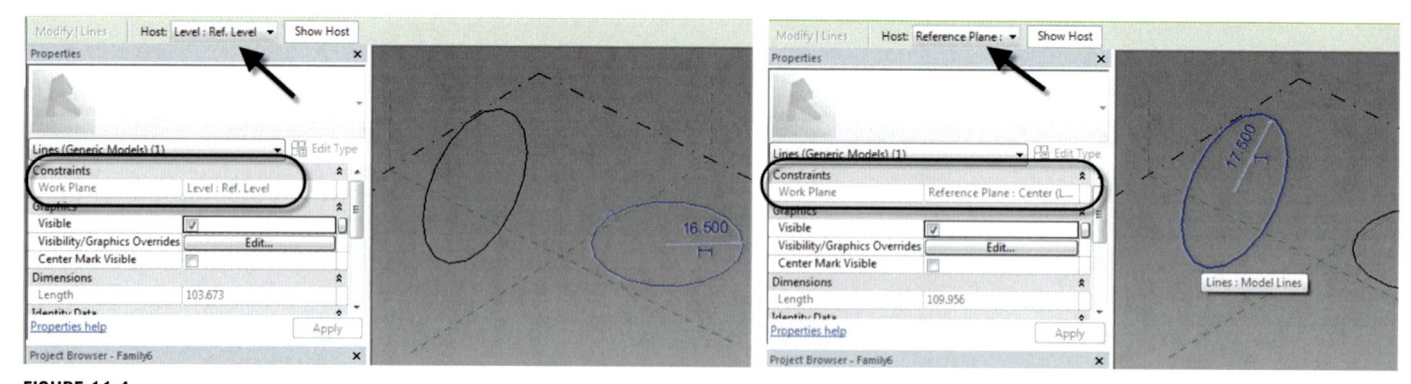

FIGURE 11.4
Select an element to see its work plane

OBJECT SELECTION IN THE MASSING ENVIRONMENT

Selection in the massing environment is a bit different as well.

1. Cancel the command and then click the level again to make it the active work plane.
2. On the Modify tab, click the rectangle button. Draw a rectangle next to the circle any size.
3. Cancel the command.
4. Move your cursor near the rectangle.

Notice that the entire rectangle highlights and the tip onscreen and/or on the Status Bar reads: "Chain of walls or lines." In the massing environment, chain selection is the default. If you want to select a single edge, of an element, use the TAB.

• Renaissance Revit •

⇨ Without clicking, keep the element highlighted and then press TAB without moving the mouse.

Only a single line will now highlight. So the TAB order is reversed in the massing environment. Other aspects of selection are unchanged. You can use CTRL and SHIFT to add and remove, you can use window and crossing box selections. Filter works, everything is the same except the TAB order. So just pay close attention to what highlights before you click.

CREATING FORM

Many forms are possible in the conceptual modeling environment. Like the standard Family editor you can create extrusions, blends, sweeps, swept blends, and revolves in both solid and void forms. In addition, in the conceptual environment, you can also create lofts, surface (or mesh) models, and even patterned surfaces. Unlike the standard Family editor, you don't need to choose a specific tool for the type of form you want to create before you create it; rather, you simply sketch the required shapes and use a single "Create Form" button to make any type of form. Revit will interpret your geometry and give you an appropriate form. When more than one form is possible, you will be offered a choice.

Let's look at some simple examples. The basic process varies in one significant way. Instead of first choosing a tool for a specific kind of form, you start by drawing the shapes you'll need. You select these shapes and then click the Create Form button. Revit will interpret your sketched lines and decide which type of form to create. If you want an extrusion, you draw a single shape. A blend you draw two shapes and select them both before Create Form. For a sweep, you would draw a shape and a path and select them together and so on. Work planes also become *very* important. It is a different way of thinking, to be sure. With a little practice you are sure to get the hang of it.

1. Select the rectangle. (A single click should select it).

   ⇨ On the Modify | Lines tab, click the Create Form button (see the top of Figure 11.5).

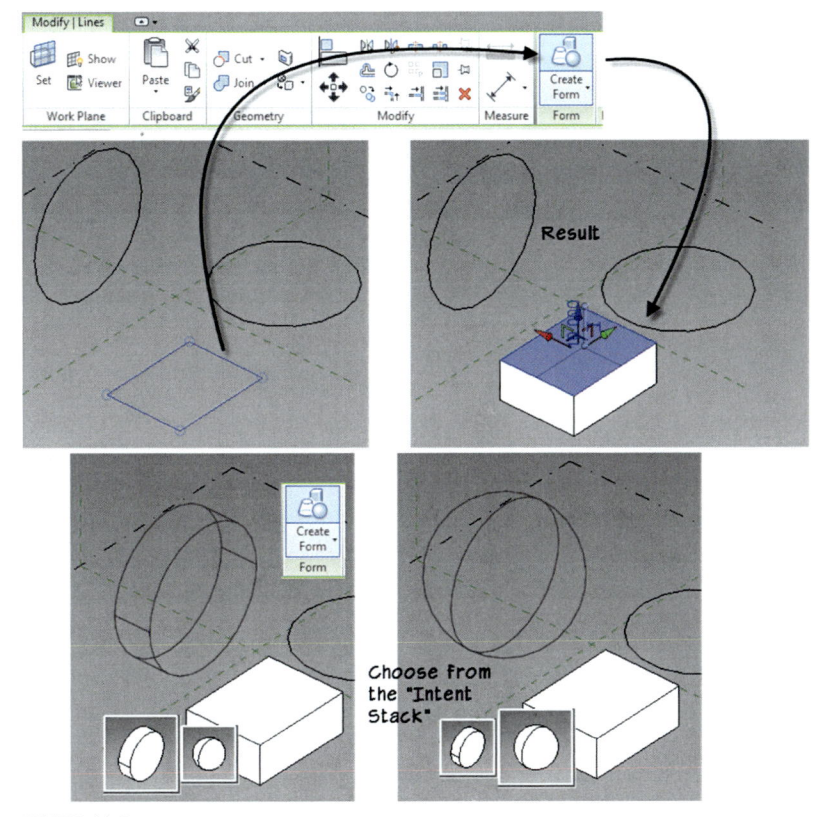

FIGURE 11.5

Select a shape and then click Create Form

• *Creating Classical Architecture with Modern Software* •

2. Repeat for one of the circles.

Notice that this time some small images will appear near the bottom of the screen. This is called the "Intent Stack." You can move your mouse and select one of the options. When it is possible for Revit to create more than one form from the selected elements, the intent stack will display so you can clarify your intent (see the bottom of Figure 11.5).

If you choose the cylinder, notice that the direction it extrudes is perpendicular to the work plane. Try the other one if you like to see it extrude the other way. Let's look at another example.

3. Draw another rectangle on the Ref. Level.

4. Highlight one edge of the rectangle and then press TAB. Click to select just that edge.

⇨ Click Create Form (see the left side of Figure 11.6).

Notice that this time you get a simple plane. In the massing environment, both solid and surface forms are possible.

5. Use TAB again and select one of the sides of the rectangle that is perpendicular to the one you just created a plane from.

⇨ Hold down the CTRL key and click to select the side parallel to it. (You'll have the two sides selected).

⇨ Create Form (see the right side of Figure 11.6).

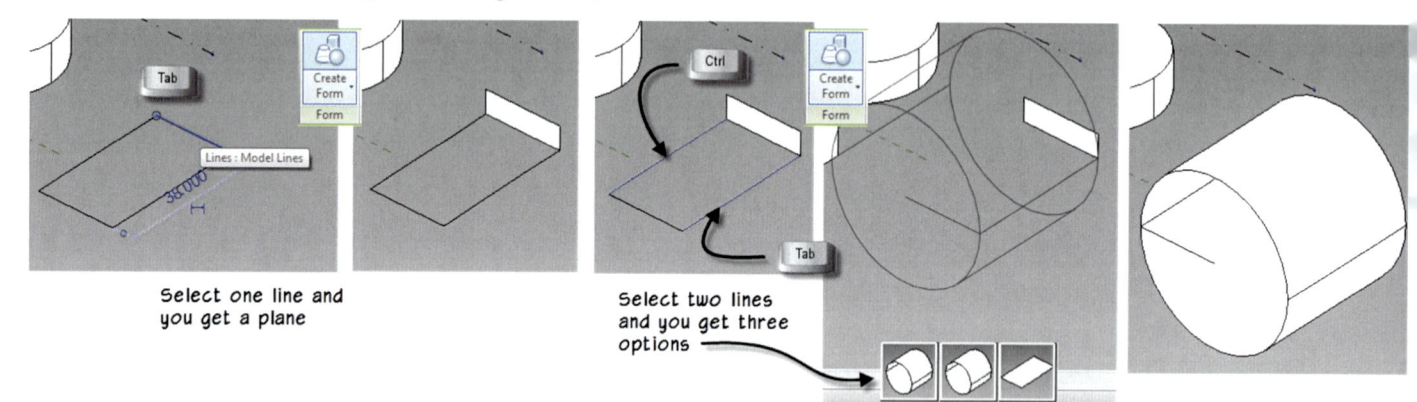

FIGURE 11.6

Create form can also create surfaces

Once again this will give you an intent stack with three options. You can revolve one line around the other (two options for that where either line can become the axis) and a third option to create a plane spanning between the two lines.

Hopefully this small exercise begins to give you a small sense of how the form making tools in the massing environment work. Feel free to try some more before continuing.

Now let's delete the forms we have. There is a catch however.

6. Click to select one of the cylinders.

Once again, we experience one of the differences of the massing environment. Depending on how you click the cylinder, you will get different selections, but each will only be part of the form. You can select the edges, or the surfaces of the form. If you delete the edge you will end up with a circular plane. To select the entire form, use the TAB key again. You can also use a window or crossing selection.

7. When you are finished experimenting, delete all of the forms, but be sure to leave the reference planes and level.

• Renaissance Revit •

The Massing Environment | 317

SAVE A SIMPLE MASSING SEED FAMILY

Before we get too far along, let's back up and configure a few settings as we did back in Chapter 2, and save this as a seed family.

1. On the Manage tab, click the Project Units button.
   ⇨ As we did in the "Set the Units" topic in Chapter 2, choose: **Decimal Feet** and **3 decimal places** of rounding and then click OK twice.
2. Click to select the level to make it the active work plane.

The extents of this template start at around 100 per side. This is obviously quite a bit larger than we need. So rather than constantly zooming in, I prefer to save a seed template where I have resized everything down smaller. You can resize the levels and reference planes directly onscreen with grip controls. But to help us in sizing, let's put an object in the middle for a sense of scale.

3. Click the circle icon and then snap the center point at the intersection of the two reference planes.
   ⇨ Begin drawing the circle but instead of clicking the radius type in: **1.500** and then press ENTER.
   A small circle will appear in the center.
4. Cancel the command, click the circle onscreen and then click Create Form. Choose the cylinder option.
   ⇨ A small temporary dimension will appear, edit it to **10.000** and then press ENTER.
5. Select the level onscreen.
   ⇨ A small blue grip handle will appear on each side.
6. Drag these grips in close to the cylinder.

You cannot snap to the cylinder, so just drag them as close as you can to the four quadrant points of the cylinder. Zoom and Orbit the view as you work to make more precise adjustments; the ViewCube works well for this.

7. Repeat the process with each of the reference planes (see Figure 11.7).

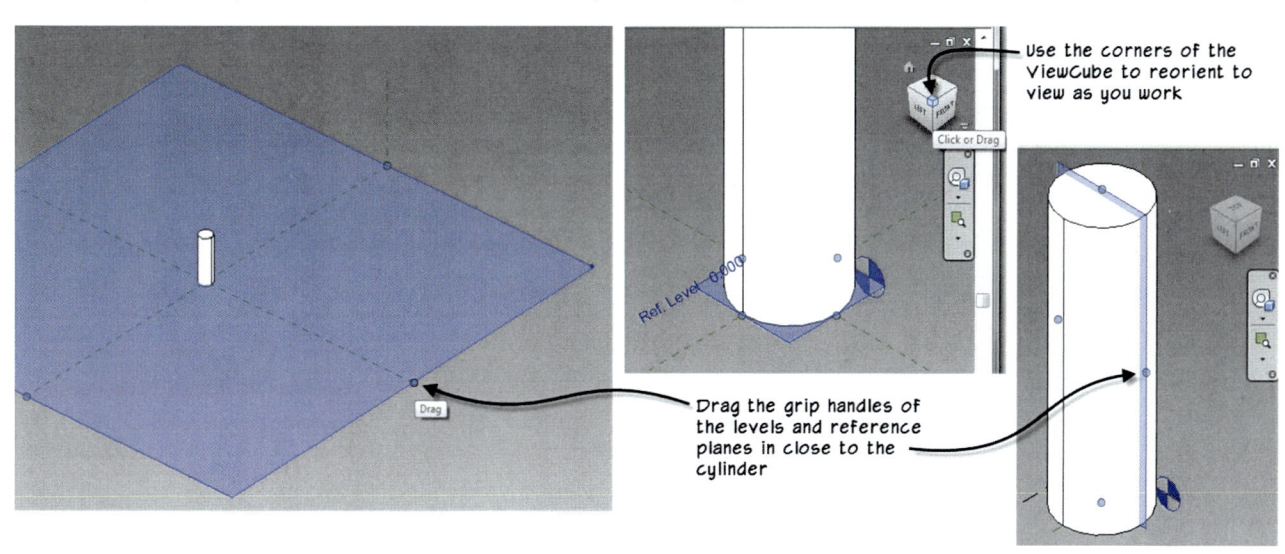

FIGURE 11.7

Adjust the extents of the existing level and reference planes

8. Increase the scale in the {3D} view. **1 ½" = 1'-0"** or **3" = 1'-0"** are good choices.

• Creating Classical Architecture with Modern Software •

⇨ Open each of the other views in this file: plan, reflected ceiling plan and four elevations, and set the same scale in each of those.

> **Note:** While you are opening and configuring views, note that the Front and Back view names are reversed in the default adaptive template. It is a good idea to rename them. First on Project browser, right-click *Front*, rename it something like: **Temp**. Then rename Back to: **Front**, finally rename Temp to: **Back**.

9. Reopen the *{3D}* view and then on the Quick Access Toolbar, click the Close Hidden Windows button.

10. Open the "Family Types" dialog and add a Base Diameter parameter set to a value of **1.000**.

⇨ Create a new Family Type named: **Flex** and then click OK.

11. From the Application menu, choose **Save As > Family**.

⇨ Browse to the *Chapter11* folder and name the family: *Family Seed (Adaptive).rfa* and then click Save.

I like to click the Options button in the Save As dialog and change the number of backups to 1. This is optional.

12. Delete the cylinder. (Remember to TAB to select it).

13. Save the file.

> **CATCH UP!** You can open a file completed to this point named: *11_Family Seed (Adaptive).rfa*.

TRADITIONAL TECHNIQUES IN THE MASSING ENVIRONMENT

As we have seen, the interface of the massing environment is quite different and everything from working with reference planes to creating forms is different. However, remember that the massing environment is the family editor. So all of the techniques covered in earlier chapters can be applied in the massing environment as well. However, not all of them will be directly applicable in the same ways.

For example, you will rely heavily on rigs when building complex forms that need to flex parametrically in the massing environment, but you will *not* be using detail items for those rigs. In fact, detail items cannot be inserted in the massing environment.

The massing environment does not support any 2D families in fact. This means that you cannot use profile families either. But the same function served by profile families in the traditional environment can be achieved with generic models in the massing environment. Build your shapes inside of Generic Model family using model lines instead. When you load a Generic Model family into a massing family or adaptive component family, any enclosed model lines in that nested Generic Model will behave in much the same way as profile families. This technique can also be used to build rigs. Rigs can be either 2D or 3D.

Other than their displaying in 3D, reference planes behave virtually the same in the massing environment. However, you will find that many massing environment modelers rely more on reference lines instead. Dimensions and parameters work in exactly the same way in both environments. You can use equality dimensions, align and lock things and add family types and flex. Automatic Sketch Dimensions are also part of the massing environment and work the same way. So much of what we have already covered is directly applicable. Some requires minor reimagining.

CREATING A MASSING PROFILE

As noted in the previous passage, the massing environment does not support 2D families. So let's run through the process to create one based on one of our profile families created in Chapter 4. To do this, we create a generic model family that matches a profile previously created. This can then be used as a profile in the massing environment.

There is really no easy process to do this. I have tried a few approaches with varying degrees of success. You cannot simply convert a profile family to a generic model. So you essentially have to recreate the shape in a new generic model family. You can build the entire thing from scratch following the procedures in Chapter 4. This is the most time-consuming but is also the most reliable approach. The other approach that I tried was to copy and paste. I had mixed success with this approach. In most cases, you have to rework some or all of the elements pasted in to get them to flex properly. Let's walk through an exercise to demonstrate.

1. Close all open files.
2. From the Application menu, choose **Open**, browse to the *Moldings* folder select *Cyma Reversa Profile (w Fillets).rfa* and then click Open.
3. Select everything onscreen (lines, dimensions and reference planes). A crossing selection works well.
   ⇨ Hold down the SHIFT key and deselect the Center (Left/Right) and Center (Front/Back) reference planes. (You aren't allowed to copy these or other "built-in" elements in a family).
   ⇨ Copy to the clipboard.
4. From the Application menu, choose **Open** again, browse to the *Seed Families* folder, select the *Family Seed (Face Based - Type Based).rfa* file and then click Open.
5. Delete the four outer reference planes.

   This will also delete the dimensions. Leaving only the Center (Left/Right) and Center (Front/Back) reference planes.
6. Save the family as: **Cyma Reversa GM Profile (w Fillets).rfa** in the *Chapter11* folder.

I added the letters "GM" here for Generic Model. This will help you distinguish this one from the original profile. Careful naming is an important habit to develop.

7. On the Modify tab, click the Paste drop-down and choose **Aligned to Current View**.
   ⇨ Change the scale to at least: **1"=1'-0"**.

The nice thing is that everything pasted in at the correct location. All of the reference planes retained their names. The dimensions and labels are all still applied and many of the locks and constraints are still applied. Unfortunately, it does *not* paste over is the formulas. Also some of the parameters, (those that were not applied to labeled dimensions) did not paste in. So all we have to do is open "Family Types" and add these missing items. But the real problem comes in when we try to flex later. Pasting saves us some rework, but the reference planes that paste in do not behave well. I found it best to recreate them. So there is still quite a bit of work to do.

8. Open the "Family Types" dialog and using Table 11.1 as a guide, add the missing parameters. (Note that the two parameters in the Constraints grouping are angle parameters).

Chapter 11

TABLE 11.1

Parameter	Value	Type of Parameter	Comments
Dimensions Grouping			
Y Mult	1.000	Number	
X Mult	0.800	Number	
Fillet Y Mult	0.150	Number	
Fillet X Mult	0.100	Number	
Depth Projection Mult	0.200	Number	
Base Diameter	1.000	Length	
Constraints Grouping			
A	38.660°	Angle	Type numbers only, Revit will add degrees
B	8.660°	Angle	Type numbers only, Revit will add degrees

⇨ Rename the parameters indicated in Table 11.2.

TABLE 11.2

Old Name	New Name	Value	Comments
Constraints Grouping			
Width	Y1	0.096	
Height	R	0.640	
Depth	D	1.281	

⇨ Close "Family Types," save the file then reopen "Family Types."

9. Using Table 11.3 as a guide, add the formulas.

TABLE 11.3

Parameter	Formula	Comments
Constraints Grouping		
Y2	Y + Y1	
Y1	R * sin(B)	Edit this one last
Y	Base Diameter * Y Mult	Edit this one first
X1	R * cos(B)	Edit this one last
X	Base Diameter * X Mult	Edit this one first
R	D / 2	
Fillet Y	Base Diameter * Fillet Y Mult	
Fillet X	Base Diameter * Fillet X Mult	
Projection	Base Diameter * Depth Projection Mult	
D	sqrt((X ^ 2) + (Y ^ 2))	
B	60° - (90° - A)	Type numbers only, Revit will add degrees
A	atan(X / Y)	Edit the angles second

• Renaissance Revit •

When inputting the formulas, put in X and Y first. Then do the two angles A then B, then do the remaining Base Diameter ones, Y2, R and D and finish with the trig functions.

> Default Elevation is built in to the face based template and does not get a formula.

⇨ Click OK to finish.

10. Return to "Family Types" and flex.

This is where it fails. I am not sure what causes it. But Revit seems unhappy with the pasted reference planes. If I delete the reference planes, redraw them and then reapply the dimensions, all works fine. So, whether or not starting by pasting really saves any effort is hard to say. I think it does save a bit of effort on the parameters and formulas, so it is probably worth doing. But it sure would be nice if we did not have to redo the reference planes.[3]

11. Make a crossing window to select everything.

⇨ On the ribbon, click the Filter button, click Check None, select only Reference Planes and then click OK.

⇨ Delete them.

> The two center ones will remain. They cannot be deleted.

12. Select all of the lines. Cut them to the clipboard, and then paste them back **Aligned to Same Place**.

Again, this is a bizarre required step. But before you do this, you cannot chain select the lines and they will misbehave. After pasting them back, it is like it resets the lines and they should chain select and behave better.

13. Use the lines onscreen to guide the creation of new reference planes.

You can snap the new reference planes directly to the existing lines. Then stretch the endpoints as appropriate. Add new dimensions. Automatic Sketch Dimensions are turned on in the file, so they will appear during this process. Re-label all the dimensions. Finally, align and lock all the lines to the new reference planes. Align and lock the centers and endpoints of the arcs (see Figure 11.8).

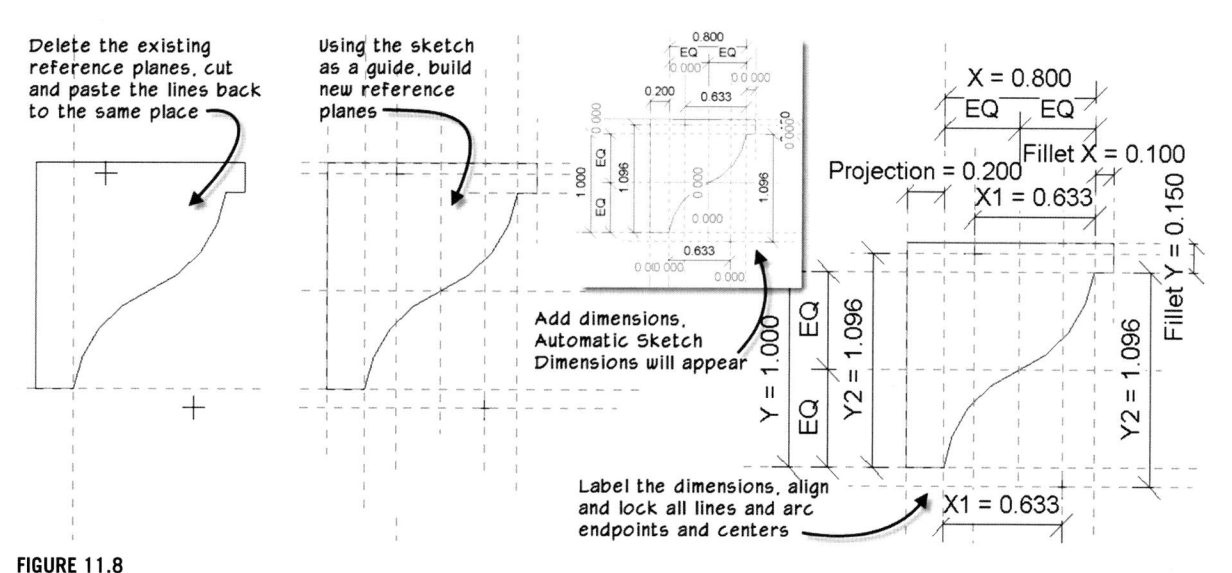

FIGURE 11.8

Finish the process of recreating the generic model version of the profile

---

[3] Interestingly, my technical editor got different results. His flexed after pasting. However he did report that many automatic sketch dimensions appeared implying that many of the constraints were broken during paste. In the end, while it is more work to recreate the family from scratch, I think that it is for the best if your goal is stable and reusable content.

• *Creating Classical Architecture with Modern Software* •

322 | Chapter 11

Once again, I am not completely convinced that this copy and paste approach is really any quicker than just rebuilding the entire family. I tried it both ways and it is almost a toss-up. I will let you be the judge. The bottom line is that like it or not, in order to use the parametric profile shapes we created back in Chapter 4 in the massing environment, we have to recreate all of them (or at least all of the ones we want to use) as generic model families. The face based seed gives the best results.

14. Be sure to flex and then save the file.

Also check the two center reference planes before closing. Make sure they both have "Defines Origin" checked.

> **CATCH UP!** You can open a file completed to this point named: *11_Cyma Reversa GM Profile (w Fillets).rfa*.

LOAD A MASSING PROFILE AND CREATE FORM

Now that we have gone to all the effort to create the generic model profile, let's load it into our adaptive seed and see how we can create form from it.

1. Open the *11_Family Seed (Adaptive).rfa* file.

   ⇨ Save it as: **Generic Model Profiles**.

2. Click on the level onscreen to make it the active work plane.

3. On the Create tab, click the Component tool.

Revit will alert you that there are no component families loaded and offer to load one for you.

   ⇨ Click Yes in the dialog that appears.

   ⇨ Browse to the *Chapter11* folder and select the *Cyma Reversa GM Profile (w Fillets).rfa* file (or choose the catch-up file).

4. On the Modify | Place Component tab, on the Placement panel, click the Place on Work Plane button.

   ⇨ Click anywhere onscreen to place an instance (see the left side of Figure 11.9).

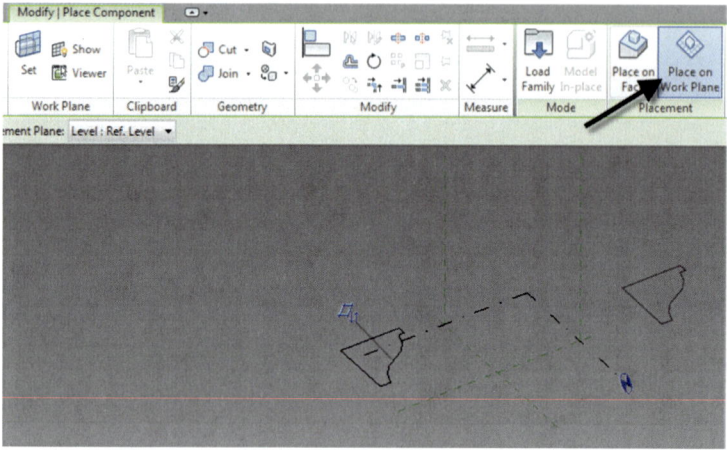

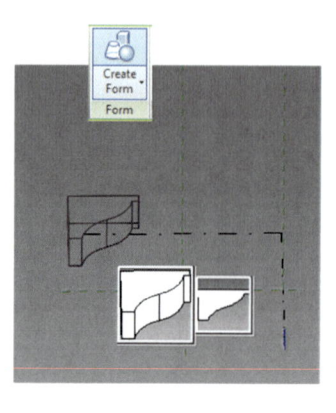

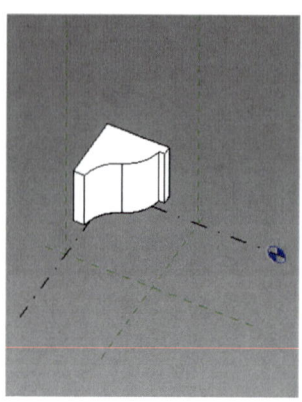

FIGURE 11.9
Load in and place the generic model profile component

5. Cancel the command. Select the generic model profile onscreen.

   ⇨ Click Create Form and then choose the extrusion option (see the right side of Figure 11.9).

We are not limited to just extrusions. You saw that we could also create a surface. But if we add some additional geometry, we can use this same shape to create revolved or swept forms.

• Renaissance Revit •

6. Click on one of the vertical reference planes to set it as the work plane.
   ⇨ Click the component button again, click on Place on Work Plane and then place an instance.

Notice that it will now be oriented with the selected work plane and be placed upright.

7. Click on the level to set it as the work plane again.
   ⇨ On the Draw panel, click the line tool and draw a chain of lines on the level.
   ⇨ Select both the path and the generic model. Create Form (see the top of Figure 11.10).

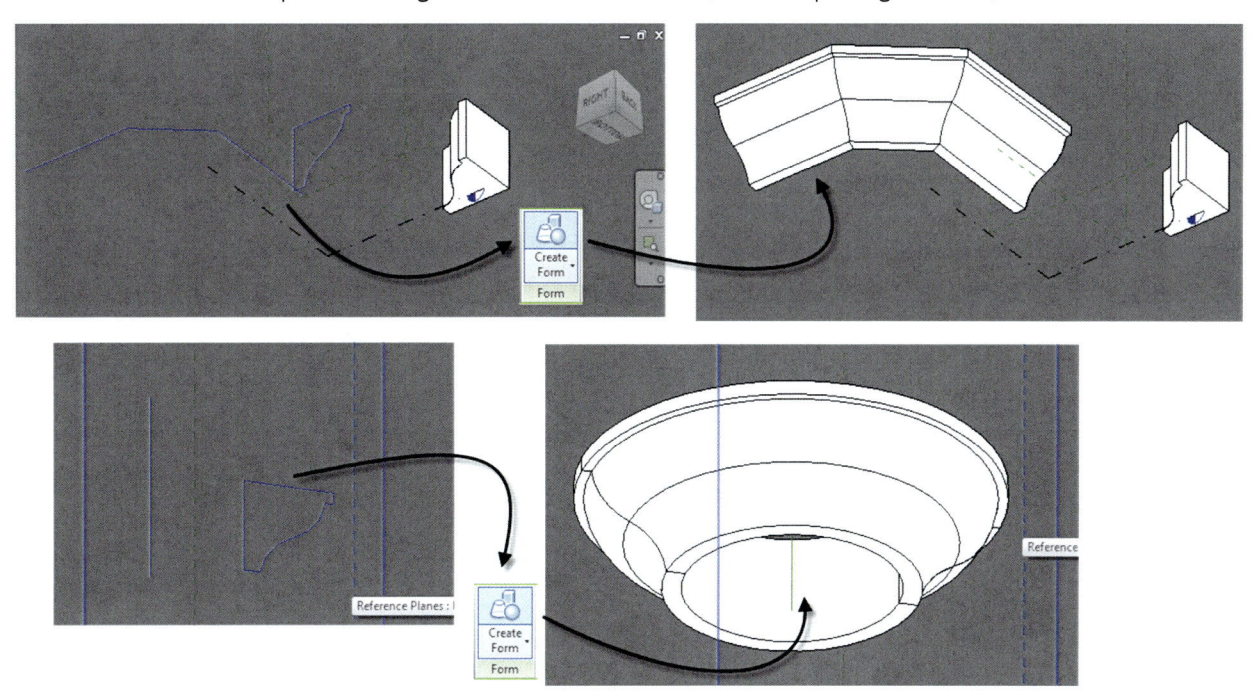

FIGURE 11.10
Create a swept form or a revolved form depending on the path you draw

This will create a sweep. You typically have to make sure that the path is perpendicular to the shape or it may fail. So if yours did not work, try adjusting the path and try again.

On the bottom of Figure 11.10, you can see what you get if you draw the path in the same plane as the shape. Revit will treat this like a revolve instead, and use the path you draw as the axis line.

REFERENCE LINES AND POINTS

Reference lines were discussed in the "Add a Swing Parameter" topic under "Controlling Rotation" in Chapter 4. If you recall, reference lines have several integral work planes that can be used to host geometry. In the Massing Environment, all sketched shapes can be created from either model lines or reference lines. When you create a form from model lines, the model lines get "absorbed" into the form. To edit the form later, you can use direct manipulation, X-Ray or Dissolve (all tools on the ribbon). When you create a form from reference lines instead, the lines are not absorbed into the form and continue to drive the shape of the form. (The form "references" the lines). Manipulating the reference line's shape directly changes the shape of the 3D form as well. While reference planes are also a part of the massing environment, these unique features of reference lines tend to mean that they play a much larger role. As such, reference lines in the massing environment are used in many of the ways that reference planes are used in the traditional environment. When you create forms from reference lines, they remain associated to the reference lines so that you can edit the forms by manipulating the reference lines.

324 | Chapter 11

The massing environment also contains Reference Points. Reference points are useful in all massing families and are an essential building block of nearly any Adaptive Component family. (They are so useful in fact, that it is a shame that they are not available in the traditional family editor or the project environment). Reference points are single point elements that you can place in the canvas. They can be moved in three-dimensional space using the integrated gizmo control. The control allows movement along each of the X, Y and Z axes (red, green and blue respectively) and also along the plane of any two of these axes by dragging the small "L" shaped portion instead of the arrow itself (see Figure 11.11).

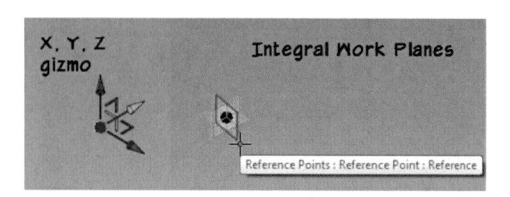

FIGURE 11.11
Point element with its gizmo visible

More importantly, reference points (like reference lines) define work planes and consequently can host geometry. This feature gives tremendous power and flexibility to the use of reference points. Reference points can also be turned into "Shape Handle Points" and "Adaptive Points." Adaptive Points are like insertion points when the family is placed in a project or other massing family. Adaptive points are considered hosts, so when you place a family with adaptive points, the geometry can actually conform to the shape of the points as you click to place them. A Shape handle point is a special kind of adaptive point that can be manipulated after initial placement. This can be used to flex the family.

SPLINE THROUGH POINTS

When you combine both reference lines and reference points, you gain some very useful advantages. There are two ways that you can host your lines (either Model or Reference) to reference points: 3D Snapping and Spline Through Points. The real key to leveraging these tools is realizing how they can work together. Using either method, we will have a construct whereby the reference points serve as the host for the reference lines, which in-turn will be used to generate the 3D forms.

Find the Spline Through Points icon on the Draw panel. You can use the tool two ways: click it first and then place several points. As you click points, a spline will appear passing through each point you click. The other method is to create several points using the point tool first (also on the Draw panel). Then select the points and click the Spline Through Points icon. It will pass a spline through all of the selected points (see Figure 11.12).

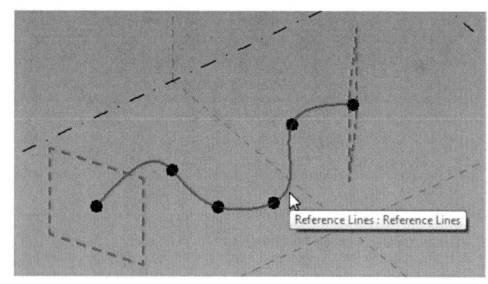

FIGURE 11.12
Spine Through Points

Let's create a spline through points and then use it to create form.

1. Click on the level onscreen to set it as the work plane again.
2. On the Draw panel, click the Reference button.
   ⇨ Click the Spline Through Points icon.
   ⇨ Click approximately four points onscreen to create an "S" shape (see Figure 11.13).

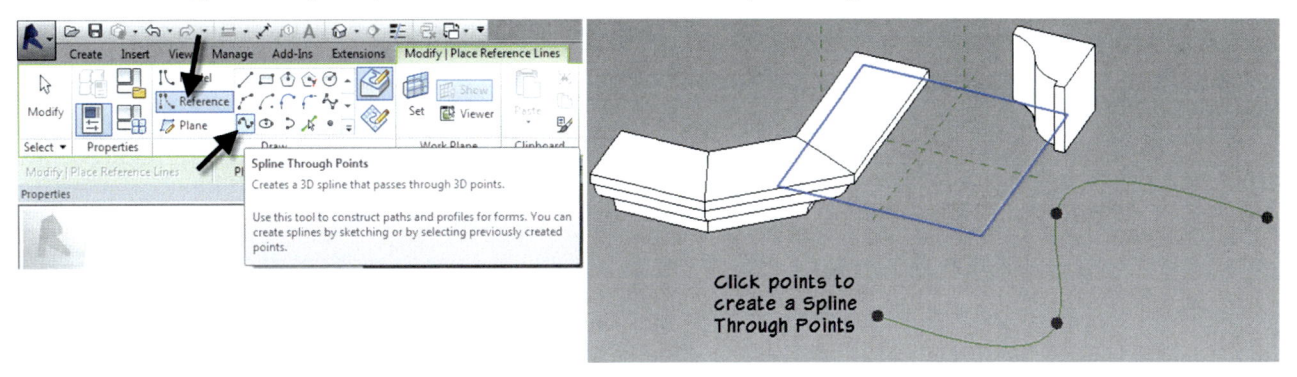

FIGURE 11.13
Create a reference line using Spline Through Points

You will know you have a reference line because it defaults to a green color. Also, if you move the cursor over it onscreen and highlight it, two work planes will appear at the ends. Model lines will appear black onscreen and will not have work planes. If you create a model line instead of a reference line, simply select it and on the Properties Palette check the "Is Reference Line" checkbox. This will convert it to a reference line.

3. Cancel the command and then select one of the points in the middle of the spline.

Notice the control gizmo that appears. You can drag these arrows and the spline will reshape. If you want to use one of these points as a work plane, use the Set button.

4. On the Work Plane panel, click the Set button.
   ⇨ Click the reference point at one end of the spline.
5. On the Draw panel, click the Reference button, then click the circle.
   ⇨ Snap directly to the same point that you just set as work plane.

Notice that the circle draws on this work plane. You can make it any size you like.

6. Set work plane at the other end and draw an ellipse on that work plane.

If you select only the circle and ellipse and then create form, you will get a straight blend between the two, but if you select the circle, the ellipse and the spline, you get a blend that follows along the path of the spline (see Figure 11.14).

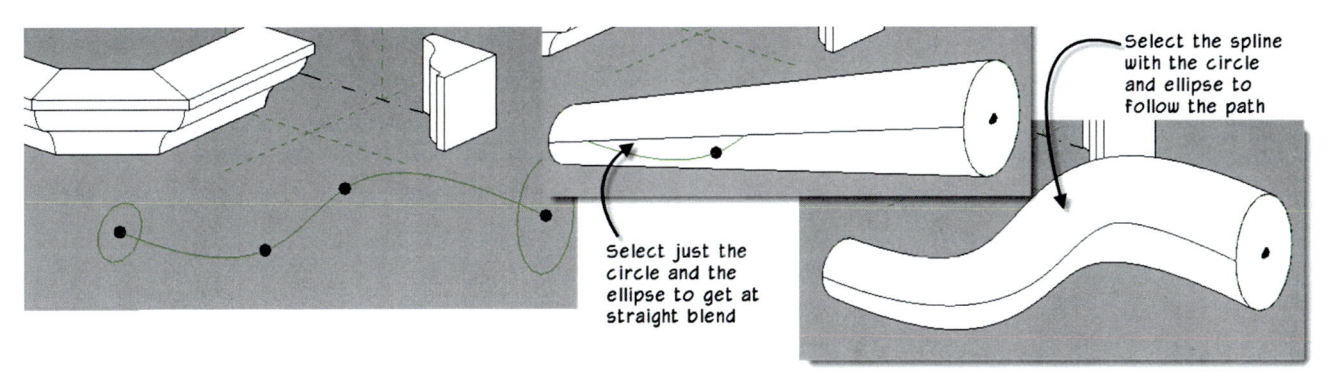

FIGURE 11.14
Create forms from splines and shapes hosted on points

• *Creating Classical Architecture with Modern Software* •

Since everything is a reference: reference lines and reference points, you can manipulate the location or shape of any of the references and the shape will adjust in real time. Try moving one of the points. Try changing the size of the circle or ellipse. Try reshaping the spline. All of these will dynamically effect the 3D form.

Another way that you can make a spline through points is to add the points first.

1. Click on the level onscreen to set it as the work plane again.
2. On the Create tab, click the Point element icon.
⇨ Click to place some points onscreen the exact locations are unimportant. Place about four points.
3. Cancel the command and then select all of the points you just placed.
⇨ On the Draw panel, click the Spline Through Points icon.

Notice that Revit will pass a spline through all of the points you just placed. If you select one of the points and move it, it will reshape the spline. You should also notice that the spline is black, not green. If you select the spline itself (not the points), it is a model line. When you use the method of placing points, then clicking Spline Through Points, you end up with a model line. This is not always undesirable. But assuming that you wanted a reference line instead, this is easy to fix. Select the spline onscreen. On the Properties palette, click the "Is Reference Line" checkbox (see Figure 11.15).

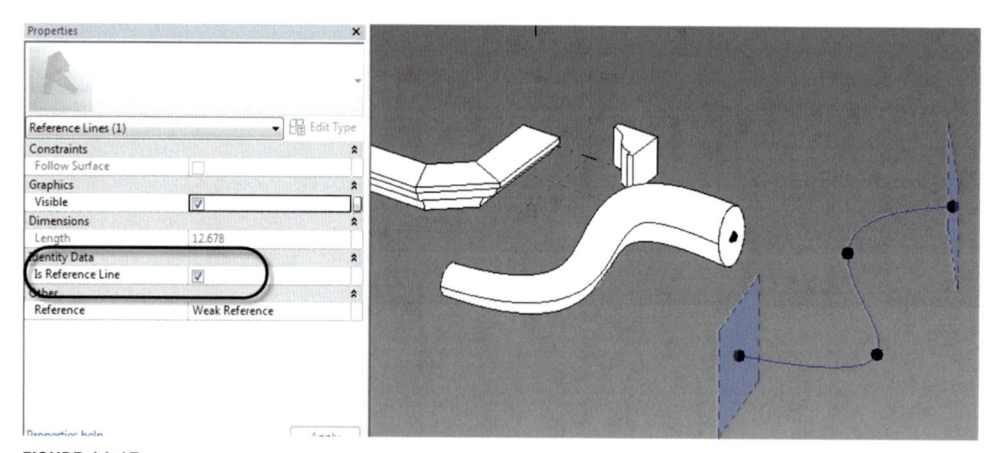

FIGURE 11.15
Convert between a model and reference line with the "Is Reference Line" checkbox

HOSTED POINTS

In both of the methods noted for creating a Spline Through Points, the points will "drive" the shape of the spline. If you move a point, the spline will reshape. However, if you place a point on an existing line (any line, straight, curved or spline) it will become hosted to the line. The line will then "drive" the point. If you use that hosted point as the host for something else, like geometry or other lines and points, you can build a complex set of relationships. (This is the essence of building rigs in the massing environment which we will look at below). Let's look at a simple example.

1. On the Draw panel, click the Point element icon.
⇨ Move the cursor over the spline.
It will highlight (see the left side of Figure 11.16). Make sure that "Draw on Face" is active, or this will not work.
⇨ Click to place the point hosted on the spline.

Sometimes the point does not show up right away. Pan or zoom the screen slightly to force a redraw and it will display.

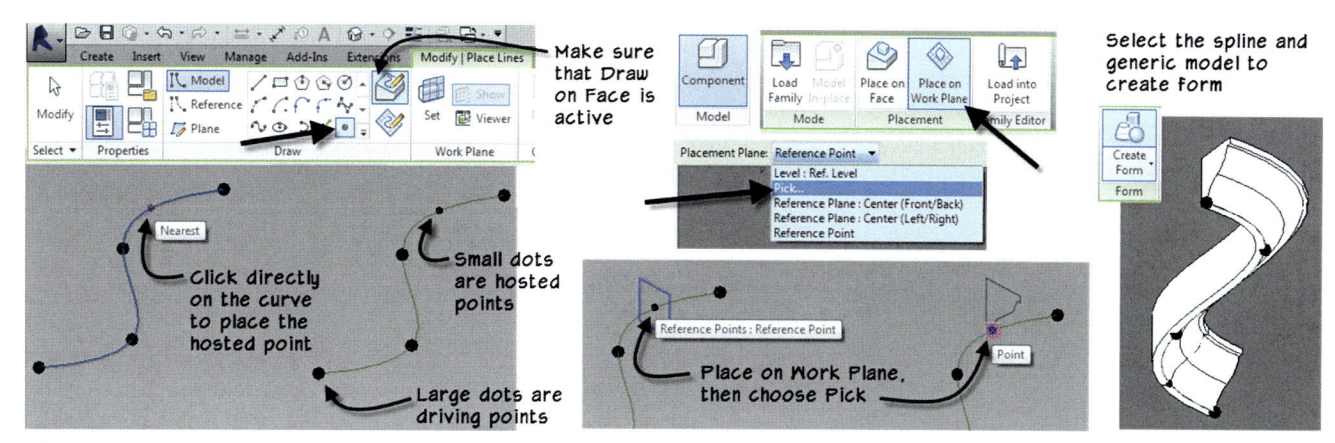

FIGURE 11.16
Points can drive the shape of geometry or be hosted by geometry. Other elements can then be hosted on the driven points

2. On the Create tab, click the Component button.

In the massing environment it is important to pay attention to the drawing mode. In many cases you can place object on faces, or on work planes. The behaviors and features available often differ in subtle ways. For example, in the previous steps, we had to ensure that we were using "Draw on Face" to get the point to host on the line. However, in this case, if we use that mode, the generic model will not host on the work planes of the points. To do that, we need to use the Place on Work Plane mode. Clear as mud?

3. On the Modify | Place Component tab, click the Place on Work Plane button.
   - On the Options Bar, click the Placement Plane drop-down and choose **Pick**.
   - Click on the work plane of the hosted point.
     It will automatically be oriented perpendicular to the path.
   - Click to place the generic model snapped to the point and then cancel.
4. Select both the spline and the generic model and then click Create Form (see the right side of Figure 11.16).

If you get an error, try adjusting the spline a little. So the basic idea behind building form in the massing environment is like constructing a skeleton. It is like the "Dem Bones" jingle: "The foot bone connected to the leg-bone, the leg bone connected to the knee bone, the knee bone connected to the thigh bone…"

In other words, you must construct a careful set of interconnected references that will ultimately give shape to and control your 3D form. It is a bit more complex to set up, but the nice thing about the massing environment is that I have built a complex hierarchy here without a single parameter. Don't be fooled however, you certainly can introduce parameters, but it is nice that you can build complex relationships that are very stable and robust without them.

Feel free to experiment further with this form before continuing. Adjust the points, which will adjust the shape of the spline which will ultimately reshape the 3D form… the hip bone connected to the back bone…

3D SNAPPING

Certain shapes in the massing environment can be drawn in three-dimensional space instead of on a particular work plane. This represents a fairly significant departure from the standard Revit operating procedure and with it comes some nice benefits as well. Elements eligible for this behavior include lines, rectangles and three-point arcs. Spline by points is always a 3D object. In other words, with the other three elements I noted, you have to turn on "3D

328 | Chapter 11

Snapping" in order to create them in 3D space. With spline through points, you are always placing the points in 3D space, so 3D snapping is not required.

Essentially what happens is that if you enable 3D Snapping, the element you are creating looks and acts much like a spline through points. It will have the large driving point elements at each of its control points. You can move these points freely in 3D space and the element will respond accordingly. Here's a few examples:

> Normally the first step is to click the work plane you want to make active. With 3D Snapping this is not as critical since the element will not be constrained to the work plane.

1. On the Draw panel, click the Reference button.

    The toolbox will default to line.

2. On the Options Bar, click the 3D Snapping checkbox (see Figure 11.17).

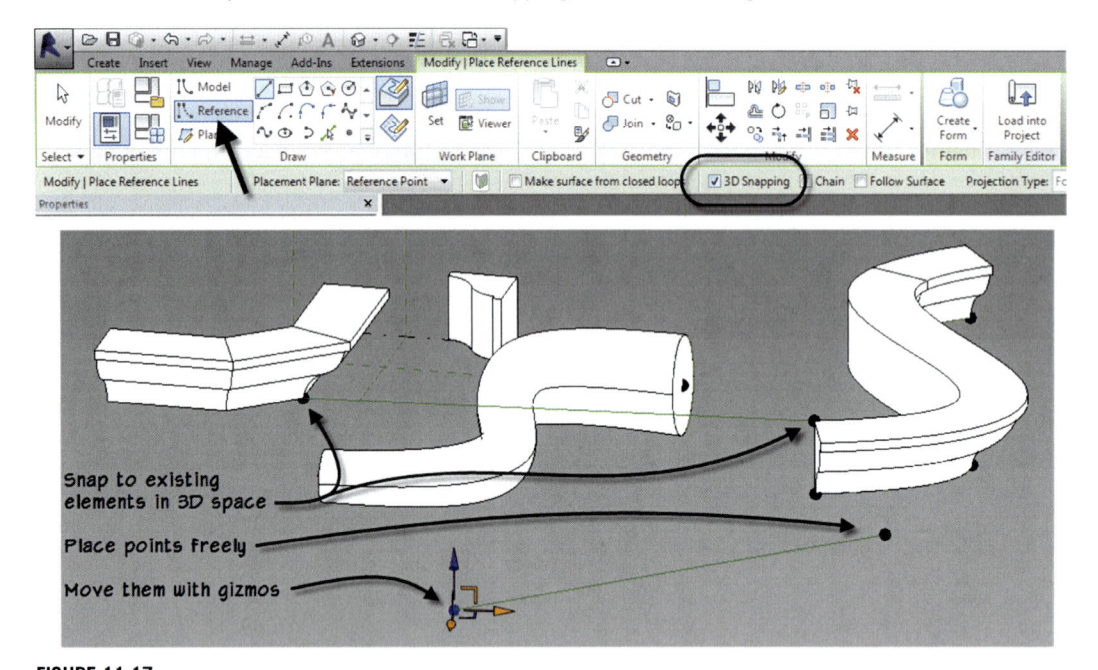

FIGURE 11.17
Enable 3D Snapping on the Options Bar

3. Click points onscreen.

You can place points freely in space. You can also snap to existing geometry. The location of the point snaps in X, Y and Z directions to the points you click. If you pick in empty space, it matches the work plane. After placement, you can select a point and manipulate its gizmo like the splines above to move it around. This will reshape the line.

4. Try a rectangle next.

Rectangles initially draw on the active work plane. So it is not a bad idea to set the work plane first. However, you can manipulate the points later so that they move out of plane with the work plane. A really interesting feature is the "Follow Surface" feature. When you check this box on the Options Bar, you can draw the shape (line, rectangle, spline or arc) directly on the surface of a 3D form and the object will follow the shape. This is very handy on curved surfaces.

5. Toggle on the "Follow Surface" option and draw a rectangle on one of the curved surfaces (see Figure 11.18).

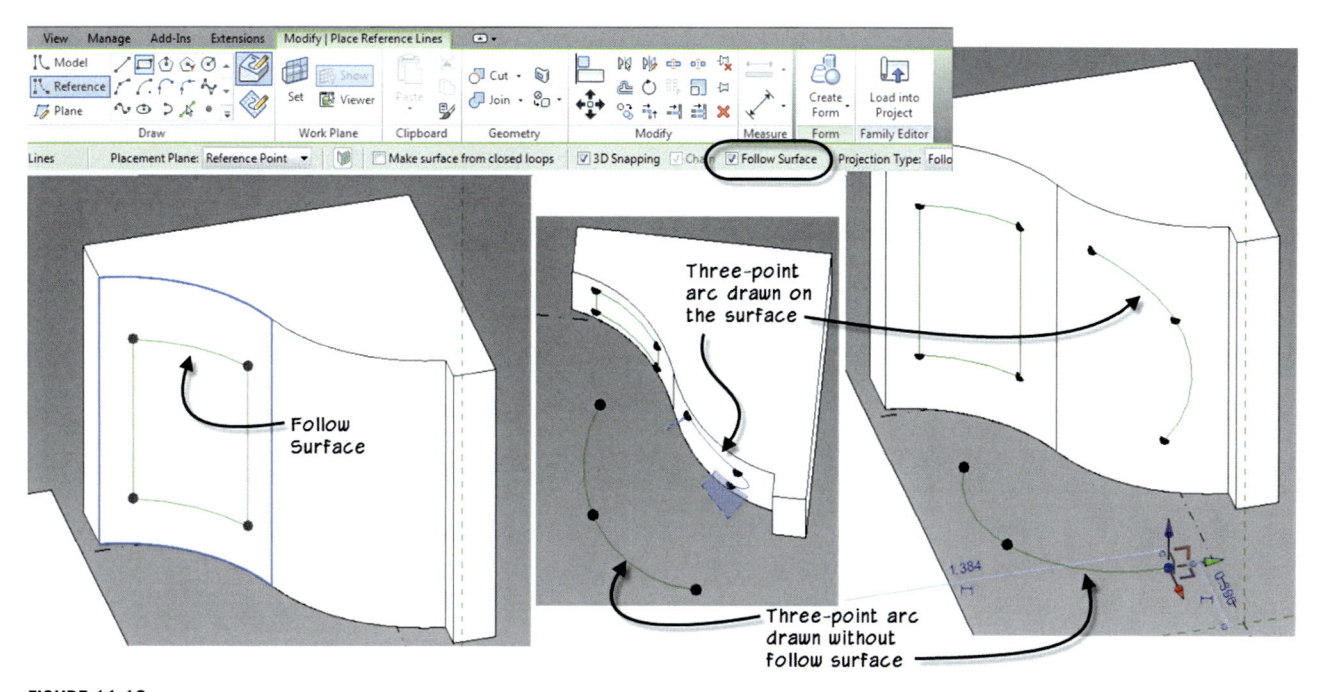

FIGURE 11.18

Try follow surface and the three-point arc

When you use follow surface, you will no longer have the gizmos for the points. They will stay attached to the surface.

6. Try a Start-End Radius (three-point) arc next.

   Make sure that the "3D Snapping" checkbox is still enabled.

This can be draw freely, snapped to other 3D points, or even with follow surface. So it works just like the other elements that support 3D snapping. Try drawing a few to see. Perhaps the best feature of this arc, is that you can easily move one of the points the arc will reshape! This is very handy.

LOFTING

One of the nicest features of the massing environment is the ability to build lofted forms. Lofts are forms that can use multiple shapes to create their form. Think of a form with multiple cross sections each blending to the next one. In a way, a blend is the simplest form of loft. Unfortunately, the traditional family editor is limited to simple blends where only two shapes are possible and the blend follows a straight path. Swept blends help a little by allowing for a curved path, but the transition from the base shape to the top shape is still linear in progression. If you look at an elevation view of a blend or swept blend, the edge is straight. If you wanted to create a complex form that required more than two cross sections, you would have to stack several blends, but the transition between them would be segmented.

With a loft, you can have two or more shapes. If there are only two it basically emulates the traditional blend. But with three or more, you start to see a curved progression along the path between the shapes. The result is a much smoother form. The transition is not segmented since it is a single continuous element. Let's explore a quick example to clarify.

1. Click on the level onscreen to set it as the work plane again.
2. On the Draw panel, click the Reference button and then click the Start-End Radius arc.

330 | Chapter 11

- ⇨ On the Options Bar, make sure that 3D Snapping is checked.[4]
- ⇨ Click three points to place the arc. (Place it in empty space, not snapped to any existing geometry).

3. On the Work Plane panel, click the Set button.

- ⇨ Highlight and then click one of the endpoints of the arc.

4. On the Draw panel, click Reference and then rectangle. Uncheck 3D Snapping.

- ⇨ Snap the first corner of the rectangle to the point you just set as the work plane and then drag out a small rectangle.

5. Repeat the process to set the work plane to the next point, draw a new rectangle of a different size and then repeat once more on the final point (see the left side of Figure 11.19).

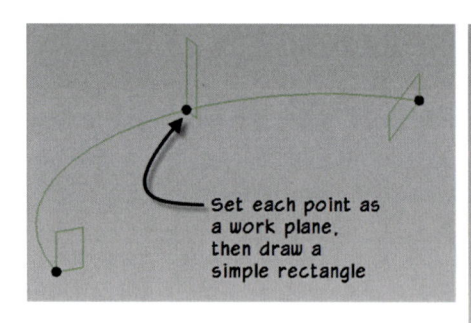

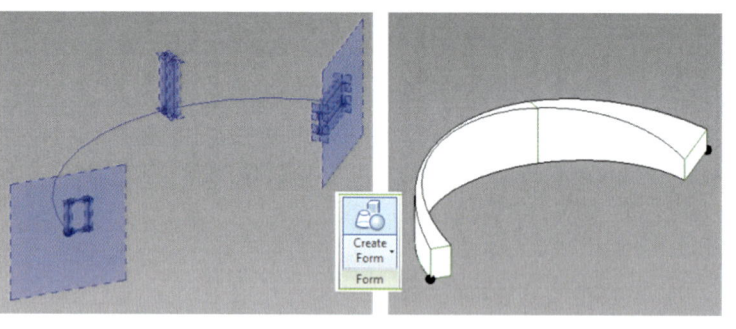

FIGURE 11.19
Create a simple lofted form

This is a simple example here, so don't be too concerned with precision. Just rough sketch the size of each rectangle. Revit may try to snap to nearby elements, try to avoid snapping for now. If you forget to click the Reference button before you draw, remember you can change the "Is Reference Line" setting on the Properties palette.

6. Select all three rectangles and the path. (You can use a window selection box).

- ⇨ Create Form.

See how smoothly it flows one shape to the next? If you need to create complex and organic forms (like perhaps acanthus leaves) this is by far the best available option in Revit. Not only that, you can actually add another profile to an existing form after it is created and reshape the form. We will see examples of this in future chapters.

BUILDING RIGS

Back in Chapter 4, in the "Using a nested rig to model traditional molding forms" topic, we discussed the use of a "rig" to help constrain the curved forms we were creating. In that chapter, the rig we used was a simple two-dimensional detail item family. I noted earlier that you cannot use detail items families in the massing environment, but building rigs is a critical part of the workflow. In fact, I first started using rigs in the massing environment and later adapted the idea to create the rigs we used in Chapter 4. Rigs in the massing environment are constructed from a collection of interconnected reference elements: lines and points and can be simple 2D constructs or very elaborate 3D scaffolds. Regardless of the level of complexity, the essential concept remains the same: create a stable form that flexes in predicable ways upon which you can build your 3D geometry. You can think of the rig as akin to the formwork used to pour concrete or the chicken wire or balloon supports used to sculpt papier-mâché.

---

[4] This feature is only available for arcs in Revit 2014 and later. If you are using an earlier version, add hosted points to the arc manually.

The secret to building rigs is the "Normalized Curve Parameter". This parameter is a numerical value that determines the precise location of a hosted point along its host line. The host can be any shape as we noted above, but it is illustrated on a straight line here for simplicity (see Figure 11.20). Rather than being an absolute measurement, Normalized Curve Parameter is a numerical value between 0 and 1: basically a percentage. This number does *not* change if the length of the line changes. So, if you start with a 10 unit long line and a normalized curve parameter of .8, your point will be 8 units from the end. Stretch the line to only 5 units long and because the normalized curve parameter remains .8, the point is now 4 units from the end. In other words, the point's location (and anything hosted to it) scales proportionally!

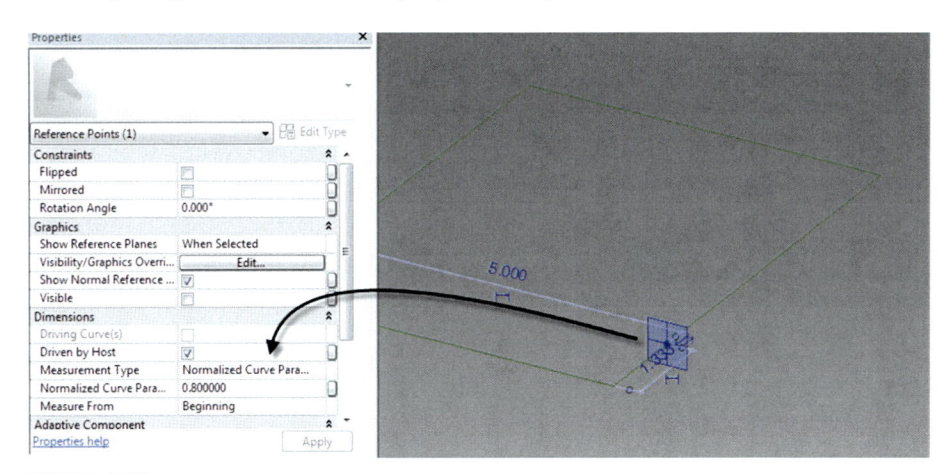

FIGURE 11.20

Normalized Curve Parameter

If proportional scaling is important to what you are building, then reference line rigs with hosted reference points can be a very powerful way to approach the task. Let's build a really simple example here, and then we'll look at more complex examples in the coming chapters.

You can continue in the same file for this simple example.

1. Click on the level onscreen to set it as the work plane again.
2. On the Draw panel, click the Point element icon.
3. Off to the side somewhere, click to place a single point and then cancel the command. (Do not snap it to anything).
    ⇨ Select the new point. On the Properties palette, from the Show Reference Planes drop-down, choose **Always**.

Three small blue reference planes will appear on the point. It can be helpful to have these displayed, so you can tell where the work planes are.

4. On the Draw panel, click the Point element icon again.
    ⇨ Before placing the point, on the Options Bar, from the Placement Plane drop-down, choose **Pick** (see the left side of Figure 11.21).
    ⇨ Click on the horizontal work plane of the point (the one parallel to the level) (see the middle of Figure 11.21).
5. Click to place the point directly on top of the first point (an object snap will confirm that you are snapping properly).
    ⇨ Click OK to ignore the warning and then cancel the command (See the right side of Figure 11.21).

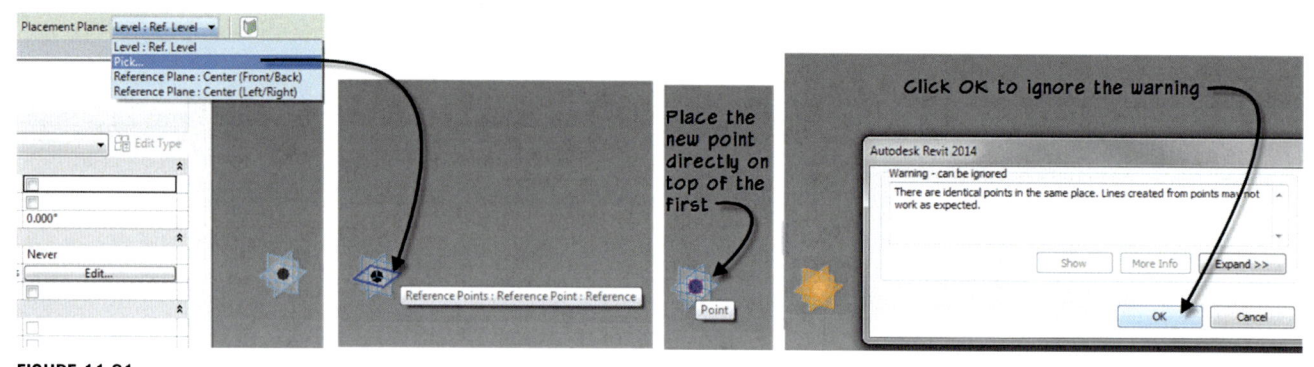

FIGURE 11.21
Create a new point directly on the work plane of the existing point

We now have two points directly on top of one another. But remember the knee bone, hip bone and thigh bone? By setting the work plane of the second point to one of the reference planes of the first point, we have established a hierarchy.

6. Click to select the new point. (This is the hosted point).

    It will be easy to tell them apart since only the first point has the work planes turned on. So be sure to click the other one.

7. On the Properties palette, for the Offset, input: **1.000**.

Notice that the second point is now 1.000 unit away from the original. However, they are still linked together. Select the original point and move it. Notice that both points move. The other important thing to realize here is that the offset property we just edited can be parameterized.

8. Select the hosted point again. On the Properties palette, next to the Offset parameter, click the Associate Family Parameter button.

    ⇨ Add a new parameter called **Z1** and grouped under **Constraints**.

    ⇨ With the point still selected, from the Show Reference Planes drop-down, choose **Always**.

9. Create another new point.

    ⇨ Repeat the procedure above to pick its Placement Plane. This time click the vertically oriented work plane on the original point.

    ⇨ Place the point directly on the point again and ignore the warning.

10. Staying in the point command, repeat one more time.

    ⇨ Pick the vertical work plane of the second point this time (the one at 1.000 unit away). Place the new point directly on the second hosted point.

    ⇨ Cancel the command.

You should now have four points. Two in the original location and two offset at 1.000 away. We are now going to select the two new points and offset them as well. But since we used the vertical work planes this time, they will offset laterally instead of vertically.

11. With the CTRL key held down, select both of the new points (remember these are the ones not showing their reference planes).

    ⇨ Set an offset of **2.000** this time and then create and associate a new parameter called **X1** (See Figure 11.22).

These four points will form the main framework of the rig. You can check that you got the hosting correct by clicking on a point and then click the Show Host button on the Options Bar. It will highlight the host onscreen.

• Renaissance Revit •

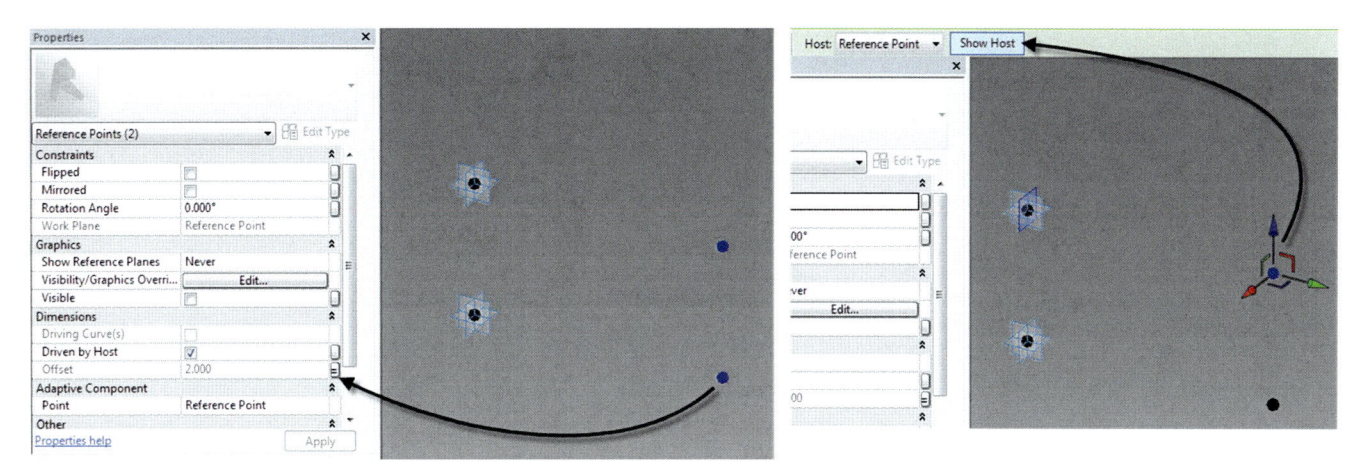

FIGURE 11.22

Create two more points with a single parameter controlling their offset. Use the Show Host button to check the setup

This next task has to be done two points at a time. If you do spline through points with only two points selected, you get a straight line. If you have three or more, you get a curve. We want to basically outline the four points with a box that will become our rig. The four points are the control points.

12. Select the first two points (the ones showing work planes). On the Draw panel click Spline Through Points.

You will get a straight line between these two points.

⇨ Repeat three more times. Select just two points each time.

When finished, you should have a rectangle. The splines are model lines. And the reference planes turned off.

13. Select the rectangle. (A single click should select the whole shape).

⇨ On the Properties palette, check Is Reference Line.

So at this point, I wouldn't blame you for wondering why we would have gone to all this trouble to create a rectangle when we could have simply draw it with the rectangle tool. The difference is in the hierarchy. The original point here is the master host. It controls the location of the second point and they both control the locations of points 3 and 4. Select the original point and move it. You see the way the entire rectangle moves? If you had just drawn it, this would not be the case. The other difference is that baked in some parameters. So let's go to "Family Types" and test.

14. Open the "Family Types" dialog.

⇨ Change the value of Z1 and then apply.

⇨ Change the value of X1 and then apply.

See how this is not your ordinary rectangle? This is our rig. Now we can "hang" geometry off of this rig, leveraging the "Normalized Curve Parameter" noted above and gain parametric control over freeform elements. Let's take a look.

⇨ Reset Z1 to **1.000** and X1 to **2.000** and then click OK.

15. On the Draw panel, click the Reference button. Then click Spline Through Points.

   Make sure the Draw on Face button is selected (shown in Figure 11.16 above).

⇨ Click four points for the spline; one on each of the four sides of the rectangle (See Figure 11.23).

⇨ Click the Modify tool to cancel.

• Creating Classical Architecture with Modern Software •

334 | Chapter 11

FIGURE 11.23

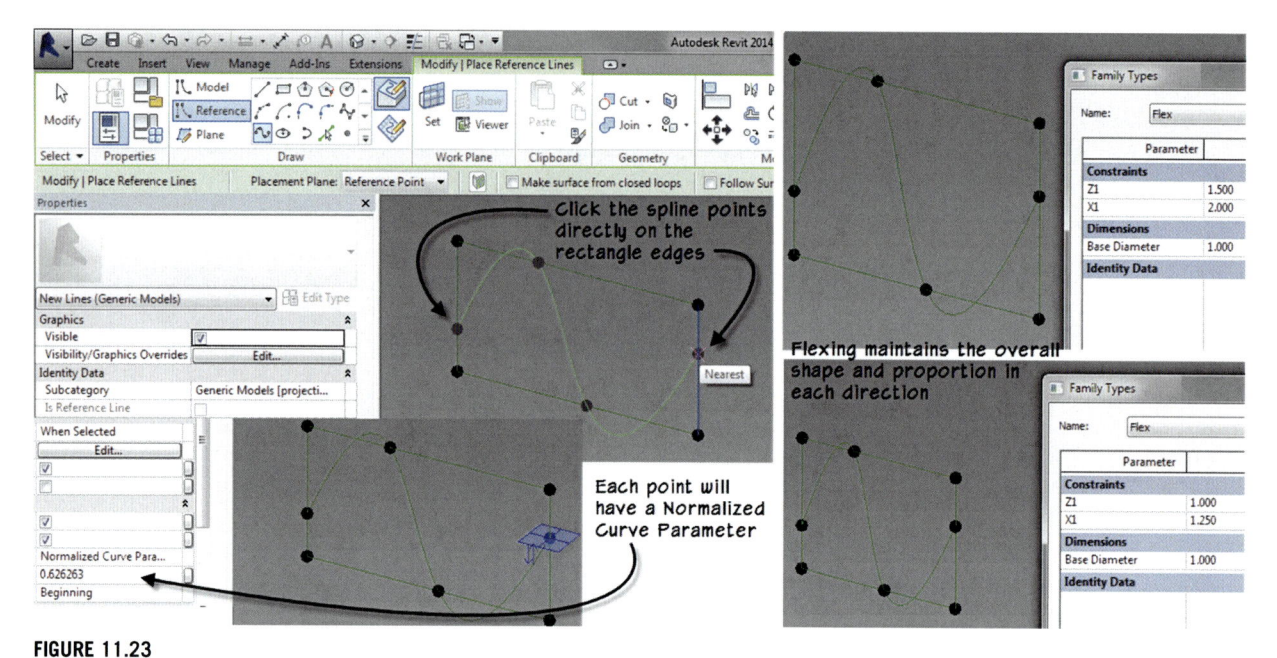

Create a spline referenced to the rig

Select one of the points of the spline and notice the Normalized Curve Parameter on the Properties palette.

16. Open the "Family Types" dialog.

   ⇨ Change the value of Z1 and then apply.

   ⇨ Change the value of X1 and then apply.

   ⇨ Reset Z1 to **1.000** and X1 to **2.000** and then apply.

As you can see, the shape is scaling proportionally in each direction. But at the moment, they are not scaling together. This is easy to remedy with a formula. Simply add a Base Diameter formula to both Z1 and X1 and they will scale at the same rate and proportion.

There is plenty more you can do with this. We have only introduced the concept of rigs here. Once you have your rig and the elements constrained to it, you can build geometry. So for example, I welcome you to build a sweep or loft on the spline we just created and then flex it.

> **Note:** The precise method used here is not the only way to build a scaling rig. I have seen it done many ways and I have tried many different approaches myself. The one that I showed you here is one of the more straight-forward methods I have seen and I owe the credit for it to Andy Milburn (Milburn 2013). You can learn more about his methods at his blog at: http://grevity.blogspot.com/. Zach Kron also has many excellent rig examples on his buildz blog as well (Kron 2012).

CATCH UP! Not so much a "catch-up" file this time as a sample file. I have provided my version of the file used in this chapter so far for you to explore: *11_Massing_General.rfa* and *11_Massing_Rig.rfa*.

USING DIVIDE AND REPEAT

I'd like to explore one more feature of the massing environment before we conclude this overview chapter. The divide and repeat feature allows us to take any path and divide it into a parametrically controlled quantity of divisions. Once we have these divisions, we can repeat elements along the path in regular patterns. This is a very powerful, if a little quirky, feature of the massing environment and provides a compelling alternative to the traditional array approach we explored in the standard family editor.

BASIC DENTIL MOLDING

I could fill an entire chapter on nearly every topic in this chapter so far. This is especially true of divide and repeat. But given space constraints, I will instead offer a couple very simple examples.[5]

1. From the *Chapter11* folder, open the file named: *Colonnade (Divide and Repeat)_Start.rfa*.
   ⇨ Save the file as **Colonnade (Divide and Repeat)**.

Let's start with the basic concept. Start with a line or curve, divide it into segments. A series of nodes (points) will appear along the line. Then apply a component to one of the nodes and repeat it. Everything remains parametric. So you can change the quantity of nodes, the spacing, and what you repeat in a variety of ways. For the first example, we'll do a quick dentil molding.

2. Select the single segment reference line near the lower-right portion of the screen.

It is just a single segment reference line 10.000 units long.

3. On the Modify I Reference Lines tab, click the Divide Path button (See Figure 11.24).

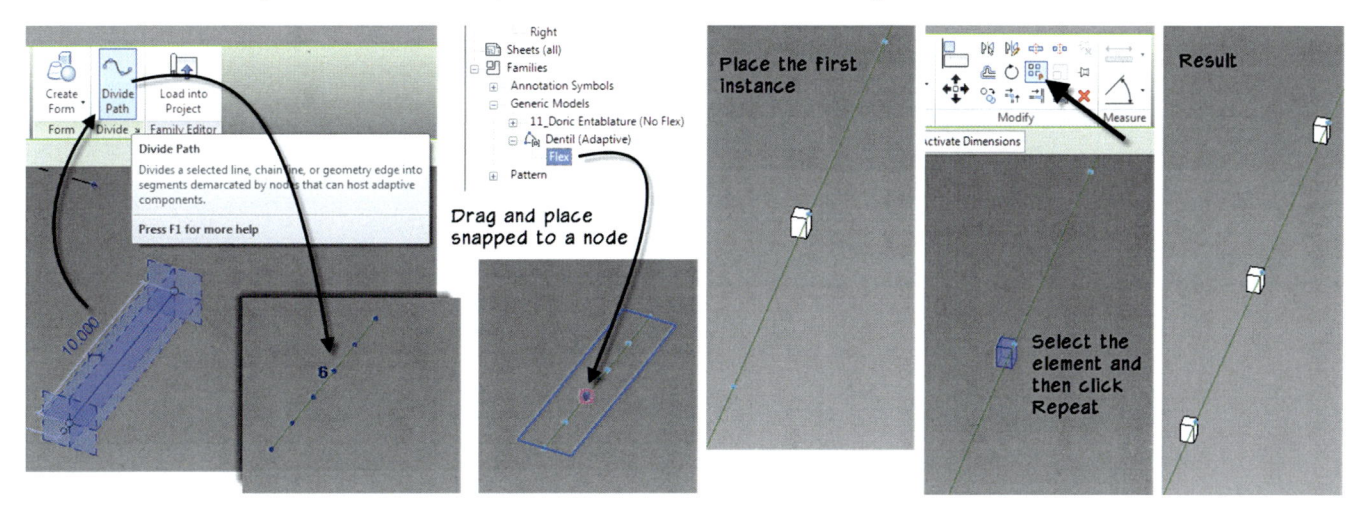

FIGURE 11.24
Divide a line with divide path add a component and then repeat it

4. On the Project Browser, beneath *Families*, expand *Generic Models > Dentil (Adaptive)*.
   ⇨ Select Flex and drag it into the canvas area.
   ⇨ Snap it directly to one of the nodes on the line.

   It does not matter which one you snap to. Just make sure it snaps to the node.

> TIP: To be sure you are snapping to the node, you can type sx; the keyboard shortcut for snap to points.

5. Select the element and then on the ribbon, click the Repeat icon (See the right side of Figure 11.24).

---

[5] Divide and Repeat is available in Revit 2013 and later. I have provided a starting file in 2012 format, but if you are using that version, you will have to add and space the points manually.

• *Creating Classical Architecture with Modern Software* •

The element will repeat to each node. As I said, this is a simple example. One of the peculiarities of the repeat feature is that the orientation of the element cannot be easily changed. One approach is the one I used here, which is to build the desired orientation of the single dentil into the dentil family. If you want to see this, right-click the *Dentil(Adaptive)* family on the Project Browser and choose **Edit**. You will see its orientation inside the family differs from how it came in here. I wish I could say that I had a good rule of thumb for this, but honestly I just did trial and error until I got it right. The other option which gives you more control is to use adaptive points. I will show this option below.

Meanwhile, let's configure the quantity and spacing. The Divide Path command defaults to a quantity of 6. The original reference line is still here, but now superimposed on top of it is the divided path element. So when editing, make sure you select the right one. In this case, we want to select the divide path in order to change the quantity and spacing. If you wanted to change the overall length of the path, you would TAB to select the original reference line instead.

6. Select the divided path.

    Take a look at the various properties on the Properties palette.

The default settings give us a path of layout of fixed number with the number set to 6. What we want is to set the spacing between the elements instead and let Revit determine how many dentils we need based on the overall length. You can set any parameter directly, but notice that most can also have an associated family parameter. Experiment with some of the values before continuing.

7. For the Layout, choose: **Fixed Distance**.
8. For the Distance, click the Associate Family Parameter button.

    ⇨ Choose Dentil Spacing and then click OK.

If you open "Family Types" you will see that Dentil Spacing is a simple length parameter that uses a distance that is 1/8 of the Base Diameter. Base Diameter in this file is 1.300.

ROUND COLONNADE

One of my favorite buildings is the Tempietto by Bramante. This little gem of a chapel is a renaissance masterpiece. It uses the Doric order but since it is round, the already strict rules of the Doric order are even stricter. I don't have the actual dimensions of the Tempietto, but looking at photographs I took my best guess. One illustration I found online had some dimensions as did Palladio's Four Books of Architecture (Palladio 1965, 97). I am not going to detail how to create a model of the Tempietto here. I do have a partially finished version which I will publish when it is more complete. Meanwhile, the colonnade in the file we are using here is loosely based on the size I determined above with a Base Diameter of 1.300 which is a close estimate. Using this number and an intercolumniation of 3.75, I was able to calculate the rough size of the circle needed. If you open "Family Types" you can see my calculations. I have provided the two circles in the file based on these calculations.

The basic strategy is to divide the circles with divided path. Set the number of nodes equal to the number of columns (16 in this case) and then repeat the column, the triglyph and the mutule. Sounds simple right? The only wrinkle is the orientation issue again. That and the fact that you can only repeat adaptive components. The adaptive component issue is easy to remedy; we can nest our traditional family from Chapter 9 directly in an adaptive component. Orientation could be tricky if we relied on trial and error like I did for the dentil. But if we use adaptive points instead, we gain the control we need over orientation.

So just what is an adaptive point? I briefly mentioned adaptive points above in the "Reference Lines and Points" topic. They are essentially custom insertion points for the family. What makes them unique and interesting is that you can have more than one in a family. In fact you can have several if you need to. When you add an adaptive family to your project, you will be prompted to place each adaptive point. Depending on how the family is constructed, the shape and form of the geometry in the family can actually morph with the placement of these adaptive points. Very powerful indeed! In our case, for the current example, we don't need to morph anything, but by using two adaptive points, we can "show" Revit the orientation we want our column to have when we insert it as a repeater. Let's set up our path first, then we'll build the repeater.

9. Select both circles.

   ⇨ On the ribbon, click the Divide Path button.

10. On the Properties palette, next to Number, click the Associate Family Parameter button, choose **Number of Columns** and then click OK.

11. Save the file.

CATCH UP! You can open a file completed to this point named: *11_Colonnade (Divide and Repeat)_A.rfa*.

CREATE AN ADAPTIVE COMPONENT FAMILY

Let's start by building the adaptive component that we'll use for the repeater.

1. From the *Chapter11* folder, open the file called: *11_Family Seed (Adaptive).rfa* (You can also use the one you created above if you prefer).

   ⇨ Save the file as: **Doric Column (Adaptive)**.

2. Open the *Ref. Level* floor plan view.

   ⇨ Create a Point element and snap it directly to the intersection of the two reference planes.

3. Open the *Front* elevation view.

   ⇨ Select the point, click the Copy icon, click any base point and then copy it straight up: **8.000** units.

4. Return to the *{3D}* view.

5. Select both points and then on the ribbon, click the Make Adaptive button (See the left side of Figure 11.25).

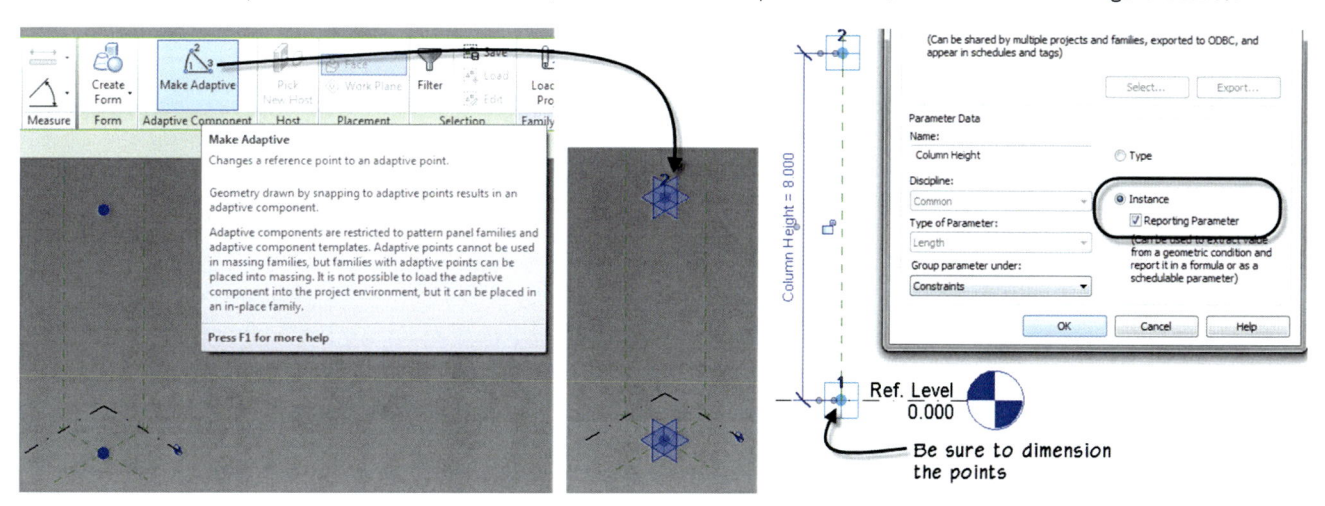

FIGURE 11.25

Create two adaptive points

• Creating Classical Architecture with Modern Software •

338 | Chapter 11

Notice that the two adaptive points have numbers. So when this family is inserted into another family or project, you will be prompted to place each adaptive point in numerical order. If you have hosted geometry to the points, the geometry will adapt accordingly. But adaptive points have another super power. They are host elements. This means that you can measure the distance between the two adaptive points and use that distance to drive formulas. So we'll nest in a column family and use this feature to drive the height of the column.

6. Open the *Front* elevation view.

7. Create a new dimension between the two points. (Make sure to dimension the points themselves.)

   ⇨ Label this with a new parameter. Call it **Column Height**, make it and Instance parameter and check **Reporting** (See the right side of Figure 11.25)

   ⇨ Return to the *{3D}* view.

8. On the Create tab, click the Component button, click Yes when prompted.

   ⇨ Browse to the *Chapter09\Railings* folder, select: *Doric Column (without Pedestal).rfa* and then click Open.

   ⇨ Click anywhere to place an instance and then cancel the command.

   It might be convenient to tile the *Ref. Level* floor plan, the *Front* elevation and the *{3D}* view onscreen together.

9. Select the column onscreen.

   ⇨ On the Properties palette, next to Top Offset, click the Associate Family Parameter button, choose **Column Height** and then click OK.

The column should adjust to match the distance between the two adaptive points. If you want test that this is working, select point 2 and using the blue arrow on the gizmo, move it up. The column will flex in real time. Let's do it more precisely. Let's try the size it will be when we load it into the other file.

10. Select point 2. This will activate the vertical dimension. Type in 10.400 and then press ENTER.

11. In the plan view, align and lock the column to the center reference planes in both directions (See Figure 11.26).

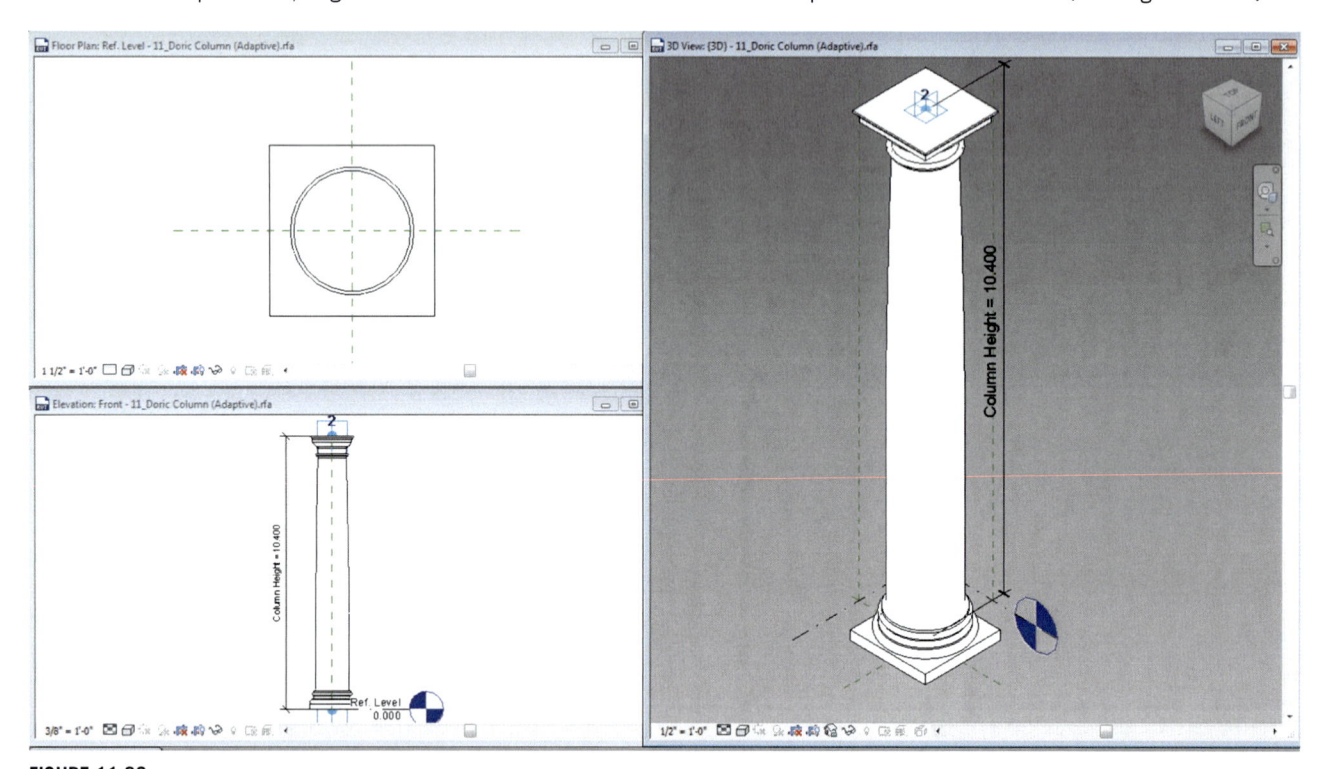

FIGURE 11.26

Configure the location and height of the nested column family

• Renaissance Revit •

⇨ Save the file.

> **CATCH UP!** You can open a file completed to this point named: *11_Doric Column (Adaptive).rfa*.

Be sure that you still have the *Colonnade (Divide and Repeat)* file open in the background, or open the catch-up file.

12. On the ribbon, click the Load into Project button.

On the Status Bar you will see the message: "Click to place a point." This is asking you to click point 1 of the adaptive component we just loaded.

13. Snap directly to one of the nodes on the bottom circle. (Use SX if necessary to ensure you snap).

On the Status Bar the prompt will repeat, this is point 2. You will not see the column appear onscreen until you click the second point.

⇨ Snap to the point directly above the previous one on the upper circle.

14. Cancel the command. Select the column and click the Repeat button (See Figure 11.27).

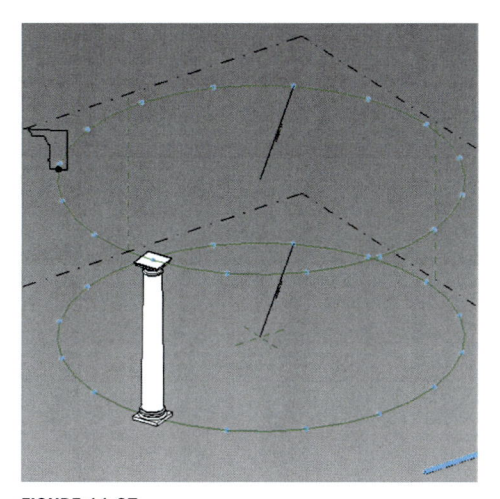

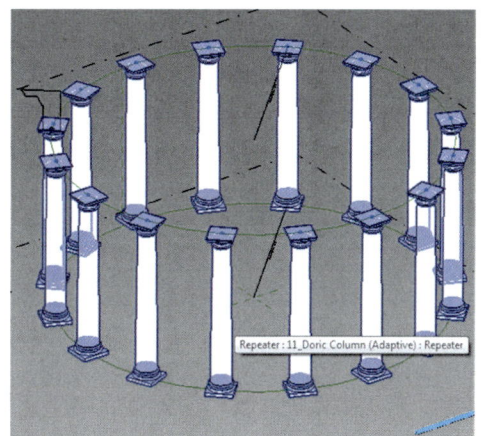

FIGURE 11.27
Complete the curved colonnade

15. Press TAB to select the circle reference line at the top (not the divided path). Hold down the CTRL key and also select the entablature shape already in the file.
16. Create Form.

I think that is enough to give you the idea of how the tool behaves. I must say that I had to cheat a little. Nesting a column family into an adaptive component gave a little bit of trouble. Columns are associated with levels but in adaptive families the adaptive points are the hosts. So the height was flexing a little odd. When I preset the height to 10.4 in the adaptive family and then loaded in, it seems to behave betters, but it is unfortunate that I had to resort to that.

> **CATCH UP!** You can open a file completed to this point named: *11_Colonnade (Divide and Repeat).rfa*.

I will leave the triglyphs and mutules to you as an additional exercise. The strategy would be similar. You might need to create another circle to host to second point in the triglyph family.

• Creating Classical Architecture with Modern Software •

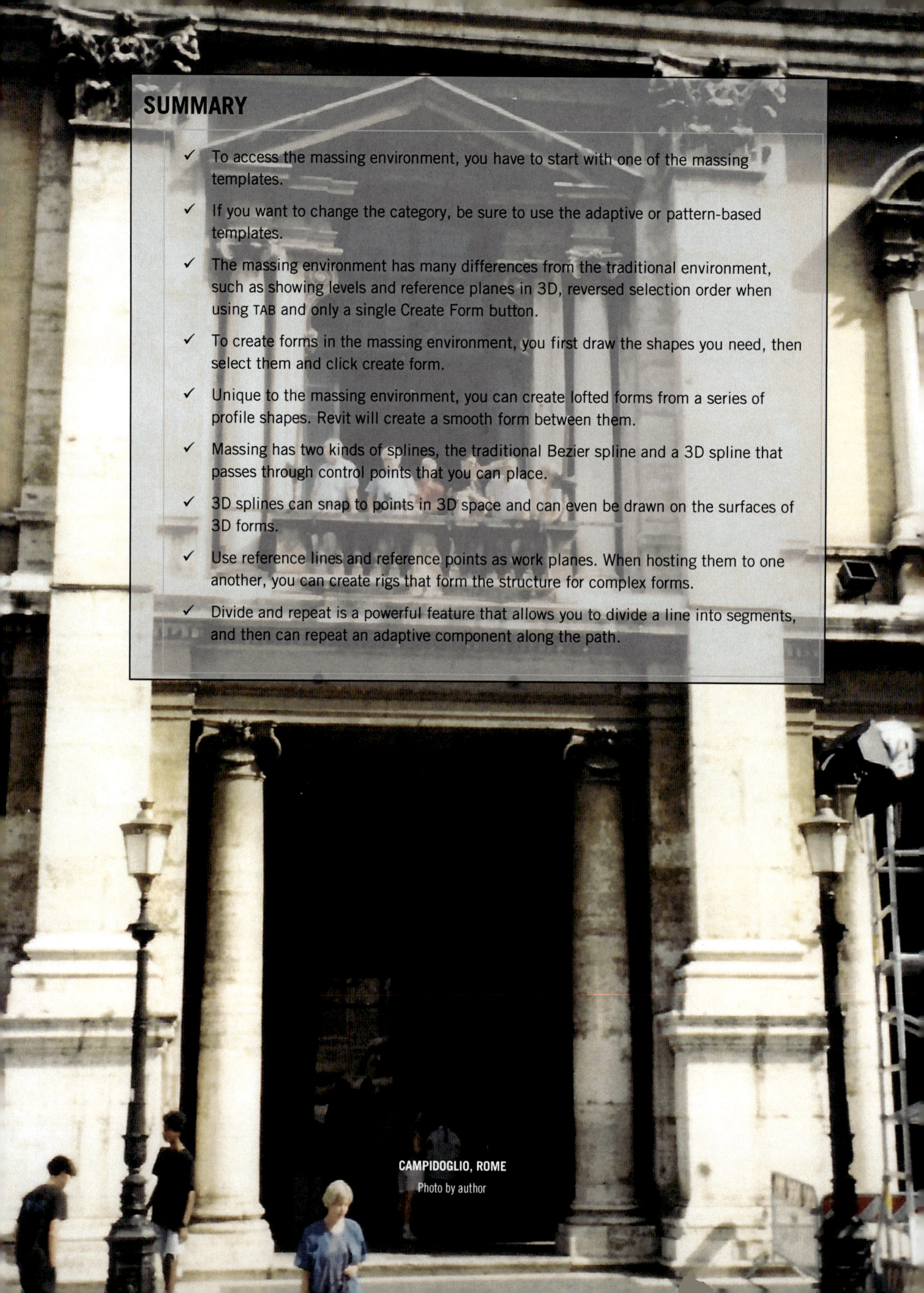

SUMMARY

- ✓ To access the massing environment, you have to start with one of the massing templates.

- ✓ If you want to change the category, be sure to use the adaptive or pattern-based templates.

- ✓ The massing environment has many differences from the traditional environment, such as showing levels and reference planes in 3D, reversed selection order when using TAB and only a single Create Form button.

- ✓ To create forms in the massing environment, you first draw the shapes you need, then select them and click create form.

- ✓ Unique to the massing environment, you can create lofted forms from a series of profile shapes. Revit will create a smooth form between them.

- ✓ Massing has two kinds of splines, the traditional Bezier spline and a 3D spline that passes through control points that you can place.

- ✓ 3D splines can snap to points in 3D space and can even be drawn on the surfaces of 3D forms.

- ✓ Use reference lines and reference points as work planes. When hosting them to one another, you can create rigs that form the structure for complex forms.

- ✓ Divide and repeat is a powerful feature that allows you to divide a line into segments, and then can repeat an adaptive component along the path.

CAMPIDOGLIO, ROME
Photo by author

Chapter 12
The Column Shaft

INTRODUCTION

This may come as a surprise to you, but of all the items I will demonstrate in this book, one of the most challenging modeling tasks for me has actually proven to be the shaft of the column. That's right, it was more difficult than modeling the Corinthian capital in the next chapter! In just the two pages of discussion that Chitham devotes to the column shaft and its diminution (Chitham 1985, 2005, 163-165), I found enough variation to fill several chapters of examples on the subject. If I broaden the look to the many other source materials available, volumes could be filled on just this topic. Remembering that classical architecture is a language and not a rigid prescription, it is important to follow the rules and guidelines adopted by our predecessors but realize that many nuances are deliberately flexible. The English language can produce works of fiction, prose, poetry, legal briefs and even tweets. Each will be recognizable (with the possible exception of tweets) as English, but the style, content and emotion conveyed would vary widely. As such, when considering the column shaft, there are key items which have established rules, and then other considerations of equal importance which have only hints and guidelines or in some cases precedent only to guide us. With such issues in mind, we will use this chapter to explore the construction of the column shaft.

OBJECTIVES

The primary goal of this chapter is the creation of a shaft family that can be used in our column families. To achieve this goal we will explore the following topics:

- Shaft height proportions
- Entasis and Diminution
- Traditional and massing environment approaches
- Fluting

SHAFT HEIGHT PROPORTIONS

As noted in the introduction, there are many variations among the published masters and in the physical structures left by our predecessors. So just how tall should the column be? Well it is well known that the Tuscan is the shortest and the orders get progressively taller as we move through Doric, Ionic and then Corinthian/Composite. However, beyond this, there is actually quite a bit of variation. Chitham has a nice set of summary plates that show the disparities graphically (Chitham 1985, 2005, 53-55). In the Tuscan order, it seems that Serlio recommended an overall height of just 6 column diameters where Scamozzi and Perrault had it closer to 7 ½. Most of the other masters have the Tuscan at 7 diameters tall, which is the height that I have adopted in this book. For Doric, Vitruvius uses 7 diameters, while Palladio and Scamozzi use closer to 8 ½. Serlio shows the shortest Ionic at 8 diameters and nearly everyone else has it at or very near 9 diameters. For Corinthian we again see a lot of variation. Vitruvius uses 9 ½, Serlio only 9 and most others at or very close to 10. I will not be showing a composite order in this book, but there is almost universal agreement on 10 diameters with Scamozzi opting for a slightly shorter 9 ¾.

So with all this variation among the masters, how do we decide what height to use? Well, it honestly depends on the context and other criteria that inform your design. What all masters do agree upon is that the proportions of the order overall should be derived from the size of the diameter as measured at the base. This is the standard that I have adopted throughout this book. All things being equal, if the proportions of the order are derived from the base diameter, then even if you vary the height of the column, the overall proportions should still feel correct. But this is exactly the point. The *rules* are not as rigid as some assume. There is plenty of room for interpretation and personal style.

For this book, I have adopted the same proportions advocated by Chitham. I used 7 diameters for Tuscan, 8 diameters for Doric, 9 diameters for Ionic and in the next chapter will use 10 for Corinthian. I would like to say that I tried all the variations noted above before deciding on my values. I must admit however that this is not the case. Nice whole numbers appeal to me, so I adopted these numbers on much simpler grounds (see Figure 12.1).

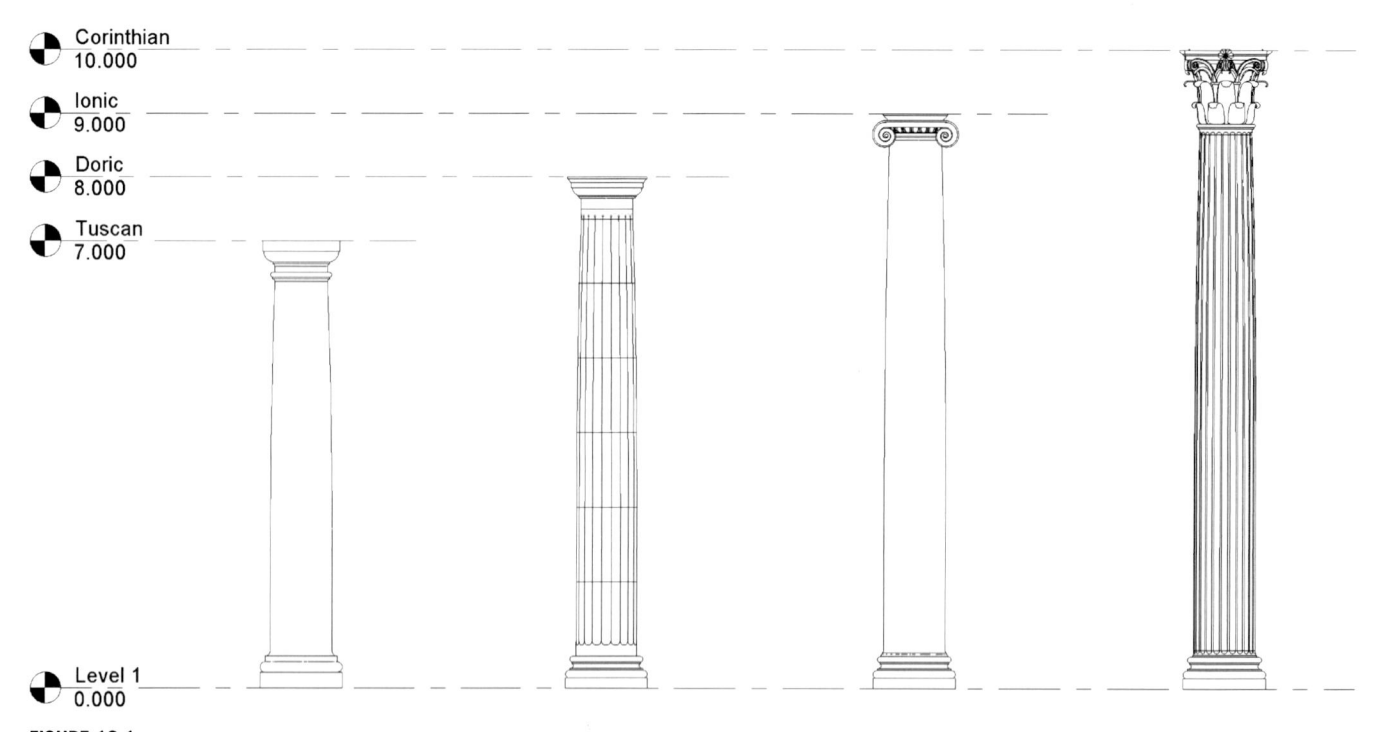

FIGURE 12.1
Progression of height for each of the orders built in this book

ENTASIS AND DIMINUTION

Column shafts are not the same diameter for their entire height. From the earliest examples we have, we can see that the height is diminished as it moves up. This is sometimes referred to as diminution and sometimes as entasis. Chitham has a very nice summary of the issue:

> "I have deliberately used the term diminution rather than entasis to describe the curved profile of the column. It is not at all clear whether the two terms are exactly synonymous. The term entasis is derived from the Greek enteino, to stretch, and means a swelling or convexity. This conveys the impression that the greatest diameter of a column is at a height some way above its base." (Chitham 1985, 2005, 164)

I like Chitham's rationale for the choice in term. And by his definition, most of the Renaissance examples use diminution rather than entasis: the first third of the column shaft is cylindrical; not diminished. The tapering or diminution occurs on the top two-thirds only. If entasis were employed, the column would taper out slightly to some point above the base where maximum thickness is achieved, and then it would taper back for the remainder to a size smaller than the base diameter. It is not clear to me from my research if this point of maximum thickness would be actually larger than the base diameter or if it would actually become the new module. It seems to me that it would have to be larger, otherwise it would be very difficult to establish the actual module with any degree of accuracy.

By Chitham's definition, I will be using diminution in my examples: specifically, the first third of the height is undiminished and then the column shaft diminishes for the top two-thirds. While I agree with Chitham that it is not clear that the terms entasis and diminution are interchangeable, that does not stop people from frequently using them interchangeably. I see both terms used, but more often it is entasis that is used in conversation, or in print to refer to diminishing column thickness. If you look up diminution in an online dictionary, the definition will refer in very general terms to the diminishing effect but the definition does not cite any particular domain. The definition can certainly can be applied to columns, but does not mention them specifically. Entasis on the other hand is almost always associated with Architecture exclusively. So while it may be true that entasis implies a subtlety that is not always present in the design of the column's particular tapering, I have no issue using either term to convey the effect. In fact, while I might use diminution at times in the text in an attempt to be slightly more precise in my choice of terms, if you see me speaking in person, don't be surprised to hear me favor entasis. (I tend to stumble on the pronunciation of "diminution;" but I have no trouble pronouncing entasis).

BUILD A SMOOTH SHAFT WITH ELLIPTICAL ENTASIS

Back in Chapter 6 we built a smooth shaft for the Tuscan column and have reused this in the lessons that followed. If you worked through that chapter and specifically the "Create the Shaft as a Sweep" topic, you may recall that we used an arc to represent the column's entasis profile. As I noted at that time, the use of an arc is almost imperceptibly close to actual curve that ought to be plotted. As you might expect, if you review the various masters and treatises you will find a few ways to plot the proper entasis. The method outlined by Chitham (and used by many other Renaissance authorities) divides the top two thirds of the shaft into equal parts; you can choose any number, I have typically used 4 or sometimes 6. Next, you draw a semicircle at the base and project a line down from the top at the narrowest point. Chitham notes that most authorities diminish the column 1/6th of its diameter. This would be about 0.840. Chitham goes with 0.850 and I have adopted this value as well. Where this vertical line meets the circle, we get an arc. Divide this arc into the same number of parts. Finally, you project lines from these points on the circle until they intersect the horizontal lines divided above. This gives you the points through which to pass your curve (See Figure 12.2).

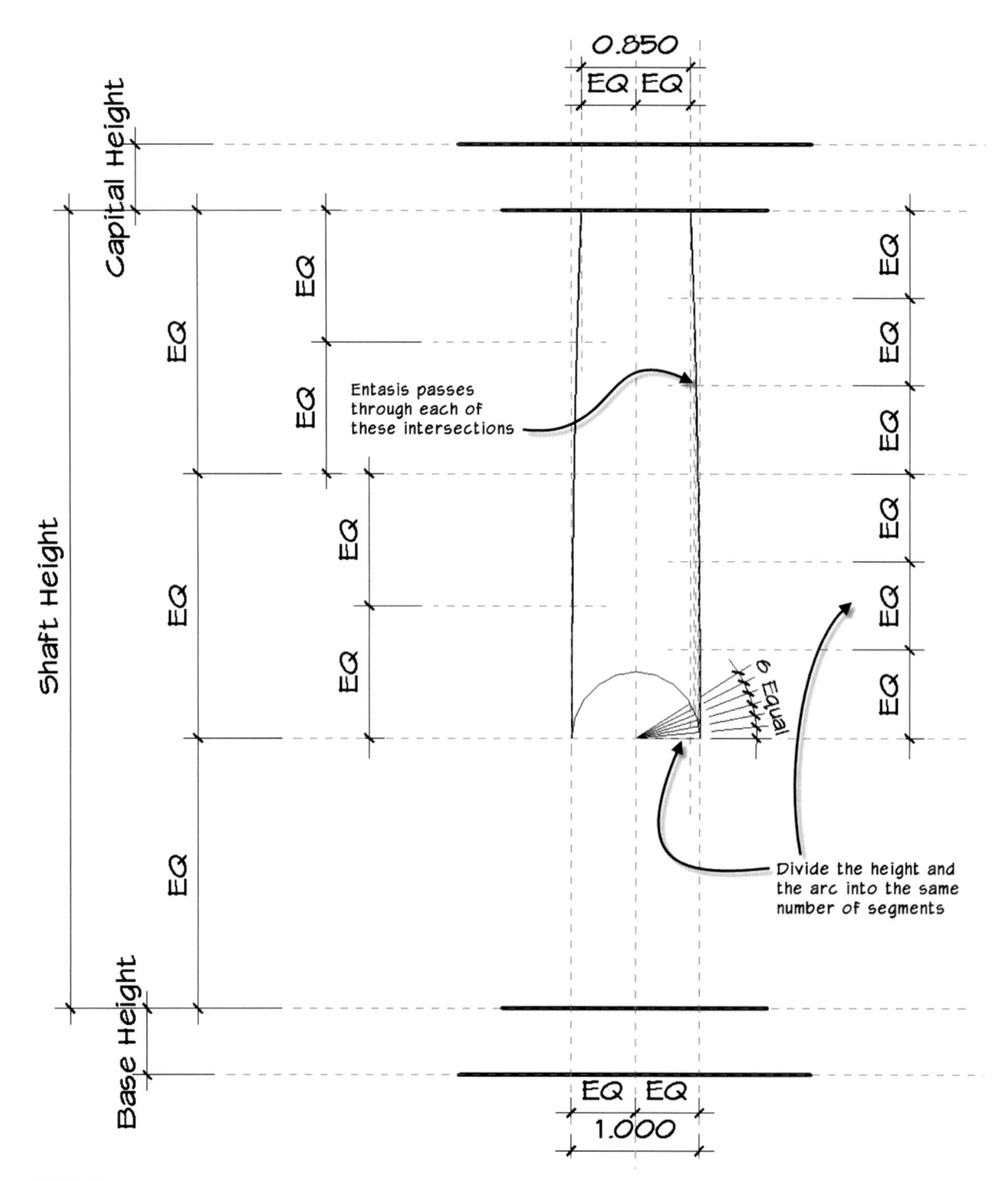

FIGURE 12.2

Constructing the shaft entasis profile curve

The arc we used in Chapter 6 would come very close to these points. Another option is to use a spline. A spline is a nice option because you can make as many control points as you need to make the shape of the spline intersect at the required points. We also saw that locking the two open ends of the spline will maintain the shape of the curve when you flex. So this can be quite effective. However, in working on the content as I was building the layout described above, it occurred to me that if you take the divided circle and imagine stretching it up vertically, you would be transforming the circle into an ellipse and the point divisions on the arc portion would continue to line up with your vertical divisions. If you stretch it far enough, you end up with a very tall and thin ellipse. This basically means that the curve profile of the entasis is actually an elliptical arc. So as an alternative to the approach we took in Chapter 6, I am going to present the steps required to build the elliptical profile here. You can also try the spline approach as an exercise on your own if you prefer.

To build an ellipse in Revit, you need to know its center and the length of each axis. For an elliptical arc, you basically need just the axis lengths. Revit determines the center automatically. So the challenge is to take the construction technique recommended by Chitham and other authorities (for hand drafting the entasis curve) and convert this to the inputs that Revit requires to create an accurate ellipse. Figure 12.3 shows a compressed diagram (I shortened it vertically) to illustrate the concepts and what inputs are needed.

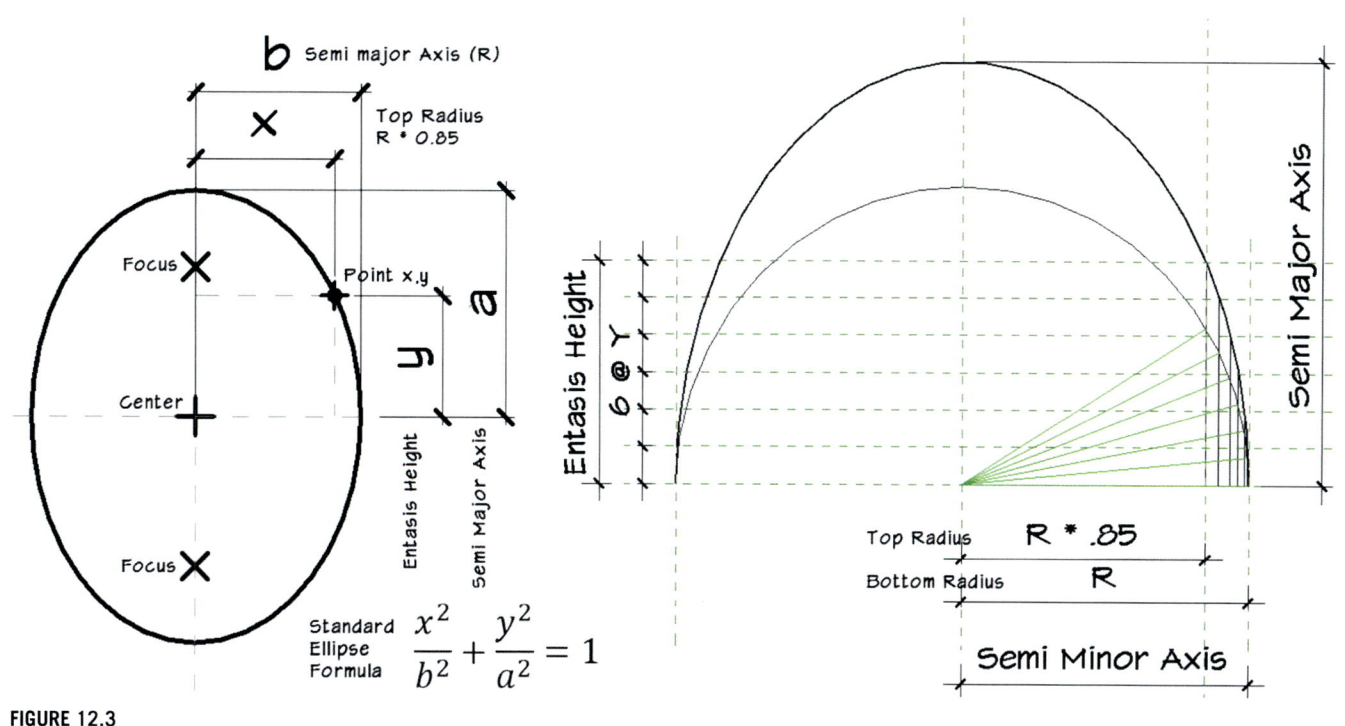

FIGURE 12.3

Applying the standard formula for an ellipse to the entasis and our known variables

I spent a lot of time trying to figure out the formula. (Maybe a little too much in retrospect). I owe thanks to many resources online (which are listed in the bibliography) and to Desirée Mackey (D. Mackey 2013) who helped me personally with the formula. The basic concept is that there is a standard mathematical formula for an ellipse. It has four inputs typically labeled a, b, x and y. The ratio of the squares of these is always constant and equal to one:

$$\frac{x^2}{b^2} + \frac{y^2}{a^2} = 1$$

On the left side of the figure I have drawn a standard ellipse diagram and labeled each part. The two axes typically get assigned the variables a and b. Some point on the ellipse is labeled as point x,y. On the right side, I have taken the diagram from Figure 12.2 and compressed it vertically to make it easier to comprehend. In our case, we have three of the required values in the formula, so we can input them into the standard formula and determine the missing value.

The total of the height of the six divisions (I chose 6, but it can be any value you choose) is the height of the top two thirds of the shaft minus any upper moldings. I called this Entasis Height. This is the y value in the standard formula. Each division is shown with a horizontal reference plane. The bottom radius: R is half of our column base (Base Diameter / 2). The top radius is 0.850 times this number (the radius at the top of the shaft minus any moldings). This gives us the b and x in our ellipse formula. You can see the diagonal lines dividing the arc equally and how these project up to intersect the ellipse at the horizontal divisions.

So our missing variable is a; the Semi Major Axis. This is required to draw the ellipse in Revit, so we must figure out what this value is in order to draw the proper ellipse. Simply input what we know into the formula and then solve for: a.

$$a = \sqrt{\frac{y^2}{1 - \frac{x^2}{b^2}}}$$

Or to put that in Revit format:

sqrt((Entasis Total ^ 2) / (1 - (Top Radius ^ 2) / (Base Radius ^ 2)))

We will need to define the parameters within the formula as well and add a reference plane for the semi major axis.

1. From the *Chapter12* folder, open the file named: *Corinthian Shaft_Start.rfa*.

   The *Front* elevation view will open. Minimize the view.

2. On the Project Browser, expand *Families > Profiles* and then right-click on *Corinthian Shaft Profile_Start* and choose **Edit**.

   ⇨ Type: WT to tile the window.

   Since there is only one window, it makes this window full screen, while leaving the original elevation window minimized.

This is a copy of the profile used for the other orders with the numbers slightly adjusted for Corinthian. It is using the arc for entasis like the others. We will delete this, create some parameters with the appropriate formulas and then draw the elliptical arc.

3. Delete the large arc.

4. Open the "Family Types" dialog and add the parameters shown in Table 12.1.

   They are all Length parameters, they should all be Type parameters and group them under Constraints.

> **Note:** Input Semi Major Axis last. Be sure all of the other parameters are in place with their formulas working before you complete Semi Major Axis. The numbers in the Value column are for your information. When you fill in the formulas, these values should automatically appear.

TABLE 12.1

Parameter	Value	Type of Parameter
Top Radius	0.425	Top Diameter / 2
Top Minus	0.105	Astragal Torus + Astragal Fillet + Transition Top
Semi Major Axis	10.368	sqrt((Entasis Total ^ 2) / (1 - (Top Radius ^ 2) / (Base Radius ^ 2)))
Entasis Total	5.462	(Shaft Height * 2 / 3) - Top Minus
Base Radius	0.500	Base Diameter / 2

There is already a Top Diameter parameter in this family. To get the Top Radius we simply half that. Likewise for the Base Radius, we half the Base Diameter. This gives us our x and b values. To calculate the Entasis Height (y in the ellipse formula), I created two separate parameters, but it is possible to merge all of this into a single formula if you prefer. Top Minus totals all of the moldings at the top of the shaft. This is subtracted from 2/3 of the shaft height (See Figure 12.4).

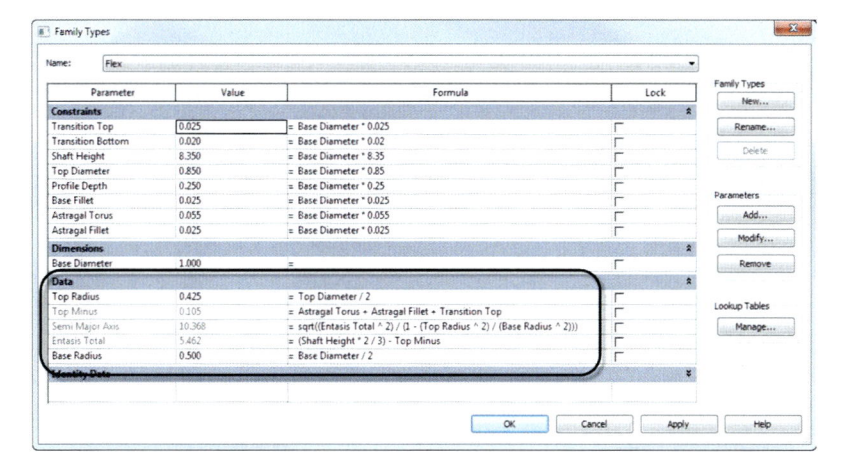

FIGURE 12.4
Create the parameters and their formulas

After inputting the others, input Semi Major Axis. It is a long and complex formula, so type it carefully. To square a value in Revit, you raise it to the power of 2. This is done with the carrot (^) symbol. You can use this symbol to raise to any power. So, 4^2 is four squared. 4 ^5 is four to the fifth power. You can substitute either number for a parameter so that M ^ N power is also easy to achieve (where M and N are parameter names). To take the square root, type: **sqrt()** and input the value in the parenthesis.

After creating the parameters and formulas, the values should match the table.

5. Click OK to dismiss "Family Types."

6. Zoom out and add a horizontal reference plane above the profile a few units away.

⇨ Add a dimension between this new reference plane and the first third (where the entasis begins).

⇨ Label it with the Semi Major Axis parameter (See Figure 12.5).

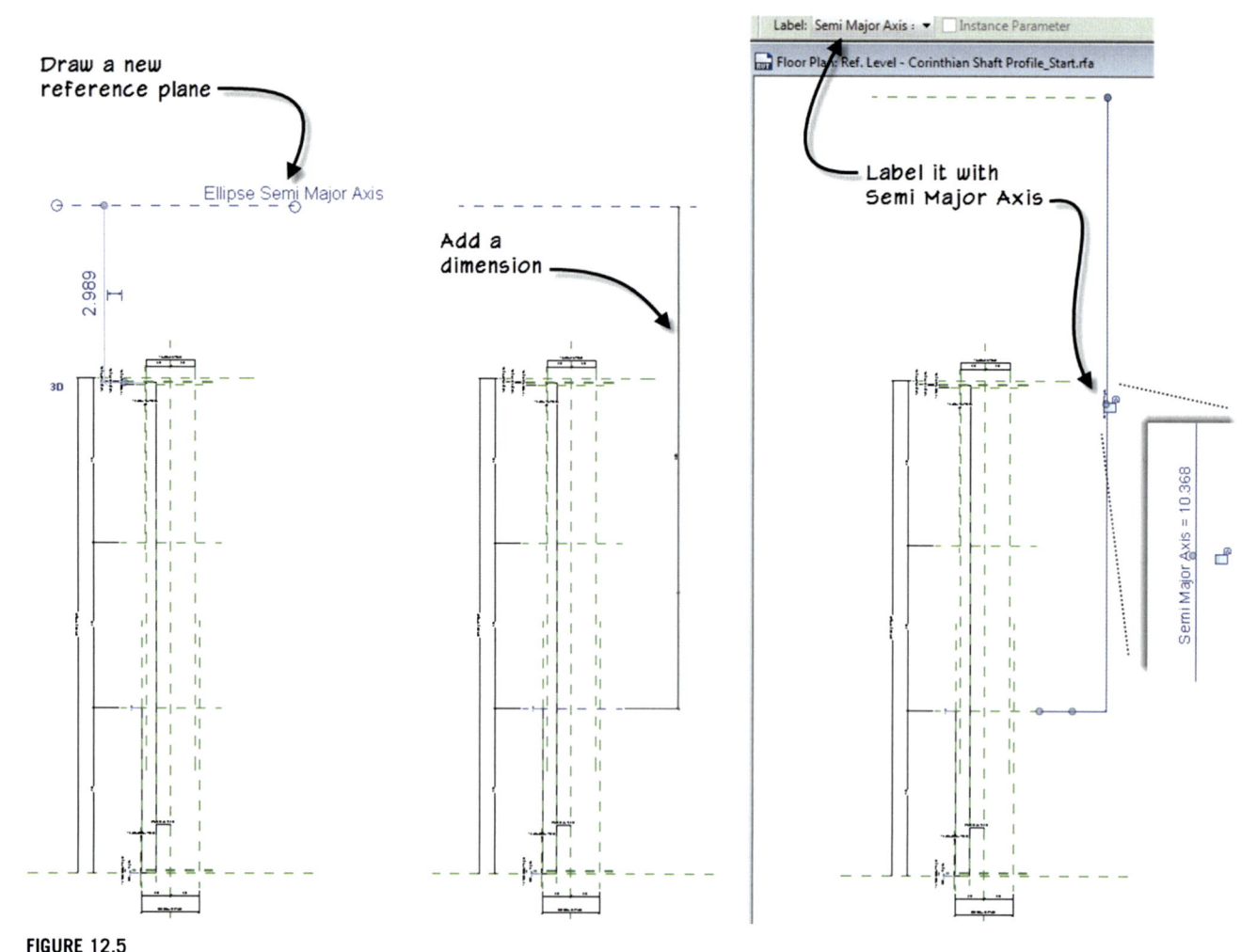

FIGURE 12.5
Add a reference plane and label it with the Semi Major Axis parameter

We are now ready to draw the ellipse.

7. On the Create tab, click the Line button. Choose the Partial Ellipse icon.

   ⇨ Snap the first two points across the width of the shaft profile snapping to the intersections of the reference planes (see the left side of Figure 12.6).

   ⇨ Snap the long axis to the horizontal reference plane at the top (Semi Major Axis).

   ⇨ Click the "Make this temporary dimension permanent" icon in both directions (see the middle of Figure 12.6).

8. Using the shape handle at the end on the right side of the elliptical arc, drag it around (over the top) and release close to the top of the shaft (see the right side of Figure 12.6).

   ⇨ Zoom in and stretch the grip handle again to snap it precisiely to the intersection of the reference planes named: H2 and Top Left (it should snap right to the endpoint fo the small arc at the transition top)

9. Label the two dimensions created in the previous step.

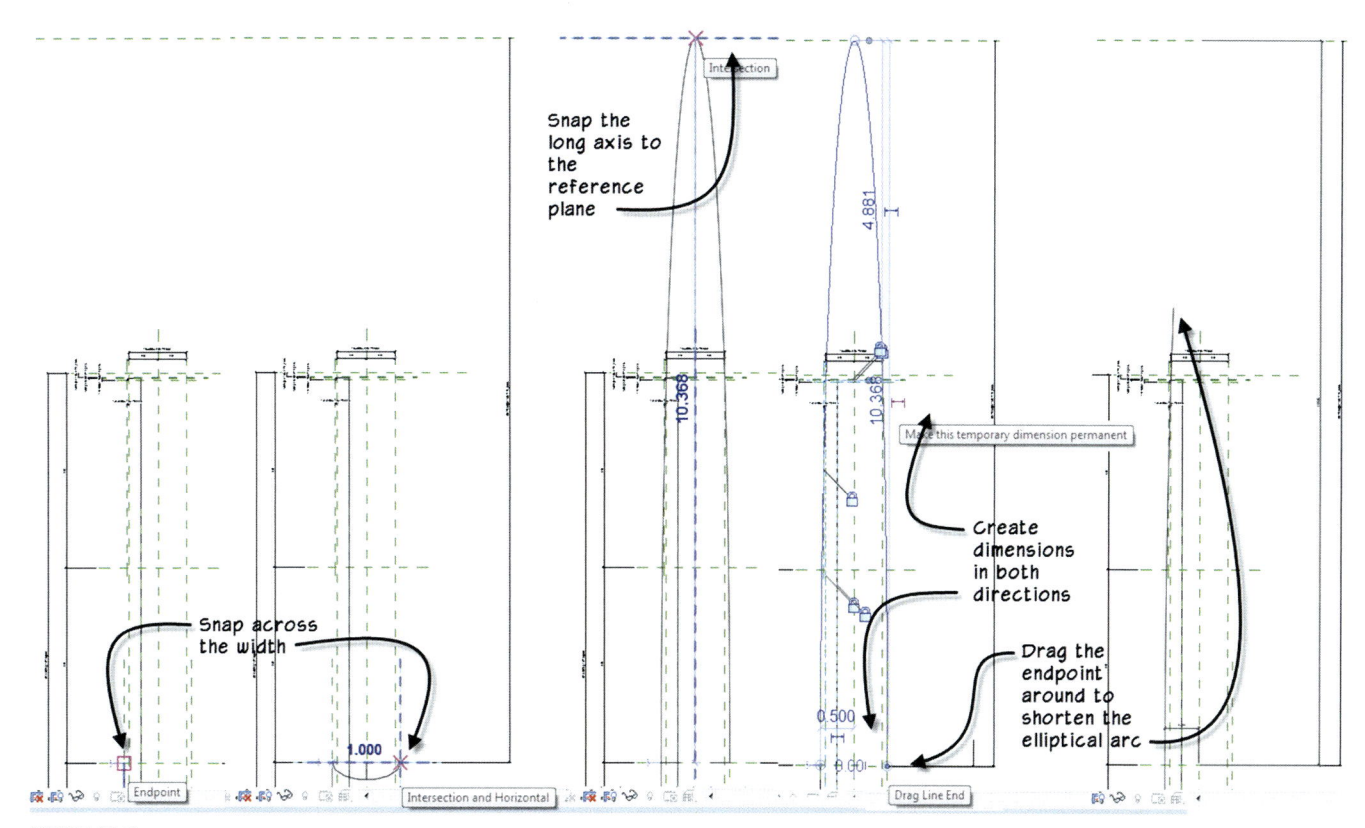

FIGURE 12.6

Draw the elliptical arc, dimension it and then adjust the length

> ⇨ Label the long vertical dimension on the ellipse with the **Semi Major Axis** parameter.
>
> ⇨ Label the short horizontal dimension with the **Base Radius** parameter.

10. Align and lock the enpoints at both ends of the ellipse to the reference planes in both directions.

> **CATCH UP!** You can open a file completed to this point named: *12_Corinthian Shaft Profile.rvt*.

11. Click Load into Project and overwirte the existing.

You will see a very slight change in the profile of the shaft. If you like, you can rename the profile on Project Browser to remove the "_Start" suffix.

12. Flex the family and then save and close the file.

> **CATCH UP!** You can open a file completed to this point named: *12_Corinthian Shaft.rfa*.

FLUTING IN THE TRADITIONAL FAMILY EDITOR

We already successfully created a smooth column shaft family in earlier chapters. Adding fluting is one of the aspects of the column shaft which really makes it challenging to model. There is much variation in fluting column shafts. These variations occur across the various orders and also when comparing ancient examples to Renaissance ones. Starting with the flute cross section shape, the Tuscan order is not fluted. Its shafts are always smooth. The Doric order often uses a 60° arc, has only 20 channels around the circumference and the channels butt right up against one another without a fillet in between. This is common in ancient Greek examples and sometimes in Renaissance examples. Ionic and Corinthian examples have a cross section that looks more like a gear. The flute cross section is a half-circle and there is a fillet in between each flute. Furthermore, there are typically 24 channels around the circumference in Ionic and Corinthian (see Figure 12.7). Some examples of Doric also use the half-round channels with fillet in between. Palladio advocates this type of fluting on the Doric.

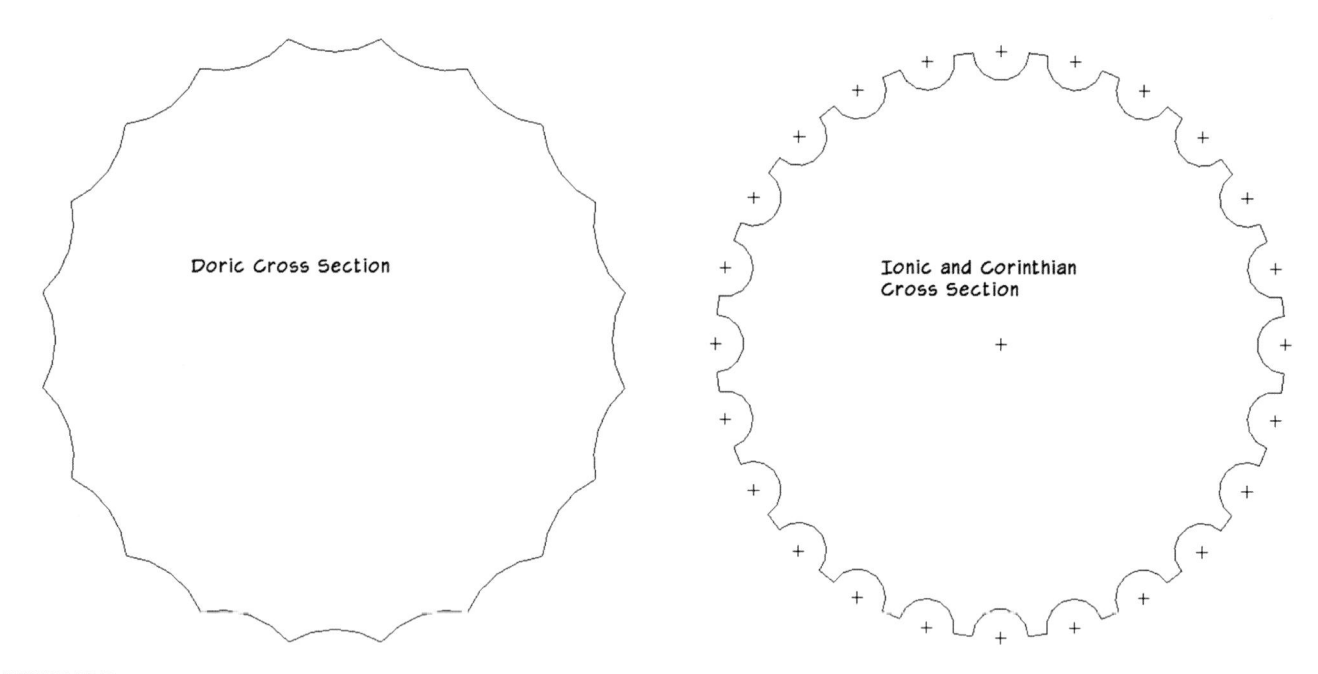

FIGURE 12.7

Fluting shape and quantity varies among the different orders

Fluting adds a level of sophistication to the look of a column but introduces a good deal of complexity when considering how to model it. Whether you are attempting to build the Doric variation or the Ionic/Corinthian one, the challenge is that you have curvature in three directions. Recall our discussions on the challenges of controlling, constraining and flexing curves back in Chapter 4. Now add curvature in the third dimension and you end up with much more complicated modeling. I have developed a few different approaches which I will showcase in the lessons here. We will look at examples of the Doric and also of the Ionic/Corinthian. Our explorations will span both the traditional and massing family editor environments.

FLUTED DORIC SHAFT (GREEK INSPIRED)

For the first example, we will look at a simple approach in the traditional family editor. The Doric order originated in ancient Greece and was quite a bit different than the Roman and Renaissance variants that came after it. For one, the Greek Doric did not have a base. The shaft simply came right to the ground. The proportions were also different with the height being shorter and therefore the column shaft being thicker overall. The entasis was typically more pronounced as well. For this example, we will use a flexible profile for the cross-section of the column and use it to create several stacked swept blends. When you look at photos of the old ruins you often see sections of the columns that have collapsed and you can see that they were created as a series of cylinders stacked up on top of each other. This approach will invoke that kind of look and feel.

Let's start by opening the starting profile family. We have seen plenty of examples of profiles that contain multiple curves and along the way have learned several techniques to help ensure that they flex properly. The cross-section of the Doric shaft has 20 separate arcs. This takes several reference planes but fortunately only a handful of formulas. This is because the shape is symmetrical about both axes and we can reuse the same five parameters a total of four times.

1. From the *Chapter12* folder, open the file named: *Doric Channels Profile_Start.rfa*.

The file was created from our profile seed family. By now you should be comfortable with adding reference planes, parameters and basic formulas, so I have completed several preliminary steps already. The reference planes in the file are all named from the center outward and use labeled dimensions with similar names. The first four arcs are already in the file as well.

I had to build this file at least a few times before I got to flex successfully. It seems that the order in which you add geometry and constraints can make a difference and Revit seems to establish some subtle difference in the way things flex based on the order they were added. So the sequence in which you add the remaining arcs is important.

The trick is to avoid any ambiguity wherever possible. So you can see that I started with the four arcs at the 90° positions. These are constrained carefully. Next we'll add the arcs near the 45° marks and constrain them. Finally we'll fill in the remaining arcs and constrain whatever points remain. In this way, we ensure that we are making our intent clear to Revit. In other words, if you build them in sequence next to each other, Revit may constrain to the neghboring arc, or it may constrain to the reference planes. It is hard to know. By building them separated from each other as much as possible we avoid much of the ambiguity.

You will also notice that instead of locking the center point this time, I have instead added a dimension for the arc angle. This dimension appears when you select the arc and then you click the "Make this temporary dimension permanent" icon. Those dimensions are also locked, which gives a similar result to locking the center points. The only reason that I did not lock the centers is that I feel there are already several reference planes. To lock the centers would require several more as well as many more parameters.

2. Select the lowest arc and its arc dimension.

3. On the ribbon, click the Rotate tool.

⇨ On the Options Bar, click the Place button (next to "Center of Rotation") or press the SPACEBAR.

⇨ Snap to the intersection of the two center reference planes for the center of rotation.

⇨ On the Options Bar, check the Copy checkbox. In the Angle field, input: **36** and then press ENTER (see Figure 12.8).

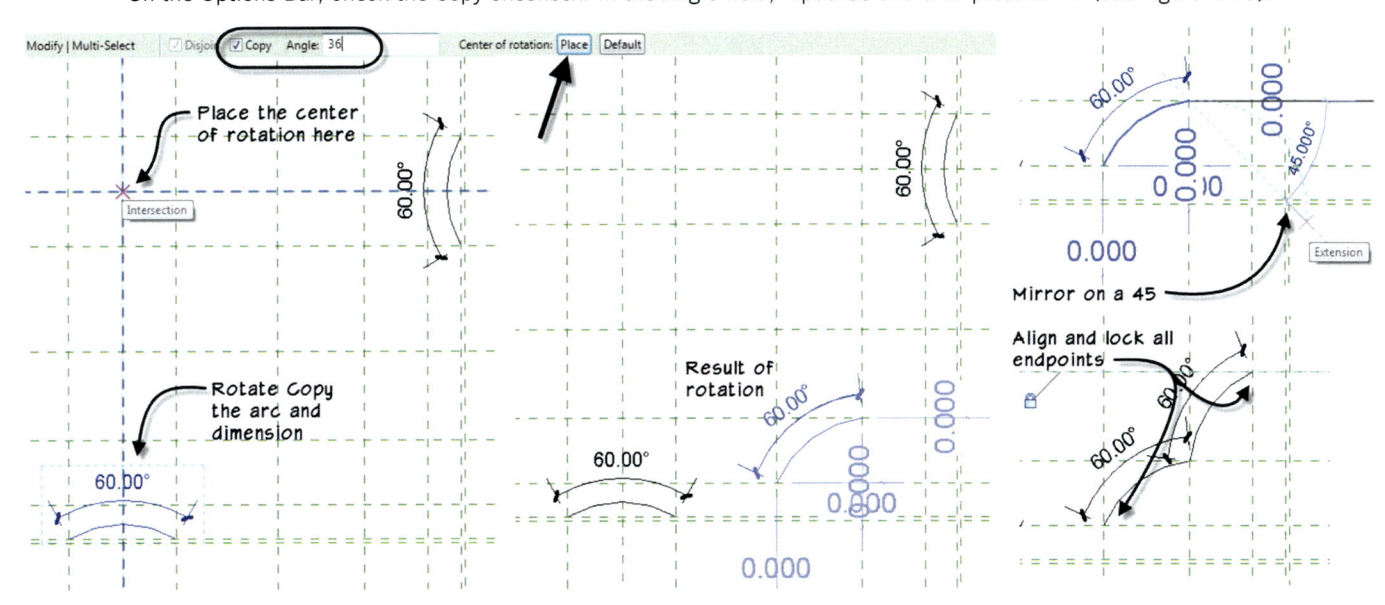

FIGURE 12.8
Rotate copy and mirror to create two more arcs. Align and lock their endpoints

Several Automatic Sketch Dimensions will appear. Before we align and lock them, make another copy with the mirror command. The elements you just copied should still be selected.

• *Creating Classical Architecture with Modern Software* •

4. With the two new elements still selected, mirror them along a 45° line.

5. Align and lock all of the endpoints of the two arcs in both directions (see the right side of Figure 12.8).

6. Select these two new arcs and their dimensions and mirror them up to the top and then again over to the left (make three copies for a total of four sets of arcs on the 45° lines).

7. Align and lock all of the endpoints in both directions (cancel any "overconstrained" warnings) (see Figure 12.9).

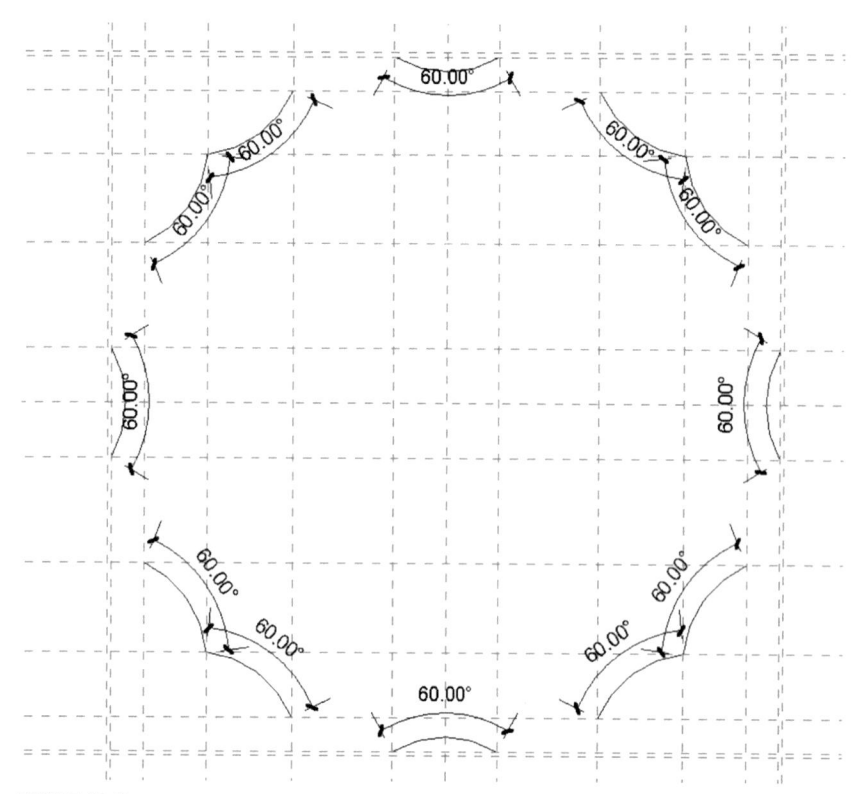

FIGURE 12.9

Mirror the two 45° arcs to each of the other positions

> **CATCH UP!** You can open a file completed to this point named: *12_Doric Channels Profile_A.rfa*.

8. Open the "Family Types" dialog.

   ⇨ Go through each of the named types from the drop-down at the top. Apply after each choice.

   ⇨ When finished, return to the type named: **Bottom** and then click OK.

9. Select the lowest arc and its dimension again and then repeat the rotate process from above.

   Remember to check Copy and Pick your center point. The rotation angle is 18°.

10. Mirror the new copies in each direction to fill in all of the missing arcs (eight total).

11. Align and lock any remaining unconstrained points. (You may get several "This would overconstrain the sketch" warnings, just click OK and keep moving all the way around until you have locked everything).

12. Flex the file and then save.

> **CATCH UP!** You can open a file completed to this point named: *12_Doric Channels Profile.rfa*.

CREATE STACKED SWEPT BLENDS

The family has five types: Bottom, Top and Entasis 1 through 3. Entasis 1 through 3 mark three intermediate points along the tapered part of the shaft. The amount of taper was calculated using the same ellipse formula we discussed

• Renaissance Revit •

above. In the images above, I divided the shaft into six parts, but for this file I used only four divisions. More divisions would make a more accurate profile, but four will certainly be enough. The final step is to create a series of stacked forms, each with a slightly different taper.

1. From the *Chapter12* folder, open the file named: *Doric Column (Greek Inspired)_Start.rfa*.

Early Greek Doric columns had shorter shafts and no bases. The capital also varies pretty considerably from its Roman and Renaissance decendants. I have simply provided the capital completed already. It is made from a simple extrusion and a sweep. You are welcome to edit this family to explore it. The shaft family already in the file is obviously incomplete. Let's open it and edit it.

2. Select the shaft onscreen. On the Modify | Generic Models tab, click the Edit Family button.

The shaft will be made from a collection of sweeps and swept blends stacked on top of each other. There are six total. The first two are sweeps because the first third of the shaft is not tapered in this example. The next four are swept blends. The strategy is quite simple. The sweeps at the bottom use the *Doric Channels Profile:Bottom* type. The first swept blend uses this same type for its bottom and then the *Entasis 1* type for its top. The next one uses *Entasis 1* for the base and *Entasis 2* for the top and so on ending with the *Top* profile. To save some effort, I have already loaded the *Doric Channels Profile* family and built the first sweep and swept blend. I have also already linked up the Base Diameter parameter for each of the types.

> **Note:** if you recall our discussion about entasis earlier, sometimes Greek columns actually taper both top and bottom making them bludge slightly at the middle. If you wanted to express the shaft this way, you could use a swept blend in place of the lower sweep.

3. Select the sweep at the bottom.

⇨ On the ribbon, click Edit Sweep.

⇨ Click the Select Profile button and then from the Profile list, choose **Doric Channels Profile:Bottom** (see Figure 12.10).

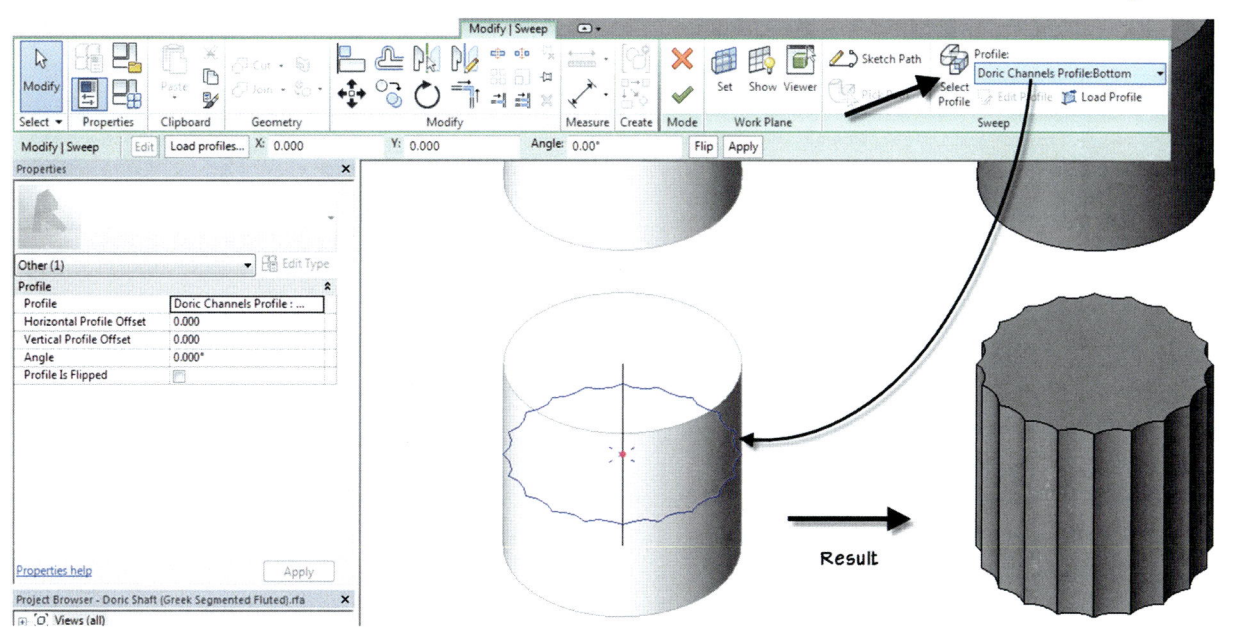

FIGURE 12.10
Change the profile of the sweep from sketch to the Doric Channels Profile

4. Click the Finish Edit Mode button.

354 | Chapter 12

5. Select the swept blend next and then on the ribbon, click Edit Swept Blend.
   ⇨ Click the Select Profile 1 button and then from the Profile list, choose **Doric Channels Profile:Bottom**.
   ⇨ Click the Select Profile 2 button and then from the Profile list, choose **Doric Channels Profile:Entasis 1**.
6. Click the Finish Edit Mode button.

The effect will be difficult to notice in 3D. Let's open an elevation to continue.

7. Open the *Front* elevation view.

The effect is still very slight. The multiplier used on the Entasis 1 profile is 0.991290. Entasis 2 and 3 will be more noticable at multipliers of: 0.964690 and 0.918644 respectively. And the Top is at 0.850 of course, so this will be the most noticable. You can check these multipliers from Project Browser. Exapnd *Families > Profiles > Doric Channels Profile* and then edit the Type Properties of each profile.and look at the Mult.

8. Select the sweep at the bottom and copy it up (snap to the reference planes to copy it precisely).
9. Repeat to copy the swept blend three times (see the left side of Figure 12.11).

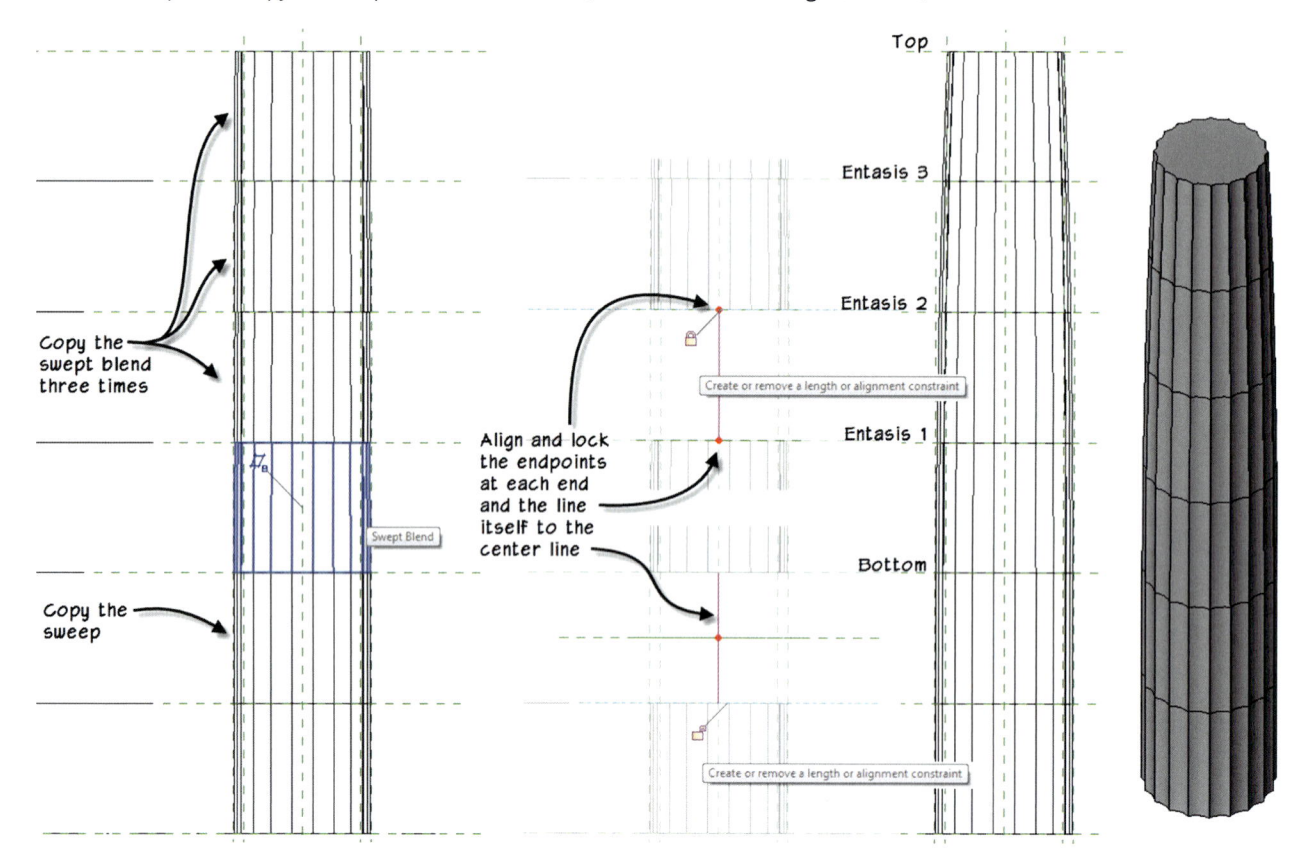

FIGURE 12.11
Copy the sweep and swept blends and then edit the paths and profiles

The copied sweep has the right profile, but we need to align and lock the path. The swept blend copies also need their paths aligned and locked and they need to have their profiles adjusted.

10. Select the copied sweep (second from the bottom) and click Edit Sweep.
    ⇨ Click Sketch Path and then align and lock the path to the Center (left/Right) reference plane.
    ⇨ Align and lock both endpoints to the horizontal reference planes as well.
    ⇨ Finish Edit Model

• Renaissance Revit •

11. Repeat this process on each swept blend. Align and lock the line itself to the Center (Left/Right) reference plane and align and lock the endpoints as well (see the middle of Figure 12.11).

12. Work your way up the shaft editing each swept blend. Change the profiles as indicated on the right side of Figure 12.11.

13. Save the file and then click the Load into Project button.

14. Overwrite the existing version (see Figure 12.12).

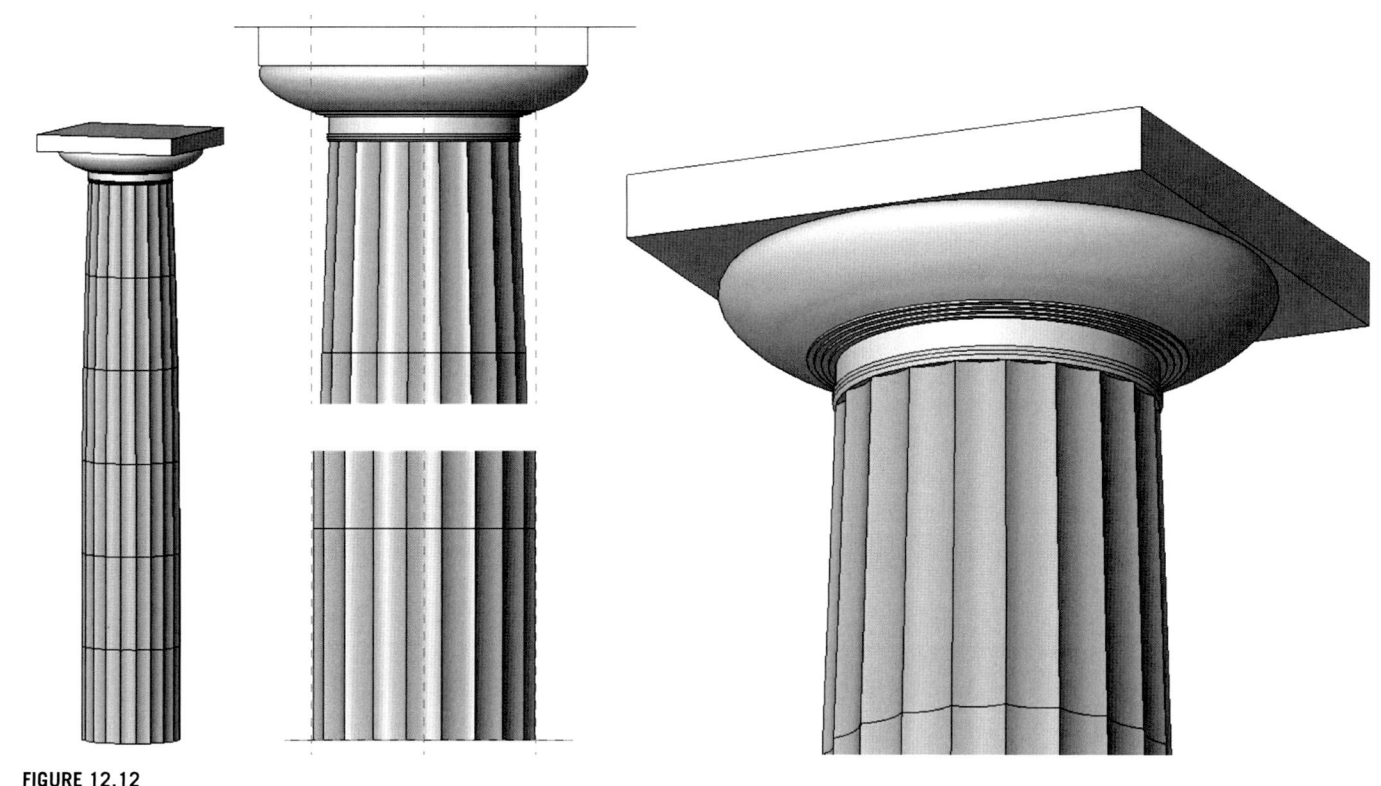

FIGURE 12.12

Complete the Greek inspired Doric

15. Save and close the file.

> **CATCH UP!** You can open a file completed to this point named: *12_Doric Column (Greek Inspired).rfa*.

There are two minor downsides to this approach. The swept blend does a straight line transition between the two profiles, so the profile edge is straight and not curved and we see the seams between each element. The seams are not that big of an issue when you consider that you can often see these seams in actual columns. So in a way, this is more accurate. To do a smoother transition between the profiles however, you must build the form as a loft in the massing environment instead. We'll look at an example of this below.

FLUTED DORIC SHAFT (PALLADIAN)

Let's look at another quick example with the stacked swept blends. This one will be closer to the shaft advocated by Palladio. Instead of the channels running the full height of the shaft, they will round out at the ends as if cut by a router blade. We can do this with a void form at the top and bottom sweeps.

1. From the *Chapter12* folder, open the file named: *Doric Shaft (Segmented Fluted)_Start.rfa*.

This file is nearly the same as our Greek version except that it is a little taller and the top and bottom elements are non-fluted sweeps with voids to cut the channels. If you zoom in on the bottom element, you see that the flutes round out at the bottom as the give way to a smooth shaft. Let's apply the same effect at the top (see Figure 12.13).

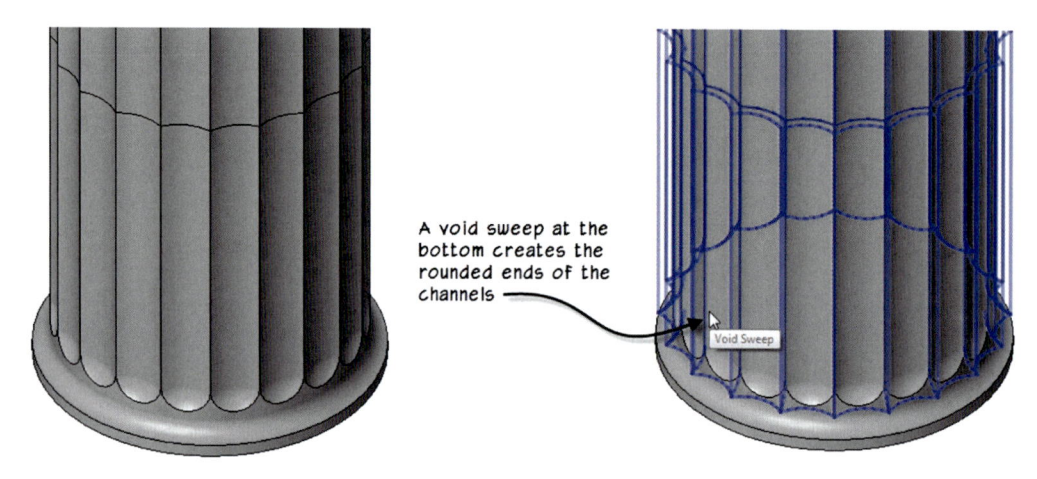

FIGURE 12.13
Rounding off the ends of the channels with a void sweep

Zoom in at the top of the shaft.

Notice that there is a small sweep here.

2. Select this small sweep and then on the View Control Bar, click the Temporary Hide/Isolate pop-up and choose: **Hide Element**. (You may have to do it twice since there is a joined extrusion here as well).

3. Create a new Void Sweep and use the Pick Path option.

   ⇨ Click on each of the arc edges at the top of the shaft (20 in all).

   ⇨ Click Finish Edit Mode.

4. From the Profile list, choose **Doric Channel Void Profile:Top**.

We have to rotate and flip the profile to make it align with the channels below it correctly.

5. On the Options Bar, click the Flip button and then type: **180** in the Angle field and click Apply (see Figure 12.14).

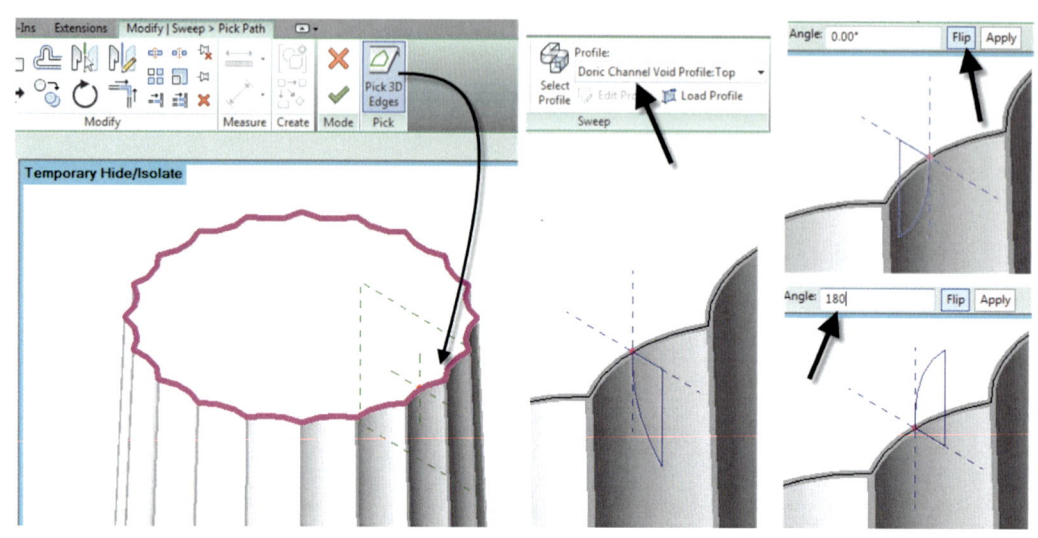

FIGURE 12.14
Create a new sweep void

6. Finish Edit Mode and then Reset Temporary Hide/Isolate.

I created the profile that we are using and included it in the file. If you like, you can select it on the Project browser and edit the family to study it. You may be wondering why we did not do the entire channel with a void sweep.

• Renaissance Revit •

The reason this does not work is the entasis. Given the tapering of the column shaft, it is very difficult to get a single void form that can run the entire height of the column shaft. I tried several attempts to make this work, but unfortunately I did not find a successful solution. The void does work for a segmented shaft like we have here, because the start and end are separate from each other and we are therefore avoiding the three-dimensional curve of the entasis by carving away from straight cylinders instead. This eliminates curvature in one direction.

> CATCH UP! You can open a file completed to this point named: *12_Doric Shaft (Segmented Fluted).rfa*.

USE THE FLUTED SHAFT AS THE FINE DETAIL VERSION

I have provided a copy of the Doric column family in the *Chapter12* folder. Open that to load this family in. We could simply do as we have in the previous exercises and reload the family replacing the shaft that is there. But in this case, I would like to consider an alternative. We have a coarse scale version in the file already. Let's leave the smooth shaft for medium and use the fluted version for fine.

1. Open the file named: *Doric Column_Start.rfa*.

   ⇨ Select the smooth shaft onscreen, copy it to the clipbard and then paste **Aligned to Same Place**.

   Ignore the warning and keep the new copy selected.

   ⇨ On the Properties palette, click the Edit Type button.

2. In the "Type Properties" dialog, at the top-right, click the Load button.

   ⇨ Browse to the Chapter12 folder and load the *12_Doric Shaft (Segmented Fluted).rfa* (or you can load the version you completed in the previous exercise).

3. Using the Associate Family Parameters buttons, link up Base Diameter and Shaft Material and then click OK.

4. Keep the shaft selected and on the Modify | Generic Models tab, click the Visibility Settings button.

5. Under Detail Levels, uncheck Medium and then click OK.

6. Use the tab key to select the smooth shaft and repeat. This time uncheck only Fine.

You may also want to open the plan view and align and lock the shaft to the center reference planes. This should not be completely necessary, but it doesn't hurt either. To flex the family, as before, open an elevation, select the upper level and change its height. Everything should flex accordingly.

7. Flex the family and then save and close the file when you are done.

I provided a completed version as a family file and in a sandbox project (see Figure 12.15).

• *Creating Classical Architecture with Modern Software* •

FIGURE 12.15

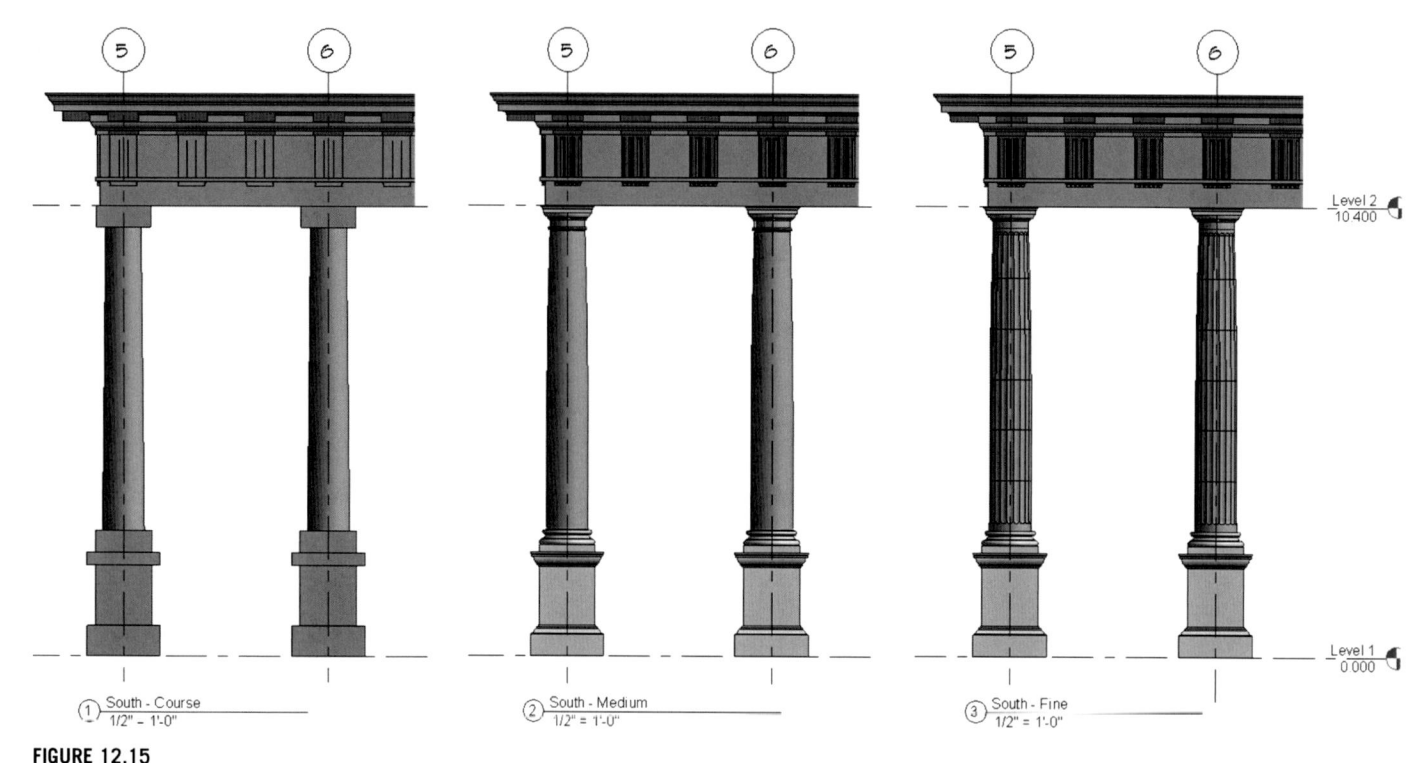

The completed Doric column with three levels of detail loaded into a sandbox file

> **CATCH UP!** You can open a file completed to this point named: *12_Doric Column.rfa* and *12_Sandbox_Colonnade_Doric.rvt*

FLUTING IN THE MASSING FAMILY EDITOR

If you want the profile of your shaft to be smooth and eliminate the seams between sections of the shaft as the profile changes, you can build it in the massing environment instead. We discussed many basic techniques for using the massing environment in the previous chapter. One of the features that the massing environment gives us is the ability to build a lofted form. A lofted form is like a blend with more than two profiles. In the massing environment, select two or more profiles, and optionally a path, and then create form. The result is that Revit will smoothly average the form using the profiles as cross sections. Think about the way an airplane wing or fuselage is created and you will have a pretty good idea about how this functions (see the "Lofting" topic in Chapter 11 for more information). In this topic, I am going to walk through the procedure that I used to create a smoothly lofted Corinthian shaft complete with fluting. I want to warn you ahead of time; the process is a bit intense. So be prepared for some tedious repetition in some of the steps.

UNDERSTANDING THE APPROACH

To complete the fluted Corinthian shaft, we need to build it in four discrete pieces (see Figure 12.16). The first thing we need is the profile of the column shaft. This will need to be parametric so that it can reduce in size as we move up the height of the column. The profile will be similar to the one that we built above for the Doric column, but we will create it as an adaptive component this time. Next we will need to load this into another adaptive family and use it to create our loft. This will be the main portion of the shaft. Then at the top and bottom where the fluting scoops out in a spherical shape (or like a plunge router bit), we need to build this separately as a solid (I used a sweep again, but a revolve would also work) and then a series of voids to cut out the negative portion. The voids really threw me for a loop. Given the compound curves involved, Revit was uncooperative with many of my early attempts. I have finally settled on an approach that works and gives a nice result. But there are a few compromises as you will see.

FIGURE 12.16

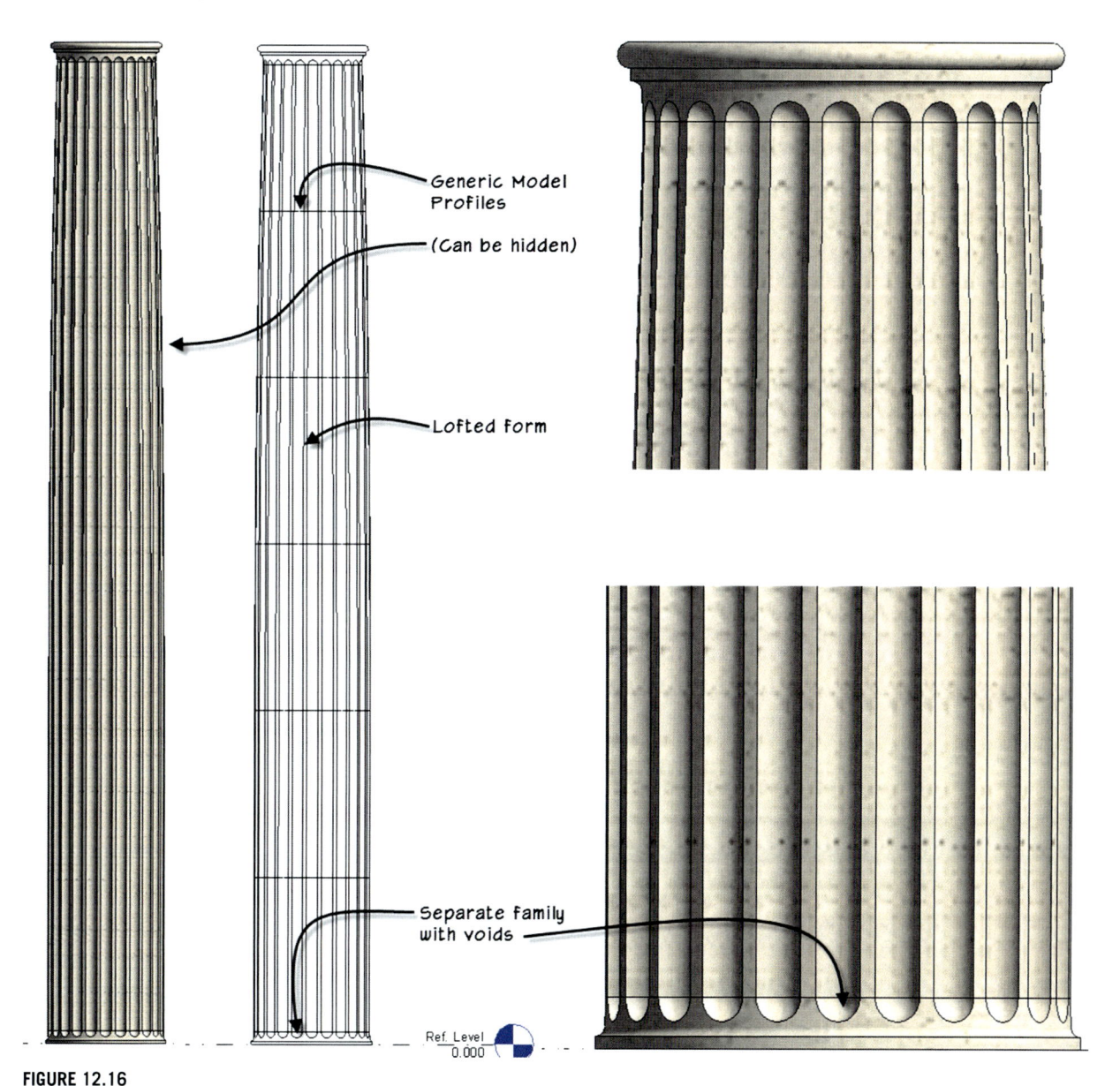

The Corinthian shaft will be constructed from a lofted form and solids with voids at top and bottom

Unfortunately, we'll be unable to get rid of the seams at the top and bottom, but all of the profiles can be hidden. So the shaft itself will be smooth.

CREATE A MASSING PROFILE

In the massing environment, you cannot load or insert two-dimensional families. This means that we cannot use Detail Item families or Profile families in our massing. However, as we saw in the "Creating a Massing Profile" topic of Chapter 11, we can create profiles using model lines in a generic model family. We can use any generic model template, including adaptive components. Adaptive components give us some features that are not available in other templates, like the ability to use hosted points and divided paths. We will use these features to create a special rig that will constrain and flex the shape of our fluted cross section.

> I have copied the seed family we built in Chapter 11 to the *Seed Families* folder.

1. From the *Seed Families* folder, open the file named: *Family Seed (Adaptive).rfa*.

2. Save the family to the *Chapter 12* folder as: **Corinthian Channels AC Profile**.

360 | Chapter 12

When I start working with adaptive components and particularly when I plan to mix adaptive components with standard families, I like to add descriptors to the names. So I have used "AC" for "Adaptive Component." I use "GM" for "Generic Model," "FB" for "Face Based" and so on.

    3. On the Manage tab, click the Project Units button, edit the Format for Length and for Rounding, choose **Custom**.

      ⇨ Set the Rounding increment to: **0.000001** and then click OK twice.

    4. From the Create tab, open the "Family Types" dialog and add three new parameters with formulas as indicated in Table 12.2.

TABLE 12.2

Parameter	Value	Type of Parameter	Type of Parameter
Mult	1.000		Number (Group under Dimensions)
Inside Diam	0.902	(Base Diameter * 0.902) * Mult	Length (Group under Constraints)
Calc Diam	1.000	Base Diameter * Mult	Length (Group under Constraints)

    5. Remain in the "Family Types" dialog and add the family types indicated in Table 12.3.

TABLE 12.3

Name	Value of Mult Parameter	Comments
Bottom	1.000000	Rename the existing type: Flex
Entasis 1	0.991290	
Entasis 2	0.964690	
Entasis 3	0.918644	
Top	0.850000	

      ⇨ Make Bottom the current type and then click OK to dismiss Family Types.

I calculated the values for the Mult parameter in another temporary family using the same ellipse formula discussed above in the "Build a Smooth Shaft with Elliptical Entasis" topic. Basically, I divided the Entasis Total (the Y value) into four equal segments. I reworked the formula to solve for X instead of semi major axis. I then plugged in the value we already calculated for semi major axis and for Y I substituted each of the values based on the four divisions. This let me solve for the three X values I needed which we used here. If you would like to see the formulas, open the file named: *Fluted Cross Section Profile.rfa*.

In the massing environment, it is typical to work in a 3D view. But other typical views are also included on the Project Browser. To build this profile, I prefer to work in plan view.

    6. On the Project Browser, open the *Ref. Level* plan view.

    7. On the Create tab, click the Reference button and then the circle icon. Create three concentric circles centered on the two reference planes.

      ⇨ Turn on the Center Marks for all three circles and then align and lock them in both directions.

      ⇨ Cancel the command and then add Diameter dimensions to the two inner circles.

      ⇨ Label these dimensions with **Calc Diam** (for the middle circle) and **Inner Diam** (for the inner circle) (see Figure 12.17).

The Column Shaft | 361

FIGURE 12.17

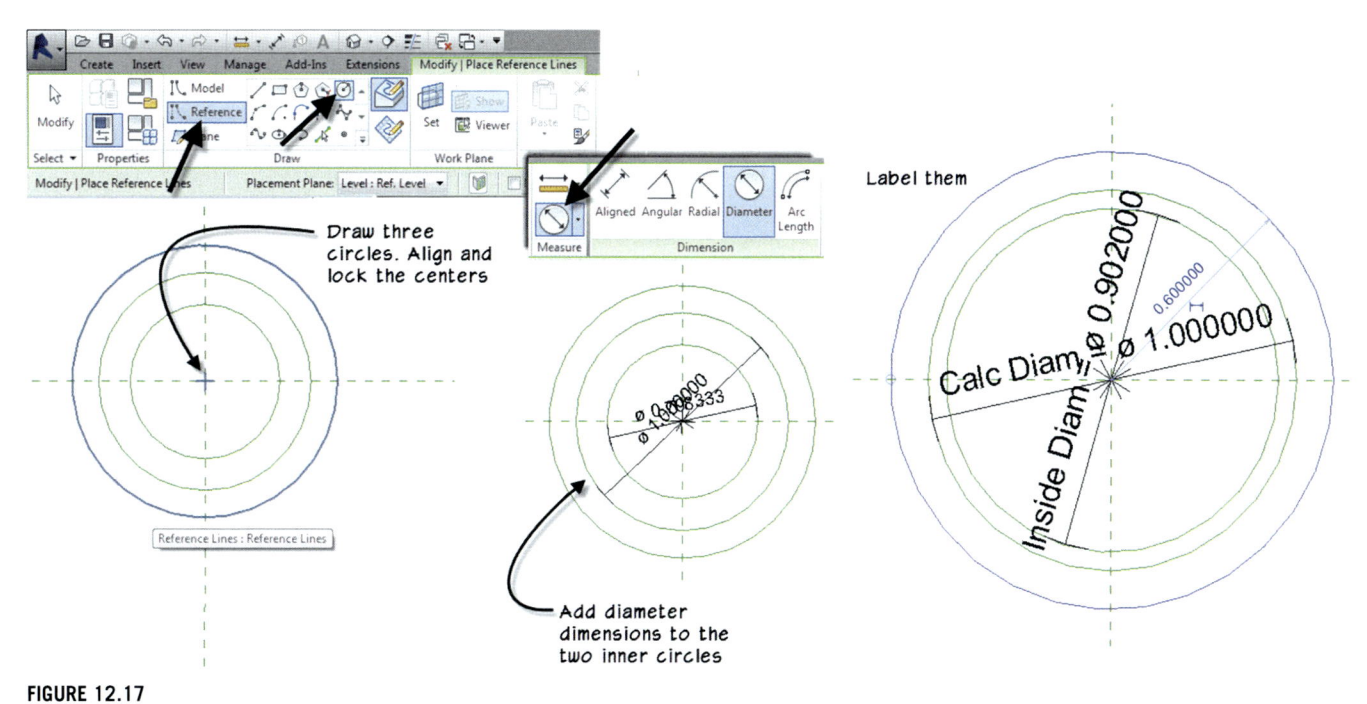

Draw three circles constrained to the centers and labeled with the parameters

The diameter of the outmost circle is not important. It should be a little larger. I used a radius of 0.600 in the figure.

Our next step is to add several hosted reference points on the two inner circles. This will be a tedious step as there is no good way to copy hosted points. So we have to add them in a mostly manual fashion and then use the properties palette to position them correctly. On the inner circle, we need 24 points. On the outer circle, we need three times this many; 96 points total (see Figure 12.18).

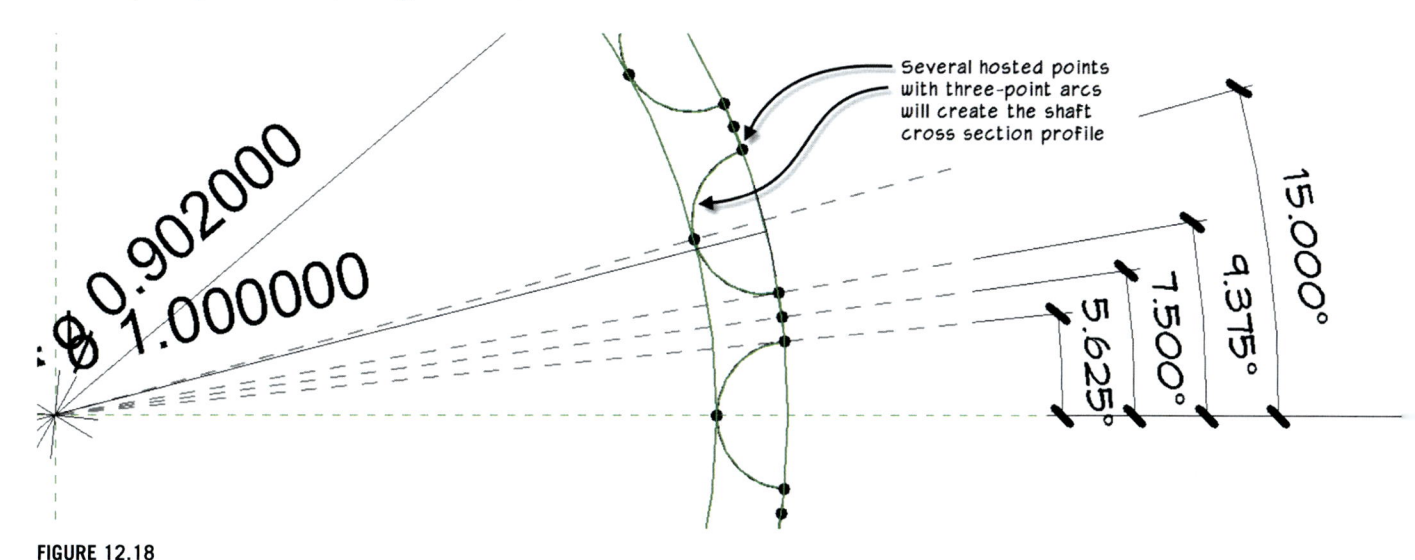

FIGURE 12.18

A detail of the reference points required

I'll give you a few tricks to speed the input, but for the most part, we have to add and position each point. Let's start with the inner circle, which is easier in both quantity and positioning.

8. On the Create tab, click the Reference Point icon and then click directly on the inner circle at zero degrees (it should snap to the quadrant).

⇨ Place another point at each of the other three quadrants.

• *Creating Classical Architecture with Modern Software* •

Remember, make sure you highlight the circle, and then click. The point should appear small. This will indicate that it is hosted.

> TIP: Make sure that the "Draw on Face" icon is selected on the ribbon. There are two mode icons on the Draw panel between the draw icons and the Set Work Plane button. Draw on Face is on top (pointed out in Figure 12.19). You cannot create hosted points if the Draw on Work Plane (below it) is active.

9. Place another 20 points on the circle. Place five in each 90° quardrant roughly equally spaced.

You have to place the hosted points first, then you can position them precisely. So just get them close to start with.

To get the points spaced correctly, there are a few options open to us. We could use a divided path to help us locate our points. (We will do this below). This approach could work here, but snapping to the points ca be tricky, so instead I recommend two alternative options for this exercise. Use the Properties palette, or draw a 24 sided polygon and snap to it.

If you want to use the Properties palette, select all 24 points. On the Properties palette, change the Measurement Type to **Angle**. In the "Building Rigs" topic in Chapter 11, we discussed the "Normalized Curve Parameter." We have 24 points that need to be equally spaced. If we divide 1.000 by 24, we get 0.041666. This is not a very convenient number to work with. Changing the Measurement Type to Angle means that each point needs to be 15° away from the previous one. These numbers will be much easier to work with. Start at the first point (it should already be at 0° since we snapped it to the quadrant, but check it just to be sure). Work your way aroudn the circle counter clockwise. Set the next one to 15°, then 30° and so on all the way around. You will have to do each point manually this way.

As an alternative, you can draw a 24 side polygon first.

10. On the Draw panel, click the Inscribed Polygon icon.

⇨ On the Options Bar, set the Sides to 24 and then draw it from the center of the circle out to the quardrant.

⇨ Zoom in on each point. Select a point, drag it and snap it to the vertex of the polygon (see Figure 12.19).

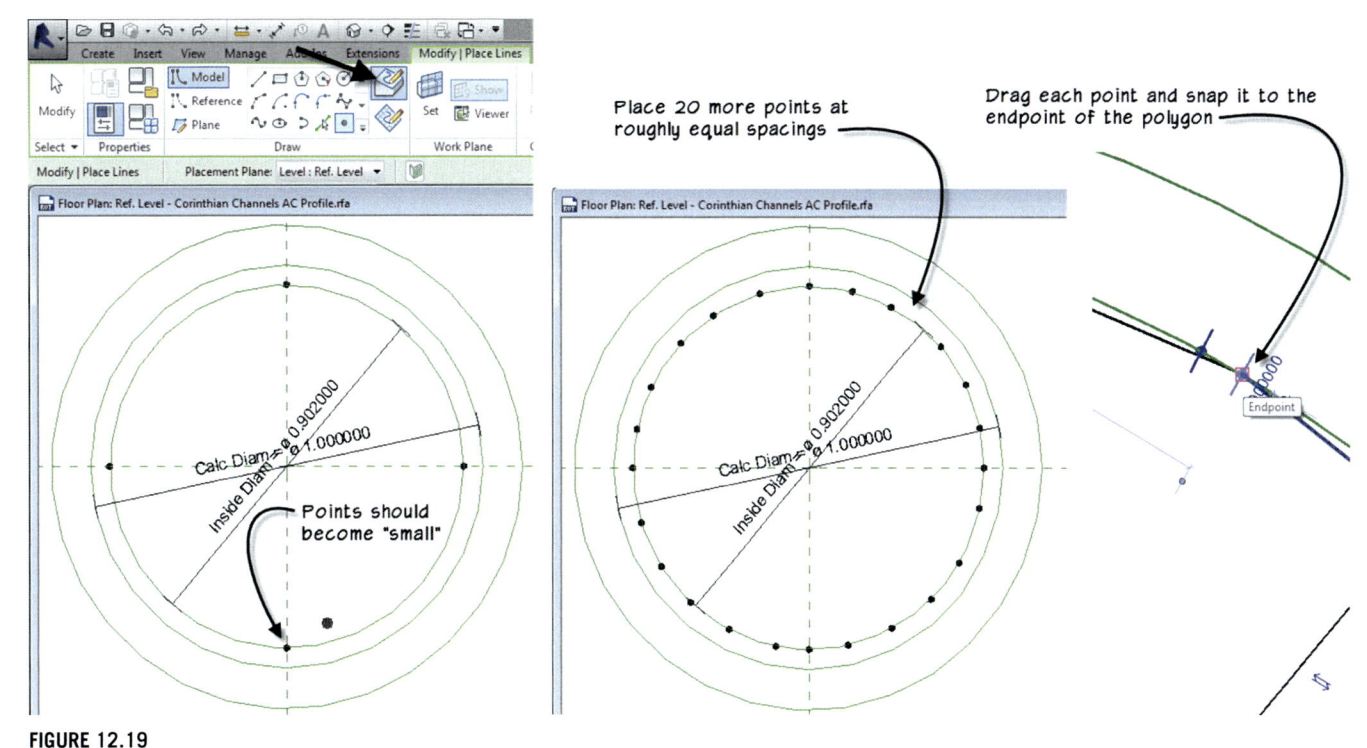

FIGURE 12.19
Add 24 equally spaced points around the inner circle

Be patient as you do this. Start dragging the point, and then pause for a moment and wait for the endpoint snap to appear. Then let go of the mouse button. I did this process both ways; with the polygon and on the Properties palette. They both took about the same amount of time and effort. So the method you use is up to you.

11. Select the polygon and delete it.
12. Save the file.

> **CATCH UP!** You can open a file completed to this point named:
> 12_Corinthian Channels AC Profile_A.rfa.

> **Note:** You may be wondering why we didn't just array, copy, mirror or rotate/copy the points. Unfortunately, certain standard and straight-forward methods don't work well in the massing environment. Array is not available in the massing environment at all. Other means of copying do work, but unfortunately not with hosted points. If you manually copy a hosted point, it looses its association to the host. So we have to add each one separately as we have done here. Or below we'll see that CTRL + dragging also works to copy them.

USING A DIVIDED PATH TO AID IN SPACING

Another tool you may be wondering about at this point is the divided path. Why wouldn't we just divde the circle into a 24 segment divided path. Well, the divided path is no problem, but unfortunatley when we later attach the arcs to it to make our profile shape, they would not flex properly. So I had to resort to adding each point. Believe me, I tried many other options first. However, we can use a divide path in this sequence to help us space the manually placed points.[6]

---

[6] Divided path is available in Revit 2013 and later. If you have 2012, a small arc with manually placed points can be substituted.

364 | Chapter 12

1. Select the outmost circle and then on the Modify I Reference Lines tab, click the Divide Path button.

   The path will divide into 6.

2. Onscreen, click right on the quantity 6 (or edit the Number field on the Properties palette). Change the Number to: **192**.

There are 24 flutes. Some authorities set the width of the fillet between channels at ¼ the size of the channel. Chitham goes with a ratio of 1/3: 2/8 for the fillet and 6/8 for the channel (Chitham 1985, 2005, 163-165). This is the ratio I have adopted here. So this means that our 24 divisions each get divided by 8 (8 x 24 =192). Next we'll draw some guide lines to help with point placement.

3. Draw three model lines. Snap each one to the center of the circle and then to the nodes on the outer circle. The first line should snap to the third point above 0°. The other two are directly above this one (see the left side of Figure 12.20).

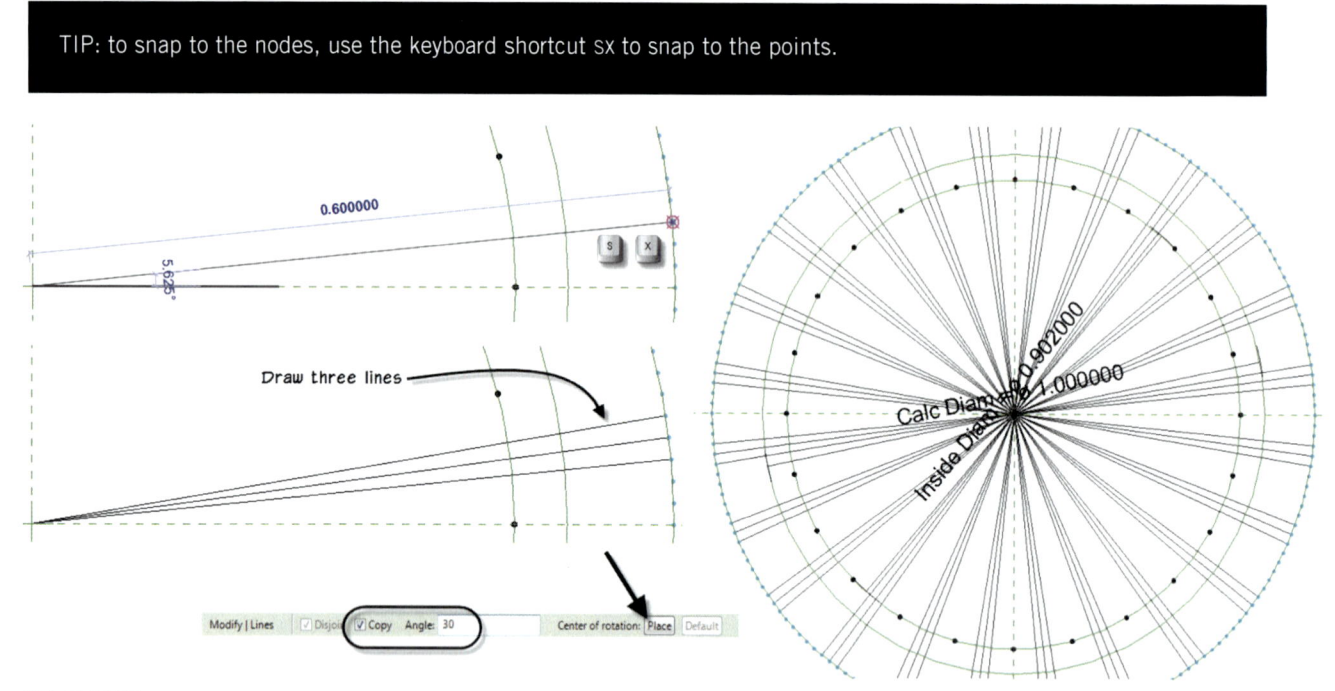

TIP: to snap to the nodes, use the keyboard shortcut SX to snap to the points.

FIGURE 12.20
Draw three guide lines and then using rotate/copy and mirror make 24 copies around the circle

Unfortunately, we don't have the array command in the massing environment. We need 24 copies of these three lines, so we'll have to use rotate/copy and mirror instead.

4. Select all three lines. Click the Rotate tool.

   ⇨ On the Options Bar, click the Place button to place the center and click at the center of the circle.

   ⇨ Check the **Copy** checkbox and then in the Angle field, type: **15** and press ENTER.

5. Select all six lines (the original and the copies) and repeat the entire process using **30** for the angle this time.

   ⇨ Leave the new copies selected, repeat the rotate/copy once more at 30 degrees.

   ⇨ Select all of the lines (18 total) and then mirror them around the centerline. Repeat in the other direction (see the right side of Figure 12.20).

We now need to add the points we need on the middle circle and we'll use these guidelines to help position them. Place the first three points on the second circle, but do *not* try to snap them yet. If you try to place and snap them at the same time, Revit is very likely to associate the points with the lines instead of the circle. We want the points

• Renaissance Revit •

hosted on the circle. Once we have them there, we can use the lines to snap them to the correct locations. Start near zero degrees (the right side of the circle) and work your way around counter clockwise.

6. Near the right quadrant of the second circle (the one dimensioned with "Calc Diam") place three hosted points. Place them randomly for now. Do *not* snap to the lines.

7. Select one of the new points.

   ⇨ On the Options Bar, click the Host Point By Intersection button. Click the intersecting line nearest to the point (see left side of Figure 12.21).

   ⇨ Repeat for the other two points.

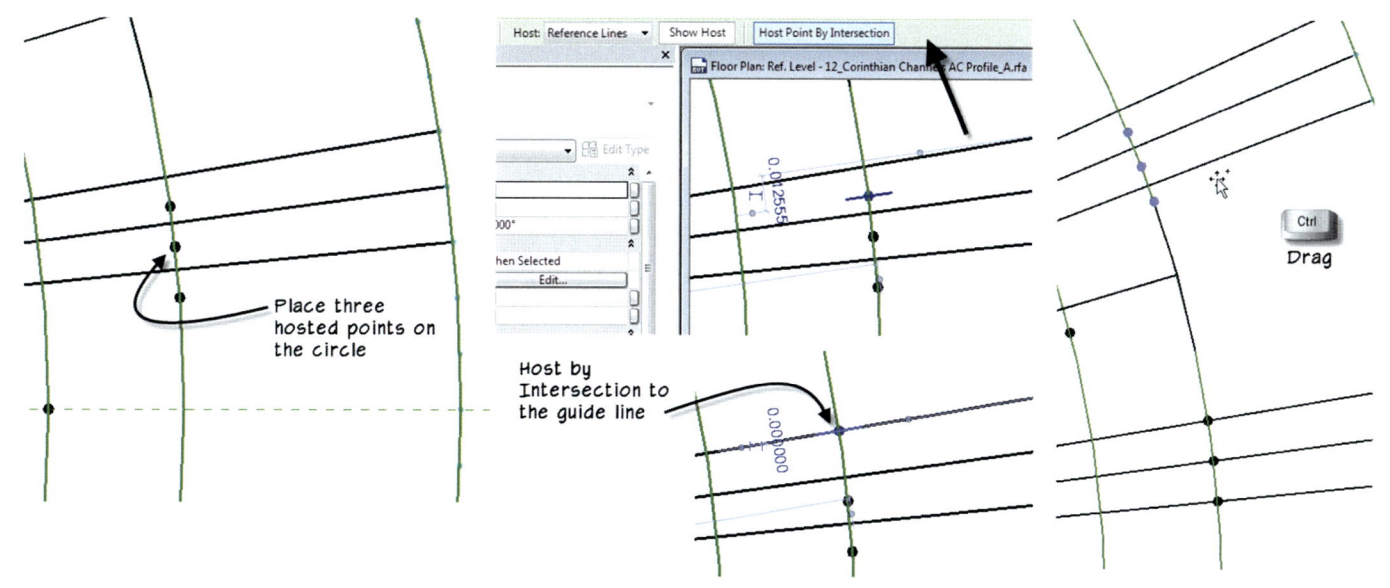

FIGURE 12.21
Align the points to the guide lines and then CTRL drag to copy them

8. Select all three points. Move your cursor next to one of the selected points.

   A move cursor will appear.

9. Hold down the CTRL key, and drag the points near to the next set of guidelines and then release.

You will now have a set of copies and notice that these will still be hosted! This is the only way to copy them and maintain the hosting to the circle.

10. Repeat the process above to host each point to the intersection with the guild lines at the new location.

    ⇨ Continue the CTRL drag and host to intersection process until you have made copies all the way around the circle.

11. Delete the divide path, the outer circle and all of the straight model lines.

> TIP: Use a crossing window to select the divide path and outer circle together. Highlight one model line, press TAB and they will all highlight. Click to select them all and then delete.

12. Save the file.

CATCH UP! You can open a file completed to this point named:
12_Corinthian Channels AC Profile_B.rfa.

CREATE HOSTED 3-POINT ARCS

So you now have 96 carefully placed reference points hosted to the two circles. If you flex the family at this point, you will see that the locations of these points follows the circle as it grows and shrinks. These points will host several arcs. The next step in the process is also manual. There is no quick way to do this. We simply have to draw each arc.

Start near zero degrees and work counter clockwise again.

1. On the Create tab, on the Draw panel, click the Start-End Radius Arc.

We want the arcs to "inherit" the hosted points and be driven by them. This is the same as how splines through points behave (see the "Spline Through Points" topic in Chapter 11). To do this, you must check the 3D Snapping checkbox on the Options Bar.[7]

2. On the Options Bar, check 3D Snapping and make sure that Chain is also checked (see the left side of Figure 12.22).

⇨ Snap to the point on the outer circle just below zero degrees.

⇨ Snap to the next point on the outer circle just above zero degrees.

⇨ Snap the final point to the point on the inner circle directly at zero degrees (see the right side of Figure 12.22).

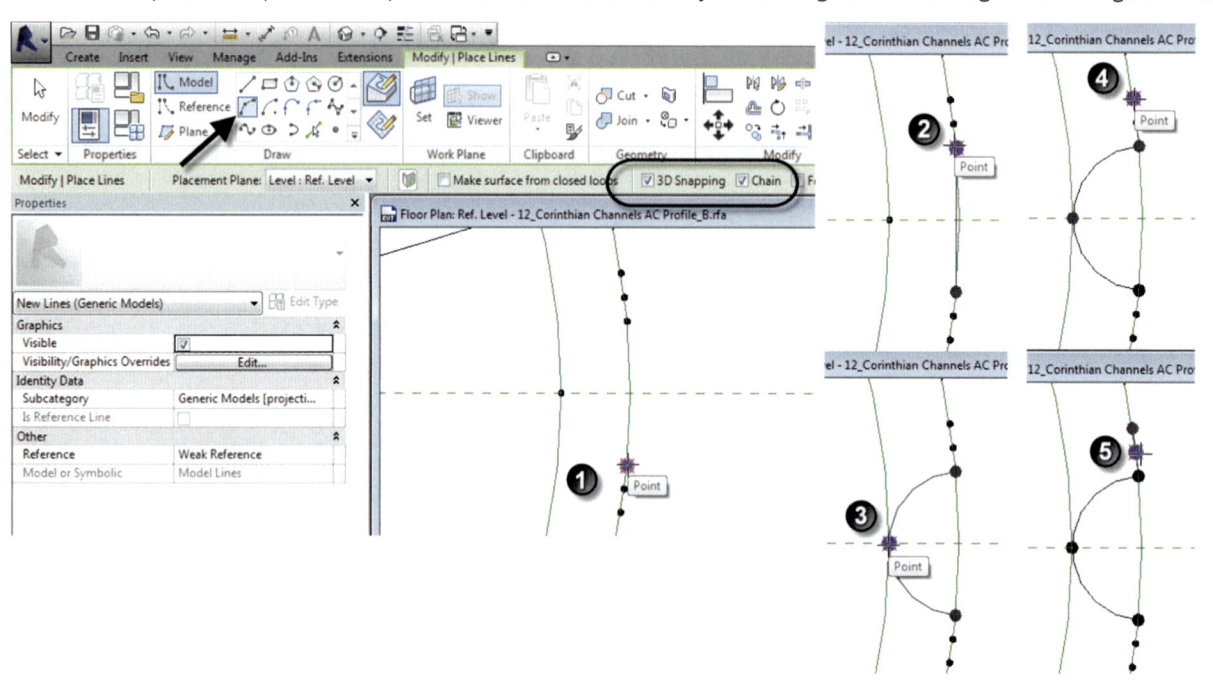

FIGURE 12.22

Create a chain of 3-point arcs snapping directly to the host points

Make sure that you are clicking directly on the points each time. Be patient and click carefully. If you miss, it will create a non-hosted point. Undo this and try again. If you have to start again, Revit will warn that you have two points on top of each other. It is safe to ignore this warning.

3. Keep the chain going all the way around the entire circle. There will be 48 arcs total.

⇨ When you click back on the original point, click the Modify tool to end to command.

---

[7] This feature is only available in Revit 2014 or later. To perform this task in prior versions, add another circle between the two we have. Then add several more points. You want five for each channel. Then use Spline Through Points instead of arcs. It gives a close approximation.

4. Open "Family Types" and move through each type to flex.

So, there's the payoff. We put in a great deal of effort to create 96 hosted points and 48 hosted arcs, but now with just four parameters, the entire thing flexes exactly as we need it to. There is one final issue to overcome however. If we were not interested in making this flex, we could delete the two circles and then load this family into a massing family. In the massing family, we could use the closed chain of model lines here to create form. The trouble is that because we do want it to flex, we need to keep the reference lines. This means that when we try to load it and create form, Revit will no longer select the chain of model lines in the nested family. This means we would have to TAB and individually select 48 separate arcs to create form. This will be nearly impossible. Fortunately there is an easy solution.

5. Highlight one of the arcs. The whole chain should highlight. Click to select the chain.

⇨ On the Properties palette, check the Is Reference Line checkbox.

6. Open the {3D} view.

7. Keep the selection and then click Create Form.

⇨ Of the two choices that appear, choose the flat plane option (see Figure 12.23).

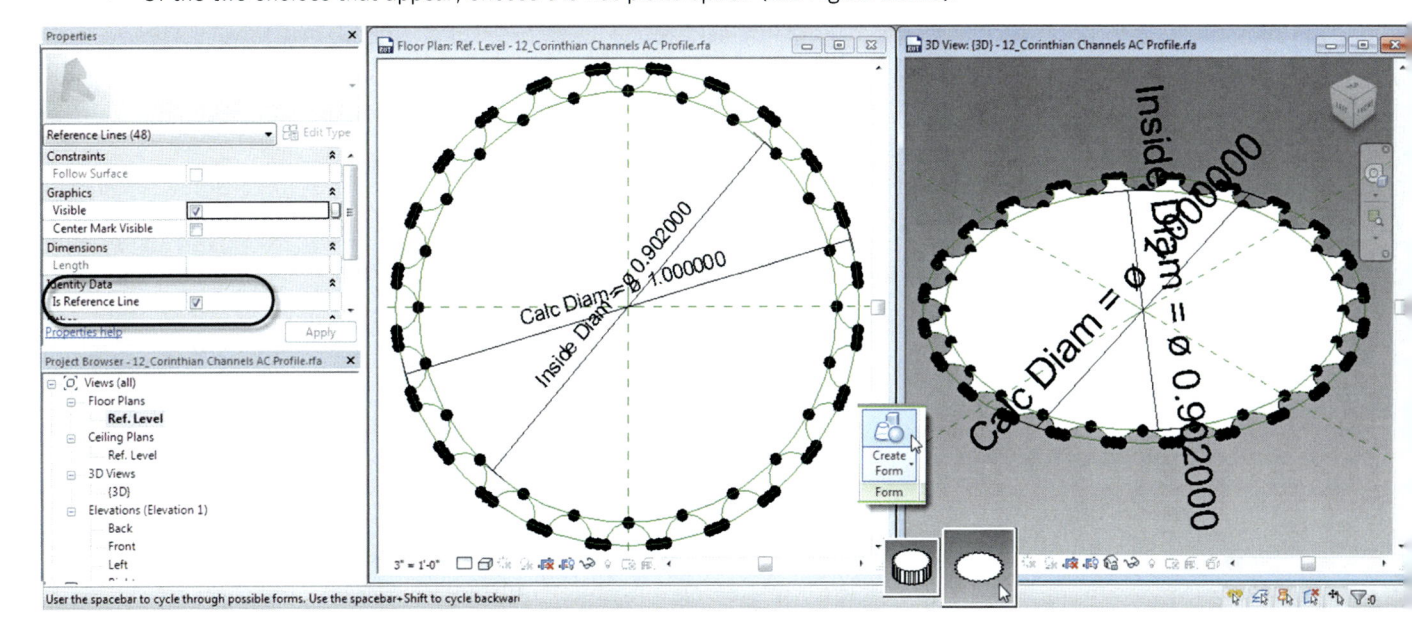

FIGURE 12.23
Create a simple planar surface from the chain of arcs

This plane can now be easily selected when we nest this family into other families to create form.

8. Save the file.

CATCH UP! You can open a file completed to this point named: *12_Corinthian Channels AC Profile.rfa*.

CREATE THE SHAFT FORM

For the rest of this model, I am only going to detail tasks we have not covered elsewhere. So to build the shaft, I have provided a file that has all the reference planes, dimensions, parameters and has a nested family for the top and bottom portion of the shaft. We will modify that family below. So for now, let's load in the profile we just completed and use it to create the lofted form of the shaft.

1. From the *Chapter12* folder, open the *Corinthian Shaft (Fluted).rfa* file.

2. On the Create tab, click the Component button.

• *Creating Classical Architecture with Modern Software* •

368 | Chapter 12

The Fluting Bottom and Top family is already loaded and Revit defaults to this one. Let's load our new profile instead.

- On the Modify I Place Component tab, click the Load Family button.
- Browse to the *Chapter12* folder and load the *12_Corinthian Channels AC Profile.rfa* file (you can load your own version instead if you prefer).

3. On the Modify I Place Component tab, on the Placement panel, click the Place on Work Plane button.

- On the Options Bar, from the Placement Plane drop-down, choose **Reference Plane : Channel Start**.
- Click to place it at the intersection of the two center reference planes (see Figure 12.24).

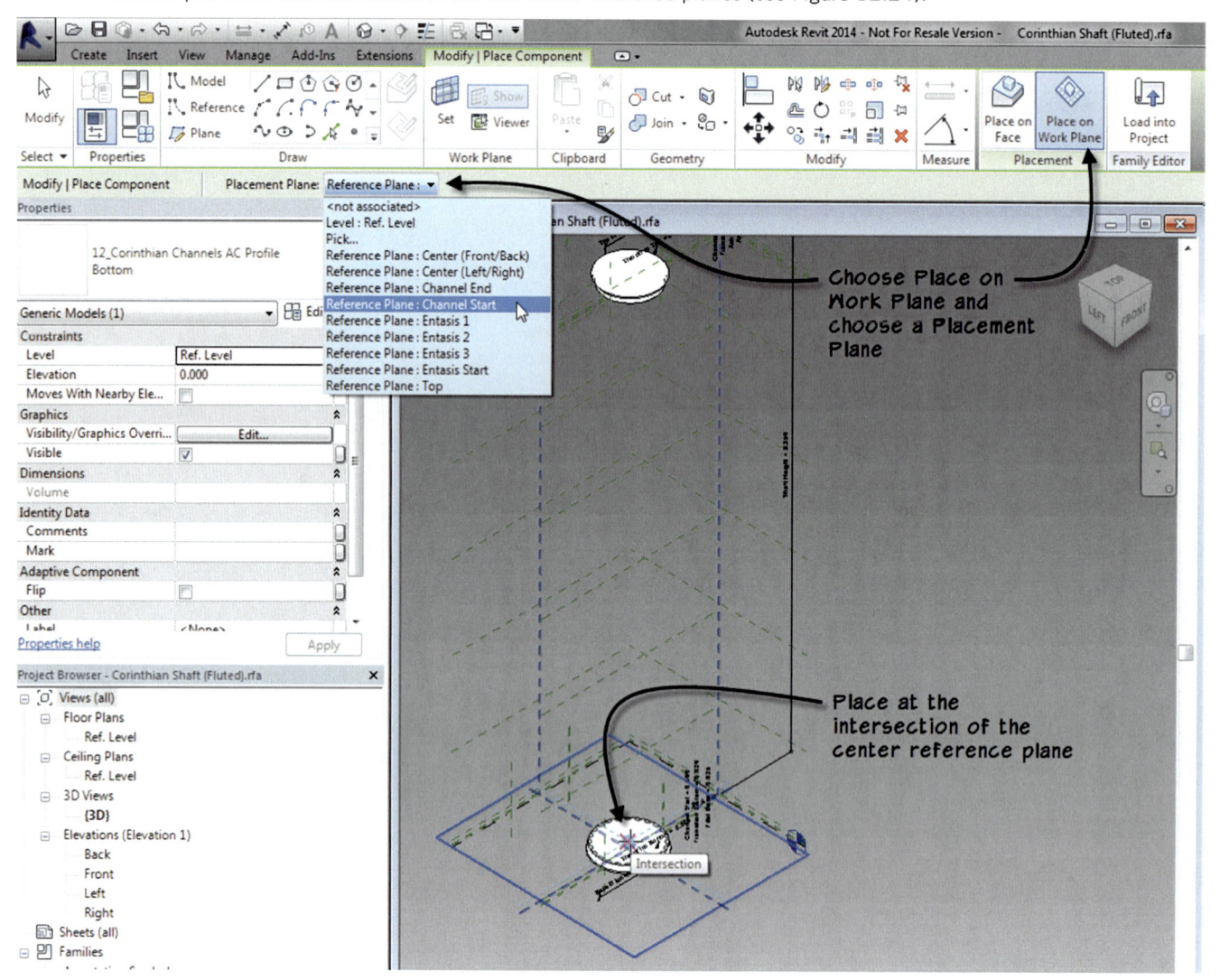

FIGURE 12.24
Place the channel profile on a specified placement plane

Stay in the Place Component command. We need to place six more profiles.

4. On the Options Bar, from the Placement Plane drop-down, choose **Reference Plane : Cylinder**.

- Click to place at the intersection of the center reference planes again.

It can be tricky to get it to highlight the reference planes. If you have a hard time, you can open the Ref. Level floor plan instead. It should be easier to snap to the intersection there.

5. Place the next instance on **Reference Plane : Entasis Start**.

• Renaissance Revit •

The first three are the same size since the lower portion of the shaft is cylindrical. Above this they taper in to form the entasis.

6. From the Type Selector at the top of the Properties palette, choose the **Entasis 1** type.

⇨ Change the Placement Plane to **Entasis 1** and then place the next profile.

7. Repeat for **Entasis 2**, then **Entasis 3** and finally **Top** (see Figure 12.25).

The profile called Top should be placed on the reference plane called: **Channel End**.

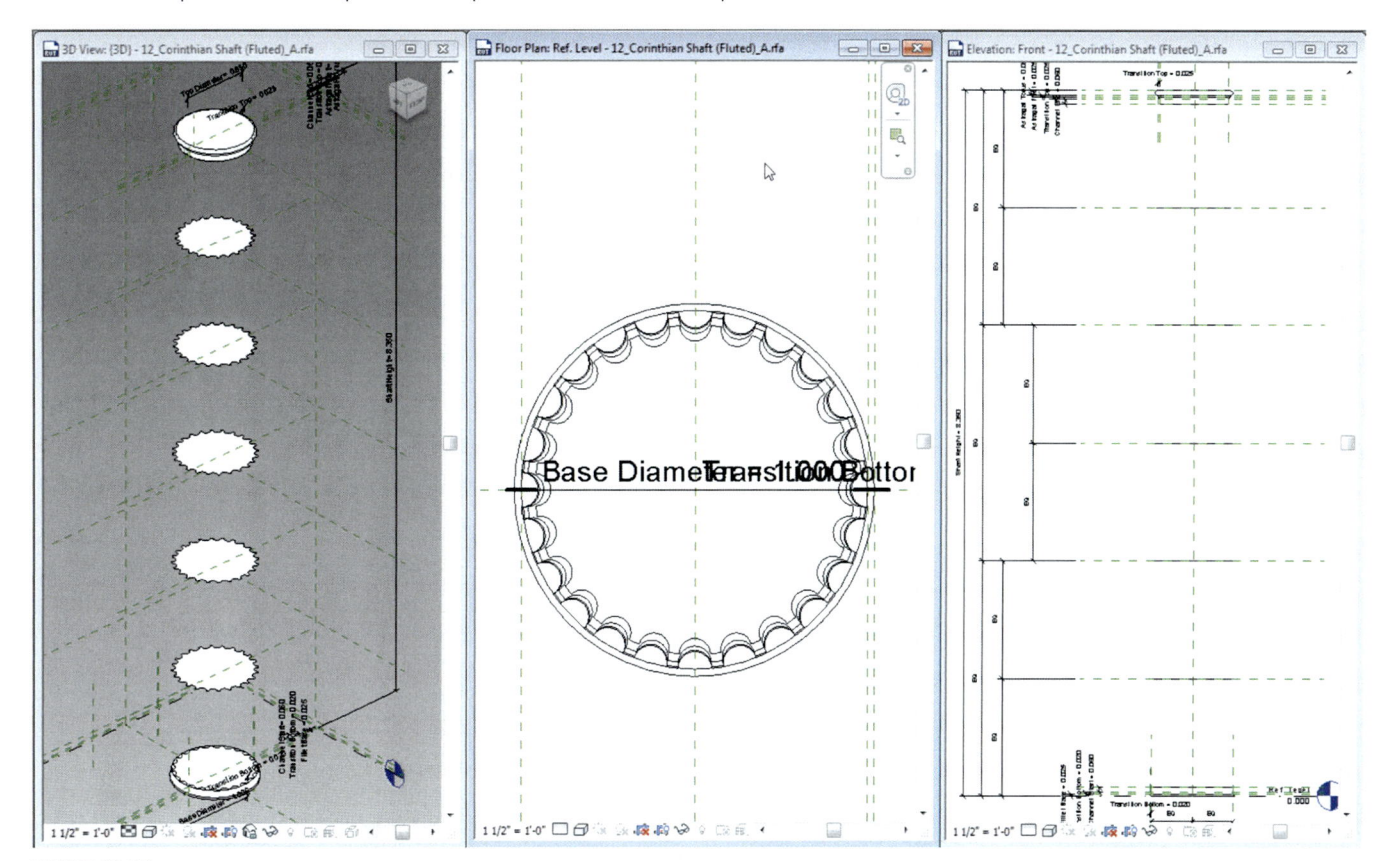

FIGURE 12.25
Place the profiles on their respective work planes

Now we need to link up the parameters and flex.

8. On the Project Browser, expand *Families* and then *Generic Models > 12_Corinthian Channels AC Profile*.

9. Double-click on the type called Bottom. Link up the Base Diameter parameter and then click OK.

⇨ Repeat for each type.

10. Open "Family Types" and flex. Return to Base Diameter **1.000** and then save the file.

CATCH UP! You can open a file completed to this point named: *12_ Corinthian Shaft (Fluted)_A.rfa*.

To create the shaft form element, we need to select the surfaces inside the nested families.

Switch to the *{3D}* view.

11. Select the Bottom and Top family element onscreen. (It is the family that was already in the file when we started).

⇨ On the View Control Bar, click the Temporary Hide/Isolate pop-up and choose **Hide Element**.

• *Creating Classical Architecture with Modern Software* •

370 | Chapter 12

12. Highlight the lowest instance Channel Profile family.

Look at the tooltip onscreen and/or on the Status Bar. It will read: *Generic Models:12_Corinthian Channels AC Profile:Bottom*.

⇨ Keep the element highlighted and press TAB one time.

Notice that the tooltip and Status Bar now reads: *Generic Models:12_Corinthian Channels AC Profile:Bottom:Face*. The important part of the message is the "Face" at the end. This is what we need to select (see Figure 12.26).

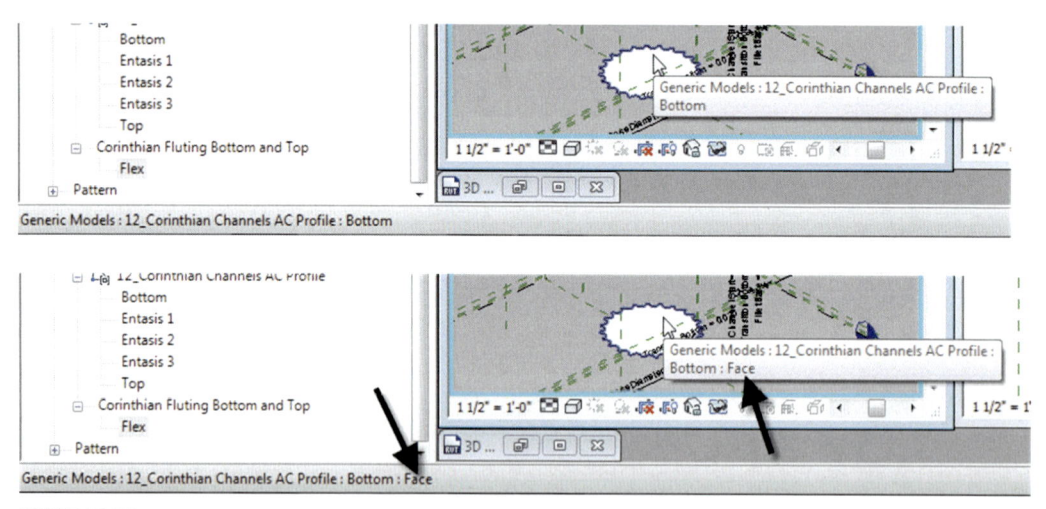

FIGURE 12.26
Use TAB to highlight the face inside the family

13. Click to select the face.

14. Highlight the next face, press TAB and when the message says "Face" hold down the CTRL and click to add the second face to the selection.

⇨ When you have all seven faces selected (the Properties palette filter list will read 7 Generic Models), click the Create Form button (see Figure 12.27).

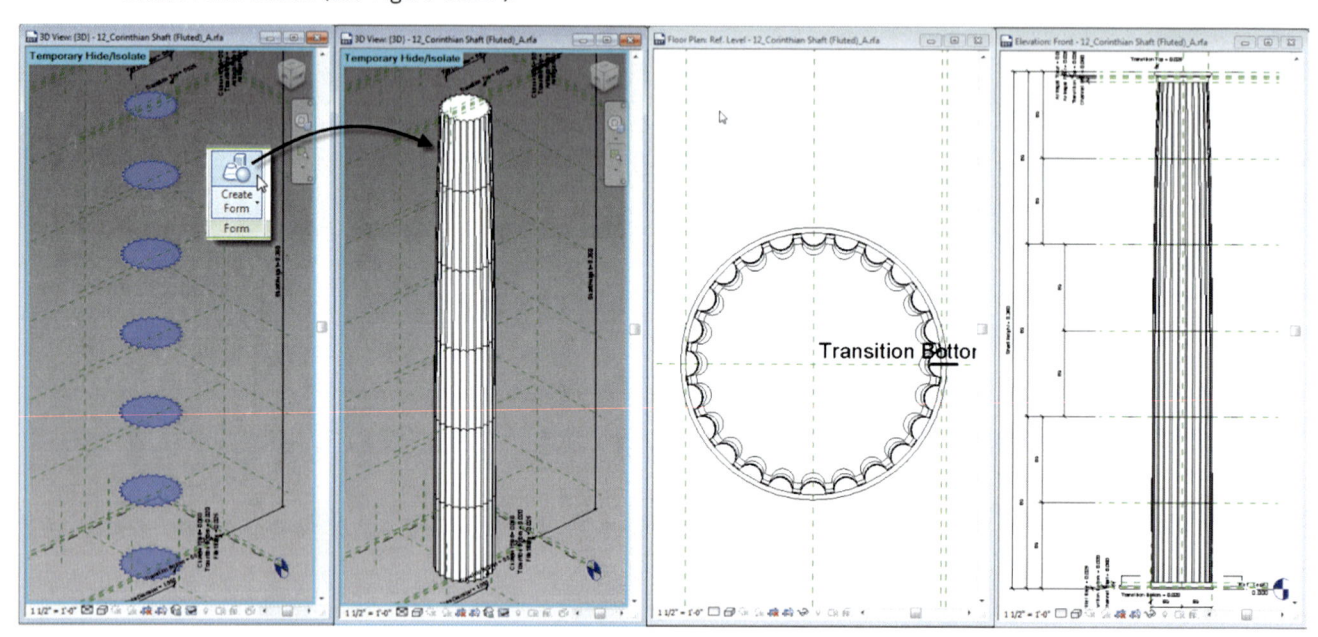

FIGURE 12.27
Use the TAB and CTRL keys to select the seven faces and then create form

• Renaissance Revit •

15. Using a window selection, surround the entire shaft.

    ⇨ Click the Filter button, check none, and then check Generic Models only.

    The quantity should be 7. We are selecting the families this time, not the faces.

    ⇨ On the Properties palette, uncheck the Visible checkbox.

Turning off the visibility means that these families will not display when this family is loaded into another family or project. We only need them to shape the shaft form. But we do not want to see the edges.

16. Reset the Temporary Hide/Isolate mode.

17. Open "Family Types" and flex. Return to Base Diameter **1.000** and then save the file.

CATCH UP! You can open a file completed to this point named: *12_Corinthian Shaft (Fluted)_B.rfa*.

USING VOIDS FOR FLUTING

Ideally, I wanted to use a void for the entire flute and then simply repeat it 24 times around the smooth shaft. This proved to be much more difficult than it sounds. When we consider the form required carefully, we actually require the form to curve in three directions. You have a half round shape for the section cut of the flute. It follows the entasis which curves it along the vertical axis and then when you add the top and bottom where it scoops in we have a curve in the third dimension as well. This makes it complicated enough but in addition, Revit stubbornly refused to cut and join the geometry of these complex forms in every one of my attempts. This is why I have settled on the approaches showcased here. As a consequence, the top and bottom portions of the fluting I have had to do as a separate form. Furthermore, I had better success with the traditional family editor for this than the massing. So if you examine the top and bottom family that is already in the file, you will notice it is a standard generic model.

If you select this family onscreen, you will notice that both top and bottom are part of a single family. Feel free to edit the family and study it a bit if you like. I took the original profile family used to create the smooth shaft in previous examples and made a copy and simply modified it slightly to include only the top and bottom moldings. I also included a small portion of the shaft on each end; enough for the start and end portions of the channels. To create these, I started with a simple sphere, created from a revolve. Ultimately I had better success with cylindrical shape with half round on one side only. Also, revolving on the vertical axis instead of either X or Y worked much better. I have provided the void family in the *Chapter12* folder. We will open it, study it a little and then load it into the shaft family and copy it as required.

Continue in the *Corinthian Shaft (Fluted)* file or open the catch-up file.

1. In the *Ref. Level* plan view, select the *Corinthian Fluting Bottom and Top* family instance onscreen.

    ⇨ From the Temporary Hide/Isolate pop-up, choose: **Isolate Element**.

2. On the Insert tab, click the Load Family button.

    ⇨ From the *Chapter12* folder, select the *Corinthian Fluting Bottom and Top Void.rfa* file and then click Open.

3. On the Create tab, click the Component tool.

    ⇨ On the Modify | Place Component tab, on the Placement panel, click the Place on Face button.

    ⇨ Click at the center of the circle to place an instance (see Figure 12.28).

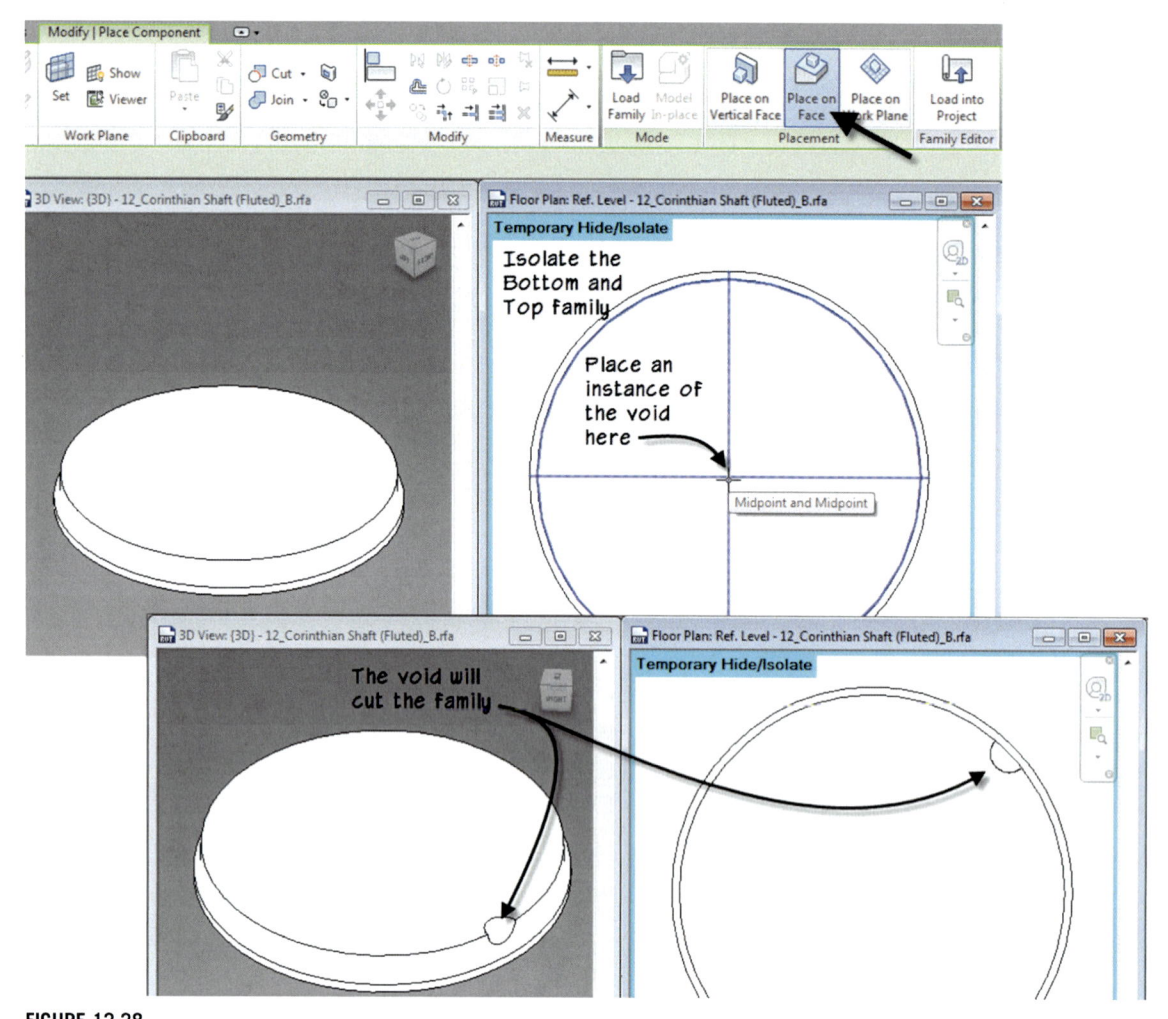

FIGURE 12.28

Place an instance of the void family

4. Click the Modify tool to cancel the command.

5. Select the void family you just placed and then on the ribbon, click the Edit Family button.

This family was created from our *Family Seed (Face Based).rfa* seed family. There is a single reference line that is locked to the center reference planes in both directions. An angular dimension is attached that allows this reference line to rotate at any angle. A dimension with parameter is also attached to the length of the reference line. Refer to the "Controlling Rotation" topic in Chapter 4 for more information. It is set up essentially the same way that you would set up a parametric door swing.

6. Open the "Family Types" dialog.

This family has the standard Base Diameter and Mult parameters. A is an angular parameter that controls the rotation of the reference line. Calc Radius drives the length of the reference line. Flute Radius is derived from parameters a and a1. Recall above that I noted using Chitham's proportions of 6/8 Base Diameter for the channel diameter. Converting this to an angle and then using simple trig formulas in the a and a1 parameters gives us the radius of the flute channel. This drives the arc in the void revolve sketch. The revolve uses the vertical work plane of the reference line as its work plane. I added a section looking at this plane to make it easier to work on (see Figure 12.29).

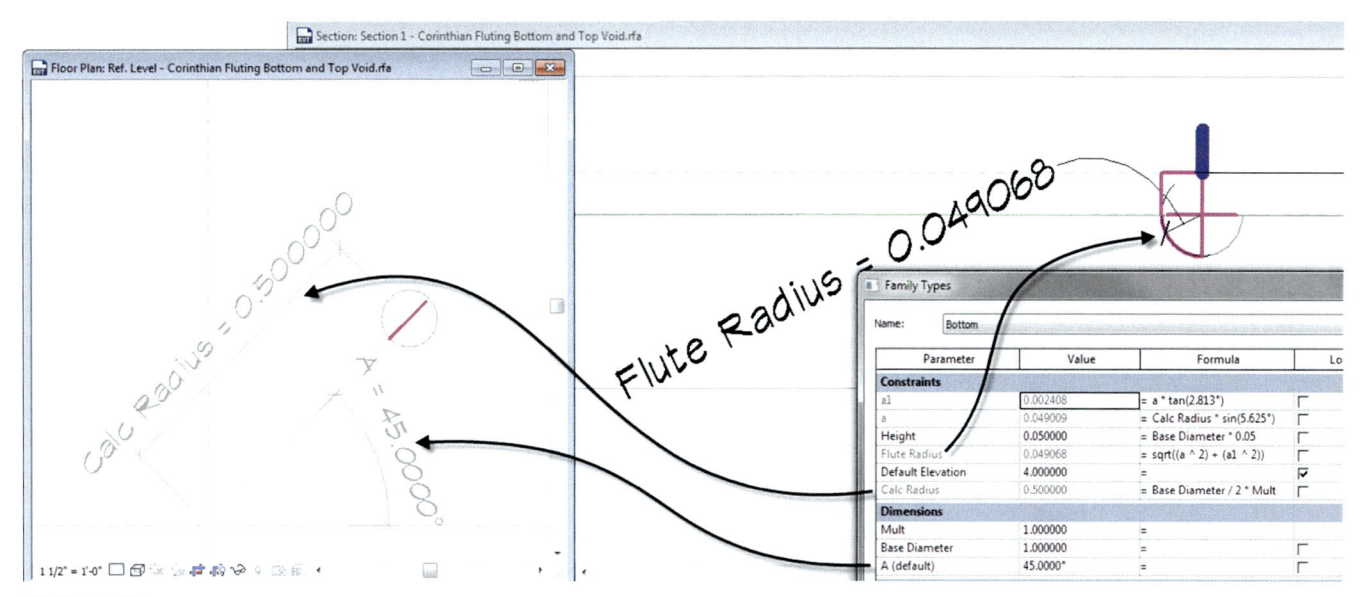

FIGURE 12.29

Understanding the fluting bottom and top void family

7. When you are finished exploring the family, you can close it without saving.

Now here is the next tedious task. We have to place 23 more instances of this family. The process that I am going to have you follow for this will at first seem a bit odd, but ultimately it is about the same amount of effort as other method and supports the way the family was constructed better.

8. Select the instance of the void family onscreen and then on the Clipboard panel, click the Copy to Clipboard button.

Void families cannot be pasted on top of each other. Remember that we do not have array in the massing environment. So as you saw when we opened the family, I built in a rotation parameter. So we'll edit the rotation, then paste, edit that rotation, paste again, etc.

9. With the void still selected, on the Properties palette, change the value of A to: **0.000**.

⇨ On the Clipboard panel, click the Paste drop-down and choose: **Aligned to Same Place**.

⇨ Change the value of A to: **15.000**.

⇨ Repeat another 22 times. Each time add 15° to the previous angle.

Skip 45°. This will be the last one you paste (see Figure 12.30).

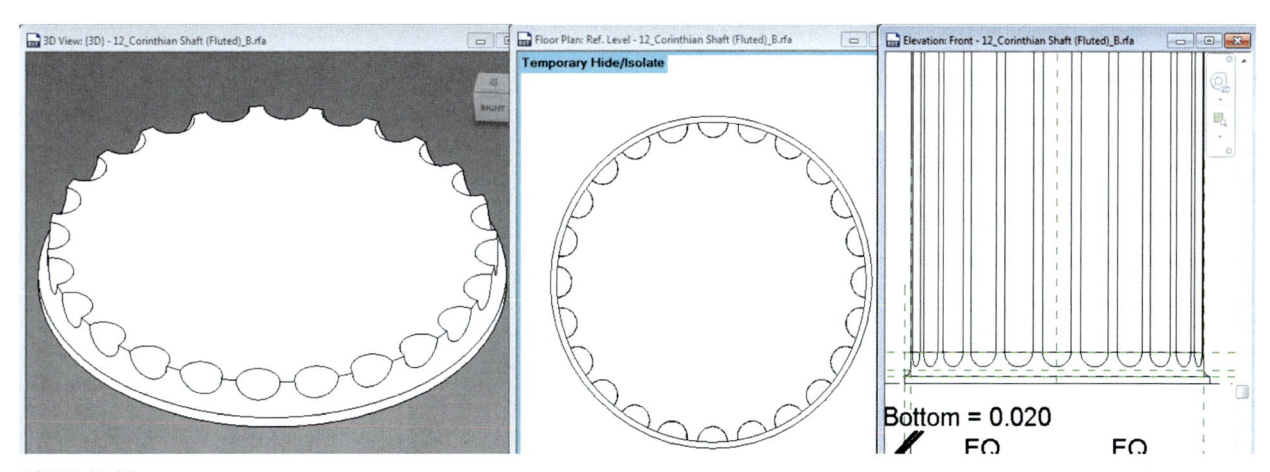

FIGURE 12.30

Paste the void aligned to the same place and then edit its angle and repeat

• Creating Classical Architecture with Modern Software •

Now that we have all 24 set at the correct angles for the bottom, we can copy and paste them all to the top. To do so, we need to change the type before copying, or when we paste the voids will fail. We will need our ceiling plan open for this next sequence.

10. On the Project Browser, open the *Ref. Level* ceiling plan, select the *Corinthian Fluting Bottom and Top* family instance onscreen.

    ⇨ From the Temporary Hide/Isolate pop-up, choose: **Isolate Element**.

11. Leave the ceiling plan open and then back in the floor plan, select all 24 voids onscreen.

    ⇨ On the Properties palette, from the Type Selector, choose the type called: **Top**.

They will all reduce in size and move closer to the center.

12. Copy them to the clipboard.

13. With all 24 still selected, return them to the **Bottom** type.

14. Choose Paste **Aligned to Current View**.

You will now have two sets, one large and one small on the same surface.

15. On the Modify |Generic Models tab, on the Work Plane panel, click the Pick New button.

The 24 selected elements will disappear. The next plane you click will become their new work plane. We want to place them on the surface of the form at the top. The ceiling plan will be best for this.

16. Switch to the ceiling plan.

    ⇨ Highlight the surface onscreen and snap to the center.

The copied voids should appear on this surface and cut the top and look like Figure 12.16 above.

17. On the Project Browser, edit the type properties of both the Bottom and Top types of the Corinthian Fluting Bottom and Top Void family and link up the Base Diameter parameter.

18. Open "Family Types" and flex. Return to Base Diameter **1.000** and then save the file.

> **CATCH UP!** You can open a file completed to this point named: *12_Corinthian Shaft (Fluted).rfa*.

MEDIUM DETAIL ALTERNATIVE

The shaft we have just completed works well for the large scale views. But it would be a little too detailed for small scale views. We have already discussed applying levels of detail to our content. In our Tuscan, Doric and Ionic examples, we built a low detail version of the model that displays in coarse scale views. In those examples, not only was the shaft smooth, but it was a simple blend that does not correctly represent the entasis. This is perfectly fine for small scale views. At intermediate scales like 1/2"=1'-0" [1:25] or 1"=1'-0" [1:10], the coarse scale version that we have will be too simplistic, but the model we just built might still be too detailed. In this case, we should consider a separate medium detail version.

For this example, we will represent each channel as a single model line drawn directly on the surface of a smooth shaft. To do this in the traditional environment, you need to have a vertical work plane to work on. If you add the lines to the coarse scale version with the tapered blend, it is pretty easy to do this since the shaft has a straight taper. If you use the swept version that uses the profile with proper entasis, you cannot draw the lines along the curved surfaces in the traditional environment. But you can do this in the massing environment!

DRAW LINES ON 3D SURFACES

To get started, you can open the *Family Seed (Adaptive).rfa* file from the *Seed Families* folder. Save it to the *Chatper12* folder as: **Corinthian Shaft Medium**. Click the Component button and when prompted, load the family: *12_Corinthian Shaft.rfa* (or your version created earlier in this chapter) and place it at the center. Align and lock it in both directions and link up the Base Diameter parameter. If you prefer not to do these initial steps, I have created the file up to this point and saved it as: *12_Corinthian Shaft Medium_A.rfa*. The steps will start with this file, but feel free to create your own version instead.

1. From the *Chapter12* folder, open the file named: *12_Corinthian Shaft Medium_A.rfa*.
2. Save the file as: **Corinthian Shaft Medium**.

Four of the shapes on the Draw panel can be drawn on the 3D surfaces: Line, Rectangle, Start-End Radius Arc and Spline Through Points. Let's try a few first to see how it works. You can use either model or reference lines for this, but in this case, we want model lines since ultimately we want the lines we draw to be visible in a project and print.

3. On the Draw panel, click the Rectangle icon.
   ⇨ On the Options Bar, check the **3D Snapping** and **Follow Surface** checkboxes.
   Leave the Projection Type set to **Follow surface UV**.
4. Click two points to define the rectangle directly on the surface of the 3D form (see Figure 12.31).

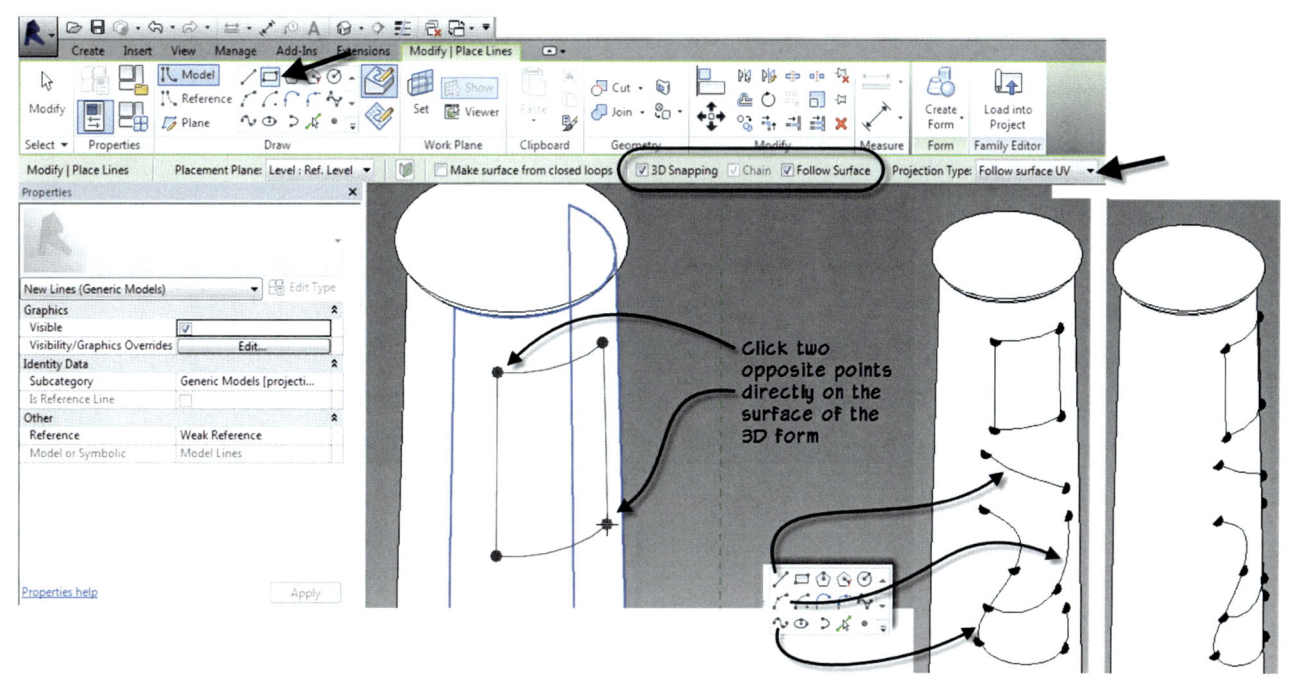

FIGURE 12.31
Follow Surface draws the shape along the curvature of the 3D form

5. Try some of the other shapes as well to get the hang of it (see the right side of Figure 12.31).
6. When you are done experimenting, delete all shapes that you drew on the surface.

One thing you might have noticed, is that the massing environment "sees" every face of the 3D form. So our shaft is actually four separate curved faces. This is important to understand if you want to draw on the surfaces because you cannot draw across two surfaces. So you will have to break your drawing at the seam and then resume on the other surface with a new drawing. This limitation is manageable but important to be aware of.

• *Creating Classical Architecture with Modern Software* •

We actually need something quite simple; we want 24 straight lines running vertically the full height of the column. We want each to mark to location of a channel in the 3D version. We want them to follow the surface of the entasis. The tricky part is drawing them that way. This feature can be a little fussy. Like the other hosted points, you have to draw them on the surface. You cannot copy them using any of the normal means except the CTRL drag option we used above. So, if you get one line drawn that you like, you can select it and CTRL drag it to make other copies. But remember, we need 24 channels total. So it is still a fairly tedious process. You can draw the two lines you need, the one on the entasis portion and the one on the lower cylindrical portion and CTRL drag them together. If you like, you can try doing just 12 and see if this provides a convincing enough representation for medium scale views.

To make this process a little more precise, the points are hosted to the surface and have two parameters: Hosted U Parameter and Hosted V Parameter. These parameters seem to be derived from the underlying curve. So, in the U direction, they go from 0 to 3.14. So it appears that Revit is measuring this direction in radians. If you divide 3.1415 by 12 you get 0.2617. So you can place these points very precisely around the curve. It will just take some time. Vertically, it looks to me like the V parameter is being derived from the ellipse in some way. So at the lower point, it is 0 and up near the top moldings of the shaft it is 0.5548. The V direction is easier because you can select all of the points after the lines are drawn and set all of their lower point V parameter to zero and their top points to 0.55 and this will get them very close to the top. I have provided a finished version in the *Chapter12* folder. I found it easier to use parameters and formulas to position the points. But you can simply input the values directly into the Properties palette as well (see Figure 12.32).

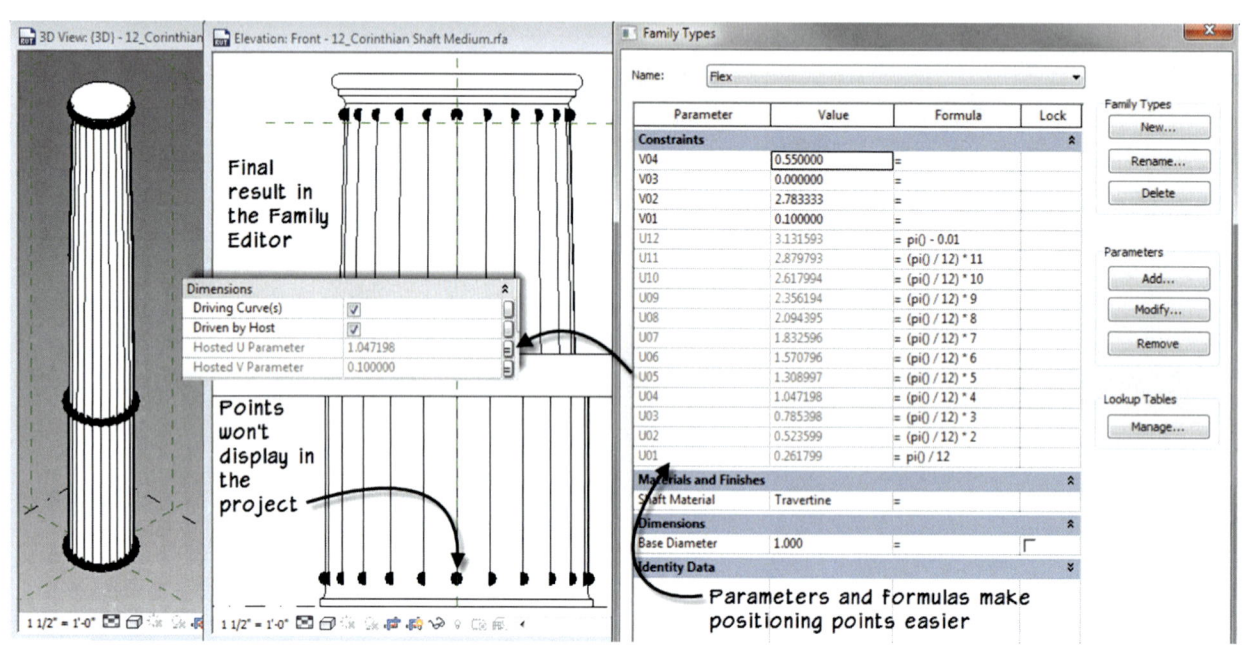

FIGURE 12.32
Completed version of the medium detail shaft with 3D lines on the surfaces

CATCH UP! You can open a file completed to this point named: *12_Corinthian Shaft Medium.rfa*.

USING A DIVIDED SURFACE FOR MEDIUM DETAIL

Let's wrap up the chapter with a much simpler example. Instead of drawing the lines on the surface, you can instead use the divided surface feature. It will divide the surfaces you select with a grid. We can leave the grid as is and simply use it instead of the 3D lines to represent the fluting at medium detail.

1. From the *Chapter12* folder, open the file named: *12_Corinthian Shaft Medium_A.rfa*.

2. Save the file as: **Corinthian Shaft Medium_Divided**.

3. In the 3D view, highlight the 3D element and then press TAB.

   One of the curved faces will highlight.

   ⇨ Click to select the curved face.

   ⇨ On the Modify I Generic Models tab, click the Divide Surface button.

   ⇨ Repeat on the remaining three curved surfaces (four total).

You will now have four divided surfaces that are divided into a 12 x 12 grid by default. You can select these surfaces separately now. You should not have too much trouble highlighting them, but use TAB if necessary.

4. Select all four divided surfaces.

   ⇨ On the Properties palette, for the U Grid, set the Number to: **1**.

That's it. We now have a grid of lines wrapping the shaft. The only downside of this much simpler approach is the seam in between the cylindrical and tapered portions of the shaft. Load it into a project and see what you think (see Figure 12.33).

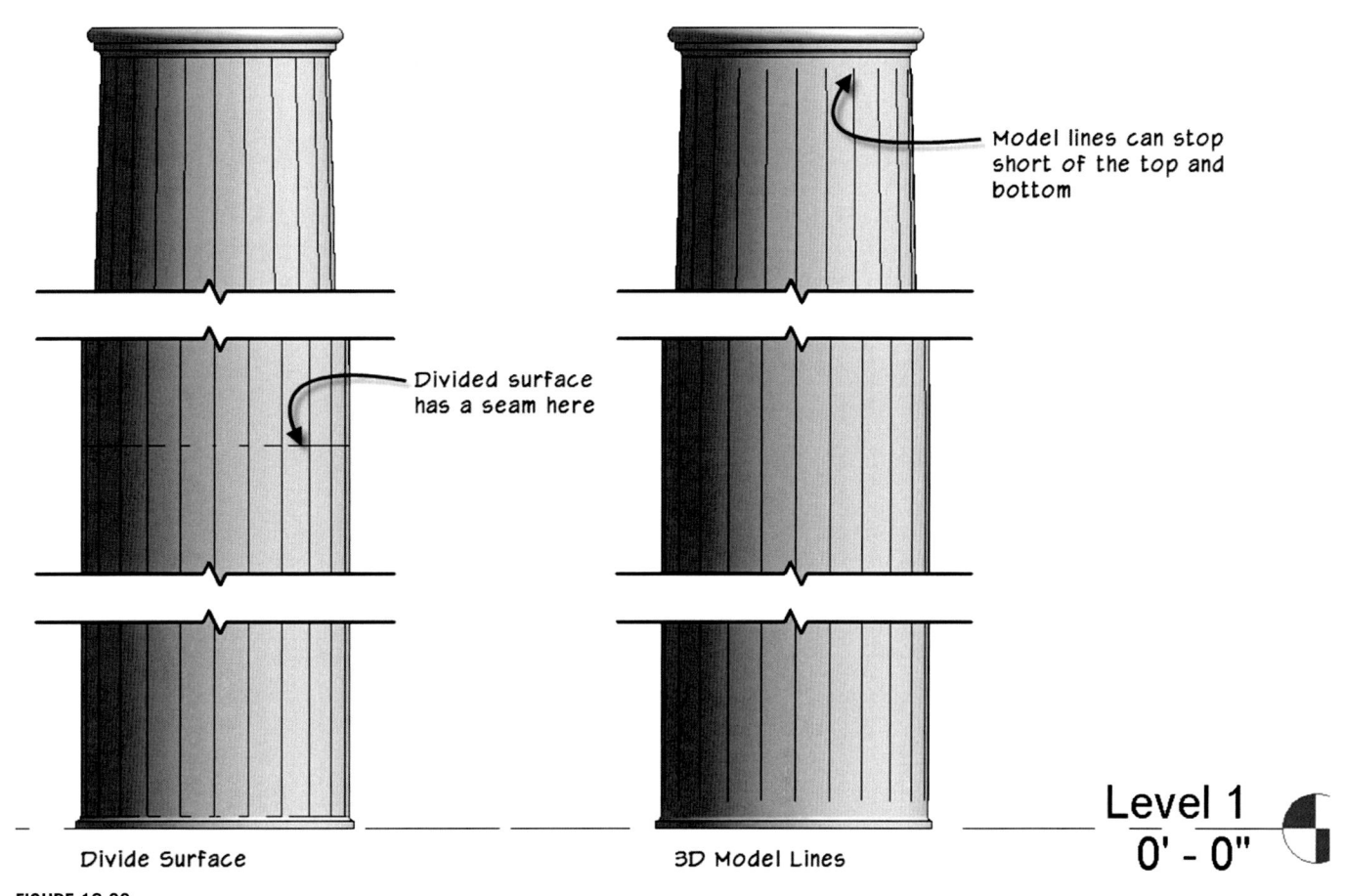

FIGURE 12.33
Comparing the Divided Surface and 3D Lines approaches

SUMMARY

- ✓ Create column shafts with properly constructed entasis can be a little challenging.
- ✓ Creating a smooth shaft with entasis can be approximated with a very large radius arc.
- ✓ An ellipse more accurately describes the shape proposed by many authorities.
- ✓ Creating a fluted shaft can be accomplished by stacking swept blends that approximate the diminution of the entasis or by lofting several profile cross sections.
- ✓ The beginning and ending routed portions of the channels can be created with voids.
- ✓ In the massing environment, a profile can be constructed from a series of hosted points and reference lines.
- ✓ The 3-point arc in the massing environment can be hosted on the points of the rig reducing the number of parameters required.
- ✓ Selecting the chain of reference lines after the profile is nested into a family is challenging. Create a plan from the reference lines first and then use this plane to build the loft in the host family.
- ✓ For lower detail representations, you can draw lines directly on the surfaces of 3D forms or use a divided surface.

FORUM ROME
Photo by author

Chapter 13
The Corinthian Capital

INTRODUCTION

The Corinthian is the most elaborate of the orders. (We are not considering Composite in this book, but it is also quite elaborate). The best way to approach the Corinthian is to break it in to several smaller pieces. There are enough components to build in just the Corinthian capital that we could have done the entire book on them alone. Naturally I wanted to show more than just the Corinthian order in this book. Therefore, with only one chapter to devote to the Corinthian capital, I have provided partially completed files as starting points for most items we will build. I have not gone over the detailed steps to create those parts that use techniques already covered elsewhere in the book. Instead I will point you to the relevant topics and chapters should you decide to build the items from scratch yourself.

OBJECTIVES

The last chapter used the tools in the massing environment to assist us in creating the complex and subtly curving forms of the fluted column shaft. In this chapter we will use the tools available in the massing environment to create the organic forms required by the Corinthian capital. Topics in this chapter include:

- Building massing environment rigs to host 3D forms.
- Building profiles hosted on reference points.
- Understanding the Normalized Curve Parameter.
- Create complex lofted forms that follow both 2D and 3D paths.
- Alternative approaches to parametric scaling such as using nested planting families.

THE CORINTHIAN DATASET FILES

If you study several Corinthian capitals, you will find quite a bit of variation. However, despite the variations, each will have some combination of standard components. There is typically two rows of leaves at the bottom. Above this is a Cauliculi, bud and button with an additional row of leaves in a flouret style. Above and behind this is are the volutes; which are smaller than those in the Ionic order. Also, there are two sets of volutes that are paired together occurring both at the corners and toward the middle. Supporting all of this is the bell form which is the same diameter as the column shaft at the top. The bell is crowned with the abacus which comes to a point at each corner. Each side of the four sided abacus is adorned by a flower (see Figure 13.1).

FIGURE 13.1

Corinthian capital examples with parts labeled (Photos by author)

Like the Ionic column in the previous chapter, I have only included the base, shaft and capital in the Corinthian column file and have omitted the pedestal. The column we will be working with contains three levels of detail: coarse, medium and fine (see Figure 13.2).

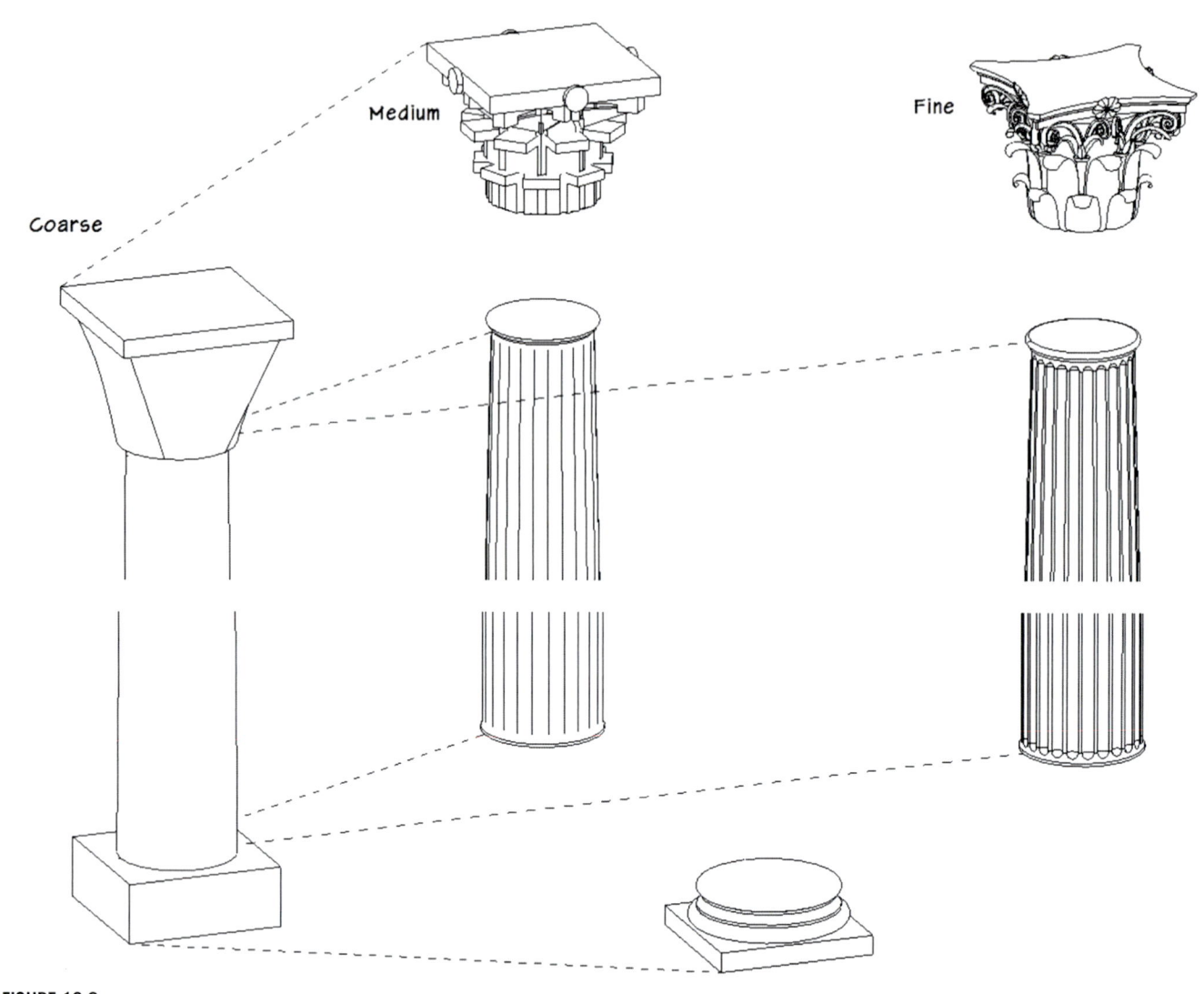

FIGURE 13.2

Understanding the Corinthian Column File

• Renaissance Revit •

Following an approach similar to the other orders we have already built, I created a simplified version for the coarse detail version using a blend topped with an extrusion. The shaft and base are saved from the other schematic versions in the other orders. The medium and fine detail versions are a bit more involved. The shaft was built in the previous chapter. I have provided a base family and a medium detail capital family which I will explain in detail in the next topic. We will build the fine detail version here in this chapter.

UNDERSTANDING THE MEDIUM DETAIL VERSION

The medium detail version contains a nested family for each major component. Most of the forms of the fine detail version will require the freeform and lofting tools of the massing environment. The medium detail version of the Corinthian capital could be built using the traditional family editor, but since we will use save as to create a copy of it for the fine detail version, I used the *Family Seed (Adaptive).rfa* file to create it instead.

The abacus is a simple extruded square. This tops a cylindrical form that represents the drum. Copied around the drum are two tiers of "L" shaped extrusions, the first tier short and the second one tall representing the two lower rows of leaves. Above this, there are two families, one representing the volutes and another representing the flouret (third tier of leaves). Finally the flowers that adorn the abacus are represented as simple cylindrical forms. I built each form as a rough approximation of the final fine detail version. These are simplified forms that can be thought of as bounding boxes for the fine detail versions that we will build below (see Figure 13.3).

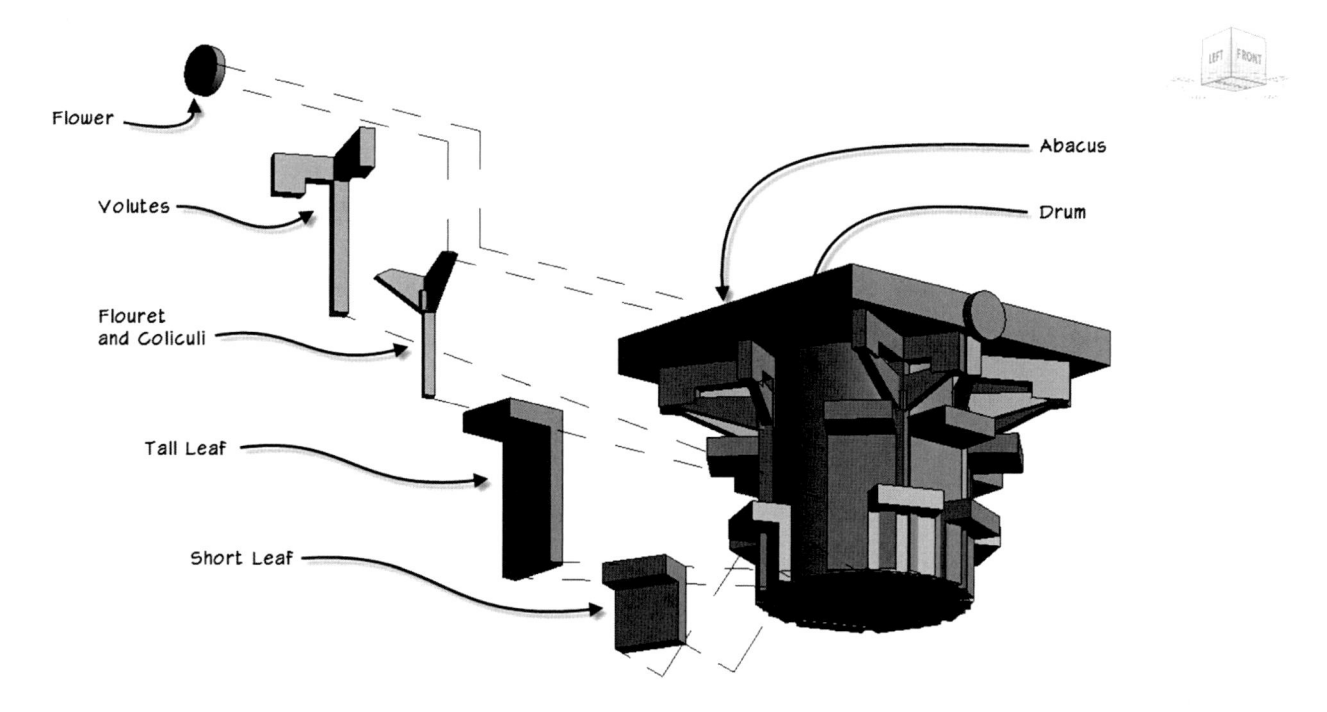

FIGURE 13.3
Understanding the provided Corinthian Medium Detail Capital

If you explore the file a little (*Corinthian Capital Medium.rfa*), you will see that there are some circles in the file that have several hosted reference points on them. The individual families are hosted to these points. This was particularly helpful for the flourets and volutes since these elements had to be rotated on their respective work planes. Once you establish the rotation and mirroring required, it will be maintained even when the family scales.

> **Note:** I'd like to say a word about divided paths. I built an earlier version of this family that used divided paths and repeated components instead of reference points. Orientation is a little trickier to set up with repeated components. Furthermore, once you repeat, all of the repeated elements will become part of the repeated element. In other words you can no longer select a single leaf or volute. These issues are not necessarily "deal killers" but just the same, I opted for the hosted reference points as it did make set up and ongoing modifications a little easier.

SAVE A FINE DETAIL VERSION

Now that you have some idea how the provided files are structured, let's get started on the fine detail version of the Corinthian capital. We'll get started with the medium detail version, copy it and then modify each of the sub-components.

1. From the *Chapter13* folder, open the file named: *Corinthian Capital Medium.rfa*.
2. From the Application menu, choose **Save As > Family**.
   ⇨ Name the new file: **Corinthian Capital Fine** and save it in the *Chapter13* folder.

At this point, we could select any other the nested families, click the Edit Family button and then save them as the fine detail version. I have provided all of the nested families as separate RFA files in the *Chapter13* folder. So we can open them directly from there instead and then proceed to save them as fine detail versions. So for now, we can close this new file we created here. We will reopen it at the end of the chapter when we are ready to assemble the column capital.

3. Close the file. (Save if prompted).

THE ABACUS AND DRUM

There are a few different techniques that I would like to share in this chapter. Beginning with the abacus and drum, we will create solid forms in the massing environment using 2D "profiles" created in the traditional family editor environment (from generic model families). I have create the generic model families and the starting point family for the abacus and drum. Each of these forms will be built from nested generic model families. But I will discuss two slightly different approaches. Let's open each file and explore them a bit before we build anything.

1. From the *Chapter13* folder, open the file named: *Bell FB Path.rfa*.

This is a very simple file. I created it from our *Family Seed (Face Based).rfa* seed family (refer to the "Create a Face Based Family Seed" topic in Chapter 2). The seed family uses instance parameters, so I had to open "Family Types" and modify each parameter to change them to Type based. I added a simple formula: Base Diameter * 0.850 to both Width and Depth. This sets them to the size of the shaft at the top of the column.

Next, leaving "Family Types," I deleted the existing box and height reference plane from any elevation view. Back in the plan view, I used the Model Line tool to draw a centered circle and add a diameter dimension. Labeled the dimension with either the Width or Depth parameter. Turned on the center mark and align and lock in both directions. This is the process followed in the "Create a Parametric Circle" topic in Chapter 4. You can review it for more information. That's it. This is a very simple file. This will be the path of the bell shape that will form the backup for all of the leaves and other complex forms in the Corinthian capital.

2. Close the file, there is no need to save.
3. From the *Chapter13* folder, open the file named: *Bell FB Profile.rfa*.

This is the shape of the bell. It will sweep around the circular path to form the 3D form. This shape is a little more complex. It uses a beak mold which is a shape we have not previously used, but as you can see a beak mold is comprised of two 90° arcs and we have seen plenty of examples of how to constrain these. Refer to the "Quarter Round and Half Round (Astragal and Torus)" topic in Chapter 4 for more details. So once the reference planes at the top were established, it was a simple matter of turning on the center marks and aligning and locking the centers and endpoints in both directions. Remember, when all of the Automatic Sketch Dimensions disappear, or if a Revit alert appears telling you that this "would over constrain the sketch;" you are done. At the bottom, the shallow curve tapers the bell in at the top of the shaft to allow room for the leaves to "sprout." This curve is another arc that is nearly identical to an ovolo, so I constrained it using the procedures covered in the "Ovolo" topic in Chapter 4. A parameter called Projection allows us to keep the inside portion of the sweep hollow and avoid any errors associated with making too tight of a sweep. I tried to keep any additional parameters to a minimum by relying on equality dimensions for the overall spacing and proportions.

4. Close the file, there is no need to save.

The final profile is one we will use to cut the moldings into the abacus. Think of it a virtual router bit.

5. From the *Chapter13* folder, open the file named: *Abacus Void FB Profile.rfa*.

This profile uses an ovolo and a corona separated by a fillet. I already mentioned the "Ovolo" topic above. The "Corona" topic is also in Chapter 4. I simplified the corona here and built it more like the quarter round. This is because the corona shape required follows a 45° angle. So there is no need for the trig or the nested detail rigs. The Projection parameter gives us the ability to increase the depth of the void to ensure it cuts all the way through the solids. The distance is somewhat arbitrary.

6. Close the file, there is no need to save.

USING GM PROFILES FOR BOTH PATH AND SHAPE

Now that we have explored each of the shapes, let's build our first form. We will start with the bell shape and create both the path and the profile by nesting in the generic model families that we just opened and studied.

1. From the *Chapter13* folder, open the file named: *Abacus and Bell.rfa*.

This is the medium detail version of the file.

2. Save the family as: **Abacus and Bell_Fine**.
3. Delete both form elements onscreen. (Delete just the forms, use TAB as necessary).
    ⇨ Delete the circle reference line as well.
    Do *not* delete the square reference lines.

Pay attention to the tooltips and/or the Status Line when you select elements in the massing environment. You want the tip to say "Form Element" not "Form Element:Surface" before you delete. Press TAB to highlight and select the right thing if necessary.

4. Click on the reference plane right beneath the level (named: Abacus Bottom) to set it as the active work plane.
5. On the Create tab, click the Component tool. When prompted to load a family, click Yes.
    ⇨ Browse to the *Chapter13* folder, select the *Bell FB Path.rfa* file and then click Open.
    ⇨ On the Modify I Place Component tab, on the Placement panel, click the Place on Work Plane button.

⇨ Move the cursor near where the intersection of the two center reference planes is.

They should highlight onscreen (see Figure 13.4).

TIP: If they do not highlight, try holding down the shift and dragging the wheel to orbit the view slightly.

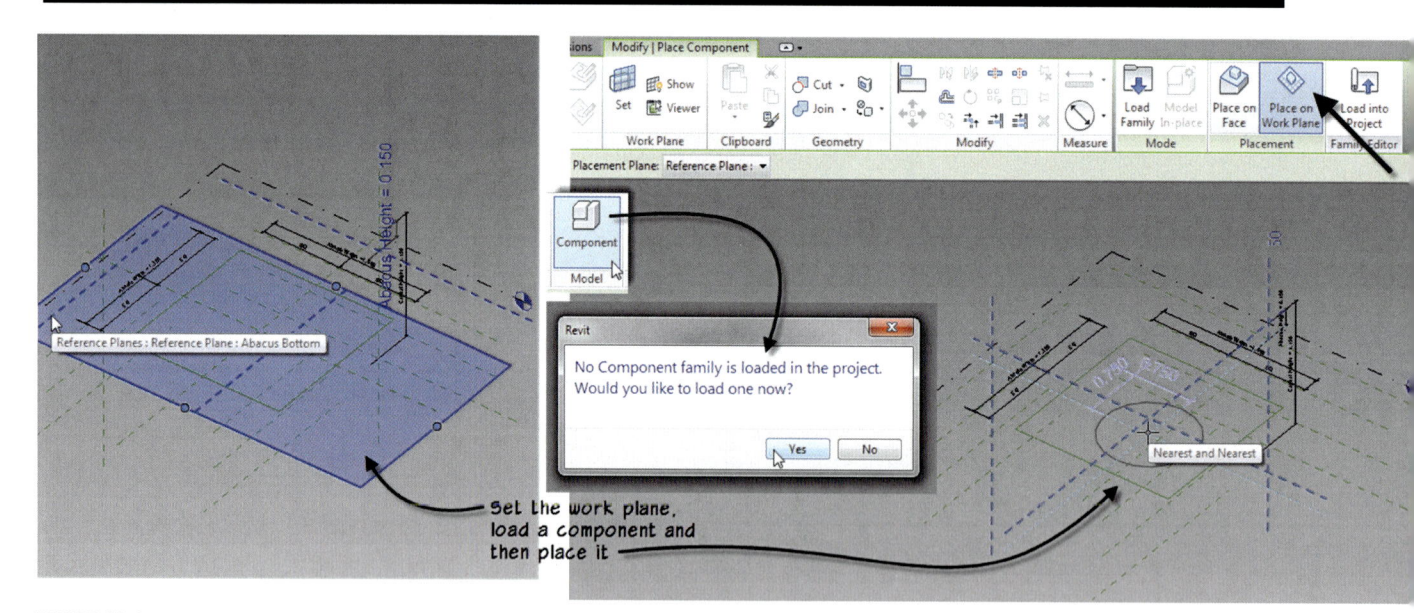

FIGURE 13.4
Load and place a component family in the massing environment on a selected work plane

6. Click to place the family at the intersection of the two center reference planes.

⇨ Click the Modify tool to cancel the command.

⇨ Select the newly placed family and then on the Options Bar, click the Show Host button.

The Abacus Bottom reference plane should highlight to indicate that it is the host.

7. Open the *Ref. Level* floor plan view and align and lock the family to the centers in both directions, then return to the *{3D}* view.

The aligning and locking is not always necessary in the massing environment, but I like to do it just the same. It takes a little practice to know when you can skip it. Just be careful not to over constrain. There is a fine line. With practice, you'll get the feel for it.

8. Click the point tool and add a hosted point on the circle. I like to place it at a quadrant point (see the left side of Figure 13.5).

Note: A little anomaly I have noticed in the massing environment, is that when placing hosted points, often the first one does not show up right away. If you roll your wheel a little, you can force a view regeneration. If you perform another action that regens, then it will usually appear as well. This is another area where it takes practice to have the confidence to trust that even though the point did not appear immediately, it is there. So be sure to only click once. You don't need two points here.

9. Click the Modify tool to cancel, then select the point to make it the work plane.

⇨ Click the Component tool again. Click the Load Family button, browse to the *Chapter13* folder and select the *Bell FB Profile.rfa* file this time.

⇨ Click the Place on Work Plane button again.

• Renaissance Revit •

⇨ Click on the point to place it. Then click the Modify tool to cancel.

Make sure that the point snap icon appears. If necessary, type SX to ensure you are snapping to the point. Not the quadrant or endpoint.

10. Tap the SPACEBAR a few times and then click the Flip Work Plane icon to orient the shape (see the right side of Figure 13.5).

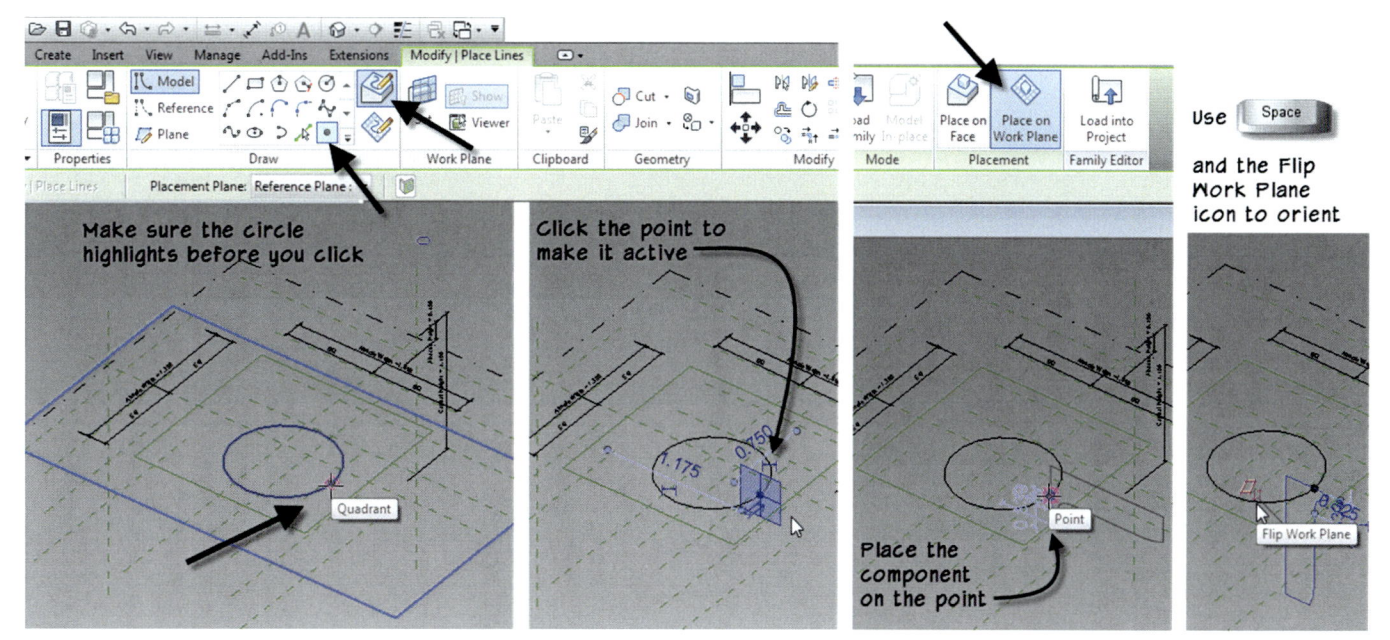

FIGURE 13.5
Add the other profile to a new hosted point on the circle family instance

11. Select both families onscreen.

⇨ On the Properties palette, uncheck the Visible checkbox and then on the ribbon, click the Create Form button.

12. On the Project Browser, expand *Families > Generic Models* and then edit the Type Properties of the type named: Flex for both families. Link up the Base Diameter parameter.

⇨ Open "Family Types" and flex. Return to **1.000** when finished.

13. Select the form and on the Properties palette, assign the Capital Material parameter to the material.

14. Save the file.

> **CATCH UP!** You can open a file completed to this point named: *13_Abacus and Bell_Fine_A.rfa.*

One more note before we move on from the bell to the abacus. I had you build this form similar to how we approached it in the traditional environment; that is sweep it along a circular path. However, we have a few more options open to us in the massing environment. So if you prefer, you can delete this form and the circle. Draw a vertical reference plane directly at the intersection of the two center reference planes. Place the profile on one of these planes and increase the Project Mult parameter to 0.425. The reference line should touch the profile edge. You can then select the reference line and the profile and create form and Revit will interpret it as a revolve. The unique feature here is that you can revolve a profile! So if you don't want your bell to be hollow, or just want to experiment, give it a try.

BUILDING THE PATH WITH A MASSING RIG

For the abacus, we'll build the path directly in the adaptive family. I already have the four reference lines forming a square shape at the top. They are dimensioned with a parameter labeled Abacus Width. In this approach, we will

386 | Chapter 13

build a reference line "rig" and no additional parameters will be required. The trick as discussed in Chapter 11 is the "Normalized Curve Parameter."

Continue in the *Abacus and Bell_Fine* file or open the catch-up file.

1. On the Create tab, click the Reference button and then the Line icon.
   ⇨ On the Options Bar, check the 3D Snapping checkbox.
   ⇨ Click directly on one of the edges of the square. Then click on the opposite side.
   Both points should be hosted to the rectangle. Don't worry if the line is not straight, we'll fix that in a minute.
2. Repeat three more times to create a total of four lines inside the original square (see the top of Figure 13.6).

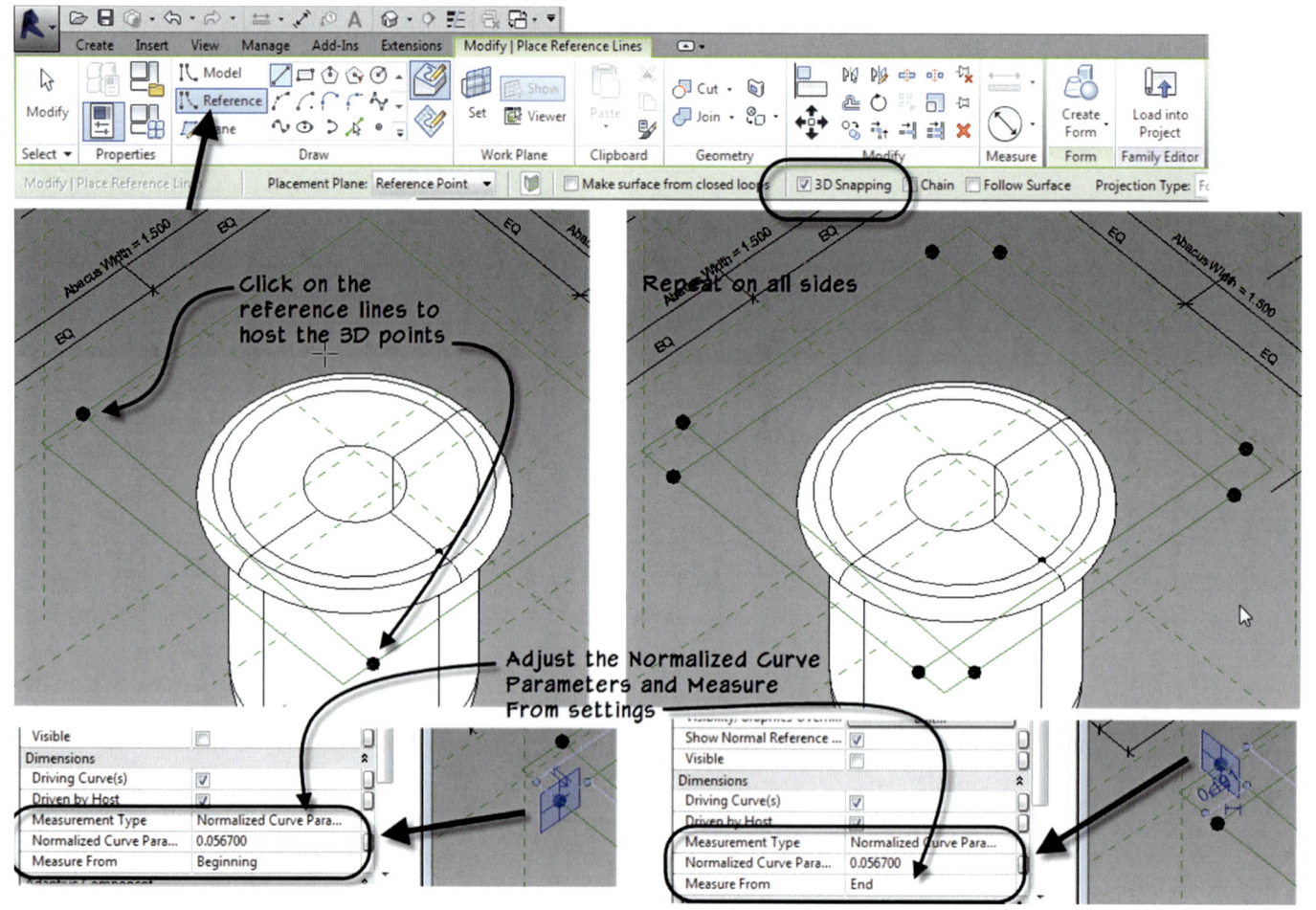

FIGURE 13.6
Add reference lines and then adjust the normalized curve parameter

3. Select one of the points.

The Normalized Curve Parameter is a value between 0 and 1. The point is measured from can be the begging or end of the line. We can change this on the Properties palette, or using the small flip measure-from end icon onscreen. We will leave all the ones that have a value close to zero measured from the beginning and change all the ones that have a value close to 1 to measure from end.

⇨ If the value of the Normalized Curve Parameter is close to zero, set it to: **0.0567**.
⇨ If the value is closer to 1.000, change the Measure From setting to **End** and then input: **0.0567** for the Normalized Curve Parameter (see the bottom of Figure 13.6).

• Renaissance Revit •

The Corinthian Capital | 387

4. Repeat for all points.

To calculate the amount of concavity of the abacus, we construct 60° lines from the corners to find the arc center. If this needed to flex, I would advocate some trig to determine the center location. But since the arc is always 60°, we can simply convert the amount of rise from the chord and add the value directly to the Normalized Curve Parameter when drawing the arcs. I calculated this by drawing a quick sketch (see Figure 13.7).

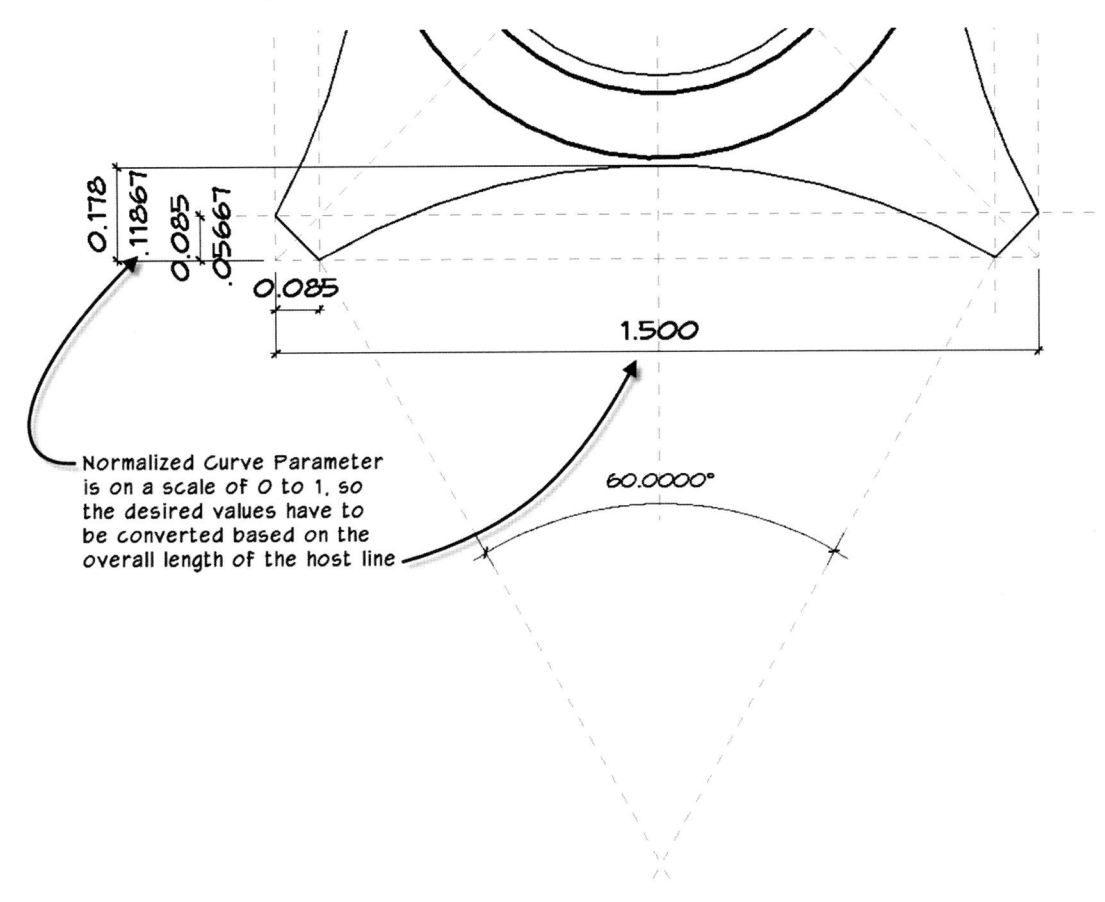

FIGURE 13.7
60° construction lines give us the curvature of the arc. You can draw a quick sketch in a project with drafting lines to determine the values

5. Draw two more reference lines bisecting the square in both directions (snap to the midpoints on all sides).

6. Using Reference Lines, click the Start-End Radius Arc. Make sure that 3D Snapping is still enabled.

⇨ Snap the start and end points directly on the hosted points on one edge of the square (the ones at the edges, not the midpoint).

⇨ Host the last point on the bisecting reference line.

⇨ Set the Normalized Curve Parameter of this third point to: **0.11867** (see Figure 13.8).[8]

---

[8] The 3-point arc with 3D Snapping is available in Revit 2014 and later. If you are using an earlier version, you will need to build an additional square rig further out to host the center points of the arcs. Use equality dimensions and a new parameter to flex this square. Host a center point element on each midpoint and use that to build the arcs. Remember that the triangles formed are equilateral (60° on a side).

• *Creating Classical Architecture with Modern Software* •

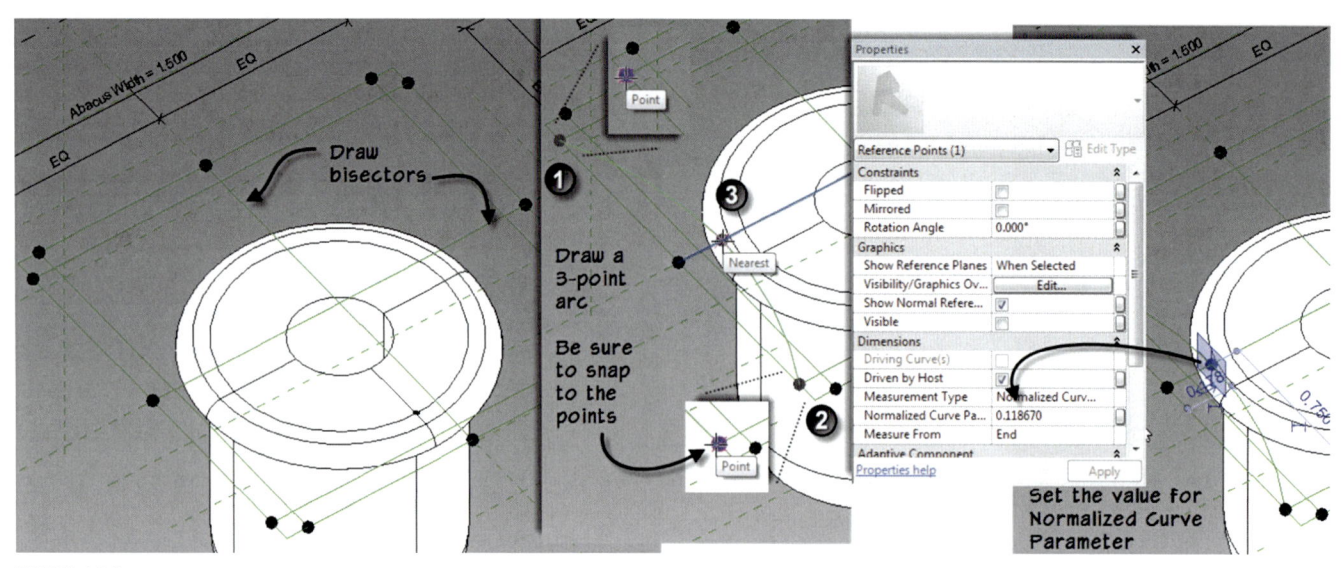

FIGURE 13.8
Create bisecting lines and then draw the arcs hosted to the rig.

7. Repeat the process to create three more arcs. Snap your points carefully to ensure you are associating with the correct hosts.

   ⇨ The Measure From for two of the arcs will need to be changed to **End**.

8. Cap off the small diagonal ends with straight reference lines.

   You can draw these with the line tool and 3D Snapping, or select the two points and then click the Spline Through Points.

9. Place a point hosted at the midpoint of one of the diagonal lines.

10. Using the Component tool, load the *Abacus Void FB Profile.rfa* file and place it on the hosted point's work plane.

    ⇨ Use the spacebar and Flip Work Plane icon to orient it properly (see Figure 13.9).

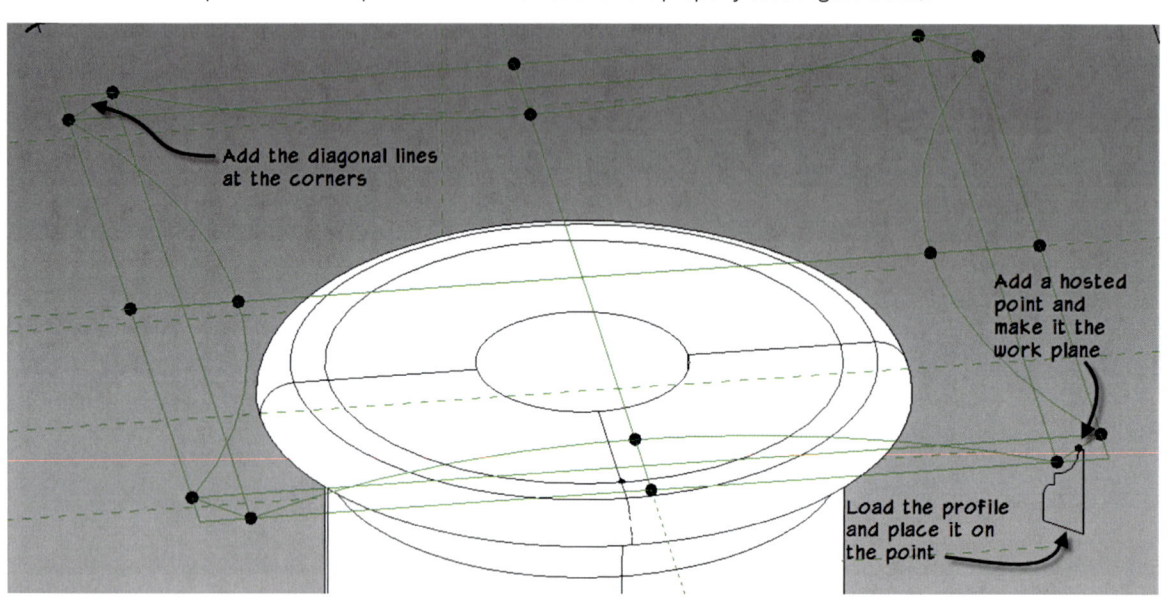

FIGURE 13.9
Complete the path and load and place the profile

11. On Project Browser, edit the Type Properties of the profile and link up the Base Diameter.

    ⇨ Flex to make sure everything is working.

• Renaissance Revit •

12. Select the four arcs and the four 45° lines. You will probably not be able to chain select these, so use the CTRL key as required.

⇨ Create Form. Choose the Extrusion option. (Don't select anything else, leave the form selected as-is).

13. On the Properties palette, change the Positive Offset to **0**.

⇨ Click the Associate Family Parameter button next to Negative Offset (see the top of Figure 13.10).

⇨ In the "Associate Family Parameter" dialog, choose Abacus Height and then click OK.

14. Right-click in the canvas area and then choose **Select Previous**.

The four arcs and four 45° lines should be selected again.

⇨ Hold down the CTRL key and select the profile family.

15. Click on the Create Form drop-down and choose Void Form (see bottom of Figure 13.10).

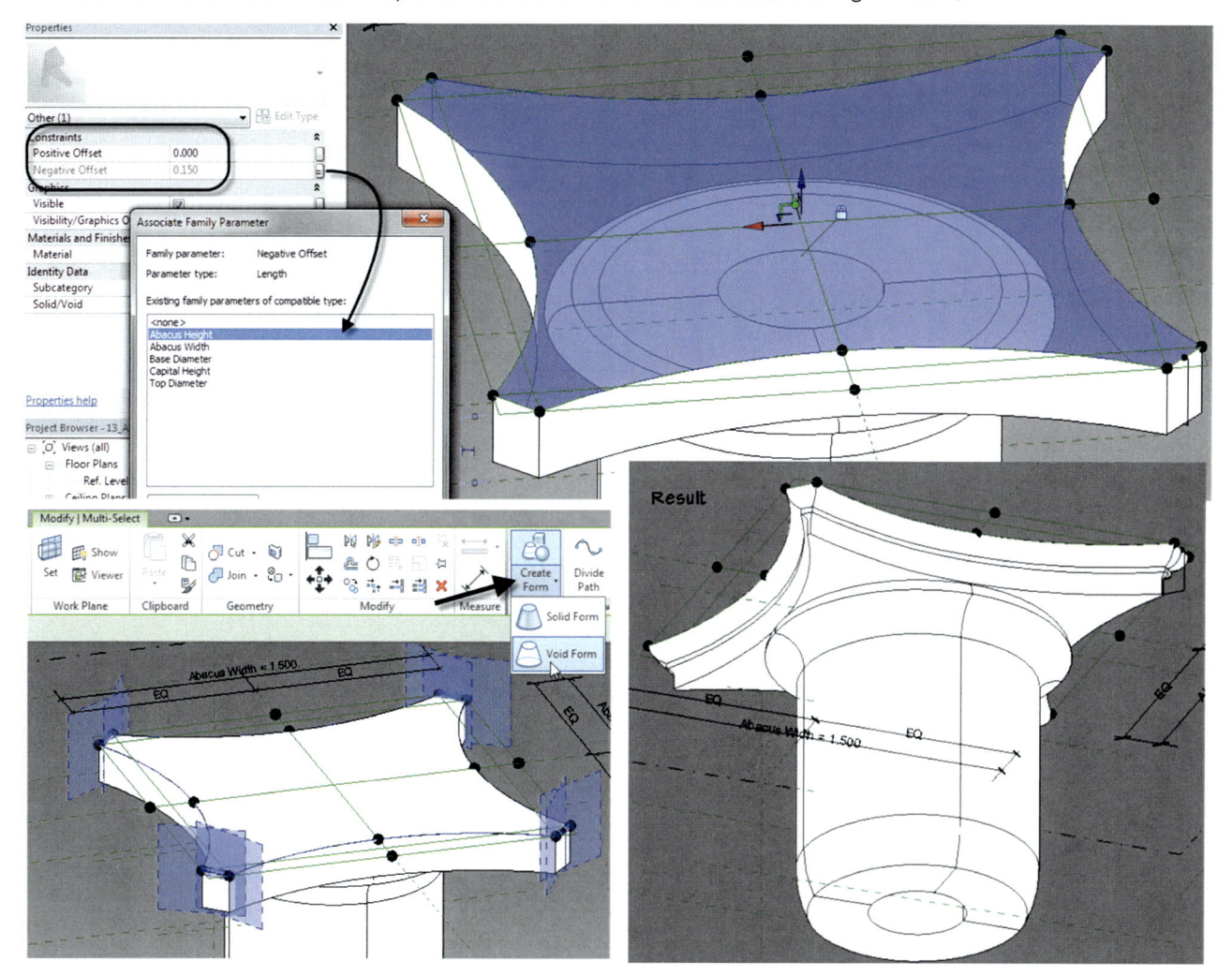

FIGURE 13.10

Create an extruded form and then cut it with a swept void form

16. Orbit the view to study the results. Open "Family Types" to flex and then save the file when finished.

17. Select the abacus form and on the Properties palette, assign the Capital Material parameter to the material.

CATCH UP! You can open a file completed to this point named: *13_Abacus and Bell_Fine.rfa*.

So far all of these forms could have been built in the traditional family editor with very similar results. In fact, you will notice that cylindrical curves in the massing environment are made in two halves with a seam in the middle. I am not particularly fond of this, but overall it is not too troublesome. If you decide to combine families, just remember that a traditional family can be nested into a massing or adaptive family, but a massing or adaptive family cannot be nested into a traditional one. So plan carefully. Now let's move on to some forms that are nearly impossible to create in the traditional environment: the Corinthian capital leaves.

ACANTHUS LEAVES

I have tried many options to build the leaves. Building a convincing looking leaf is not too challenging. Making it flex proportionally, making the file size manageable, making it a solid model instead of surface model and most importantly; simplifying the process to recreate it were the real challenges.

1. From the *Chapter13* folder, open the file named: *Leaf.rfa*.

This is the medium detail version of the file.

2. Save the family as: **Leaf_Fine**.
3. Delete the form element onscreen.

   Keep the rest for now.

THE LEAF PATH

The "L" shaped set of reference lines were used in the medium detail version to give a very rough outline of the form. Here they will guide us to draw the path (basically the stem) of the leaf. As you know, the massing environment (for which adaptive components like this one are a part) contains two splines: spline through points and spline. Spline through points is a 3D spline. The spline is the traditional spline available in the standard family editor that uses a Bezier curve. I have tried both for this and while many (if not most) creators of adaptive components would likely favor the spline through points, I got better results from the standard spline. So this is what we will use for the path. It is also pretty common when working in the massing environment for folks to work exclusively in 3D, but I like to use my orthographic views too.

4. Open the *Left* elevation view.
   - Select any dimension onscreen, right-click and choose **Select All Instances > Visible in View**.
   - On the View Control Bar, from Temporary Hide/Isolate (sunglasses), choose **Hide Element**.

   Zoom in close on the "L" shape.

5. On the Create tab, click the Reference button and then click the Spline icon. (*Not* Spline Through Points).
   - Using the left side of Figure 13.11 as a guide, sketch a spline inside the "L" shape.

   Be sure to leave space around the edges, do not snap to anything.

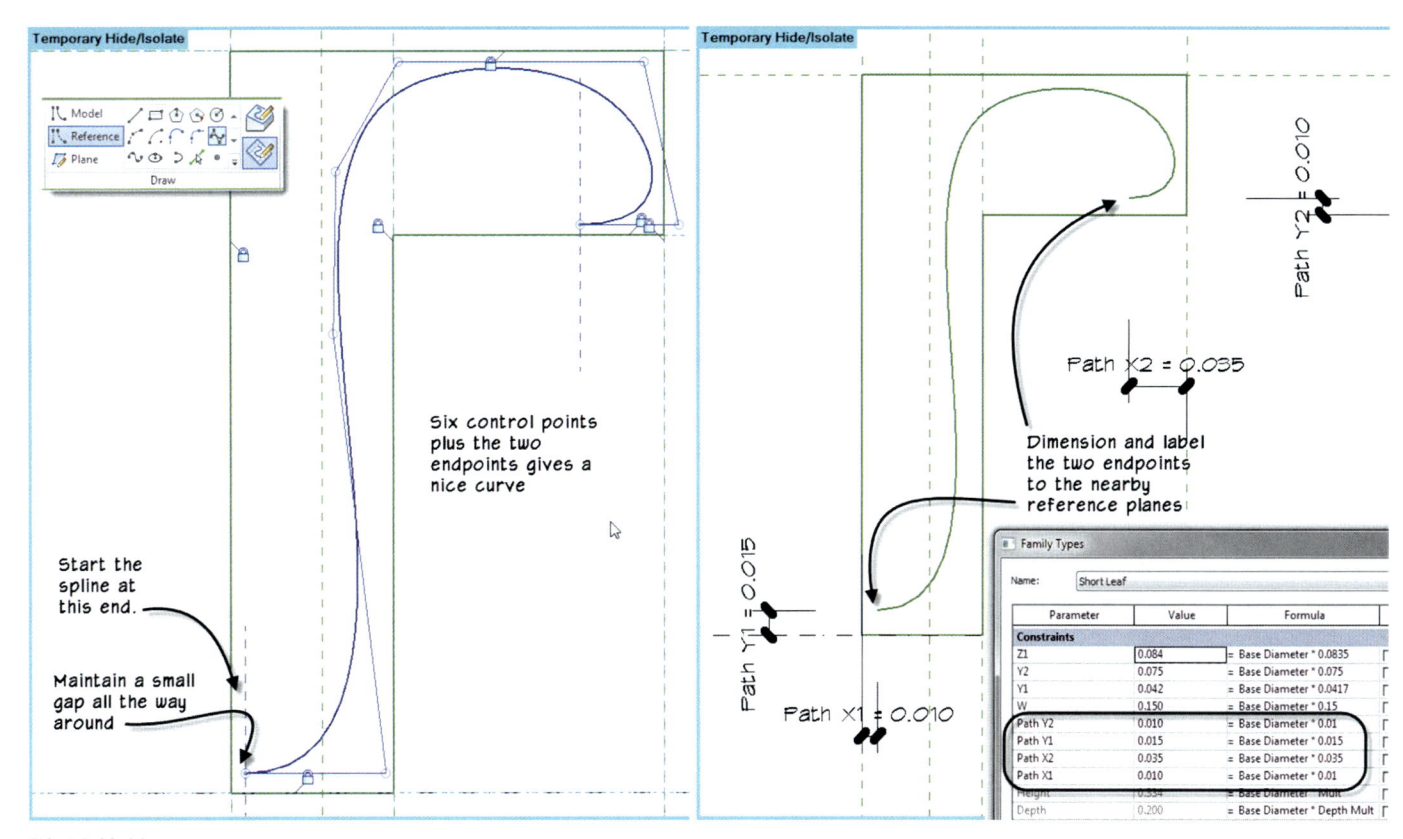

FIGURE 13.11

Sketch a spline curve for the shape of the leaf path

Remember, if we want it to flex, we have to secure the endpoints. Normally we would use reference planes for this. You are welcome to do that here. But if you recall, in the 3D view, all of the reference planes display. So it can get a little cluttered. So instead, I am going to simply add dimensions directly to the endpoints.

6. Add dimensions to the endpoints in each direction (see the right side of Figure 13.11).

⇨ Label the dimensions with new parameters (see Table 13.1).

TABLE 13.1

Parameter	Value	Type of Parameter
Path X1	0.010	Base Diameter * 0.010
Path X2	0.035	Base Diameter * 0.035
Path Y1	0.015	Base Diameter * 0.015
Path Y2	0.010	Base Diameter * 0.010

7. Fine tune the position of any of the points.

8. Flex the file and then save it.

If you need to move the endpoint, remember to TAB first. Otherwise, when you stretch the point, the whole curve will rescale.

CATCH UP! You can open a file completed to this point named: *13_Leaf_Fine_A.rfa*.

• *Creating Classical Architecture with Modern Software* •

ADDING HOSTED POINT RIGS

Now that we have the path, we need to create several cross sections along this path to build a lofted form for the leaf. This can theoretically be done by loading in nested families for the profile or by drawing the profiles directly in this file. The advantage of the nested families is that it simplifies the setup a bit. We can bury the parameters that flex the shape of the profile inside the nested family and control them from a couple control parameters. However, I enjoyed much better success when building everything directly in this adaptive family.

Continue in your *Leaf_Fine* family or open the catch-up file.

1. Place a point hosted on the spline near the bottom end. Do not put it right at the end, just close by.

   ⇨ Click the Modify tool to cancel.

2. Open the {3D} view.

3. Select the point, and then on the Properties palette, for the Show Reference Planes option, choose **Always**.

   ⇨ Uncheck the "Show Normal Reference Plane Only" checkbox.

We are now going to build a series of reference points that are hosted on this point. These points will each be offset from the host point in various directions. This will allow a single point to control and drive the geometry required by the cross section. It must be set up very carefully in order to function properly.

4. On the Create tab, click the Point button.

   Do not click yet.

   ⇨ On the Work Plane panel, click the Set button.

   ⇨ Highlight the point (the main work plane will highlight).

   ⇨ TAB to highlight the one that runs opposite the path. Click to set the plane.

5. Click directly on the existing point to add the new one.

   ⇨ In the warning that appears when placing the point, click OK to dismiss the dialog (see Figure 13.12).

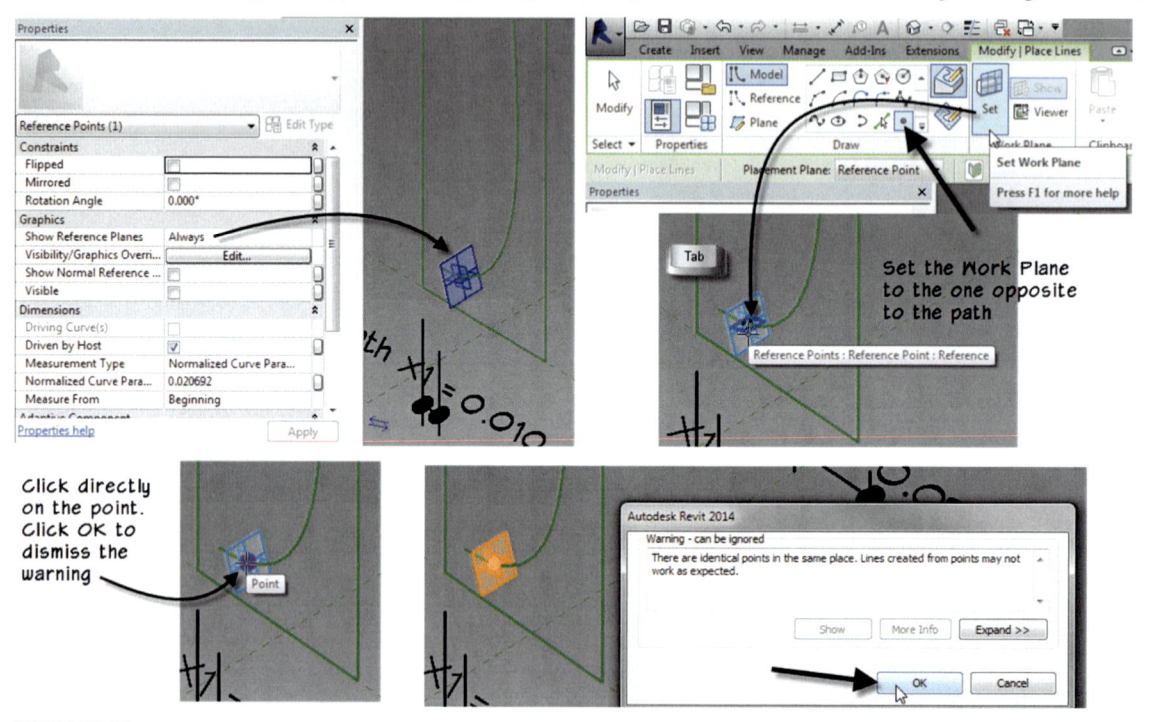

FIGURE 13.12

Set a work plane on the hosted point and the place a point directly on the point

Revit warns us that unexpected results can come from multiple points in the same place. In the next step we'll move the point, so this is not an issue.

6. Click again in the same spot to place a second point. Click OK to dismiss the warning.
7. Click the Modify tool to cancel the command.
8. Click on the point you just added.
   ⇨ On the Properties palette, next to Offset, type: **0.005** and then apply.

   The point will move down and away from the host point.

   ⇨ Keep the point selected. Next to Offset, click the Associate Family Parameter button.
   ⇨ Create a new type-based parameter grouped under **Constraints** called: **Profile V1**.
9. Select the other point that we created, set its Offset to: **0.025** and then add a parameter for it called: **Profile V2**.

> **Note:** I am using the letter "V" here for the "Y" direction and I will later use "U" for the "X" direction. This is standard practice in 3D modeling to designate "local" coordinates as opposed to absolute coordinates which use X, Y and Z directly.

We will add formulas to these parameters later. For now, we just want to make sure that we have them all assigned and hosted properly.

10. Drag the main host point (the one showing the work planes) slightly.

The point will slide along the spline and take the two hosted points with it. The two vertical parameters will keep the offsets constant as the points move along the spline.

11. Add two more points on the main host point.
    ⇨ This time, we want to set the work plane that is parallel to spline current.
    ⇨ Offset one point to: **0.100** and the other to **-0.100**.
    ⇨ Assign them new parameters named: **Profile U1 Pos** and **Profile U1 Neg** (see Figure 13.13).

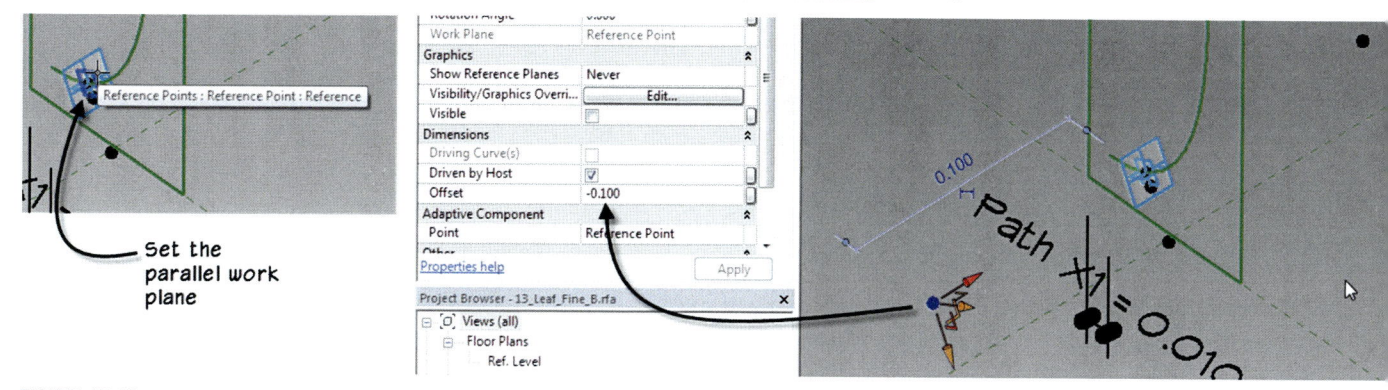

FIGURE 13.13
Add two more points hosted on the parallel work plane and assigned to two new parameters

If you drag the point again, all four points will travel with it. Now we can use the CTRL + drag method to make copies of the points.

12. Select all five points, the main host point and the four points hosted to its work planes.
    ⇨ Hold down the CTRL key and then drag the point along the spline and release.

• *Creating Classical Architecture with Modern Software* •

394 | Chapter 13

You should have a copy of all the points and the newly copied sub-points will be hosted to the copied main point. Refer to the "Using a Divided Path to Aid in Spacing" topic in Chapter 12 for another example of this technique.

13. On the newly copied points, select the two "U" points and one of the "V" points.

    ⇨ Click the Spline Through Points icon.

    ⇨ Select the two "U" points again, and then the other "V" point and create a second spline through points (see Figure 13.14).

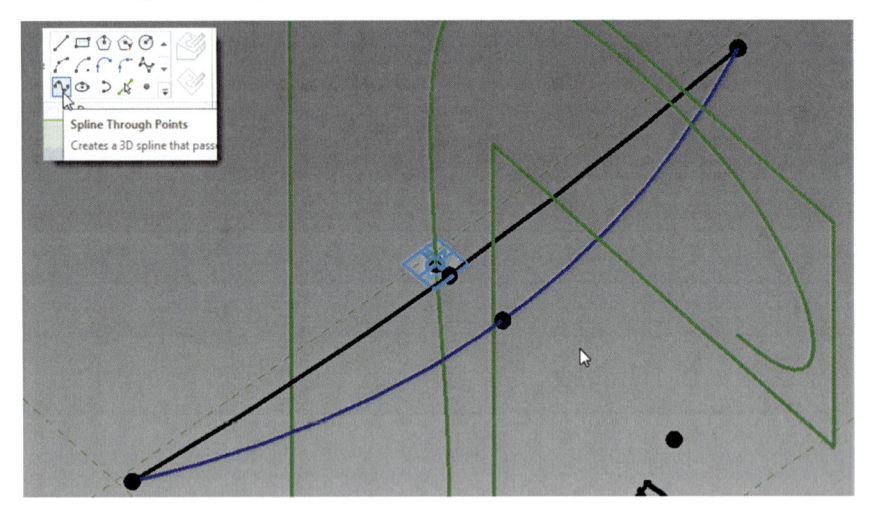

FIGURE 13.14
Create two splines through points

14. Select both splines and on the Properties palette, check the Is Reference Line checkbox.

    Try dragging the host point again to ensure everything is still functioning properly.

We will now repeat this entire process several times. Unfortunately the hosting breaks if you try to create the splines before you CTRL drag. So the process is: CTRL + drag the points. Create the splines, make them reference lines. Drag the host to test. Then repeat.

15. Repeat the CTRL + drag from the original points (the ones you have not made into splines yet).

    ⇨ Create three more sets of points and splines roughly equally spaced on the lower half of the spline.

    Do not create splines from the original points yet (see the left side of Figure 13.15).

16. Copy another set of points from the original with the CTRL + drag method.

    ⇨ Deselect everything, select the newly copied main host point.

    ⇨ On the Properties palette, set the Rotation Angle to **180** (see the middle of Figure 13.15).

Don't make splines from the new copies yet. The rest of the copies also need the 180° rotation, so we will use them to copy the remaining point groups we need.

17. Select the newly copied and rotated set of points and CTRL + drag another copy. Don't drag too far.

Revit does an odd thing at the top of the spline. You cannot drag a point on the last quarter of the curve. If you try, it always snaps to the end of the spline. So for the remaining copies, keep them in the vertical portion of the curve before it wraps around the top.

18. Create the splines, then CTRL + drag two more copies and make splines.

    ⇨ Make splines from any remaining points including the original ones.

• Renaissance Revit •

⇨ Check the Is Reference Plane box to make all the splines reference lines (see the right side of Figure 13.15).

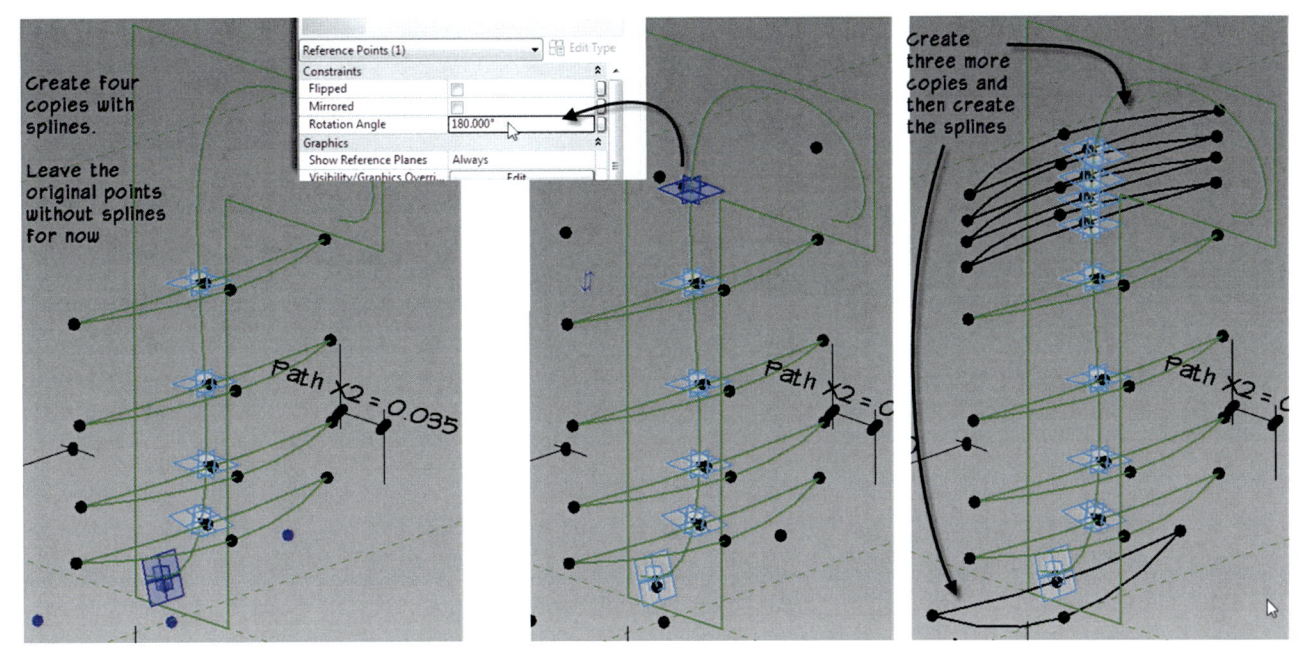

FIGURE 13.15

Using ctrl + drag you can create copies of the points and then use spline through points to complete the profiles

> **CATCH UP!** You can open a file completed to this point named: *13_Leaf_Fine_B.rfa*.

CREATE PARAMETERS AND ADJUST PROFILES

We have the basic framework we need, but in order to make the lofted leaf look more organic, we want to adjust the size and location of each profile. This will take some effort and is somewhat tedious. So be forewarned. We'll leave the profile at the bottom alone. So let's start with the second profile.

Continue in the same file or open the catch-up file.

1. Select one of the points at the end of the second profile. Click the Associate Family Parameter button, click the Add Parameter button and create a new parameter. Repeat this for all endpoints (see Figure 13.16).

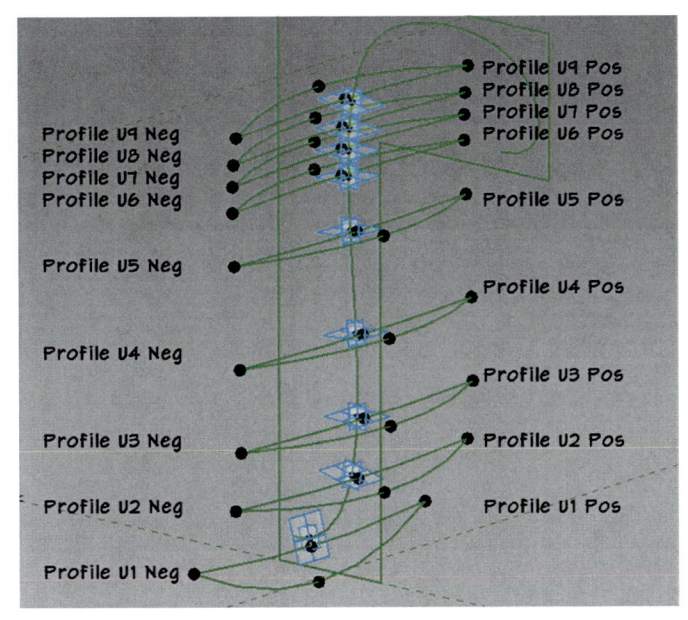

FIGURE 13.16

Create and assign new parameters to the endpoints of all the profiles

• *Creating Classical Architecture with Modern Software* •

Now we want to link together the positive and negative parameters so that they change the same. We also need formulas to tie everything to the Base Diameter. And we want to position the host points precisely along the spline. Let's start with moving the host points.

2. Select the first host point at the bottom.

    ⇨ On the Properties palette, change the Normalized Curve Parameter to: **0.001**.

This places the point very near to, but not exactly at the end. For this example, it would be fine to place it right at the end. But many times your lines when building rigs will have control points at each end. So it is good to get in the habit of setting the host points slightly away from the ends to make it easier to make selections when more than one point is involved. So let's consider 0.001 "best practice."

3. Using the same logic, we'll place the last point at **0.999**.

4. Work your way through the rest of the host points, using Normalized Curve Parameters of: **0.050**, **0.180**, **0.230**, **0.340**, **0.650**, **0.800** and **0.920**.

It might be easier to start with the high numbers and work backwards. Please note that I have arrived at these values through trial and error. If you prefer, you may want to adjust them slightly more to your liking.

5. Open the "Family Types" dialog and input formulas for all of the parameters indicated in Table 13.2.

TABLE 13.2

Parameter	Value	Type of Parameter
Profile V2	0.025	Base Diameter * 0.025
Profile V1	0.005	Base Diameter * 0.005
Profile U9 Pos	0.045	Base Diameter * 0.045
Profile U9 Neg	-0.045	-Profile U9 Pos
Profile U8 Pos	0.061	Base Diameter * 0.061
Profile U8 Neg	-0.061	-Profile U8 Pos
Profile U7 Pos	0.074	Base Diameter * 0.074
Profile U7 Neg	-0.074	-Profile U7 Pos
Profile U6 Pos	0.106	Base Diameter * 0.106
Profile U6 Neg	-0.106	-Profile U6 Pos
Profile U5 Pos	0.136	Base Diameter * 0.136
Profile U5 Neg	-0.136	-Profile U5 Pos
Profile U4 Pos	0.144	Base Diameter * 0.144
Profile U4 Neg	-0.144	-Profile U4 Pos
Profile U3 Pos	0.146	Base Diameter * 0.146
Profile U3 Neg	-0.146	-Profile U3 Pos
Profile U2 Pos	0.140	Base Diameter * 0.14
Profile U2 Neg	-0.140	-Profile U2 Pos
Profile U1 Pos	0.129	Base Diameter * 0.129
Profile U1 Neg	-0.129	-Profile U1 Pos

I arrived at these numbers by sketching a spline in the front view and then measuring where each point ended up. There was some trial and error, but mostly this approach gave good values (see Figure 13.17).

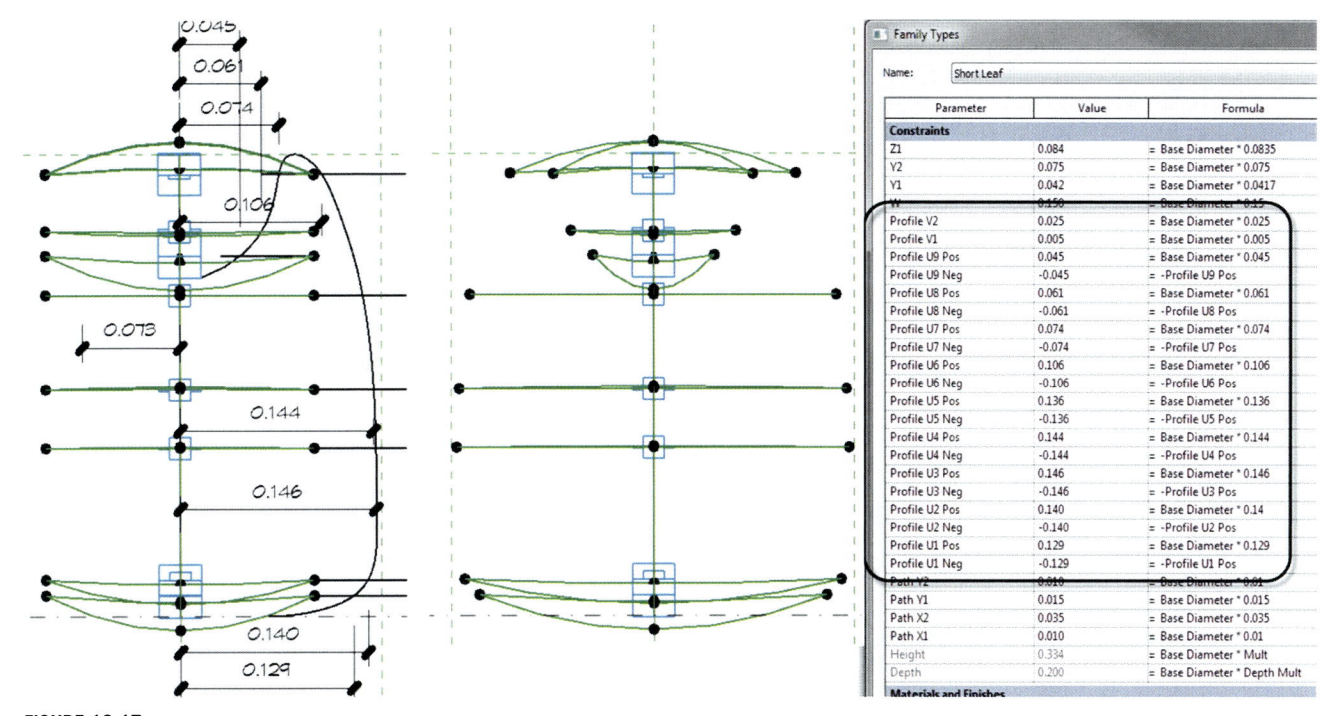

FIGURE 13.17

To determine the values of the numbers in the formulas draw a spline in front view and measure where it intersects each profile

6. Fine tune the position of any of the points if desired. Flex the file and then save it.

CATCH UP! You can open a file completed to this point named: *13_Leaf_Fine_C.rfa*.

CREATE THE LOFTED FORM

We are ready to see the fruits of our labor. There are a few finishing touches and then we can create the lofted form. If you return to the Left elevation view, you can get a sense of what the final form will look like. Remember that the original "L" shaped reference lines in the file determine the bounding box. As much as possible, we want the leaf to fall within this shape. As you can see, the parameter Profile V2 puts the thickness of the leaf a little past the edge particularly on the top and leading edge. Also, the curvature could use a slight adjustment so that the end does not terminate abruptly. I think the best way to deal with these issues is to add a couple more parameters to allow more variation in the height/thickness of the leaf and make a slight adjustment at the curled end.

Continue in the same file or open the catch-up file.

1. Open the *Left* elevation and then select the spline.

   ⇨ On the Modify | Reference Lines tab, click the Add Control button.

To add a control point, you click on the straight line of the control handle, *not* on the curved edge of the spline itself.

   ⇨ Click on the horizontal control handle adjacent to the spline endpoint (see the middle of Figure 13.18).

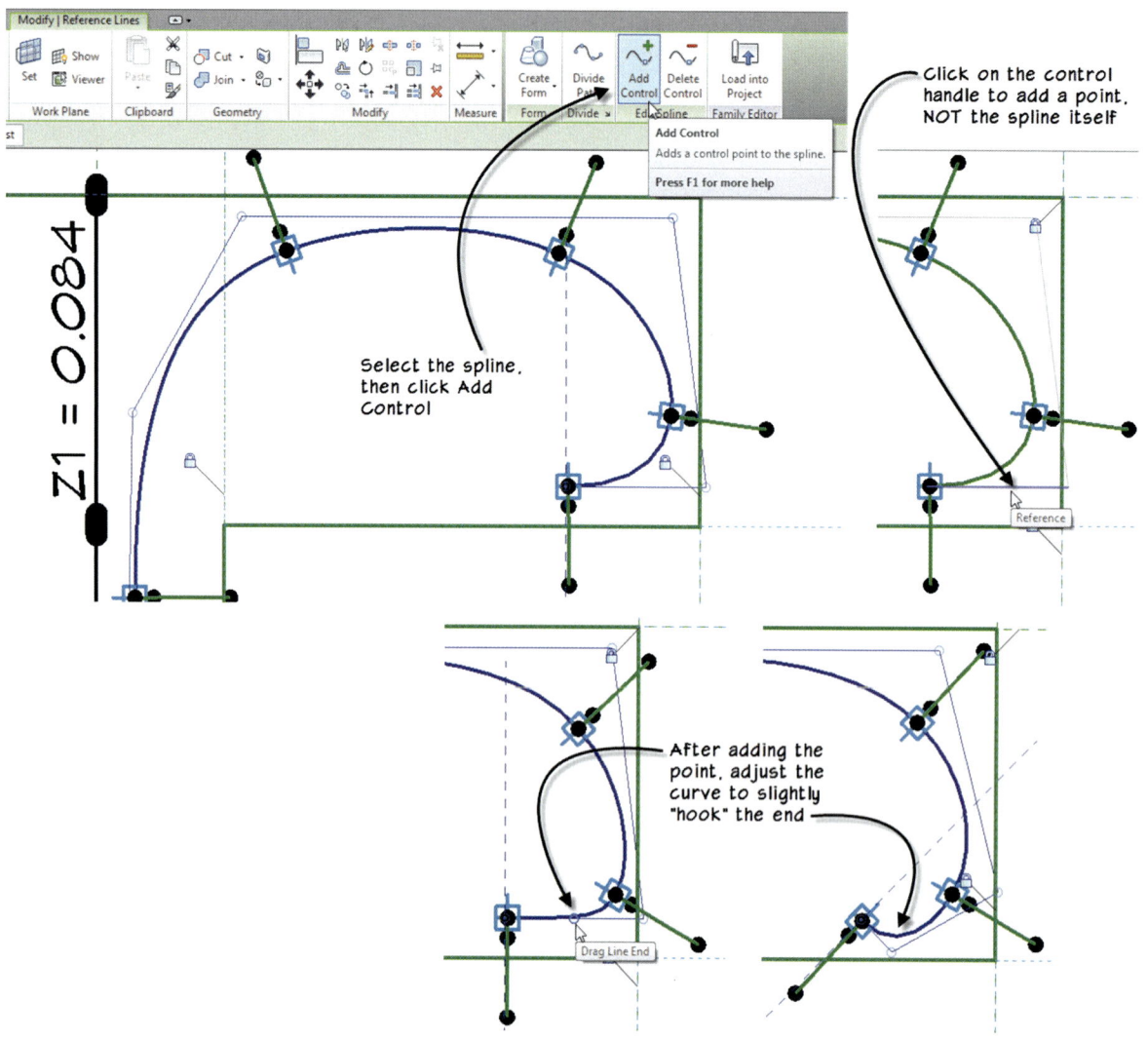

FIGURE 13.18

Add a control point near the end of the spline

2. Drag the new point to add a slight upward hook to the curve (see the left side of Figure 13.18).

3. Open the "Family Types" dialog and create the parameters listed in Table 13.3.

TABLE 13.3

Parameter	Value	Type of Parameter
Profile V0	0.003	Base Diameter * 0.003
Profile V3	0.010	Base Diameter * 0.010
Profile V4	0.015	Base Diameter * 0.015

4. Return to the *{3D}* view, and select the reference points at the ninth profile.

   ⇨ For the one closest to the host point, associate it with: **Profile V0**.

   ⇨ For the other one, associate it with the existing **Profile V1**.

5. Repeat for the other points indicated in Figure 13.19.

• Renaissance Revit •

FIGURE 13.19

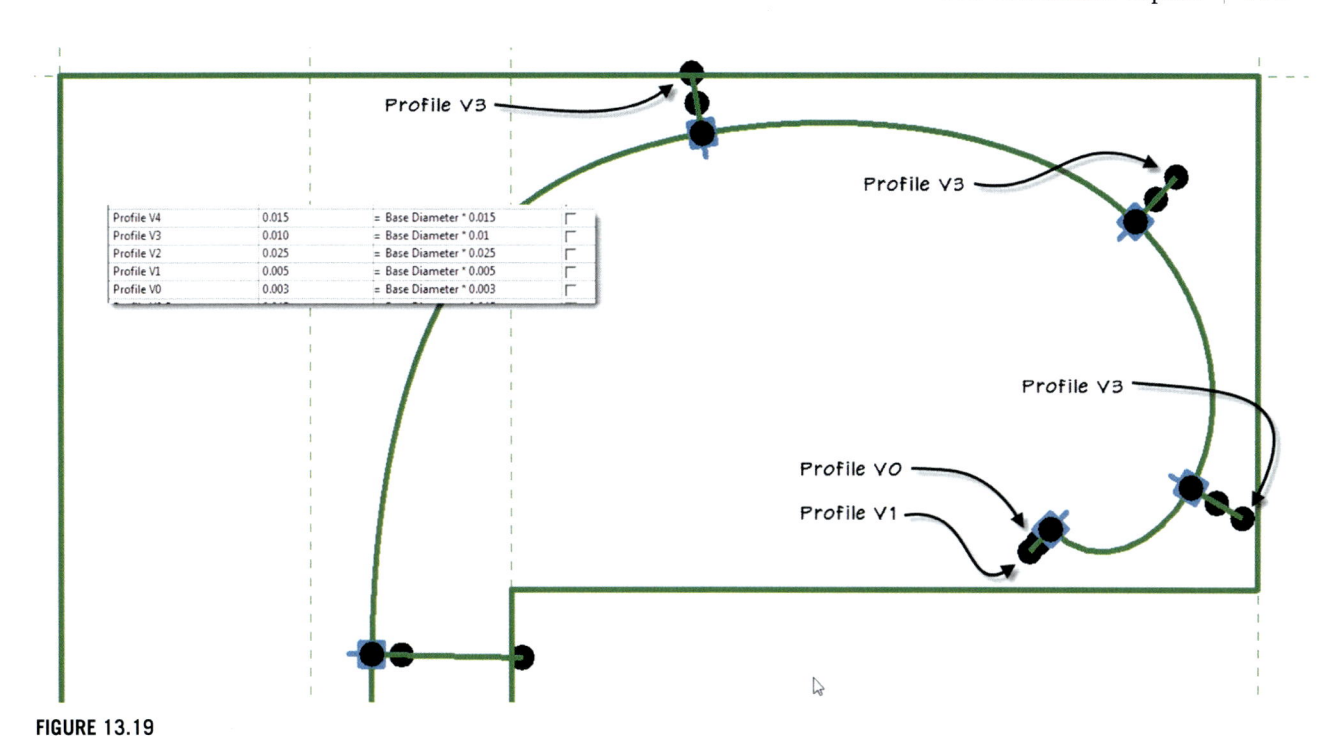

Fine-tune the positions/thickness of the profiles

You can perform the next step in the *Left* elevation or the *{3D}* view. In elevation, the profiles look like lines. However, since chain selection is the default mode in adaptive components and the massing environment, we can click on the line and the whole profile chain will select.

6. Starting at the top where the profile curls in, select the ninth profile, then hold down the CTRL key and select the eighth.

   Zoom in as necessary and watch the screen tips to be sure you are selecting chains of reference lines and not points.

   ⇨ Click Create Form.

Notice that we get a form, but it is not what we were expecting. Since we only selected two profiles, we get a straight blend between the two. Now let me show you one of the more frustrating error messages that Revit can display.

7. Click the newly created form and with the CTRL key, also select another profile chain.

   ⇨ Click Create Form.

Revit will fail to create a form and instead will display a message reading: "Unable to create form element: self-intersecting or singular geometry would result." It might also be the one about "self-intersecting geometry and a supposed "reorder profiles" button. Either way, I wish I could say that I have only seen this once or twice, but alas that is not the case. In my experimentations with the massing environment, I have received this message *many* more times than I would care to.

   ⇨ Click the Cancel button to dismiss the warning and then undo to reverse the creation of the blend.

Sometimes the error is caused by having bad geometry. But in this case, the selection is the problem.

8. Select the "L" shaped reference line chain and hide it with temporary hide.

9. Using a window selection, surround the curved spline and all of the profiles.

   ⇨ On the Modify | Multi-Select tab, click the Filter button. Check Reference Lines only and then click OK.

   ⇨ Click Create Form.

⇨ Study the result in the {3D} view (see Figure 13.20).

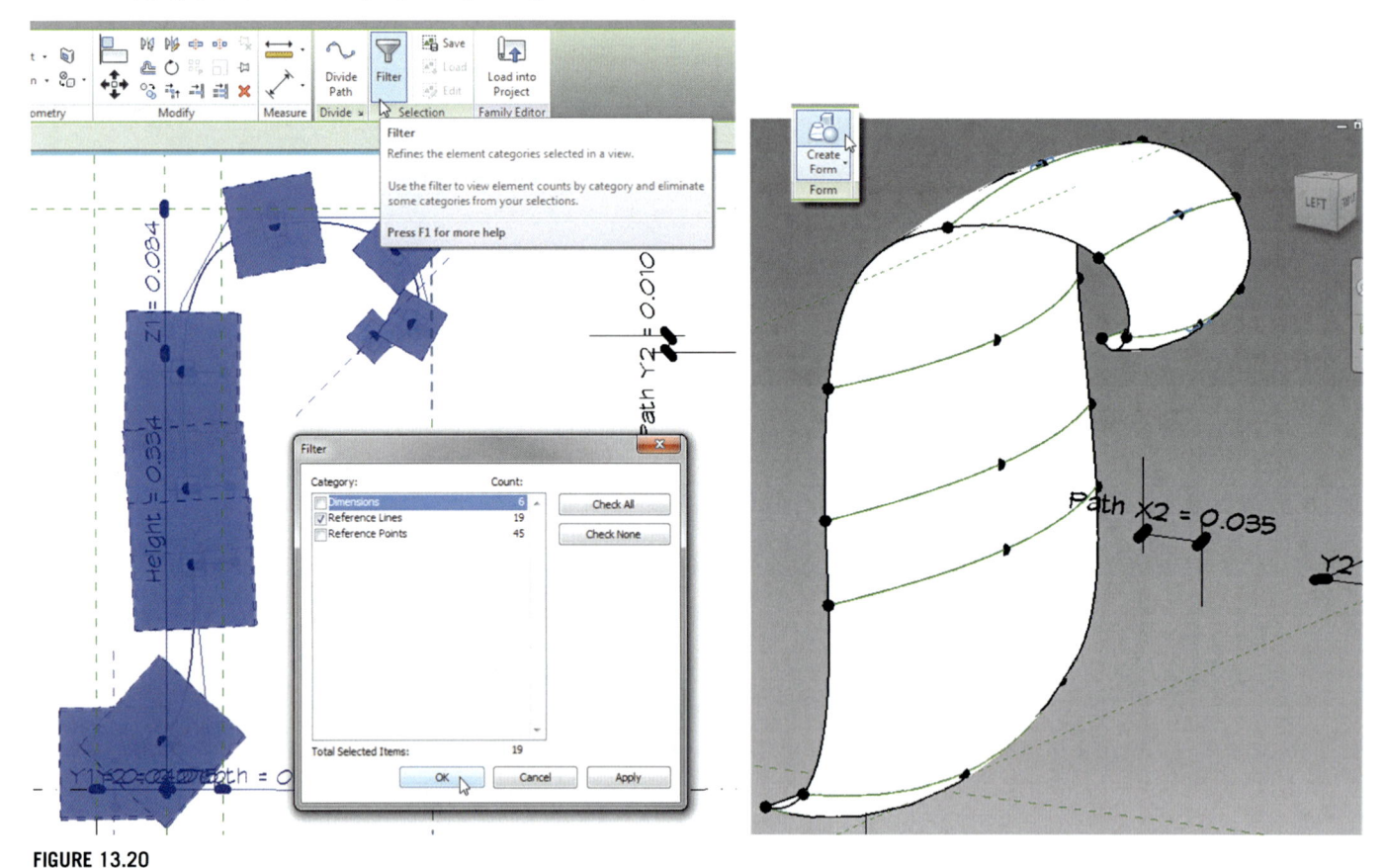

FIGURE 13.20
Selecting both the path and the profiles gives much better results for Create Form

Notice that the form now creates with no trouble. Take a look at it in the 3D view as well. If you have hidden anything, reset the temporary hide and select all reference lines. For the Is Reference property, set them to **Not a Reference**.

At this point, we could either add additional multiplier parameters to "Family Types" so that we can vary the values for a short or tall leaf, or we can simply save the family as a new name and make two families instead. There are pros and cons to each. We have created quite a few formulas and parameters in this family already. So adding several additional multiplier parameters would be undesirable at this point. Furthermore, the spline curve shape needs to vary for each leaf. So it would be difficult with the traditional spline we used to pull this off in a single family. For these reasons, I have saved the catch-up file as a short leaf only and made a copy for the tall leaf.

CATCH UP! You can open a file completed to this point named: *13_Leaf_Short_Fine.rfa*.

CREATE THE TALL LEAF

I have created a starting file for the tall leaf. It is just a copy of the short leaf with the height and other overall parameters adjusted already. We need to adjust the shape of the spline first. Once we have that to our liking, we open "Family Types" and adjust the formulas to reshape the leaf as required.

1. From the *Chapter13* folder, open the file named: *13_Leaf_Tall_Fine_Start.rfa*.

2. Open the *Left* elevation view and temporarily hide the 3D form.

3. Select the spline and adjust the control points until it is shaped to your liking and fits within the bounding "L" shape again.

• Renaissance Revit •

Take your time. It can take a while to get the curve just right. You can hide the 3D form to make it easier.

4. Open the Front elevation view and "Family Types" and slowly make adjustments to the formulas to reshape the form.

I reduced the values for the lower points to taper in the lower portion of the leaf a bit. This will make it less likely to overlap the small leaves in front of it when we load into the capital family (see Figure 13.21).

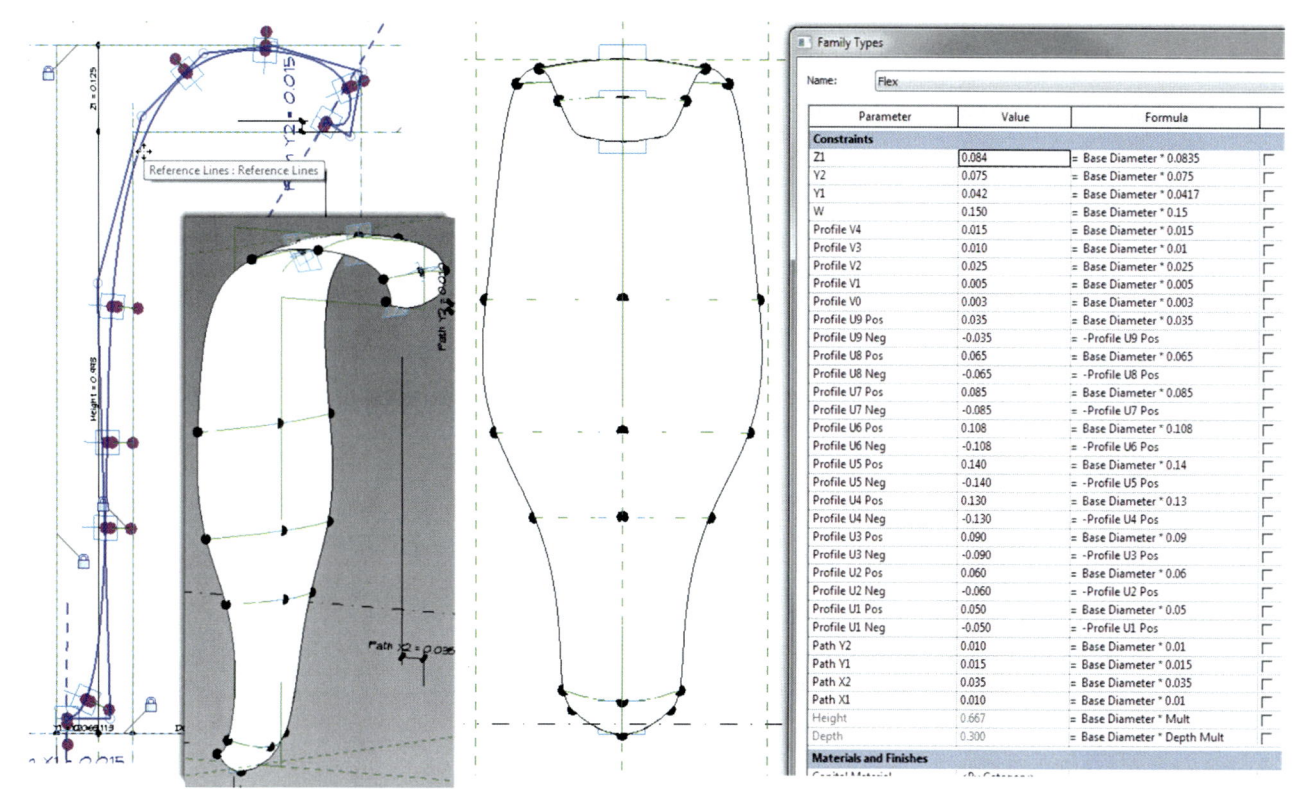

FIGURE 13.21
Once you have one leaf, modify a few formulas to easily shape the tall one

5. Flex and save the file.

CATCH UP! You can open a file completed to this point named: *13_Leaf_Tall_Fine.rfa*.

CORINTHIAN VOLUTES

There is another tier of leaves above the second row and below the volutes. To help make sure that this tier of leaves fits into its allotted space properly, let's shift our attention to the volutes next. There are sixteen total; eight at the corners and eight in the middle of face of the capital. They are all in pairs, so the total eight is actually four pairs at the corners and four pairs on the sides. The volutes at the corners are longer since they run along the diagonal and the ones on the sides are more flattened out. If you take a small and large volute together, we can build this as a family and then repeat it eight times. At a schematic level, the small and large volute form close to a 90° to one another. They are slightly curved in plan, so this is only approximate. But I looked at several examples and most were similar in this respect. I have a starting file like the ones we used for the leaves that has the basic form and relationships in it.

The approach we are going to use is actually quite similar to the leaves. We'll have a spline for the volute spiral path and then loft shapes along it. For this example, I have included the profiles already as face based generic model families. Remember that we can use generic model families in the same way as profiles in the traditional family editor. Let's open the profiles and look at them first.

• *Creating Classical Architecture with Modern Software* •

1. From the *Chapter13* folder, open the *Volute Fillet GM Profile.rfa* file.

Notice that the shape is a simple rectangle. There is a Depth and Width parameter, both tied to the Base Diameter in "Family Types." Take note of the two offset parameters. Parameters can have positive or negative values, but labeled dimensions cannot use both. Dimensions must be positive. So if you want to allow a negative offset, you have to do it formulaically.

2. Open the "Family Types" dialog.

I have an Offset Mult parameter. This is a numerical parameter and can take either a positive or negative value. This is multiplied by the Base Diameter to yield an Offset parameter that can also be either negative or positive. However, this parameter does not drive any dimensions directly. Instead, the Total Offset parameter adds the Offset parameter to the Neg Offset parameter. Neg Offset drives a dimension that is always positive and below the center reference plane. Total Offset measures from here directly to the bottom of the profile, making it possible for the profile to move above or below the centerline.

The last thing to take note of in "Family Types" is that there are several named types in this family. Profile 1 through Profile 4 and Profile A through C. These will be used on the two volutes as we loft from one profile to another.

3. From the *Chapter13* folder, open the *Volute GM Profile.rfa* file.

This one is very similar. Its shape is nearly rectangular, but has a spline at one end to soften the edge of the profile. There are several types here as well. This profile has both a vertical and horizontal offset set up much like the other profile.

4. From the *Chapter13* folder, open the *Volutes.rfa* file.
5. Save the file as: **Volutes_Fine**.

The 3D forms in this file are very schematic, but the underlying reference lines give the basic extents of the volutes. As you can see, the large and small volute forms are set at 90° to one another. Let's start by deleting these solid forms.

6. Select and delete the solids onscreen.

    Leave all of the reference lines and dimensions.

Corinthian volutes are a little less precise to construct than their Ionic counterparts. None of my resource materials in fact makes any mention of how to construct Corinthian volutes and instead simply show a completed example. In his book: "The Architectural Orders of the Greeks and Romans," J. M. Mauch provides 100 intricately detailed plates of absolutely stunning quality (Mauch 1910, 1845, 67 & 73). Of the several Corinthian examples he includes, I settled on two that are instantly recognizable as the quintessential Corinthian order. Palladio's example and the plate depicting the temple of Nerva in Rome. Using these samples as my primary resource, I sketched the spiral curve of the volute using a spline.

7. Select all of the reference lines onscreen (there are two chains, so they should be easy to select with a CTRL + click).

    ⇨ Open the *Front* elevation view. (The elements should still be selected, if they aren't, just right-click and choose **Select Previous**).

    ⇨ From the Temporary Hide/Isolate pop-up, choose **Hide Element**.

8. Beginning on the right at the intersection of the Center (Left/Right) and Volute Start Hor reference planes, draw a spline in the spiral shape shown on the left side of Figure 13.22.

    ⇨ Snap the final endpoint to the intersection of the Eye Center Vertical and Lrg Volute Eye Center reference planes.

    ⇨ Align and lock the endpoints both horizontal and vertical at both ends.

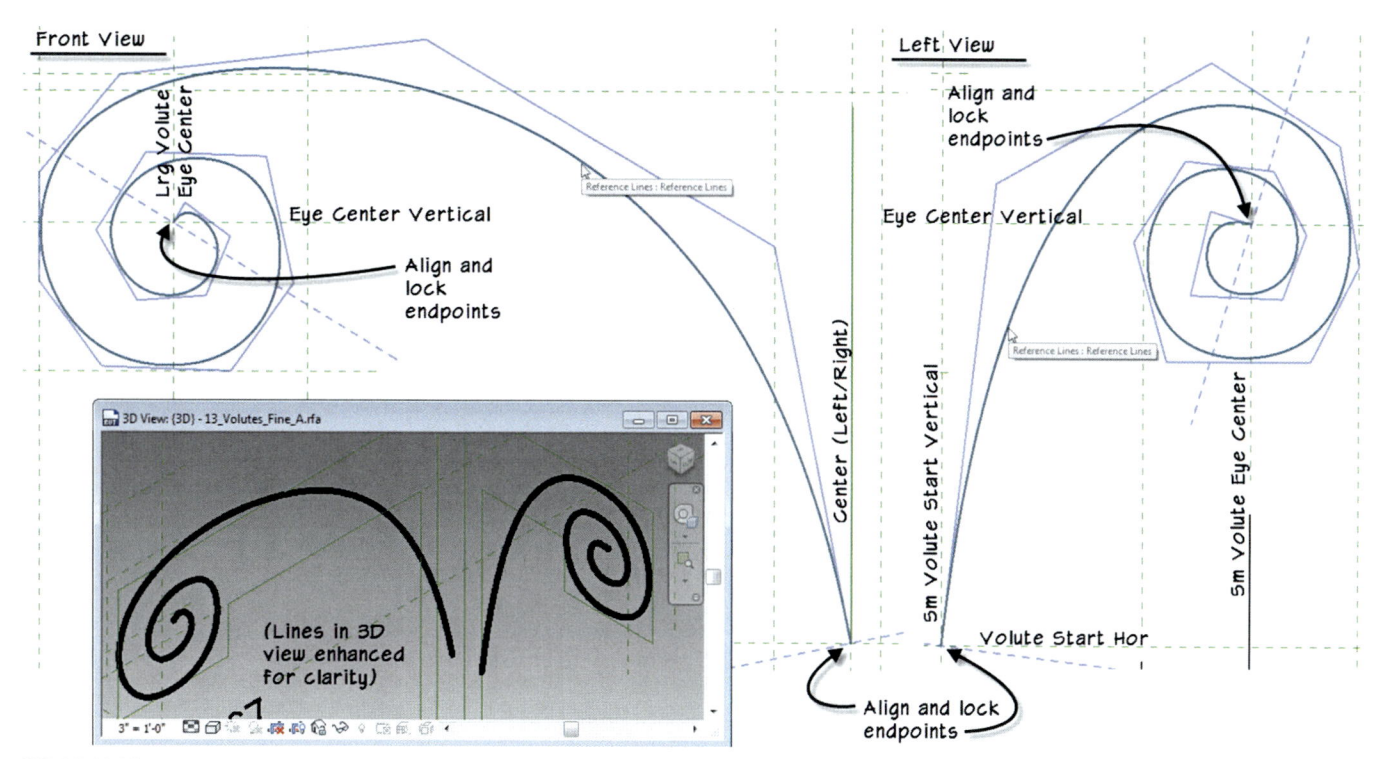

FIGURE 13.22

Sketch the splines in the Front and Left elevation views and align and lock the endpoints

9. Open the Left elevation view and repeat the process locking the start point to the intersection of the Sm Volute Start Vertical and Volute Start Hor reference planes.

   ⇨ Lock the end point at the intersection of the Sm Volute Eye Center and Eye Center Vertical reference planes (see the right side of Figure 13.22).

It takes some trial and error to get the curve just right. Make it as close as you can to the figure, or open the catch-up file.

> **CATCH UP!** You can open a file completed to this point named: *13_Volutes_Fine_A.rfa*.

ADD HOSTED PROFILES TO A PATH

As noted above, the angle between the small and large volutes of the typical Corinthian column is about 90°. Building a rig that allows angular rotation is certainly an option that we have available to us, but it can get complicated. Instead, I have opted for the offsets in the profiles (that we explored in the previous steps). The offsets allow the profiles to move off of the path which has the effect of opening up the angle between the two forms. It also introduces some subtle curvature.

   Continue in the previous file or open the catch-up file.

1. On the Insert menu, choose Load Family, browse to the Chapter13 folder and load both of the profiles discussed above: *Volute Fillet GM Profile.rfa* and *Volute GM Profile.rfa*.

2. Open the *{3D}* view and zoom in near the top of the large volute curve.

3. Add a hosted point directly on the curve, near the top.

   ⇨ Cancel the command, select the point and then on the Properties palette, change the Normalized Curve Parameter to: **0.250**.

4. On the Project Browser, expand *Families > Volute Fillet GM Profile* and then drag *Profile B* into the model canvas (see the left side of Figure 13.23).

404 | Chapter 13

⇨ On the Modify | Place Component tab, on the Work Plane panel, click the Set button and then click on the work plane of the hosted point (see the middle of Figure 13.23).

5. On the Modify | Place Component tab, click the Place on Work Plane button.

⇨ Highlight the point.

The profile will be oriented incorrectly, do not click yet.

⇨ Tap the SPACEBAR twice to rotate the component and then snap it directly to the hosted point to place the component (see the right side of Figure 13.23).

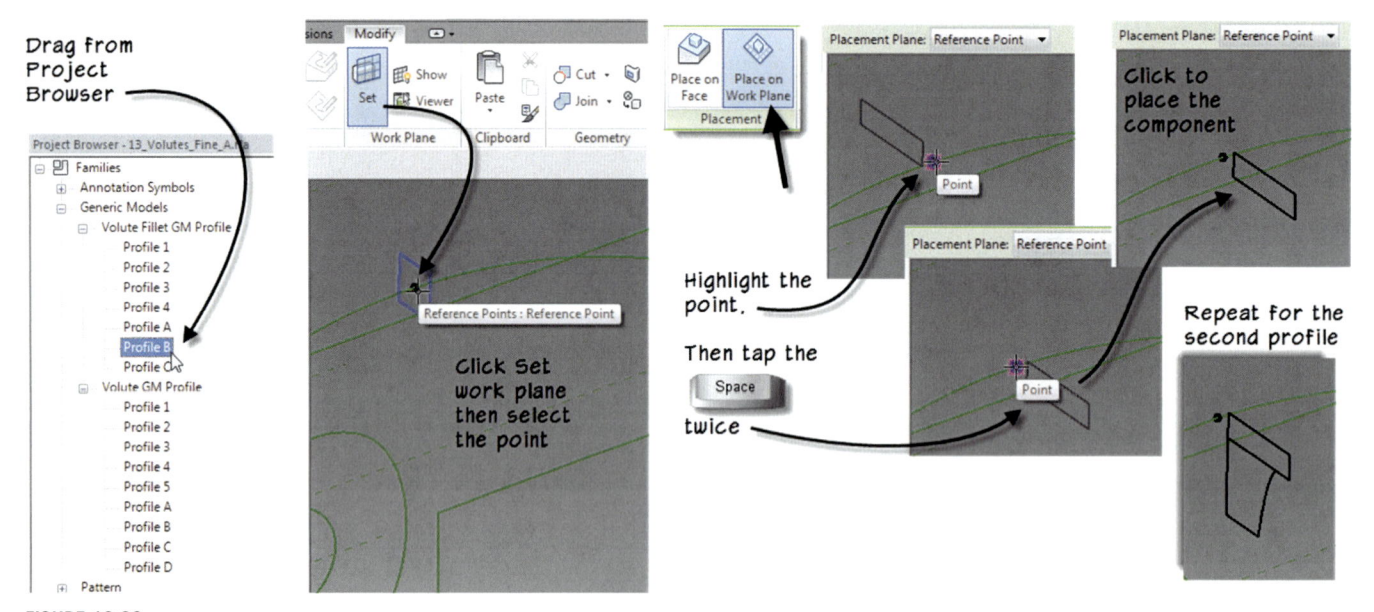

FIGURE 13.23
Place a profile on a hosted point

We need to place a second profile on the same point.

6. On the Project Browser, expand *Families > Volute GM Profile* and then drag *Profile B* into the model canvas.

⇨ Use the SPACEBAR again to orient it and click to place it on the same point (see the far right side of Figure 13.23).

We need to repeat this process a few more times to create the remaining host points with profiles on this path. Let's do the point at the start of the path next.

7. Repeat the entire process, starting with creating a new hosted point. Set its Normalized Curve Parameter to: **0.001**.

TIP: remember, setting the point a little away from the end makes it easier to select the endpoint later if required.

⇨ Repeating the procedure of the last few steps add the *Profile A* type from both the *Volute GM Profile* and the *Volute Fillet GM Profile* families. Use the SPACEBAR again to rotate them 180°.

With just these profiles, you can begin to see how this process will work. If you select the path and then one of the fillet profiles (the rectangular ones), and then click Create Form, it will give you a nice spiral form that is offset from the path. Undo this and try the other profile and you get a similar shape with different offset and proportions. If you undo again and select both profiles and the path, you get an even more interesting form that tapers from Profile A to Profile B. If you try this with one of the profiles from the from the *Volute GM Profile* family, it will fail because the profile is too big to go all the way along the path as it spiral in. But if you select both profiles and then create form, it will work as it will only loft between the two shapes (see Figure 13.24).

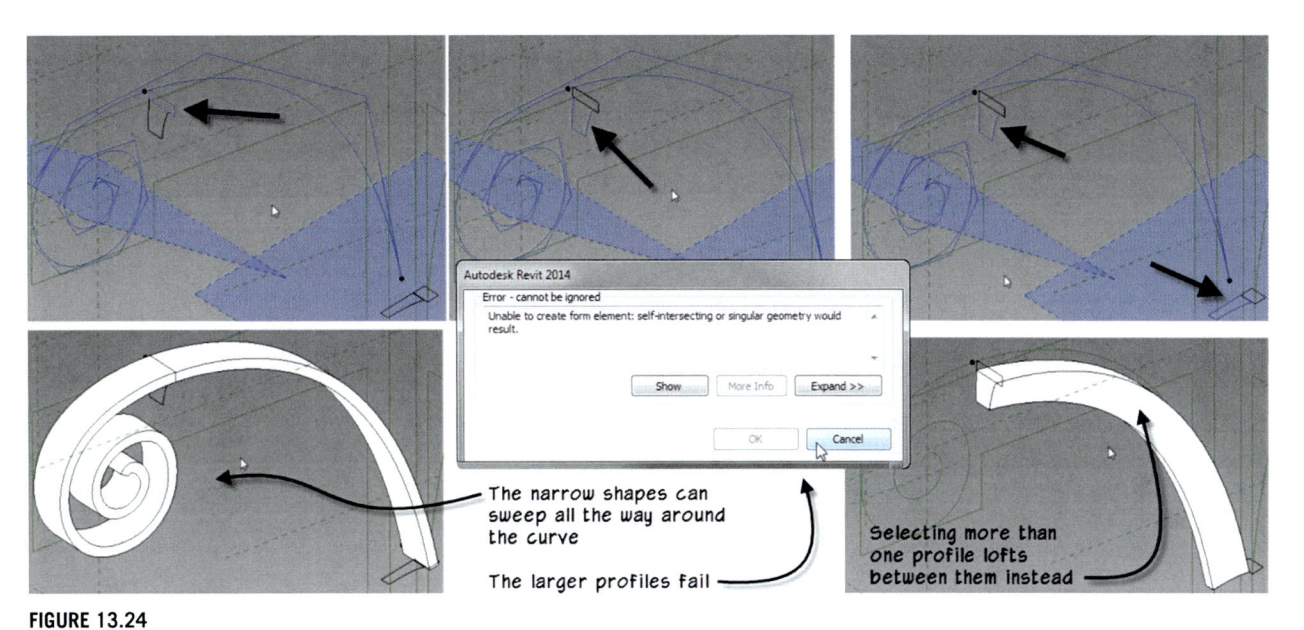

FIGURE 13.24
Experiment with Create Form and the profiles we have so far

You can edit the profile's type parameters to vary the size of the profile and the amount of the offset. I have already done the necessary trial and error to determine what offsets and sizes are needed to get a pleasing volute shape, but you are free to experiment further to fine-tune the shape to your preference if you wish.

Undo any form creation experiments you did and let's continue adding profiles.

As the curve tightens, we only need one more fillet profile, but the other (wider curved face) profile needs two more to negotiate the smaller space. Also, in the center of the spiral, I had to resort to creating a separate form as spiral curve became too tight for the profile to follow.

8. Add three more hosted points at: **0.480**, **0.900** and **1.000**.

On these spiraling curves, I find that towards the center, the points always want to snap to the end. Go ahead and let one of the points snap to the end and leave it at 1.000, for the other two, click back toward the middle of the curve first and then change the value of the Normalized Curve Parameter to set them at the desired locations numerically.

9. Using the procedure above, place the *Volute Fillet GM Profile:Profile C* family type at the 1.000 point.

⇨ Place the *Volute GM Profile:Profile C* family type at point 0.480 and the *Volute GM Profile:Profile D* family type at the 0.900 point (see Figure 13.25).

If necessary, use the keyboard shortcut SX to be sure you are snapping to the point and don't forget the SPACEBAR to rotate.

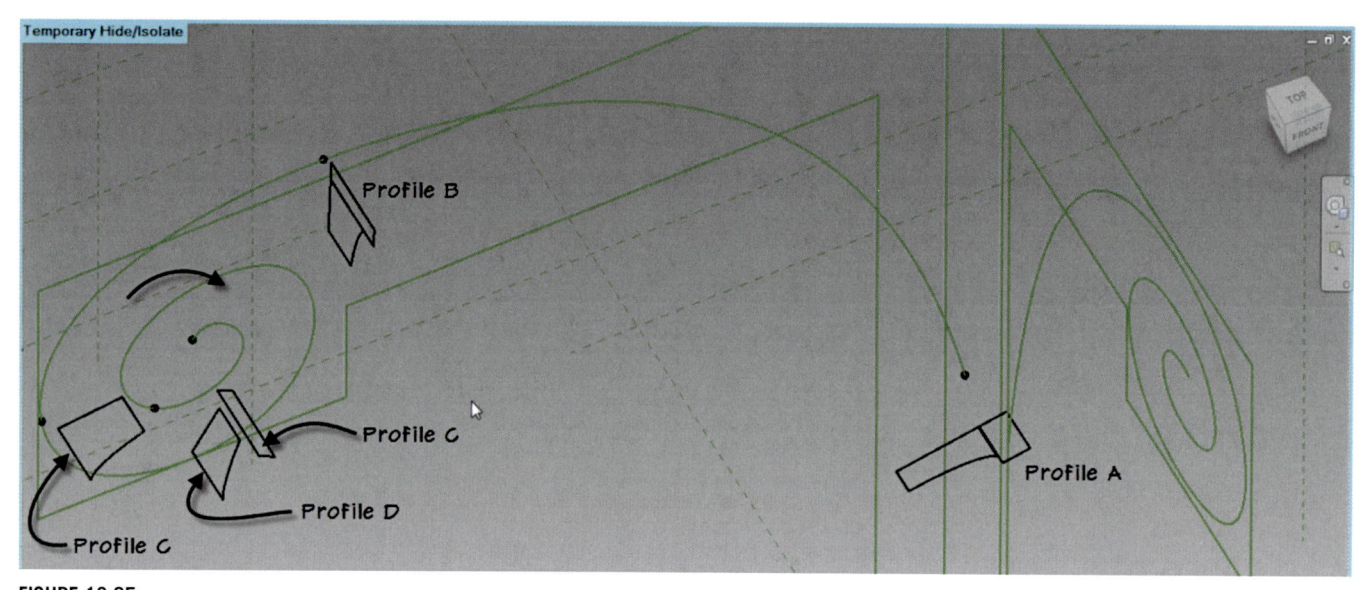

FIGURE 13.25
Place the remaining profiles

10. Select all of the Generic Models (7) and then on the Properties palette, uncheck the Visible checkbox.

This will make the edges of the profiles invisible when we load this family into other families and project later. We are ready to begin creating form and see some results.

> **CATCH UP!** You can open a file completed to this point named: *13_Volutes_Fine_B.rfa*.

CREATE FORMS

To make the main volute geometry, we have everything we need.

Continue in the previous file or open the catch-up file.

1. Select the three fillet profiles and the path, and then click Create Form.
2. Select the four remaining profiles and the path and create form again (see Figure 13.26).

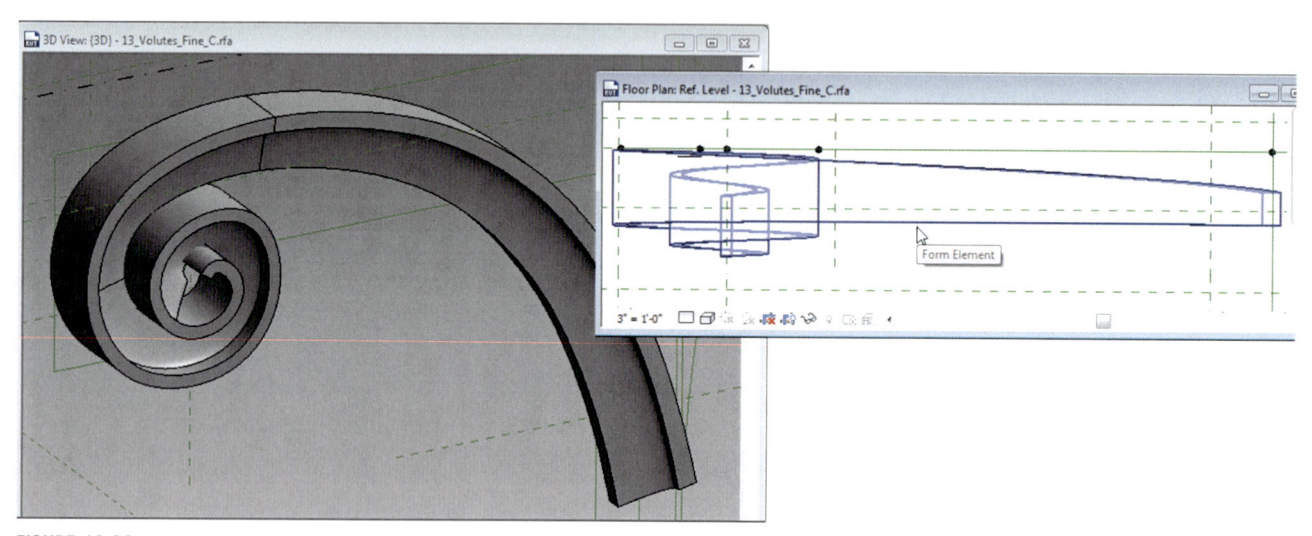

FIGURE 13.26
Create forms to complete the basic volute shape

• Renaissance Revit •

If the form fails, tweak the spline a little and try again. This gives us the overall geometry we need. Notice if you study from different angles, even though we used a 2D spline path, the form has a nice subtle curve in three dimensions. This is because of the offsets built into the profiles. Feel free to revisit the profile families and vary the settings a little to experiment with different results. If you vary the numbers too much, the form might fail, so preform a little trial and error until you get comfortable with how far you can vary the parameters and fine-tune the results.

3. On the Project Browser, edit the type properties of ALL types for both profile families, (16 total) and link up the Base Diameter parameter for each one.

4. Open the "Family Types" dialog and flex. When satisfied, return to 1.000 and save the file.

To make the eye of the volute, we'll have to add an additional form. The curve here turns in too sharply for us to continue the loft. However, what we can do is create another form using the same profile as we have at the 0.900 point.

5. Select the two 3D forms and temporarily hide them.

   Zoom in on the profile on point 0.900. We are going to draw a reference line along the top edge.

6. On the Create tab, click the Reference button, then on the Options Bar, check the "3D Snapping" checkbox. Draw a reference line across the upper edge and then cancel the command (see the left side of Figure 13.27).

7. Click the Set work plane button.

   ⇨ Click to select the first point of the reference line (the one at the top of the straight, not curved, edge).

   ⇨ Place a reference point directly on this point, click OK to ignore the warning.

8. Cancel the command, select the new point and change the Offset to **0.009**. (Use -0.009 if necessary).

   ⇨ Click the Associate Family Parameter button and create a new parameter for this offset called: **Eye Center**.

   ⇨ Open "Family Types" and set the Formula to: **Base Diameter * 0.009** (see the right side of Figure 13.27).

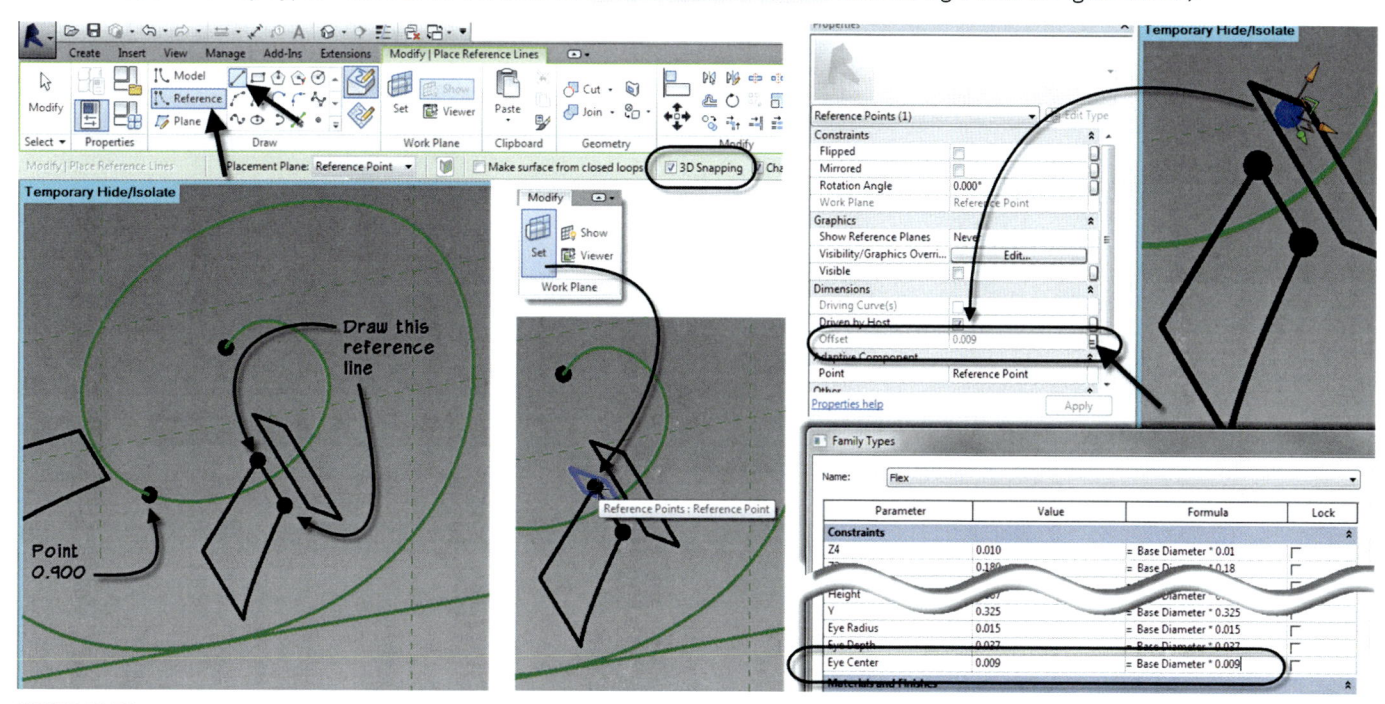

FIGURE 13.27
Add a reference line along the profile and then host a point on the work plane of the endpoint

The reference line we just drew will be the axis for a revolved form. The point will locate the center of the circle for the eye of the volute.

• *Creating Classical Architecture with Modern Software* •

9. Select the new point and on the Properties palette, set the Work Plane Visible parameter to **Always**.

   ⇨ Use Set work plane again and choose the work plane of this point that is parallel to the spline. (Use TAB if necessary).

   ⇨ Using the Reference tool, draw a circle at this point and label its radius with the existing **Eye Radius** parameter (see the left side of Figure 13.28).

10. Select the profile (at point 0.900) and the reference line that we drew along its edge.

    ⇨ Create Form.

    You'll get a revolved form in a full circle.

    ⇨ Select the new form and on the Properties palette, change the End Angle to: **152**.

    ⇨ Select the circle and click create form. This time associate the family parameter Eye Depth to the Positive Offset property (see the right side of Figure 13.28).

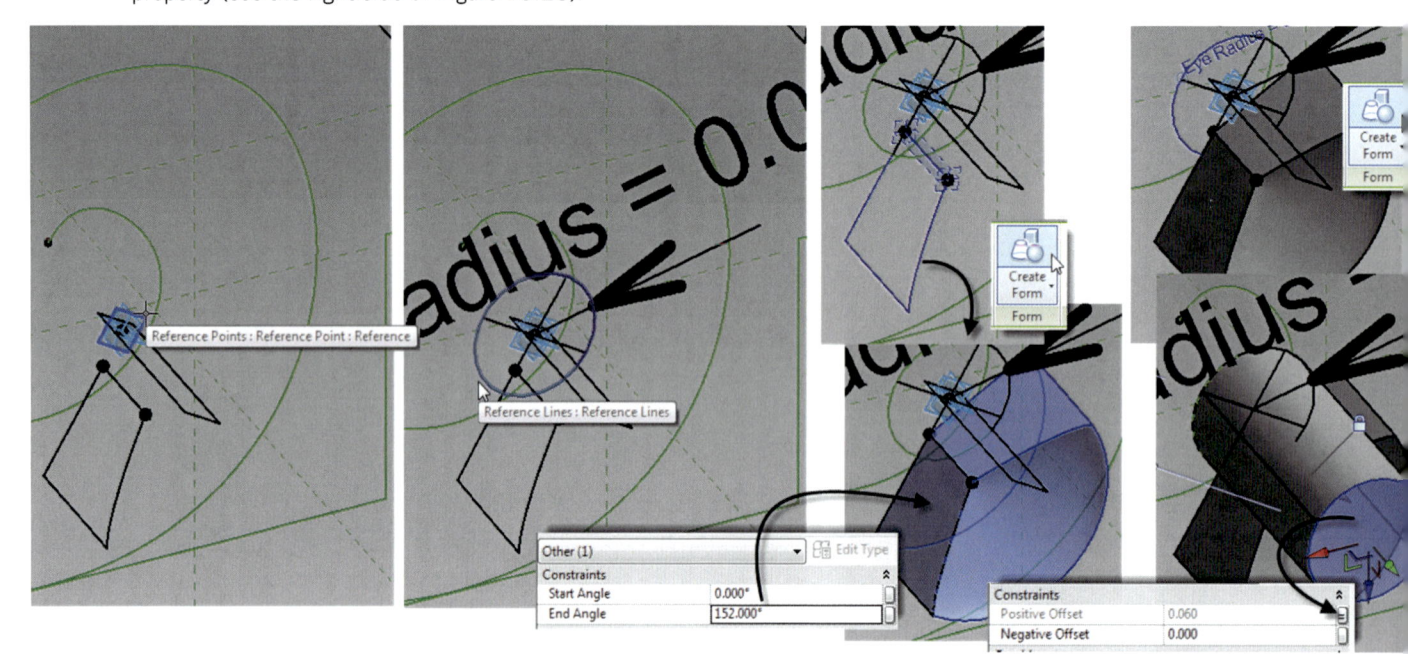

FIGURE 13.28
Using the new reference lines create the remaining forms and adjust their parameters

At this point you can reset the temporary hide mode to see all of the forms. Feel free to make any fine-tune adjustments and flex the family.

CATCH UP! You can open a file completed to this point named: *13_Volutes_Fine_C.rfa*.

CREATE THE SMALL VOLUTE

To create the small volute, we repeat the previous steps. I will give you an outline of the process, but leave the specifics to you as a challenge exercise.

Start by hiding all of the geometry, path and profiles of the large volute. This will make it easier to work. Add hosted points along the spline at locations indicated in Table 13.4. Also using Table 13.4, set work planes and then place profile indicated at each point.

TIP: Place all of the hosted profiles on each of their respective points first. When all done, select all of the profiles (Generic Models) and then press the SPACEBAR twice to flip them all to the correct orientation in a single operation.

• Renaissance Revit •

TABLE 13.4

Point Location (Normalized Curve Param)	Show Reference Planes	Volute Fillet GM Profile	Volute GM Profile	Comments
0.001	Always	Profile 1	Profile 1 (Mirrored)	
0.150	Always	Profile 2	Profile 2 (Mirrored)	
0.500	Always	Profile 3	Profile 3 (Mirrored)	
0.920	Always	None	Profile 4 (Mirrored)	
1.000	Always	Profile 4	None	

Set the Show Reference Planes option to Always and uncheck the Show Normal Reference Plane Only setting. Each of the Volute GM Profiles in the table is listed as mirrored. In order to reuse the same profile family for both volutes, we have to flip or mirror each of these profiles after placement. To do this, you can zoom out and look for the small flip work plane icon. It is sometimes far away from the profile. Alternatively you can mirror. To mirror, set the host point as the active work plane. Make sure that the work planes are visible and that the Show Normal Reference Plane Only setting is toggled off. Select the profile and click the mirror tool. On the Options Bar, uncheck the Copy option and then mirror about the perpendicular work plane. This will flip it about the axis of the point. If you end up with a copy, delete the original. Repeat for all five profiles.

On point 0.920 build a reference line with 3D snapping and host a point for the circle of the eye like we did above. Follow the same process as outlined for the large volute eye and use the same parameters. Create all of the same solid forms to complete the volute (see Figure 13.29).

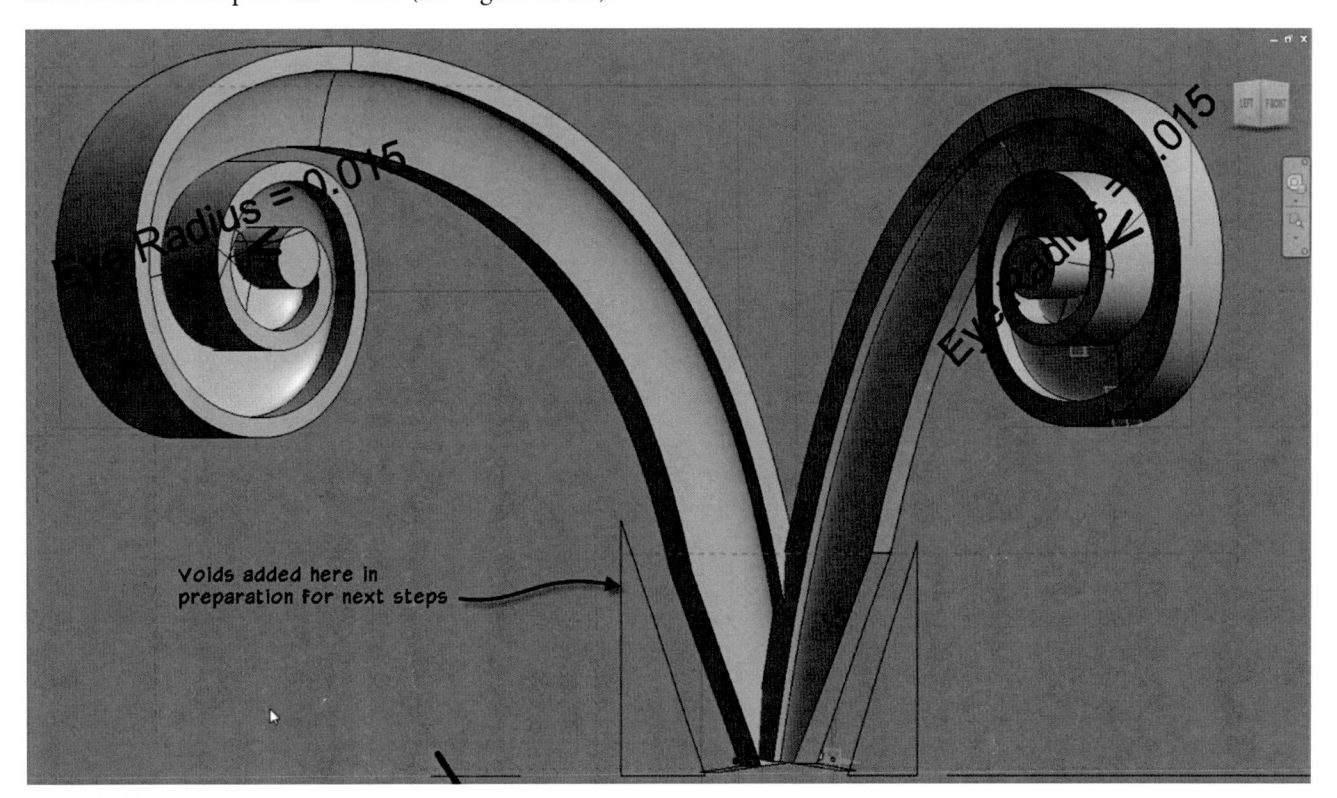

FIGURE 13.29

Complete the small volute using the same process as the large one

Remember to select all of the Generic Models and uncheck Visible on the Properties palette. Flex the file before saving and closing. There are two catch-up files. One has just the profiles, points and reference lines. The other contains the completed volutes. In the completed version I fine-tuned it slightly and added two voids at the base.

In the steps below, we will be adding leaves at the base of these volutes and carving away some of the form gives us more room to work with the leaves.

> CATCH UP! You can open a file completed to this point named: *13_Volutes_Fine.rfa*.

CAULICULI

Between the rows of leaves and the volutes is the flourets and cauliculi. The cauliculus looks like a long thin vase from which the flourets and the bud and button spring. The starting low detail file has a simple mass like the other starting files for this entire portion of the capital. Although it is often desirable to avoid nesting too many level deep, to make construction of this item a bit simpler, I will present the cauliculi (the vase-like portion) as a separate family. If you have been following along through all of the lessons in this book, it is a very simple form. There are four profiles that vary in size to form a lofted form. Top this with another lofted form that wraps around the shape of the first form. I have provided the files to speed up the process. Several examples of generic model families used as profiles have already been discussed in this chapter. But if you like, feel free to open the files and explore before continuing.

1. From the *Chapter13* folder, open the file named *Cauliculi.rfa*.

As you can see, not only are the profiles already loaded, I have inserted them in the file so you can see them. The four rounded forms will stack on the points already in the file to form the vase-like form. I have placed the first one. The other two profiles form a molding around the top. I have placed the first two of those as well. I have also built the rig and created the necessary parameters.

2. Click the Component tool, choose **Profile A** and then click the Set work plane button.
   ⇨ Set the second point from the top as the work plane and then click the Place on Work Plane button.
   ⇨ Place the profile snapped to the point. (Type the keyboard shortcut SX if necessary)
3. Repeat for Profile B and C. Use the SPACEBAR if necessary to keep them all oriented the same way.
4. Select the four profiles and the vertical straight reference line and then create form (see the left side of Figure 13.30).

There is one more point at the top of the reference line. It is the host for three more points that form structure to define the 3-point arc floating above the form. This arc has several points hosted on it at regular spacing. As you can see, I have already placed two of the profiles on these points.

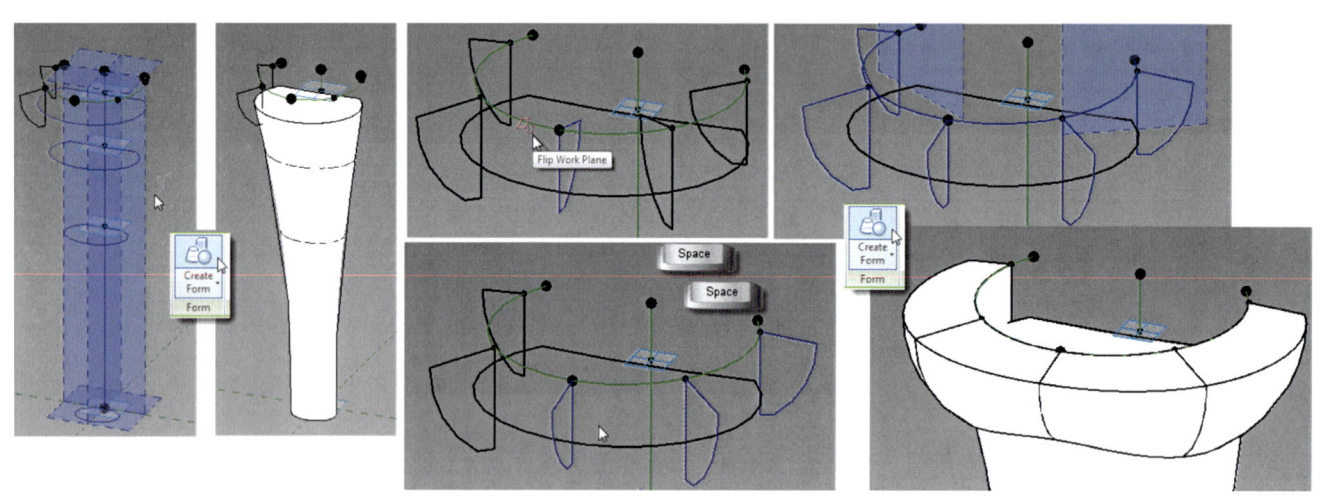

FIGURE 13.30
Place all the profiles and then create the forms

5. Place a Small profile on the midpoint and on the far hosted point.

⇨ Place a Big profile on the other hosted point. Do not place any on the two endpoints.

6. You will have to flip the profiles and then rotate them twice with the SPACEBAR.

7. Select the five profiles and the curved path and then create form (see the right side of Figure 13.30).

8. Delete the extra profiles that were already in the file on the ground.

9. Select all of the profiles used in the form and on the Properties palette uncheck Visible.

10. Apply a material parameter to both forms and then save and close the file.

CATCH UP! You can open a file completed to this point named: *13_Cauliculi.rfa*.

FLOURET

The flouret[9] is a series of leaves that spring from the Cauliculi and wrap up under the volutes. They are more organic in form and trickier to build than the rows of leaves below. I tried many variations for these leaves to try and get them just right. I have settled on the approach we will use here as the most repeatable. But I will note some alternatives along the way and you are encouraged to explore on your own and see what variations you can achieve.

The leaves on the rows below were also organic in form, but since the curved path for their loft could be drawn in a single plane, it made their construction a bit easier. The basic approach for the flouret leaves is the same as the other leaves. First we draw a path and host some points and profiles on it. We then create a loft from the profiles that follows the freeform path. What will be different in this case is that we will use a 3D spline (Spline Through Points) instead of a 2D Spline for the path. This will allow the path and leaf form to be a bit more organic. I have limited my examples here to 3 profiles for each leaf and we will build three forms total; two leaves and one bud. We will also use a loaded component for the profile instead of drawing them directly which will help simplify the onscreen clutter and reduce the number of parameters. And speaking of limiting the parameters, when you open the starting file, you will find very few parameters in the file. For this example, we will use a totally different approach to scale it proportionally. The approach will be detailed below, but requires the use of nested families using the Planting category instead of parameters. See the "Scaling Families with the Planting Category" topic below for more details.

CREATE 3D SPLINES

As with some of the other components we have built in this chapter, I have provided a starting file with some of the basic framework already established. This will save us time and effort. As always, you are encouraged to try building these items from scratch on your own later if you wish. The starting file is a copy of the medium detail Flouret family with some modifications made.

1. From the *Chapter13* folder, open the file named: *Flouret_Start.rfa*.

As noted above, I removed most of the parameters from this file. I also removed the medium detail solid geometry and some of the reference planes. I have not yet deleted the reference lines that the medium detail forms were created from as there shape will provide some assistance in forming the 3D splines. The guide lines and circle on the level are also there for reference. The two diagonal lines define the angle that this component will sit at when loaded into

---

[9] I have seen various spellings for "Flouret" and "Cauliculus," including: "Floret" and "Cauliocolus." I have chosen one set of spellings which I have tried to use consistently.

412 | Chapter 13

the Corinthian capital. This give some context. Also for context, I have loaded the Cauliculi and Volutes families that we built above. We'll delete much of this later.

I have provided also provided some additional guide items in this family. In the location where the leaves will go, I have created a surface from. This was created by lofting three arcs (see Figure 13.31). On the level, there are some diagonal lines. The middle one marks the centerline of the Cauliculi. This line has points hosted on it running vertically. The arcs are hosted on these points.

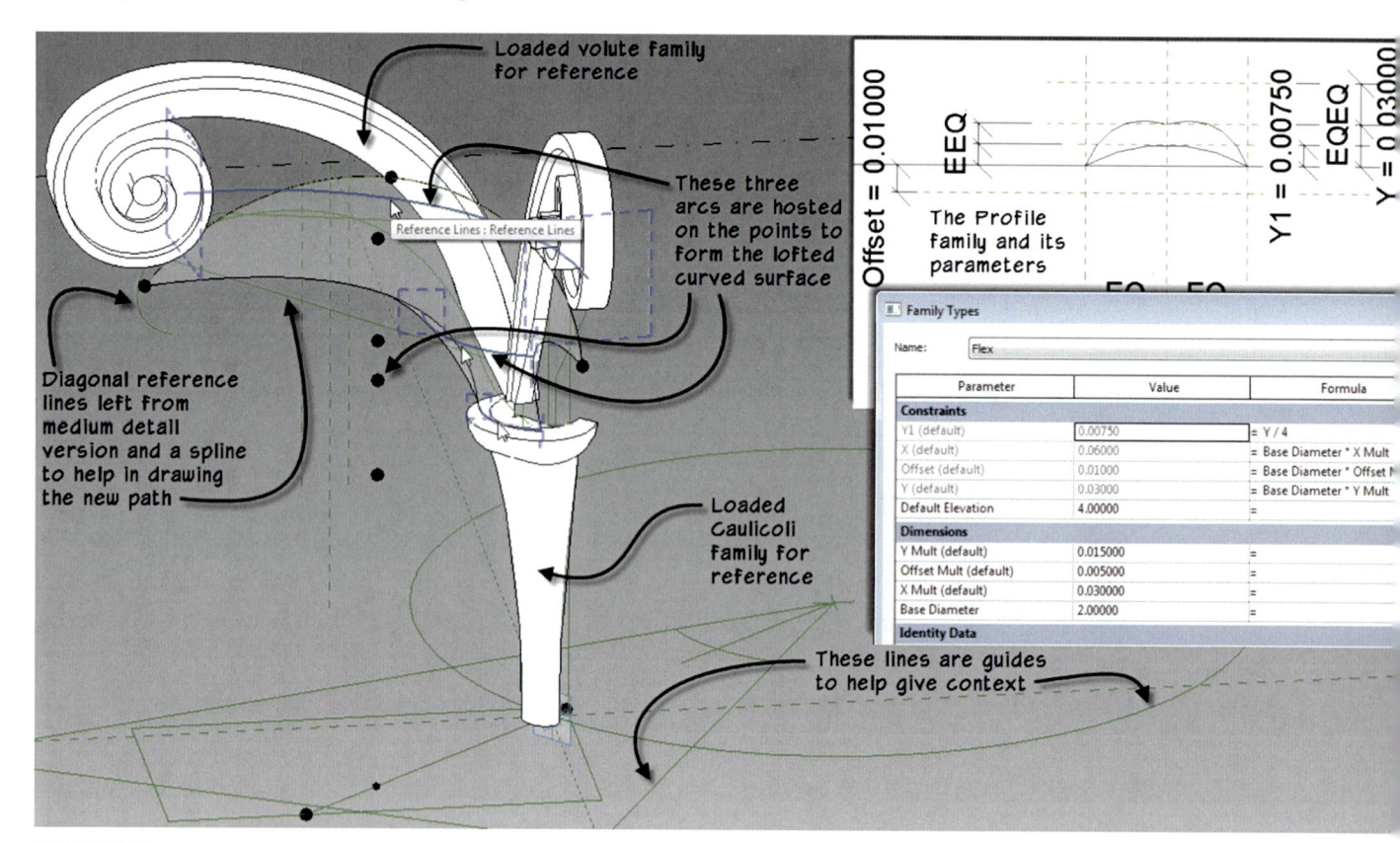

FIGURE 13.31
Understanding the starting files

Let's open the profile family next and take a quick look at how it is set up.

    2. From the *Chapter13* folder, open the file named: *Flouret Leaf Cross Section FB Profile.rfa*.

    ⇨ Open the Ref. Level floor plan and zoom in (see the right side of Figure 13.31).

The shape is very similar to the profile we used for the lower leaves except I added an extra curve with a slight indentation to suggest the stem of the leaf. These two upper curves are splines the one below is an arc. They are all aligned and locked and the formulas keep everything flexing proportionally. One other point to note is that in contrast to most of the other families in this book, I made these parameters instance based. That will make it easier for use to manipulate them interactively.

    ⇨ Click the Load into Project button to load the profile into the *Flouret* family.

    ⇨ Cancel the command after it is loaded. You don't have to place an instance yet.

    3. Switch windows back to the profile family and close it.

          This leaves just the *Flouret_Start* family open.

    4. Save the family as: **Flouret_Fine**.

• Renaissance Revit •

For the creation of the 3D splines, you might want to have several windows open and tiled. I recommend the *Ref. Level* floor plan, the *Front* and *Left* elevation view and the *{3D}* view.

There are a few basic approaches that we can take here. We can work between the plan and elevation views placing points and slowly tweaking them, and we can actually draw right on the 3D curved surface as we did back in the "Draw Lines on 3D Surfaces" topic in the last chapter.

5. On the Create tab, click the Reference button, and then click the Spline Through Points button.
   - On the Options Bar, check the Follow Surface box.
   - Click about seven points directly on the transparent surface up and under the large volute making a curved shape that flows down toward the Cauliculus (see the left side and middle of Figure 13.32).

Try to avoid snapping to other geometry in this first pass. If you do snap to other geometry, it will pull the point off of the curved surface. For now, you want to follow the surface only. If you have trouble with this, you can cancel, isolate the curved surface and then try again.

6. Orbit the 3D view so you can see the small volute and repeat to create a second spline on the other side (see the right side of Figure 13.32).

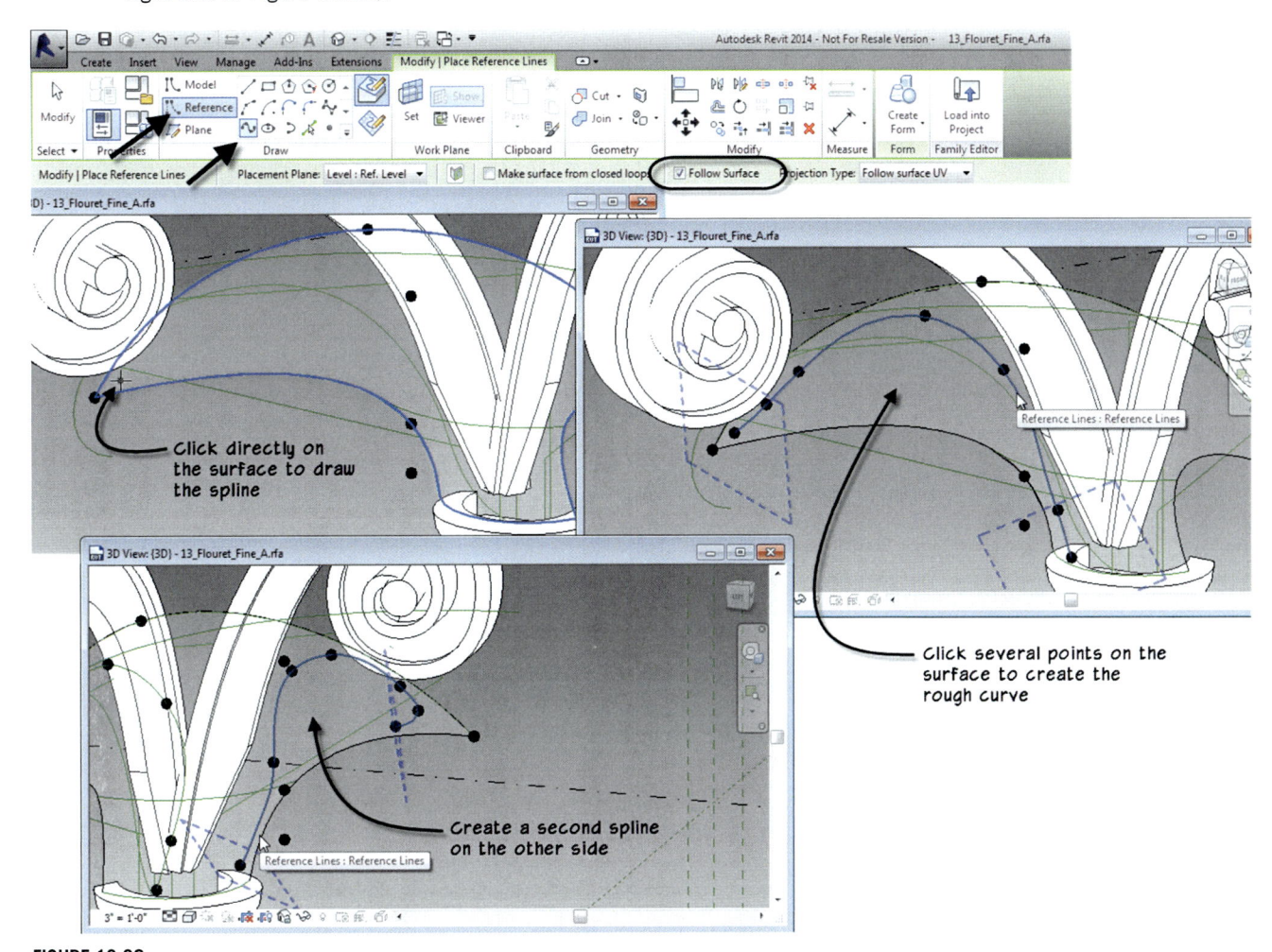

FIGURE 13.32
Draw two rough splines directly on the 3D curved surface

At this point, you should orbit the 3D view to see the new splines from several angles. They are still very rough, but you can see the way they follow the curved surface. If you want to fine-tune the placement of any of the points, simply drag them. You can also modify them numerically on the Properties palette if you like. There is a Hosted U Parameter and a

414 | Chapter 13

Hosted V Parameter. These numbers take a little trial and error, but offer a more precise way to move the points than simply dragging does. You can also nudge the points using the arrow keys on your keyboard. Select a point and then press one of the arrows. It will move slightly and you will see the numbers on the Properties palette also adjust. As you zoom in and out, the amount of nudging increases and decreases, so for fine control, zoom in, for more coarse movements, zoom out. If you hold down the SHIFT key and then press an arrow, it nudges 10 times (see Figure 13.33).

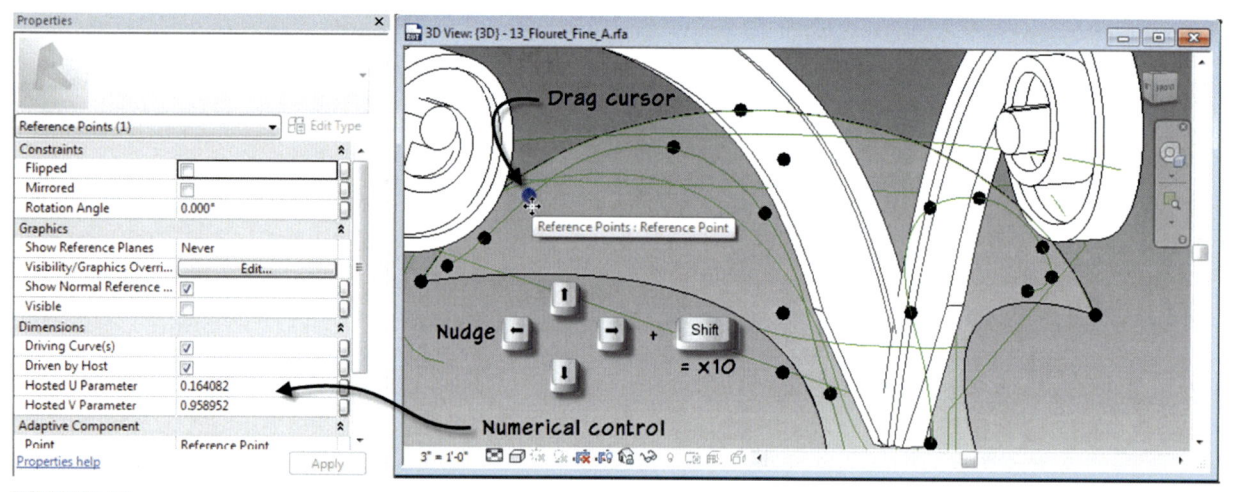

FIGURE 13.33

Fine-tune point placement

7. Adjust the points as much as you can on the surface of the form.

Work between elevation, plan and 3D views nudging and adjusting as you go. The goal is a nice smooth curve that represents the stem of the leaf. Use a photograph like those in Figure 13.1 above to guide you, or search for some examples online.

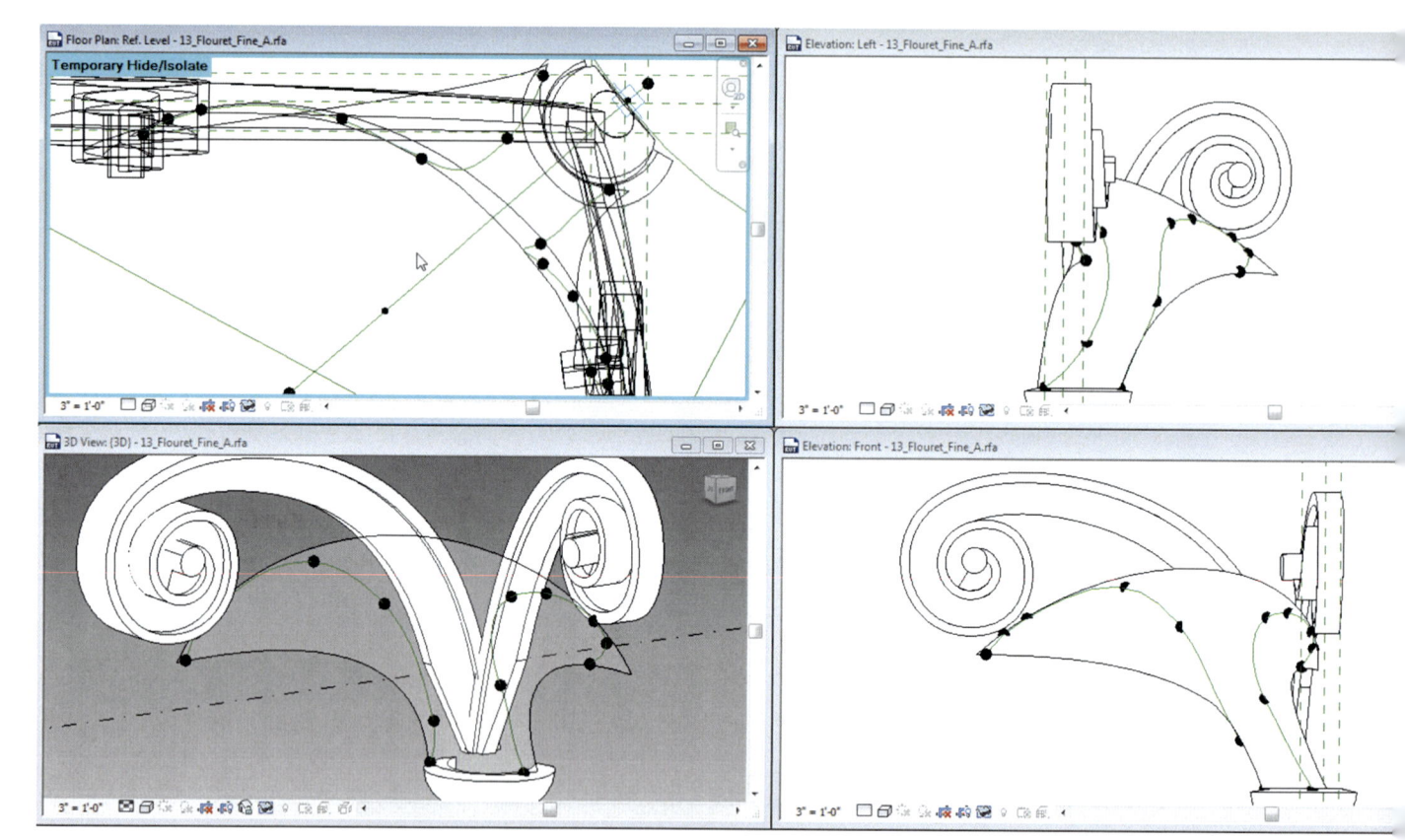

FIGURE 13.34

Using the arrow keys, the Properties palette or dragging onscreen, adjust the points to fine-tune the shape of the curves

• Renaissance Revit •

The Corinthian Capital | 415

Some of the views can be quite busy as you work. You can use temporary hide to hide items that are in your way in each view. Also it can sometimes be helpful to change the Visual Style to Wireframe to make it easier to see concealed items, and Shading to check your progress. Don't be afraid to change these settings frequently.

> Be patient. This is a slow process. You nudge a little, look at all the views, switch to another view, nudge some more and continue until the curve is to your liking (see Figure 13.34).

We will take another pass at these points, but if you like I have provided a catch-up file.

Catch Up! You can open a file completed to this point named: *13_Flouret_Fine_A.rfa*.

ADJUST POINTS WITH GIZMO CONTROLS

You may have noticed that the points we are manipulating do not have the nice control gizmos we discussed in the "Reference Lines and Points" topic in Chapter 11. This is because they are hosted to the surface and controlled by its U and V coordinates. However, we can disassociate the points from the surface as required to move them freely in 3D space. Once you disassociate, you cannot re-associate them to the surface, so make sure you have manipulated them on the surface as much as you can before continuing. I am going to recommend disassociating the points near the ends of the splines so that we can extend them beyond the curve and add more of a curl to the ends at the volutes and pull the other ends close the Cauliculus in closer.

1. Near the bottom of the curve, at the top of the Cauliculus, select the last point on either spline (use TAB if required).

2. On the Properties palette, uncheck Driven by Host.

Important: Do not uncheck Driving Curve(s). This setting would prevent the point from controlling the spline.

An orange gizmo should appear on the point.

3. In the plan view, use the orange arrow and drag the point closer to the center of the Cauliculus (see Figure 13.35).

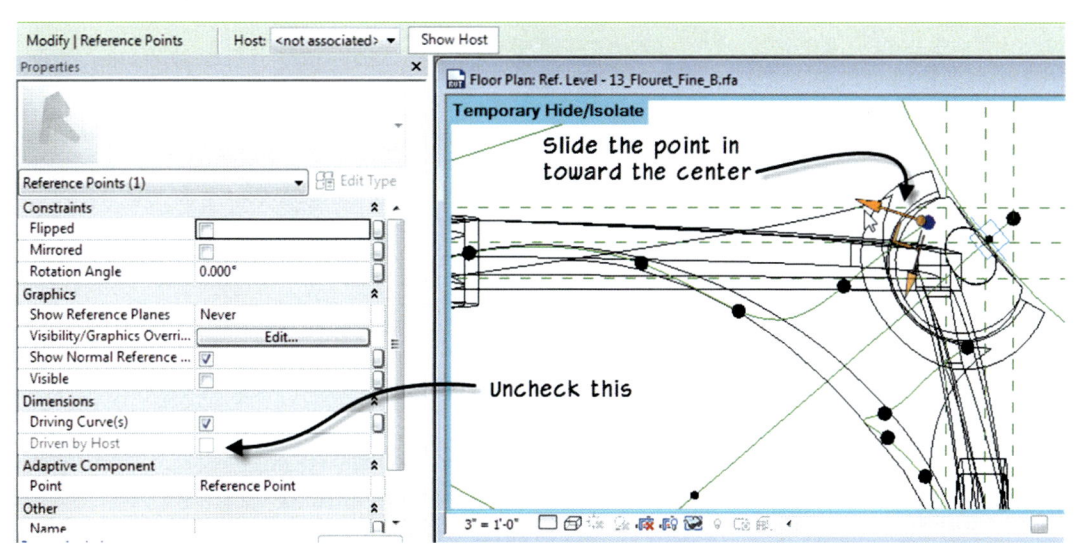

FIGURE 13.35

Turn off Driven by Host and then use the gizmo to move the point

4. Repeat for the endpoint on the other spline.

5. Switch to one of the elevation views.

• *Creating Classical Architecture with Modern Software* •

Notice that the point is still selected, but its orange arrows are skewed from the view. This is because even though we disassociated the point from the surface, it still has "memory" of its previous orientation. This is helpful for us as we fine-tune because you can toggle between this orientation and the orthogonal (X, Y and Z) orientation using the SPACEBAR.

- ⇨ Tap the SPACEBAR and then drag the blue arrow down slightly so that the height of the point is just below the top edge of the cauliculus.
- ⇨ Repeat for the other point.

6. Move to the other end of the splines now and disassociate the endpoints and the two points next to it (three total).

- ⇨ Fine-tune their positions using either the X, Y, Z (red, green, blue) or U, V, W (orange) gizmos to add a curve "hook like" end to each spline (see Figure 13.36).

   Adjust in all views.

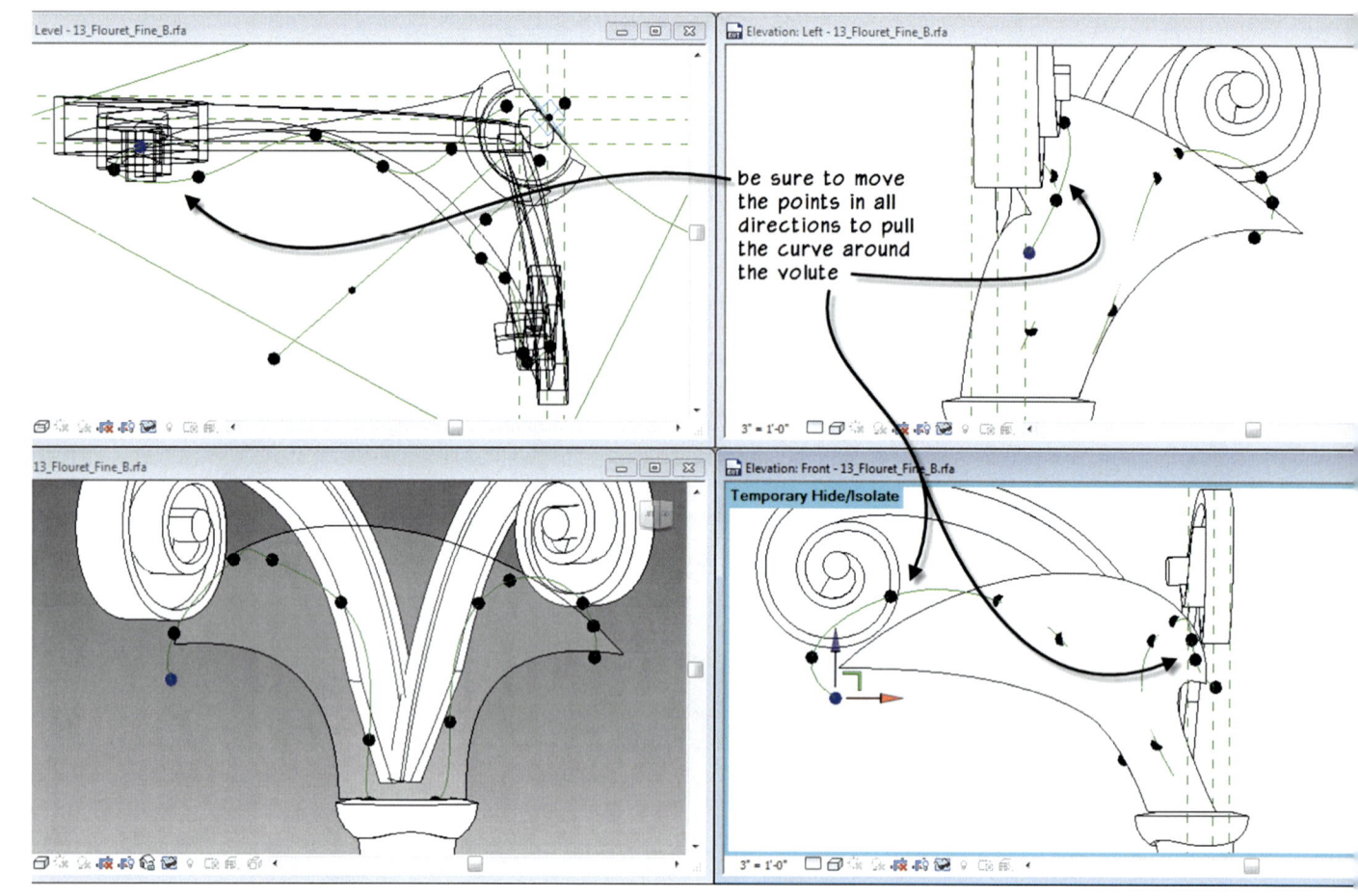

FIGURE 13.36
Adjust the splines in 3D space

Continue to fine-tune the points to your liking.

We have one more spline to make. This one can be created with either a 2D or 3D spline. It is for the bud which appears directly above the Cauliculus. It is often expressed as a symmetrical leaf between the two freeforms we have just sketched out. It is sometimes given other forms as well. We are going to draw this path on the work plane of the diagonal reference line at the base of the Cauliculus. You can work in the 3D view, or create a section parallel to the diagonal. Getting the work plane set is tricky though. Be sure to use TAB and hide other geometry.

7. Create a section view parallel to the diagonal line running through the middle.

⇨ Open the new view. Keep the 3D view visible.

It is often necessary to adjust the crop region height, sometimes the scale and possibly hide some items in the view. Set your work plane first.

8. Select the rectangular chain of reference lines in the 3D view, then click over to the section and hide them.

You may also have to repeat on the other angled reference lines. We want to set the center reference line as the work plane, so hiding all others makes this easier.

9. Set the work plane to the vertical work plane of the diagonal reference line running through the center of the Cauliculus.

⇨ Up near the top of the Cauliculus, draw a simple spline shape curving out slightly.

Draw it out in empty space first to avoid snapping to (and thereby associating with) nearby geometry. After drawing, you can move it to the proper location (see Figure 13.37).

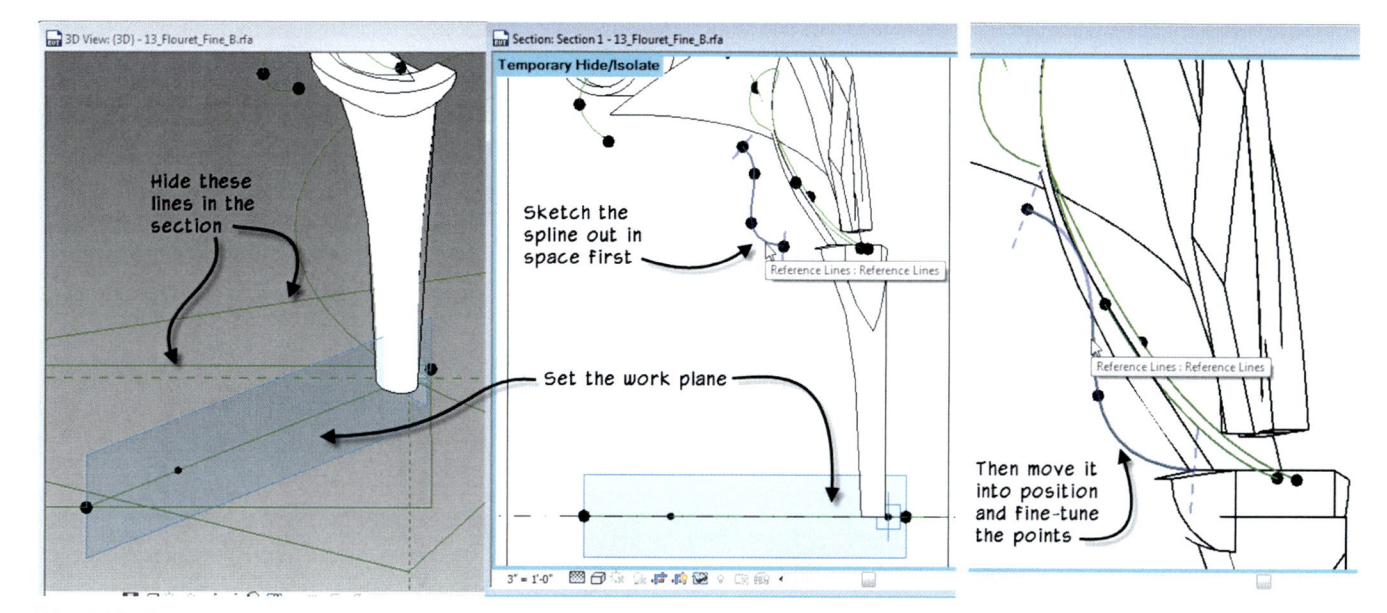

FIGURE 13.37
Completing the final spline

We now have our three splines. If you like you can continue in your file or use the catch-up file.

CATCH UP! You can open a file completed to this point named: *13_Flouret_Fine_B.rfa*.

ADD HOSTED POINTS AND PROFILES

The next step is to add hosted points to each spline, add the generic model profiles to these points and then create the lofts. Once we have the basic form, we can continue to refine it. It will be easiest to work mostly in 3D for this part of the exercise. Also, it is a good idea to hide as much as you can to make it easy to focus on just the parts we are editing. In fact, I recommend hiding everything except the three splines and the volutes.

1. Add three hosted points to each spline. One near each end and one at the midpoint.
2. Set the Normalized Curve Parameter of the endpoints to **0.005** and **0.995**. Set the middle one to **0.500**.

⇨ For all nine hosted points (three on each spline) set the Show Reference Planes to **Always** and uncheck the Show Normal Reference Plane Only box (see Figure 13.38).

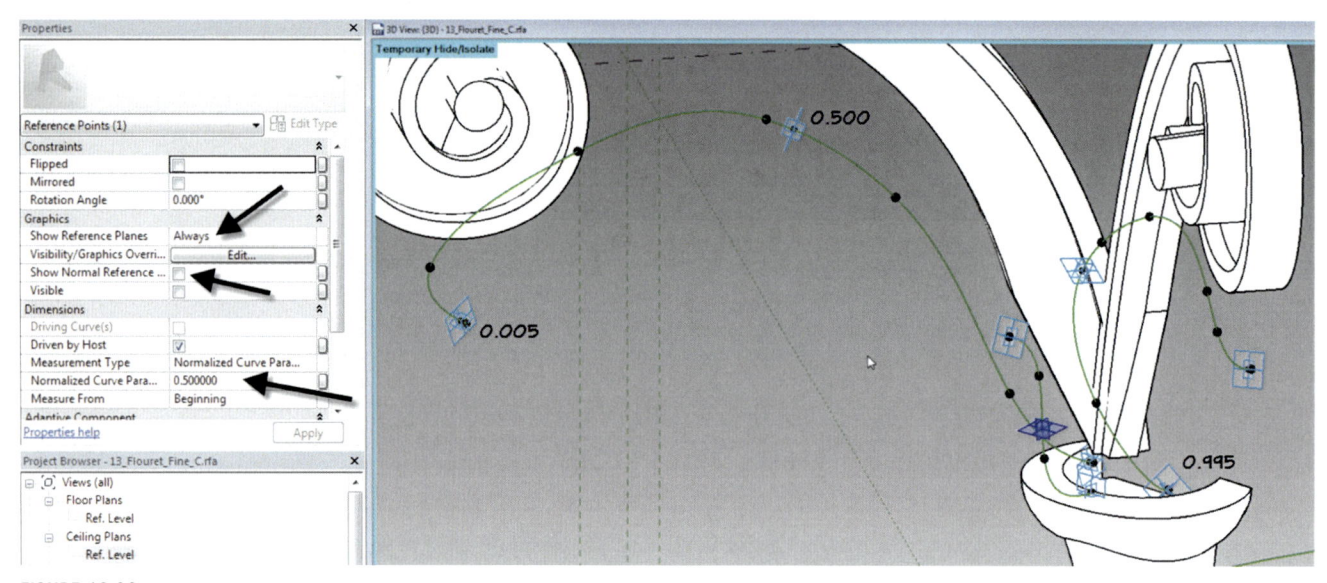

FIGURE 13.38
Set up the hosted points

Let's now add the profiles to the nine points using the procedures we used above in the "Add Hosted Profiles to a Path" topic. Here's a summary of the steps:

3. On the Create tab, click the Component tool.

   ⇨ From the Type Selector make sure that **Flouret Leaf Cross Section FB Profile:Flex** is chosen.

   ⇨ Set the work plane on one of the points and then place the profile.

   Remember to choose the Place on Work Plane button and use the keyboard shortcut SX to make sure you are snapping to the point. Tap the SPACEBAR to rotate if necessary (see Figure 13.39).

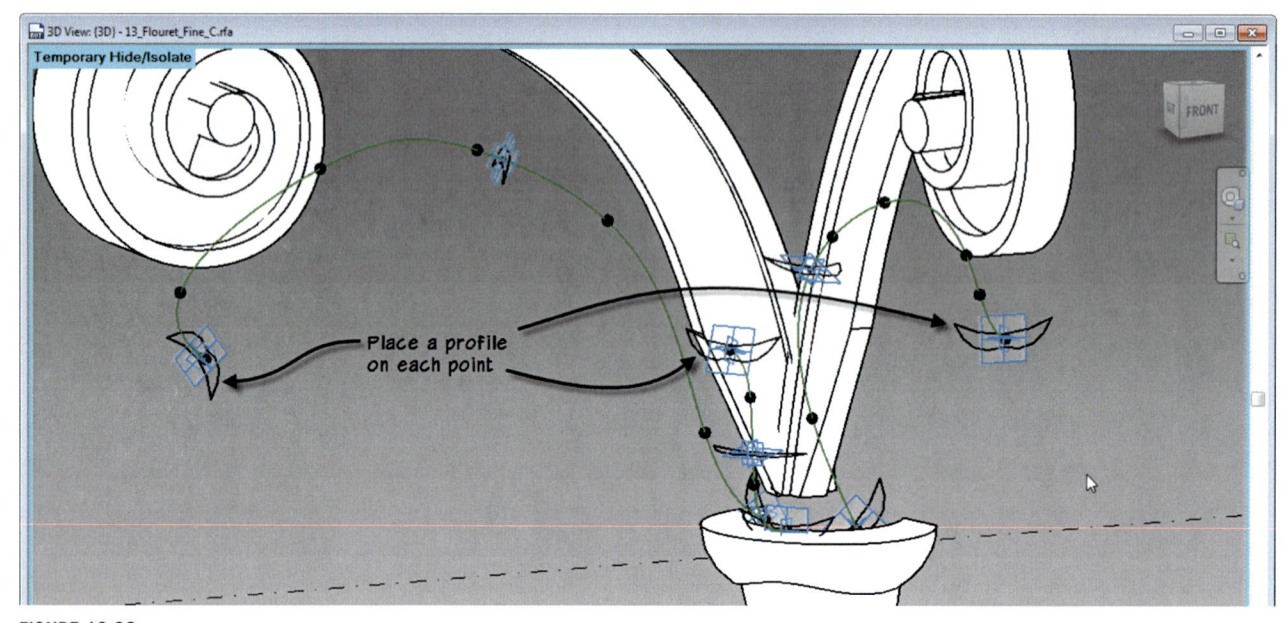

FIGURE 13.39
Add profiles to the points

As you may recall from above, the parameters in these profiles are instance based. This means that we can adjust each one individually directly on the Properties palette without having to make duplicate types. Using Table 13.5 and Figure 13.40, select each profile and edit its values as indicated. (The numbers in the table correspond to the locations in the figure).

• Renaissance Revit •

The Corinthian Capital | 419

TABLE 13.5

#	Profile	Y Mult	Offset Mult	X Mult	Host Point Rotation Angle	Comments
Large Volute Spline						
1	Start (0.005)	0.015	0.005	0.020	45°	
2	Midpoint	0.020	0.005	0.045	125°	
3	End (0.995)	0.015	0.005	0.025	0°	
Middle Spline						
4	Bottom (0.005)	0.025	0.010	0.025	0°	
5	Midpoint	0.038	0.010	0.035	0°	
6	Top (0.995)	0.010	0.005	0.012	0°	
Small Volute Spline						
7	Start (0.005)	0.0075	0.005	0.011	5°	
8	Midpoint	0.015	0.005	0.035	25°	
9	End (0.995)	0.0075	0.005	0.010	25°	

The screen is looking a little busy; stick with it. We are almost ready to make the forms. If you are wondering how all these numbers were determined, it was much trial and error. There really is no scientific way to calculate these values. You simply try the numbers see what it gives you and then adjust and repeat. I settled on the values in the table as giving good results. You are welcome to make any adjustments you wish.

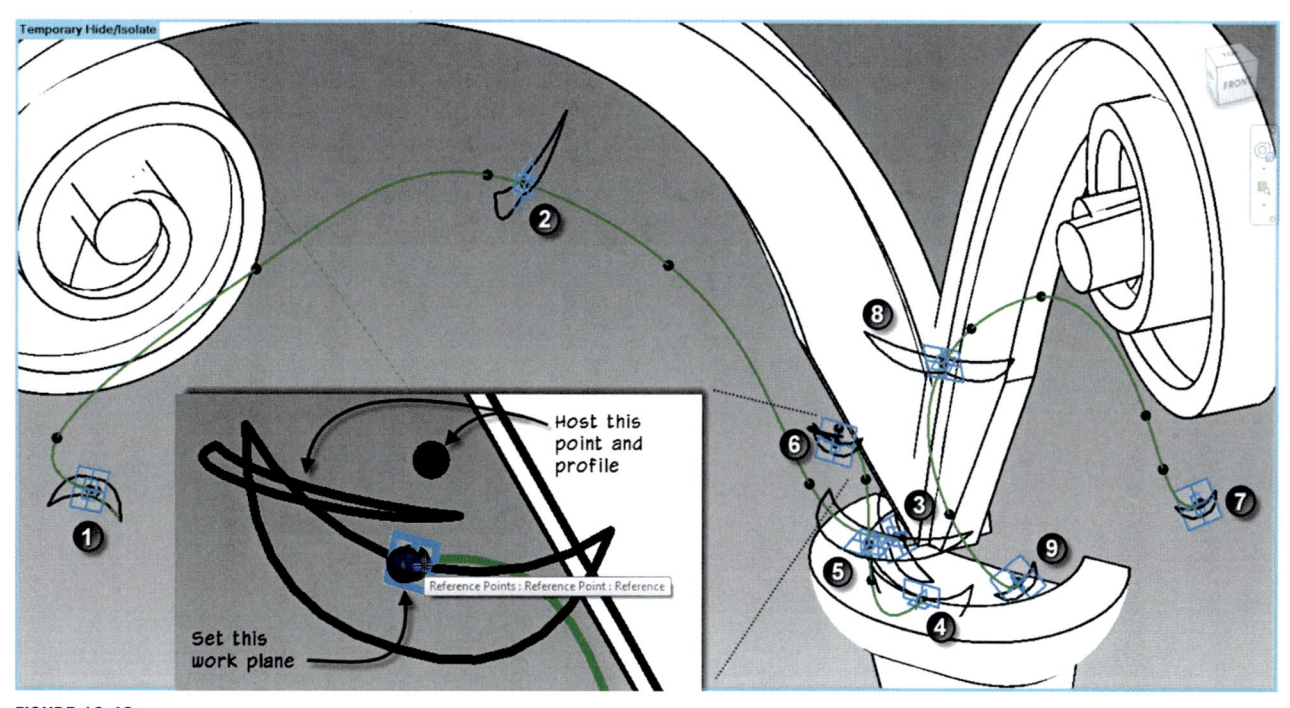

FIGURE 13.40

Host and adjust all of the splines

We are going to add one more profile at the top of the middle spline. If you loft the profiles that we have so far, it looks pretty good, but it ends a little abruptly. I think it will look a little better if we round off the end a little. I will propose two methods to do this. For this middle leaf, we can host another profile on the last point, but on a different work plane. This will put the two profiles at a right angle to each other which will affect the way it lofts.

• *Creating Classical Architecture with Modern Software* •

Zoom in at the top of the middle spline.

4. Create a new point and then set the work plane. Pick the perpendicular work plane on the top host point.
   ⇨ Place the point and ignore the warning about double points. Use the gizmo or properties palette to shift the offset of the new point to **0.006**.
   ⇨ Add a profile to this new point as shown in the inset of Figure 13.40.
   ⇨ For the Y Mult, and X Mult, use: **0.008** and the Offset Mult, use: **0.020**.

CATCH UP! You can open a file completed to this point named: *13_Flouret_Fine_C.rfa*.

CREATE FORMS FROM GM PROFILES

We are ready to create the forms.

1. Using the numbers in Figure 13.40 to assist you, select profiles 1, 2 and 3. Select the spline that passes through these three as well.
   ⇨ Create Form.

You should get a nice sweeping organic form. As noted above, it ends a little abruptly. Also, you may want to fine-tune the positions of some of the control points to make refinements. Let's create the other forms first and then make a final pass at all the points.

2. Select profiles 7, 8 and 9 and their spline.
   ⇨ Create form.
   ⇨ Orbit the 3D view and view from all angles.

The small volute leaf looks a little smoother than the large one. Also, they are kind of close together and do not allow a lot of room for the middle leaf. Let's create the middle leaf and then we'll make our final pass of adjustments.

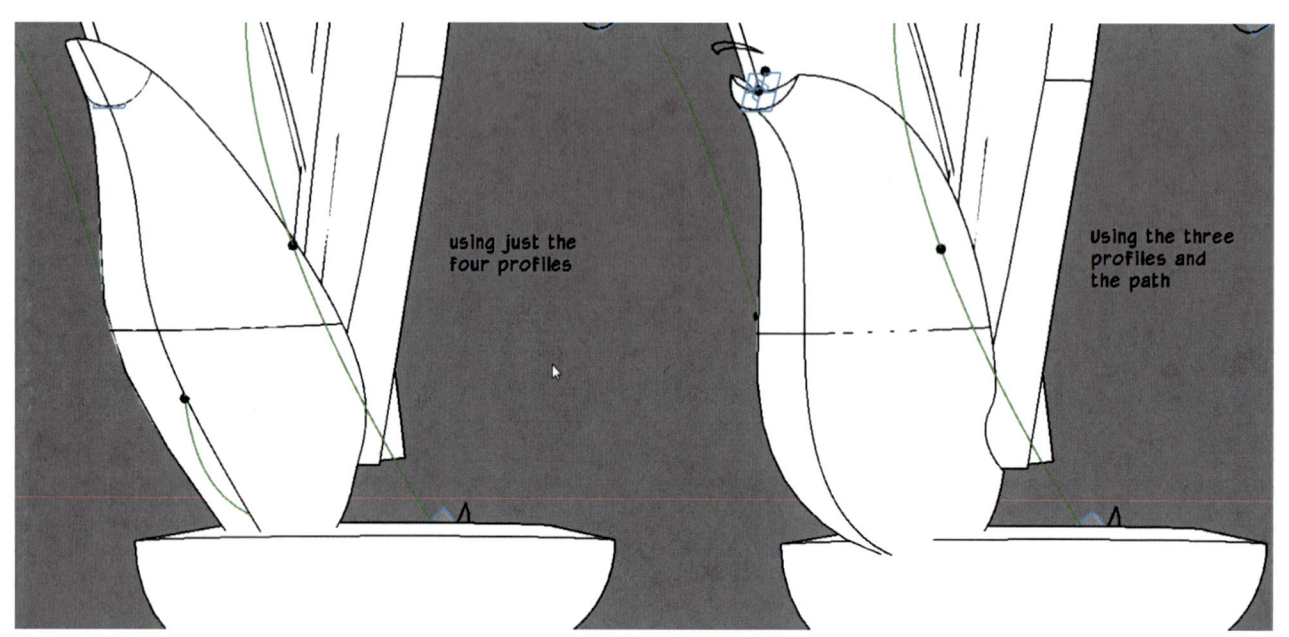

FIGURE 13.41
Two alternatives to creating the middle leaf

For the middle leaf, since we added the fourth profile at the right angle, we cannot use the path in the form. You actually get interesting results by selecting either; the path and profiles 4, 5 and 6, or by selecting the four profiles

The Corinthian Capital | 421

only without the path. Go ahead and hide the two large leaves, then try create the form each way. Undo in between each. I like the termination at the top when using just the four profiles better. But I like the bulge at the base when using the three profiles and path better. So it is a bit of a toss-up, but I think I favor the four profile option. You are free to use whichever one you like better (see Figure 13.41).

3. Reset the temporary Hide/Isolate mode.

At this point, it is clear that the curved surface upon which some of our path points still rely is making the shapes a little awkward. I think it is time to clean up the file a little and delete this surface and some of the other reference lines that are no longer necessary.

4. Delete the curved transparent surface and the three arcs that shape it.

> **Important:** Be sure to not delete the paths of any of their control points or any of the profiles. Use temporary Hide to assist you if necessary.

This will release all of the hosted points making it possible to move them freely.

5. Work between the elevation, plan and 3D views and make small methodical adjustments to the points controlling each spline.

   Take your time and be sure to check progress in multiple views as you work. Wireframe can sometimes be helpful (see Figure 13.42).

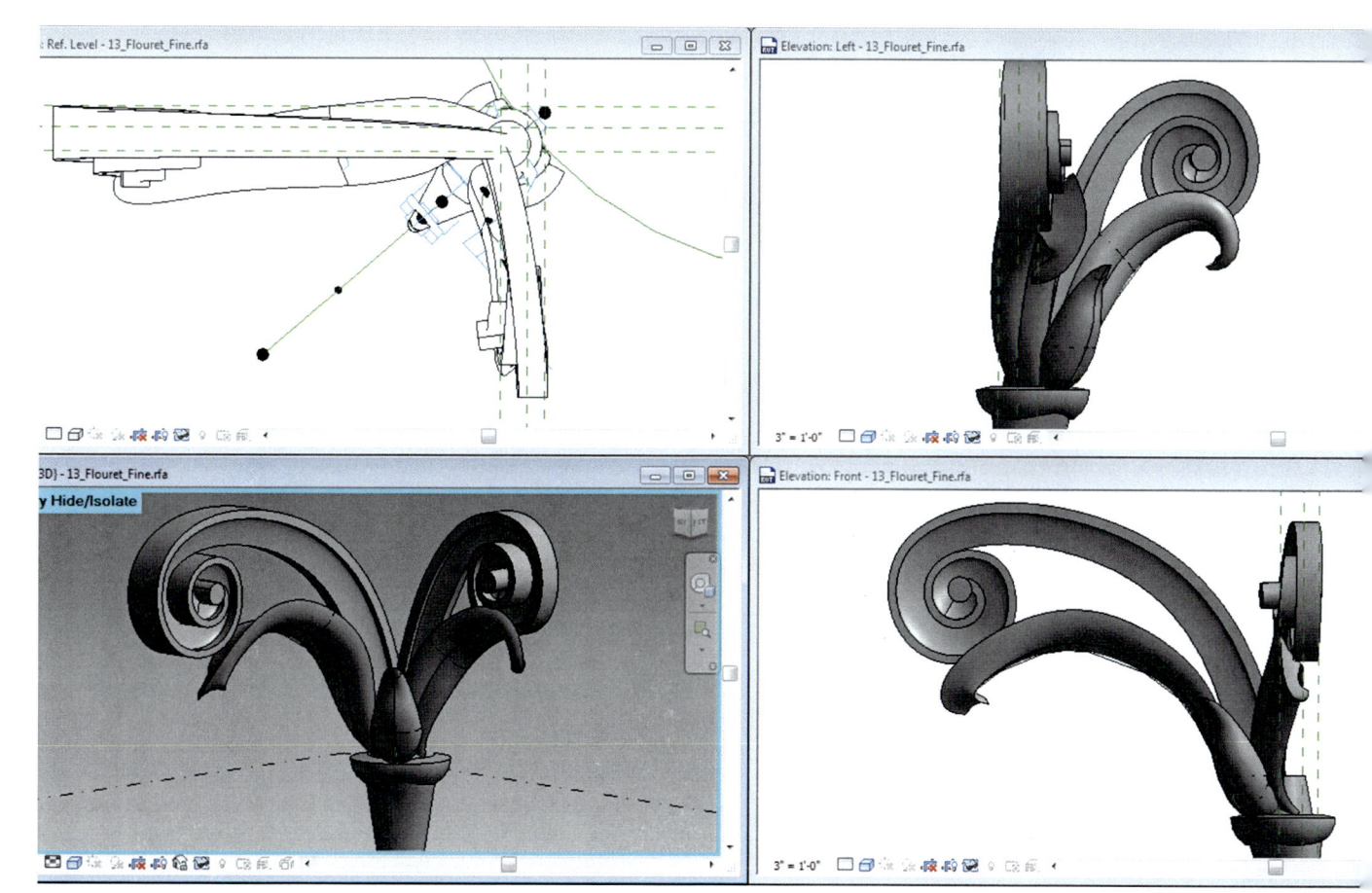

FIGURE 13.42

Finish the leaves by making final adjustments to the path points

• *Creating Classical Architecture with Modern Software* •

6. On the Project Browser, beneath *Families > Generic Models > Flouret Leaf Cross Section FB Profile*, right-click on *Flex* and choose **Select All Instances > In Entire Project**.

   ⇨ On the Properties palette, uncheck Visible.

7. Save the file.

> **CATCH UP!** You can open a file completed to this point named: *13_Flouret_Fine.rfa*.

In the catch-up file I added a small solid behind the leaves to fill in the open area. I also decided to add another profile to the form of the middle leaf. To do this is easy, just add another hosted point and profile. Select the existing form and the new profile and then click create form. The form will be recreated with the new profile incorporated into it.

Another optional item you can do is cap off the ends. I did this by sketching some reference lines on the work plane of the points at each end. Set the point's work plane active. Use the pick lines option to create the lines and trim everything to make a shape that is half the profile. Draw another straight line for the axis line and then create form. It will revolve a full 360° but you can edit the angles on the Properties palette to make it only go half of a full revolution (see Figure 13.43).

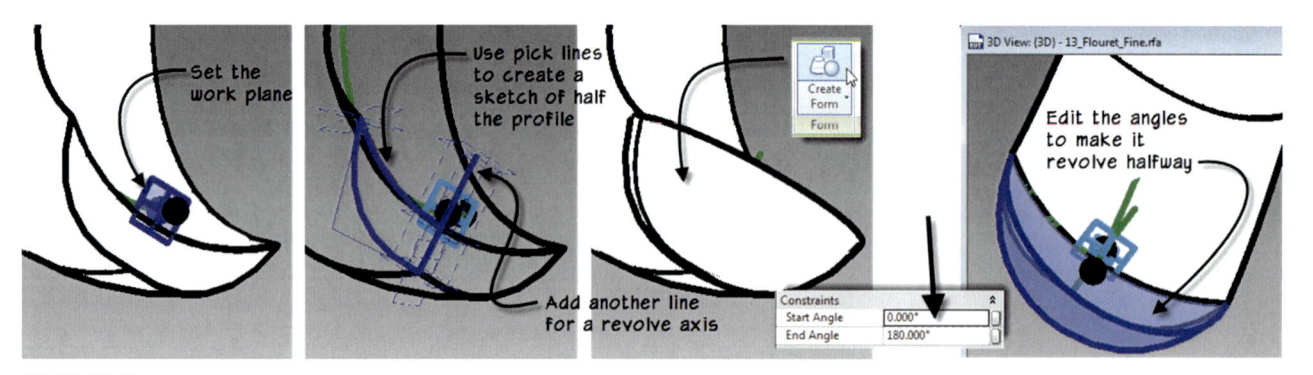

FIGURE 13.43
Add a simple revolved form at the ends of the two volute leaves

SCALING FAMILIES WITH THE PLANTING CATEGORY

At the start of the previous topic, I noted that we would be scaling it using a different technique. If you have been building Revit family content for a while, you have likely noticed that there are many family templates from which to choose. These templates sometimes vary considerably from one another. Templates set the category of a new family, its hosting behavior and many other sometimes subtle behaviors. A few months back I read a post on Kelvin Tam's Revit Swat blog which discussed a special "super power" of the Planting category (Tam 2013). Mr. Tam discovered that when you flex the built-in Height parameter in a planting family that it scales the entire family proportionally! It almost feels like cheating.

There is always a catch however. To make this trick work, it turns out that the planting family has to be "double nested" before it will work its magic. In this topic we'll take the family that we built in the last exercise and nest it into a planting family to enable this special scaling behavior.

   Open the *13_Flouret_Fine.rfa* file or continue in your own version of the file.

1. On the ribbon, on the Properties panel, click the Family Category and Parameters button.

   ⇨ Choose the Planting category. Click OK to dismiss the warning (see Figure 13.44).

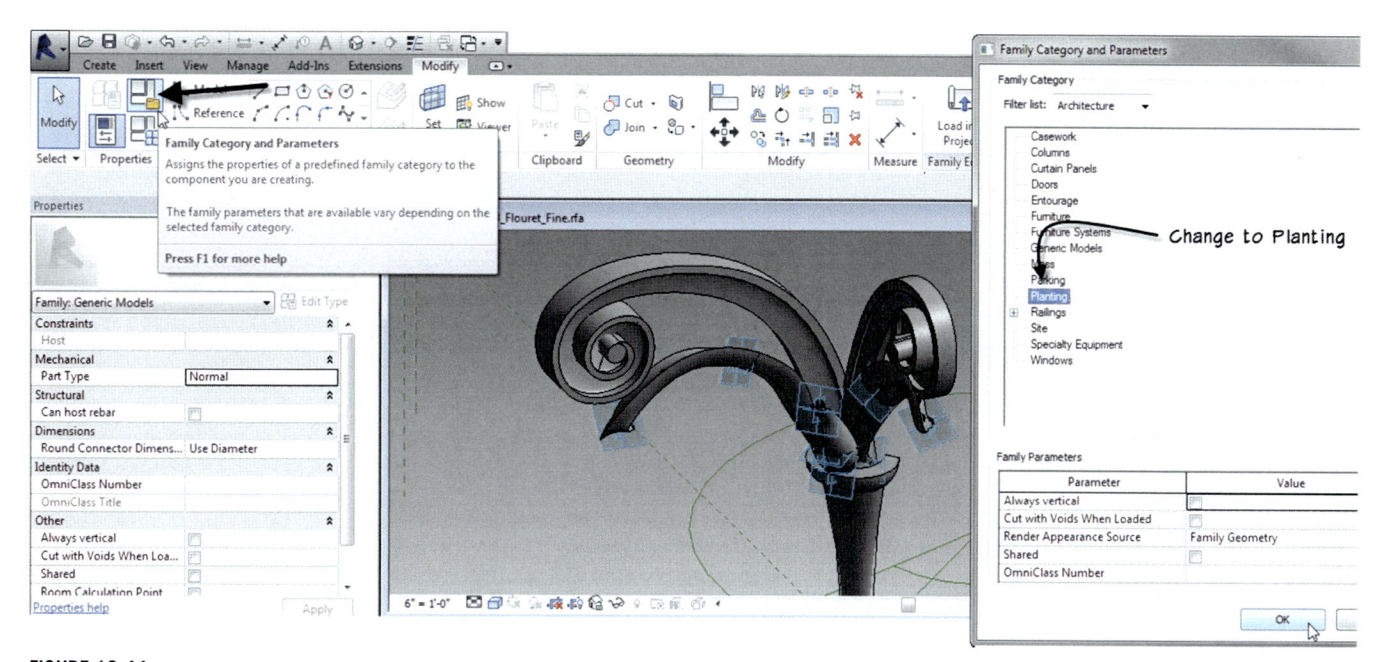

FIGURE 13.44

Change to the Planting category

So our family is now a planting family. The next step is to ensure that it scales at the correct amount. Revit looks at the height of any geometry in the file and treats that as the base height. So later when you scale the height, the ratio is calculated from the extents of the existing geometry. So in the current file, the geometry is about 0.667 tall. This value will be used in conjunction with the height parameter to determine scaling. We could develop a multiplier parameter to get everything to scale properly, or we can build our geometry at the desired starting height. In other words, since our controlling dimension is the Base Diameter, all we need to do is add an object in the file that is the height of the Base Diameter. Since this is 1.000 to start with, this new geometry will be the tallest thing in the file and will be used by Revit to determine the scale factor.

One small snag I ran into in my tests was that the geometry that you are using for scaling has to be visible. To overcome this, we will create a cylinder that is 1.000 tall in the center of the column. If you recall the bell that we modeled at the start of the chapter, it is hollow so this cylinder will serve to control the scaling of the flouret and have the added benefit of filling in the hollow portion of the capital. I provided some lines in the file for us to use to create this form. We will actually be creating more of a pie slice; 1/8 of the cylinder. This is because we will be repeating this family eight times in the final Corinthian capital.

2. Using Trim/Extend to a Corner, trim the two diagonal lines to the small arc at the center of the circle. This will create a pie shaped set of reference lines (see the top left side of Figure 13.45).

⇨ Select the shape and create form.

⇨ On the Properties palette, next to Positive Offset, click the Associate Family Parameter button and choose the parameter **Z2**.

⇨ Repeat for the Negative Offset choosing **Z1** this time (see top right side of Figure 13.45).

424 | Chapter 13

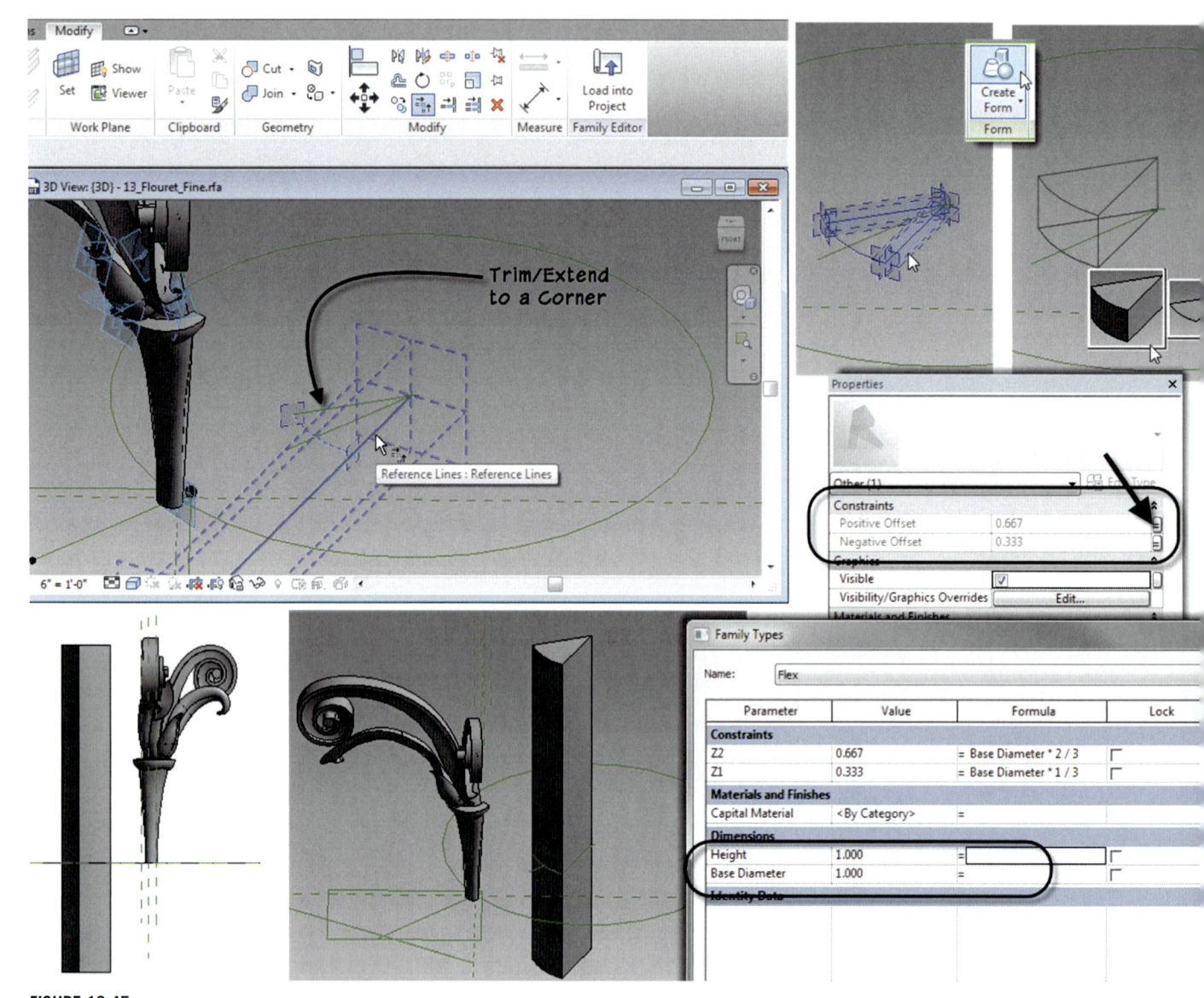

FIGURE 13.45

Create a 1.000 unit tall extrusion

I have preconfigured these two parameters in the file to multiply the Base Diameter by 2/3 and 1/3 respectively. This makes the overall height of the extrusion 1.000 unit tall.

3. Open the "Family Types" dialog.

⇨ Set the Height parameter to: **1.000** and then click OK (see the bottom of Figure 13.45).

Before we finish this family, let's delete and purge out the volutes family. The current file size of the flouret family is about 3.25 MB. This is not tremendously large considering its complexity, but it is considered large for a family. Even though the volutes instance is currently set to be invisible, it still makes the file larger. If you remove it, we can get the file down to about 2.5 MB. Still on the larger side, but definitely better. I should note that in general, adaptive component families are larger than their traditional family editor counterparts.

4. On the Project Browser, right-click and delete the *13_Volutes_Fine* file. Confirm the deletion by clicking Yes.

5. Save the file as: **Flouret_Fine_PLNT**.

6. From the *Seed Families* folder, open the *Family Seed (Adaptive).rfa* file.

• Renaissance Revit •

7. Save this file to the Chapter13 folder and call it: **Flouret_Fine_PLNT_Host**.

8. Follow the procedure above and change this family's category to **Planting** as well.

9. Open the "Family Types" dialog, set the Height parameter to: **1.000** and then click OK.

10. Switch windows back to the *Flouret_Fine_PLNT* family.

    ⇨ Click Load Into Project.

    Revit will switch over to the other family and run the place component command.

11. On the ribbon, click the Place on Work Plane button, on the Options Bar, choose Level: Ref. Level from the Placement Plane drop-down and then snap the instance to the intersection of the two reference planes.

    ⇨ Cancel out of the command.

12. Save the file.

> **CATCH UP!** You can open a file completed to this point named: *13_Flouret_Fine_PLNT_Host.rfa*.

We are ready to test it out. In the next topic, we will bring all the pieces together into a single host family and test it all out, including flexing our new planting family.

ASSEMBLE THE CAPITAL

We now have all of the required components of our fine detail Corinthian capital. To assemble it, we'll save a copy of the medium detail version and swap out all the families.

1. From the *Chapter13* folder, open the file named: *Corinthian Capital Fine.rfa*. (We created this in the "Save a Fine Detail Version" topic above).

At the start of this chapter, we created this file from the medium detail version. Now that we have created a fine detail version for each of the nested families in this file, let's import them all in to replace the simplified versions we have here.

2. On the Project Browser, expand *Families > Generic Models*.

    ⇨ Right-click on *Abacus and Bell* and choose **Reload**.

    ⇨ From the *Chapter13* folder, choose *13_Abacus and Bell_Fine.rfa* and then click Open.

    If you prefer, select your saved version of this file created above instead.

    ⇨ When prompted, choose Overwrite the existing version.

Unfortunately, when you do this, we will lose the four flowers around the abacus. This is because they were face hosted and the faces they were hosted to are no longer there. We can create a new work plane for the flowers by drawing a reference line with 3D snapping that is hosted to the abacus.

3. On the Create tab, click the Reference button and then on the Options Bar, check the 3D Snapping checkbox.

    ⇨ Snap to the midpoint of the lower curved edge of the abacus.

    ⇨ Snap to the upper midpoint of the curved edge of the abacus

    ⇨ Add a hosted point at the midpoint of this new line (see the left side of Figure 13.46).

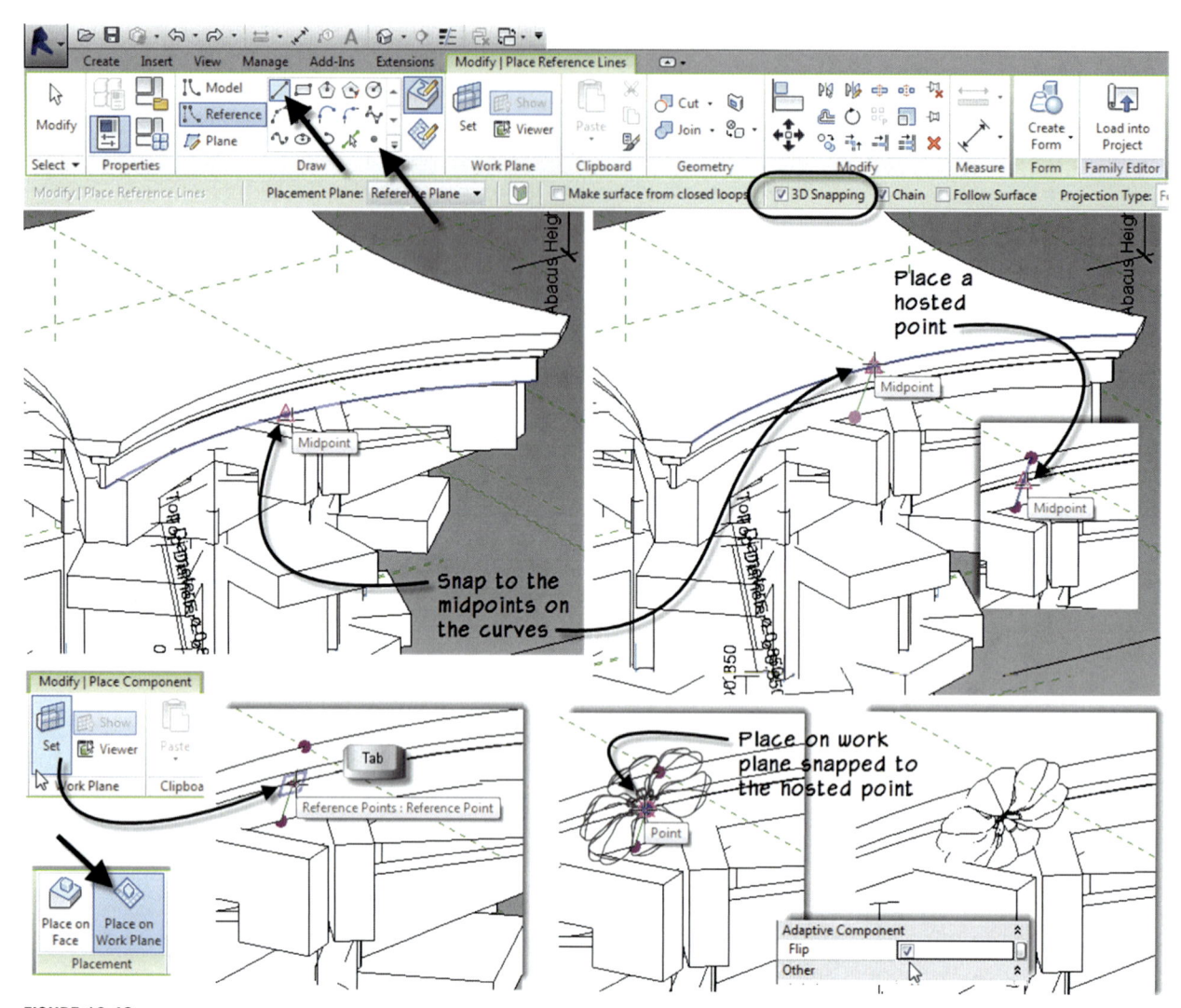

FIGURE 13.46

Create new work planes and add the flowers

4. On the Project Browser, beneath *Families > Generic Models*, right-click on *Flower* and choose **Reload**.

    ⇨ From the *Chapter13* folder, choose *13_Flower_Fine.rfa* and then click Open.

    ⇨ When prompted, choose Overwrite the existing version.

This file was created using the same procedures we used above to create the flouret. In fact, the same profile family was used in this file and the planting family trick was also employed to control its scaling.

5. On the Project Browser, beneath the *Planting* category, expand the *13_Flower_Fine* family and then drag *Flex* into the model canvas area.

    ⇨ Snap it to the work plane of the point hosted on the reference line.

6. On the Properties palette, beneath the Adaptive Component grouping, check the Flip checkbox.

    ⇨ Repeat the process on the other three sides. When drawing the 3D lines, always snap the points from the lower are first to the upper arc.

> TIP: If any of your flowers end up pointing the wrong way, select it and then on the Properties palette, check the Flip checkbox. You can also select the hosted point and set its rotation to 180° instead.

7. Flex the family to be sure that the hosted 3D reference lines and flowers are working correctly. Return to Base Diameter **1.000** before continuing.

I set up the planting family height a little differently in the flower family. Recall that in the previous exercise, we built a one unit tall extrusion and set the Height in the planting family to 1.000 to facilitate the scaling. In the flower, I instead set the height using a formula based on Base Diameter. (Specifically, Base Diameter * 0.025). You can open the flower family to see this if you wish. It turns out that this is just as effective in controlling the scaling ratio.

> **CATCH UP!** You can open a file completed to this point named: *13_Corinthian Capital Fine_A.rfa*.

Let's replace the two rows of leaves next. They currently use two types from the same family. When we built the fine detail versions above however, we saved them as separate families. So to replace them, we have to approach it slightly differently.

8. Right-click one of the short leaves at the bottom row and choose **Select All Instances > Visible in View**.
9. On the Properties palette, click the Edit Type button.
   ⇨ At the top of the "Type Properties" dialog, click the Load button.
   ⇨ Browse to the *Chapter13* folder, select the *13_Leaf_Short_Fine.rfa* file and then click Open.
   If you prefer, select your saved version of this file created above instead.
10. Stay in "Type Properties," scroll down and link up the Capital Material and Base Diameter parameters and then click OK.

This approach effectively separates these eight leaves to a different family. Now we can use the reload approach on Project Browser to swap out the tall leaves.

11. On the Project Browser, beneath *Families > Generic Models*, right-click on *Leaf* and choose **Reload**.
    ⇨ From the *Chapter13* folder, choose *13_Leaf_Tall_Fine.rfa* and then click Open.
    If you prefer, select your saved version of this file created above instead.
    ⇨ When prompted, choose Overwrite the existing version.
12. Repeat the reload process on the last two nested families: Flouret and Volutes.

    Load files: *13_Flouret_Fine_PLNT_Host.rfa* and *13_Volutes_Fine.rfa*, or select your saved versions of these files created above instead (see Figure 13.47).

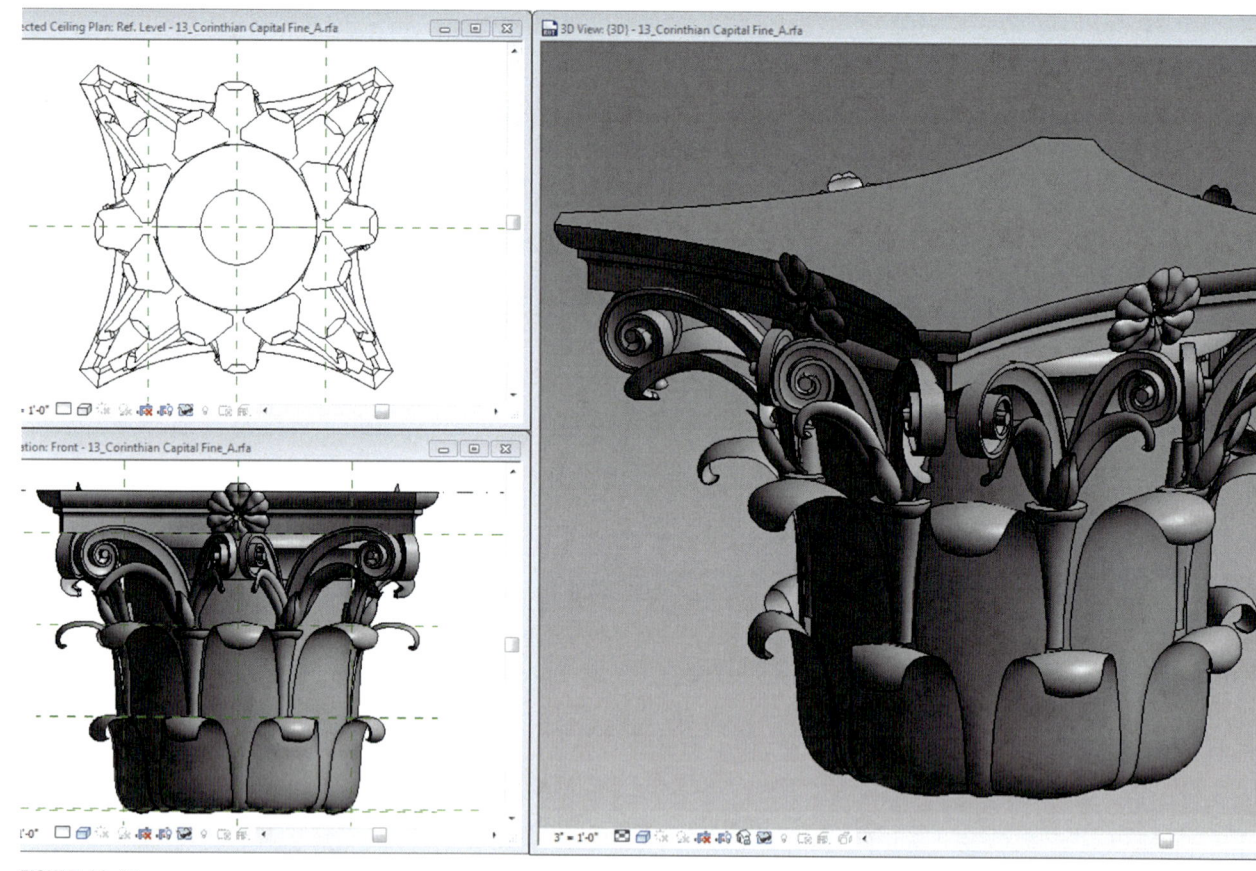

FIGURE 13.47

The completed Corinthian capital

13. Edit each family's type and make sure that the Base Diameter and material is properly linked up.

    For the *13_Flouret_Fine_PLNT_Host.rfa* family, we will link the parameters a little differently. We want the Base Diameter parameter in the current file to drive the nested family's "Height" parameter.

14. On Project Browser, beneath *Families > Planting > 12_Flouret_Fine_PLNT_Host*, right-click Flex and choose **Edit**.

    ⇨ Next to Height, click the Associate Family Parameter button and link it up with Base Diameter and then click OK.

15. Flex the family.

Assuming that everything flexed OK, congratulations! You now have a fully parametric Corinthian capital.

16. Save the file.

> **CATCH UP!** You can open a file completed to this point named: *13_Corinthian Capital Fine.rfa*.

LOAD INTO PROJECT

As always the final test is to load the family into a project. A version of the column is provided that just needs the new fine detail version loaded in.

1. From the *Chapter13* folder, open the *Corinthian Column (without Pedestal).rfa* file.

2. On the Project Browser, beneath *Families > Generic Models*, right-click *Corinthian Capital Fine* and choose **Reload**.

   ⇨ Browse to the *Chapter13* folder and choose the *13_Corinthian Capital Fine.rfa* file (or choose the version that you built in this chapter instead).

• Renaissance Revit •

⇨ When prompted, choose Overwrite Existing Version.

Check the settings for Coarse, Medium and Fine and be sure that each component is configured properly.

⇨ Save and close the file.

When I assembled this file, I had to change a few of the basic settings from how they were configured in previous chapters. We are using adaptive components here. It is possible to change an adaptive component to the Columns category, but unfortunately it will not gain a second reference level. This means that when we use this family in a project, it will not have a Top Constraint. Instead, I had to use a formula to derive the height from the Base Diameter. This is applied to the Top Offset in the coarse scale version. For the medium and fine versions of the capital, I made them Work Plane Based, then associated them to a reference plane that is driven by the Column Height parameter.

3. From the *Chapter13* folder, open the *13_Sandbox_Colonnade_Corinthian.rvt* file.

4. On the Project Browser, beneath *Families > Columns*, right-click *Corinthian Column* and choose **Reload**.

⇨ Browse to the *Chapter13* folder and choose the *13_Corinthian Column (without Pedestal).rfa* file (or choose the version that you just saved instead).

⇨ When prompted, choose Overwrite Existing Version.

This is going to take a while. Unfortunately as you will see adaptive components can become quite large. The exact amount of time will depend on the speed of your system. But the completed versions of these files are large. So you will want to use them in large scale views and rely on the medium and coarse detail versions in smaller scales. I'll discuss performance a bit more in the next chapter.

CATCH UP! You can open a file completed to this point named: *13_Sandbox_Colonnade_Corinthian_A.rvt*.

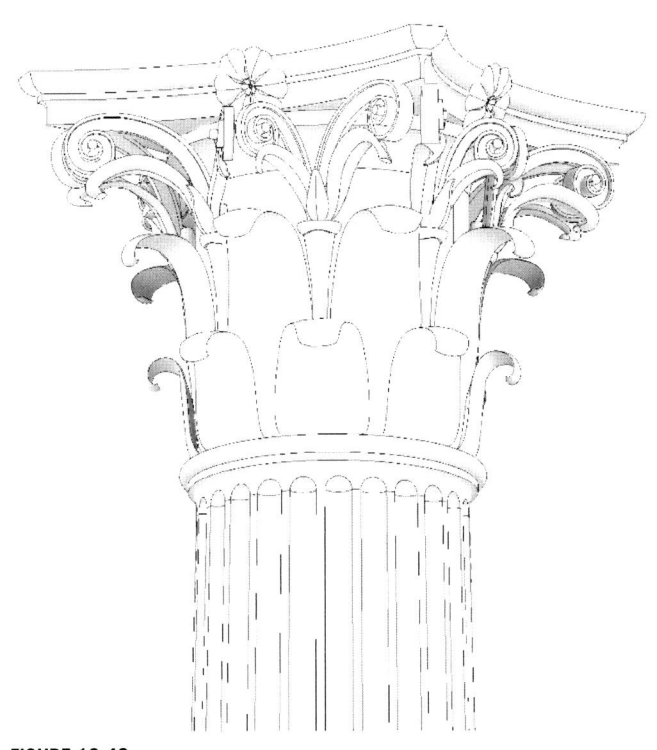

FIGURE 13.48
With Ambient Shading enabled

SUMMARY

- ✓ Begin constructing complex orders like the Corinthian by creating the schematic version first.

- ✓ The Corinthian capital is broken into several smaller nested families.

- ✓ Using adaptive components, we can construct the organic forms required by the Corinthian order.

- ✓ Use generic model families with closed loops drawn from model lines to form the same function as profile families.

- ✓ Using reference lines and hosted points a detailed flexible rig can be constructed that will form the basis for a complex lofted form element.

- ✓ Add parameters to the rig points to make the form fully parametric.

- ✓ 2D or 3D splines can be used for the path of the lofted forms.

- ✓ Selecting the profiles and paths will give different results than just selecting the profiles without the path. Be sure to experiment with both.

- ✓ An alternative scaling method involves using nested families set to the planting category. The planting category automatically scales based on its own built-in height parameter.

- ✓ Be sure to include all three levels of detail in complex families like the Corinthian. This will give you flexibility when using a family of this size and complexity at various scales.

FORUM ROME
Photo by author

Chapter 14
File Management Techniques

INTRODUCTION

When building family content it is important to have a good management strategy for your files. In this chapter we will wrap up our Revit family editor journey through classical architecture with some practical considerations about file size, saving options and management techniques.

OBJECTIVES

Topics in this chapter include:

- Managing file size
- Incorporating two-dimensional data in 3D families
- File save options

MANAGING FILE SIZE

A common concern with family content is managing file size. The larger a family file becomes, the more of an impact it can potentially have on overall file size and performance in a project. The trouble with this concern however is that file size is not the only, nor always the best indicator of file performance in a program like Revit. That being said, keeping file size as small as possible is always a desirable goal. Naturally the complexity of the geometry within the family is one of the primary factors, and as you have probably noticed, some of our families in this book have become quite large. Without becoming consumed by the task of file size reduction, there are some strategies that you can do to manage the size of your families.

Purge Unused—As you work in a family file, you may create types or import families and style items that you don't actually put into use. These items can be purged out of the file. Every family and type definition takes up space, so deleting those that are not used can help to reduce the size of the file. The Purge Unused command is located on the Manage tab (see Figure 14.1). When you run this command, it will display a list of the items that are not used and you can check the ones you wish to purge. I would recommend checking the file size before and after purge. Sometimes there is not much difference, so this might mean instead of purging everything, you focus on large unused items. Some smaller items might not really impact the file size and might prove useful later. For example, you might want to retain extra text, dimension and view tag types.

432 | Chapter 14

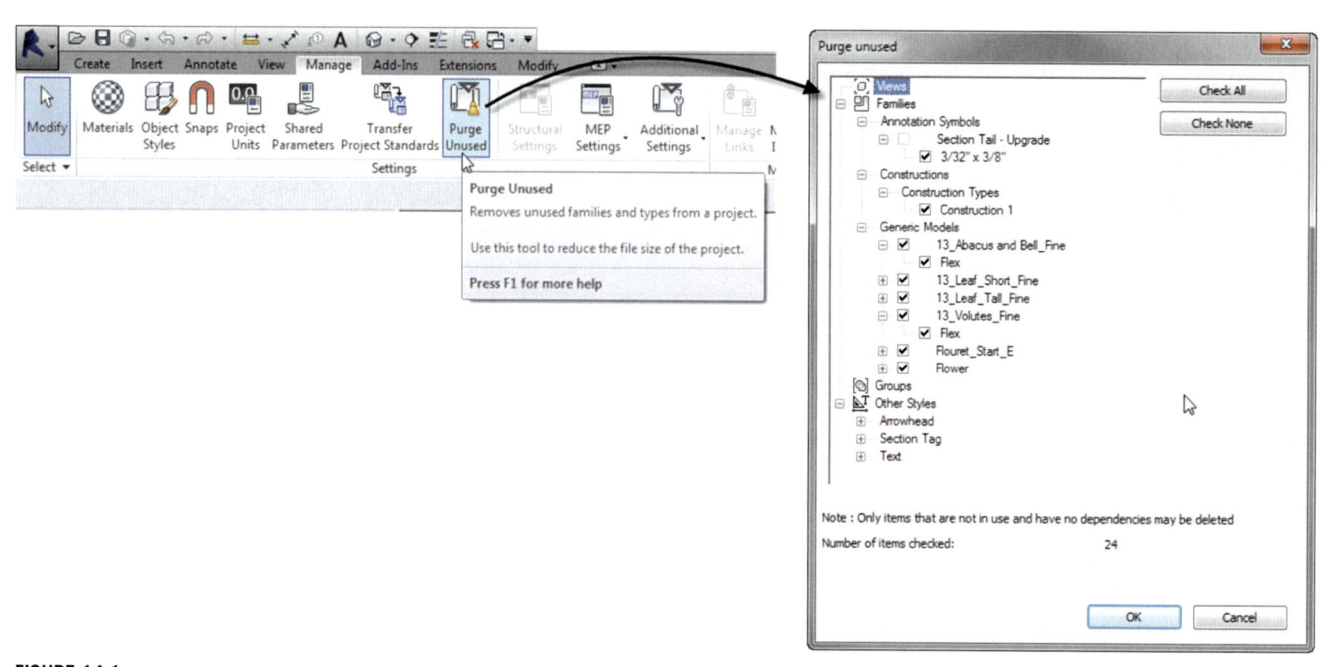

FIGURE 14.1

Purge Unused is accessible from the Manage tab

Deleting from Project Browser—If you want to purge just a few items, instead of using purge unused, you can right-click an item directly on the Project Browser and delete them there. This is sometimes all you need to do instead of the Purge Unused. I frequently use this technique to delete families and types I am no longer using in the family or project (see Figure 14.2).

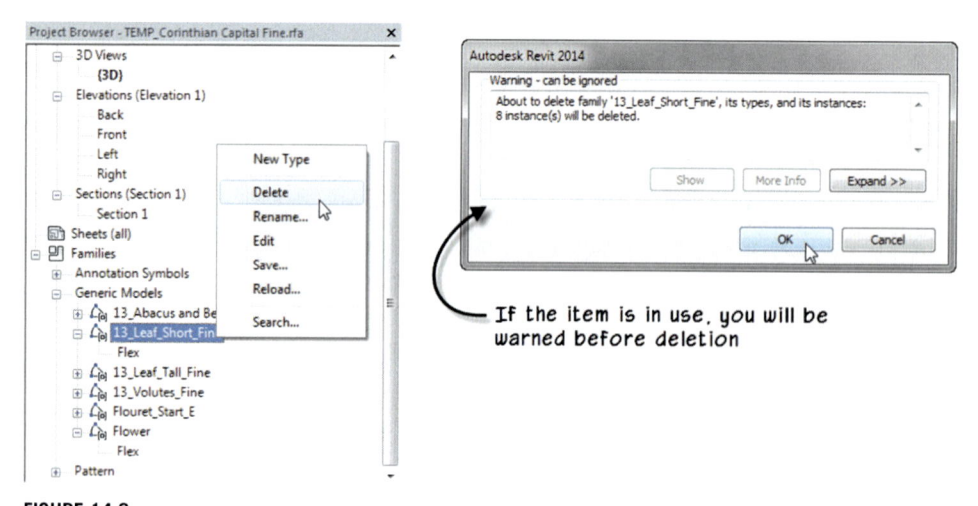

FIGURE 14.2

You can delete used or unused families from the Project Browser

An important difference in this technique is that you can use this method to delete items that are in use! So be careful. As you can see in the figure, you will get a warning if the item is being used. If you click OK, it deletes the definition from the Project Browser and all instances in the model. Cancel if this is not what you want. In the figure, I am right-clicking the family itself. The same technique can be done by right-clicking the type instead. So if you want to keep the family and just delete an unwanted type, right-click it instead.

Compact File—when saving a file, you can choose Save As and then in the "Save As" dialog, click the Options button (see Figure 14.3). In the "File Save Options" dialog, check the Compact File checkbox. This will compress

File Management Techniques | **433**

the file a bit and cleanup its internal database. It does not always reduce file size, but it does help ensure the integrity of the file, so it's not a bad idea to do this regularly.

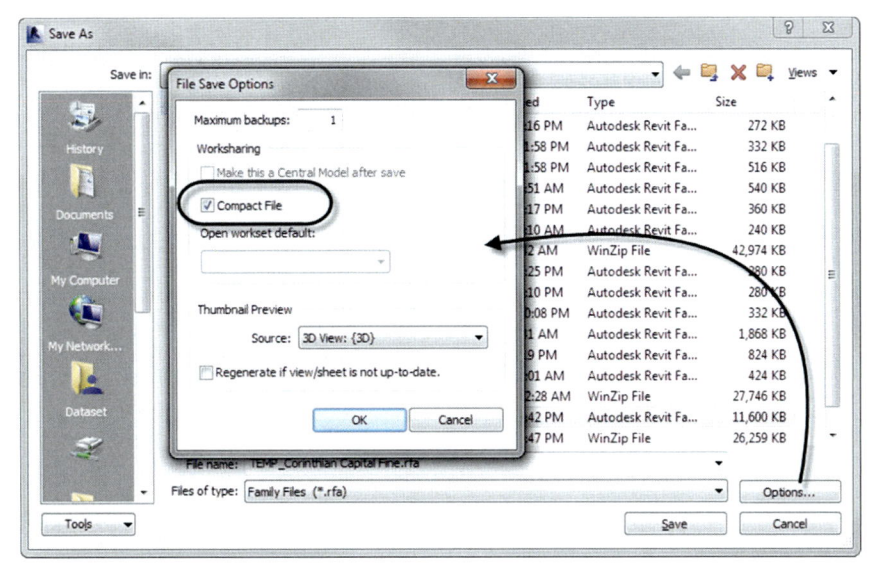

FIGURE 14.3
Access Compact File from the Save As Options

Audit—similar to compact file, audit is a maintenance operation. It is available when you open a file in the "Open" dialog. Just check the Audit checkbox (see Figure 14.4) before clicking Open. A confirmation warning will display. Click Yes to confirm it. Audit will check the file for problems. Again, it may not do anything to reduce the file size, but if there is any corruption in the file, it can help clean it out.

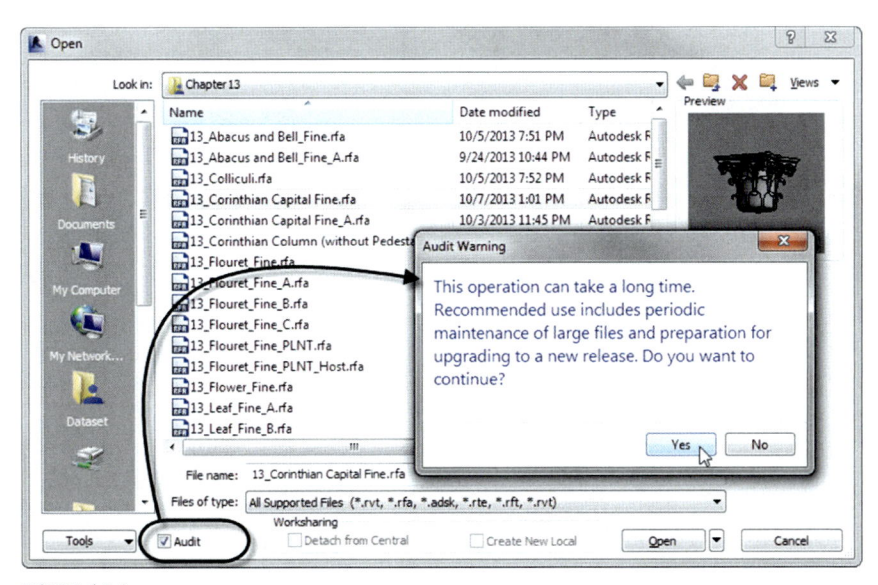

FIGURE 14.4
Run an Audit from the Open dialog

Deleting unneeded views—sometimes you will create extra views in your family files. If you delete any unneeded views, it can reduce the file size a little. Consider carefully however, as deleting views can make it more difficult to edit the file later. So the small reduction in file size may not be worth leaving your file with only minimal views. On the other hand, if you created numerous sections and 3D views while working, deleting the ones you no longer need can help slim the file down a bit (see Figure 14.5).

434 | Chapter 14

FIGURE 14.5

Quantity of views sometimes impacts the file size in unpredictable ways

Interestingly and somewhat counterintuitively, sometimes the adding or deleting views does not impact file size at all, or can actually do the opposite of what you expect. In my tests, I added a new view and in some cases, this actually reduced the file size a little. While this is not typical, it is again another reason that you should treat file size recommendations as a guideline and not allow yourself to become consumed with the task of reducing a file's size as sometimes you will only be thwarted in your attempts.

Using traditional instead of massing families—in my experience, families created in the massing environment, especially adaptive components and files that use 3D splines, are significantly larger than traditional families. Consider our two most complex families created in this book: the Ionic column family and the Corinthian family. Best practice recommendations say we typically want to keep family size at around half a MB to as much as one MB. This is a good goal, but not always achievable. For example, the Ionic weighs in at about 4.8 MB. This is large for a family to be sure and nearly five times the recommended size. The fine version of the Corinthian capital alone logs in at a whopping 10 plus MB. When it is loaded into the column family, it balloons to around 30 MB, which is *very* large for a family. (I have had entire projects that were smaller than this). I am not sure why the column is three times larger than the capital alone. Before the fine detail version of the capital is loaded into the column family it is only 3.6 MB. After loading the capital it jumps in size. So this brings me to my other point about file size: it is often tough to pin down. So despite many of the above best practice recommendations, sometimes your families will resist your attempts to slim them down (see Figure 14.6).

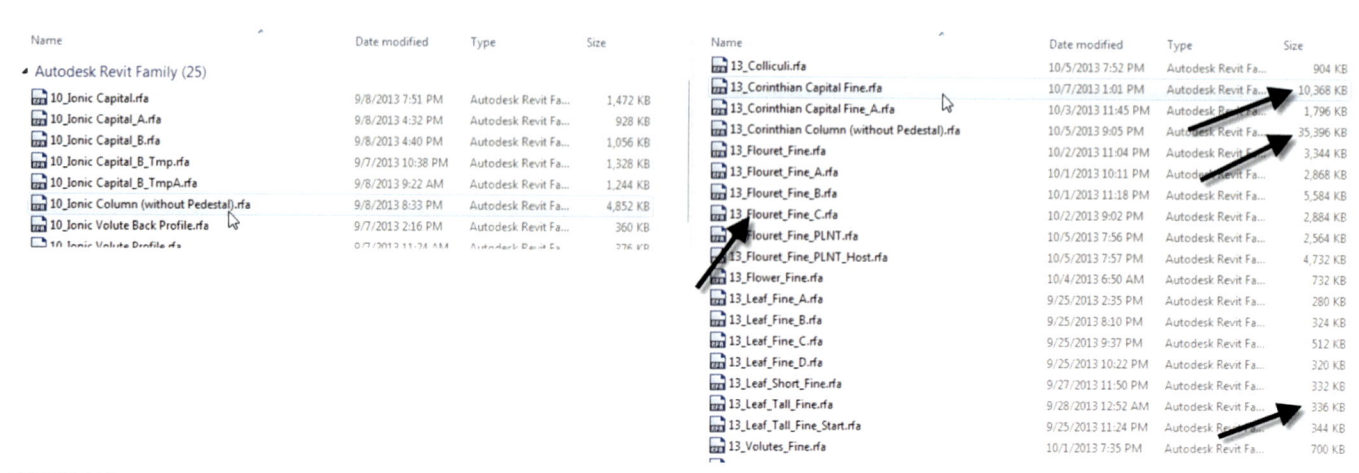

FIGURE 14.6

The complexity of the geometry in the family has a big impact on the file size

3D splines seem to make a big difference. Consider the two leaf families, (short and tall) which are each about 330 KB. But the flouret family jumps to ten times this size. Now the cauliculi family is nested in here which contributes as well, but the use of 3D splines seems to have a biggest impact. This is one of the reasons that I have tried to favor the use of 2D splines for paths. That and because I tend to get fewer errors when attempting to make complex lofted forms. But it you imagine the leaves in the flouret, it would have been difficult to find a 2D path that would have given the same 3D form. So sometimes the use of 3D splines is simply the best tool for the job. Voids can also have an impact. If you can create the same form without a void, it is usually smaller. But you can't always avoid voids. So once again, if file size is your primary concern, it could run in direct odds to what you are trying to build.

Nesting and Formulas—Some other factors that contribute to overall file size are the multi-level nesting and large quantities of formulas within the parameters. Ultimately the most important issue is performance. If you have a large file, but you are having no trouble loading it, then the issue is not as great as when the file loads very slowly or does not load at all. So the best you can do is try to keep file size in check and test your content frequently to make sure it is performing well. If you remove all nesting and formulas in an attempt to speed up a file and reduce its size, you might make it very difficult or impossible to flex. So there always has to be a balance between the sometimes competing goals.

Level of Detail—large files take a while to load. So there is certainly an advantage to keeping your content as small as possible. However, another strategy that I have been advocating throughout this book is to use the level of detail feature: coarse, medium and fine. This can help a great deal to make your content more useful. When you are working in small scale overall views, you often only need a simple representation of the column or other element.

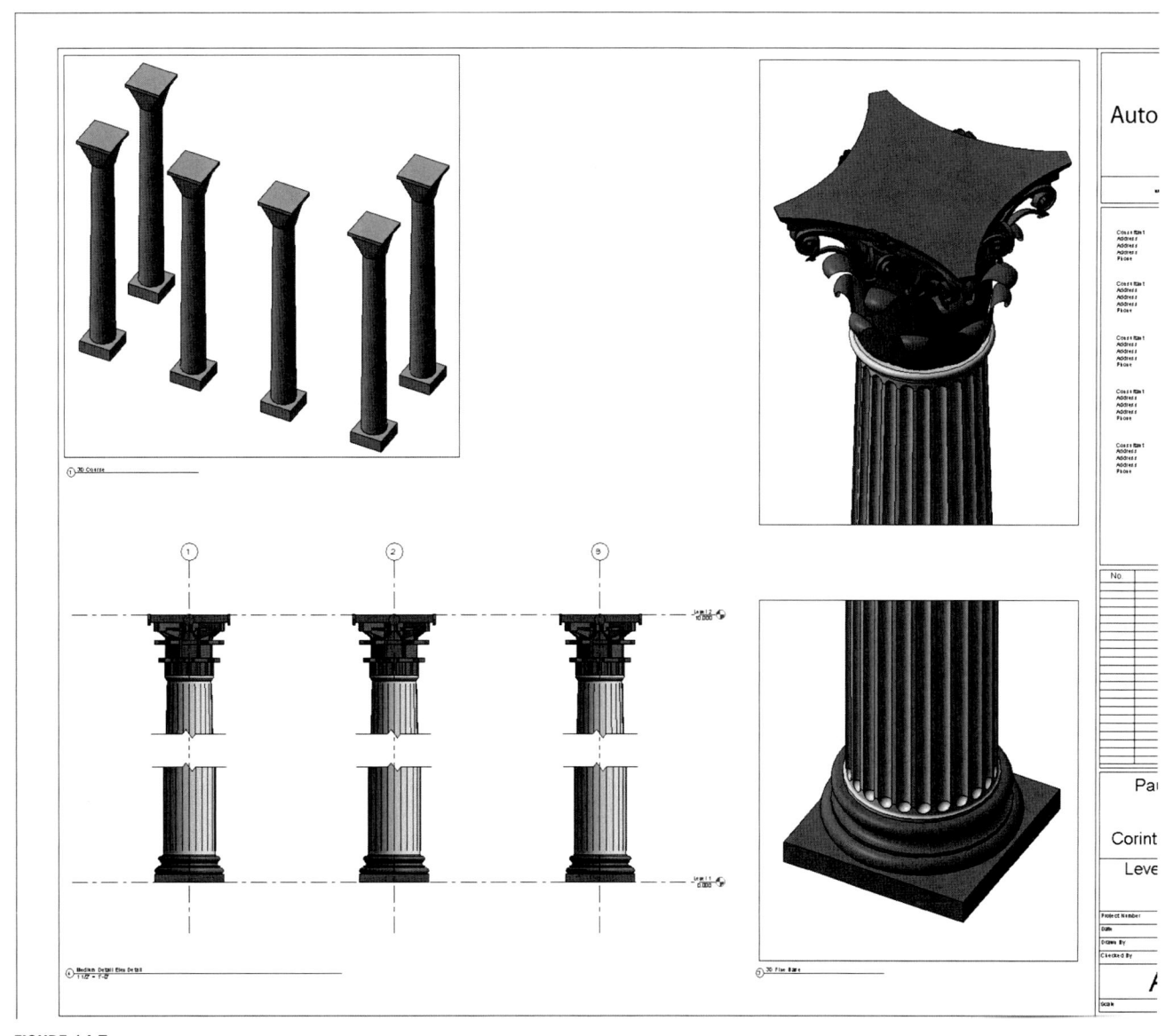

FIGURE 14.7

Three levels of detail helps contain detail to large scale views only

• *Creating Classical Architecture with Modern Software* •

Recall our schematic versions of the columns which show very little detail. These will load much more quickly than the medium or fine detail versions. So by managing which version displays in your project views you can often mitigate some of the otherwise poor performance you might experience from using the highly detailed versions. If used carefully, you may only see the fully detailed Corinthian capital in enlarged scale detail views where the focus is on only one or two capitals. So while the file size of the capital may be prohibitive using it on the small scale views, the reality is that at small scales you would never make out all the details anyway. So using well thought-out coarse, medium and fine versions is essential management strategy for content like the items we are building in this book (see Figure 14.7).

Swapping Families—a more manual approach to managing high and low detail versions of the same family is to literally swap them out with one another. I prefer to use three levels of detail directly in the family and then rely on coarse, medium and fine display. However, there are times when this might not be very practical. First, level of detail is controlled first at the view level and then can be overridden in Visibility/Graphics. It cannot be overridden at the object level. So if you only want some elements of a particular category to display fine, while the rest display medium or coarse, you cannot do this. The other scenario is for very large families like our Corinthian capital, even with coarse, medium and fine displays, the sheer file size might make it difficult to load. So if you only intend for example to use the fine detail version for renderings, you can create a version that only has the high detail and only load it in when needed to do renderings in a certain area. The process is manual and not ideal, but in some cases might be the only way to effectively manage things. But families have to be built properly to do this effectively. If references are not properly configured, it can really do a number on dimensions and alignments. You will have to do some trials on your own system to be sure.

TWO-DIMENSIONAL MODEL FAMILIES

Sometimes the best way to manage the file size issue is use two-dimensional families. You can embed two-dimensional representations of a complex family directly into the model family. These representations can be displayed in the elevations and sections and will typically render much more quickly than a true three-dimensional view. Furthermore, you can more easily abstract a two-dimensional view to remove those elements you don't wish to see in elevations or sections and make fine-tuning adjustments to lineweights and other graphical characteristics. If managed properly, there are many positives to the approach. There are of course negatives as well. The 2D information, while it might be derived from the 3D, is not typically linked to the 3D. So if the 3D changes, the 2D has to be adjusted separately. Sometimes you can simply use a parametric Detail Item family. In the case of our classical forms, the complexity of these forms would make it difficult to create 2D Detail Items that flex properly. Also, the 2D items only display or look correct when viewed head-on. So if you have your columns on a curved colonnade or along an angle, it is very difficult to use 2D effectively. There are some work arounds that can overcome some of these limitations, but as with any work around, there are trade-offs. Let's consider an example.

EXPORT TO CAD TO CREATE A 2D VERSION

So what if you want to show the high detail version but don't want to bring in the overhead? For 3D views, there is not much you can do, but in elevations and sections you have an alternative. In this topic, we'll walk through the process to create a 2D version of our fine detail capital. As always I have provided completed versions along the way.

1. From the *Chapter13* (last chapter) folder open the *13_Corinthian Capital Fine.rfa* file.
2. On the Project Browser, open the *Front* elevation view.

The easiest way to create a two-dimensional version of your 3D model is to export it to CAD.

3. From the Application menu, highlight **Export**, then slide over to **CAD Formats** and then finally choose **DWG** (see the left side of Figure 14.8).

File Management Techniques | **437**

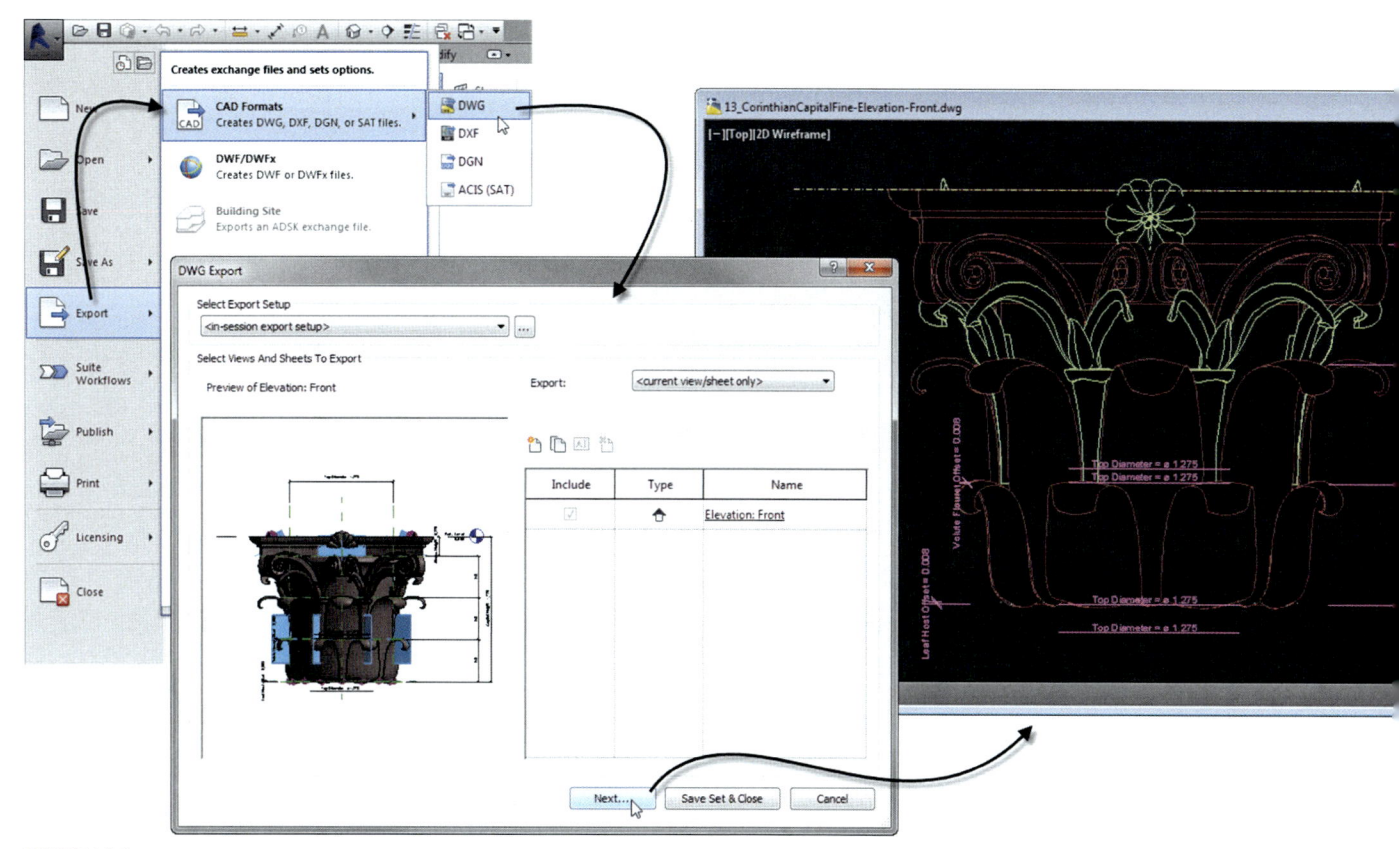

FIGURE 14.8

The completed Corinthian capital

⇨ In the "DWG Export" dialog, click the Next button.

⇨ Accept the default file name and then click OK.

Optionally, you can choose a different file format. Revit defaults to the latest version of DWG, but if you prefer an older one, you can choose it from Files of Type. The naming is always a little odd with exporting from Revit. You are not really naming the file, but rather choosing the name prefix. So you can change it if you like, but I prefer to just rename it in Windows Explorer later.

The file will require some cleanup to help optimize it. You can skip this step if you like. The 2D version created will still be quicker than the 3D model version, but if optimization is your goal, it is recommended that you open the file and clean it up. You can do this directly in Revit, but it is kind of tricky. Preferably if you have a copy of AutoCAD, it will be easier and faster to clean it up there first.

4. If you have AutoCAD, open the file (see the right side of Figure 14.8).

There are obviously items in here we can delete right away.

5. Delete the dimensions and the level.

Each nested family in the file has been exported as a block in AutoCAD. We need to explode all of these and then proceed to delete as many small redundant lines as we can find. This will take a while. You have to zoom in, make small window selections and look for double lines. You do not want to be too aggressive about deleting or you will lose important detail. But you want to get rid of as many double lines as possible.

6. Select everything remaining onscreen and explode. The Explode command is on the Modify panel of the Home tab, or you can simply type EXPLODE at the command line.

• *Creating Classical Architecture with Modern Software* •

438 | Chapter 14

⇨ Take your time and work systematically around the drawing (see Figure 14.9).

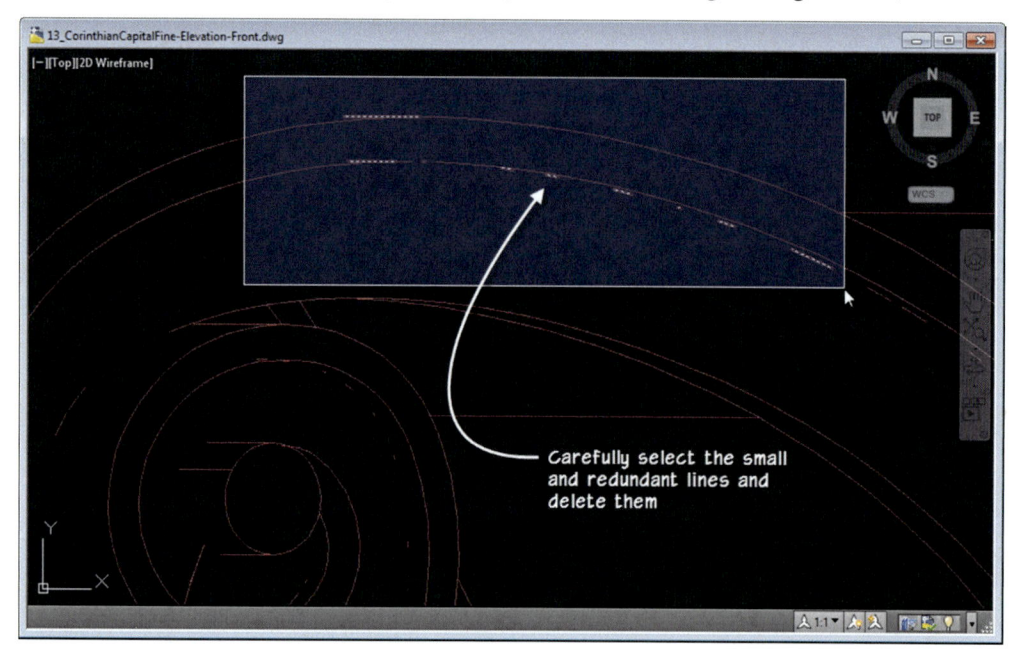

FIGURE 14.9
Spend some time selecting and deleting the small redundant lines

At a minimum, delete all the stray and double lines. If you wish to draw new lines to fill in some of the gaps or make other edits, this is your choice. You may also wish to purge unused layers. When you are done, save the file.

7. Back in Revit, in the plan view, create a section running at a 45° angle.

8. Repeat the entire process to export another CAD file along the 45°. Clean this one up too.

> **CATCH UP!** You can open a file completed to this point named: *Corinthian Elevation 90.dwg* and *Corinthian Elevation 45.dwg*.

> **Note:** You do not need AutoCAD to perform the cleanup. You can do it directly in Revit. To do so, work in a temporary file first such as our *Family Seed (Type Based).rfa* seed family. On the Insert tab, you can insert the CAD file into an elevation view. Select the imported CAD file and then on the ribbon, choose Full Explode. You will be warned about this affecting performance. It is certainly slower to do the cleanup here as compared to AutoCAD in my experience. But you want to do basically the same process and delete all of the extraneous lines. When finished, select all remaining lines and change them to a lines style like Thin Lines. You will then copy and paste these lines to a new family to ensure that you leave all of the unnecessary stuff behind. Ultimately, we still need a DWG for the next step, so you will want to repeat the export process again to resave your cleaned up version as a new DWG.

BUILDING A TWO-DIMENSIONAL ELEVATION VERSION

Once you have your cleaned up DWG files, you can import them into a generic model family.

1. From the *Seed Families* folder, open the *Family Seed (Type Based).rfa* file.

⇨ Delete box onscreen.

⇨ Save the family as: **Corinthian 2D Capital 90**.

2. Make the *Front* view active.

⇨ On the Insert tab, click the Import CAD button.

• Renaissance Revit •

File Management Techniques | 439

3. Browse to the *Chapter14* folder and select the *Corinthian Elevation 90.dwg* file.

   ⇨ For Colors, choose **Black and White**.

   ⇨ For Positioning, choose **Auto – Origin to Origin**.

   ⇨ Check the "Current view only" checkbox and then click Open (see Figure 14.10).

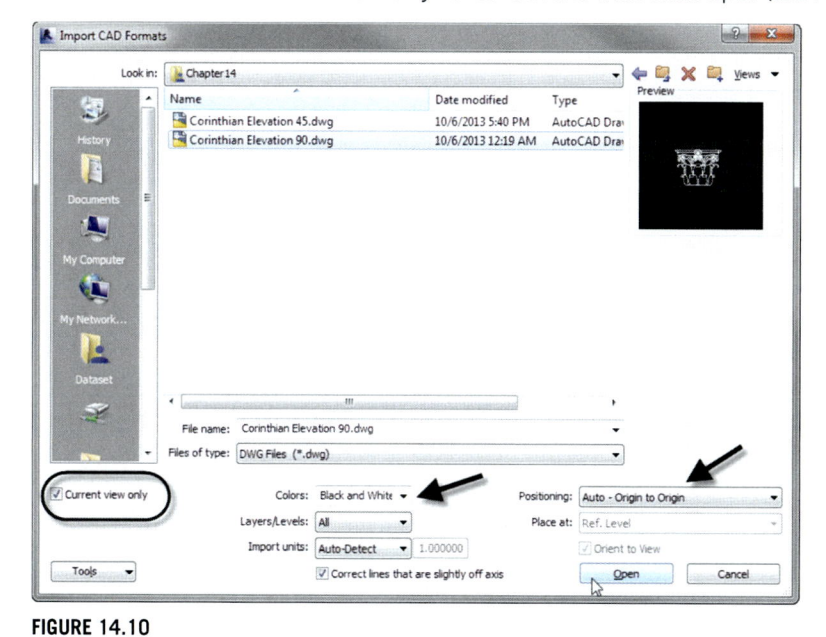

FIGURE 14.10

Import the CAD file to the Front elevation

Current view only is the most important setting. It makes Revit treat the CAD file like symbolic lines. Symbolic lines in the family editor are 2D lines that show only in views parallel to the one in which they were originally drawn. So in this case, this CAD file will show only when we look at a view parallel to the *Front* or *Back* elevation views.

4. Open the *Left* elevation and repeat the same process with the same settings.

5. In the *Front* elevation view, move the horizontal reference plane (labeled with Height) down below the level and align to the bottom edge of the import.

   The Height parameter should flex to 1.150 when you move it (see Figure 14.11).

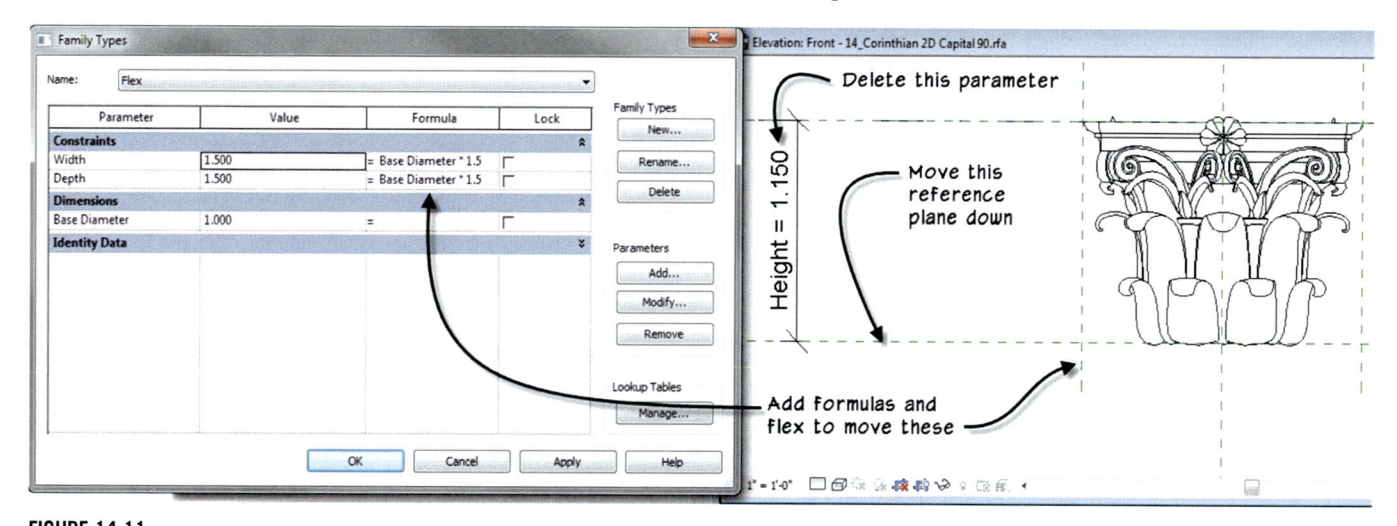

FIGURE 14.11

Adjust the reference planes and parameters

• Creating Classical Architecture with Modern Software •

6. Open "Family Types" and add formulas to the parameters:
    ⇨ For Width and Depth: **Base Diameter * 1.500**.
    ⇨ Remove the Height parameter.

The formulas put the reference planes in expected locations. Also since their "Is Reference" setting is set to Weak Reference, you will be able to snap and dimension to these locations. To make everything scale, we will be relying on the Planting family trick from the last chapter. So this means that Revit will create a Height parameter. So removing this one will avoid confusion later.

One other consideration when building 2D families is that we have to add masking regions to make them hide geometry. If you load this family into a project as it stands right now, view it in elevation and place it in the foreground in front of other objects, those objects will show right through this family. So the solution is to create a masking region in the shape of the outline in each elevation. Creating this is time consuming. There really is no short cut to tracing over the outline using arcs, lines or splines. Unfortunately, Pick Lines does not work for most of the edges in these DWGs, so it is better to just trace the outline. I traced half and then simply mirrored it.

7. In the *Front* elevation, on the Annotate tab, click the Masking Region button.
    ⇨ Set the Subcategory to **<Invisible Lines>**.
    ⇨ Trace the outside edges around the CAD file.
    ⇨ Before finishing, select all of the edges and copy them to the clipboard.
8. When finished, click the green Finish Edit Mode (checkmark) button.
9. Switch to the Left elevation view and start the Masking Region command again.
    ⇨ Paste from clipboard and position it relative the DWG in this view.
    ⇨ Finish Edit Mode.
10. On the Properties panel, click the Family Category and Parameters button.
    ⇨ Set the Category to Planting and click Close to dismiss the warning. Click OK again.
11. Save and close the family.

CATCH UP! You can open a file completed to this point named: *14_Corinthian 2D Capital 90.rfa*.

12. Repeat the entire process to create another family with the *Corinthian Elevation 45.dwg* file.
    ⇨ Change the formulas for Width and Depth to: **Base Diameter * 2.000**.
    ⇨ Trace the DWG with a Masking region and then copy it to the other view again.
    ⇨ Change the category to Planting.

CATCH UP! You can open a file completed to this point named: *14_Corinthian 2D Capital 45.rfa*.

CREATE A CAPTIAL FAMILY USING THE 2D PLANTING FAMILIES

There is a little trick to getting the 45° versions of the capital to display. We have to insert both of the families we previously created into another family. Then when you load this into a project, it will display the 90° versions when viewed from a standard orthographic view (front, left, right and back). If you view on a 45° angle, it will display the nested 45° version instead. Theoretically, you could build in other angles as well, but at some point there might be a diminished return or practical limit. If you recall our use of the planting technique in the previous chapter required nesting two levels deep as well.

1. From the *Chapter14* folder, open the *Corinthian Capital 2D_PLT.rfa* file.
2. Make the *Ref. Level* plan view active.
3. On the Create tab, click the Component button. When prompted choose Yes.
   - Browse to the *Chapter14* folder and select both of the families you just completed in the previous exercise, (or choose the catch-up files).
   - Place an instance of *14_Corinthian 2D Capital 90* at the center of the reference planes.
4. Place an instance of *14_Corinthian 2D Capital 45* at the center of the reference planes as well.
   - Rotate this instance 45° about the center

If you want to test that this is working correctly open one of the section views in this file. They are cut at 45°. You will see the 45° version only in the section view and the 90° version only in the elevations.

5. On the Properties panel, click the Family Category and Parameters button.
   - Set the Category to Planting and click Close to dismiss the warning. Click OK again.
6. Open the "Family Types" dialog and add a formula next to Height: **Base Diameter * 1.189**.

> CATCH UP! You can open a file completed to this point named: *14_Corinthian Capital 2D_PLT.rfa*.

IMPORT THE 2D FAMILY AND LOAD IT INTO A PROJECT

At this point, everything is ready to test and should be functioning properly. If you don't want the capital family to be a planting family, you can nest it one level deeper. I have provided a file called: *Corinthian Capital 2D.rfa* which you can use for this purpose. However, I would also like to caution you on nesting too many levels deep. So you can skip that file as well. There is another version of the Corinthian column family in this folder. It does not contain the fine detail 3D version. You can nest the planting family directly into there and it will not be evident in the final family that there is a planting file.

1. From the *Chapter14* folder, open the file named: *Corinthian Column (Low Detail).rfa*.
2. On the Project Browser, open the Ref. Level floor plan view.
3. On the Insert tab, click Load Family.
   - Load the *14_Corinthian Capital 2D_PLT.rfa* file (or your own version of same if you prefer).
4. On the Create tab, click the Component tool.
   - On the ribbon, click the Place on Work Plane button.
   - On the Options Bar, from the Placement Plane drop-down, choose: **Reference Plane: Capital Top**.
   - Place an instance of the planting family at the center of the reference planes.
5. Cancel the command. Align and lock the new instance in both directions.
6. Edit its Type Properties and link up the Base Diameter.
7. Open the *Front* elevation.
   - Select the medium detail version (3D family).
   - Copy and paste it using **Aligned to Same Place**. Ignore the warning.
8. With the new copy still selected, on the ribbon, click the Visibility Settings button.
   - In the "Family Element Visibility Settings" uncheck *all* boxes and check *only* Fine (see Figure 14.12).

• Creating Classical Architecture with Modern Software •

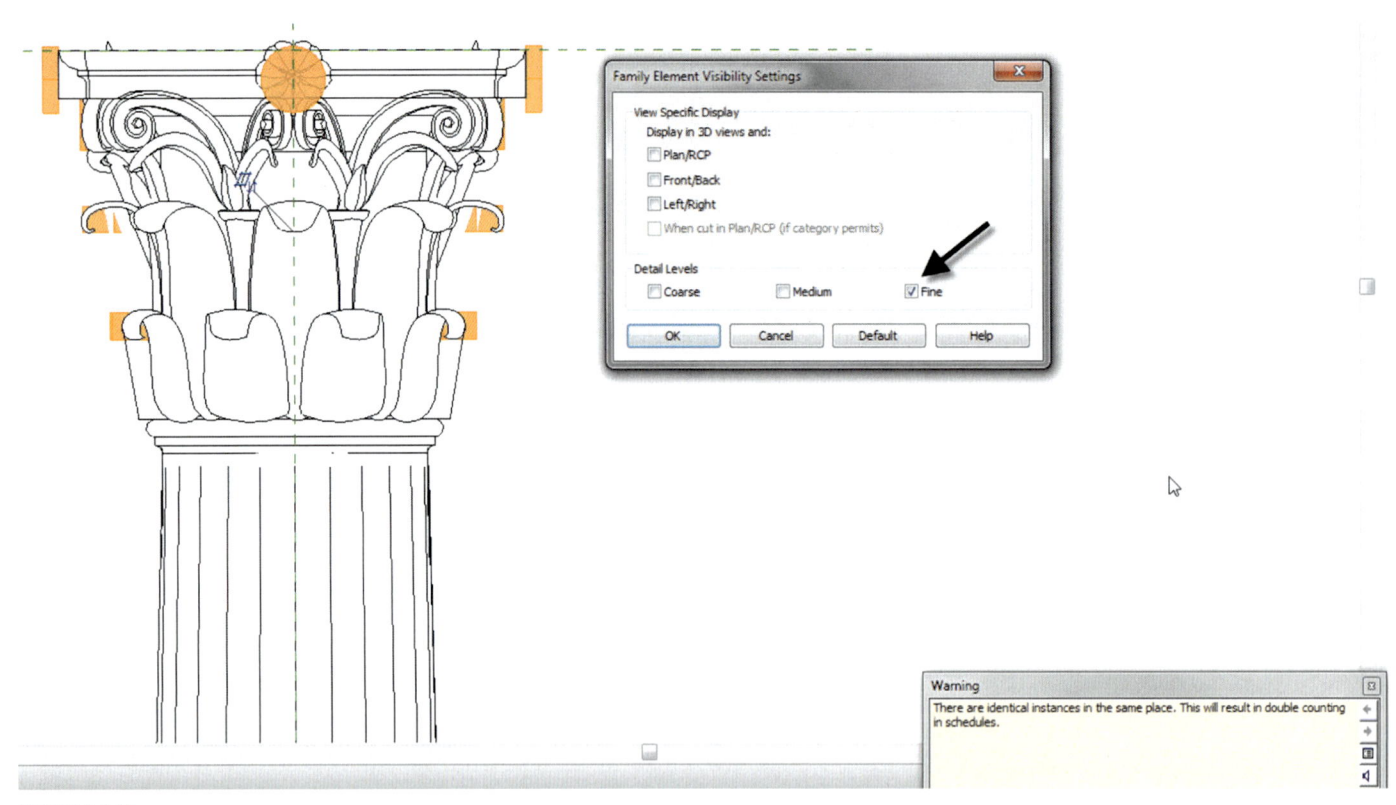

FIGURE 14.12
Create a copy of the medium detail for use in 3D views only

9. Select the medium detail capital again, on the Properties palette, click the Associate Family Parameter button next to the Visible checkbox.

⇨ Create a new parameter grouped under Graphics called: **Show Medium Capital**. Make it an Instance parameter.

Doing this makes the medium detail version display in 3D views for fine level of detail, but not plans and elevations. This way, if you set a 3D view to fine, you will still see something displayed in the absence of the 2D fine detail elements. However, we added the checkbox parameter to manually override this in those cases where we end up with both the medium and fine versions showing at the same time.

10. Select the 2D planting family.

⇨ Click Visibility Settings again and uncheck Coarse and Medium.

11. Save and close the file.

CATCH UP! You can open a file completed to this point named: *14_Corinthian Column (Low Detail).rfa*.

Now let's open a sandbox file and try it out.

12. From the *Chapter14* folder, open the *14_Sandbox_Colonnade_Corinthian.rvt* file.

13. On the Project Browser, beneath *Families > Columns*, right-click on *Corinthian Column (Simple)* and choose **Reload**.

⇨ Browse to the *Chapter14* folder and select the *14_Corinthian Column (Low Detail).rfa* file (or choose your version created here instead).

⇨ Overwrite the existing version.

There are four open windows: *South* elevation, *20 Degree Section*, *45 Degree Section* and the *View1* 3D view. *South* is set to medium detail. The others are currently set to Coarse.

• Renaissance Revit •

14. In each view, toggle through Coarse, Medium and Fine (see Figure 14.13).

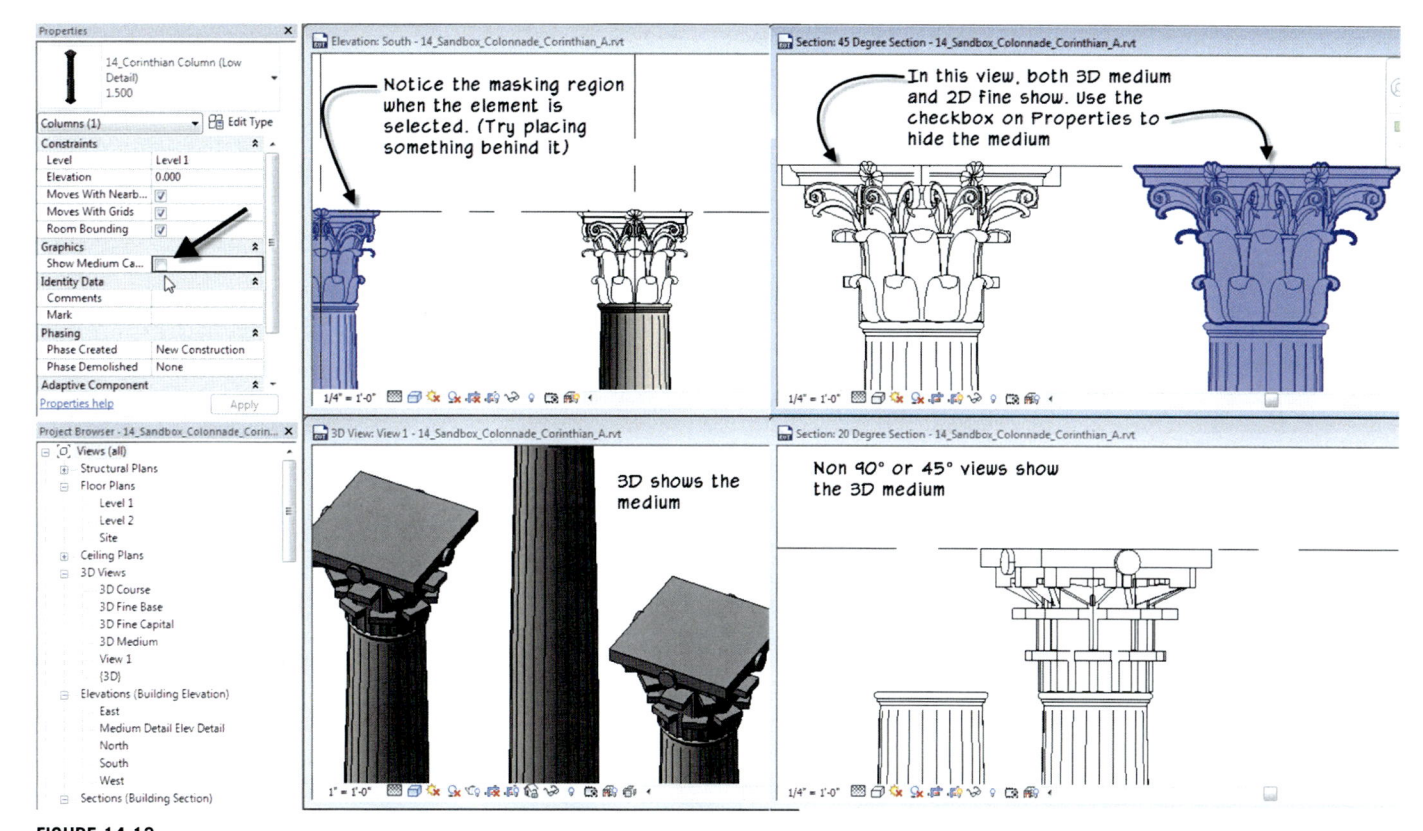

FIGURE 14.13
Load into sandbox and try out different levels of detail

> **CATCH UP!** You can open a file completed to this point named: *14_Sandbox_Colonnade_Corinthian_A.rvt*.

This solution is not ideal in many respects. There are tradeoffs. But if most of your elevations are on 90° or 45° lines, then this solution can work effectively. The final file size of this column is 3.2 MB. This is about a tenth of the 3D version. So perhaps use this one regularly and then swap in the 3D version in those cases that need it. I should reiterate though that file size is not the only determinant in performance, and 2D geometry is often a poor substitute for true 3D elements. If you have an elevation at an angle other than 90° or 45°, if you want it to cast shadows, if you want to tag it with material tags or render it, you cannot do any of these things with this solution. So you really have weigh just how much you are giving up against whatever advantage the 2D might bring. There isn't a single "correct" option all the time, but in general I would prefer the true 3D model with coarse, medium and fine over a 2D version in most cases.

SAVING OPTIONS

From the Application Menu, choose **Save As > Family**. In the "Save As" dialog, near the lower right corner, click the Options button. A variety of options are available here. We already discussed the "Compact File" checkbox above. Let's take a quick look at the remaining options.

BACKUPS

At the top of the window is the quantity of maximum backups. This setting is available for both projects and families. The default is 3 backups. This is a good setting in most cases for projects. For families, I often set the number of backups to just 1. You cannot set it less than 1. I think a single backup for families is usually sufficient.

• *Creating Classical Architecture with Modern Software* •

This is particularly true when building lots of content. If you browse a folder full of families and there are three backups to every one family, it can make it difficult to find the one you need. (The backups show up in Windows Explorer with numbers at the end of their names). I have a small batch file that I run that deletes all of the backups in a folder. Before doing this, make sure that you have a good backup of all your important files somewhere else, like the daily company backup, an online backup service or just a separate copy on a removable drive.

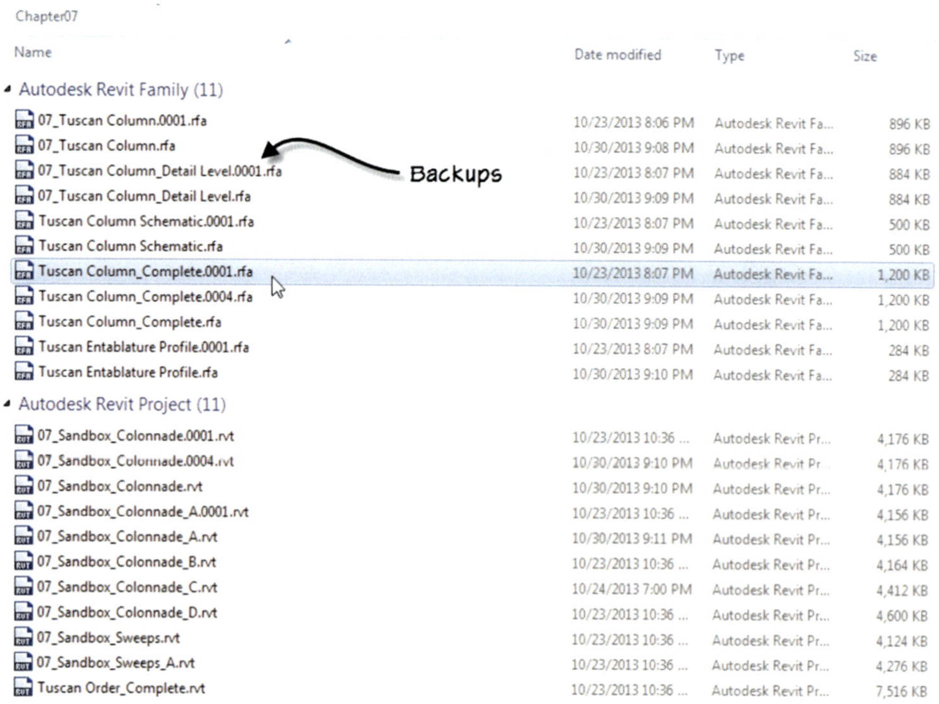

FIGURE 14.14
Backup files have a numbered suffix appended to the file name

PREVIEWS

When you browse files with the open command, or view them in Windows Explorer, a preview image is displayed. This preview is generated from one of the views in your file. You can indicate which view is used to create the thumbnail preview at the time of saving. Simply choose it from the source dropdown. You will probably notice that much of the out-of-the-box Autodesk content uses the default 3D view, often called View 1 or {3D} for this purpose. You can continue this practice or create your own view for this. Just remember that each view you add can impact file size. Non-3D families use other views for preview and they often have the annotation categories turned off. This can be confusing when you first open them, so typically one of the first things to do when opening a family is check VG to see what is hidden. This could be a good reason to make a special view just for the preview that way the other views can continue to display annotation and reference planes without affecting the preview. Particularly so in the massing environment.

If you notice that the preview does not seem to match the view, use the checkbox here to regenerate it on the next save (see Figure 14.15).

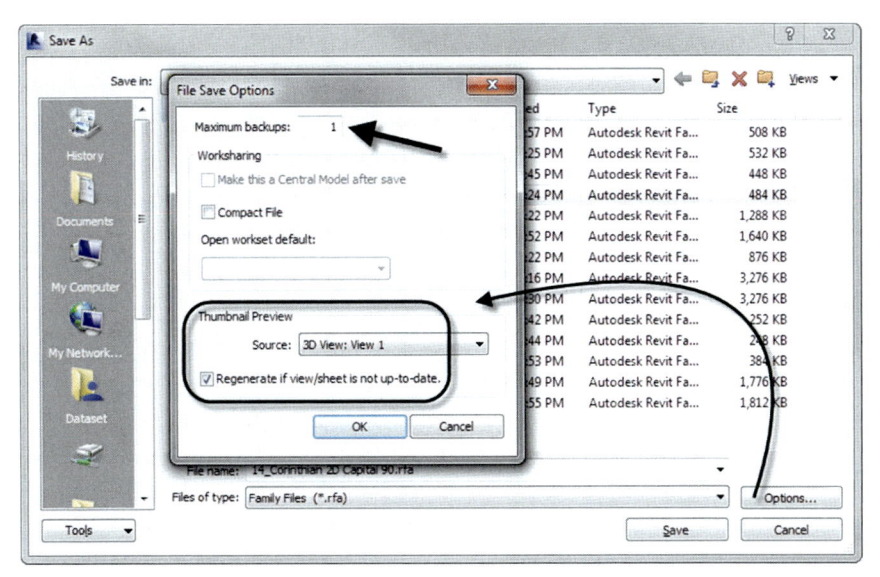

FIGURE 14.15

Set your preferred number of backups and save previews in the save as options dialog

Feel free to continue experimenting with these files. If you want to add additional 2D only components, you can draw them directly using the Symbolic line tool. Symbolic lines display in views parallel to the one in which they were drawn in the family editor. So if you want to create a custom 2D plan version, draw with filled regions, masking regions or symbolic lines in a plan view. If you want to add 2D to an elevation, do the same in an elevation view. You can even create complete 2D families using the Detail item template. These families can be fully parametric and embedded into your 3D families, or used independently in projects directly. The symbolic line, detail components and region tools are only available in the traditional family editor. The massing environment only supports 3D entities. So if you want to draft elements two-dimensionally, you must use model lines and then hide them in views where you don't want them displayed.

SUMMARY

- ✓ Revit includes several tools to help you manage file size.
- ✓ Use purge unused or delete from Project Browser to remove unused items.
- ✓ Compact and Audit are options available during save an open to help keep file healthy.
- ✓ Deleting unneeded views can help reduce the file size.
- ✓ Choosing between massing and traditional environments can be an important consideration.
- ✓ Use 2D splines instead of 3D splines when possible.
- ✓ Try to minimize the quantity of nested families, formulas and parameters.
- ✓ To help improve performance in 2D views, consider embedding two dimensional versions of your family that display in place of the 3D in elevations and sections.
- ✓ Be sure to check you save settings like backups and previews when saving files.

FORUM ROME
Photo by author

Conclusion

I hope you have enjoyed taking this exploration of classical architecture through the lens of Autodesk Revit with me. For me this is the culmination of a journey that began over ten years ago. I have always looked at the work of the ancients with awe and respect. As I write these words and bring this book to a close, I am left with an even deeper appreciation of their legacy and achievements. So much more so since they did not have the benefit of a computer!

Regardless of whether your primary focus is an interest in classical architecture or an interest in creating Revit content, I sincerely hope that you have found the lessons in these chapters useful, informative and most of all that you have enjoyed the ride. I know that I have enjoyed the process of bringing it to you tremendously.

If you have any questions about this book or Revit in general, you can use the contact form at **www.paulaubin.com** to send me an email.

Follow me on twitter: **@paulfaubin**

Appendix

INTRODUCTION

This appendix includes resources that support the information in the main text. It is meant to be a simple reference as you work on your projects.

MOLDING TYPES

Here is an illustration of many standard molding types:

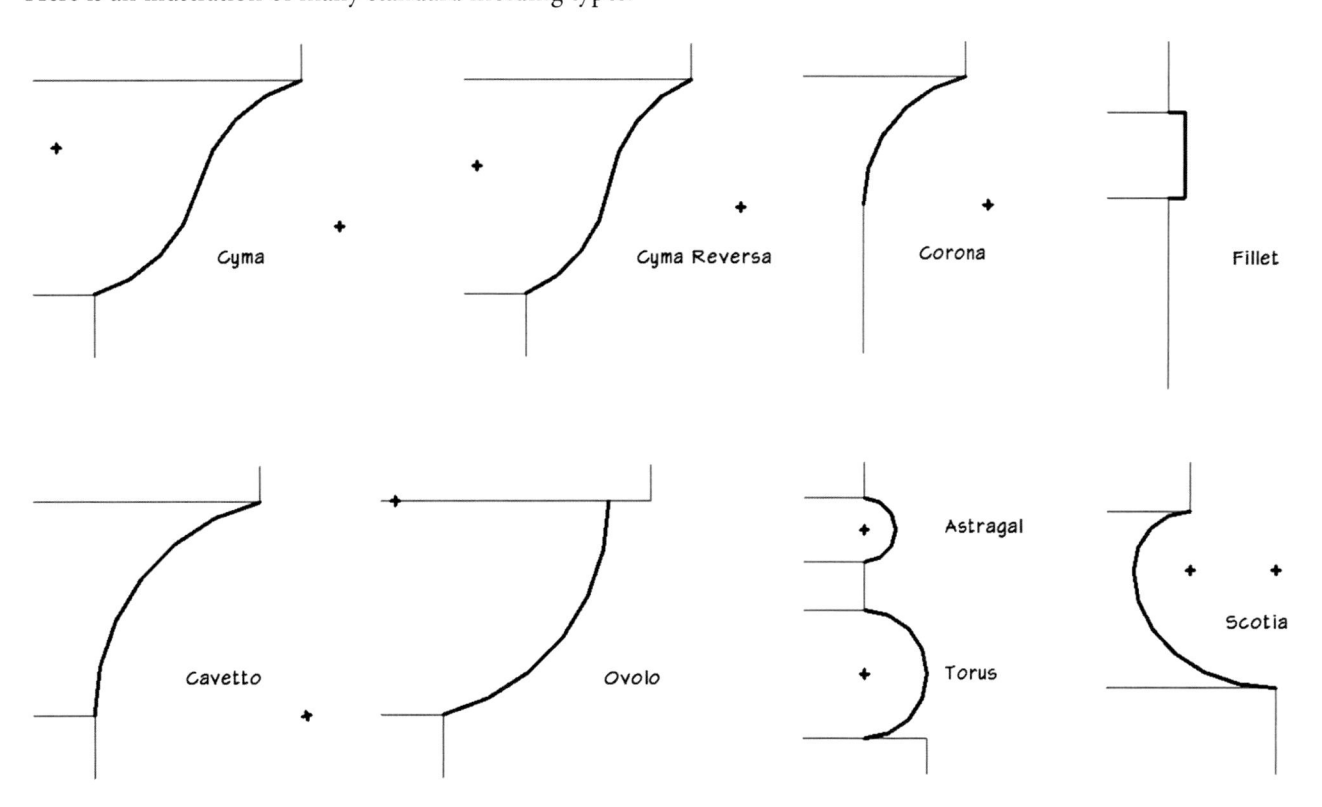

TRIGONOMETRY RESOURCE

When you first start using the family editor, you are thrilled to simply create a family that flexes without breaking. But as you get deeper into it, it won't be long before you want to go deeper. Over the years using Revit, I have had to re learn my high school trigonometry. There are countless online resources to assist in this. I have listed some here. My favorite is on the Revit Forum website in a post title: "Revit Formulas for Everyday usage." With the permission of the author: Klaus Munkholm I have reproduced a portion of the post here. You can find the complete post, which contains many examples of several other types of formulas here:

Reproduced from: http://www.revitforum.org/tutorials-tips-tricks/1046-revit-formulas-everyday-usage.html

TRIGONOMETRY CHEAT SHEET FOR REVIT

To solve a triangle, you need to know at least two of the following values. From any two values, you can solve for the other parts. Using the diagrams, figure out which parts are known, then plug in the appropriate formula in your Revit families. (Remember that formulas in Revit are case sensitive).

Which parts are known?

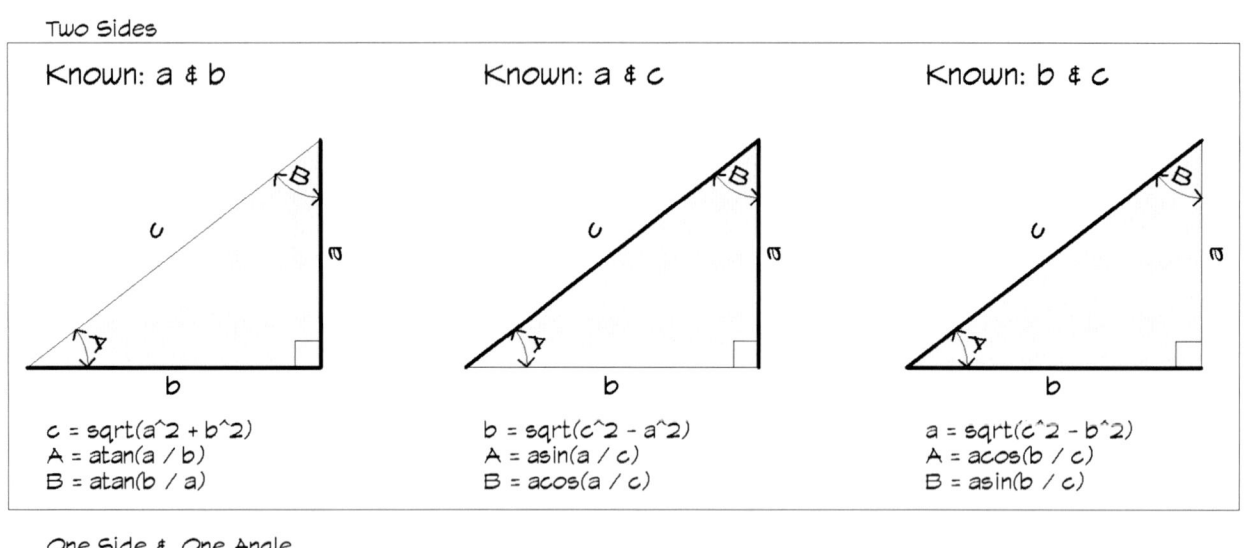

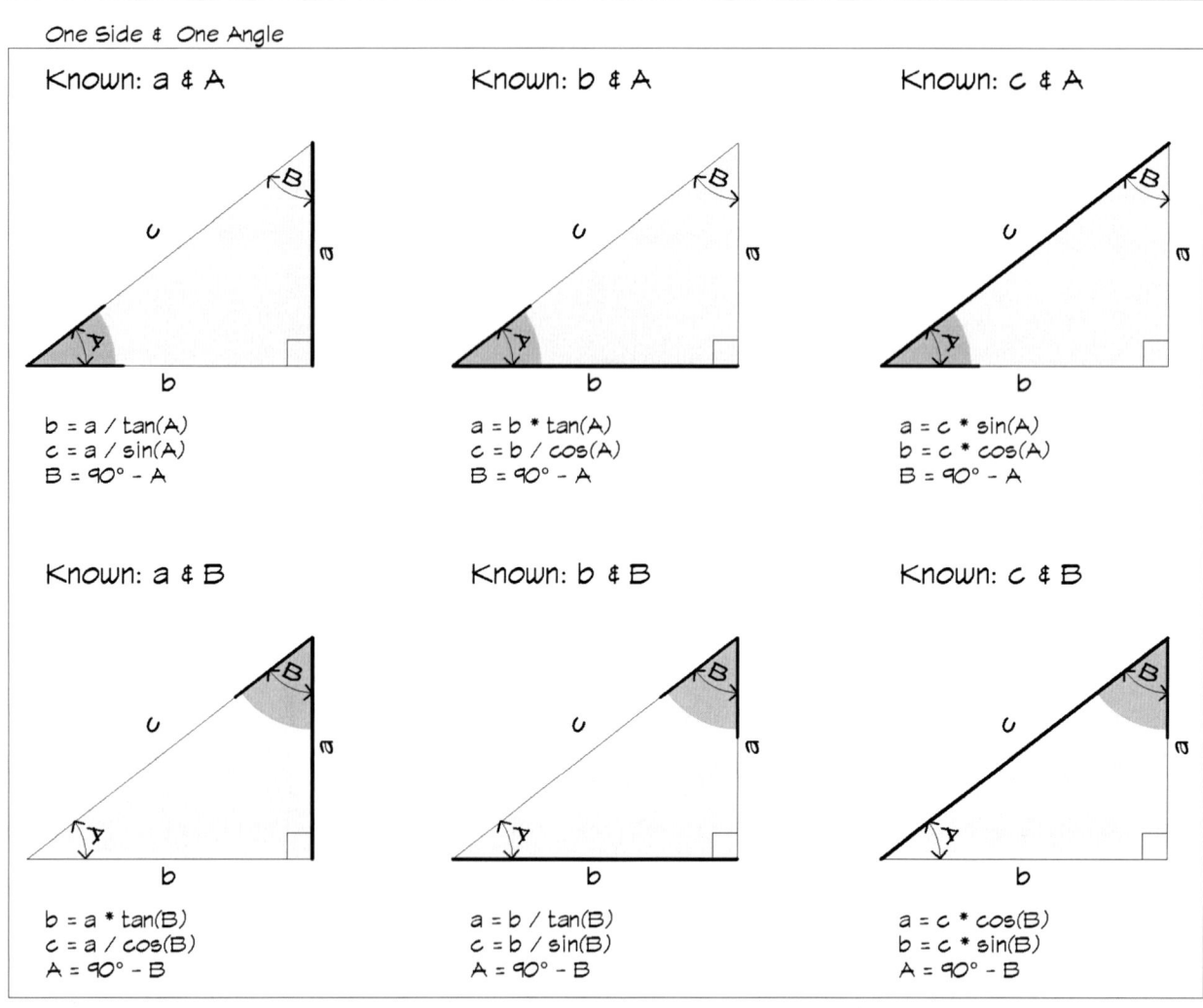

Two Sides

Known: a & b

c = sqrt(a^2 + b^2)
A = atan(a / b)
B = atan(b / a)

Known: a & c

b = sqrt(c^2 - a^2)
A = asin(a / c)
B = acos(a / c)

Known: b & c

a = sqrt(c^2 - b^2)
A = acos(b / c)
B = asin(b / c)

One Side & One Angle

Known: a & A

b = a / tan(A)
c = a / sin(A)
B = 90° - A

Known: b & A

a = b * tan(A)
c = b / cos(A)
B = 90° - A

Known: c & A

a = c * sin(A)
b = c * cos(A)
B = 90° - A

Known: a & B

b = a * tan(B)
c = a / cos(B)
A = 90° - B

Known: b & B

a = b / tan(B)
c = b / sin(B)
A = 90° - B

Known: c & B

a = c * cos(B)
b = c * sin(B)
A = 90° - B

Reproduced with permission

• Renaissance Revit •

CREATING THE COVER RENDERING

I wanted to take a few moments to discuss how I created the rendering that you see on the front cover of the book. The Corinthian capital that you see is the one that we built in this book. For the entablature, I created it following the same procedures that we used in the "Creating a Complex Profile" topic in Chapter 9 except that I built it in the massing environment, so the profile is a face based generic model. The file was begun from our *Family Seed (Face Based - Type Based).rfa* template file. A considerable number of dimensions, reference planes and parameters are required. I have provided two versions of the completed profile In the *Appendix* folder; a medium detail version named: *Corinthian Entablature FB Profile_Medium.rfa* that contains only straight lines, no curves and a fine detail version with all of the curves: *Corinthian Entablature FB Profile.rfa*. I also provided the *Console.rfa* file. I am not completely satisfied with family, but since it was not a primary focus of the rendering, I left it rough. It does not flex. For the dentils, I used the techniques and files discussed in the "Basic Dentil Molding" topic in Chapter 11. For the pineapple at the corners, I made a copy of the dentil file, and then built a very simple loft from a stack of circles. I then selected the surfaces of this form and made divided surfaces. I applied the rhomboid pattern to those surfaces to get the pineapple skin effect. Both of these files are in the *Appendix* folder: *Pineapple.rfa* and *Dentil (Adaptive).rfa*.

There is a really interesting feature of Divide and Repeat that I have not mentioned previously. You can divide the edges of *any* form! To apply the dentils, I used tab until I had just one edge of the entablature selected. I divided this and then configured it to fixed distance on the Properties palette. This allowed for exact spacing of the dentils as required, but places it exactly where it is needed in the model.

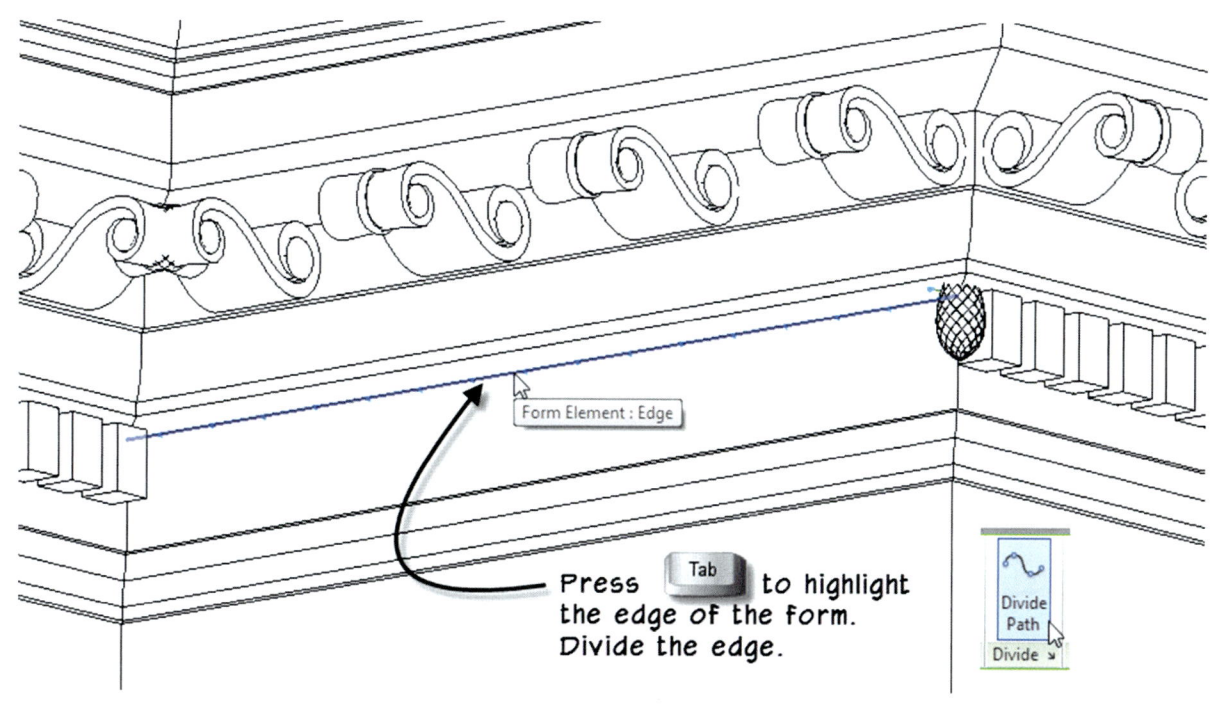

I did not provide the final model due to file size considerations, but with all of the pieces, you should be able to assemble your own version. For the rendering I assigned the out-of-the-box Travertine material to everything. I made no changes to this material. I set up sun light and rendered with an out-of-the-box preset directly in the product. No Photoshop or post production.

• *Creating Classical Architecture with Modern Software* •

Bibliography

BOOKS AND REFERENCES

Aubin, Paul F. 2012. *Advanced Modeling in Revit Architecture.* May 28. www.lynda.com/paulaubin.

—. 2012. "Autodesk® Revit® Families: Step-by-Step Advanced Concepts." *Autodesk University 2012.* Las Vegas. 19-30. www.paulaubin.com/au.

—. 2011. *Revit Architecture: The Family Editor.* September 21. www.lynda.com/paulaubin.

—. 2013. *The Aubin Academy Master Series: Revit Architecture 2013 and beyond.* Clifton Park, NY: Delmar, Cengage Learning.

Brandwein, Martin, and M. Gunnison Collins. n.d. *Classical Architecture: A Handbook of the Tradition for Today.* http://www.classicist.org/publications-and-bookshop/handbook/.

Chambers, William. 2003, 1791. *A Treatise on the Decorative Part of Civil Architecture.* Dover edition, is an unabridged reprint of the third edition of the work (first published in 1759) published by Joseph Smeeton, London, 1791. Mineola, NY: Dover. Accessed August 2013.

Chitham, Robert. 1985, 2005. *The Classical Orders of Architecture, Second Edition.* New York: Rizzoli International Publications, Inc.[10]

Gibbs, James. 1732. *Rules for drawing the several parts of architecture, in a more exact and easy manner... by which all fractions, in dividing the principal members and their parts are avoided.* Reprint edition. London: Ecco Print Editions.[11]

John Fleming, Hugh Honour, Nikolaus Pevsner. 1980. *The Penguin Dictionary of Architecture.* Third Edition. London.

---

[10] This book is unfortunately out of print. I have copies of both the first and second edition. The second edition is expanded to include 96-part orders more compatible with imperial units. For use in Revit, I found the decimal measures actually easier to work with even though I am comfortable with imperial units. There is a Kindle edition still available, but I highly recommend trying to locate a second hand copy of an original physical book.

[11] The edition I have is a very low quality reprint. The illustrations look to be very useful, if you can find a good quality reprint. Unfortunately the copy I have is almost illegible.

Kron, Zach. 2012. *Buildz.* December 8. Accessed December 2012. http://buildz.blogspot.com/2012/12/tool-making-way-better-bezier-ish-by.html.[12]

Light, David. 2009. *Revit - Everything Autodesk Revit & BIM.* September 18. Accessed June 2013. http://autodesk-revit.blogspot.com/2009/09/gaudi-form.html.

Mackey, Brian. 2013. *Mackey Consulting.* http://bdmackeyconsulting.com/.

Mackey, Desirée. 2013. *Ellipse.* email. August 24.

Mattison, Harry. 2013. *Boost Your BIM.* March 28. Accessed March 2013. boostyourbim.wordpress.com.

Mauch, J. M. 1910, 1845. *THe Architectural Orders of the Greeks and Romans: 100 Plates.* Folio Edition. Edited by Pavl Wenzel and Maurice Krakow. Translated by E.R.A. Litzau. New York, NY: Architectural Book Publishing Co., Inc.[13]

Milburn, Andy. 2013. *Shades of Grey.* July 18. Accessed July 2013. http://grevity.blogspot.com/2013/07/snake-oil-rig.html.[14]

Munkholm, Klaus. 2011. *Revit Formulas for "everyday" usage.* March 23. Accessed 2012. http://www.revitforum.org/tutorials-tips-tricks/1046-revit-formulas-everyday-usage.html.

Palladio, Andrea. 1965. *The Four Books of Architecture.* Dover Edition. Mineola, NY: Dover.

Realtor. 2001. *Types of Arches.* May 1. Accessed August 2013. http://www.realtor.org/rmoprint.nsf/pages/arch36.

Sgambelluri, Marcello. 2013. "Size Matters - Learn How to Scale Any Family in Revit." *Revit Technology Conference, North America 2013.* Vancouver. 7 - 14.

Tam, Kelvin. 2013. *Revit Swat.* June 2. Accessed June 2013. http://revitswat.wordpress.com/2013/06/02/class-34-s-m-l-xl-how-to-scale-a-family/.

The Classical Orders.com. n.d. *The Elements of Classical Architecture.* Accessed October 10, 2013. http://theclassicalorders.com/.

Vignola, Giacomo Barozzi Da. 2011, 1669. *Canon of the FIve Orders of Architecture.* Dover edition, first published in 2011, is an unabridged republication of "The Regular Architect: or the General Rule of the Five Orders of Architecture", printed for William Sherwin, London, in 1669. Translated by John Leeke. Mineola, NY: Dover. Accessed August 2013.

Vitruvius. 1960, 1914. *The Ten Books of Architecture.* Dover Edition, unabridged reproduction of the first edition of the English translation by Morris Hicky. Translated by Morris Hicky. New York, NY: Dover.

---

[12] Zach's blog is a treasure trove of information on the use of the Revit massing environment. It should be on your "must read" list for sure.
[13] This book is long out of print, but I was able to locate a used copy. You can also find scanned reproductions, but they do not do it justice. If you want to truly appreciate the book, try to find an original or original reprint. The edition I have is folio format, no binding. The dimensions are10 x 13 and each plate is printed on heavy card stock.
[14] Andy's is another blog that is an absolute gold mine of information on Revit and the Revit massing environment. Be sure to search the site for various post on making rigs in the massing environment and be sure to check out Andy's post on the annual parametric pumpkin contest. Definitely not to be missed.

Ware, William R. 1994, 1977, 1903. *The American Vignola – A Guide to the Making of Classical Architecture.* Dover edition, unabridged republication of the edition first published by W. W. Norton & Company, Inc. New York. Dover.

WEBSITES AND BLOGS

This is by no means a comprehensive list, but I have included sites with information directly related to my research for this book, and some of my favorite "go to" Revit-related sites as well.

http://www.classicist.org/ (Lots of useful information and publications. Memberships available.)

http://www.doric-column.com/index.html

http://www.doric-column.com/glossary_classical_architecture.html

http://www.realtor.org/rmoprint.nsf/pages/arch36

http://theclassicalorders.com/theclassicalorders.html

http://www.classicist.org/publications-and-bookshop/handbook/ionic-order/

http://www.youtube.com/watch?v=BW_76G46798

http://mathforum.org/library/drmath/sets/select/dm_ellipse.html

http://sites.csn.edu/istewart/mathweb/Math127/ellipses/ellipses.htm

http://malleristicrevitation.blogspot.com/2013/03/the-helen-of-geometry.html

http://tinyurl.com/l8ufahv

http://do-u-revit.blogspot.com/2011/10/face-painting-in-family-editor-fixed.html

Index

<

<Family Types> parameter, 55, 199

A

abacus, 113, 117, 123, 214, 215, 216, 219, 294, 295, 302, 379, 381, 382, 383, 385, 387, 425
adaptive components. *See* components: adaptive
Architectural Desktop, 1
associate family parameter, 51, 52, 107, 119, 121, 122, 136, 137, 159, 166, 167, 169, 198, 199, 201, 217, 222, 233, 237, 238, 262, 283, 332, 336, 337, 338, 389, 393, 395, 407, 423, 428, 442
astragal. *See* moldings: astragal
AutoCAD Architecture, xi, 1, 3, 4

B

bell, 379, 382, 383, 385, 423
blend, 26
Bramante, 209, 336
Building Design Suite, x
buildz, 334

C

categories: component, 6
cavetto. *See* moldings: cavetto
center mark visible, 63, 69, 75
Chambers, ix, 8, 281, 452
Chitham, Robert, 7, 35, 111, 113, 143, 147, 181, 209, 281, 282, 283, 303, 341, 342, 343, 345, 364, 372
coliculi, 379, 410, 411, 434
components: adaptive, 6, 249, 311, 359, 390, 399, 429, 434
Composite order, 4
Corinthian order, **7**, **379**, **402**
corona. *See* moldings: corona
cyma. *See* moldings: cyma
cyma reversa. *See* moldings: cyma reversa

D

dentils, 244, 336, 451
die, 130, 212, 235
Die, 212
dimensions: add, 15; automatic sketch, 64, 67, 87, 254, 258, 285, 286, 290, 318, 321, 351, 383; make temporary permanent, 79; temporary, 71
diminution. *See* entasis
displace elements tool, 313
Doric order, **161**, **181**, **209**, **224**, **263**, **279**, **336**, **349**, **350**

E

echinus, 214, 215
entablature, 2, 3, 4, 93, 143, 144, 161, 162, 163, 174, 175, 176, 177, 187, 188, 189, 190, 191, 192, 193, 194, 203, 204, 209, 210, 243, 244, 245, 246, 247, 248, 249, 250, 257, 262, 263, 264, 266, 269, 272, 273, 274, 276, 277, 291, 292, 451; adaptive components and, 250; alternate approaches, 193; beams and, 243; coarse scale, 206; Corinthian, 451; creating from complex profile, 250; curtain walls and, 246; Doric, 188, 209; height, 190; level of detail and, 196; line based, 246; options, 168; railings and, 247; Tuscan, 143, 161; walls and, 244
entasis, 43, 57, 100, 144, 145, 151, 154, 176, 341, 342, 343, 344, 345, 346, 347, 350, 353, 357, 369, 371, 374, 376, 378
equality dimensions, 286
extrusion: creating, 16; flexing, 46; void, 33

F

face normal direction, 71
family content, 1, 9, 11, 12, 56, 59, 174, 177, 184, 422, 431
family editor, 4; basic skills, 11; massing, 5, 6, 399; traditional, 4, 6
family types, 16, 19, 38, 53, 93, 97, 105, 174, 223, 244, 282, 318, 336, 382, 400, 402; Flex, 19, 20, 38, 53, 103, 164, 174
Family Types parameters. *See* <Family Types> parameter
file size, 313, 431

fillet. *See* moldings: fillet
flex, 16, 19, 25, 30, 33, 38, 42, 43, 46, 52, 55, 57, 60, 61, 62, 63, 64, 65, 67, 69, 72, 73, 75, 78, 79, 80, 84, 93, 94, 97, 100, 101, 105, 107, 109, 121, 124, 126, 129, 131, 132, 135, 153, 155, 157, 158, 159, 164, 168, 171, 172, 174, 179, 193, 195, 198, 206, 223, 224, 233, 234, 250, 258, 262, 267, 269, 270, 271, 275, 283, 285, 290, 301, 302, 305, 306, 311, 318, 319, 324, 330, 334, 338, 339, 344, 350, 357, 359, 363, 366, 367, 387, 390, 391, 392, 408, 412, 422, 425, 428, 435, 436, 449, 451
Flex. *See* family types:Flex
flexing. *See* flex
flouret, 379, 381, 410, 411; approach, 411; file size, 424, 434; scaling, 423
flower, 379, 427
fluting: adding, 349; in the massing environment, 358; never applied to Tuscan, 144; representing with lines, 376; tops and bottoms, 371
formulas, 153, 193, 264, 268, 279, 282, 396, 412; adding, 127, 158, 213, 217; adjusting, 215; and performance, 435; cannot add to system families, 244; do not paste, 319; driving points, 376; driving with adaptive points, 338; editing, 225, 228, 229, 251, 255, 265, 320; elliptical, 346; online resource, 449; reusing, 350; trig cheat sheet, 450; with trig, 372
frieze, 209, 246, 247, 263, 268, 271

G

Gibbs, ix, 8, 35, 113, 147, 281, 452
guttae, 264

I

intercolumniation, 4, 181, 188, 262, 336
Ionic order, **279, 280, 308, 379**

K

Kron, Zach, 334

L

leaf: Corinthian, 390, 392, 395, 397, 400, 414; file size, 434; flouret, 416, 419, 420, 422
level of development, 7
LOD. *See* level of development

M

Mackey, Desirée, 345
Maller, Aaron, 103
Mass.rft template: don't use, 5
massing environment. *See* family editor, massing
massing environment, the, 5
Mauch, J. M., 303, 402
metopes, 209, 244, 263, 268, 273, 276
Michelangelo, 3, 4

Milburn, Andy, viii, 2, 334
moldings, 2, 4, 7, 39, 80, 93, 100, 108, 113, 115, 117, 130, 131, 137, 145, 164, 171, 173, 175, 193, 195, 197, 198, 200, 216, 219, 229, 230, 234, 237, 238, 239, 243, 244, 246, 250, 252, 265, 294, 345, 347, 371, 376, 383, 449; astragal, 66, 69, 143, 147, 149, 227; beak, 383; cavetto, 80, 85, 143, 149, 212, 214, 217, 235; corona, 93, 94, 95, 99, 113, 119, 120, 121, 217, 253, 254, 383; cyma, 88, 92, 130, 135, 235, 251, 252, 253; cyma reversa, 88, 91, 92, 104, 131, 212, 223, 240, 294, 295; fillet, 93, 95, 104, 116, 124, 127, 129, 131, 143, 147, 164, 223, 224, 252, 254, 256, 282, 285, 286, 288, 289, 292, 349, 364, 383, 404, 405; ovolo, 80, 104, 113, 114, 115, 116, 117, 120, 122, 123, 214, 216, 235, 253, 254, 294, 295, 383; scotia, 94, 231; torus, 66, 69, 124, 126, 127, 129, 143, 147, 224, 231
Munkholm, Klaus, 449
mutules, 244, 245, 248, 263, 266, 267, 270, 271, 273, 274, 339

N

necking, 3, 214, 215, 217, 218

O

Orders, understanding, 2
ovolo. *See* moldings: ovolo

P

Palladio, viii, ix, 8, 35, 113, 147, 177, 209, 281, 336, 341, 350, 355, 402, 453
parametric, ix, 4, 11, 12, 18, 27, 33, 39, 59, 60, 62, 69, 73, 75, 80, 92, 94, 99, 101, 105, 209, 247, 267, 281, 310, 318, 322, 333, 335, 358, 372, 428, 436, 445
Piazza del Campidoglio, 3
plinth, 124, 126, 127, 235
profiles, 161; can't use in revolves, 116; importing, 113; nested, 123; understanding, 30; using for sweeps and swept blends, 31
project: load into, 17, 32, 55, 86, 122, 152, 160, 172, 178, 180, 201, 211, 212, 214, 223, 227, 228, 234, 240, 241, 262, 272, 339, 349, 355, 412

R

reference lines, 5, 59, 60, 324, 326, 367, 385, 394, 397, 402, 411, 417; built in workplanes and, 69; Is Reference setting, 400; profile families and, 80, 85; rotating, 73, 74, 78; sketching on workplanes, 422
reference planes, 4, 18, 19, 23, 47, 52, 59, 60, 64, 65, 68, 70, 75, 79, 81, 85, 89, 92, 104, 113, 124, 129, 130, 134, 145, 147, 149, 156, 161, 162, 184, 204, 220, 225, 261, 264, 266, 281, 299, 302, 303, 306, 313, 318, 319, 350, 357, 372, 383, 385, 391, 411, 440, 444, 451; aligning to, 69; creating, 14; equality dimensions and, 94; flexing, 25, 46, 86; Is Reference setting, 184; locating profiles and, 168; locking

endpoints to, 78; pasting, 319; profile families and, 80; resizing, 317; rotation and, 69
reference points, 324, 326; hosted, 331, 361, 366, 381, 392; show reference planes, 409
reload family, 97, 154, 176, 202, 213, 357, 425, 426, 427, 428, 429, 442
reporting parameters, 53
Revit 2012, x
Revit 2013, x
Revit API, 66
Revit LT, x
revolve, 26

S

scotia. *See* moldings: scotia
seed families, 19, 20, 21, 23, 27, 76, 161, 283; adding Base Diameter, 39; beginning with, 47; choice of, 243; creating, 18; massing, 317; omitting geometry, 25
shaft: channels, 349, 355, 356, 371, 376
shared family, 52, 312
sweep, 26
swept blend, 26

T

Tam, Kelvin, 422
Tempietto, 209, 336
template files: adaptive, 310, 311; baluster, 275; beams and braces, 161, 174, 206; column, 47; custom, 21, 23; default settings, 317; default view orientation, 318; detail item, 85, 445; door, 70, 102; face based, 21, 75; family, 13; generic annotation, 282; generic model, 359; levels and, 51; line based, 247; massing, 310; out-of-the-box (OTB), 21, 30; pattern based, 310; planting, 422; profile, 31, 102; project, 12, 178; project settings, 185; renaming, 21; scale in, 26; wall based, 22
temporary dimension, 78
torus. *See* moldings: torus
trig. *See* trigonometry
triglyph: channels, 209, 264
triglyphs, 209, 244, 245, 248, 263, 266, 267, 268, 270, 273, 275, 277, 339
Triglyphs, 269, 271
trigonometry, 80, 81, 84, 87, 89, 92, 95, 254, 282, 449
Tuscan order, **42**, **47**, **111**, **142**, **143**, **156**, **161**, **177**, **181**, **210**, **224**, **341**, **349**

U

units, x, 13, 38, 40, 48, 162, 178, 257; imperial, 178; metric, x

V

Vasari, x
Vignola, ix, 35, 143, 281, 453, 454
visibility/graphics, 249
Vitruvius, 8, 35, 177, 181, 341, 453
volute, 406; Corinthian, 401, 408; eye, 286, 407, 409; fillet, 288; Ionic, 281; layout, 282; profile, 291, 306; scroll, 300, 303; spiral, 283, 402; sweeps, 296

• Renaissance Revit •

Made in the USA
Las Vegas, NV
02 February 2023